Fodor's

MOSCOW AND ST. PETERSBURG

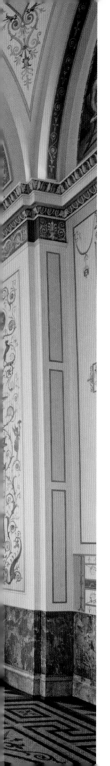

WELCOME TO MOSCOW AND ST. PETERSBURG

Russia's grandest cities may be steeped in history, but they continue to move full speed into the future. From Moscow's energy and influence to St. Petersburg's elegance and charm, these two very different cities never cease to surprise. The colorful onion domes of St. Basil's Cathedral rise over the trendy art galleries that replaced Soviet factories, and vigorous capitalism has ushered in chic restaurants, nightclubs, and shops that take luxury to a new level. In modern Russia, it seems anything is possible.

TOP REASONS TO GO

★ **Opulent Palaces**: The homes and summer retreats of Russia's former rulers dazzle.

★ **Top Museums:** Cultural riches abound, from the Hermitage to the Armory Chamber.

★ **Architecture:** Tsarist and Soviet history can be traced through distinctive buildings.

★ **Posh Eateries:** You can sip vodka and dine with Russia's new millionaires.

★ **Royal Theaters:** Ballet and opera are performed in theaters literally built for kings.

★ **Scenic Countryside:** Short day trips let you explore quaint riverside villages.

12
TOP EXPERIENCES

Moscow and St. Petersburg offer terrific experiences that should be on every traveler's list. Here are Fodor's top picks for a memorable trip.

1 Peterhof Palace

In St. Petersburg, this opulent palace and its elaborate gardens, lavish fountains, and cascading waterfalls (all designed by Peter the Great) offer a glimpse of just how extravagantly the tsars lived. *(Ch. 8)*

2 Nevsky Prospekt

Often compared to the Champs-Elysées in Paris, this is
St. Petersburg's busiest street and prime real estate for
people-watching, dining, and shopping. *(Ch. 8)*

3 Moscow Metro

Moscow's fast and efficient metro system is used by more
than 8 million people each day. The stations contain stunning
Soviet mosaics and statues glorifying the proletariat. *(Ch. 2)*

4 Peter and Paul Fortress

St. Petersburg's oldest building has stunning interiors and serves as the final resting place for the Russian tsars. *(Ch. 8)*

5 Gorky Park

The park is *the* place to be on a nice day in Moscow. Stroll past modern art galleries and cafés, or rent a bike or paddleboat to explore the grounds. *(Ch. 2)*

6 White Nights

St. Petersburg comes alive in the summer, when the sun barely sets and local pride in the city's beauty is contagious. You'll be tempted to stay up all night. *(Ch. 8)*

7 Borscht

A bowl of Russia's traditional soup (made primarily from beets) will fill you up after a long walk around the city; it's especially satisfying on cold winter nights. *(Ch. 3 and 9)*

8 Red Square/Kremlin

Centuries of Russian history fill Moscow's famous square, inviting you to linger in the shadows of the iconic onion domes and the stunning facade of the Armory Chamber. *(Ch. 2)*

9 Ballet at the Bolshoi

Revel in one of the country's most respected arts by seeing a Russian classic, like Tchaikovsky's *Swan Lake*, at Moscow's oldest and grandest theater. *(Ch. 2)*

10 Lenin Mausoleum

The founder of Russian communism is entombed in Moscow. Millions viewed him after he died in 1924, and Soviet history buffs still visit his embalmed body. *(Ch. 2)*

11 State Hermitage Museum

St. Petersburg has one of the world's renowned art collections. The lavish halls here contain works by European masters including Rembrandt, Matisse, and others. *(Ch. 8)*

12 Canal Cruise

Cruising the myriad waterways takes you past St. Petersburg's top attractions and provides a look at the details of the city's ornate buildings and bridges. *(Ch. 8)*

CONTENTS

CONTENTS

MAPS

ABOUT THIS GUIDE

Fodor's Recommendations

Everything in this guide is worth doing—we don't cover what isn't—but exceptional sights, hotels, and restaurants are recognized with additional accolades. Fodor's Choice ★ indicates our top recommendations; and **Best Bets** call attention to notable hotels and restaurants in various categories. Care to nominate a new place? Visit Fodors.com/contact-us.

Trip Costs

We list prices wherever possible to help you budget well. Hotel and restaurant price categories from $ to $$$$ are noted alongside each recommendation. For hotels, we include the lowest cost of a standard double room in high season. For restaurants, we cite the average price of a main course at dinner or, if dinner isn't served, at lunch. For attractions, we always list adult admission fees; discounts are usually available for children, students, and senior citizens.

Hotels

Our local writers vet every hotel to recommend the best overnights in each price category, from budget to expensive. Unless otherwise specified, you can expect private bath, phone, and TV in your room. For expanded hotel reviews, facilities, and deals visit Fodors.com.

Restaurants

Unless we state otherwise, restaurants are open for lunch and dinner daily. We mention dress code only when there's a specific requirement and reservations only when they're essential or not accepted. To make restaurant reservations, visit Fodors.com.

Credit Cards

The hotels and restaurants in this guide typically accept credit cards. If not, we'll say so.

Top Picks
★ Fodor's Choice

Listings
⊠ Address
⊠ Branch address
☎ Telephone
🖷 Fax
⊕ Website
✉ E-mail
🎫 Admission fee
🕑 Open/closed times
Ⓜ Subway
✛ Directions or Map coordinates

Hotels & Restaurants
🏨 Hotel
🛏 Number of rooms
🍴 Meal plans
✕ Restaurant
🍸 Reservations
👔 Dress code
🚫 No credit cards
Ⓢ Price

Other
⇨ See also
☞ Take note
🏌 Golf facilities

1

EXPERIENCE
MOSCOW AND
ST. PETERSBURG

MOSCOW AND ST. PETERSBURG TODAY

Russia has come a long way since the breakup of the Soviet Union in 1991, and now visitors have more access to what makes the country so enticing—its rich history, vast expanses of land, and hospitable people. The country is at once exciting, overwhelming, and inviting.

Economy

Moscow and St. Petersburg aren't budget travel destinations. There's unimaginable wealth in the two cities, despite unnerving poverty in some of the farther regions of Russia's vast expanse. In Russia, oil and gas are still the biggest games in town, and economic development is directly dependent upon their prices. Despite several economic crises during the past 15 years, Russia's economy has bounced back and remains fairly stable, meaning the rich do indeed keep getting richer. The infamous business oligarchs who made their money during the post-Soviet privatization of Russia are still around, but the next generation, too, have acquired multimillionaire and billionaire status. All this opulent wealth can't hide the persistent poverty of these cities. Central Asian immigrants, in particular, come seeking economic stability and a better life only to find they can barely survive on the low wages of street cleaners and construction workers. The Kremlin's attempts and promises to diversify the economy have, so far, been slow to bring significant results. However, there has been some trickle down, and Russia's middle class continues to grow. And as their incomes continue to rise, so, too, do the prices in Moscow and St. Petersburg.

Politics

If you can't remember whether Vladimir Putin is president or prime minister, don't worry. It's confusing to many Russians, too, since Putin has held one of the two positions since 1999. As of this writing, Putin was again the president of Russia—his third term after a break in between consecutive term limits to switch places with his successor and serve as prime minster.

But whatever his title, Putin's political strength and influence call the shots in Russia. Western pundits criticize Putin's erosion of Russia's young democracy, but ask most Russians about how they feel about him, and they're likely to tell you that they admire him and what he's done for the country. Russians won't hesitate to complain about the bureaucracy and poor state of much of the cities' infrastructure, however, and critical voices do exist, although their dissent is usually quashed when it gets too loud, as it happened during the protests that followed the parliamentary elections of 2011. Hundreds of thousands took to the streets of Moscow and other large Russian cities with their symbolic white ribbons pinned to their heavy coats to rally against what they said was a rigged election. Hundreds of the protesters were arrested, and the Kremlin quickly imposed harsher regulations for conducting public protests. When Putin was reelected as president in March 2012, the protests were smaller and lacked the previous vigor—with the notable exception of members of the feminist punk-rock group Pussy Riot, several of whom were arrested for staging and filming a performance in an Orthodox Church to protest its leadership's support of Putin.

Meanwhile, anti-American rhetoric amped up after the U.S. said it would ban visas to Russians accused of human rights violations. The Kremlin responded with a ban on all adoptions of Russian orphans by U.S. citizens. The good news is that

most visitors are unlikely to be affected by the tit-for-tat between Washington and Moscow, and most Russians will avoid uncomfortable political talk with guests.

In 2013, President Putin signed a bill into law that criminalized so-called homosexual "propaganda." This caused controversy when it happened, and time will reveal the consequences.

Olympic Fever

The Olympic committee surprised the world when it chose the southern Russian city of Sochi to host the 2014 Winter Games. Russians greeted the news with less surprise, however. Sochi was a favorite winter destination during Soviet times, and was repopularized when Putin's ski trips there were broadcast on state news channels. The remaking of Sochi and its surroundings continues with much to-do about controversial government spending and questionable project tenders. Some estimates put a $15-billion price tag on the project of turning Sochi into a smooth-running Olympic operation. But in Moscow and St. Petersburg, Olympic pride has taken hold. Bosco Sports, a Russian sports clothing line and one of the official sponsors of the events, has opened stores around the country to sell some of the Team Russia paraphernalia.

Religion

The Russian Orthodox Church is experiencing a new surge in believers after having an on-again, off-again relationship with its congregation for decades. During the years of the Soviet Union, the church—and religion in general—was forbidden at times and used to manipulate nationalist sentiment during others. Today, many previously destroyed churches have been reconstructed, the most notable of these being the sparkling Cathedral of Christ Our Savior in Moscow. Ethnic Russians make up about 80% of the country's 142 million population, and polls show that some 90% of them say they're part of the Orthodox Church. This holds true even with the younger crowd. It's not uncommon to see hip, twentysomethings standing in line at the Kazan Cathedral in St. Petersburg to kiss an icon, or trying to squeeze a place inside a golden-domed church in Moscow during a crowded Easter service. Religion can still get political in Russia. State-run news channels don't hesitate to show Putin in photo ops with heads of the church.

Tearing Down the Past

It's not immediately apparent that there's a vicious war raging behind the massive amounts of construction happening in both St. Petersburg and Moscow. What some see as progress, others see as the destruction of Russian architectural heritage. Preservationists accuse the St. Petersburg government of giving the go-ahead to Gazprom and other big investors to build modern office buildings that will ruin Peter the Great's European feel. In Moscow, the fight has been particularly contentious as the city's skyline continues to be dominated by massive construction cranes. Former Mayor Yuri Luzhkov, who lost his job in 2010, was in office during the destruction of some 400 architecturally significant buildings in the capital. Lushkov's billionaire wife, Elena Baturina, and her construction company, Inteco, contributed to the lucrative buildup of the city, adding to accusations of corruption. In both cities, activist groups have formed to try to put a stop to the great teardown.

WHAT'S WHERE

1 Moscow. Cosmopolitan in flavor, Russia's capital exudes prosperity and vigor. From Stalin's carved-marble metro stations to the sprawl of modern business complexes, Moscow flaunts its ambition with a penchant for going over the top. It's an all-night-party town whose days offer endless opportunities for those who can keep up. A merchant capital by birth, Moscow was fashioned for big spenders, and money has always made the wheels go 'round here. Now counted as one of the world's most expensive cities, the only possible limit is the size of your wallet.

2 Moscow Environs and the Golden Ring. In the 12th to 14th centuries, the Golden Ring cities were the most important political, religious, and commercial centers in Russia before Moscow usurped all power. Nowadays these ancient enclaves are perfect destinations for rolling back the centuries. A visit to their medieval convents, ancient trade chambers, and kremlins is like stepping into a living encyclopedia of Russian culture, complete with picture-postcard views of onion-domed churches set on the banks of the Volga River.

3 St. Petersburg. Serenity and reflection reign in this city. Tsars don't rush—it would be undignified. St. Petersburg

was founded as the new capital of the Russian Empire in 1703 by Peter the Great and still carries itself with austere regal grace. The city built on the marshy banks of the Neva River today attracts more tourists than anywhere else in Russia. A brilliant fusion created by Italian and French architects, St. Petersburg invites comparisons with Amsterdam, Venice, and Stockholm. The big attractions here are the pastimes of the nobility—artwork, classical concerts, ballet, and idyllic promenading in the 19th-century landscape.

4 Summer Palaces and Historic Islands. Several of St. Petersburg's imperial summer residences have been meticulously restored to their original splendor, and the sheer opulence is stunning. Peterhof's (Petrodvorets) park is Russia's answer to Versailles, while Catherine's Palace at Pushkin (Tsarskoye Selo) houses the legendary Amber Room. Lomonosov (Oranienbaum), a UNESCO World Heritage Site, and the Konstantine Palace have both undergone restoration and are great places for a summer stroll or picnic. The islands of Kronshtadt and Vallam showcase another side of the city's history.

TOP ATTRACTIONS: MOSCOW

Red Square

No matter how many times you walk on the uneven cobblestones of Red Square, the view is awe-inspiring and the experience monumental. Stand in the center and let your mind wander as centuries of Russian history unfold in the architecture. Tsars were crowned and traitors beheaded just outside of St. Basil's Cathedral's colorful domes. Soviet tanks once rolled ceremoniously across as Stalin surveyed from the sidelines, and Lenin's mausoleum is still guarded by stern-faced soldiers.

The Kremlin and Armory Chamber

The first walls of the Kremlin were erected more than 850 years ago and continue to symbolize Russian power today. Don't miss the Tomb of the Unknown Soldier in Alexander Gardens, a popular place for newlyweds to have their first photo taken. The Armory Chamber is the jewel of the Kremlin and contains one of the richest collections of silver, gold, diamonds, and Fabergé eggs in the country. Several halls display more than 4,000 artifacts dating back to the 12th century, including diamond-encrusted coronation thrones and extravagant Russian armor.

Bolshoi Theatre

Moscow's oldest—and most famous—theater recently reopened after a complete renovation that took six years. Watching a ballet performance of a Russian classic, such as Tchaikovsky's Nutcracker, on the main stage is unforgettable.

Tretyakov Gallery

Wander through the rooms of Old Tretyakov's extraordinary collection of famous Russian icons, landscapes, and portraits housed in an early-20th-century building that feels more like a castle. The museum boasts one of the largest and most renowned collections of work from the prerevolutionary Russian realists known as the Wanderers.

Gorky Park

After a recent renovation, this "Park of Culture" has once again become a very popular spot for Muscovites. The dilapidated Soviet buildings and Ferris wheel have been torn down and replaced with modern art galleries, cafés, and playgrounds. Young and old will find plenty to do here, from simply strolling around the vast green space to renting paddleboats, bicycles, or rollerblades. There are concerts and art shows in the summer, and snowboarding and ice skating in the winter.

Lenin Mausoleum

If the imposing marble exterior of this Soviet-era iconic structure doesn't intimate you, the soldiers standing guard inside might. The stern guards are there to watch over Vladimir Lenin's embalmed body and ensure visitors maintain a respectful silence around the former leader of the Russian Revolution. Gigglers will be scolded. While admittedly morbid, the experience of seeing one of modern history's most noteworthy figures is certainly a can't-miss Moscow sight.

Pushkin Museum of Fine Arts

Opened in 1912, the museum holds Moscow's largest collection of European art. Broken up into several wings, it contains both rotating and permanent collections of fine art and archeological treasures from Central Asia to Europe. The private collections wing has some outstanding art collected over the years by prominent Russian collectors.

TOP ATTRACTIONS: ST. PETERSBURG

Palace Square and the State Hermitage Museum

Russia's other historic square is the heart of its imperial past, as well as the host to pivotal moments in Tsarist Russia's demise. On Bloody Sunday in 1905, palace guards shot dead hundreds of peaceful protestors here, sparking the first of Russia's revolutions. Housed in the pastel green and white Winter Palace, the Hermitage museum contains one of the world's most important art collections. On par with the Louvre, the collection is housed in what was once the tsars' family residence.

Peter and Paul Fortress

Peter the Great built the fortress in 1703 to defend Russia from the Swedes, making it the oldest building in the city. Inside the fortress walls, the cathedral's gilded 400-foot spire is one of the city's most recognizable landmarks.

St. Isaac's Cathedral

It took more than 40 years to complete the world's third-largest domed cathedral, now the dominant feature of St. Petersburg's skyline. Climb up the 262 steps of the colonnade to get a spectacular panoramic view of the city.

Nevsky Prospekt

This main drag is the center of the action (day or night) in Russia's second city. Frequently described by Dostoyevsky in *Crime and Punishment,* the street is often compared to Paris's Champs-Élysées and contains some of St. Petersburg's most impressive imperial Russian buildings, including the Stroganov Palace and the Kazan Cathedral. Don't miss the shopping arcade at Gostiny Dvor.

Alexander Nevsky Lavra

Peter the Great had this Russian Orthodox monastery built in 1710 and named it after the Russian prince who defeated invading Swedes in 1240. Today the lavra still contains impressive baroque churches and a neoclassical cathedral. Most visitors go to see the graves of several of Russia's greatest names, including Tchaikovsky and Dostoyevsky.

The State Museum

Housed in a former grand duke's palace, the Russian Museum (as it's known to locals) doesn't get the attention that the Hermitage collection does, but in most Russians' minds, it should. The museum is best known for its collection of paintings, which contains some of Russian art's greatest masters, such as Kandinsky and Chagall. The park behind the museum makes a lovely spot to reflect on what tsarist St. Petersburg might have been like.

Peterhof and Pushkin summer palaces

A hydrofoil cruise on the Gulf of Finland to Peterhof's cascading fountains and lavish gardens gets you in an imperial mood. The ornate, golden interiors and recently reconstructed Amber Room of the 18th-century Catherine's Palace at Pushkin (Tsarskoye Selo) offer a look into the extravagance of the Russian royal family.

QUINTESSENTIAL MOSCOW AND ST. PETERSBURG

Festivals

Rio and Venice may have their colorful carnivals, but Russians have something no less amazing up their sleeves—Maslenitsa, or Shrovetide, celebrated on the last week before Lent on the Julian calendar.

Today Shrovetide is a rambunctious outdoor spring festival where Russians indulge in dressing up and wild singing and dancing. Russian *blini* (pancakes), golden and round to symbolize the sun, are served in virtually every eatery across the nation during this week.

The White Nights Festival takes place in St. Petersburg at the end of June. Named in honor of the remarkably long days around the summer solstice, the festival features performances by Russia's top ballet, opera, and musical ensembles, as well as a massive fireworks display once the sun finally does set.

Epic Food

In Russian folk tales, amorous admirers ply their sweethearts with *pryaniki pechatnie* (printed gingerbreads). This ancient Russian culinary delight is a baked sweet pastry filled with honey or jam and flavored with spices; try it at any bakery.

While gingerbread might have done the trick in the olden days, caviar is one of the preferred methods of impressing your darling in modern Russia. It's sold everywhere, from grocery stores to local markets called *rynoks*. The best caviar comes from the beluga variety of sturgeon. It's silvery gray, uniform in size and shape, and tastes like a million bucks.

Another favorite is *kvas,* a refreshing nonalcoholic drink. Kvas, which literally translates as "sour drink," is made with fermented rye bread and is a renowned hangover remedy.

Experience Russia with all your senses and discover what "Russianness" means. We guide you through some of the most exciting pursuits, basic rituals, and beloved symbols of this country.

Vodka

Social lubricant and vice of choice for centuries, the national drink is produced by hundreds of brands and comes in many flavor varieties. A few of the best labels are Flagman, Russky Standart, Beluga, and Beloye Zoloto. If straight shots aren't your thing, flavored vodkas can help take the edge off. *Limonnaya*, slightly sweet lemon-flavor vodka, is particularly tasty, as is spicy *pertsovka*, infused with peppercorns and chilies.

At the bar, toasts such as *Vashe zdorovie!* (To your health!) and clinking glasses accompany every shot as do zakuski (appetizers) chasers, which vary from humble pickles to fine caviar. For reasons shrouded in the mists of time, empty bottles are considered bad luck and are immediately discarded or put on the floor, so watch your step and mind your manners.

Banya

Sweaty people whipping themselves with wet bundles of birch twigs in a room full of steam may sound like purgatory or sadomasochism. But for Russians the *banya* experience is the way to nirvana and longevity. Most people in Russia believe the excruciating wet heat of the banya makes you shed toxins ultrafast, through heavy sweating, and that it rejuvenates the internal organs. If you're willing to give it a try, Moscow's ornate Sandunovskiye bani is the gold standard.

The banya also appears in an ancient Russian legend. In the year 945, Olga, widow of Kievan prince Igor, lured his murderers—the elite corps of an East Slavic tribe of Drevlyane—into a banya and set the bathhouse on fire. Meet Russia's first saint.

IF YOU LIKE

Palaces and Estates

Lovers of all things beautiful and luxurious shouldn't miss Russia's imperial estates and palaces. Far from frugal, the tsars truly went all out when it came to their residences. Hiring the world's best architects and using literally tons of gold, marble, and semiprecious stones was only the beginning—these palaces and estates are truly Russian in size as well. Most were built close to Moscow and St. Petersburg as the tsars' summer residences and are therefore just a day trip away from the major cities.

Peterhof (Petrodvorets). Nicknamed the "Russian Versailles," the elaborate interiors, formal gardens, and beautiful fountains of Peter the Great's summer palace live up to their moniker. This is St. Petersburg's most famous imperial residence, located in the suburbs about 40 minutes away.

Pushkin (Tsarskoye Selo). This St. Petersburg palace, with its richly decorated baroque facade, was the favorite residence of the last Russian tsar, Nicholas II. Its main draw is the turquoise and gold Catherine's Palace, home to the sumptuous Amber Room.

Romanov Palace Chambers in Zaryadye. Located in Moscow's historic Kitai Gorod neighborhood, this palace-museum gives a taste of the luxurious boyar lifestyle, including period costume, furniture, and household items.

Kuskovo. Pastel pink and neoclassical in style, this estate just outside of Moscow was once the summer residence of the Sheremetyevs, one of Russia's wealthiest and most distinguished families. It also houses the celebrated Kuskovo State Ceramics museum.

Ballet

Classical ballet is the only art form that never really went dissident in Russia. The last tsar, Nicholas II, fell for the charms of ballerina Matilda Kshessinskaya, and from then on, through the Communist era and into the Putin years, ballet and especially ballerinas have been beyond criticism and free from oppression. As ballet has continued to thrive under state sponsorship, it's become an essential part of any official visit, as much a part of protocol as a trip to the war memorials.

Russian ballet is known for its exquisite blend of expressiveness, technique, and ethereal flair. Visiting ballet professionals envy both coordination and torso, the two strongest elements of Russian ballet training. Russian classical ballet, with its antique poetic charm, has preserved its precious legacy without becoming old-fashioned. New stars, such as the amazing Nikolai Tsiskaridze, inject new life into one of Russia's oldest and most respected arts.

Swan Lake. See this signature ballet at the Bolshoi (Moscow) or Mariinsky (St. Petersburg) theaters.

Sleeping Beauty. This marvel of 19th-century choreography has been meticulously restored in its original form at the Mariinsky Theatre in St. Petersburg.

The Nutcracker. The Bolshoi, Mariinsky, and other companies perform this Christmas classic year-round.

Vaganova Ballet Academy in St. Petersburg. Russia's most prestigious classical ballet academy is alma mater to Anna Pavlova, George Balanchine, and Mikhail Baryshnikov. It has a wonderful museum.

Exploring the Communist Legacy

Attitudes toward Soviet times are complex, with many people of all ages regarding them as "the good old days." Soviet themes and symbols are everywhere, from old monuments and inscriptions on buildings to the red star, which is still the symbol of the Russian armed forces.

Gulag Museum, Moscow. The small museum provides a harrowing look into one of Russia's most brutal histories. Tens of millions of Soviet citizens were subjected to the harsh life of these labor camps, which played a major role in the USSR's political oppression.

Lenin's Mausoleum, Moscow. Vladimir Lenin has lain in state here since his death in 1924.

Museum of the Contemporary History of Russia, Moscow. If you're a Soviet history buff, you'll enjoy this museum's collection of USSR propaganda posters, velvet flags, and socialist worker's medals.

The Seven Sisters, Moscow. The seven legendary skyscrapers that dominate Moscow's skyline were constructed just after World War II by Stalin as a symbol of Soviet power at the beginning of the Cold War.

Russian Political History Museum, St. Petersburg. The museum documents all aspects of the Communist past, from the paraphernalia of spying to propaganda.

All-Russian Exhibition Center, Moscow. This exhibition park, also known by its Russian acronym VDNkH, is the ultimate example of Soviet glorification. The center opened in 1959, with each former Soviet republic building its own pavilion to show off their achievements in agriculture, industrialization, and communization.

Porcelain and Folk Art

When Catherine the Great ordered her elaborate dinner service from the renowned Imperial Porcelain Manufacturer, porcelain was the exclusive preserve of aristocrats. But since then it's become almost every Russian's favorite gift.

In addition to porcelain, Russia also has a large number of other folk handicrafts, such as Gzhel ceramics, Palekh boxes, and, of course, the ubiquitous *matryoshka* nesting dolls.

Lomonosov Porcelain Factory. Arguably the most famous porcelain manufacturer in Russia, this St. Petersburg gem was founded in 1744 and owned for a time by the Romanovs. Its patented and instantly recognizable cobalt-blue pattern lends a distinctly Russian flavor to any event.

Palekh Boxes. These beautiful hand-painted lacquer boxes are handicrafts of the Golden Ring towns. Typically a fairy-tale scene adorns the box top, but images of landscapes, battle scenes, or even poetry can be found. They require about two months to create and the finer details are drawn using a special brush made from a squirrel's tail.

Gzhel Ceramics. First manufactured in the village of Gzhel outside Moscow in the 6th century, this famous white-and-blue pottery may be Russia's oldest folk art.

Matryoshka. Dating from 1890, these nesting dolls are a relatively new Russian handicraft. The largest wooden doll opens to reveal ever-smaller wooden figures inside. They usually depict red-cheeked, brightly dressed peasant women, although matryoshkas can be purchased featuring everyone from Soviet leaders to *Star Wars* characters.

RUSSIAN CRUISES

The Volga River is the longest river in Europe and it's so important to the Russian psyche that it is often referred to as the Mother Volga. Its majestic waterways wind through some of Russia's most scenic and historical cities, passing golden onion domes of centuries-old monasteries and white brick walls of kremlins that once held equal power to Moscow's.

Exploring the heart of Russia on a river cruise is a memorable—and relaxing—part of any trip to the region—and it's an excellent alternative to train or plane travel between Moscow and St. Petersburg. Cruises are usually eight to 14 days long, working their way along the Volga and Neva Rivers and their tributaries, and making stops along the way for guided tours of the sites.

Whether you start in Moscow or St. Petersburg, your cruise is likely to make the same stops and will include some of Russia's most impressive countryside scenes and classic architectural gems. Many of the cruise lines offer elaborate meals and accommodations, but the scenery is sure to be the highlight of the cruise.

Popular Stops

Uglich. This Golden Ring city was once a small princedom of its own until it was sold to the Duchy of Moscow in the 13th century. Today it's most famous as the site of the mysterious murder of Ivan the Terrible's son inside the kremlin walls. Apart from the kremlin, there are several other stunning examples of medieval Russian artchitecutre, including the Assumption three-tented church.

Yaroslav. One of Russia's most well-known Golden Ring cities, Yaroslav was founded in the 11th century by its namesake, Yaroslav the Wise. It is now a World Heritage Site known for its impressive examples of old Russian church architecture.

Kirillo-Belozersky Monastery. Saint Cyril founded this spectacular structure in the 14th century. It was once the largest monastery in Northern Russia.

Kizhi. This island in Lake Onega is famed for its breathtaking wooden churches with silver domes.

Planning Your Cruise

Most cruise lines offer tours between May and October. Prices range between $1,500 and $10,000, depending on the length of the cruise and the level of luxury. Most cruises can be booked directly through the cruise company or by a travel agent. Either way, plan well in advance since trips in high season can get booked up as much as a year in advance.

Viking Cruises and Volga Dream are two of the better known companies operating the Moscow-St. Petersburg route. Contact the companies or a travel agent for booking information and availability.

Viking Cruises ☎ 855/338-4546
⊕ www.vikingcruises.com.

Volga Dream ☎ 703/763-4614
⊕ www.volgadream.com.

BANYA

Few of Russia's traditions are as steeped in ritual than a trip to the banya, a sauna-style bathhouse where the steam is produced by throwing a steady supply of water over heated rocks. In fact, for many banya lovers a trip to the bathhouse is almost a religious experience, complete with birch twigs for self-flagellation (to open pores and promote circulation). The banya is a cultural tradition that became popular in the 17th century, when attending a communal bath was the only way for many Russians to stay clean. Today, it's still believed to have therapeutic benefits and is also valued as a place to relax, socialize, and even do business. Many find that a visit to one is a highlight of a trip to Russia.

BANYA BASICS

Keep in mind that men and women are separated, although families and couples can hire a private bath for use together, and soap is strictly forbidden (the steam is supposed to clean you). To prepare best for the Russian banya, go to the Sandunovskiye bani's website (⊕ *www.sanduny.ru*) and read the "secrets" section (available in English). Here are a few easy steps that will help you get the best steam possible:

1. Check yourself: If you have low or high blood pressure, a heart ailment, or some other health issue, you may want to stay away. Pregnant women and asthma sufferers are advised to do the same.

2. Check In: After paying the entrance fee, your valuables are handed to a special attendant who puts them in a locker and watches over them. Theft is rare, but you may be better off leaving valuables in a hotel safe. Tipping is customary, generally 50R–150R for the attendant, 300R–500R for a good masseur. You'll

then be given a towel and assigned a locker for your clothes. Bring a pair of flip-flops to walk around in.

3. Sweat it out: Banya fans believe that steaming helps combat respiratory problems, aids in circulation, and opens the pores to help rid you of "toxins"—that's why the steam room is kept at a toasty 90°C (194°F). Have a seat on one of the benches lining the walls. You can wrap yourself in a towel but most bathers in gender-segregated rooms go nude. Towels are, however, very useful for sitting on. And don't overdo it: 10–15 minutes is more than enough for your first time.

4. Cool down: Once you feel sufficiently steamed, dunk yourself in the pool, barrel, or bucket of icy water provided. If you don't get your body temperature down, your next trip to the steam room won't be much fun.

5. Relax: The banya will probably have a relaxation zone with couches, cold drinks, and even meals. While the ultra-Russian ambience might seem ideal for doing a shot or two of vodka, keep in mind that you'll be dehydrated. Stick to beer, juice, or best of all, water.

6. Repeat steps 3–5: Once you're rested, reenter the steam room. You'll likely sweat more this time. Repeat the process as many times as you see fit, and when you're done, give your neighbors the traditional post-banya salutation: *s lyokhim parom*—may your steam be light!

For information on individual banyas, ⇨ *Shopping in Chapter 6 for Moscow and Chapter 12 for St. Petersburg.*

MOSCOW AND ST. PETERSBURG MADE EASY

Airports and Visas

All foreigners, except citizens of some former Soviet republics, need a visa to visit Russia. An official invitation is required to apply for a visa. The invitation can be issued by a Russian citizen, or, more commonly, from an official tour agency or company. Processing fees, times, and additional visa application needs vary according to the issuing consulate or embassy. ⇨ *See Travel Smart Moscow and St. Petersburg for more details.*

Flying into Russia has gotten remarkably easier, thanks to several major U.S. and European carriers that now have direct flights from hub cities like New York, Atlanta, Washington, D.C., London, and Frankfurt. Moscow's airports make international travel even easier with airport trains that whisk you to the center of the city within 30–40 minutes. St. Petersburg's newly expanded Pulkovo Airport is catching up with the number of international carriers flying in.

Customs of the Country

Russians, particularly Muscovites, have a reputation for being cold and unfriendly, but extremely hospitable to guests invited into their homes. This is indeed the case, and should you be invited to a meal at a Russian friend's house be sure to say yes; you're likely to make friends for life. Russians tend to dress more formally than in the West. You won't see super baggy jeans even on teenagers. Men don't always wear a coat and tie, but they'll usually wear a jacket to upscale restaurants. Women dress femininely, and rarely adopt the casual, tomboyish look popular in the West. They take great pride in how they appear, even in winter when the attire is heavy fur coats, hats, scarves, and gloves; they often wear heels even when there's an inch of ice on the sidewalk.

Eating Out

While only the wealthy dine out in the Russian provinces, in Moscow and St. Petersburg you'll likely need a reservation for many restaurants. Most restaurants are open from noon to 11 pm, and Russians tend to dine around 8 pm or later. Your choices of cuisine are plentiful, but sushi has been all the rage for several years. It's not uncommon to see a separate sushi menu, even at an Italian restaurant. Business lunches are popular in the cities, and you can often get good deals on set menus that include a soup, salad, and main dish, as well as coffee or tea. Breakfasts tend to be smaller, except in some hotels that offer "American-style" breakfast. Otherwise, simple omelets, fried eggs, yogurt, and pastries are common menu items. Cafés are springing up everywhere and can easily provide a quick snack or simple meal.

Greetings

Russian men shake hands for business, and may throw one hand around the back of a friend for a brotherly, quick hug. Some Russian men have adopted the European habit of kissing a woman's cheeks, but it's not that common on the first meeting. Russians consider it bad luck to shake hands or pass anything across a threshold, so be sure to step inside first. And if you're presenting flowers to a Russian, remember that an even number of flowers in a bouquet is for funerals only, so skip the dozen roses.

Language

Russian is the national language. Outside of Moscow and St. Petersburg, you'll have a hard time getting by without knowing a little more than the basics. In the cities, however, many people, particularly those under 40, use English in their daily lives. In hotels and more popular restaurants, you're not likely to have a problem communicating the essentials. But public transportation and smaller museums and shops will be a challenge. While the Cyrillic alphabet looks daunting, it's actually not that difficult to learn enough to find your way around, particularly in the metro. Russians know their language is difficult and appreciate foreigners' efforts to try to speak it. In both cities, you're likely to run into people who are more than happy to practice their English with you.

Money and Shopping

The Russian ruble has had its ups and downs over the last decade, but is—for now—stable at about 30R to the $1. Moscow and St. Petersburg are expensive, and it's easy to run up high restaurant bills. Other things, like public transportation, are extremely affordable. Russian law dictates that all prices be quoted in rubles. Tip in rubles; smaller dollar bills are harder to exchange so most Russians would rather have their own currency. Using ATMs to withdraw cash from your bank account back home is preferable to using traveler's checks, which aren't always accepted outside of the larger hotels. You'll pay an 18% VAT on hotels and services, and Moscow tacks on an additional 1% to that rate. ⇨ *See Travel Smart Moscow and St. Petersburg for more details.*

Safety

Use caution in Moscow and St. Petersburg just as you would in any major metropolitan or urban center. Avoid walking alone on empty streets at night, particularly if you're a woman. As a foreigner, you'll be targeted at tourist spots by pickpockets and scam artists. Use common sense, and keep a close eye on your belongings, particularly in crowds. Moscow has been the scene of several terrorist bombings, so you should heed any warnings from public announcements about avoiding crowded, public spaces during these times, including the metro. However, the days of violent outbreaks between rival gangs in downtown Moscow are long over.

When to Go

The climate in Russia changes dramatically with the seasons. Both Moscow and St. Petersburg are best visited in May or late August. In Moscow, summers tend to be hot, and thunderstorms and heavy rainfall are common in July and August. In St. Petersburg, on the other hand, it rarely gets very hot, even at the height of summer, though you'll likely need an umbrella. Try to visit St. Petersburg during the White Nights (June to early July), when the northern day is virtually endless. In winter months both cities are covered in an attractive blanket of snow, but only the hardiest travelers should visit between late November and early February when the days are short, dark, and bitterly cold.

GREAT ITINERARIES

Russia may span 11 time zones and two continents, but it's still possible to take in the sights of two major cities and a bit of countryside in just a few days.

MOSCOW ITINERARY

Day 1: The Kremlin, Moscow

Devote this day to exploration of the Kremlin museums and cathedrals. Stroll through Red Square, St. Basil's Cathedral, and the shopping arcades of GUM. Admire the crowns of the Russian tsars at the Armory Chamber. If you're into treasures, don't miss the notorious 190-carat Orlov Diamond at the Diamond Fund. Going inside Lenin's Mausoleum is optional, but the novelty of it can make it worth it. Take a ride on the world's most opulent and ornate metro, with its marble columns, mosaic panoramas, elaborate chandeliers, and quirky Soviet-era monuments. If you have any energy left, spend the evening at the Bolshoi Theatre.

Logistics: The most fascinating metro stations are on the brown circle line (#5). Mayakovskaya and Ploshchad Revolutsii are also exciting. The Armory is closed on Thursday, and the Mausoleum, open Tuesday through Thursday, closes at 1 pm.

Day 2: Old Moscow

Discover old Moscow: wander through the winding narrow streets and visit the ancient churches of Kitai Gorod and pass through the cheerful Old Arbat. Make a pilgrimage to the sad and stately 1524 New Maiden's Convent, a refuge for exiled noble women in the tsarist era. Be sure to see the Romanov Palace Chambers in Zaryadye, the impressive 16th-century palace of the Romanov boyars, and the home of the Romanov family before they made it to the throne. End your day with a steam at a banya—the palatial, venerable Sandunovskiye bani has been considered the best in Russia since the 19th century.

Logistics: The Romanov palace is open to groups with reservations during the week and Saturday; Sunday is the best day for individual visitors. It costs from 1,700–2,100 rubles per person to visit Sandunovskiye bani.

Day 3: Tretyakov Gallery and Cathedral of Christ Our Savior

Spend the morning at the Tretyakov Gallery, which has one of the world's finest collections of Russian art. To feel the vigor of the new Moscow, head to the resurrected Cathedral of Christ Our Savior, demolished in 1931 and rebuilt from scratch.

ST. PETERSBURG ITINERARY

Day 1: St. Petersburg from Above and the Hermitage

For an invigorating start, climb the 260 steps to the colonnade of St. Isaac's Cathedral for a fabulous all-around panorama of the historical center. Then head to the State Hermitage Museum. But don't try to rush through this huge place all in one go. Make a list of your favorite things and return when you can. In the evening attend a performance at the Mariinsky Theatre, and take a short detour before the start of the show to visit the magnificent 18th-century St. Nicholas (patron saint of sailors) Cathedral.

Logistics: The Hermitage is free on the first Thursday of every month.

Day 2: Icons, Onion Domes, and Peter and Paul Fortress

Culture vultures should begin the day at the State Museum of Russian Art, home to the world's largest collection of Russian art, from icons to avant-garde to socialist realism. The brightly colored onion domes of the Church of the Savior on Spilled Blood are just around the corner. In good weather, spend an hour observing the city from the water on one of many boat trips on offer. Visit the Peter and Paul Fortress in the late afternoon. Sightseeing can be continued even during a meal. The Bessonnitsa ("Insomnia") restaurant next to the fortress overlooks the Hermitage, Admiralty, and Strelka.

Logistics: The quickest way to get to the Peter and Paul Fortress from Nevsky prospekt is to travel one stop by metro and get off at Gorkovskaya. When you get out of the station, turn right and walk through a little park until you reach the fortress.

Day 3: A Palace Visit

Devote the day to a trip to one of the former royal residences. Choose Pushkin (Tsarskoye Selo) in winter and Peterhof (Petrodvorets) in summer.

Logistics: It takes 30 minutes to get to Peterhof by hydrofoils departing in the summer from several quays along Dvortsovaya embankment, near the Hermitage and the Bronze Horseman.

TIPS

■ All top tourist sights and central metro stations in both cities are notorious for pickpockets. Be extra careful.

■ To save time and money, buy tickets for Moscow's Bolshoi and St. Petersburg's Mariinsky theaters online at ⊕ www.bolshoi.ru and ⊕ www.mariinsky.ru.

■ Be sure to bring an umbrella. According to the latest research, St. Petersburg boasts a pathetic 30–40 cloudless days a year.

■ Consider staying in one of St. Petersburg's more than 200 mini-hotels—small, 8- to 10-room guesthouses that offer an intimate alternative to the city's major hotels. Most are centrally located, reasonably priced, and if you travel in a group, you could have the property all to yourselves.

■ Alcohol counterfeiting, which can lead to alcohol poisoning, is a problem, so try to purchase vodka from a reputable-looking store or, if buying from a kiosk, check to see that the seal hasn't been broken.

■ In some museums, galleries, and palaces, such as the Tretyakov Gallery, you may be asked to put on plastic booties, similar to the kind surgeons wear, over your shoes before entering the gallery. When entering a Russian home, always remove your shoes at the entryway.

A WALK THROUGH MOSCOW'S HISTORIC CENTER

Moscow can at once overwhelm and awe. The city's sights are somewhat spread out, meaning you'll need a few days to see them. The outlined walk is designed to weave you around the city center for an introduction to the city, allowing you to pick and choose where to spend more time later.

Ulitsa Tverskaya: Moscow's Main Drag

The **statue** of Russia's most beloved poet, Pushkin, is a popular meeting spot for Muscovites and a great starting point. **Ulitsa Tverskaya**, in various forms, has been the main drag of Moscow for centuries. Shops and government buildings line the sides of its wide street, which is often blocked with Moscow's worst inhabitant—traffic. Stroll south, making sure to stop and browse in **Yeliseyevsky Grocery** at No. 14. Despite its ornate chandeliers and stained glass, the store's prices are reasonable, making it a favorite of Muscovites.

The **mayor's office** is just another block down, housed in a red building with white Corinthian columns across the street from a commanding **statue** of Moscow's founder, Yuri Dolgoruky.

Pereulok Kamergersky to Kuznetsky Most

You can while away a day sitting at one of this pedestrian street's sidewalk cafés. Making your way east, Kuznetsky Most is chock-full of interesting, prerevolutionary architecture, such as the art-nouveau apartment building at **3 Kuznetsky Most**. Look up at the colorful mosaics on the facade. The intersection at **ulitsa Petrovka** is the heart of Moscow's high-end shopping district. Take note of the Central Department Store, or **TsUM**, which has been completely remodeled and now serves as a hub for expensive Russian and foreign labels. Continue on Kuznetsky most as it winds up past more high-end shops, cafés, and student hangouts. **Secreti Bulochka** at ploshchad Vorovskovo is a cozy café with cakes and sandwiches if you need a break.

Ploshchad Lubyanskaya to Ploshchad Teatralnaya

On the northeast side of ploshchad Lubyanskaya, the yellow stone building was once the **KGB headquarters** and notorious **Lubyanka prison**. It remains the offices of Russia's security services, as well as the starting point for exploring Kitai Gorod's winding streets and trendy bars and restaurants. Down proyezd Teatralny, you'll pass **Destky Mir** (Children's World), a store dear to every Soviet childhood, as well as the luxury-shopping lane, **pereulok Tretyakovsky,** on your left. The 19th-century remodeled archway bumps up against 16th-century walls that once fortified the ancient Kitai Gorod. Farther down, the **Metropol Hotel** stands across from ploshchad Teatralnaya and the pink **Bolshoi Theatre.**

Ploshchad Teatralnaya to Red Square

You're now entering some of the oldest parts of Moscow. Facing Zhukov atop his horse, you can enter **Red Square** from the right or left of the red **State Historical Museum**. Either way, coming onto the square is breathtaking. The walls of the **Kremlin, St. Basil's Cathedral, Lenin's Mausoleum,** and **GUM** surround you as you absorb the centuries of history that have unfolded here.

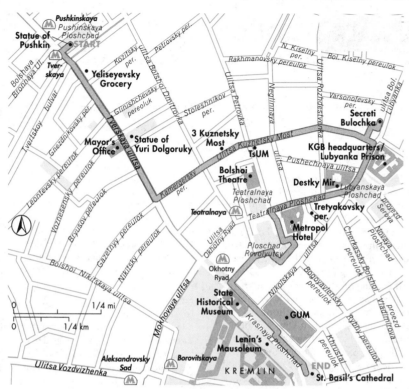

Highlights:	Posh shopping streets, people-watching from sidewalk cafés, prerevolutionary architecture, the former KGB headquarters, Bolshoi Theatre, and Red Square.
Where to Start:	Take the metro to Pushkinskaya, Tverskaya, or Chekovskaya stations and follow the signs to ploshchad Pushkinskaya (Pushkin Square) on ulitsa Tverskaya.
Length:	Between 2 and 4 hours, depending on shopping. About 2 1/2 miles in all.
Where to Stop:	Red Square
Best Time to Go:	Midday during the week for the best people-watching.
Worst Time to Go:	Shops can get crowded on weekends.
Best Views:	After the walk, get an impressive view of Red Square and ulitsa Tverskaya from the O2 Lounge (⌗ 3/5 ulitsa Tverskaya) at the top of the Ritz-Carlton.

A WALK THROUGH ST. PETERSBURG'S HISTORIC CENTER

Many of St. Petersburg's top attractions are located in the historical center of the city and within walking distance of each other. The following walk is designed to get you oriented in Peter the Great's "Window to the West."

Palace Square to the Church of the Savior on Spilled Blood

Visitors and locals use picturesque **Palace Square** and the central Alexander Column as a meeting point. The green and white **Winter Palace** occupies the north side of the square. Take a romantic stroll through the arch of the **General Staff Building** on the southern side of the square. Leave the square on the northeast corner via ulitsa Millionnaya. Be sure to get a shot taken with one of the muscular Atlases holding up the columns of the pink **State Hermitage Museum** here. The delicate bridge here is another good photo opportunity if you get the Neva River in the background through the arch. This area of the Moika River has seen the residents change over the centuries from wealthy nobles to beloved poets (don't miss **Pushkin's Apartment Museum**) and eventually Soviet-era communal flats, many of which have been redeveloped into luxurious apartments. The run-down pink **Imperial Stables** once housed the imperial horses. Wander around the colorful and impressive **Church of the Savior on Spilled Blood.**

Square of the Arts to Kazan Cathedral

Continue to the **Square of the Arts** (ploshchad Iskusstv). St. Petersburgers use the park in front of the **State Museum of Russian Art** for a peaceful lunch break. International and Russian bankers and movers-and-shakers frequent the über-luxurious **Grand Hotel Europe** for fine dining. The intersection with Nevsky prospekt is a good starting point for taking in the pulse of St. Petersburg's main drag. The street has a wide range of shopping and dining, as well as several historical churches and buildings, such as the **Kazan Cathedral.** Don't miss the stunning facade of the former Singer building, which now holds **Dom Knigi** (House of Books).

Along the Moika River to St. Isaac's Cathedral

Turn left onto Naberezhnaya moika past the **Stroganov Palace,** walk alongside the canal, and cross over **Krasny Most** (Red Bridge). The buildings on Bolshaya Morskaya once housed the city's banking and insurance industries. The golden dome of **St. Isaac's Cathedral** dominates the scene, but be sure to notice the **Siniy Most** (Blue Bridge) to the south of the square. It's the widest bridge in the city. North of the cathedral is the green area that makes up **Decembrists' Square** and the **Admiralty** gardens. Newlyweds often have their first photos taken in front of the **Bronze Horseman statue** depicting Peter the Great.

Neva riverbank to Strelka

Take advantage of nice weather with a stroll along the Admiralty embankment. Crossing over the river, you'll come onto **Vasilievsky Island.** Standing on the **Strelka** with its red columns behind you, you'll get a city view that includes the **Winter Palace** and the **Peter and Paul Fortress.**

Highlights:	Palace Square, the nobilities' houses along the Moika River, St. Isaac's Cathedral's golden dome, the golden spire of the Admiralty, Kazan Cathedral, and Nevsky prospekt.
Where to Start:	Take the metro to Nevsky prospekt and walk west. Palace Square will be on your right.
Length:	This 2 1/2-mile walk will take from 2 to 4 hours, depending on your pace and refueling stops.
Where to Stop:	Strelka on the tip of Vasilievsky Island.
Best Time to Go:	If it's summer, anytime since there's plenty of daylight.
Worst Time to Go:	A late evening stroll isn't optimal because stores and sites will be closed.
Best place to Refuel:	Sip cappuccinos and watch the world go by on Nevsky prospekt at Café Singer (⊠ 28 Nevsky pr.) in the old Singer building.

VODKA: A TASTE OF RUSSIA

The national drink is an inseparable part of Russian social life. Vodka is drunk everywhere, with the intention of breaking down inhibitions and producing a state of conviviality Russians refer to as *dusha-dushe* (soul-to-soul). When a Russian taps the side of his throat, beware: it's impossible to refuse this invitation to friendship. If you have a cold, sore throat, or any such minor ailment, don't be surprised if someone prescribes a shot of vodka—even for a hangover. The Russian belief in the curative and preventative powers of this drink is almost limitless.

Choosing Vodka

There are hundreds of brands of vodka in Russia, as a glance into any store will show. Some of these are rough and best left alone; three of the best are Flagman, Beluga, and Russky Standart, although there are many acceptable cheaper brands. Alcohol counterfeiting, which can lead to alcohol poisoning, is a big problem, so you should always purchase vodka from a reputable-looking store, and be sure the seal on the bottle hasn't been broken.

The Vodka Procedure

When you're drinking vodka, there's some etiquette involved. In North America and Great Britain, vodka is generally associated with cocktails and martinis. In Russia, mixing vodka with anything else is considered a waste, unless the mixer is beer, which produces a fearsome beverage known as *yorsh*. Vodka is meant to be gulped down in one go, not sipped. Since this can give you a bit of a kick, Russians always have some zakuski, or snacks (including pickles, herring, boiled potatoes, and black bread), to chase the shot. You may witness something called the "vodka procedure," which, if you want to try it yourself, goes roughly as follows. Prepare a forkful of food or chunk of bread. Inhale and exhale quickly, bringing the food to your nose. Breathe in and tip the vodka down your throat. Now breathe out again, and eat your food.

A Toast

Vodka shots (unlike beer and wine) are downed collectively, and always preceded by a toast. You'll score points if you propose toasts—it doesn't matter if they're in English, particularly if you wax long and eloquent. Drinking before a toast is considered a faux pas of the first order. Although you're expected to gulp down the first couple of shots, no one will mind if you take it a little easier after that—saying *choot'-choot'*, *pozhaluista* (just a little, please) is a polite way of asking for a smaller refill. Vodka is also considered predominantly a man's drink, so it's more acceptable for women to take things easier.

If all this sounds like an ordeal, rest assured that vodka drinking can be an extremely pleasurable experience, involving good food, great company, and a unique sense of mild inebriation that can last for hours. It's a memorable taste of Russia in more ways than one.

FLAVORS OF MOSCOW AND ST. PETERSBURG

The variety of international cuisine in Moscow and St. Petersburg might make you think that traditional Russian food ended with the Soviet Union. Luckily, sushi and ostrich burgers haven't completely replaced the hearty classic dishes that have satisfied everyone from tsars to Soviet collective farm workers. Russians know how to do comfort food right, and most meals consist of meat, potatoes, and a variety of typically Eastern European vegetables such as cabbage, beets, carrots, and onions. These days there are more choices for vegetarians, but don't expect a large variety. Russians don't tend to go overboard with spices, but do expect garlic, onions, dill, and mayonnaise to play a large part in your flavor palate. What Russian dishes lack in exotic ingredients they make up for in satisfying taste.

Zakuski

If you're lucky enough to be invited to a Russian's house for a meal, you'll be greeted by a tableful of *zakuski,* or appetizers. They're usually eaten before the main meal or soup, and preferably accompanied with vodka. A few typical zakuski you might find on the menu at Russian restaurants are *olivie* salad—think potato salad with pickles, boiled eggs, green peas, and lots of mayonnaise. Another staple salad is *shuba,* a layered combination of herring, boiled eggs, beets, carrots, potatoes, and, of course, mayonnaise. This is sometimes called herring in shuba, or *selyodka pod shuboy,* which roughly translates as "herring under a fur coat." On special occasions, you might be offered some *salo,* which is cured pork fat. Russians say the best salo comes from Ukraine. It looks like lard, but tastes like bacon and is the perfect chaser after a shot of peppered vodka.

Pelmeni

Every Eastern European nation seems to have its own form of the dumpling. Russians call them *pelmeni*, and they're sometimes referred to as Siberian pelmeni. The flour-based dough is stuffed with a mixture of meat (usually beef and pork mixed together) and onions, and then boiled. They're generally served with a dollop or *smetana*, or sour cream, on top. Don't confuse pelmeni with Ukrainian *vareniki*, which can be stuffed with potatoes and mushrooms, cabbage, cottage cheese, or cherries. It's not unusual to see both vareniki and pelmeni on the same menu.

Borscht

The beet-based soup is packed with carrots, onions, potatoes, meat, and sometimes beans. It's not as thick as stew, but it's nonetheless a good remedy for tired legs after a long walk around the city, particularly in winter. Borscht is usually followed by a main course, although a large bowl is sometimes filling enough on its own. Whisk in a heaping spoonful of sour cream and slurp it down with a slice of brown bread.

Georgian Cuisine

Russia and Georgia may have heated territorial disputes, but there's one thing they can agree on—Georgian cuisine is delicious and a favorite of most Russians. Both Moscow and St. Petersburg have plenty of Georgian restaurants. Be sure to try *khachapuri* (a baked bread stuffed with salty cheese) and eggplant slices stuffed with walnuts, followed by succulent kebabs. Georgia also makes good wine, both dry and sweet.

EXPLORING
MOSCOW

Updated by
Sabra Ayres

Moscow is a city of tremendous power and energy. Hulking gothic towers loom over broad avenues that form a sprawling web around the Kremlin and course with traffic day and night. The Soviet past looms large, but the city embraces capitalism with gusto. Although Muscovites are protecting some of their architectural heritage, they're also creating a new, often controversial legacy in the form of soaring skyscrapers and shopping malls. With a population of more than 11 million, Moscow is Russia's largest city and, indeed, the largest—and one of the most rapidly changing—cities in Europe.

Founded in the 12th century as the center of one of several competing principalities, Moscow eventually emerged as the heart of a unified Russian state in the 15th century. One hundred years later it had grown into the capital of a strong and prosperous realm, one of the largest in the world. But under Peter the Great (1672–1725), the city was demoted. Influenced by his exposure to the West, Peter deliberately turned his back on the old traditions and established his own capital—St. Petersburg—on the shores of the Baltic Sea. Yet Moscow continued to thrive as an economic and cultural center, and more than 200 years later, within a year of the Bolshevik Revolution in 1917, the young Soviet government restored its status as the nation's capital.

The city became the undisputed political and ideological center of the vast Soviet empire. And even though it has been nearly two decades since that empire broke apart, the city retains its political, industrial, and cultural sway as Russia's capital. It's the home of some of the country's most renowned cultural institutions, theaters, and film studios. It's also the country's most important transportation hub—even today many flights to the former Soviet republics are routed through Moscow's airports.

To fortify and spur forward Russia's giant economy, the government and city's business communities actively court outside investments and set ambitious economic agendas. For visitors, this translates into a modern, fast-paced city with an increased availability of Western-style services and products. But even as Moscow becomes a hub of international business activity, it's determinedly holding onto its Russian roots. Restaurant kitchens, many of which strove to satisfy Russians' thirst for foreign tastes in the '90s, are turning back to the country's native cuisine, serving gourmet borscht and delicious *pelmeni* (bite-sized dumplings). Retro Soviet nostalgia is chic with young hipsters who were barely born before the Soviet Union split up. Business deals may no longer be made over a banquet table and sealed with a shot of

TOP REASONS TO GO

See the spectacle of Red Square at Night: The heart of Russia is transformed at night by the glowing red stars atop the Kremlin towers and the lit-up fairy-tale onion domes of St. Basil's Cathedral.

Choose from Chekhov to Tchaikovsky: Tapping into the thriving arts scene in Moscow is easy; fitting in your many options—a play at the Moscow Art Theater, opera or ballet at the Bolshoi, or art at the Tretyakov Gallery—is the hard part.

Find the Hidden City: If you can conquer your fear of getting lost, wandering through the intricate side streets can be a rewarding experience. You may accidentally bump into architectural wonders, like the Melnikov House, hidden away on pereulok Krivoarbatsky, or find a quiet square or park you can call your own.

Eat well: Whether sharing drinks and *zakuski* (appetizers) with friends, grabbing a *blin* (thin pancake) on the run, or sitting down to a bowl of borscht and *pelmeni* (meat dumplings), dining in Moscow is a heartwarming experience.

Get fashionable: Moscow offers more for shoppers than just stacking dolls and Soviet-era souvenirs. Russian designers are making a name for themselves, and the boutiques around the city carry many original designs.

vodka, but Muscovites take hospitality seriously, as a visit to any private home will show you. This tradition of welcoming with open arms has persisted alongside a less generous Soviet mentality, however: stubborn indifference remains the default attitude of staff at some hotels, restaurants, and stores. This is gradually fading, but you might still be faced with surly ticket sellers or even ungracious hotel employees, especially if trying to communicate strictly in spoken English.

As Russia enters its third decade of post-Soviet life, development and reconstruction are at an all-time high. Parts of Moscow, especially within the Boulevard Ring (*Bulvarnoye Koltso*), are now clean, safe, and well kept. Many of these buildings are designed to be harmonious with the ancient Russian style, but there are a growing number of shockingly modern steel-and-glass office towers, particularly in central Moscow. The decades ahead promise more change and hurdles to overcome. But this city has survived devastating fires, an invasion by Napoléon, and more than half a century of alternating demolition and breakneck construction by the Soviets. Moscow is ready for anything.

ORIENTATION AND PLANNING

GETTING ORIENTED

The best way to orient yourself in Moscow is via the city's efficient and highly ornate metro system. ■TIP→ **Most of the sights in this chapter are located on or within the metro's brown line (#5) which circles the old historic center.** Learning the Cyrillic alphabet will prove infinitely useful in helping you to distinguish between metro stops. When asking locals for directions, it's often more fruitful to discuss locations by the nearest metro stop than by neighborhood names.

Moscow is laid out in a series of concentric circles that emanate from its heart—the Kremlin/Red Square area. This epicenter, encircled by the tree-lined Boulevard Ring (*Bulvarnoye Koltso*), is rich with palaces and churches. Although the individual streets that make up the Boulevard Ring have different names, most of them have the word for boulevard, *bulvar*, in their names. The Boulevard Ring passes by stations Arbatskaya, Pushkinskaya, and Chistye Prudy on its way around the city. Much of your time is likely to be spent near metro stop Pushkinskaya, a few hundred yards up ulitsa Tverskaya, the city's main street, which goes north directly from the Kremlin.

Marking the outer edge of the city center is the Garden Ring (*Sadovoe Koltso*), a wide boulevard that has lost all the trees for which it was once famous. The metro's brown (#5) line almost follows the route of the Garden Ring. Metro stations Smolenskaya, Barrikadnaya, Mayakovskaya, Sukharevskaya, Krasniye Vorota, Taganskaya, Paveletskaya, Oktyabrskaya, and Park Kultury are all located on the Garden Ring road.

The Kremlin and Red Square. The ancient heart of the city stands out for its grand palaces, towers, and some of the country's most sacred churches, including St. Basil's and Assumption Cathedral. In addition to the historical sights, there are also modern shopping centers and a lively atmosphere in this most central area.

Kitai Gorod. North and east of the Kremlin/Red Square area and within the Boulevard Ring, this neighborhood began as an outgrowth of the Kremlin. Its sights include the Bolshoi Theatre and Sandunovskiye Bani, as well as some of the city's best restaurants.

Ulitsa Tverskaya. North of the Kremlin is the famous northern road to St. Petersburg, ulitsa Tverskaya, which extends from the Kremlin through the Boulevard Ring and out to the Garden Ring. This is Moscow's main shopping street. The Museum of the Contemporary History of Russia, just north of the Boulevard Ring, provides an interesting look at Moscow's evolution.

Ulitsa Bolshaya Nikitskaya. This main thoroughfare is lined with some stunning old mansions and the Tchaikovsky Conservatory. The area around Patriarch's Ponds (Patriarshy Prudy) is full of posh cafés and shops and reminiscent of New York's Greenwich Village.

The Arbat. Two streets radiating out of the Kremlin to the west are the *Stary Arbat* (Old Arbat) and the *Novy Arbat* (New Arbat). The Stary Arbat is referred to by Russians simply as "the Arbat" and is a cobblestone pedestrian street with cafés, street performers, and all manner of souvenir shops. Novy Arbat is a modern thoroughfare with shopping malls and upscale restaurants.

The Kropotkinsky District. Southwest of the Kremlin, the Kropotkinsky District is home to the monumental Church of Christ Our Savior, where the Russian Patriarch leads mass on the most important holidays. Also here are the venerable Pushkin Museum of Fine Arts and the Tolstoy Memorial Museum.

Zamoskvoreche. This area is best known for its many churches, especially along the long north–south street Bolshaya Ordynka. Also here is the Tretyakov Gallery, the country's best art museum and the entrance to the recently revamped Gorky Park.

Moscow Outskirts. Four magnificent monasteries are the main points of interest south and east of the city center. The can't-miss among them is New Maiden's Monastery, with its colorful battle towers and peaceful pond. To the west and south, parks and former estates outside the city give you a glimpse of the verdant Russian countryside. Perfect for a visit on a day with fine weather, these spots draw masses of picnicking Muscovites all summer long. For those on a tight schedule, and with an interest in World War II, the sprawling Victory Park is just a quick trip from the center on the Moscow metro.

PLANNING

WHEN TO GO

Far and away the best time to visit Moscow is in the late spring or summer. During the months of May to September, the weather is usually balmy, with averages in the 70s. It should be said that in recent years, it has also become uncomfortably and even dangerously hot at stretches. Even so, the warm temperatures and long days are ideal for enjoying outdoor terraces at restaurants, music festivals at countryside estates, and lounging in the city's parks. From October to April, the weather is unpredictable, usually with a lot of rain and snow, making it inconvenient for touring the city on foot.

GETTING HERE AND AROUND

AIR TRAVEL

As the most important transportation hub in the Commonwealth of Independent States (CIS, a quasi-confederation of states that includes most of the former Soviet Union), Moscow has several airports. Most international flights from the United States arrive at Sheremetyevo, about 29 km (18 miles) north of the city center. One of the most modern airports in Russia when it was built in 1979, Sheremetyevo's terminals have undergone a huge upgrade. There are five passenger terminals, known by letters B through F; most international flights are served by terminals E and F. (There's a terminal A as well, used for business air traffic.) The Russian carrier Aeroflot operates flights from

Sheremeyevo to just about every capital of Europe, as well as to Canada and the United States, and codeshares with Delta Airlines. The airline also serves numerous domestic destinations.

Domodedovo, one of the largest airports in the world by passenger volume and Russia's busiest, is some 48 km (30 miles) southeast of Moscow. British Airways, Swiss, and Lufthansa fly in and out of Domodedovo. Flights also depart from Domodedovo to the republics of Central Asia and other parts of Russia.

Vnukovo, 29 km (18 miles) southwest of the city center, has become more popular in the last several years after an extensive upgrade. Several international carriers, including Turkish Airlines, Virgin, and Lufthansa, use the airport. Vnukovo also serves regional flights to Georgia, the southern republics, and Ukraine.

> ## STALIN'S EIGHTH SISTER?
>
> You may notice a new stepsister to the Seven Gothic Sisters on the drive in from Sheremetyevo airport. Triumph Palace, near the Sokol metro station, is a modern copy of the original skyscrapers. This expensive block of apartments, some of the tallest residential buildings in Europe at 866 feet (264 meters), has been criticized by architects, but its huge size and similarity to the original buildings that Stalin built will likely make it another city symbol.

For general information on arriving international flights, call the airline directly or check the airports' websites—all three airports have made theirs more user friendly. Calling the airports usually takes longer and fewer people speak English.

It's necessary to pass through metal detectors and bag scanners at the entrances to terminals at all three airports. As a result, you should budget extra time when departing (up to three hours for international flights), as the lines to enter the buildings, as well as those at ticket counters, passport control, and security, can be long.

Airport Information Domodedovo. This easy-to-use airport is located about 48 km (30 miles) south of the city center. The Aeroexpress train from Paveletsky train station gets you to the airport terminal in 40 minutes, allowing you to avoid the heavy traffic on the shosse Kashirskoe. Several major international carriers fly into Domodedova (DME), including British Airways, Swiss Air, and Lufthansa. Flights to other parts of Russia and the former Soviet republics of Central Asia also depart from here. The website has up-to-date arrival and departure information. ⊠ *Domodedovo* ☎ *495/933–6666* ⊕ *www.domodedovo. ru/en.* **Sheremetyevo.** Most direct flights from the U.S. arrive at Russia's second busiest airport (after Domodedovo), including those on Delta and its codeshare partner, Aeroflot. Sheremetyevo (SVO) is also the main hub for Aeroflot's domestic destinations, most of which leave from the new Terminal D. The Aeroexpress train connects the airport with Belorussky train station and takes about 35 minutes each way. ⊠ *Khimki* ☎ *495/578–6565, 800/100–6565* ⊕ *www.svo.aero/en.* **Vnukovo.** More international carriers, such as Virgin and Turkish Airlines, have begun flying into Vnukovo (VKO), and some of Luftahansa's flights now use the airport. With less passenger travel than the other two major Moscow airports, the facilities can seem a bit more user-friendly. It's easy to reach via the Aeroexpress train to and from Kievsky train station. ✉ *12 ul. 1st Reysovaya* ☎ *495/937–5555* ⊕ *www.vnukovo.ru/eng.*

TRANSFERS   You can make arrival a lot easier by arranging in advance for your transfer from the airport. Most hotels will provide airport transfers (for a fee, usually about 4,500R) upon advance request by a phone call or fax (which you should confirm). Various private taxi companies charge considerably less (1,500R to 2,000R, depending on the airport), usually have English-speaking drivers available, and can be booked online ahead of time.

If you don't have many bags and feel comfortable navigating public transport straight off the plane, consider using the airports' newly spiffed-up Aeroexpress trains to get into the city. You'll see arrows pointing to the small stations from which they leave when you exit customs at each airport. A regular ticket (320R) takes you to one of the city's central train stations—Belorussky station from Sheremetyevo, Paveletsky station from Domodedovo, and Kievsky station from Vnukovo—from which you can take a cab or the metro to wherever you're staying. When heading to the airport on these trains, you can sometimes check into your flight at the train station (it depends on which airline you're using) and even hand off any baggage you want to check.

There are plenty of unofficial gypsy cabs available at the airports, but there's always a risk of being swindled. (If you do take one, be sure to bargain, bargain, bargain.) It's better to use the services offered on the airports' ground floors. These private firms are less risky, they can provide you with a receipt, and you may find their prices more reasonable than those of the gypsy cabs. The prices are still not cheap, however, ranging from 1,500–2,000R depending on your destination. Traveling to the airport from the city is cheaper. It's best to book a taxi in advance to do this. The rate is typically 1,000R–1,500R.

The cheapest options for getting to and from the city's airports are buses and *marshrutka* (minibuses), which shuttle back and forth from various outlying metro stations. Those going to Sheremetyevo leave from metro station Rechnoy Vokzal (at the northern end of the green line); and those going to Domodedovo leave from metro station Domodedovskaya (also on the green line but in the south). Those headed to Vnukovo leave from metro station Yugo-Zapadnaya, a name that translates as South-West, as it's at the southwestern end of the red metro line. It can be confusing trying to find the next bus leaving, but you can usually just follow someone else carrying luggage once you're outside the metro station. The buses each take about 30 minutes to get to the different airports. Traffic is unpredictable, though, and it can take longer, sometimes significantly so. The road to Sheremetyevo is particularly notorious for traffic, often becoming gridlocked for hours during the commuter rushes in morning and early evening.

Aeroexpress. The website provide schedules and ticket information for this handy service that links Paveletsky train station with Domodedovo airport, Belorussky station with Sheremetyevo airport, and Kievsky station with Vnukovo airport. ⊕ *www.aeroexpress.ru.*

BOAT TRAVEL

Moscow has a river-taxi service that runs from Kiev train station to the Southern River Terminal from April to October, with stops at Gorky Park and the bottom of Sparrow Hills. The open-top boats are more of a tourist attraction than a form of commuter transport, although they can beat the traffic snarls. Tickets cost 300R for adults and 150R for children, and the timetable can be found at the ferry stops. Trips last about 1½ hours, and it's possible to buy drinks and snacks on board. The same company organizes longer tours in and around Moscow.

BUS, TRAM, AND TROLLEY TRAVEL

You're unlikely to want to travel by long-distance bus in Russia, since trains are frequent, cheap, and reliable. Most bus services go to provincial towns that lack good rail links.

For travel within Moscow, the municipal buses, trams, and trolleys all use the same tickets (30R), which you can buy in special kiosks, usually near metro stations. The tickets come in various denominations, ranging from one ride to 60 rides. You have to get on at the entrance next to the driver and put the ticket through an electronic turnstile, front-side down. Single-ride tickets are valid for a ride on one bus only; if you transfer to another bus or to a tram or trolley, you must pay another fare.

At metro stations, you can purchase smart cards in various denominations for multiple uses, including the "Troika" card introduced in 2013, which is good for all forms of city transportation both above and below ground. Another version of the smart card allows unlimited travel on buses, trams, trolleys, and the metro within 24 hours for 200R or 11 trips for 300R. Buses, trams, and trolleys operate from 5:30 am to 1 am, although service in the late-evening hours and on Sunday tends to be unreliable. Trolleys are connected to overhead power lines, trams to metal rails.

Newspaper kiosks sell a map that shows all of Moscow's transport routes: it's called *karta Moskvy so vsem transportom.*

The tram can be a fun way to take in part of the city while also resting your legs. A nice tram ride is the 39, which goes from Universitet metro station on the red line in the southwest of the city to Chistiye Prudy metro station, past Donskoy Monastery and Danilovsky Market. The B trolley bus runs around the Garden Ring and can be a pleasant way to see the Ring when the traffic's not heavy.

Bus, Tram, and Trolley Contacts Mosgortrans. This organization runs all the city's bus, trolley, and tramcar lines. The website has schedules and maps in Russian only. ☎ 495/950-4204 ⊕ www.mosgortrans.com. **Moskovsky Avtovokzal** (*Moscow Central Bus Station*). This is Moscow's central bus station, serving towns and cities in the oblast as well as those farther out. The website is Russian only. ✉ 2 ul. Uralskaya, Eastern Outskirts ☎ 499/748–8029, 499/748–8964 ⊕ turizm. mostransavto.ru Ⓜ Shchelkovskaya.

CAR TRAVEL

You can reach Moscow from Finland and St. Petersburg by taking the Helsinki–St. Petersburg Highway through Vyborg and St. Petersburg and continuing from there on the Moscow–St. Petersburg Highway. Using a car for getting around Moscow isn't advised, though, as driving in Russia is invariably more of a hassle than a pleasure. Roads are very poorly maintained, and many streets in the city center are one-way. Renting a car can also be much more expensive than in the U.S. To top it all off, Moscow traffic police are infamous for seeking out bribes, especially from foreigners, and they'll often demand that you pay a *shtraf* (fine) whether you have all the proper documents or not. If you do decide to drive, be sure to carry a notarized translation of your current license.

METRO TRAVEL

The Moscow metro, which opened in 1935, ranks among the world's finest public transportation systems. With more than 300 km (186 miles) of track, the Moscow metro carries an estimated 8 million passengers daily. Even though it scrapes by with inadequate state subsidies, the system continues to run efficiently, with trains every 50 seconds during rush hour. It leaves New Yorkers green with envy.

If you're not traveling with a tour group or if you haven't hired your own driver, taking the metro is the best way to get around the Russian capital. You'll be doing yourself a big favor and saving yourself a lot of frustration if you learn the Russian (Cyrillic) alphabet well enough to be able to transliterate the names of the stations. This will come in especially handy at transfer points, where signs with long lists of the names of metro stations lead you from one major metro line to another. You should also be able to recognize the entrance and exit signs *(⇨ English–Russian Vocabulary, at the end of this book).*

Pocket maps of the system are available at newspaper kiosks and sometimes from individual vendors at metro stations. Be sure that you obtain a map with English transliterations in addition to Cyrillic. If you can't find one, try any of the major hotels. Plan your route beforehand and have your destination written in Russian and its English transliteration to help you spot the station. As the train approaches each station, the station name will be announced over the train's public-address system; the name of the next station is given before the train starts off. Reminders of interchanges and transfers are also given. All trains have the transliterated names of stations on line maps, and newer trains have electronic displays next to the doors that show the names of all the stations on the line and the train's progress.

Stations are built deep underground (they were built to double as bomb shelters); the escalators are steep and run fast, so watch your step. If you use the metro during rush hour (8:30–10 am, 5–7 pm), be prepared for some pushing and shoving. In a crowded train, just before a station, you're likely to be asked, *"Vy vykhódíte?"* or whether you're getting off at the next station. If not, you're expected to move out of the way. Riders are expected to give up seats for senior citizens and small children.

FARES AND SCHEDULES The metro is easy to use and amazingly inexpensive. Stations are marked with a large illuminated "M" sign and are open daily 5:30 am to 1 am. The fare is the same regardless of distance traveled, and there are many stations where lines connect and you may transfer for free. You purchase a magnetic smart card (available at all stations) for 1, 5, 10, 20, or more journeys and hold it near the yellow circle on the right side of the entry gate. Wait until you see the red light replaced by a green one, signaling that your card has registered, then walk through.

A single ride costs 30R and discounts are available for multiple-journey cards—for instance, unlimited travel on the metro as well as on buses, trams, and trolleys within 24 hours for 200R, or 11 trips for 300R. You can purchase smart cards at any metro station.

TAXI TRAVEL

Exercise caution when using taxis. There are standard taxis of various makes and colors, but professional ones all have taxi lights on top. Official taxis also have a "T" and checkered emblem on the doors (but there aren't many of them). When you enter a cab, check to see if the meter is working; if it isn't, agree on a price beforehand. Everyone with a car is a potential taxi driver in Moscow, and there are huge masses of people who make extra money or even their entire livelihood driving people in their private vehicles (often beat-up Soviet models), so you never have to wait long for someone to stop. This is generally a safe practice, but it's best to avoid it, particularly if you don't speak Russian, as most drivers will try to swindle you. Some private drivers also don't know the city very well and may not be able to reach your destination without directions from you. If you do choose to take a ride in an ordinary car, take some precautions: never get in a car with more than one person inside, and if the driver wants to stop for another fare, say no or get out of the car.

The easiest thing to do if you want a cab is to order one by phone or through your hotel. Moscow has numerous cab companies, most with 24-hour service. There's sometimes a delay, but a cab usually arrives within the hour. If you order a cab in this way, you usually pay a set rate for the first 20–40 minutes (around 350R–500R) and then a set rate per minute (usually around 10R per minute) after that. Always ask for an approximate price when you telephone for a cab. Unfortunately, most operators don't speak English, so when possible ask your hotel concierge (or a restaurant's maître d') to order one for you. Formula Taxi provides city cabs (typically silver Renault sedans) as well as airport service from hotels or private residences. Novoye Zhyoltoye Taksi (New Yellow Taxi) is a cab firm with a good reputation. Yandex Taxi is a smartphone app and a website that allows you to locate the closest cab, depending on your location.

Taxi Contacts Formula Taxi ☎ *495/777–5777* ⊕ *www.formula-taxi.ru/en.* **Novoye Zhyoltoye Taksi.** This is one of the larger taxi companies operating in Moscow and St. Petersburg. Prices start at 22 rubles a kilometer. Bookings can be made on the phone or via the online system. ☎ *495/940–8888* ⊕ *www. nyt.ru/en.* **Welcome Taxi.** English-speaking drivers make airport pick-ups and trips around the city. They'll purchase a mobile SIM card for you and meet you at the airport with it. Bookings may be made online. ☎ *499/922–0674, 499/553–0158* ⊕ *welcometaxi.ru.* **Yandex Taxi.** This site, with a smartphone app, allows customers to book a taxi online. The system uses Yandex maps to locate your phone, and then allows you to choose a taxi service that's closest to your location. The site is in Russian, but you can type your location in English. ⊕ *taxi.yandex.ru.*

2

TRAIN TRAVEL

Moscow is the hub of the Russian railway system, and the city's several railway stations handle nearly half a billion passengers annually. There are several trains daily to St. Petersburg, and overnight service is available to Kiev, Helsinki, Riga, and Tallinn. All the major train stations have a connecting metro stop, so they're easily reached by public transportation. The most important stations are Belorussky station, for trains to Belarus, Lithuania, Poland, Germany, and France; Kazansky station, for points south and to Central Asia and Siberia; Kievsky station, for Kiev and western Ukraine, Moldova, Slovakia, the Czech Republic, and Hungary; Kursky station, for eastern Ukraine, the Crimea, and southern Russia; Leningradsky station, for St. Petersburg, northern Russia, Estonia, and Finland; Paveletsky station, for eastern Ukraine and points south; Rizhsky station, for Latvia; and Yaroslavsky station, for points east, including Mongolia and China. Trains to Vladivostok on the Trans-Siberian Railway depart from Yaroslavsky station. Both overnight trains and high-speed day trains depart from Leningradsky and Kursky stations for St. Petersburg. The daytime high-speed Sapsan trains take four hours and leave at various times throughout the day. Of the numerous overnight trains, the most popular is train number 2, the *Krasnaya Strela* (Red Arrow), which leaves Moscow at 11:55 pm and arrives the next day in St. Petersburg at 7:55 am. The *Grand Express* has a similar schedule, departing Moscow at 11:40 pm and arriving in St. Petersburg at 8:35 am. There are half a dozen categories of accommodation; the higher-class compartments have showers, and some have satellite TV and other amenities.

FARES AND SCHEDULES Note that although there are phone numbers for each station, it's all but impossible to get through to them. If you want to check schedules and ticket prices ahead of time, you can use the booking function on the Russian Trains website. The system can be finicky, but should improve over time. You can also purchase tickets at the railway stations, but expect long lines and brusque clerks, most of whom have little patience for those who speak no Russian. The easier route is to ask your hotel for help, as they typically have a connection with a travel agency who can arrange tickets for you. In either case, have your passport or a photocopy with you. You need it to buy tickets (they print your name and your passport number on the ticket), and you'll need to show your passport to the attendant on the train.

Train Information **Russian Railways.** Every train station in Moscow has a ticket counter, and other ticket agencies are located around the city. You can also buy tickets online, but only through the Russian pages of the website. ✉ *5 pl. Komsomolskaya* ☎ *800/775-0000* ⊕ *www.rzd.ru* Ⓜ *Chistiye Prudy.*

Train Station Information **Belorussia station** (*Belorussky Vokzal*). ✉ *pl. Tverskaya Zastava, Northern Outskirts* ☎ *495/266-0300* Ⓜ *Belorusskaya.* **Kazan station** (*Kazansky Vokzal*). ✉ *pl. Komsomolskaya, Northern Outskirts* ☎ *495/266-2300* Ⓜ *Komsomolskaya.* **Kiev station** (*Kievsky Vokzal*). ✉ *pl. Kiyevsky, Krasnaya Presnya* ☎ *499/240-7071* Ⓜ *Kievskaya.* **Kursk station** (*Kursky Vokzal*). ✉ *pl. Kursky, Eastern Outskirts* ☎ *495/266-5310* Ⓜ *Kurskaya.* **Leningrad station** (*Leningradsky Vokzal*). ✉ *pl. Komsomolskaya, Northern Outskirts* ☎ *495/262-9143* Ⓜ *Komsomoskaya.* **Pavelets station** (*Paveletsky Vokzal*). ✉ *pl. Paveletskaya, Southern Outskirts* ☎ *495/950-3700*

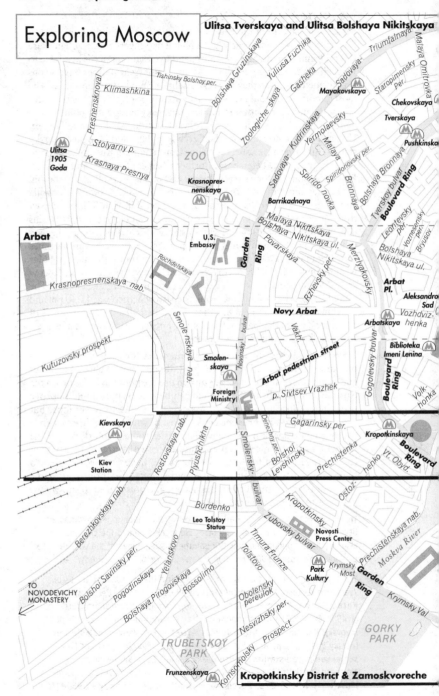

Exploring Moscow

Ulitsa Tverskaya and Ulitsa Bolshaya Nikitskaya

Arbat

Kropotkinsky District & Zamoskvoreche

2

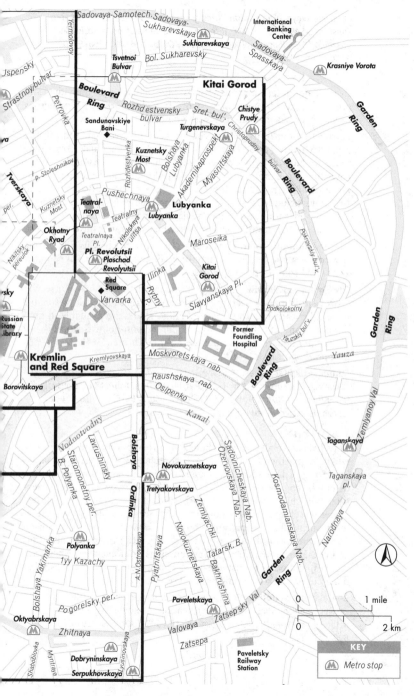

International
Banking
Center

(M) Krasniye Vorota

Sadovaya-Samotech. Sadovaya-
Sukharevskaya

(M) Sukharevskaya

Tsvetnoi
Bulvar

Bol. Sukharevsky

Sadovaya-
Spasskaya

Yermolovoy

Jspensky

Strastnoybulvar

Kitai Gorod

**Boulevard
Ring**

Rozhdestvensky
bulvar

Sret. bul'.

Chistye
Prudy

Garden
Ring

Petrovka

Sandunovskiye
Bani ◆

Turgenevskaya (M)

Christoprudny

ya

Rozhdestvenka

Kuznetsky
Most

Bolshaya
Lubyanka

Akademikaprospekt

Myasnitskaya

bulvar
**Boulevard
Ring**

P. Stoleshnikov

Tverskaya

Kuznetsky
Most

per.

Pushechnaya

Teatral-
naya (M)

Teatralny

Teatralnaya
Pl.

Nikolskaya
ulitsa

Lubyanka

Lubyanka (M)

Pokrovsky bul'v.

Okhotny
Ryad (M)

Pl. Revolutsii
(M) Ploschad
Revolyutsii

Maroseika

Nikitsky
pereulok

Ilinka

Red
Square ◆

Rybny
P.

Kitai
Gorod

Slavyanskaya Pl.

Podkolokolny

Yauzsky bul'v.

Varvarka

sky

Russian
State
.ibrary

**Kremlin
and Red Square**

Kremlyovskaya

Former
Foundling
Hospital

Moskvoretskaya nab.

Boulevard
Ring

Yauza

Garden

Ring

Zemlyanoy Val

Borovitskaya

Raushskaya nab.

Osipenko

Taganskaya (M)

Vodootvodny

Lavrushinsky

Kanal

Staromonetny per.

B. Polyanka

Bolshaya Ordinka

Novokuznetskaya (M) (M)

Tretyakovskaya

Sadovnicheskaya Nab.
Ozervovskaya Nab.

Kosnodamianskaya Nab.

Taganskaya
pl.

Narodnaya

Bolshaya Yakimanka

Polyanka (M)

1yy Kazachy

A.N.Ostrovskovo

Pyatnitskaya

Novokuznetskaya

Zemlyachki

Tatarsk. B.

Bakhrushina

(N)

Shabolovka

Po.gorelsky per.

Oktyabrskaya (M)

Zhitnaya

Pavetetskaya (M)

Zatsep.sky Val

Garden
Ring

0 — — — — 1 mile

0 — — — — 2 km

Myntaya

Valovaya

Zatsepa

Dobryninskaya (M)

Lysinovskaya

Serpukhovskaya (M)

Pavetetsky
Railway
Station

KEY
(M) Metro stop

M Paveletskaya. **Riga station** *(Rizhsky Vokzal). ⊠ pl. Rizhskaya, Northern Outskirts ☎ 495/631-1588 M Rizhskaya.* **Yaroslav station** *(Yaroslavsky Vokzal). ⊠ 5 pl. Komsomolskaya, Northern Outskirts ☎ 495/266–6300 M Komsomolskaya.*

TOUR OPTIONS

Every major hotel maintains a tourist bureau that books individual and group tours to Moscow's main sights. In addition, there are numerous private agencies that can help with your sightseeing plans.

Patriarshy Dom Tours conducts unusual day and overnight tours in and around Moscow and St. Petersburg for groups or individuals. Among the tours are Novodevichy Convent and Cemetery and the Andrei Sakharov Museum, literature and architectural walks, and the space-flight command center. Capital Tours handles group and individual tours in Moscow, including a guided trip through the most interesting metro stations and a tour of a former Soviet nuclear command bunker. They can also arrange custom tours or even whole itineraries through Russia.

The new hop-on, hop-off bus tour service operated by City Sightseeing Moscow is a good, cheap option for getting your bearings in Moscow and seeing some of the major sites.

City Sightseeing Moscow. Moscow's new hop-on, hop-off bus tour service gives visitors a good overview of the city's main sights at a reasonable price. The route has 18 stops, and audio guides are available in English, German, and Russian. A good jumping-on point is stop No. 10 on Theater Square across from the Bolshoi Theater. ☎ *495/227–7996* ⊕ *hoponhopoff.ru* ⊠ *600R* ⊙ *Daily 10–10.*

Contacts Capital Tours ⊠ *4 ul. Ilyinka, Kremlin/Red Square ☎ 495/232–2442* ⊕ *www.capitaltours.ru M Kitai-Gorod.* **Patriarshy Dom Tours** ⊠ *6 per. Vspolny, Ulitsa Bolshaya Nikitskaya ☎ 495/795–0927, 650/678–7076 in U.S. ⊕ www. toursinrussia.com M Barrikadnaya.*

VISITOR INFORMATION

Travel agents in all the major hotels offer their guests (and anyone else willing to pay their fees) various tourist services, including help in booking group or individual excursions, making a restaurant reservation, or purchasing theater or ballet tickets. The Moscow city government offers very little assistance to tourists, in part because the established Soviet travel service monopoly, Intourist, was sold off by the government during the '90s privatization spree. However, there's an official Moscow tourist office that runs a hotline you can call to ask questions and obtain information regarding museums, tour agencies, emergency services, and other tourist activities. The operators speak English, but don't count on them for a great deal of detailed information.

Contact Tourist Hotline. This service is hit or miss in terms of getting the answer you want. They usually have information about the major sights in the city, however. English is spoken. ☎ *495/690–1301, 800/220–0001, 800/220–0002.*

EXPLORING MOSCOW

Moscow is an in-your-face metropolis that can overwhelm you with monstrous-size avenues, unbearable traffic jams, and a 24-hour lifestyle that will leave you exhausted and wanting more at the same time. Behind the brash facade, however, is a city that also allows for quiet moments of serenity and beauty.

Even Muscovites often find themselves in new corners of the city that they've never before seen. Don't be afraid to wander off the beaten track, for the city, despite its disorganized and chaotic edge, has a straightforward layout. Russians often call Moscow a *bolshaya derevnya,* or "big village," and the center itself is more compact and vital than those of many other world capitals.

KREMLIN/RED SQUARE КРЕМЛЬ И КРАСНАЯ ПЛОЩАДЬ

Fodor'sChoice
★

Few places in the world possess the historic resonance of the Kremlin, the walled ancient heart of Moscow and the oldest part of the city. The first wooden structure was erected on this site some time in the 12th century. As Moscow grew, the city followed the traditional pattern of Russian cities, developing in concentric circles around the elevated fortress at its center (*kreml* means "citadel" or "fortress"). After Moscow emerged as the center of a vast empire in the late 15th century, the Kremlin came to symbolize the mystery and power of Russia, as it has ever since. Before the black-suited men of the Bolshevik Revolution took over, tsars were ceremoniously crowned and buried here. In the 20th century the Kremlin became synonymous with the Soviet government, and "Kremlinologists," Western specialists who studied the movements of the politicians in and around the fortress, made careers out of trying to decipher Soviet Russian policies. Much has changed since the Soviet Union broke up, but the Kremlin itself remains mysteriously alluring. A visit to the ancient Kremlin grounds reveals many signs of the old—and new—Russian enigma.

You can buy tickets for the Kremlin grounds and cathedrals at the two kiosks at the base of the Kutafya Tower in Alexander Garden (Aleksandrovsky Sad). Tickets, which cost 350R, grant you access to all the churches and temporary exhibits within the Kremlin. Tickets to the Armory Chamber (Oruzheynaya Palata) and Diamond Fund (Almazny Fond) cost extra (700R and 500R, respectively); you can buy them at the kiosks or at the entrances to these buildings. Tickets for the Diamond Fund are limited in number and are sold 1½ hours before the four showings each day. Between April and October tickets are also available for a changing-of-the-guard ceremony, which takes place on Saturday at noon. Ignore scalpers selling tickets. Keep in mind that you need to buy a 50R ticket if you wish to take pictures with your camera, and that video cameras aren't allowed. All heavy bags must be checked for about 60R at the *kamera khraneniya,* which is in Alexander Garden, to the right down and behind the stairs from the ticket kiosks.

GREAT ITINERARIES

You can get a decent introduction to the capital in just a few days, leaving time to travel to St. Petersburg.

IF YOU HAVE 3 DAYS

Start with a stroll across Red Square, a tour of St. Basil's Cathedral, the shopping arcades of GUM, and, if you're a devoted student of Soviet history and/or embalming techniques, the Lenin Mausoleum. Then walk through Alexander Garden to reach the tourist entrance to the Kremlin. Plan on spending the better part of your first day exploring the churches, monuments, and exhibits within the grounds of this most famous of Russian fortresses. On the second day, spend the morning sightseeing and shopping on ulitsa Tverskaya. In the afternoon, head to Kitai Gorod; this neighborhood has churches and historic buildings on ulitsa Varvarka, which extends from the eastern edge of Red Square, just behind St. Basil's. Try also, toward the end of the day, to squeeze in a stroll across ploshchad Teatralnaya to see the Bolshoi and Maly theaters. If there's time, don't miss the Gulag Museum. Devote the third morning to the Tretyakov Gallery, which has the finest collection of Russian art in the country. In the afternoon stroll down the Arbat, where you can find plenty of options for haggling over Russian souvenirs.

IF YOU HAVE 7 DAYS

Follow the three-day itinerary above. On the fourth day explore ulitsa Bolshaya Nikitskaya and the surrounding neighborhood, with its enchanting mansions, and the chic and attractive neighborhood around Patriarch's Ponds. Devote the fifth day to the Pushkin Museum of Fine Arts, the Cathedral of Christ Our Savior, and an exploration of some of the streets in the surrounding Kropotkinsky District. Come back the next day and walk from the Russian State Library to the Kropotkinsky District. Be sure to include the Pushkin Memorial Museum and a walk along the naberezhnaya Kremlyovskaya (the embankment of the Moskva River) in the late afternoon for the spectacular views of the cupolas and towers of the Kremlin. Depending on whether your interests tend toward the religious or the secular, you could spend your last day visiting either the New Maiden's Convent and the adjoining cemetery or Gorky Park and the Tolstoy House Estate Museum, where the legendary author of Russian classics once lived.

GETTING HERE AND AROUND

If you're staying outside the Boulevard Ring, the best way to get to the Kremlin/Red Square area is to take the metro to one of the following stations: Ploschad Revolyutsii, Alexsandrovsky Sad, Borovitskaya, or Teatralnaya. If you're closer in, it's a pleasant walk to this central circle of the city, especially if you're coming from the north (you have to cross traffic-heavy bridges if walking up from the south). Many of the surrounding neighborhoods are easily walked to from here as well; the metro is advisable only if you're traveling more than a few stops.

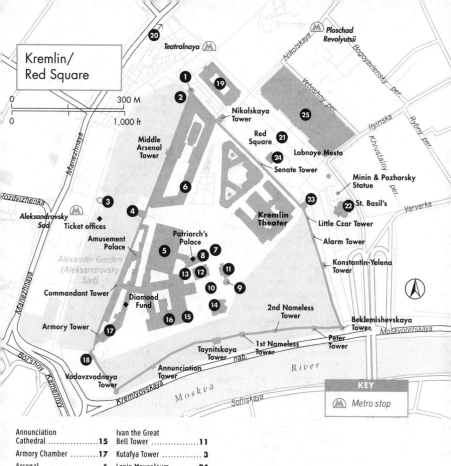

Kremlin/ Red Square

TIMING Plan to spend half a day, at the very least, touring the Kremlin; budget a full day or more if you want to linger at the museums. The Kremlin grounds and cathedrals are open 10 to 5 every day except Thursday. The Armory Chamber and Diamond Fund are also closed on Thursday. Note that the Kremlin occasionally closes on other days for official functions. Check with your hotel concierge.

If you don't want to tackle all of this solo, you should consider a tour of the Kremlin grounds, which includes the Armory Chamber, available from virtually any tour service in Moscow. Plan to come back in the evening, when Red Square and its surrounding buildings are beautifully illuminated.

> **FABERGÉ EGGS**
>
> Intricate, playful, and exuberantly luxurious, Fabergé eggs were created by the 19th-century jeweler Carl Fabergé for the tsarist family. Alexander III began the tradition by ordering a bejeweled egg as an Easter present for his wife. Sixty-eight eggs in all were created before the Bolshevik Revolution; each one is unique and contains an Easter surprise inside. On display in the Armory Palace are two eggs, one with a train dedicated to the Trans-Siberian Railway, the other with a cruiser ship to commemorate a sea journey made by the Royal Family in 1890.

TOP ATTRACTIONS

Annunciation Cathedral (Благовещенский Собор *Blagoveshchensky Sobor*). This remarkable monument of Russian architecture, linking three centuries of art and religion, was the private chapel of the royal family. Its foundations were laid in the 14th century, and in the 15th century a triangular brick church in the early Moscow style was erected on the site. Partially destroyed by fire, it was rebuilt in the 16th century during the reign of Ivan the Terrible, when six gilded cupolas were added. Tsar Ivan would enter the church by the southeast-side porch entrance, built especially for him. He was married three times too many (for a total of six wives) and was therefore, under the bylaws of the Orthodox religion, not allowed to enter the church through its main entrance. The interior is decorated by brilliant frescoes painted in 1508 by the Russian artist Feodosy. The polished tiles of agate jasper covering the floor are said to be a gift from the Shah of Persia. Most striking of all is the chapel's iconostasis. The fine icons of the second and third tiers were painted by some of Russia's greatest masters—Andrei Rublyov, Theophanes the Greek, and Prokhor of Gorodets. ⊠ *Kremlin, Kremlin/Red Square* ⬚ *350R Kremlin ticket* ☉ *Fri.–Wed. 10–5* Ⓜ *Aleksandrovsky Sad or Borovitskaya.*

Fodor's Choice **Armory Chamber (Оружейная Палата** *Oruzheynaya Palata*). The oldest
★ and richest museum in the Kremlin was founded in 1806 as the Imperial Court Museum, which was created out of three royal treasuries: the Court Treasury, where the regalia of the tsars and ambassadorial gifts were kept; the Stable Treasury, which contained the royal harnesses and carriages used by the tsars during state ceremonies; and the Armory, a collection of arms, armor, and other valuable objects gathered from the country's chief armories and storehouses. The Imperial Court Museum was moved to the present building in 1851 and enhanced and expanded

after the Bolshevik Revolution with valuables taken from wealthy noble families as well as from the Patriarchal Sacristy of the Moscow Kremlin. The roughly 4,000 artifacts here date from the 12th century to 1917, and include a rare collection of 17th-century silver. Tickets for the Armory are sold separately at the main box office and allow you to enter at a specific time. Halls (*zal*) VI–IX are on the first floor, Halls I–V on the second.

Hall I displays the works of goldsmiths and silversmiths of the 12th through 19th centuries, and **Hall II** contains a collection of 18th- to 20th-century jewelry. One of the most astounding exhibits is the collection of Fabergé eggs on display in Hall II (Case 23). Among them is a silver egg whose surface is engraved with a map of the Trans-Siberian Railway. The "surprise" inside the egg, which is also on display, was a golden clockwork model of a train with a platinum engine, windows of crystal, and a headlight made of a tiny ruby. ■TIP➔ **Feeling overwhelmed by everything to see at the Armory Chamber? If nothing else, be sure to see the Fabergé eggs. If the weather is too good to spend all day indoors, check out the splendor of the Cathedral Square and come back to see the Armory another day.**

Hall III contains Asian and Western European arms and armor, including heavy Western European suits of armor from the 15th to 17th centuries, pistols, and firearms.

Hall IV showcases a large collection of Russian arms and armor from the 12th to early 17th centuries, with a striking display of helmets. The earliest helmet here dates from the 13th century. Here, too, is the helmet of Prince Ivan, the son of Ivan the Terrible. The prince was killed by his father at the age of 28, an accidental victim of the tsar's unpredictable rage. The tragic event has been memorialized in a famous painting by Ilya Repin now in the Tretyakov Gallery, showing the frightened tsar holding his mortally wounded son.

Hall V is filled with foreign gold and silver objects, mostly ambassadorial presents to the tsars. Among the displays is the "Olympic Service" of china presented to Alexander I by Napoléon after the signing of the Treaty of Tilsit in 1807.

Hall VI holds vestments of silk, velvet, and brocade, embroidered with gold and encrusted with jewels and pearls. Also on display in this section are several coronation dresses, including the one Catherine the Great wore in 1762. Notice how small some of the waists are on the dresses. A pair of Peter the Great's leather riding boots are also on display—take note of their huge size.

Hall VII contains regalia and the imperial thrones. The oldest throne, veneered with carved ivory, belonged to Ivan the Terrible. The throne of the first years of Peter the Great's reign, when he shared power with his older brother Ivan, has two seats in front and one hidden in the back. The boys' older sister, Sophia (1657–1704), who ruled as regent from 1682 to 1689, sat in the back, prompting the young rulers to give the right answers to the queries of ambassadors and others. Among the crowns, the oldest is the sable-trimmed Cap of Monomakh, which dates to the 13th century.

Hall VIII contains dress harnesses of the 16th through 18th centuries.

Hall IX has a marvelous collection of court carriages. Here you'll find the Winter Coach that carried Elizaveta Petrovna (daughter of Peter the Great and someone who clearly liked her carriages; 1709–62) from St. Petersburg to Moscow for her coronation. ✉ *Kremlin, Kremlin/Red Square* ☎ *495/695–3776 main Kremlin museum number, 495/697–4611 excursions* ⊕ *kreml.ru/en/museums/armoury/* 🎫 *700R, tickets sold separately from Kremlin ticket and available 1 hr before each entry session* ⊗ *Fri.–Wed. entry times at 10, noon, 2:30, and 4:30* Ⓜ *Aleksandrovsky Sad.*

Assumption Cathedral (Успенский Собор *Uspensky Sobor*). This dominating structure is one of the oldest edifices of the Kremlin, built in 1475–79 by the Italian architect Aristotle Fioravanti, who had spent many years in Russia studying traditional Russian architecture. Until the 1917 revolution, this was Russia's principal church, where the crowning ceremonies of the tsars took place, a tradition that continued even after the capital was transferred to St. Petersburg. Patriarchs and metropolitans were enthroned and buried here.

Topped by five gilded domes, the cathedral is both austere and solemn. The ceremonial entrance faces Cathedral Square; the visitor entrance is on the west side (to the left). After visiting the Archangel and Annunciation cathedrals, you may be struck by the spacious interior here, unusual for a medieval church. Light pours in through two rows of narrow windows. The cathedral contains rare ancient paintings, including the icon of the Virgin of Vladimir (the work of an 11th-century Byzantine artist), the 12th-century icon of St. George, and the 14th-century Trinity icon. The carved throne in the right-hand corner belonged to Ivan the Terrible, and the gilt wood throne to the far left was the seat of the tsarina. Between the two is the patriarch's throne.

After the revolution the church was turned into a museum, but in 1989 religious services were resumed on major church holidays. ✉ *Kremlin, Kremlin/Red Square* ☎ *495/697–3776 main number for Kremlin museum* ⊕ *kreml.ru/en/museums/dormite* 🎫 *350R Kremlin ticket* ⊗ *Fri.–Wed. 10–5* Ⓜ *Aleksandrovsky Sad.*

Cathedral of the Archangel (Архангельский Собор *Arkhangelsky Sobor*). This five-dome cathedral was commissioned by Ivan the Great (1440–1505), whose reign witnessed much new construction in Moscow and in the Kremlin in particular. The cathedral was built in 1505–09 to replace an earlier church of the same name. The architect was the Italian Aleviso Novi, who came to Moscow at the invitation of the tsar; note the distinct elements of the Italian Renaissance in the cathedral's ornate

2

decoration, particularly in the scallop-shaped gables on its facade. Until 1712, when the Russian capital was moved to St. Petersburg, the cathedral was the burial place of Russian princes and tsars. Inside there are 46 tombs, including that of Ivan Kalita (Ivan "Moneybags"; circa 1304–40), who was buried in the earlier cathedral in 1340. The tomb of Ivan the Terrible (1530–84) is hidden behind the altar; that of his young son, Dmitry, is under the stone canopy to your right as you enter the cathedral. Dmitry's death at the age of seven is one of the many unsolved mysteries in Russian history. He was the last descendant of Ivan the Terrible, and many believe he was murdered because he posed a threat to the ill-fated Boris Godunov (circa 1551–1605), who at the time ruled as regent. A government commission set up to investigate Dmitry's death concluded that he was playing with a knife and "accidentally" slit his own throat. The only tsar to be buried here after 1712 was Peter II (Peter the Great's grandson; 1715–30), who died of smallpox while visiting Moscow.

The walls and pillars of the cathedral are covered in frescoes that tell the story of ancient Russian history. The original frescoes, painted right after the church was built, were repainted in the 17th century by a team of more than 50 leading artists from several Russian towns. Restoration work in the 1950s uncovered some of the original medieval frescoes, fragments of which can be seen in the altar area. The pillars are decorated with figures of warriors; Byzantine emperors; the early princes of Kievan Rus' (the predecessor of modern-day Russia and Ukraine), Vladimir and Novgorod; as well as the princes of Moscow, including Vasily III, the son of Ivan the Great. The frescoes on the walls depict religious scenes, including the deeds of Archangel Michael. The carved baroque iconostasis is 43 feet high and dates from the 19th century. The icons themselves are mostly 17th century, although the revered icon of Archangel Michael is believed to date to the 14th century. ⊠ *Kremlin, Kremlin/Red Square* ☎ *495/695–3776 main number for Kremlin Museum* ⊕ *kreml.ru/en/museums/archangel* ☜ *350R Kremlin ticket* ☽ *Fri.–Wed. 10–5* Ⓜ *Aleksandrovsky Sad.*

Prime Star (Прайм Стар). This citywide chain is one of the few trustworthy spots to get fresh, tasty food on the fly, including low-cost wraps, salads, soups, and even sushi. There's also a pastry case with good fresh-baked cinnamon rolls, and a worthy chocolate mousse. When it's warm, sit under a patio umbrella here, on a pedestrian street near Red Square, and watch every class of Muscovite go by. ⊠ *1 ul. Bolshaya Dmitrovka, 7/5 bldg., Kremlin/Red Square* ☎ *495/692–5011* ⊕ *www.prime-star.ru* Ⓜ *Okhotny Ryad or Teatralnaya.*

Cathedral Square (Соборная Площадь *Ploshchad Sobornaya*). The Kremlin's ancient center is framed by three large cathedrals in the old Russian style, the imposing Ivan the Great Bell Tower, and the Palace of Facets. A changing-of-the-guard ceremony takes place in the square every Saturday at noon in summer. ⊠ *Kremlin, Kremlin/Red Square* ⊕ *kreml.ru/en/museums/scheme* Ⓜ *Aleksandrovsky Sad.*

Diamond Fund (Алмазный Фонд *Almazny Fond*). In 1922 the fledgling Soviet government established this amazing collection of diamonds, jewelry, and precious minerals. The items on display within the Armory Chamber date from the 18th century to the present. Highlights of the collection are the Orlov Diamond, a present from Count Orlov to his mistress, Catherine the Great (1729–96); and the Shah Diamond, which was given to Tsar Nicholas I (1796–1855) by the Shah of Persia as a gesture of condolence after the assassination in 1829 of Alexander Griboyedov, the Russian ambassador to Persia and a well-known poet. Tickets to view the exhibit are sold for specific times, and viewings begin every 20 minutes. They are sold at the entrance to the Fund (inside the Armory Chamber), not at Kutafiya Tower, where tickets for other Kremlin museums can be bought. ⊠ *Armory Chamber, Kremlin/Red Square* 🖾 *500R, separate from the Kremlin and Armory Chamber tickets* ☉ *Fri.–Wed. 10–1 and 2–5, entry times every 20 mins* Ⓜ *Aleksandrovsky Sad.*

Great Kremlin Palace (Большой Кремлевский Дворец *Bolshoi Kremlyovsky Dvorets*). The palace actually consists of a group of buildings. The main section is the newest, built between 1838 and 1849. Its 375-foot-long facade faces south, overlooking the Moskva River. This was for centuries the site of the palace of the grand dukes and tsars, but the immediate predecessor of the present building was badly damaged in the major fire of 1812. It's currently closed to the general public.

The other buildings of the Great Kremlin Palace include the 17th-century **Terem** (Tower Chamber), where the tsarina received visitors, and the 15th-century **Granovitaya Palata** (Palace of Facets). Both of these buildings are also closed to the public. ⊠ *Kremlin, Kremlin/Red Square* 🕾 *495/695–3776 main Kremlin Museum number* ⊕ *kreml.ru/ en/kremlin/buildings/BKD* Ⓜ *Aleksandrovsky Sad.*

GUM (ГУМ). Pronounced "goom," the initials are short for Gosudarstvenny Universalny Magazin, or State Department Store. This staggeringly enormous emporium, formerly called the Upper Trading Rows, was built in 1889–93 and has long been one of the more famous sights of Moscow. Three long passages with three stories of shops run the length of the building. A glass roof covers each passage, and there are balconies and bridges on the second and third tiers. Another series of passages runs perpendicular to the three main lines, creating a mazelike mall. It all feels like a cavernous turn-of-the-20th-century European train station. There are shops (both Western and Russian) aplenty here now, with all the world's big-name boutique brands crowding the first floor, and a saunter down one of the halls is enjoyable. One can't-miss spot is the newly restored Gastronom No. 1, which runs the length of one side of the ground floor. It's a nostalgic supermarket with pricey caviar and champagne, as well as lowbrow canned meats that Russian World War II vets would recognize. In the adjacent hall, the store also runs a row of small cafés that serve affordable and tasty eclectic fare. Back across the ground floor from the market is the elegant Bosco restaurant, which has a small summer terrace that looks out onto Red Square. ⊠ *3 Red Sq., Kremlin/Red Square* 🕾 *495/788–4343* ⊕ *www. gum.ru* ☉ *Daily 10–10* Ⓜ *Ploshchad Revolutsii.*

2

Historical Museum (Исторический Музей *Istorichesky Muzey*). You may recognize these twin towers if you've ever caught clips of Soviet military parades on television. Against the backdrop of the pointed spires, the tanks and missiles rolling through Red Square seemed to acquire even more potency. The redbrick museum, built in 1874–83 in the pseudo-Russian style, combines a variety of backward-looking architectural styles and houses extensive archaeological and historical collections and interesting temporary exhibits outline. ✉ *1 Red Sq., Kremlin/Red Square* ☎ *495/692–4019, 495/692–3731 guided tours* ⊕ *www.shm.ru* 💳 *250R* ⊙ *Wed., Fri.–Mon. 10–6, Thurs. 11–8; closed 1st Mon. of month* Ⓜ *Ploshchad Revolutsii, Okhotny Ryad, or Teatralnaya.*

Ivan the Great Bell Tower (Колокольня Ивана Великого *Kolokolnya Ivana Velikovo*). The octagonal main tower of the tallest structure in the Kremlin rises 263 feet and, according to a tradition established by Boris Godunov, no building in Moscow is allowed to rise higher. The first bell tower was erected on this site in 1329 and was replaced in the early 16th century, during the reign of Ivan the Great (hence the bell tower's name). But it was during the reign of Boris Godunov that the tower received its present appearance. In 1600 the main tower was rebuilt, crowned by an onion-shaped dome and covered with gilded copper. For many years it served as a watchtower; all of Moscow and its environs could be observed for a radius of 32 km (20 miles). The annex of the bell tower is used for temporary exhibits of items from the Kremlin collection. ✉ *Cathedral Sq., Kremlin, Kremlin/Red Square* ☎ *495/697–0349* 💳 *500R in addition to 350R Kremlin ticket* ⊙ *Fri.–Wed., entrance by tour at 10, 11:15, 1:30, and 2:45* Ⓜ *Aleksandrovsky Sad.*

Kutafya Tower (Кутафья Башня *Kutafya Bashnya*). This white bastion, erected in 1516, once defended the approach to the drawbridge that linked Alexander Garden to the Kremlin. In Old Slavonic, *kutafya* means "clumsy" or "confused"; this adjective was applied to the tower because it so differs in shape and size from the other towers of the Kremlin. Kutafya Tower marks the main public entrance to the Kremlin, which opens promptly at 10 am every day except Thursday. You can buy tickets to the Kremlin grounds and cathedrals at the kiosks on either side of the tower. The guards may ask where you're from and check inside your bags; there's a small security checkpoint to walk through, similar to those at airports. ✉ *ul. Manezhnaya, Kremlin/Red Square* ⊕ *kreml.ru/en/kremlin/towers/Kutafyay* 💳 *350R Kremlin ticket* ⊙ *Fri.–Wed. 10–5* Ⓜ *Aleksandrovsky Sad.*

Lenin Mausoleum (Мавзолей Ленина *Mavzolei Lenina*). Except for a brief interval during World War II, when his body was evacuated to the Urals, Vladimir Ilyich Lenin (1870–1924) has lain in state here since his death. His body is said to be immersed in a chemical bath of glycerol and potassium acetate every 18 months to preserve it. Whether it's really Lenin or a wax look-alike is probably one of those Russian mysteries that will go down in history unanswered. From 1924 to 1930 there was a temporary wooden mausoleum, which has been replaced by the pyramid-shaped mausoleum you see now. It's made of red, black, and gray granite, with a strip of black granite near the top level symbolizing a band of mourning. Both versions of the mausoleum were designed by one of Russia's most prominent architects, Alexei Shchusev, who also designed the grand Kazansky train station.

In the Soviet past, there were notoriously endless lines of people waiting to view Lenin's body, but this is now rarely the case, although if a large tourist group has just encamped the wait may be long. Now only the curious tourist or the ardent Communist among Russians visits the mausoleum. A visit to the mausoleum, however, is still treated as a serious affair. The surrounding area is cordoned off during visiting hours, and all those entering are observed by uniformed police officers. It's forbidden to carry a camera or any large bag. The interior of the mausoleum is cold and dark and it's considered disrespectful to put your hands inside your pockets (the same applies when you visit an Orthodox church).

Outside the mausoleum you can look at the Kremlin's burial grounds. When Stalin died in 1953, he was placed inside the mausoleum alongside Lenin, but in the early 1960s, during Khrushchev's tenure, the body was removed and buried here, some say encased in heavy concrete. There is discussion almost every year of finally burying Lenin as well, and though this would still be a controversial move in today's Russia, momentum has steadily been gaining for the mausoleum to be closed. Also buried here are such Communist leaders as Zhdanov, Dzerzhinsky, Brezhnev, Chernenko, and Andropov. The American journalist John Reed, friend of Lenin and author of *Ten Days That Shook the World,* an account of the October revolution, is buried alongside the Kremlin wall. Urns set inside the wall contain ashes of the Soviet writer Maxim Gorky; Lenin's wife and collaborator, Nadezhda Krupskaya; Sergei Kirov, the Leningrad Party leader whose assassination in 1934 (believed to have been arranged by Stalin) was followed by enormous purges; the first Soviet cosmonaut, Yury Gagarin; and other Soviet eminences. ⊠ *Red Sq., Kremlin/Red Square* 🎫 *Free* 🕑 *Tues.–Thurs. and weekends 10–1* Ⓜ *Ploshchad Revolutsii.*

Lobnoye Mesto (**Лобное Место**). The name of the strange, round, white-stone dais in front of St. Basil's Cathedral literally means "place of the brow," but it has come to mean "execution site," for it is next to the spot where public executions were once carried out. Built in 1534, the dais was used by the tsars as a podium for public speeches and the proclamation of imperial *ukazy* (decrees). When the heir apparent reached the age of 16, he was presented to the people from this platform. ⊠ *Red Sq., Kremlin/Red Square* Ⓜ *Ploshchad Revolutsii.*

Minin and Pozharsky statue (**Памятник Минину и Пожарскому**). In 1818 sculptor Ivan Martos built this statue honoring Kuzma Minin (a wealthy Nizhni-Novgorod butcher) and Prince Dmitry Pozharsky, who drove Polish invaders out of Moscow in 1612 during the Time of Troubles. This period of internal strife and foreign intervention began in approximately 1598 with the death of Tsar Fyodor I and lasted until 1613, when the first Romanov was elected to the throne. This was the first monument of patriotism funded by the public. The inscription on the pedestal reads, "To citizen Minin and Prince Pozharsky from a thankful Russia 1818." The statue originally stood in the center of the square, but was later moved to its current spot in front of St. Basil's. In 2005, November 4 was named a new public holiday in honor of Minin and Pozharsky, replacing the old Communist November 7 holiday, which celebrated the anniversary of the Bolshevik Revolution. ⊠ *Red Sq., Kremlin/Red Square* Ⓜ *Ploshchad Revolutsii.*

Fodor's Choice ★ **Red Square** (Красная Площадь *Krasnaya Ploshchad*). Famous for the grand military parades staged here during the Soviet era, this vast space was originally called the Torg, the Slavonic word for marketplace. Many suppose that the name "Red Square" has something to do with Communism or the Bolshevik Revolution. In fact, the name dates to the 17th century. The adjective *krasny* originally meant "beautiful," but over the centuries the meaning of the word changed to "red," hence the square's present name. The square is most beautiful and impressive at night, when it's entirely illuminated by floodlights, with the ruby-red stars atop the Kremlin towers glowing against the dark sky. There are five stars in all, one for each of the tallest towers. They made their appearance in 1937 to replace the double-headed eagle, a tsarist symbol that is again an emblem of Russia. The glass stars, which are lighted from inside and designed to turn with the wind, are far from dainty: the smallest weighs a ton. ⊠ *Red Sq., Kremlin/Red Square* Ⓜ *Ploshchad Revolutsii.*

Resurrection Gates (Воскресенские Ворота *Voskresenskiye Vorota*). These gates, which formed part of the Kitai Gorod defensive wall, were named for the icon of the Resurrection of Christ that hangs above them. However, the gates are truly "resurrection" gates; they have been reconstructed many times since they were first built in 1534. In 1680 the gates were rebuilt and a chapel honoring the Iberian Virgin Mary was added. In 1931 they were destroyed by the Soviets. Stalin ordered their demolition partly so that tanks could easily make their way onto Red Square during parades. They were most recently rebuilt in 1994–95. Today the redbrick gates with the bright-green-and-blue chapel are truly a magnificent sight and a fitting entrance to Red Square. The bronze compass inlaid in the ground in front of the chapel marks Kilometer Zero on the Russian highway system. ⊠ *Red Sq., Kremlin/Red Square* ⊙ *Chapel daily 8 am–10 pm* Ⓜ *Ploshchad Revolutsii.*

Fodor's Choice ★ **St. Basil's Cathedral** (Покровский Собор *Pokrovsky Sobor*). The proper name of this whimsical structure is Church of the Intercession. It was commissioned by Ivan the Terrible to celebrate his conquest of the Tatar city of Kazan on October 1, 1552, the day of the feast of the Intercession. The central chapel, which rises 107 feet, is surrounded by eight towerlike chapels linked by an elevated gallery. Each chapel is topped by an onion dome carved with its own distinct pattern and dedicated to a saint on whose day the Russian army won battles against the Tatars.

The cathedral was built between 1555 and 1560 on the site of the earlier Trinity Church, where the Holy Fool Vasily (Basil) had been buried in 1552. Basil was an adversary of the tsar, publicly reprimanding Ivan the Terrible for his cruel and bloodthirsty ways. He was protected, however, from the tsar by his status as a Holy Fool, for he was considered by the Church to be an emissary of God. Ironically, Ivan the Terrible's greatest creation has come to be known by the name of his greatest adversary. In 1558 an additional chapel was built in the northeast corner over Basil's remains, and from that time on the cathedral has been called St. Basil's.

Very little is known about the architect who built the cathedral. It may have been the work of two men—Barma and Postnik—but now it seems more likely that there was just one architect, Postnik Yakovlyev, who went by the nickname Barma. Legend has it that upon completion of the cathedral, the mad tsar had the architect blinded to ensure that he would never create such a masterpiece again.

After the Bolshevik Revolution, the cathedral was closed and in 1929 turned into a museum dedicated to the Russian conquest of Kazan. Although services are held here on Sunday at 10 am, the museum is still open. The antechamber houses displays that chronicle the Russian conquest of medieval Kazan as well as examples of 16th-century Russian and Tatar weaponry. Another section details the history of the cathedral's construction, with displays of the building materials used. After viewing the museum exhibits, you're free to wander through the cathedral. Compared with the exotic exterior, the dark and simple interiors, their brick walls decorated with faded flower frescoes, are somewhat disappointing. The most interesting chapel is the main one, which contains a 19th-century baroque iconostasis. ✉ *Red Sq., Kremlin/ Red Square* ☎ *495/698–3304* ⊕ *www.saintbasil.ru/en/* 💷 *250R adults* ☉ *Daily 11–5 winter, 10-7 summer* Ⓜ *Ploshchad Revolutsii.*

Tomb of the Unknown Soldier (Могила Неизвестного Солдата *Mogila Neizvestnovo Soldata*). Dedicated on May 9, 1967, the 22nd anniversary of the Russian victory over Germany in World War II, this redgranite monument within Alexander Garden contains the body of an unidentified Soviet soldier, one of those who, in autumn 1941, stopped the German attack at the village of Kryukovo, just outside Moscow. To the right of the grave there are six urns holding soil from the six "heroic cities" that so stubbornly resisted the German onslaught: Odessa, Sevastopol, Stalingrad (the current Volgograd), Kiev, Brest, and Leningrad (now St. Petersburg). Very likely, no matter what time of year you are visiting, you'll see at least one wedding party. The young couple in full wedding regalia, along with friends and family, customarily stops here after getting married, leaving behind flowers and snapping photographs along the way. The gray obelisk just beyond the Tomb of the Unknown Soldier was erected in 1918 to commemorate the Marxist theoreticians who contributed to the Bolshevik Revolution. It was created out of an obelisk that had been put up three years earlier, in honor of the 300th anniversary of the Romanov dynasty. ✉ *ul. Manezhnaya, Kremlin/Red Square* Ⓜ *Ploshchad Revolutsii.*

Tsar Bell (Царь-Колокол *Tsar Kolokol*). The world's largest bell is also the world's most silent: it has never rung once. Commissioned in the 1730s, the bell was damaged when it was still in its cast. It weighs more than 200 tons and is 20 feet high. The bas-reliefs on the outside show Tsar Alexei Mikhailovich and Tsarina Anna Ivanovna. ⊠ *Kremlin, Kremlin/Red Square* Ⓜ *Aleksandrovsky Sad.*

Tsar Cannon (Царь-Пушка *Tsar Pushka*). This huge piece of artillery (*pushka*) has the largest caliber of any gun in the world, but like the Tsar Bell that has never been rung, it has never fired a single shot. Cast in bronze in 1586 by Andrei Chokhov, it weighs 40 tons and is 17½ feet long. Its present carriage was cast in 1835, purely for display purposes. ⊠ *Kremlin, Kremlin/Red Square* Ⓜ *Aleksandrovsky Sad.*

> **HISTORY OF THE ONION DOME**
>
> Historians argue over the origin of the onion dome commonly associated with Russian churches. One theory for the dome shape is that it was simply a way to ensure the snow slid off the church in the winter. Others say that the style was borrowed from the Mongols. St. Basil's Cathedral is topped by the most famous onion domes in the world.

WORTH NOTING

Alexander Garden (Александровский Сад *Aleksandrovsky Sad*). Laid out in the 19th century by the Russian architect Osip Bove, this garden named after Alexander I stretches along the northwest wall of the Kremlin, where the Neglinnaya River once flowed. The river now runs beneath the garden, through an underground pipe. Bove added the classical columns topped with an arc of chipped bricks; in the 19th century such "romantic" imitation ruins were popular in gardens. Today this mock ruin is blocked by a gate, but in eras past it was a famous place for winter sledding. A few pleasant outdoor cafés opposite the garden on the side of the Manezh building provide a nice place to rest after a tour of the Kremlin. ⊠ *ul. Manezhnaya, Kremlin/Red Square* ☉ *Fri.–Wed. 10–5* Ⓜ *Aleksandrovsky Sad.*

Amusement Palace (Потешный Дворец *Poteshny Dvorets*). Behind the State Kremlin Palace stands this smaller palace used by *boyarin* (nobleman) Alexei in the 17th century as a venue for theatrical productions. Stalin and Trotsky had apartments here, now closed to the public. ⊠ *Kremlin, Kremlin/Red Square* ☎ *495/695–3776* ⛨ *350R Kremlin ticket* ☉ *Fri.–Wed. 10–5* Ⓜ *Aleksandrovsky Sad.*

Arsenal (Арсенал). Commissioned in 1701 by Peter the Great, the weapons arsenal was partially destroyed by the fire that greeted Napoléon as he stormed the city in 1812 (some say the Russian army set fire to the city intentionally). Its present form dates from the early 19th century, when it was given its yellow color and simple but impressive shape by Osip Bove (the same architect who designed the Alexander Garden). Notable on the building's facade are arched windows framed in white granite and statuettes built into the walls flanking the main entrance. Once planned to be the site of a museum dedicated to the Napoleonic wars, today it houses government offices and is closed to the public. ✉ *Kremlin, Kremlin/Red Square* ⊕ *kreml.ru/en/kremlin/ buildings/Arsenal* 🎟 *350R Kremlin ticket* Ⓜ *Aleksandrovsky Sad.*

Borovitskaya Tower (Боровицкая Башня *Borovitskaya Bashnya*). The main entrance to the Kremlin rises to more than 150 feet (46 meters). At its base a gate pierces the thick walls, and you can still see the slits for the chains of the former drawbridge. Black Volgas (now replaced by top-of-the-line Mercedes and BMWs) once whizzed through the vehicular entrance, carrying government employees to work. ✉ *ul. Manezhnaya, Kremlin/Red Square* ⊕ *kreml.ru/en/kremlin/towers/Borovitskaya* Ⓜ *Borovitskaya.*

Cathedral of the Twelve Apostles (Собор Двенадцати Апостолов *Sobor Dvenadtsati Apostolov*). Built in 1655–56 by Patriarch Nikon, this was his private church. An exhibit here displays icons removed from other Kremlin churches destroyed by the Soviets. The silver containers and stoves were used to make holy oil. Next door to the church is the Patriarch's Palace. ✉ *Kremlin, Kremlin/Red Square* ☎ *495/695–3776* ⊕ *kreml.ru/en/kremlin/buildings/Patriarshie_Palaty* 🎟 *350R Kremlin ticket* ⊙ *Fri.–Wed. 10–5* Ⓜ *Aleksandrovsky Sad.*

Church of the Deposition of the Virgin's Robe (Церковь Ризоположения *Tserkov Rizopolozheniya*). This single-dome church was built in 1484–86 by masters from Pskov. It was rebuilt several times and restored to its 15th-century appearance by Soviet experts in the 1950s. Brilliant frescoes dating to the mid-17th century cover the church's walls, pillars, and vaults. The most precious treasure is the iconostasis by Nazary Istomin. On display inside the church is an exhibit of ancient Russian wooden sculpture from the Kremlin collection. ✉ *Kremlin, Kremlin/Red Square* ☎ *495/695-3776* ⊕ *kreml.ru/en/museums/church_riza* 🎟 *350R Kremlin ticket* ⊙ *Fri.–Wed. 10–5* Ⓜ *Aleksandrovsky Sad.*

Patriarch's Palace (Патриарший Дворец *Patriarshy Dvorets*). Adjoining the Cathedral of the Twelve Apostles, the Patriarch's Palace houses the **Museum of 17th-Century Applied Art.** The exhibits here were taken from the surplus of the Armory Palace and include books, tableware, clothing, and household linen. ✉ *Kremlin, Kremlin/Red Square* ☎ *495/695-3776* ⊕ *kreml.ru/en/museums/patriarchal* 🎟 *350R Kremlin ticket* ⊙ *Fri.–Wed. 10–5* Ⓜ *Aleksandrovsky Sad or Borovitskaya.*

Sobakina Tower (Собакина Башня *Sobakina Bashnya*). More than 180 feet high, the Sobakina (formerly Arsenal) Tower at the northernmost part of the thick battlements that encircle the Kremlin was an important part of the Kremlin's defenses. It was built in 1492 and its thick walls concealed a secret well, which was of vital importance during times of siege. It isn't open for touring. ✉ *ul. Manezhnaya, Kremlin/Red Square* 🎟 *350R Kremlin ticket* Ⓜ *Ploshchad Revolutsii.*

State Kremlin Palace (Государственный Кремлевский Дворец *Gosudarstvenny Kremlyovsky Dvorets*). In 1961 this rectangular structure of glass and aluminum was built as the Dvorets Syezdov (Palace of Congresses) to accommodate meetings of Communist Party delegates from across the Soviet Union. Today it's affiliated with the Bolshoi Theatre and is used for concerts, fashion shows, and ballets. Big names such as Tom Jones, Elton John, and Rod Stewart have played here. A sizable portion of the palace is underground: the architect designed the structure this way so that it wouldn't be higher than any of the other Kremlin buildings. Apart from attending a concert, the building is of no real interest. ⊠ *Kremlin, Kremlin/Red Square* ☎ *495/695–3776* ⊕ *kreml.ru/ en/kremlin/buildings/GKD* Ⓜ *Aleksandrovsky Sad.*

Tower of the Savior (Спасская Башня *Spasskaya Bashnya*). Until Boris Yeltsin's presidency (1991–99) this 1491 tower served as the main entrance to the Kremlin. Indeed, in the centuries before Communist rule, all who passed through it were required to doff their hats and bow before the icon of the Savior that hung on the front of the tower. The icon was removed, but you can see the outline of where it was. The embellished roof and the first clock were added in 1625. President Vladimir Putin uncharacteristically used the Spasskaya Tower exit in May 2003 when hurrying to a Paul McCartney concert on Red Square. ⊠ *Red Sq., Kremlin/Red Square* ☎ *495/695–3776 main Kremlin museum number* ⊕ *kreml.ru/en/kremlin/towers/Spaskaya* Ⓜ *Ploshchad Revolutsii.*

Troitskaya Tower (Троицкая Башня *Troitskaya Bashnya*). Rising 240 feet, this is the tallest *bashnya* (tower) in the Kremlin wall and is linked to the Kutafya Tower by a bridge that once spanned a moat. Its deep, subterranean chambers were once used as prison cells. Napoléon supposedly lost his hat when he entered the Kremlin through this gate in 1812. ⊠ *Aleksandrovsky Sad, Kremlin/Red Square* ☎ *495/695-3776* ⊕ *kreml.ru/en/kremlin/towers/Troitskaya* 🎫 *350R Kremlin ticket* ⊗ *Fri.–Wed. 10–5* Ⓜ *Aleksandrovsky Sad.*

KITAI GOROD КИТАЙ-ГОРОД

Kitai Gorod, with its winding streets, is the oldest section of Moscow outside the Kremlin. The literal translation of Kitai Gorod is "China Town," but there has never been a Chinese settlement here. The origin of the word *kitai* is disputed; it may come from the Tatar word for fortress, but most likely it derives from the Russian word *kita,* in reference to the bundles of twigs that were used to reinforce the earthen wall that once surrounded the area.

Kitai Gorod begins to the east of where Red Square ends. Settlement of this area began in the 12th century, around the time that the fortified city of Moscow was founded on Borovitsky Hill (the site of the present-day Kremlin). By the 14th century Kitai Gorod was a thriving trade district, full of shops and markets. At that time it was surrounded by earthen ramparts, which were replaced in the 16th century by a fortified wall, remnants of which still remain. As Moscow grew, so did Kitai Gorod. At the time of the Bolshevik Revolution it was the city's most important financial and commercial district, with major banks, warehouses, and trading companies concentrated here. These days the multitude of shops, restaurants, and banks demonstrates the area's reasserted role as an energized commercial center.

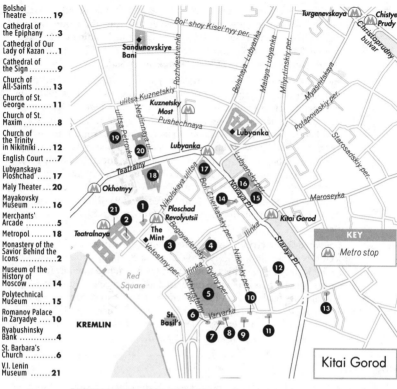

GETTING HERE AND AROUND

Kitai Gorod can be reached by the Kitai Gorod, Lubyanka, Kuznetsky Most, Turgenevskaya, Chistiye Prudy, and Tsvetnoi Bulvar metro stations. The central street in the neighborhood, ulitsa Maroseika, originates in the west at ploschad Staraya, sloping gently uphill and east. It becomes ulitsa Pokrovka after the intersection with the Boulevard Ring and runs all the way to the Garden Ring. The only way to get around the side streets here is on foot, but tram number 39 and a few others run the length of the boulevards that run north to metro station Chistiye Prudy and south across the Moskva River.

TOP ATTRACTIONS

FAMILY

Fodor'sChoice

★

Bolshoi Theatre (Большой Театр). Moscow's biggest (*bolshoi* means "big") and oldest theater, formerly known as the Great Imperial Theater, was completely rebuilt after a fire in 1854. Lenin made his last public speech here in 1922. The splendor of tapestries, balconies, crystal chandeliers, and gold-leaf trim is matched by the quality of the resident opera and ballet troupes, two of the most famous performing-arts companies in the world. If you want to see a performance at the Bolshoi, be sure to book one of its 2,155 seats as far ahead as possible because performances can sell out quickly. To the left of the Bolshoi is the **RAMT** (Russian Academic Youth Theater), which puts on performances with a talented group of young actors. This is where you'll find the Bolshoi's main ticket office. The plaza, with fountains and fine wooden benches, is a nice spot for a relaxing look at the theater. ✉ *1 pl. Teatralnaya, Kitai Gorod* ☎ *495/495–5555 tickets* ⊕ *www.bolshoi.ru/en* Ⓜ *Teatralnaya.*

Coffeemania. Good coffee and food make this spot just around the corner from the Bolshoi Theatre a favorite with theatergoers (you'll find other branches all around Moscow). The coffee is considered by many to be the best in the city, the cakes and pastries are excellent, there's a large menu of well-prepared international dishes, and if you're looking for a big salad, this is the place to go. ✉ *6/9 ul. Rozhdestvenka, Kitai Gorod* ☎ *495/624–0075* ⊕ *www.coffeemania.ru* Ⓜ *Kuznetsky Most.*

Kamchatka. For a fun, retro-Soviet experience, step into this new hot spot owned by one of Moscow's best-known restauranteurs for a cold beer and a caviar sandwich. The menu and price list are reminiscent of a typical Soviet beer bar with a modern touch of today's Moscow scene. ✉ *7 ul. Kuznetsky Most, Kitai Gorod* ☎ *495/624–8825* Ⓜ *Teatralnaya or Kuznetsky Most.*

Cathedral of Our Lady of Kazan (Казанский Собор *Kazansky Sobor*). Built between 1633 and 1636 to commemorate Russia's liberation from Polish occupation during the Time of Troubles, this church was purposely blown up in 1936, at the beginning of a planned remodeling of all Kitai Gorod that was to help usher in a new industrial era. The centerpiece of the area was to be a monumental House of Industry, but neither the House nor the plan ever came to fruition. The current cathedral is a replica, rebuilt and fully restored in 1993. Its salmon-and-cream–painted brick and gleaming gold cupolas are now a colorful magnet at the northeast corner of Red Square, between the Historical Museum and GUM. Inside and outside hang icons of Our Lady of Kazan; every inch of the impressive interior is covered in frescoes and whorled floral patterns. Many worshippers visit throughout the day. ✉ *8 ul. Nikolskaya, at Red Sq., Kitai Gorod* ☎ *495/698–2726* ⊕ *kazanski-sobor.ru* 🎫 *Free* ☉ *Daily 8–7, except Mon., when it closes at end of 5 pm vespers service. Sun. services at 7 and 9:30 am* Ⓜ *Ploshchad Revolutsii.*

English Court (Английский Двор *Anglisky Dvor*). Built in the mid-16th century, this white-stone building with a steep shingled roof and narrow windows became known as the English Court because Ivan the Terrible—wanting to encourage foreign trade—presented it to English merchants trading in Moscow. It then took on the role of England's first embassy. In 1994 Queen Elizabeth II presided over the opening of the building as a branch of the Museum of the History of Moscow. Displays about Russian–British trade relations over the centuries are probably most interesting to visitors from the United Kingdom. ✉ *4a ul. Varvarka, Kitai Gorod* ☎ *495/698–3952* 🎫 *45R* ☉ *Tues. and Wed.–Sun. 10–6, Thurs. 1–9* Ⓜ *Ploshchad Revolutsii or Kitai Gorod.*

Mayakovsky Museum (Музей Маяковского *Muzey Mayakovskovo*). This collection honoring one of Russia's great revolutionary poets (1893–1930) is suitably among the most imaginative and revolutionary installations in the city, housed in the building he inhabited opposite the headquarters of the KGB. The collection includes archival documents, photos, manuscripts, paintings, and letters, including the poet's hand-written suicide note, that trace his early revolutionary activities, complicated love affairs, and death. ✉ *3/6 proyezd Lyubansky, bldg. 4, Kitai Gorod* ☎ *495/621–9387, 495/628–2569* ⊕ *www.mayakovsky. info* 🗪 *100R* ◷ *Mon., Tues., and Fri.–Sun. 10–5, Thurs. 1–8; closed last Fri. of month* Ⓜ *Lubyanka.*

> **WORD ON THE STREET**
>
> The following Russian words are useful to know when finding addresses in Moscow:
>
> ■ *pereulok* (per.)–lane
>
> ■ *ulitsa* (ul.)–street
>
> ■ *prospekt* (pr.)–avenue
>
> ■ *ploshchad* (pl.)–square

Merchants' Arcade (Гостиный Двор *Gostinny Dvor*). This former market, which takes up an entire block between ulitsas Ilinka and Varvarka, just east of Red Square, is made up of two imposing buildings. Running the length of pereulok Khrustalny is the Old Merchant Arcade, erected by the Italian architect Quarenghi between 1791 and 1805; on the other side of the block, bordering pereulok Rybny, is the New Merchant Arcade, built between 1838 and 1840 on the site of the old fish market. The complex now houses a number of restaurants, art galleries, and shops, though none of them are worth making a special trip to visit. Besides the facade, the only parts of the building of historical interest are the capacious glass-topped arcade inside and a small exhibition of the structure's old molding and other features, displayed simply in a set of rooms on the western side of the complex. ✉ *4 ul. Ilinka, Kitai Gorod* ☎ *495/698–1202* ⊕ *www.mosgd.ru/en* ◷ *Daily 10–10* Ⓜ *Ploshchad Revolyutsii or Kitai Gorod.*

Metropol (Метрополь). Built at the turn of the 20th century in preparation for the celebrations commemorating 300 years of the Romanov dynasty, the Metropol underwent reconstruction in the late 1980s to restore its brilliant art nouveau facade to its original colorful guise. The ceramic mosaics are especially arresting when the sun bounces off the tiles. Look for the Princess "Greza" panel made by Mikhail Vrubel, as inspired by the plays of the French writer Edmond Rostand, and a mosaic depicting the four seasons. The hotel was the focus of heavy fighting during the revolution, and it was also the venue of many historic speeches, including a few by Lenin. For some time the Central Committee of the Russian Soviet Federal Republic met here under its first chairman, Yakov Sverdlov. The small café-bar is a sophisticated spot for tea, coffee, and a selection of delicious cakes and pastries. The expense is worth the calming effect of comfy, padded seats and intimate service. ✉ *1/4 pro. Teatralny, Kitai Gorod* ☎ *499/501–7800* ⊕ *www. metropol-moscow.ru* Ⓜ *Ploshchad Revolutsii or Teatralnaya.*

Museum of the History of Moscow (Музей Москвы *Muzey Istorii Goroda Moskvy*). In a former 19th-century warehouse, exhibits explore Moscow's architectural and cultural history through paintings, artifacts, and amusing life-size dioramas. Unfortunately there is no written information in English, making it difficult to glean much from the exhibits unless you read Russian or have a guide. ⊠ *2 bul. Zubovsky, Krasnaya Presnya* ☎ *499/766–4196* ⊕ *www.mosmuseum.ru* ☏ *50R* ☾ *Tues., Wed., and Fri. 10–6, Thurs. 11–9, weekends 11–6; closed last Fri. of month* Ⓜ *Park Kultury.*

Ploshchad Lubyanskaya (Лубянская Площадь). Now called by its prerevolutionary name, this circular "square" had been renamed Dzerzhinsky Square in 1926 in honor of Felix Dzerzhinsky, a Soviet revolutionary and founder of the infamous CHEKA, the forerunner of the KGB. His statue once stood in the center of the square but was toppled in August 1991, along with the old regime. It now resides in the sculpture garden next to the Central House of Artists in the Kropotkinsky District. Instead, a slab of stone now stands in the middle of the square, as a tribute to those who were oppressed by the Soviet government. The stone comes from the Solovetsky Islands, once home to an infamous prison camp. The large yellow building facing the square, with bars on the ground-floor windows, was once the notorious Lubyanka Prison and KGB headquarters. The KGB Museum, which chronicles the history of espionage in Russia, is in an annex of this building. However, it has been closed for several years, fittingly, for an undisclosed reason. ⊠ *Kitai Gorod* Ⓜ *Lubyanka.*

St. John's Convent (Ивановский Монастырь *Ivanovsky Monastyr*). Among the noblewomen who were forced to take the veil here were Empress Elizabeth's illegitimate daughter, Princess Augusta Tarakanova, and the countess Dariya Saltykova, who was imprisoned here after she murdered 138 of her serfs, most of them young women. Built in the 16th century and restored in the 19th century, this convent was used as a prison in the Stalinist era and was in shambles for many years after that. The convent is open for services. ⊠ *4 ul. Zabelina, Kitai Gorod* ☎ *495/624–7521* ☏ *Free* ☾ *Daily 7:30 am–8 pm; services daily at 5* Ⓜ *Kitai Gorod.*

Fodor'sChoice
★ **Sandunovskiye Bani** (Сандуновские Бани). This impeccably clean banya, known also simply as "Sanduny," is probably the city's most elegant bathhouse, with a lavish blue-and-gold-painted interior dating to the early 1800s. The entrance is marked by wrought-iron lamps and a circular marble staircase. The VIP section has a pool surrounded by marble columns and a lounge with leather booths. Note that the banya essentials of a towel and a sheet to sit on in the steam room cost extra; you can also bring your own. You can also purchase birch branches, which you may be able to convince a fellow bather to beat you with (or you can hire a trained masseuse to do it). This is a classic Russian banya procedure that's supposedly good for the skin. There is a thorough list of rules and recommendations printed in English at the ticket booth. On-site facilities include a beauty parlor and, of course, more traditional massage. ⊠ *14 ul. Neglinnaya, Kitai Gorod* ☎ *495/625–4631* ⊕ *www.sanduny.ru* ☏ *1,700R–2,100R* ☾ *Daily 8 am–11 pm* Ⓜ *Kuznetsky Most.*

Cathedral of the Epiphany (Собор Богоявления *Sobor Bogoyavleniya*). This church is all that remains of the monastery that was founded on this site in the 13th century by Prince Daniil of Moscow. A good example of the Moscow baroque style, the imposing late-17th-century cathedral sits among former mansions and current government buildings near Red Square. One exit of the Ploshchad Revolutsii metro station is directly across the street. The entire church, both inside and out, has been restored in recent years, though the rather plain interior pales in comparison to the bright pink bell tower and walls of the facade. ⊠ *2/4 per. Bogoyavlensky, Kitai Gorod* ☎ *495/698–3771* 🎫 *Free* ☉ *Daily 8–8* Ⓜ *Ploshchad Revolutsii.*

Cathedral of the Sign (Знаменский Собор *Znamensky Sobor*). This solid redbrick church, topped with one gold and four green onion domes, was part of the monastery of the same name, built on the estate of the Romanovs in the 17th century, right after the establishment of the Romanov dynasty. The church was indeed a sign of hope, as the election of the young Mikhail Romanov as tsar by the Boyar Council brought an end to the so-called Time of Troubles, as the dark period marked by internal strife and foreign intervention that set in after the death of the last heir to Ivan the Terrible was known. ⊠ *8a ul. Varvarka, Kitai Gorod* Ⓜ *Kitai Gorod.*

Church of All-Saints in Kulishki (Церковь Всех Святых на Кулишках *Tserkov Vsekh Svyatykh na Kulishkakh*). This fine example of 17th-century religious architecture was built in honor of the Russian forces who won the decisive Battle of Kulikovo three centuries earlier between Muscovy and the Tatar Golden Horde. Standing at the southern end of Slavyanskaya Square below a sloping park, the graceful church is one of the few survivors of the Soviet reconstruction of the area. Inside it's rather dark and the walls highly gilded; every inch of the ceilings are covered in frescoes. Morning (8:30) and evening (5:30) services are held daily. ⊠ *2 pl. Slavyansky, Kitai Gorod* ☎ *495/623–7566* ☉ *Mon.–Sat. 8–8, Sun. 8–6* Ⓜ *Kitai Gorod.*

Church of St. George on Pskov Hill (Церковь Георгия на Псковской Горке *Tserkov Georgiya na Pskovskoy Gorke*). This majestic five-dome church with blue cupolas studded by gold stars, built in 1657 by merchants from Pskov, stands right next to the Romanov Palace Chambers in Zaryadye. The bell tower is an addition from the 19th century. The interior of the church is somewhat bare, though there are a few impressive old icons and frescoes. ⊠ *12 ul. Varvarka, Kitai Gorod* Ⓜ *Kitai Gorod.*

Church of St. Maxim the Blessed (Церковь Максима Блаженного *Tserkov Maksima Blazhennovo*). In 1698 this white-stone church was built on the site where the Holy Fool Maxim was buried. It's between St. Barbara's and the Cathedral of the Sign (in front of the northern side of the bare field where the Hotel Rossiya once stood). The church's exterior is in a sad state, dingy with exhaust from the cars that speed by on ulitsa Varvarka, and the interior is currently closed to visitors. ⊠ *4 ul. Varvarka, Kitai Gorod* Ⓜ *Kitai Gorod.*

Church of the Trinity in Nikitniki (Церковь Троицы в Никитниках *Tserkov Troitsy v Nikitnikakh*). Painted with white trim and topped by five green cupolas, this lovely redbrick creation—one of the most striking churches in the city—mixes baroque decoration with the principles of ancient Russian church architecture. Its handsome semblance is unfortunately hidden from view from the nearby

Staraya Ploshchad, tucked away as it is among presidential administration buildings. The church was built between 1628 and 1634 for the merchant Grigory Nikitnikov; the private chapel on the south side was the family vault. The murals and iconostasis were the work of Simon Ushakov, a famous icon painter whose workshop was nearby in the brick building across the courtyard. The church has two areas for worship, one on the ground floor and the other up a set of stairs; the upper one is used only on holidays. The lower area is open daily. The shop inside sells candles, icons and other small items. ☒ *3 per. Nikitnikov, Kitai Gorod* ☎ *495/698–5018* ☻ *Daily noon–8* Ⓜ *Kitai Gorod.*

Gulag Museum (Музей истории Гулага *Muzei Istorii Gulaga*). After being yanked from their beds in the middle of the night and loaded onto cattle cars, many of those purged by Stalin were shipped off to the camps of the infamous Gulag. The Soviet Union's network of prison camps is the focus of this small but moving museum. The entrance to the museum is through a simulated gauntlet with metal gates, barbed wire, and a guard tower. Inside the crumbling building are six rooms with paintings of camp scenes, many of which were done by former prisoners. Glass cases hold prisoners' personal effects, including handicrafts they made, such as walrus-tusk cups and a metal cigarette case, and other Gulag-related documents and pictures. The bottom floor has a life-size diorama of typical camp bunks and an isolation cell. There are often excellent temporary exhibits here as well. Guided tours are available in English but must be booked in advance. ☒ *16 ul. Petrovka, Kitai Gorod* ☎ *495/621–7310 main number, 495/621–7346 to book tours* ⊕ *www.gmig.ru* ☒ *150R, free every third Sun. of the month* ☻ *Fri.–Wed. 11–7, Thurs. 12–8; closed last Fri. of month* Ⓜ *Teatralnaya.*

Maly Theater (Малый Театр). Writer Maxim Gorky (1868–1936), known as the father of Soviet socialist realism, once called this theater famous for its productions of Russian classics "the Russian people's university." It opened in 1824 and was originally known as the Little Imperial Theater (*maly* means "little"). Out front stands a statue of a beloved and prolific playwright whose works are often performed here, the 19th-century satirist Alexander Ostrovsky. ☒ *1 pl. Teatralnaya, bldg. 1, Kitai Gorod* ☎ *495/624-4046* ⊕ *www.maly. ru* Ⓜ *Teatralnaya.*

Monastery of the Savior Behind the Icons (Заиконоспасский Монастырь *Zaikonospassky Monastyr*). The monastery was founded at the beginning of the 17th century by Boris Godunov. Russia's first institution of higher learning, the Slavonic-Greco-Latin Academy, was opened in this building in 1687. Many an illustrious scholar studied here, including scientist and poet Mikhail Lomonosov (1711–65) from 1731 to 1735. Hidden inside the courtyard is the monastery's cathedral, **Spassky Sobor**, built in 1600–61 in the Moscow baroque style. The tower of the church is under ongoing renovation, but the interior is intact, and services are held daily. ⌧ *7–9 ul. Nikolskaya, Kitai Gorod* ⊕ *zaikonospasskij-monastyr.ru* Ⓜ *Ploshchad Revolutsii.*

Museum of Russian Icons (Музей русской иконы). One of the largest private collections of Eastern Christian art in the world displays icons and other Christian pieces dating back to the first century. Many of the Russian icons have been beautifully restored and the work continues under a resident master icon restorer. ⌧ *3 ul. Goncharnaya, Kitai Gorod* ☎ *495/221–5283* ⊕ *www.russikona.ru* ⌧ *free* ⊙ *Thurs.–Tues. 11–7* Ⓜ *Kitai Gorod, Taganskaya.*

FAMILY **Polytechnical Museum (Политехнический Музей** *Politekhnichesky Muzey*). The achievements of science and technology, including an awesome collection of early-20th-century Russian cars, fill an entire Moscow block. The monumental building that houses the museum was built in 1875 by Ippolit Monigetti, a Russian of Italian birth whose day job was designing annexes on the royal family's country estates. The endless series of exhibits—miners' lamps, Soviet televisions, even a full-scale replica of the USSR's first atomic bomb—can be overwhelming and esoteric, but kids love it. There are also many good temporary exhibits, as well as the movie museum (mostly Soviet animation films) and a small planetarium at the southern entrance. ⌧ *3/4 pl. Novaya, Kitai Gorod* ☎ *495/623–0756* ⊕ *www.polymus.ru* ⌧ *150R* ⊙ *Tues.– Sun. 10–6; closed last Fri. of month* Ⓜ *Lubyanka.*

Romanov Palace Chambers in Zaryadye (Палаты Романовых в Зарядье *Palaty Romanovykh v Zaryadye*). It's believed that Mikhail Romanov (1596–1645), the first tsar of the Romanov dynasty, was born in this house. Today the mansion houses a lovely museum devoted to the boyar lifestyle of the 16th and 17th centuries. Period clothing, furniture, and household items furnish the rooms, illustrating how the boyars, a feudal aristocracy, lived. During the week the museum is often open only to groups with advance reservations—these are typically throngs of school children—but if you ask, you may be allowed to join. Tours are available in English, but you must make reservations. ⌧ *10 ul. Varvarka, Kitai Gorod* ☎ *495/698–1256* ⌧ *150R* ⊙ *Mon. and Thurs.–Sun. 10–6, Wed. 11–7; closed 1st Mon. of month* Ⓜ *Kitai Gorod.*

ULITSA TVERSKAYA ТВЕРСКАЯ УЛИЦА

As the line of the road that led from the northern tip of the Kremlin to the ancient town of Tver, ulitsa Tverskaya had been an important route for centuries. Later that road was extended all the way to the new capital on the Baltic Sea, St. Petersburg. Ulitsa Tverskaya is Moscow's main shopping artery, attracting shoppers hungry for the latest trends. The lovely, wide boulevard, a tribute to the grandiose reconstruction projects of the Stalinist era, is lined with cafés, banks and exchanges, shops, and hotels. Some of the city's best and biggest stores are on the ground floors of massive apartment buildings, some quite attractive and graced by a fine art nouveau style. On a sunny day, Tverskaya is an especially pleasant walk. Ploshchad Pushkinskaya is about halfway up the street from the Kremlin, and it is a popular meeting point for Muscovites. Tverskaya was given its present form in the mid-1930s—until then it was narrow and twisting, lined in places with wooden houses. From 1932 to 1990 the road was known as Gorky Street, in honor of the writer Maxim Gorky, the father of Soviet socialist realism. In 1990 the first section of the street, leading from the heart of town to ploshchad Triumfalnaya, was given back its prerevolutionary name of ulitsa Tverskaya. A year later, the second section, ending at the Belorussian railway station, was also returned to its old name of Tverskaya-Yamskaya.

GETTING HERE AND AROUND

The area around ulitsa Tverskaya can be reached through the Tverskaya, Pushkinskaya, Chekhovskaya, Mayakovskaya, and Okhotny Ryad metro stations. Once here, unless you're traveling north all the way to Belorusskaya metro station, which sits at the north end of ulitsa Tverskaya-Yamskaya past the Garden Ring, you're best off walking the web of streets in this neighborhood. The distances can be long at times, but other transportation options—with the exception of a car—aren't convenient for moving around here.

TIMING If you stay in Moscow for more than a few days you'll always end up on or near ulitsa Tverskaya. Consider spending half a day if you'd like to visit the museums in this neighborhood.

TOP ATTRACTIONS

Church of the Resurrection (Церковь Воскресения *Tserkov Voskreseniya*). Built in 1629, this is one of the few lucky churches to have stayed open throughout the years of Soviet rule. As a survivor, the church was the recipient of many priceless icons from less fortunate churches destroyed or closed by the Soviets. Services are still held here daily. Be sure to look at the beautiful frescoes on the ceilings in the chapels on either side of you as you enter. Two famous icons, depicting the Coronation of the Virgin Mary and the Assumption of the Blessed Virgin Mary, hang in the vaults on either side of the vestibule. ✉ *15/2 per. Bryusov, Ulitsa Tverskaya* ☎ *495/629–6616* Ⓜ *Tverskaya.*

Hotel National (Гостиница Националь). The ornate art nouveau splendor of the National, built in 1903, belies its revolutionary function as the pre-Kremlin residence for Lenin and subsequent home for Communist Party operatives and fellow travelers, such as author John Reed. Beautiful mosaics adorn the hotel facade; inside, the luxurious rooms and restaurants conjure up the National's prerevolutionary elegance. A plaque on the outside of the hotel commemorates the five killed in December 2003, when a female suicide bomber blew herself up just outside the hotel's entrance. The bombing was attributed to Chechnya's separatist war. ✉ *15/1 ul. Mokhovaya, Ulitsa Tverskaya* ☎ *495/258–7000* ⊕ *www.national.ru* Ⓜ *Okhotny Ryad.*

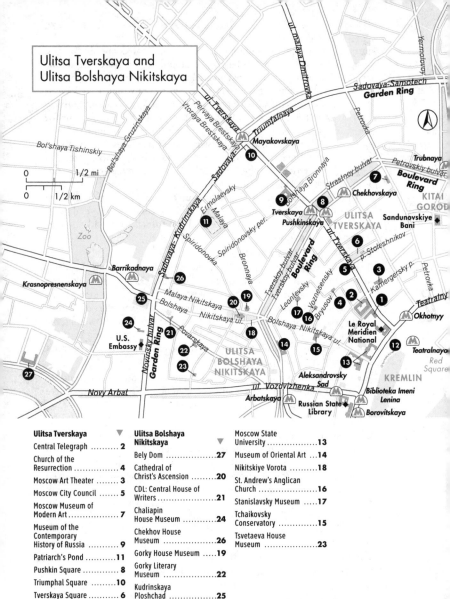

Ulitsa Tverskaya and Ulitsa Bolshaya Nikitskaya

Moscow Art Theater (Московский Художественный Театр *MKhAT*). One of Moscow's most historically important theaters, this performance space is renowned for its productions of the Russian classics, especially those of Anton Chekhov (1860–1904). Founded in 1898 by the celebrated actor and director Konstantin Stanislavsky (1863–1938) and playwright and producer Vladimir Nemirovich-Danchenko (1858–1943), the theater staged the first productions of Chekhov's and Maxim Gorky's (1868–1936) plays. It was here that Stanislavsky developed the Stanislavsky Method, based on the realism in traditional Russian theater. After the successful production of Chekhov's *The Seagull* (the first staging in St. Petersburg had bombed), the bird was chosen as the theater's emblem. An affiliated, more modern theater, with a seating capacity of 2,000, also confusingly called the Moscow Art Theater, was opened in 1972 on Tverskoi bulvar, near Stanislavsky's home. The mural opposite the old theater depicts Anton Chekhov, as does the statue at the start of Kamergersky pereulok. Book ahead for tours in English. ✉ *3 per. Kamergersky, Ulitsa Tverskaya* ☎ *495/692–6748* ⊕ *www.art.theatre.ru* Ⓜ *Okhotny Ryad.*

Moscow City Council (Моссовет *Mossoviet*). This impressive structure was built at the end of the 18th century by Matvey Kazakov for the Moscow governor-general. During the reconstruction of Tverskaya ulitsa in the 1930s, the building was moved back about 45 feet in order to widen the street. The top two stories—a mirror image of the mansion's original two stories—were added at that time. The building now houses the city government and mayor's office. Across the street there is a statue of the founder of Moscow, Yuri Dolgoruky, astride his horse. ✉ *22 ul. Tverskaya, Ulitsa Tverskaya* Ⓜ *Tverskaya.*

Museum of the Contemporary History of Russia (Музей Современной Истории России *Muzey Sovremennoi Istorii Rossii*). This is a good place to start if you want a refresher course on Soviet history. Originally built by Giliardi in 1787, the mansion was rebuilt in the classical style after the Moscow Fire of 1812; it was once the social center of the Moscow aristocracy and its entrance is flanked appropriately by two smirking lions. The building housed the Museum of the Revolution from 1926 to the late 20th century, at which time the museum was converted to its present purpose. Although the museum retains many of the former exhibits—heavily imbued with Soviet propaganda—they have been updated to reflect the changing political climate in Russia. The permanent exhibit, on the second floor, begins with a review of the first workers' organizations in the 19th century. The exhibits outlining the 1905 and 1917 revolutions include the horse-drawn machine-gun cart of the First Cavalry Army, the texts of the first decrees of the Soviet government on peace and land, dioramas and paintings portraying revolutionary battles, and thousands of other relics. The next rooms outline the history of Soviet rule, with extensive material devoted to Stalin's rise to power before whizzing through the short post-Soviet history.

With a huge archive and the country's best collection of political posters and medals, the museum has a reputation for hosting excellent temporary exhibits. Explanations are only in Russian, but you can arrange a tour in English by calling ahead. The fine gift shop sells

Russian souvenirs (including some beautiful amber) and great vintage items like flags and political-rally posters. ✉ *21 ul. Tverskaya, Ulitsa Tverskaya* ☎ *495/699–6724* ⊕ *www.sovr.ru* 💳 *250R* ⊗ *Tues., Wed., and Fri. 10–6, Thurs. 12–9, weekends 11–7; closed last Fri. of month* Ⓜ *Tverskaya, Pushkinskaya.*

Patriarch's Ponds (Патриаршие Пруды *Patriarshy Prudy*). The beginning of Russian satirist and novelist Mikhail Bulgakov's (1891–1940) novel *The Master and Margarita* is set in a small park surrounding these ponds, named after the patriarch of the Orthodox Church, who once owned the area. Shaded by trees and with plenty of benches, it's a nice spot for a break, and there are several good restaurants nearby, including a pavilion near the ponds where they serve kitschy Soviet cuisine in an opulent setting. In winter the pond is used as a skating rink. The surrounding neighborhood has become one of Moscow's poshest. ✉ *ul. Malaya Bronnaya, Ulitsa Tverskaya* Ⓜ *Mayakovskaya.*

Pushkin Square (Пушкинская Площадь *Ploshchad Pushkinskaya*). The most popular meeting place in town is located at the intersection of ulitsa Tverskaya and the Boulevard Ring. Every evening in good weather you will see crowds milling by the bronze statue of Alexander Pushkin (1799–1837), which stands at the top of a small park. It's the work of Alexander Opekushin and was erected by public subscription in 1880. It is impossible to underestimate Russia's love for the poet, who is credited with founding modern Russian literature. One of his most famous lines, from his novel in verse *Eugene Onegin* (1823), is about Moscow: "Moscow, how many strains are fusing / in that one sound, for Russian hearts! / what store of riches it imparts!" Summer and winter, fresh flowers on the pedestal prove that the poet's admirers are still ardent and numerous. Also at this site is the country's first McDonald's, once the busiest in the world, and a restaurant and shop called Armenia, which sells that country's famed Ararat brandy and other delicacies. ✉ *Junction between Tverskaya and Boulevard Ring, Ulitsa Tverskaya* Ⓜ *Pushkinskaya.*

Triumphal Square (Триумфальная Площадь *Ploshchad Triumfalnaya*). This major intersection is where the grand boulevard of Moscow, the Garden Ring, crosses Tverskaya ulitsa. In the center of the square stands a statue of the revolutionary poet Vladimir Mayakovsky (1893–1930), who it's generally believed committed suicide after he became disillusioned with the revolution he had so passionately supported.

The square is a center of Moscow's cultural life—and lately it's also become the political opposition's preferred site for anti-Putin rallies. (In order to prevent the latter, city authorities occasionally cordon off much of the square, supposedly to undertake emergency construction

---

METRO 2

Moscow's metro is one of the deepest in the world, but below it, if you believe the Soviet legend, is a second even deeper metro system, Metro 2. This metro was purportedly built for Stalin as a private line for top party officials. One of the lines supposedly led from the Kremin to the Lubyanka, the home of the feared KGB.

work.) The **Tchaikovsky Concert Hall,** which opened in 1940, stands on one corner (in its foyer are various food outlets); the **Satire Theater** is next door, on the Garden Ring; and the **Mossoviet Theater** is nearby, at 16 Bolshaya Sadovaya. The multitiered tower of the elegant **Peking Hotel,** opened in 1956 as a mark of Sino-Soviet friendship, rises nearby.

While you're here, it's worth riding the escalator down for a peek at the spectacular interior of the **Mayakovskaya metro station,** which, like many early stations, lies deep underground (it doubled as a bomb shelter during World War II). Stalin made a famous speech here on the 24th anniversary of the Bolshevik Revolution, at the height of the Siege of Moscow. Colorful, pastel mosaics depicting Soviet achievements in outer space decorate the ceiling. ✉ *Junction between Tverskaya and the Garden Ring, Ulitsa Tverskaya* Ⓜ *Mayakovskaya.*

WORTH NOTING

Moscow Museum of Modern Art (Московский Музей Современного Искусства). A collection founded in 1999 by controversial sculptor Zurab Tsereteli, best known for his enormous statue of Peter the Great on the Moskva River, is gaining respect in a city suddenly enamored with contemporary art. Works by the likes of Picasso and Dalí and, especially, artists from the Russian avant-garde movement form the core of the museum's holdings. Special exhibitions range from retrospectives of eminent Russian émigrés to debut collections to experimental video art to interactive exhibitions. The museum's main building is a restored 18th-century mansion, but there are five other branches that are also in the city center. One ticket admits you to all of the branches for the day. ✉ *25 ul. Petrovka, Ulitsa Tverskaya* ☎ *495/694–2890, 495/231–4406 guided tours* ⊕ *www.mmoma.ru* 🎫 *300R, free every 3rd Sun. of month* 🕙 *Mon.–Wed. and Fri.–Sun. noon–8, Thurs. 1–9; closed 3rd Mon. of month* Ⓜ *Pushkinskaya.*

Ulitsa Tverskaya-Yamskaya (Тверская-Ямская улица). This last section of ulitsa Tverskaya leads to Belorussky railway station, which also has two interconnecting metro stations. The entrances to all three stations are spread along the edge of sprawling ploshchad Tverskaya Zastava, known for its gnarled traffic patterns caused by construction projects that have occupied it for years. Lately, the area surrounding the square has become home to a number of popular restaurants, including the gastropub favorite Ragout and a midrange steakhouse called Torro Grill. Belorussky station is where trains roll in from Western Europe (and from Sheremetyevo airport on the Aeroexpress) and is the site of the former Triumphal Gates, built in the 19th century by the architect Osip Bove to commemorate the Russian victory in the war with Napoléon. The gates were demolished in a typical fit of destruction in the 1930s. A replica of the original gates was erected in 1968 near Poklonnaya Hill, at the end of Kutuzovsky prospekt. ✉ *Ulitsa Tverskaya* Ⓜ *Mayakovskaya.*

CLOSE UP

Moscow's Magnificent Metro

Even if you don't plan on using the metro to get around Moscow, it's still worth taking a peek at this wonder of the urban world. The first line opened in 1935, and the earliest stations—in the city center and along the ring line—were built as public palaces. Many of the millions of commuters using the system each day bustle past chandeliers, sculptures, stained-glass windows, beautiful mosaics, and pink, white, and black marble. With its rich collection of decorative materials, the metro has often been called a museum; it's even been said that no geological museum in the world has such a peculiar stone library.

Mayakovskaya station, opened in 1938, may well be the jewel in the crown of the Moscow metro. The vaulted ceiling of the grand central hall has 33 mosaic panels, based on the theme "One Day of Soviet Skies,"

by Russian artist Alexander Deineka. **Novoslobodskaya,** opened in 1952, sparkles, thanks to its light-backed stained glass. Several other stations—such as **Ploshchad Revolutsii,** with its bronze figures from the socialist world order (farmers, soldiers, and such)—are tourist attractions in their own right.

In the past, Moscow's metro architects won international architecture awards for their designs. Designs of new stations, however, have departed from these grand old stations; they lack brass sculptures and intricate stained glass, for example. But with indirect lighting, exquisite marble, and an open, airy feeling, these new stations reflect modern life in a way that the monumental Soviet displays of past glories don't. Moscow's metro is one of the top three most heavily used metro systems in the world.

ULITSA BOLSHAYA NIKITSKAYA
БОЛЬШАЯ НИКИТСКАЯ УЛИЦА

Bolshaya Nikitskaya is one of the many old streets radiating from the Kremlin, spokelike, just like ulitsa Tverskaya to the northeast and Novy Arbat to the southwest. The street was laid out along the former road to Novgorod, an ancient town northwest of Moscow, and is divided into two sections. The first part is lined with 18th- and 19th-century mansions and also includes the Tchaikovsky Conservatory and Moscow State University buildings; it begins at Ploshchad Manezhnaya, across from the fortification walls of the Kremlin. The second section, notable for its enchanting art nouveau mansions, starts at ploshchad Nikitskiye Vorota, where ulitsa Bolshaya Nikitskaya intersects with Bulvarnoye Koltso (the Boulevard Ring).

GETTING HERE AND AROUND
Bolshaya Nikitskaya is served by the Krasnopresnenskaya, Barrikadnaya, Okhotny Ryad, Arbatskaya, and Biblioteka Imeni Lenina metro stations. You can approach the street from ploshchad Pushkin walking south along the Boulevard Ring; from metro station Arbatskaya walking north, also on a boulevard; or from ploshchad Manezhnaya, where the eastern end of the street is. It's a bit of a trek to get to the street from any metro station except Biblioteka Imeni Lenina, so plan accordingly.

TIMING   This neighborhood is spread over quite a bit of territory and includes detours down crooked streets, so it's best to allow a full day to see everything at a leisurely pace. If you start out at the Okhotny Ryad metro station and walk through the sights to end at the Barrikadnaya station, you'll have walked roughly 3 km (2 miles).

TOP ATTRACTIONS

Bely Dom (Белый Дом *White House*). This large, white, modern building perched along the riverbank is the headquarters of the Russian government and the prime minister. Before the August 1991 coup, the "White House" was the headquarters of the Russian Republic of the USSR. In October 1993 the building was shelled in response to the rioting and near-coup by Vice President Alexander Rutskoi and parliamentarians. They had barricaded themselves in the White House after Boris Yeltsin's decision to dissolve parliament and hold new elections. Today the building is also known as the Dom Pravitelstvo, or Government House. It sits directly across the Moskva River from the Radisson Royal Hotel, once the Ukraina, one of the seven "Stalin Gothic" skyscrapers built in Moscow in the mid-20th century. ✉ *2 nab. Krasnopresnenskaya, Ulitsa Bolshaya Nikitskaya* ☎ *495/605–5329* Ⓜ *Krasnopresnenskaya.*

Cathedral of Christ's Ascension in Storozhakh (Храм Вознесения Господня в Сторожах *Hram Vozneseniya Gospodnya v Storozhakh*). Like Moscow State University, this classical church was designed by Matvei Kazakov and built in the 1820s. The church is most famous as the site where the Russian poet Alexander Pushkin married the younger Natalya Goncharova; Pushkin died six years later, in a duel defending her honor. There is a kitschy and much despised statue of the couple on the square outside the church. (History has judged Natalya harshly; she was probably not guilty of adultery, although she did enjoy flirting.) The statue in the park to the left of the church as you face it is of Alexey Tolstoy, a relative of Leo's and a well-known Soviet writer of historical novels. The church stood empty and abandoned for many years, but after major repairs, religious services have resumed. ✉ *36 ul. Bolshaya Nikitskaya, Ulitsa Bolshaya Nikitskaya* ☎ *495/690–5936* Ⓜ *Arbatskaya.*

CDL: Central House of Writers (Центральный Дом Литераторов *Tsentralny Dom Literatorov*). It's believed that Leo Tolstoy (1828–1910) used this large mansion, the administrative offices of the Writers' Union, as a model for the Rostov home in *War and Peace*. A statue of Tolstoy stands in the courtyard. Mikhail Bulgakov (1891–1940) set part of his satire of Soviet life, *The Master and Margarita,* here. The beautiful wood-paneled dining room is open to the public. ✉ *50 ul. Povarskaya, Ulitsa Bolshaya Nikitskaya* ☎ *495/691–1515* ⊕ *www.cdlrestaurant.ru* Ⓜ *Barrikadnaya.*

Chaliapin House Museum (Дом-музей Шаляпина *Dom-muzey Chaliapina*). Fyodor Chaliapin (1873–1938), one of the world's greatest opera singers, lived in this beautifully restored manor house from 1910 to 1922. Chaliapin was stripped of his Soviet citizenship while on tour in France in 1922; he never returned to Russia again. The Soviets turned his home into an apartment building, and until restorations in the 1980s,

The Seven Gothic Sisters

With their spookily lit cornices dominating the skyline since the mid-20th century, the "Seven Sisters" (also known as the "Stalin Gothics") are as much a part of the Moscow experience as the Empire State Building is in New York. The neo-Gothic buildings are often called "wedding cake" skyscrapers because their tiered construction creates a sense of upward movement and grandeur, like a rocket on standby.

The seven buildings—the Ministry of Foreign Affairs; the Ukraina and Leningradskaya hotels; the residential buildings at ploshchad Kudrinskaya (Kudrinsky Square), naberezhnaya Kotelnicheskaya (Kotelnicheskaya Embankment), and Krasniye Vorota; and the imposing Moscow State University on Sparrow Hills—were constructed when the country lay in ruins, just after World War II. Stalin ordered the skyscrapers to be built in 1947, on the 800th anniversary of Moscow's founding, as a symbol of Soviet power. German prisoners of war were forced to work on several of the buildings.

An eighth skyscraper was planned (before the others were started) but never built: this was the grandiose Palace of Soviets, which was meant to replace the Kremlin as the seat of government power. It was intended to be the tallest building in the world, with a height of 1,378 feet topped by a 300-foot statue of Lenin. The site

of the Cathedral of Christ Our Savior on the Moskva River was chosen, and the church was demolished in 1931. Only later did builders realize that the ground was too wet to support such an enormous structure. The plans were abandoned, and the area was turned into a swimming pool until the cathedral was rebuilt in 1997.

According to the Soviet propaganda of the time, most of the new buildings were part of the government's drive to replace slums with better housing. In truth, residents were mainly party members, actors, writers, and other members of the elite. With few ordinary people living in or having access to the buildings, legendary stories developed around the Seven Sisters. The Ukraina's spire was said to hide a nuclear-rocket launcher, while Moscow State University was rumored to have a secret tunnel leading to Stalin's dacha. The university was also said to run as deep underground as it did above, concealing secret study centers and a metro connection. The building at ploshchad Kudrinskaya overlooks the U.S. embassy. It was said that KGB spies kept an eye on the embassy compound from certain windows.

Today you can easily visit most of the skyscrapers, particularly the Ukraina and Leningradskaya hotels, now the Radisson Royal and Hilton Moscow Leningradskaya hotels, respectively.

the building contained 60 communal apartments. With help from Chaliapin's family in France, the rooms have again been arranged and furnished as they were when the singer lived here. The walls are covered with works of art given to Chaliapin by talented friends, such as the artists Mikhail Vrubel and Isaac Levitan. Also on display are Chaliapin's colorful costumes, which were donated to the museum by his son. When you reach the piano room, you'll hear original recordings of Chaliapin singing his favorite roles. Entrance is from inside the courtyard.

English-language tours are available and should be reserved ahead of time. ✉ *25 bul. Novinsky, Ulitsa Bolshaya Nikitskaya* ☎ *495/605–6236* ⊕ *www.shalyapin-museum.org* ✆ *150R* ☉ *Tues. 10-6; Wed. and Thurs. 11:30-7; Sat. 10-6; Sun. 10–4:30.* Ⓜ *Barrikadnaya.*

Chekhov House Museum (Дом-музей Чехова *Dom-muzey Chekhova*). The sign "Dr. Chekhov" still hangs from the door of this home where Chekhov resided from 1886 to 1890. The rooms are arranged as they were when he lived here, and some of the furniture, such as two sturdy desks covered in green felt, belonged to the author's family. One room showcases photos and memorabilia from Chekhov's trek to the island of Sakhalin in the Russian Far East. Overall, the materials on display at the museum are not particularly enthralling, so unless you are a Chekhov diehard, this is far from an essential stop. ✉ *6 ul. Sadovaya-Kudrinskaya, Ulitsa Bolshaya Nikitskaya* ☎ *495/691–6345* ✆ *100R* ☉ *Tues., Wed., Fri.–Sun.11–6; Thurs. 1–8; closed last day of the month.* Ⓜ *Barrikadnaya.*

Cook Street (Поварская улица *ulitsa Povarskaya*). This street is where the tsars' cooks lived, and hence the Russian name, Povarskaya. After the revolution the street was renamed Vorovskovo, in honor of a Soviet diplomat who was assassinated by a Russian, but it returned to its prerevolutionary name in the 1990s. It's an important center of the Moscow artistic community, with the film actors' studio, the Russian Academy of Music (the Gnesin Institute), and the Tsentralny Dom Literatorov (Central House of Writers) all located here. Many of the old mansions have been preserved, and the street retains its prerevolutionary tranquillity and charm. In the first flush days of summer your walk is likely to be accompanied by a rousing drum set or tinkling piano sonata issuing from the open windows of the music school. Note the other streets in this small neighborhood have similar culinary names such as Bread (Khlebny), Table (Stolovy), and Tablecloth (Skaterny) lanes. ✉ *Ulitsa Bolshaya Nikitskaya* Ⓜ *Arbatskaya.*

Gorky House Museum (Дом Рябушинского *Dom Ryabushinskovo*). This marvelous and wonderfully preserved example of Moscow art nouveau was the home of Maxim Gorky from 1931 to 1936. Sometimes called the Ryabushinsky Mansion, it was built in 1901 for the wealthy banker of that name and designed by the architect Fyodor Shektel. (If you arrived in Moscow by train, you may have noticed the fanciful Yaroslav station, another of his masterpieces, just opposite the Leningrad railway station.) Although Gorky was a champion of the proletariat, his home was rather lavish. Gorky himself apparently hated the *style moderne,* as art nouveau was termed back then. Those who don't, however, are charmed by this building of ecru brick and stone painted pink and mauve atop gray foundations. A mosaic of irises forms a border around the top of most of the house, and a fanciful yet utilitarian iron fence matches the unusual design of the window frames. The spectacular interior includes a stained-glass roof and a twisting marble staircase that looks like a wave of gushing water. Tours in English are available. ✉ *2 ul. Malaya Nikitskaya, bldg. 6, Ulitsa Bolshaya Nikitskaya* ☎ *495/690–0535* ✆ *Free* ☉ *Wed.–Sun. 11–5:30; closed last Thurs. of month* Ⓜ *Arbatskaya.*

Nikitskiye Vorota (Никитские Ворота). This square was named after the *vorota* (gates) of the white-stone fortification walls that once stood here. On one side of the square is a modern building with square windows; this is the office of ITAR-TASS, once the official news agency of the Soviet Union and the mouthpiece of the Kremlin. In the park in the center of the square stands a monument to Kliment Timiryazev, a famous botanist.

The busy road intersecting Bolshaya Nikitskaya ulitsa at one end of the square is the **Bulvarnoye Koltso** (Boulevard Ring), which forms a semicircle around the city center. It begins at the banks of the Moskva River, just south of the Kremlin, and after curving eastward, then south, it reaches the riverbank again after several miles, near the mouth of the Yauza River, northeast of the Kremlin. Its path follows the lines of the 16th-century white-stone fortification wall that gave Moscow the name "White City." The privilege of living within its walls was reserved for the court nobility and craftsmen serving the tsar. The wall was torn down in 1775, on orders from Catherine the Great, and was replaced by the current Boulevard Ring. The perfect way to get a good view of the inner city is to slowly walk along the ring—this is best done on the weekend or late at night to avoid traffic on the boulevard. Running along its center is a broad strip of trees and flowers, dotted with playgrounds and benches. Summer brings out a burst of outdoor cafés, ice-cream vendors, and strolling lovers along the boulevard. ⊠ *Ulitsa Bolshaya Nikitskaya* Ⓜ *Arbatskaya.*

Ploshchad Kudrinskaya (Кудринская Площадь *Kudrinsky Square*). Along one side of this square, cars race along the Garden Ring, the major circular road surrounding Moscow. If you approach the ring from Bolshaya Nikitskaya ulitsa or Povarskaya ulitsa, the first thing to catch your eye will be the 22-story skyscraper directly across Novinsky bulvar. One of the seven Stalin Gothics, this one is 525 feet high. The ground floor, home to a grand supermarket in Soviet times, is now occupied by clothing stores and a cafeteria called Central Restaurant House—this is worth peeking into to admire the towering ceilings and stained-glass windows inside. The rest of the building contains apartments. This area saw heavy fighting during the uprisings of 1905 and 1917 (the plaza was previously called Ploshchad Vosstaniya, or Insurrection Square). The Barrikadnaya (Barricade) metro station is very close by. Cross the ulitsa Barrikadnaya and bear right and down the hill; you'll see people streaming into the station to your right. ⊠ *Ulitsa Bolshaya Nikitskaya* Ⓜ *Barrikadnaya.*

Stanislavsky Museum (Музей Станиславского *Muzey Stanislavskovo*). Konstantin Stanislavsky (1863–1938) was a Russian actor, director, and producer, as well as the founder of the Stanislavsky Method, the catalyst for method acting. He was also one of the founders of the Moscow Art Theater. Stanislavsky lived and worked in this house, an elegant 19th-century building with stunning painted ceilings, during the last 17 years of his life. The house has been kept as it was while he lived here, showcasing a small practice theater, the various leather chairs he preferred, a few of his old theater costumes, and other memorabilia. The entrance to the museum is through the courtyard. ⊠ *6 per. Leontyevsky, Ulitsa Bolshaya Nikitskaya* ☎ *495/629–2855* 💰 *120R* ⊙ *Wed. and Fri. 12–7, Thurs. and weekends 11–6; closed last Thurs. of month* Ⓜ *Pushkinskaya.*

Tchaikovsky Conservatory (**Консерватория имени Чайковского** *Konservatoriya imeni Chaykovskovo*). The famous Tchaikovsky Music Competition takes place every four years in this prestigious music school's grand performance space. Rachmaninoff, Scriabin, and Tchaikovsky are among the famous composers who worked at the conservatory, founded in 1866 and at its current location since 1870. Concerts are performed almost daily in the school's various performance spaces, which include the smaller Rachmaninovsky and Maly Halls. Both of these host chamber music concerts. Tickets, almost always affordable, are sold at a small window directly on the sidewalk on ulitsa Bolshaya Nikitskaya east of the main hall. If you'd rather not attend a performance, you can also just sit back with a coffee and listen to rehearsals and concerts from the summer garden of the Coffeemania here, near a statue of Tchaikovsky designed by Vera Mukhina, a famous Soviet sculptor. ⊠ *13/6 ul. Bolshaya Nikitskaya, Ulitsa Bolshaya Nikitskaya* ☎ *495/629–9401* ⊕ *www. mosconsv.ru* ☉ *Box office 10–10* Ⓜ *Okhotny Ryad or Arbatskaya.*

WORTH NOTING

Gorky Literary Museum (**Литературный Музей Горького** *Literaturny Muzey Gorkovo*). Letters, manuscripts, and pictures of the great proletarian writer will be of great interest to Gorky fans. There are also portraits by Nesterov and Serov and a remarkable photograph of Gorky playing chess with Lenin on the Italian island of Capri, where Gorky made his home for many years both before and after the Soviets took power. Gorky never lived here, but there is a miniature wooden reproduction of his childhood home, complete with village yard and outbuildings. ⊠ *25a ul. Povarskaya, Ulitsa Bolshaya Nikitskaya* ☎ *495/690–5130* ☑ *Free* ☉ *Mon., Tues., and Thurs. 10–5, Wed. and Fri. noon–7; closed 1st Thurs. of month* Ⓜ *Barrikadnaya.*

Museum of Oriental Art (**Музей Искусства Народов Востока** *Muzey Iskusstva Narodov Vostoka*). Glass cases filled to capacity with artwork and clothing from the Central Asian republics, China, Japan, and Korea make up the museum's large permanent collection. The museum itself is a cool and calm place to take a leisurely stroll. Most of the placards in the museum are in Russian, but there are a few annotations in English. ⊠ *12a bul. Nikitsky, Ulitsa Bolshaya Nikitskaya* ☎ *495/691– 0212* ⊕ *www.orientmuseum.ru* ☑ *250R* ☉ *Tues., Wed., Fri.–Sun. 11–8, Thurs. noon–8.* Ⓜ *Arbatskaya.*

St. Andrew's Anglican Church. Moscow's only Anglican church, built in 1884, served the British-expatriate community for more than 40 years, including a mass for Queen Victoria after her death in 1901. No bells were rung then, however, because only Orthodox churches were allowed to have them. Instead the tower was used as a strong room for British merchants. The 1917 revolution ended both spiritual and secular functions, however, and the church was closed. The pews are believed to have been burned in the harsh winters of the early 1920s, and the stained glass was replaced when the building was converted into a recording studio. Today the Church of England has reacquired the property, and it's again a vibrant, working church and a gathering place for the community. Regular services include morning prayer on Sundays at 8 am and evening prayer on Wednesdays and Sundays at 6:30 pm.

✉ *8 per. Voznesensky, Ulitsa Bolshaya Nikitskaya* ☎ *495/629–9889* ⊕ *www.standrewsmoscow.org* ⊙ *Services Wed. 6:30 pm and Sun. 8 am and6:30 pm* Ⓜ *Okhotny Ryad.*

Tsvetaeva House Museum (Дом-музей Цветаевой *Dom-muzey Tsvetaevoy*). Marina Tsvetaeva (1892–1941), the renowned poet, lived in an apartment on the second floor of this building from 1914 to 1922. Today the building houses not only a museum dedicated to her but also a cultural center that arranges international literary evenings, musical events, and annual conferences covering the poet and the Silver Age (1890s–1917) in general. You must ring the bell to enter the museum, which begins on the second floor. Although the rooms are decorated in the style of the early 1900s, they are not as they were when Tsvetaeva lived here. The poetry written on the wall in her bedroom has been re-created. The children's room has some stuffed animals in place of the real animals—a dog, a squirrel, and a turtle, to name a few—that Tsvetaeva kept in her home. ✉ *6 per. Borisoglebsky, Ulitsa Bolshaya Nikitskaya* ☎ *495/695–3543* 🖼 *100R* ⊙ *Mon.,Wed. and Fri.–Sun. noon–8, Thurs. noon–9; closed last Fri. of month* Ⓜ *Arbatskaya.*

ARBAT АРБАТ

Two of downtown Moscow's most important avenues are the Arbat (also known as the Stary Arbat, or Old Arbat) and Novy Arbat (New Arbat), which are two more spokelike routes leading away from the Kremlin. The pedestrian-only Stary Arbat is revered by many Muscovites, who usually refer to it simply as "the Arbat." The area is an attractive, cobbled pedestrian precinct lined with gift shops and cafés; it used to be packed with souvenir stands as well, but they've all been moved indoors. It's a carnival of portrait artists, poets, and musicians, as well as the enthusiastic admirers of their work. One of the oldest sections of Moscow, the Arbat dates from the 16th century, when it was the beginning of the road that led from the Kremlin to the city of Smolensk. At that time it was also the quarter where court artisans lived, and several of the surrounding streets still recall this in such names as Plotnikov (Carpenter), Serebryany (Silversmith), and Kalashny (Pastry Cook). Early in the 19th century the Arbat became a favorite district of the aristocracy, and a century later it became a shopping street.

Novy Arbat has both a different history and spirit. For almost 30 years it was named Kalinin prospekt, in honor of Mikhail Kalinin, an old Bolshevik whose prestige plummeted after 1991. The stretch from the Kremlin to ploshchad Arbatskaya has been given back its prerevolutionary name of ulitsa Vozdvizhenka. The second section—which begins where Vozdvizhenka ends and runs west for about a mile to the Moskva River—is now called Novy Arbat. In contrast to ulitsa Vozdvizhenka, which has retained some of its prerevolutionary charm, and the Arbat, which is actively re-creating the look of its past, Novy Arbat is a modern thoroughfare. It's now something of an entertainment area, with flashy shopping malls and lots of decent restaurants.

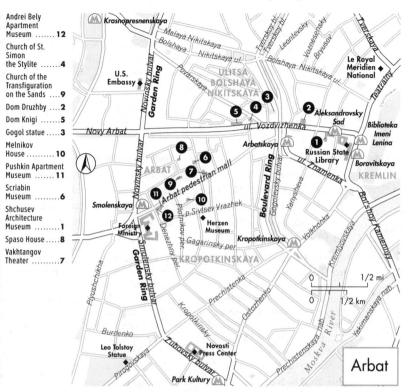

Arbat

GETTING HERE AND AROUND

You can reach the Arbat via the Arbatskaya, Smolenskaya, and Biblioteka Imeni Lenina metro stations. Novy Arbat is an enormous avenue packed with traffic and therefore not very pleasant to walk along; it's best to have a specific destination in mind if going there. It's easy to get lost in the side streets off Stary Arbat, but you inevitably make your way to a recognizable major thoroughfare, whether it's back to Stary Arbat, to Novy Arbat to the north, the Garden Ring on the western edge, or ulitsa Prechistinka to the south, which is another spoke heading southwest from the Kremlin.

TIMING   You can easily spend a whole day exploring the Arbat, especially if you go souvenir shopping at the shops and street kiosks you'll see along the way. There are numerous charming side streets just off the Old Arbat and plenty of cafés to stop in for a break. If you want to avoid crowds, check this neighborhood out on a weekday; the pedestrian zone in the Old Arbat, in particular, draws big crowds on the weekends. The museums in this neighborhood are all fairly small; you'll need no more than an hour for each of them.

TOP ATTRACTIONS

Church of St. Simon the Stylite (Церковь Симеона Столпника *Tserkov Simeona Stolpnika*). This bright white 17th-century church stands out in stark contrast to the modern architecture that dominates the area. During the reconstruction of the neighborhood in the 1960s, many old churches and buildings were destroyed, but this one was left purposely standing as a reminder of the past. For years it housed a conservation museum, but now it's been returned to the Orthodox Church and is active. Nothing remains, however, of the original interiors. ⊠ *4 ul. Novy Arbat, Arbat* Ⓜ *Arbatskaya.*

QUICK BITES

Zhiguli (Жигули). Among the numerous cafés along the Arbat where you can take a break and have a drink is this quirky place that feeds on nostalgia for the Soviet Union. Fortunately the service and the food are better than they were in the old days. There's a large dining room and a small, cafeteria-style cafe for light and quick snacks. ⊠ *11 ul. Novy Arbat, bldg. 1, off Arbatsky per., Arbat* ☎ *495/691–4144* ⊕ *zhiguli.net/ru* Ⓜ *Arbatskaya.*

Church of the Transfiguration on the Sands (Храм Спаса Преображения на Песках *Khram Spasa Preobrazheniya na Peskakh*). Built in the 17th century, this elegant church was closed after the 1917 revolution and turned into a cartoon-production studio. Like many churches throughout Russia, however, it has been returned to its original purpose. The church is depicted in Vasily Polenov's well-known canvas *Moskovsky Dvorik* (*Moscow Courtyard*), which now hangs in the Tretyakov Gallery. ⊠ *4a per. Spasopeskovsky, Arbat* ⌚ *Free* ☉ *Daily 8–8* Ⓜ *Smolenskaya.*

Dom Druzhby Narodov (Дом Дружбы Народов *Friendship of Nations House*). One of Moscow's most interesting buildings—it looks like a Moorish castle—was built in the late 19th century by the architect V.A. Mazyrin for the wealthy (and eccentric) industrialist Savva Morozov (Tolstoy mentions this home in his novel *Resurrection*). Today its rooms are used by the federal government for meetings and conferences and are not open to the public. ⊠ *16 ul. Vozdvizhenka, Arbat* Ⓜ *Arbatskaya.*

Melnikov House (Дом Мельникова *Dom Melnikova*). This cylindrical concrete building was designed by the famous Constructivist architect Konstantin Melnikov in the late 1920s. The house is currently in a state of major disrepair but remains remarkable for its wall-length windows and spiral staircases inside that link the three floors. Plans to open the house as a museum have been in motion for years but look nowhere near completion, as arcane issues regarding the house's ownership are still being settled. The architect's granddaughter lives in the house. ⊠ *10 per. Krivoarbatsky, Arbat* ⊕ *www.melnikovhouse.org* Ⓜ *Smolenskaya.*

Pushkin Apartment Museum (Музей-квартира Пушкина *Muzey-kvartira Pushkina*). The poet Alexander Pushkin lived here with his bride, Natalya Goncharova, for several months in 1831, right after they were married. Experts have recreated the original layout of the rooms and interior decoration. The first floor presents various trinkets and poems, plus information on Pushkin's relationship with Moscow; the second floor is a reconstruction of a typical early-19th-century home.

The apartment museum is one of several for the beloved Russian poet around Moscow. ✉ *53 ul. Arbat, Arbat* ☎ *499/241–9295* ⊕ *www. pushkinmuseum.ru* ✉ *100R* ⊙ *Wed. and Fri.–Sun. 10–6, Thurs. 12–9; closed last Fri. of month* Ⓜ *Smolenskaya.*

Scriabin Museum (Музей Скрябина *Muzey Scriabina*). This charming apartment was the last home of composer Alexander Scriabin's (1872–1915), where he died of blood poisoning in 1915. The rooms are arranged and furnished just as they were when Scriabin lived here. Visitors are scarce because foreign tourist groups are not usually brought to the museum. Downstairs there's a concert hall where accomplished young musicians perform his music, usually on Tuesday and Wednesday evenings. ✉ *11 per. Bolshoi Nikolopeskovsky, Arbat* ☎ *499/241–1901* ⊕ *anscriabin.ru* ✉ *150R* ⊙ *Tues., Wed., Fri., Sat. and Sun. 11-6, Thurs. 1–9; closed last Fri. of month* Ⓜ *Smolenskaya, Arbatskaya.*

Shchusev Architecture Museum (Музей Архитектуры имени Щусева *Muzey Arkhitektury imeni Shchuseva*). The rooms of an 18th-century neoclassical mansion display works by some of the best and most controversial architects in Russia and around the world. Temporary exhibits focus on Moscow architecture from ancient through contemporary times. The museum also offers a varied selection of walking tours and lectures in Russian. ✉ *25 ul. Vozdvizhenka, bldg. 5, Arbat* ☎ *495/691–2109* ⊕ *www.muar.ru* ✉ *100R* ⊙ *Tues., Wed. and Fri.–Sun. 11–7, Thurs. 1–9* Ⓜ *Biblioteka Imeni Lenina.*

WORTH NOTING

Andrei Bely Apartment Museum (Музей-квартира Андрея Белого *Muzey-kvartira Andreya Belovo*). On display are artifacts from the life of the writer Andrei Bely (1880–1934), considered to be one of the great Russian Symbolists—he's most famous for his novel *Petersburg.* The "Lines of Life" drawing on the wall of the first room shows the "energy" of Bely's life (the blue line in the middle) marked by dates and names of people he knew during specific times. The keepers of the museum offer exhaustive tours of the apartment, but they are in Russian only. ✉ *55 ul. Arbat, Arbat* ☎ *499/241–7702* ⊕ *kvartira-belogo. guru.ru* ✉ *80R* ⊙ *Wed. and Fri.–Sun. 10–6, Thurs. 12-9; closed last Fri. of month* Ⓜ *Smolenskaya.*

Gogol statue (Памятник Гоголю). This statue of a melancholy Nikolai Gogol (1809–52) originally stood at the start of Gogolevsky bulvar but was replaced by a more "upbeat" Gogol. The statue now stands inside a courtyard near the apartment building where the writer spent the last months of his life. The statue actually captures Gogol's sad disposition perfectly. He gazes downward, with his long, flowing cape draped over his shoulder, protecting him from the world. Gogol is perhaps best known in the West for his short stories, his novel *Dead Souls,* and for his satirical drama *Revizor* (*The Inspector General*), about the unannounced visit of a government official to a provincial town. Characters from his works are engraved on the pedestal. ✉ *7 bul. Nikitsky, Arbat* Ⓜ *Arbatskaya.*

Spaso House (Спасо-Хаус). The yellow neoclassical mansion behind the iron gate is the residence of the American ambassador. It was built in the early 20th century for a wealthy merchant. The building's front looks on a small square between Arbat and Novy Arbat that features an undersized statue of Pushkin in the center and is a pleasant place to take a break. ✉ *pl. Spasopeskovskaya, Arbat* ⊕ *moscow.usembassy. gov* Ⓜ *Smolenskaya.*

Vakhtangov Theater (Театр имени Вахтангова *Teatr imeni Vakhtangova*). An excellent traditional theater is housed within this impressive structure named after the great acting teacher Stanislavsky's pupil Evgeny Vakhtangov (1883–1922). The gold statue of Princess Turandot and stone fountain to the right of the theater were created in honor of the 850th anniversary of Moscow in 1997; they are loved and hated by an equal proportion of Muscovites. ✉ *26 ul. Arbat, Arbat* ☎ *499/241–1679* ⊕ *www.vakhtangov.ru* Ⓜ *Arbatskaya.*

KROPOTKINSKY DISTRICT РАЙОН КРОПОТКИНСКОЙ

This picturesque old neighborhood is known as the Kropotkinsky District after the famous Russian anarchist Prince Pyotr Kropotkin. Heading out of the district's metro station, which is also named in honor of him, you'll find yourself at the intersection of the Boulevard Ring and the area's main street, ulitsa Prechistenka, which leads southwest out to the Garden Ring. This is yet another ancient section of Moscow with a history that dates back nearly to the foundation of the city itself. Almost none of its earliest architecture has survived; the area suffered badly during the 1812 conflagration of Moscow, so most of its current buildings date to the postwar period of reconstruction, when neoclassicism and the so-called Moscow Empire style were in vogue. Before the revolution, the area was the favored residence of Moscow's old nobility, and along its thoroughfares you'll find many of their mansions and homes, often called "nests of the gentry." It was also the heart of the literary and artistic community, and there were several famous literary salons here. Prince Kropotkin compared it to the Saint-Germain quarter of Paris.

GETTING HERE AND AROUND

The Kropotkinsky District is served by the Kropotkinskaya, Borovitskaya, Biblioteka Imeni Lenina, and Park Kultury metro stations. The central landmark in the area is Cathedral of Christ Our Savior, its imposing white corpus rising up along the Moscow River next to the southwestern end of the Boulevard Ring. The Kropotkinsky District is about a 20-minute walk from the Kremlin; the easiest way to reach it from there is either along the river embankment or on ulitsa Volkhonka, which runs directly from Aleksandrovsky Sad to the Kropotkinskaya metro station.

TIMING   Taken at a leisurely pace, you could cover the neighborhood in three to four hours, but the area warrants at least half a day; with stops at any of the various museums here, your exploration could easily expand to two days (the Pushkin Museum of Fine Arts alone is worth a day). If you're definitely interested in visiting some of the museums in this district, do *not* head out on a Monday, as most of the museums are closed that day.

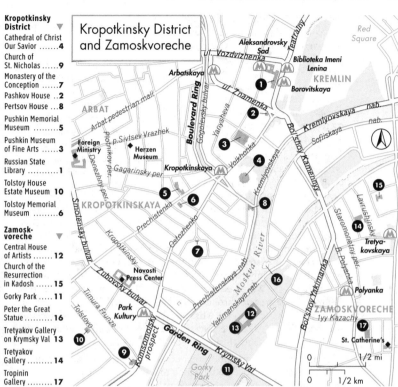

TOP ATTRACTIONS

Cathedral of Christ Our Savior (Храм Христа Спасителя *Khram Khrista Spasitelya*). Moscow's largest Orthodox cathedral has a colorful past of destruction and reconstruction. Built between 1839 and 1883 as a memorial to the Russian troops who fell fighting Napoléon's forces in 1812, the cathedral was for more than a century the largest single structure in Moscow, and it dominated the city's skyline. It took almost 50 years to build what only a few hours would destroy: on December 5, 1931, the cathedral was blown up. Under Stalin, the site had been designated for a mammoth new "Palace of Soviets," intended to replace the Kremlin as the seat of the Soviet government. Plans called for topping the 1,378-foot-tall structure with a 300-foot statue of Lenin that would have spent more time above the clouds than in plain view if the plans had ever materialized. World War II delayed construction, and the entire project was scrapped when it was discovered that the land along the embankment was too damp to support such a heavy structure.

The site lay empty and abandoned until 1958, when the Moscow Pool, one of the world's largest outdoor swimming pools, was built. Divided into several sections, for training, competition, diving, and public swimming, it was heated and kept open all year long, even in the coldest days of winter. The pool was connected to the locker rooms by covered tunnels, and you could reach it by swimming through them. The pool was dismantled in 1994. Then—in perhaps one of architectural history's stranger twists—the cathedral was resurrected in 1997 from the ruins at a cost of more than $150 million.

You enter a hallway lined with writing that surrounds the central chamber. These marble panels covered in prerevolution Russian script

> **CATHEDRAL OF CHRIST OUR SAVIOUR**
>
> On your way to the Cathedral of Christ Our Savior, stop in the Kropotkinskaya metro station to see what's left of the original cathedral, which was bombed by the Bolsheviks in 1931. The interior of the station is decorated using marble stripped from the old cathedral before it was destroyed.

describe the Napoléonic invasion of Russia in 1812. Hundreds of battles are detailed, beginning with the French army's first steps into Russian territory and ending with Napoléon's downfall in Paris and the reinstatement of peace in Europe. The immense main hall is covered in frescoes. Look straight up into the central cupola to see a dramatic painting of the Holy Father with baby Jesus in his hands. Across from the figures is the word "elohim" (meaning "God") written in Hebrew. Off to one side are two thrones behind a short fence. These are symbolic seats for Saint Nicholas the Miracle-Maker and the legendary Russian war hero Prince Alexander Nevsky, who has been honored as a saint by the Orthodox Church since his death in 1243.

The cathedral has been at the center of several controversies. A consumer watchdog group has accused the fund that oversees the church of profiting on the Orthodox Church's property by allowing a car wash, parking lot, dry cleaner, conference center, and café to operate underneath the huge structure. In 2012, the all-female, Russian punk band Pussy Riot performed a now-notorious protest concert inside the church. The stunt landed three of the members behind bars after a trial critics claimed was the Kremlin's harsh punishment for dissent. ✉ *15 ul. Volkhonka, on the bank of the Moskva River, Kropotkinsky District* ☎ *495/637–1276* ⊕ *www.xxc.ru* ⊗ *Tues.–Sun. 8–7:30* Ⓜ *Kropotkinskaya.*

Monastery of the Conception (Зачатьевский Монастырь *Zachatievsky Monastyr*). Though this working monastery was founded in the 16th century, only the redbrick Gate Church remains of the original buildings. The monastery was established by the last surviving son of Ivan the Terrible, in what amounted to a plea to God for an heir (hence its name). He and his wife failed to have a son, however, and Boris Godunov became the next Russian leader. A sparkling church, with star-spangled silver domes and gold-rimmed eaves, is a recent addition, dating to 2010. ✉ *2 per. 2nd Zachatievsky, Kropotkinsky District* Ⓜ *Kropotkinskaya.*

Pashkov House (Дом Пашкова *Dom Pashkova*). Designed by Vasily Bazhenov, one of Russia's greatest architects, this mansion was erected between 1784 and 1786 for the wealthy Pashkov family. The central building is topped by a round belvedere and flanked by two service wings. In the 19th century it housed the Rumyantsev collection of art and rare manuscripts. Following the 1917 revolution, the museum was closed and the art collection was transferred to the Hermitage in St. Petersburg and the Pushkin Museum of Fine Art. The manuscripts were donated to the Russian State Library, which now owns this building. Now, after 20 years of restoration, Pashkov House is open, but only to those with a State Library card. ⊠ *26 ul. Mokhovaya and ul. Znamenka, Kropotkinsky District* Ⓜ *Borovitskaya.*

Pertsov House (Дом Перцова *Dom Pertsova*). One of the finest examples of Moscow art nouveau was built in 1905–07 by the architects Schnaubert and Zhukov. The facade of the steep-roofed and angled building, which is closed to the public, is covered in colorful mosaics. Before the revolution, Peter Pertsov and his wife lived in an apartment in the building and rented out studios for artists. ⊠ *5 pro. Soymonovsky, Kropotkinsky District* Ⓜ *Kropotkinskaya.*

Fodor'sChoice
★

Pushkin Museum of Fine Arts (Музей Изобразительных Искусств имени Пушкина *Muzey Izobrazitelnykh Iskusstv imeni Pushkina*). One of the finest art museums in Russia, the Pushkin is famous for its collection of works by Gauguin, Cézanne, and Picasso, among other masterpieces. Founded by Ivan Vladimirovich Tsvetayev (1847–1913) of Moscow State University, father of poet Marina Tsvetaeva, the museum was originally established as a teaching aid for art students, which explains why some of the collection is made up of copies. The original building dates from 1895 to 1912 and was first known as the Alexander III Museum. It was renamed for Pushkin in 1937, on the centennial of the poet's death.

The first-floor exhibit halls display a fine collection of ancient Egyptian art (Hall 1); Greece and Rome are also well represented. The museum's great masterpieces include a fine concentration of Italian works from the 15th century (Room 5), among them Botticelli's *The Annunciation,* Tomaso's *The Assassination of Caesar,* Guardi's *Alexander the Great at the Body of the Persian King Darius,* and Sano di Pietro's *The Beheading of John the Baptist.* Rembrandt's *Portrait of an Old Woman* is in Room 10, and paintings by Murillo, Rubens, and Van Dyck are in Room 11. There are also frequent exhibits of collections on loan from other prominent European art museums. ⊠ *12 ul. Volkhonka, Kropotkinsky District* ☎ *495/609–9520, 495/697–9578* ⊕ *www.arts-museum.ru* ✉ *400R* ☯ *Tues., Wed., and Fri.–Sun. 10–7, Thurs. 10–9* Ⓜ *Kropotinskaya.*

The Museum of Private Collections. A worthy assortment of impressionist, postimpressionist, and modern art, as well as Russian icons, are spread out over two floors and include paintings, sculptures, and drawings by Russian and European artists collected during the Soviet era. Some of the more notable pieces include those from the collection of the museum's major contributors, Ilya Silberstein. The museum regularly hosts temporary exhibits. ⊠ *10 ul. Volkhonka, Kropotkinsky District* ☎ *495/697–1610* ⊕ *artprivatecollections.ru* ✉ *100R* ☯ *Wed. and Fri.–Sun. noon–7, Thurs. 12–9.*

Russian State Library (Российская Государственная Библиотека *Rossiyskaya Gosudarstvennaya Biblioteka*). Once called Biblioteka Imeni Lenina, or the Lenin Library, this is Russia's largest library, with more than 30 million books and manuscripts. The modern building was built between 1928 and 1940. Bronze busts of famous writers and scientists adorn the main facade. The portico, supported by square black pillars, is approached by a wide ceremonial staircase. A 12-foot statue of Dostoyevsky was erected in front of the library in 1997 in honor of the 850th anniversary of Moscow. The great novelist, sculpted by Alexander Rukavishnikov, sits where the Soviets once considered erecting a giant Lenin head. In theory, anyone can visit the library as a day visitor, but you need some persistence to fill in forms and deal with the bureaucracy (bring your passport). It's arguably worth it, though, to see the grand main hall. ⊠ *5 ul. Vozdvizhenka, bldg. 3, Kropotkinsky District* ☎ *495/695–5790* ⊕ *www.rsl.ru* ⊗ *Mon.–Fri. 9–8, Sat. 9–7; closed last Mon. of the month* Ⓜ *Biblioteki Imeni Lenina.*

Fodor's Choice
★ **Tolstoy House Estate Museum** (Музей-усадьба Толстого *Muzey-usadba Tolstovo*). Tolstoy bought this house in 1882, at the age of 54, and spent nine winters here with his family. In summer he preferred his country estate in Yasnaya Polyana. The years here were not particularly happy ones. By this time Tolstoy had already experienced a religious conversion that prompted him to disown his earlier great novels, including *War and Peace* and *Anna Karenina*. His conversion sparked a feud among his own family members, which manifested itself even at the dining table: Tolstoy's wife, Sofia Andreevna, would sit at one end with their sons, while the writer would sit with their daughters at the opposite end.

The ground floor has several of the children's bedrooms and the nursery where Tolstoy's seven-year-old son died of scarlet fever in 1895, a tragedy that haunted the writer for the rest of his life. Also here are the dining rooms and kitchen, as well as the Tolstoys' bedroom, in which you can see the small desk used by his wife to meticulously copy all of her husband's manuscripts by hand.

Upstairs you'll find the Tolstoys' receiving room, where they held small parties and entertained guests, who included most of the leading figures of their day. The grand piano in the corner was played by such greats as Rachmaninoff and Rimsky-Korsakov. When in this room, you should ask the attendant to play the enchanting recording of Tolstoy greeting a group of schoolchildren, followed by a piano composition written and played by him. Also on this floor is an Asian-style den and Tolstoy's study, where he wrote his last novel, *Resurrection*.

Although electric lighting and running water were available at the time to even the lesser nobility, Count Tolstoy chose to forgo both, believing it better to live simply. The museum honors his desire and shows the house as it was when he lived there. Inside the museum, each room has signs in English explaining its significance and contents. ⊠ *21 ul. Lva Tolstovo, Kropotkinsky District* ☎ *499/246–9444* ⊕ *tolstoymuseum. org* ⊠ *200R* ⊗ *Tues., Wed., Fri., and weekends 10–6, Thurs. noon–8; closed last Fri. of month* Ⓜ *Park Kultury.*

Tolstoy Memorial Museum (Музей Толстого-Литературная экспозиция *Muzey Tolstovo–Literary Exposition*). Architect Afanasy Grigoriev designed this mansion, a fine example of the Moscow Empire style (1822–24). The minor poet Lopukhin, a distant relative of Tolstoy's, lived here, and the mansion was converted into a museum in 1920. The exhibit halls contain a rich collection of manuscripts and photographs of Tolstoy and his family, as well as pictures and paintings of Tolstoy's Moscow. Even if you don't know Russian, you can learn about the writer's life through the photographs, and in each room there's a typed handout in English to help explain its holdings. Note the picture of 19th-century Moscow in the second hall (on the left-hand wall). The huge cathedral taking up more than half the photograph is the Cathedral of Christ Our Savior—the original 19th-century structure that was torn down and subsequently re-created. ⊠ *8 ul. Prechistenka, bldg. 11, Kropotkinsky District* ☎ *495/637–7410* ⊕ *www.tolstoymuseum.org* 🖾 *200R* ⊘ *Tues., Wed., Fri., and weekends 10–6, Thurs. 12–9; closed last Fri. of month* Ⓜ *Kropotkinskaya.*

Gavroche. Baguette sandwiches and a large selection of wines by the glass are on offer at this French place favored by Moscow's burgeoning foodie community. Its covered summer terrace is a pleasant place to rest your legs. ⊠ **11 ul. Timura Frunze, bldg. 19, wing 8, Kropotkinsky District** ☎ **495/558–0838** ⊕ **www.thewinebar.ru** Ⓜ **Park Kultury.**

WORTH NOTING

Church of St. Nicholas in Khamovniki (Церковь Николы в Хамовниках *Tserkov Nikoly v Khamovnikakh*). Built between 1679 and 1682 and remaining open throughout the years of Communist rule, what looks like a frosted gingerbread house has been well preserved. The elegant bell tower is particularly impressive, and five gilded domes sit atop a white facade with tangerine and forest-green trim. In fact, the design was meant to suggest a festive piece of woven cloth, for weavers who settled in considerable numbers in this quarter in the 17th century commissioned the building of this church. The interior, containing a wealth of icons, is one of the most ornate in the city. ⊠ *Komsomolsky pr. and ul. Lva Tolstovo, Kropotkinsky District* Ⓜ *Park Kultury.*

Multimedia Art Museum (Мультимедиа Арт Музей). Rotating collections of modern art, photography, video, and sculpture by an impressive array of mainly Russian and European artists change frequently. The museum is operated in conjunction with the Moscow House of Photography and often hosts guest lecturers, film premieres, and master classes. ⊠ *16 ul. Ostrozhenka, Kropotkinsky District* ☎ *495/637–1100* ⊕ *mamm-mdf.ru* 🖾 *300R* ⊘ *Tues.–Sun. noon–9* Ⓜ *Kropotkinskaya.*

Pushkin Memorial Museum (Музей Пушкина *Muzey Pushkina*). Aleksandr Pushkin (1799–1837) never lived here and probably never even visited this fine yellow mansion built in the 19th century by architect Afanasy Grigoriev. Even so, several rooms surrounding a beautiful atrium showcase the author's sketches, letters, and personal effects. ⊠ *2 ul. Prechistenka, bldg. 12, Kropotkinsky District* ☎ *495/637–5674* ⊕ *www.pushkinmuseum.ru* 🖾 *140R* ⊘ *Tues., Wed., and Fri.–Sun. 10–6, Thurs. noon–9; closed last Fri. of the month* Ⓜ *Kropotinskaya.*

ZAMOSKVORECHE ЗАМОСКВОРЕЧЬЕ

Zamoskvoreche ("beyond the Moskva River") applies to the southern area of the old city opposite the Kremlin. Until modern times Zamoskvoreche had a sleepy rural feel—even today the old twisting streets give it a character all but obliterated in other parts of the city. By the 17th century Zamoskvoreche was well settled by artisans serving the court; it was also the first line of defense against the Tatars. In the 19th century members of the most distinctive of classes, the Moscow merchants, built their homes here. They also sponsored artists and after time created Russia's first art museum, the Tretyakov Gallery.

Gorky Park, popularized by Martin Cruz Smith's Cold War novel of the same name, is situated along the right bank of the Moskva River, just beyond Krymsky Most (Crimea Bridge). Aside from the park and the Tretyakov Gallery, ulitsa Bolshaya Ordinka is a draw for its many Russian Orthodox churches.

GETTING HERE AND AROUND

Zamoskvoreche is served by the Tretyakovskaya, Polyanka, and Oktyabrskaya metro stations. It's better to take the metro or other transportation to this neighborhood, as opposed to walking, because the only way across the Moskva River at most points is over a large, traffic-filled bridge. The main exception to this is the pleasant pedestrian bridge on one side of the Cathedral of Christ Our Savior. Once in the neighborhood, it's most efficient to walk between sights, though you should give yourself plenty of time for doing so, as Zamoskvoreche covers a large area.

TIMING There's a lot to see in this area so it might be worth spending a day or even two on the sights. To truly enjoy the Tretyakov Gallery, it's probably best to plan a separate visit. A full exploration of Gorky Park could also easily take an afternoon. Note that many of the sights are closed on Monday.

TOP ATTRACTIONS

Central House of Artists (Центральный Дом Художников *TsDKh; Tsentralny Dom Khudozhnikov*). The street entrance of this huge, modern building leads to the exhibit halls of the Artists' Union, where members display their work on three floors. This is a great place to find a sketch or watercolor to take home with you. There's also a tiny movie theater that shows old international cinema as well as a concert hall with pop and rock performances almost nightly. Massive exhibitions on everything from books to fur coats to architecture take over the building periodically, and some are worth checking out. The cavernous space also has room enough to house the modern branch of the Tretyakov Gallery. Next door is the **Art Park,** where contemporary sculpture and old statues of Soviet dignitaries stand side by side. It's a pleasant place for a stroll. ✉ *10 Krymsky Val, Zamoskvoreche* ☎ *499/238–9843, 499/238–9634* ⊕ *www.cha.ru* ✉ *300R* ☉ *Tues.–Sun. 11–8* Ⓜ *Park Kultury or Oktyabrskaya.*

Church of the Resurrection in Kadosh (Церковь Воскресения в Кадашах *Tserkov Voskreseniya v Kadashakh*). Because a high fence surrounds it, this colorful church is best viewed from far away. Look for a red-and-white brick bell tower and a large gold onion dome surrounded by three smaller ones. Built in 1687, the church is an excellent example of the Moscow baroque style. ⊠ *7 per. Kadashevksy 2-y, Zamoskvoreche* ☎ *495/953–1319* ⊕ *www.kadashi.ru* Ⓜ *Tretyakovskaya.*

Krasny Octyabr. The large, redbrick compound on the island in the Moskva River across from the Kremlin was once one of the Soviet Union's beloved chocolate factories, Krasny Oktyabr, or Red October. Whiffs of sweet chocolate used to fill the air around the factory, and its chocolate bars were presented as gifts to visiting dignitaries to the Kremlin. Today the factory is closed, and the sprawling complex has been renovated to house several of Moscow's hippest restaurants and bars. It's worth strolling around the island and stopping in for a bite to eat or a drink. ⊠ *Zamoskvoreche.*

Fodor'sChoice
★

Tretyakov Gallery (**Третьяковская Галерея** *Tretyakovskaya Galereya*). On view are some of the world's greatest masterpieces of Russian art, spanning the 11th through the 20th centuries. The works include sacred icons, stunning portrait and landscape art, the famous Russian Realists' paintings that culminated in the Wanderers' Group, and splendid creations of Russian Symbolism, impressionism, and art nouveau.

In the mid-1800s, a successful young Moscow industrialist, Pavel Mikhailovich Tretyakov, was determined to amass a collection of national art that would be worthy of a museum of fine arts for the entire country. In pursuit of this high-minded goal, he began to purchase paintings, drawings, and sculpture. He became one of the—if not *the*—era's most valued patrons of the arts. In 1892 he donated his collection to the Moscow city government, along with a small inheritance of other fine works collected by his brother Sergei. The holdings have been continually increased by subsequent state acquisitions, including the seizure of privately owned pieces after the Communist revolution.

The rich collection of works completed after 1850 pleases museumgoers the most, for it comprises a selection of pieces from each of the Russian masters, sometimes of their best works. Hanging in the gallery are paintings by Nikolai Ge (*Peter the Great Interrogating the Tsarevich Alexei*), Vasily Perov (*Portrait of Fyodor Dostoyevsky*), Vasily Polenov (*Grandmother's Garden*), Viktor Vasnetsov (*After Prince Igor's Battle with the Polovtsy*), and many others. Several canvases of the beloved Ivan Shishkin, with their depictions of Russian fields and forests—including *Morning in the Pine Forest,* of three bear cubs cavorting—fill one room. There are also several paintings by the equally popular Ilya Repin, including his most famous painting, *The Volga Boatmen.* Later works, from the end of the 19th century, include an entire room devoted to the Symbolist Mikhail Vrubel (*The Princess Bride, Demon Seated*); Nestorov's glowing *Vision of the Youth Bartholomew,* the boy who would become St. Sergius, founder of the monastery at Sergeyev-Posad; and the magical pieces by Valentin Serov (*Girl with Peaches, Girl in Sunlight*). You'll also see turn-of-the-20th-century paintings by Nikolai Konstantinovich Roerich (1874–1947), whose New York City home is a museum.

The first floor houses the icon collection, including the celebrated *Holy Trinity* painted by the late-14th- and early-15th-century master Andrei Rublyov. Also on display are some of the earliest icons to reach ancient Kievan Rus', such as the 12th-century *Virgin of Vladimir,* brought from Byzantium.

The second floor holds 18th-, 19th-, and 20th-century paintings and sculpture and is where indefatigable Russian art lovers satisfy their aesthetic longings. A series of halls of 18th-century portraits, including particularly fine works by Dmitry Levitsky, acts as a time machine into the country's noble past. Other rooms are filled with works of the 19th century, embodying the burgeoning movements of romanticism and naturalism in such gems of landscape painting as Silvester Shchedrin's *Aqueduct at Tivoli* and Mikhail Lebedev's *Path in Albano* and *In the Park.* Other favorite pieces to look for are Karl Bryullov's *The Last Day of Pompeii,* Alexander Ivanov's *Appearance of Christ to the People,* and Orest Kiprensky's well-known *Portrait of the Poet Alexander Pushkin.*

When you leave the gallery, pause a moment to look back on the fanciful art nouveau building itself, which is quite compelling. Tretyakov's home still forms a part of the gallery. Keep in mind that the ticket office closes an hour before the museum closes. There are no English-language translations on the plaques here, but you can rent an audio guide or buy an English-language guidebook. ✉ *10 per. Lavrushinsky, Zamoskvoreche* ☎ *499/238–1378, 499/951–1362* ⊕ *www.tretyakovgallery.ru* 🖃 *380R* ☉ *Tues., Wed., Sat., and Sun. 10–6, Thurs. and Fri. 10–9* Ⓜ *Tretyakovskaya.*

Tretyakov Gallery on Krymsky Val (Третьяковская Галерея на Крымском Валу *Tretyakovskaya Galereya na Krymskom Valu*). This branch of the Tretyakov Gallery shares a building with the Tsentralny Dom Khudozhnikov (Central House of Artists) across from Gorky Park. Often called the "New Branch," it has a permanent exhibit entitled "Art of the 20th Century" that spans from prerevolutionary work by Chagall, Malevich, and Kandinsky to the socialist realist, modern, and postmodern periods. ✉ *10 ul. Krymsky Val, through sculpture-garden side entrance, Zamoskvoreche* ☎ *499/238–1378, 499/951–1362* ⊕ *www.tretyakovgallery.ru* 🖃 *360R* ☉ *Tues.–Sun. 10–7:30* Ⓜ *Park Kultury.*

QUICK BITES

Coffee Bean. In convivial and laid-back surroundings north of Novokuznetskaya metro station heading toward the river, you can enjoy a large selection of well-prepared tarts and cakes. Some say their coffee is among the best in the city. ✉ *5 ul. Pyatnitskaya, Zamoskvoreche* ☎ *495/953–6726* Ⓜ *Novokuznetskaya.*

WORTH NOTING

FAMILY **Gorky Park** (Парк Горького). The official name of this park laid out in 1928 and covering an area of 275 acres is actually the Central Park of Culture and Leisure. It was made famous to Westerners by its other name in Martin Cruz Smith's Cold War novel *Gorky Park,* and Muscovites refer to it by yet another name, Park Kultury (Park of Culture). The welcome swath of greenery has undergone a remarkable makeover in post-Soviet years. Gone are the dilapidated rides and unkept lawns littered with passed-out drunks. Today, Muscovites come to the park for yoga and tango lessons, paddleboat rides and bike rentals, picnics on the lawns, a selection of cafés and eateries, and in the winter, snowboarding and ice skating. The park often hosts concerts, and the Garage Center for Contemporary Art features up-and-coming Russian contemporary artists. In summer, boats leave from the pier for excursions along the Moskva River. ⊠ *9 ul. Krymsky Val, Zamoskvoreche* Ⓜ *Oktyabrskaya.*

Peter the Great statue (Памятник Петру Великому). An enormous figure of the tsar stands at the helm of a ship, symbolizing his role as the founder of the Russian naval force in the 1700s. Most Muscovites agree that the statue, by Zurab Tsereteli, is an eyesore and has no place in Moscow—after all, Peter the Great moved the capital to St. Petersburg. Ongoing movements are afoot to remove the statue, but for the time being, it's here. When you finally set eyes on the colosso you'll probably understand why common nicknames for it are "Cyclops" and "Gulliver." A red light atop the 325-foot-tall monument is a warning beacon for airplanes. ⊠ *ul. Krymskaya nab., Zamoskvoreche* Ⓜ *Park Kultury.*

NORTHERN OUTSKIRTS

Easily accessible to both the city center and as a starting point for any side trips to Moscow environs, the northern outskirts of the city offer affordable hotels and hip nightlife.

Dostoyevsky Memorial Apartment (Музей-квартира Достоевского *Muzey-Kvartira Dostoevskovo).* Fyodor Dostoyevsky (1821–81) lived here until he was 16, on the grounds of the hospital where he was born and where his father, Mikhail Andreevich, resided and worked as a doctor. The museum has kept things much as they were, from family pictures to the neat, middle-class furniture. ⊠ *2 ul. Dostoevskovo, Northern Outskirts* ☎ *495/681–1085* 🎫 *100R* ☉ *Tues. and Wed., Fri.– Sun. 11–6; Thurs. 1–8; closed last day of month* Ⓜ *Dostoyevskaya.*

SOUTHERN OUTSKIRTS

South of the city center are some of Moscow's most notable holy sites. The New Maiden's Convent, southwest of the city center, is one of Moscow's finest and best-preserved ensembles of 16th- and 17th-century Russian architecture. It's interesting not only for its impressive cathedral and charming churches but also for the dramatic chapters of Russian history that have been played out within its walls. It stands in a wooded section bordering a small pond, making this a particularly pleasant place for an afternoon stroll. Attached to the convent is a fascinating cemetery where some of Russia's greatest literary, military, and political figures are buried. A few metro stops away is another fabled religious institution, Donskoy Monastery, founded in the 16th century by Boris Godunov, with a cathedral commissioned a century later by the regent Sophia, Peter the Great's half-sister.

GETTING HERE AND AROUND

Donskoy and New Maiden's Convent can be reached via the Sport-ivnaya and Shabolovskaya metro stations. It will take you about 45 minutes to reach the area from downtown Moscow. To get to Kolo-menskoye, take the metro to Kolomenskaya station; a 10-minute walk up a slight hill brings you to the park's entrance. Tsaritsyno is close to the metro station of the same name, which is three metro stops south of Kolomenskoye.

Fodor's Choice **Donskoy Monastery** (Донской Монастырь *Donskoy Monastyr*). In
★ 1591, the Russian army stood waiting for an impending attack from Tatar troops grouped on the opposite side of the river. According to legend, the Russians awoke one morning to find the Tatars gone. Their sudden retreat was considered a miracle, and Boris Godunov ordered a monastery built to commemorate the miraculous victory. The mon-astery, now in a secluded, wooded area in the southwest section of the city, was named in honor of a wonder-working icon of the Virgin of the Don that Prince Dimitry Donskoy had supposedly carried during his campaign in 1380 in which the Russians won their first decisive victory against the Tatars.

The monastery grounds are surrounded by a high defensive wall with 12 towers, the last of the defense fortifications to be built around Moscow. When you enter through the western gates, the icon looks down on you from above the entrance to the imposing **New Cathedral,** built in the late 17th century by Peter the Great's half-sister, the regent Sophia. The smaller **Old Cathedral** was built between 1591 and 1593, during the reign of Boris Godunov. After the plague swept through Moscow in 1771, Catherine the Great forbade any more burials in the city center and the monastery became a fashionable burial place for the well-to-do, and many leading intellectuals, politicians, and aristocrats were buried here in the 18th, 19th, and 20th centuries.

From 1934 to 1992, a branch of the Shchusev Architecture Museum kept architectural details of churches, monasteries, and public buildings destroyed under the Soviets inside the monastery walls. Bits and pieces of demolished churches and monuments remain, forming a graveyard of destroyed architecture from Russia's past. ⊠ *1 pl. Donskaya, Southern Outskirts* ☎ *495/952–1481* ⊕ *www.donskoi.org* ⊠ *Free* ☉ *Daily 7–7* Ⓜ *Shabolovskaya.*

Kolomenskoye (Коломенское). If you want to spend an afternoon in the great Russian outdoors without actually leaving the city, Kolo-menskoye, on a high bluff overlooking the Moskva River, is just the right destination. The estate was once a favorite summer residence of Moscow's grand dukes and tsars. Today it's a popular public park with museums, a functioning church, old Russian cottages, and other attrac-tions. It's also the site of the city's main celebration of the holiday Maslenitsa, or Butter Week, which usually falls at the end of February or beginning of March. Traditional Russian amusements such as mock fistfights, bag races, and tug-of-war are held on the park's grounds, with heaps of hot blini served as reminders of the spring sun.

As you approach Kolomenskoye, the first sights you see are the striking blue domes of the **Church of Our Lady of Kazan,** a functioning church that's open for worship. It was completed in 1671. Opposite the church there once stood a wooden palace built by Tsar Alexei, Peter the Great's father. Peter spent much time here when he was growing up. Nothing remains of the huge wooden structure (Catherine the Great ordered it destroyed in 1767), but there's a scale model at the **museum,** which is devoted to Russian timber architecture and folk crafts. The museum lies inside the front gates of the park, at the end of the tree-lined path leading from the main entrance of the park.

The most remarkable sight within the park is the **Church of the Ascension,** which sits on the bluff overlooking the river. The church dates from the 1530s and was restored in the late 1800s. Its skyscraping tower is an example of the tent or pyramid-type structure that was popular in Russian architecture in the 16th century. The view from the bluff is impressive in its contrasts: from the 16th-century backdrop you can look north across the river to the 20th-century concrete apartment houses that dominate the contemporary Moscow skyline. In summer you'll see Muscovites bathing in the river below the church, and in winter the area abounds with cross-country skiers.

Examples of wooden architecture from other parts of Russia have been transferred to Kolomenskoye, turning the estate into an open-air museum. In the wooded area near the site of the former wooden palace you'll find a 17th-century prison tower from Siberia, a defense tower from the White Sea, and a 17th-century mead brewery from the village of Preobrazhenskaya. One of the most attractive original buildings on the site is the wooden cottage where Peter the Great lived while supervising the building of the Russian fleet in Arkhangelskoye. The cottage was relocated here in 1934.

There are several tour options available, including a "Fairy Tale Tour," troika sleigh rides, and horseback riding tours. Call the excursions desk for more information. ✉ *39 Andropova pr., Southern Outskirts* ☎ *495/232–6190, 499/612–2768* ⊕ *www.mgomz.com* ✉ *Free entrance to park* ⊘ *Sept.–Mar. daily 9–7, Apr.–Aug. daily 9 am–10 pm* Ⓜ *Kolomenskoye.*

Fodor's Choice
★
New Maiden's Convent (Новодевичий Монастырь *Novodevichy Monastyr*). Tsar Vasily III (1479–1533) founded this convent in 1524 on the road to Smolensk and Lithuania. Due to the tsar's initiative, it enjoyed an elevated position among the many monasteries and convents of Moscow and became a convent primarily for noblewomen. Little remains of the original structure. Enclosed by a crenellated wall with 12 colorful battle towers, today's complex dates largely from the 17th century, when the convent was significantly rebuilt and enhanced.

Among the first of the famous women to take the veil here was Irina, wife of the feebleminded Tsar Fyodor and the sister of Boris Godunov, in the 16th century. Godunov was a powerful nobleman who exerted much influence over the tsar and when Fyodor died, Godunov was the logical successor to the throne. Rather than proclaim himself tsar, he followed his sister to Novodevichy. Biding his time, Godunov waited until the clergy and townspeople begged him to become tsar. His election took place at the convent, inside the Cathedral of Smolensk.

In the next century, Novodevichy became the residence of Sophia, the half-sister of Peter the Great, who ruled as his regent from 1682 through 1689, while he was still a boy. She didn't want to give up her position when the time came for Peter's rule and was deposed by him. He kept her prisoner inside Novodevichy. Even that wasn't enough to restrain the ambitious sister, and from her cell she organized a revolt of the *streltsy* (Russian militia). The revolt was summarily put down, and to punish Sophia, Peter had the bodies of the dead streltsy hung up along the walls of the convent outside Sophia's window. He left the decaying bodies hanging for more than a year. Yet another of the convent's later "inmates" was Yevdokiya Lopukhina, Peter's first wife. Peter considered her a pest and rid himself of her by sending her to a convent in faraway Suzdal. She outlived him, though, and eventually returned to Moscow. She spent her final years at Novodevichy, where she's buried.

You enter the convent through the arched passageway topped by the **Preobrazhensky Tserkov** (Gate Church of the Transfiguration), widely considered one of the best examples of Moscow baroque. To your left as you enter is the ticket booth, where tickets are sold to the various exhibits housed in the convent. Exhibits include rare and ancient Russian paintings, both ecclesiastical and secular; woodwork and ceramics; and fabrics and embroidery. There's also a large collection of illuminated and illustrated books, decorated with gold, silver, and jewels. The building to your right is the Lophukin House, where Yevdokiya lived from 1727 to 1731. Sophia's prison, now a guardhouse, is to your far right, in a corner of the northern wall.

The predominant structure inside the convent is the huge five-dome **Sobor Smolenskoy Bogomateri** (Cathedral of the Virgin of Smolensk), dedicated in 1525 and built by Alexei Fryazin. It was closely modeled after the Kremlin's Assumption Cathedral. Inside, there's a spectacular iconostasis with 84 wooden columns and icons dating from the 16th and 17th centuries. Simon Ushakov, a leader in 17th-century icon art, was among the outstanding Moscow artists who participated in the creation of the icons. Also here are the tombs of Sophia and Yevdokiya. Yet another historic tale connected to the convent tells how the cathedral was slated for destruction during the War of 1812. Napoléon had ordered the cathedral dynamited, but a brave nun managed to extinguish the fuse just in time, and the cathedral was spared.

To the right of the cathedral is the **Uspensky Tserkov** (Church of the Assumption) and **Refectory,** originally built in 1687 and then rebuilt after a fire in 1796. It was here that the blue-blooded nuns took their meals.

A landmark feature of Novodevichy is the ornate belfry towering above its eastern wall. It rises 236 feet and consists of six ornately decorated tiers. The structure is topped by a gilded dome that can be seen from miles away. ⊠ *1 proyezd Novodevichy, Southern Outskirts* ☎ *499/246–8526* ✉ *250R* ☉ *Museum Wed.–Mon. 10–5:30, convent daily 10–7; closed first Mon. of month* Ⓜ *Sportivnaya.*

Novodevichy cemetery (Новодевичье кладбище). For more than a generation, this cemetery—a fascinating collection of graves, tombstones, and other memorials—was closed to the general public in large part because Nikita Khrushchev (1894–1971) is buried here, rather than on Red Square, like other Soviet leaders. Thanks to glasnost, the cemetery was reopened in 1987, and now anyone is welcome to visit its grounds.

Khrushchev's grave is near the rear of the cemetery, at the end of a long tree-lined walkway. If you can't find it, any of the *babushki* (caretakers) will point out the way. Krushchev was deposed in 1964 and lived his next and last seven years in disgrace, under virtual house arrest. The memorial consists of a stark black-and-white slab, with a curvilinear border marking the separation of the two colors. The contrast of black and white symbolizes the contradictions of his reign. The memorial caused a great furor among the Soviet hierarchy when it was unveiled. It was designed by the artist Ernst Neizvestny, himself a controversial figure. In the 1960s Khrushchev visited an exhibit of contemporary art that included some of Neizvestny's works. Khrushchev dismissed Neizvestny's contributions as "filth," and asked the name of their artist. When Neizvestny (which means "Unknown") answered, Khrushchev scornfully said that the USSR had no need for artists with such names. To this the artist replied, "In front of my work, I am the premier." Considering the times, it was a brave thing to say to the leader of the Soviet Union. Neizvestny eventually joined the ranks of the émigré artists; he now lives in the United States.

Many of those buried in the cemetery were war casualties in 1941 and 1942. Among the memorials you might want to look for are those to the composers Prokofiev and Scriabin and the writers Chekhov, Gogol, Bulgakov, and Mayakovsky. Chekhov's grave is decorated with the trademark seagull of the Moscow Art Theater, the first to successfully produce his plays (including, naturally, *The Seagull*). Recent burials include Russia's first president Boris Yeltsin and cellist and conductor Mstislav Rostropovich. You can request a tour in English from the cemetery's excursion bureau; call and reserve ahead as they usually need advance warning. In light of the bountiful history and scant English translations, these tours can be very rewarding. ✉ *2 proyezd Luzhnetsky, Southern Outskirts* ☎ *499/246–6614* ⊕ *novodevichye.com/* ✉ *Free* ☉ *Daily 9–5* Ⓜ *Sportivnaya.*

Tsaritsyno (Царицыно). This popular boating and picnicking spot is the site of the 18th-century summer palace that was started but never completed for Catherine the Great. The empress pulled down the work of her first architect; the second building phase was never completed, probably for financial reasons, and her heirs took no interest in Tsaritsyno. Now the kitchen, Gothic Revival main palace, and grounds have been restored, and a collection of porcelain, paintings, and sculptures are on display in the theater. ✉ *1 ul. Dolskaya, Southern Outskirts* ☎ *495/321–0743* ⊕ *www.tsaritsyno-museum.ru* ✉ *Museum 250R* ☉ *Park 6 am–midnight; museum Tues.–Fri. 11–6, Sat. 11–8, Sun. 11–7* Ⓜ *Tsaritsyno.*

QUICK BITES
U Pirosmani. This well-known restaurant specializing in the spicy cuisine of Georgia is across the pond from the convent. If you're visiting on a weekend, you may want to book ahead. ✉ *4 proyezd Novodevichy, Southern Outskirts* ☎ *499/255–7926* ⊕ *upirosmani.ru/index.php* Ⓜ *Sportivnaya.*

EASTERN OUTSKIRTS

There are three ancient monasteries along the banks of the Moskva River, in the southeast section of Moscow. They date to Moscow's earliest days, when it was the center of a fledgling principality and constantly under threat of enemy attack. Two of these monasteries were built across the river from the Kremlin as part of a ring of defense fortifications.

Formerly suburban, this area didn't fare well as the city grew. Beginning in the 19th century, factories were built along the banks of the river, including the famous Hammer and Sickle metallurgical plant. This industrial center is long gone, and these quaint monasteries remain and are being slowly restored.

GETTING HERE AND AROUND

The monasteries can be reached via the Proletarskaya and Taganskaya metro stations. Kuskovo is just outside the ring road marking the city boundary (known by the acronym MKAD, pronounced em-KAT). Take the metro to Ryazansky Prospekt station and then Bus 208 or 133 six stops to Kuskovo Park.

Andronik Monastery (Андроников Монастырь *Andronikov Monastyr*). A stroll inside the heavy stone fortifications of this monastery, founded in 1360 by Metropolitan Alexei and named in honor of its first abbot, St. Andronik, is an excursion into Moscow's past. The loud crowing of birds overhead drowns out the rumble of the city. Even the air seems purer here, perhaps because of the old birch trees growing on the monastery grounds and just outside its walls. The site was chosen not only for its strategic importance—on the steep banks of the Moskva River—but also because, according to legend, it was from this hill that Metropolitan Alexei got his first glimpse of the Kremlin.

The dominating structure on the monastery grounds is the **Spassky Sobor** (Cathedral of the Savior), Moscow's oldest stone structure. Erected in 1420–27 on the site of an earlier, wooden church, it rests on the mass grave of Russian soldiers who fought in the Battle of Kulikovo (1380), the decisive Russian victory that eventually led to the end of Mongol rule in Russia. Unfortunately, the original interiors, which were painted by Andrei Rublyov and another famous icon painter, Danil Chorny, were lost in a fire in 1812. Fragments of some frescoes have been restored, however.

The building to your immediate left as you enter the monastery is the former abbot's residence. It now houses a permanent exhibit titled "Masterpieces of Ancient Russian Art," with works from the 13th through 16th centuries. The next building, to the left and across the pathway from the Cathedral of the Savior, is the **Refectory**, built during the reign of Ivan the Great, between 1504 and 1506 and housing icons from the 19th and 20th centuries. Attached to the Refectory is

the **Tserkov Archangela Mikhaila** (Church of St. Michael the Archangel), another example of the style known as Moscow baroque. It
was commissioned by the Lopukhin family—relatives of Yevdokiya
Lopukhina, the first, unloved wife of Peter the Great—as the family
crypt in 1694. But there are no Lopukhins buried here, as Peter had
Yevdokiya banished to a monastery in faraway Suzdal and her family
was exiled to Siberia.

The last exhibit is in the former monks' residence and is devoted to
3rd-century saint Nikolai the Miracle Worker (270–343), better known
in the West as St. Nicholas, the inspiration for Santa Claus. Icons here
depict his life and work. ✉ *10 pl. Andronevskaya, Eastern Outskirts*
☎ *495/678–1467* 🖃 *Free* ☉ *Daily 8–8* Ⓜ *Ploshchad Ilyicha.*

Krutitskoye Ecclesiastical Residence (Крутицкое Подворье *Krutitskoye
Podvorye*). The name comes from the word *kruta,* meaning "hill," and
a small monastery built here sometime in the 13th century was used
for defense against the Tatar-Mongol invaders. At the end of the 16th
century the monastery's prestige grew when it became the suburban
residence of the Moscow metropolitan. The church and grounds were
completely rebuilt, and the current structures date from this period.
The period of flowering was short-lived; the monastery was closed in
1788 on orders from Catherine the Great, who secularized many church
buildings. In the 19th century it was used as army barracks, and it's said
that the Russians accused of setting the Moscow fire of 1812 were tortured here by Napoléon's forces. In the 20th century, the Soviets turned
the barracks into a military prison. Although the buildings have been
returned to the Orthodox Church, the prison, now closed, remains on
the monastery grounds.

To your left as you enter the monastery grounds is the five-dome, redbrick **Uspensky Sobor** (Assumption Cathedral), erected at the end of
the 16th century on the site of several previous churches. It's a working
church, undergoing restoration like many of its counterparts throughout the city. Still very attractive inside, it has an assemblage of icons,
lovely frescoes, and an impressive all-white altar and iconostasis. The
cathedral is attached to a gallery leading to the **Teremok** (Gate Tower),
a splendid example of Moscow baroque. It was built between 1688
and 1694, and its exterior decoration is the work of Osip Startsev. The
gallery and Teremok originally served as the passageway for the metropolitan as he walked from his residence (to the right of the Teremok)
to the cathedral. You should go through the gate tower to take a full
walk around the tranquil grounds. ✉ *11–13 ul. Kruititskaya, Eastern
Outskirts* ☎ *495/676–3093* ⊕ *www.krutitsy.ru* ☉ *Daily 8–8; closed 1st
Mon. of month* Ⓜ *Proletarskaya.*

Kuskovo Estate and Palace Museum (Кусково). In the 18th and 19th centuries the country estate of Kuskovo was a summer playground for the
Moscow aristocracy. It belonged to the Sheremetyevs, one of Russia's
wealthiest and most distinguished families, whose holdings numbered
in the millions of acres. (Today, Moscow's international airport, built
on land that once belonged to one of their many estates, takes their
family name.)

The Sheremetyevs acquired the land of Kuskovo in the early 17th century, but the estate, often called a Russian Versailles, took on its current appearance in the late 18th century. Most of the work on it was commissioned by Prince Pyotr Sheremetyev, who sought a suitable place for entertaining guests in the summer. The park was created by Russian landscape artists who had spent much time in Europe studying the art. They dotted the French-style gardens with buildings representing the major architectural trends of Europe: the Dutch cottage, the Italian villa, the grotto, and the exquisite hermitage, where, as was the showoffy fashion at that time, dinner tables were raised mechanically from the ground floor to the second-floor dining room. The centerpiece of the estate is the **Kuskovo Palace,** built in the early Russian classical style by the serf architects Alexei Mironov and Fedor Argunov. Fronted by a grand horseshoe staircase and Greek-temple portico, this building exemplifies Russian neoclassical elegance and overlooks a man-made lake. It's been a house museum since 1918, and its interior decorations, including fine parquet floors and silk wall coverings, have been well preserved. Ballroom extravaganzas once took place in the White Hall, with parquet floors, gilt wall decorations, and crystal chandeliers. On display in the inner rooms are paintings by French, Italian, and Flemish artists; Chinese porcelain; furniture; and other articles of everyday life from the 18th and 19th centuries. The palace also houses a collection of 18th-century Russian art and a celebrated ceramics museum with a rich collection by Russian, Soviet, and foreign artists.

You can reach Kuskovo by public transit, but you may find it more convenient to book a tour that includes transportation. However you plan to get here, be sure to phone ahead before making the trek because the estate often closes when the weather is very humid or very cold. ✉ *2 ul. Yunosti, Eastern Outskirts* ☎ *495/370–0160* ⊕ *www.kuskovo. ru* 🖾 *40R* ☽ *Nov.–Mar., Wed.–Sun. 10–4; Apr.–Oct., Wed.–Sun. 10–6; closed last Wed. of month* Ⓜ *Ryazansky Prospekt.*

New Savior Monastery (Новоспасский Монастырь *Novospassky Monastyr*). This monastery with a yellow belfry dates to the 13th century, when it was inside the Kremlin. Ivan the Great, who wanted to free up space in the Kremlin for other construction, ordered it rebuilt here in 1462, though none of the monastery's original 15th-century structures survived the move. The present fortification wall and most of the churches and residential buildings on the grounds date from the 17th century. In more modern times, a site just outside the monastery's walls was one of the mass graves for those executed during Stalin's purges.

You enter the monastery at the nearest entrance to the left of the **Bell Tower Gate,** which was erected in 1786. The first thing you see as you enter the grounds is the massive white **Sobor Spasa Preobrazheniya** (Transfiguration Cathedral). You may notice a resemblance, particularly in the domes, to the Kremlin's Assumption Cathedral, which served as this cathedral's model. The structure was built between 1642 and 1649 by the Romanov family, commissioned by the tsar as the Romanov family crypt. The gallery leading to the central nave is decorated with beautiful frescoes depicting the history of Christianity in Kievan Rus'.

In front of the cathedral, on the right-hand side, is the small red **Nadmogilnaya Chasovnya** (Memorial Chapel), marking the grave of Princess Augusta Tarakanova, the illegitimate daughter of Empress Elizabeth and Count Razumovsky. The princess lived most of her life as a nun in Moscow's St. John's Convent, forced to take the veil by Catherine the Great. During her lifetime her identity was concealed, and she was known only as Sister Dofiya. The chapel over her grave was added in 1900, almost a century after her death.

To the right as you face Transfiguration Cathedral stands the tiny **Pokrovsky Tserkov** (Church of the Intercession). Directly behind the cathedral is the **Tserkov Znamenia** (Church of the Sign). Painted in the dark yellow popular in its time, with a four-column facade, the church was built between 1791 and 1808 by the wealthy Sheremetyev family and contains the Sheremetyev crypt. In the rear right-hand corner of the grounds, running along the fortification walls, are the former monks' residences. ⊠ *10 pl. Krestyanskaya, Eastern Outskirts* ☎ *495/676–9570* ⊕ *www.novospasskiymon.ru* ✉ *Free* ☉ *Daily 7–7* Ⓜ *Proletarskaya.*

WESTERN OUTSKIRTS

Within easy reach of half-day excursions, the emblematic Russian countryside offers majestic museums and parks. To see them to the best advantage you should try to make your visits in spring or summer.
■ TIP→ **All of these sights can be reached by metro, though you may have to take a connecting bus or trolley.**

Arkhangelskoye Estate Museum. This striking assemblage was begun at the end of the 18th century for Prince Golitsyn by the French architect Chevalier de Huerne. In 1810 the family fell upon hard times and sold the estate to a rich landlord, Yusupov, who used it to house his extraordinary art collection. The collection includes paintings by Boucher, Vigée-Lebrun, Hubert Robert, Roslin, Tiepolo, Van Dyck, and many others, as well as antique statues, furniture, mirrors, chandeliers, glassware, and china. Much of the priceless furniture once belonged to Marie Antoinette and Madame de Pompadour. There are also samples of fabrics, china, and glassware that were produced on the estate itself.

Allées and strolling lanes wind through the **French Park,** which is populated with statues and monuments commemorating royal visits. There's also a monument to Pushkin, for whom Arkhangelskoye was a favorite retreat. In the western part of the park is an interesting small pavilion, known as the Temple to the Memory of Catherine the Great, that depicts the empress as Themis, goddess of justice.

Back outside the estate grounds on the right-hand side of the main road stands the **Estate (Serf) Theater,** built in 1817 by the serf architect Ivanov. Currently a museum, the theater originally seated 400 and was the home of the biggest and best-known company of serf actors in Russia, who first appeared in Russia in the mid-18th century and disappeared after 1861, when Tsar Alexander II freed the serfs. In his summer serf theater, Prince Nikolai Yusupov favored weekly opera performances as well as dance shows with rich stage decorations. The well-preserved stage decorations are by the Venetian artist Pietrodi Gonzaga.

The main palace has been under restoration for many years and only some rooms are open. To go by public transit, take Bus 541 or 549 from the Moscow metro station Tushinskaya to the Arkhangelskoye stop, or minibus 151 to the Sanatory stop. To get there by car, go west on shosse Novorizhskoye and look for the signs for the estate. ☒ *Arkhangelskoye, Western Outskirts, Arkhangelskoye* ☎ *495/363–1375* ⊕ *www.arkhangelskoe.ru* ✉ *100R* ⊗ *Palace Wed.–Fri. 10:30–5, weekends 10–6; park Wed.–Sun. 10–8; closed last Wed. of month.*

Victory Park (**Парк Победы** *Park Pobedy*). In 1812 Napoléon allegedly waited in vain for the keys to Moscow atop Poklonnaya Gora, a hill razed in the 1970s to build Triumphal Arch, a World War II memorial unveiled in 1995 in time for the 50th anniversary of the victory over Nazi Germany. The memorial is the centerpiece of the 335-acre park that also houses a World War II museum, a chapel, and an outdoor display of vintage weaponry. Victory Park is a popular spot for festivities on public holidays, including Victory Day, Orthodox Easter, and Christmas. On a warm day, expect to see strolling couples and hordes of rollerbladers. The park is near the Park Pobedy metro station, on the dark-blue line about 20 minutes from the city center. ☒ *7 ul. Bratyev Fonchenko, Poklonnaya Gora, Western Outskirts* ☎ *499/142–5994* ⊕ *poklonnayagora.ru* ✉ *Museum 250R* ⊗ *Tues.–Sun. 10–7, Thurs. 10–8; closed last Thurs. of month* Ⓜ *Park Pobedy.*

3

MOSCOW
WHERE TO EAT

Updated by
Catherine
Blanchard

In a city where onion domes and Soviet-era monoliths bespeak a long, varied, and storied past, it's easy to forget that the dining scene is relatively new, having emerged with democratization in 1991. Now, nearly twenty-five years later, the Moscow restaurant scene is still going through growing pains and has yet to find its pace. This is good news for adventurous diners. You might still find yourself being served by pantaloon-and-ruffled bedecked "serfs" beneath glittering chandeliers in one of the showy, re-created settings that arose in the post-Soviet era—and that even a tsar would find to be over the top.

But many restaurants now approach their food sensibly and seriously. A new crop of chefs is serving traditional Russian fare, often giving it some innovative twists. One European cuisine to invade the city anew is Italian, and scores of dark-haired chefs from the Mediterranean are braving the cold to bring Muscovites minestrone and carbonara. Other ethnic restaurants have long since arrived as well, and you can sample Tibetan, Indian, Chinese, Latin American, or Turkish cuisine any night of the week.

One welcome, long-standing Russian tradition that remains in place is a slow-paced approach to a meal. It's common for people to linger at their tables long after finishing dessert, and you're almost never handed the bill until you ask for it. Keep in mind that chef turnover is high in Moscow, which means restaurants can change quickly—and that there's always a new culinary experience to be had in this ever-evolving city.

PRICES

Moscow restaurant prices have moderated and even dropped in recent years, though in some top dining rooms that cater to the country's wealthy elite you might pay more for a meal than you would in the United States. Sometimes you'll be paying to be part of a scene rather than for the quality of the food. If it's an affordable gourmet experience you're after, join affluent Muscovites and head to one of the city's expensive hotels for a Sunday brunch, where you can enjoy haute cuisine in elegant surroundings at prices that are usually much lower than those at dinner. The really good news is that you can find fantastic low-cost food all over the city at any time. For as little as a few hundred rubles you might enjoy your favorite meal of the trip.

Prices in the reviews are the average cost of a main course at dinner or, if dinner is not served, at lunch.

RESTAURANT REVIEWS

Use the coordinate (✛ B2) at the end of each review to locate a site on the Where to Eat in Moscow map.

KREMLIN/RED SQUARE

$$
ITALIAN
✕ **Academiya (Академия).** This reliable Italian chain with outlets throughout Moscow may not whisk you away to a Roman piazza or the Tuscan countryside, but you can expect a well-cooked risotto and efficient if unenthusiastic service in slick environs. In the Kremlin branch, a very popular terrace that overlooks ulitsa Tverskaya is great for sipping a beer and watching the crowds in summer. Portions can be a bit small—an entrée may not fill you up if you're famished—but everything is very fresh. Ⓢ *Average main: 500R* ✉ *1 per. Kamergerkiy, bldg. 2, Kremlin/Red Square* ☎ *495/692–9649* ⊕ *www.academiya.ru* Ⓜ *Teatralnaya* ✛ *E2.*

$$
ITALIAN
✕ **Bosco Café.** One of the very few places in Moscow with a terrace on Red Square is on the first floor of the GUM department store. You pay for the view, but the Mediterranean fare is tasty, and you can just order a coffee if you're not hungry for a meal. The terrace closes once it gets cold. Ⓢ *Average main: 700R* ✉ *3 Red Sq., Kremlin/Red Square* ☎ *495/929–3182* ⊕ *www.bosco.ru/restoration/bosco_cafe* Ⓜ *Ploshchad Revolutsii* ✛ *E3.*

$$$
BRASSERIE
✕ **Brasserie Most.** While some may complain that this reincarnation of a Moscow institution is only a pale imitation of its former self, the famously massive chandeliers are still in place and now illuminate bistro-style booths where diners enjoy creative takes on rich stews and other brasserie classics. This is a popular spot for weekend brunch and for meals before and after performances at the Bolshoi Theatre. Ⓢ *Average main: 800R* ✉ *3 ul. Kuznetsky Most, bldg. 6/3, Kremlin/ Red Square* ☎ *495/660–0706* ⊕ *www.brasseriemost.ru* ⌲ *Reservations essential* Ⓜ *Teatralnaya* ✛ *E2.*

$
RUSSIAN
Fodor'sChoice
★
✕ **Kamchatka (Камчатка).** This upstairs cafeteria-style café is a throwback to the Soviet era, packed with students drinking cheap beer, pensioners reminiscing over meat-filled pancakes, and business people of all ages from the offices nearby. A larger downstairs room gets rowdy on weekends. The no-smoking policy is a huge plus and a rarity in Moscow, but you may have to walk through a cloud of smoke to get near the door. Ⓢ *Average main: 300R* ✉ *7 ul. Kuznetsky Most, Kremlin/Red Square* ☎ *495/624–8825* ▭ *No credit cards* Ⓜ *Teatralnaya or Kuznetsky Most* ✛ *E2.*

$$$$
EUROPEAN
✕ **Metropol (Метрополь).** Recalling the splendor of prerevolutionary Russia, the opulent interiors of the Metropol hotel's grand dining hall are a stunning memorial to Russian art nouveau. The nearly three-story-high dining room is replete with stained-glass windows, marble pillars, and a leaded-glass roof. Among the famous guests to have dined here are George Bernard Shaw, Vladimir Lenin, and Michael Jackson. The menu is laden with French and Russian delicacies, such as the popular fried duck with wild-cherry sauce and a baked apple. Cap your meal off with wine from the extensive list and cheese. There is also live music

BEST BETS FOR DINING IN MOSCOW

With hundreds of restaurants to choose from, how will you decide where to eat? Fodor's writers and editors have selected their favorite restaurants by price, cuisine, and experience in the Best Bets lists below. In the first column, Fodor's Choice properties represent the "best of the best" in every price category. You can also search by neighborhood for excellent eats—just peruse our reviews on the following pages.

Fodor's Choice ★

Dukhan Chito-Ra, $, p. 121
Gusyatnikoff, $$$$, p. 122
Hachapuri, $, p. 117
Kamchatka, $, p. 109
Pavilion, $$$$, p. 117
Ragout, $$$, p. 117
Shinok, $$$$, p. 122
Vatrushka, $$, p. 119

By Price

$

Dukhan Chito-Ra, p. 121
Filial, p. 111
Hachapuri, p. 117
Kamchatka, p. 109
Lyudi Kak Lyudi, p. 111
Mu-mu, p. 114

$$

Chaikhona No. 1, p. 115

$$$

Brasserie Most, p. 109
Delicatessen, p. 116
Jean-Jacques, p. 119
Ragout, p. 117

$$$$

Café Pushkin, p. 115
Pavilion, p. 117
Les Menus Par Pierre Gagnaire, p. 120
Shinok, p. 122
Turandot, p. 118

By Cuisine

RUSSIAN

Café Pushkin $$$$, p. 115
Kamchatka $, p. 109
Vatrushka $$, p. 119

ITALIAN

Buono $$$$, p. 122

UZBEK

Chaikhona No. 1 $$, p. 115
Uryuk $$$, p. 118

FRENCH

Brasserie Most $$$, p. 109

GEORGIAN

Dukhan Chito-Ra $, p. 121
Hachapuri $, p. 117
U Pirosmani $$$$, p. 121

By Experience

GREAT VIEWS

Bosco Café $$, p. 109
Buono $$$$, p. 122
Strelka Bar $$, p. 120

CREATIVE CUISINE

Bistronomia $$, p. 111
Delicatessen $$$, p. 116
Ragout $$$, p. 117

HOT SPOTS

Café Pushkin $$$$, p. 115
Kamchatka $, p. 109
Strelka Bar $$, p. 120
Vatrushka $$, p. 119

MOST ROMANTIC

Buono $$$$, p. 122
Gogol-Mogol $, p. 120
Staraya Ploshchad $$, p. 111

OUTDOOR SEATING

Café Pushkin $$$$, p. 115
Strelka Bar $$, p. 120

at breakfast and in the evenings. $ *Average main: 1000R* ✉ *Metropol Hotel, 4 pr. Teatralny, bldg. 1, Kremlin/Red Square* ☎ *499/270–1061* ⊕ *www.metropol-moscow.ru* 🍴 *Reservations essential* 🎩 *Jacket and tie* Ⓜ *Ploshchad Revolutsii or Teatralnaya* ✠ *E3.*

$$ ✕ **Staraya Ploshchad** (**Старая Площадь**). Photographs of candelabra-
EUROPEAN filled imperial-era restaurants greet you in the foyer, and candlestick sconces and red velvet festoon the walls. Deferential white-shirted waiters serve Continental, Russian, and vaguely Asian cuisine, with such classics as salade Olivier (a mayonnaise-dressed salad of meat, potatoes, and lettuce) and a sumptuous crab gratin. The hot cherry pie here is a highly memorable dessert. $ *Average main: 600R* ✉ *8 per. Bolshoy Cherkassky, Kremlin/Red Square* ☎ *495/698–4688* ⊕ *osquare. ru* Ⓜ *Lubyanka* ✠ *F3.*

KITAI GOROD

$$ ✕ **Beloye Solntse Pustyni** (**Белое Солнце Пустыни**). The name comes
ASIAN from a legendary Soviet film from 1970, *White Sun of the Desert*, and the specialty is Uzbek food, which incorporates Russian, Persian, and Chinese elements. Sun-bleached walls instantly sweep you down to Central Asia and the illusion continues with a diorama with a ship marooned in the desert, waitresses dressed as Uzbek maidens, and intricately carved wooden doors. The Dastarkhan, a set meal, overwhelms you with food—unlimited access to the salad bar, a main course such as mutton kebabs and *manty* (large mutton ravioli), *plov* (a Central Asian rice pilaf), and numerous desserts. $ *Average main: 700R* ✉ *14 ul. Neglinnaya, bldg. 29,Kitai Gorod* ☎ *495/625–2596* ⊕ *www.bsp-rest.ru* 🍴 *Reservations essential* Ⓜ *Trubnaya* ✠ *E2.*

$$ ✕ **Bistronomia** (**Бистрономия**). Steps away from ploshchad Lubyanka,
ECLECTIC chef Marc de Passorio serves pared-down takes on his haute- fusion cuisine for reasonable prices. The long menu includes now-familiar international dishes like chicken quesadillas and beef spring rolls, as well as such Russian classics as borsch and beef Stroganoff. Especially noteworthy are some of the more creative options, such as grilled goat cheese and fig salad. $ *Average main: 500R* ✉ *10 ul. Nikolskaya, Kitai Gorod* ☎ *495/787–1101* Ⓜ *Lubyanka* ✠ *F3.*

$ ✕ **Filial** (**Филиал**). Students and a sizeable portion of the local office-
ECLECTIC worker population flock here for the three-course lunch special, and in the evening, the low lighting and soft wood tones provide a warm and intimate setting. The eclectic menu veers from the Alps to the Andes, and the salade niçoise and the steak with peppercorn sauce are stand-outs. $ *Average main: 400R* ✉ *1 per. Bolshoy Krivokolenny, bldg. 3, Kitai Gorod* ☎ *495/621–2143* ⊕ *www.filialmoscow.com* 🚫 *No credit cards* Ⓜ *Lubyanka* ✠ *F2.*

$ ✕ **Lyudi kak lyudi** (**Люди как Люди**). Some of the new Russian elite
CAFÉ undoubtedly have closets bigger than this hole-in-the-wall student hang-out. But what this jammed little place lacks in size it makes up in hipster-bohemian charm. The menu offers many options ideal for a late-night snack or a late-morning pick-me-up—along the lines of salmon-and-spinach pie, Russian-style sweet-cheese pancakes, and fruit smoothies. Service can be inconsistent and hectic, but a no-smoking policy might

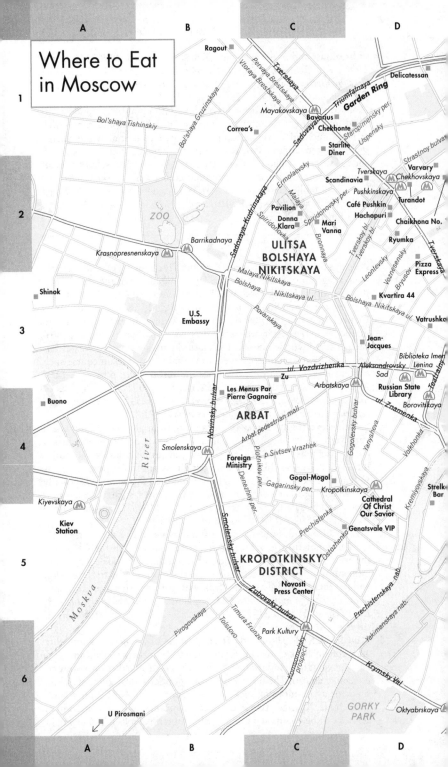

Where to Eat in Moscow

Ragout

Tverskaya

Pervaya Brestskaya

Vtoraya Brestskaya

Bol'shaya Gruzinskaya

Bol'shaya Tishinskiy

Triumfalnaya

Garden Ring

Delicatessan

Mayakovskaya

Bayarius

Chekhonte

Staropimensky per.

Uspensky

Correa's

Sadovaya

Starlite
Diner

Strastnoy bulvar

Ermolaevsky

Tverskaya

Scandinavia

Varvary

Chekhovskaya

Malaya

Spiridonovsky per.

Pushkinskaya

Café Pushkin

Turandot

ZOO

Pavilion

Donna
Klara

Spiridonovka

Mari
Vanna

Hachapuri

Chaikhona No.

Bronnaya

Ryumka

Barrikadnaya

Sadovaya-Kudrinskaya

**ULITSA
BOLSHAYA
NIKITSKAYA**

Tverskoy bl.

Tverskoy bl.

Krasnopresnenskaya

Leontevsky

Vozensensky

Bryusov

Pizza
Express

Malaya Nikitskaya

Bolshaya

Nikitskaya ul.

Bolshaya Nikitskaya ul.

Kvartira 44

Shinok

Povarskaya

**U.S.
Embassy**

Vatrushko

Jean-
Jacques

Biblioteka Imen
Lenina

ul. Vozdvizhenka

Aleksandrovsky
Sad

Zu

Arbatskaya

**Russian State
Library**

Les Menus Par
Pierre Gagnaire

Buono

ARBAT

Novinsky bulvar

Arbat pedestrian mall

Borovitsky

ul. Znamenka

Volkhonka

River

Smolenskaya

p.Sivtsev Vrazhek

Ploitnikov per.

Gogalevsky bulvar

Yanysheva

Strelke
Bar

**Foreign
Ministry**

Denezhny per.

Gagarinsky per.

Gogol-Mogol

Kropotkinskaya

Kremlyovskaya

Kievskaya

Smolensky bulvar

Cathedral
Of Christ
Our Savior

**Kiev
Station**

Prechistenka

Genatsvale VIP

Moskva

**KROPOTKINSKY
DISTRICT**

Novosti
Press Center

Ostozhenko

Prechistenskaya nab.

Zubovsky bulvar

Pirogovskaya

Timura Frunze

Tolstovo

Park Kultury

Krymsky Val

prospect

Yakimanskaya nab.

**GORKY
PARK**

Oktyabrskaya

U Pirosmani

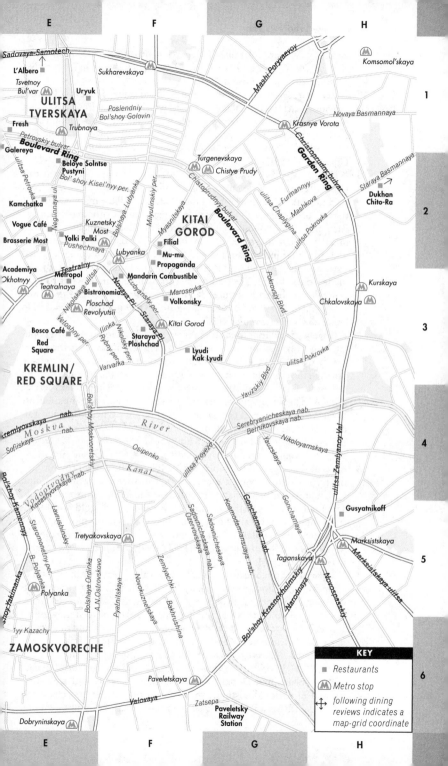

make a wait more tolerable. [$] *Average main: 400R* ✉ *1/4 tupik Soly-ansky, Kitai Gorod* ☎ *495/621–1201* ⊕ *www.ludikakludi.com* ⊟ No credit cards [M] *Kitai Gorod* ✛ *F3*.

$$$ ✕ **Mandarin Combustible (Мандарин).** Gilded ceilings and low lighting
ASIAN FUSION   provide a dark and romantic setting in which to enjoy fresh Pan-Asian cuisine that appears to be irresistible to a smart crowd. A long list of cocktails prepared by expert bartenders keeps the place hopping late into the night. [$] *Average main: 700R* ✉ *2 per. Malaya Cherkassky, Kitai Gorod* ☎ *495/745–0700* ⚱ *Reservations essential* [M] *Lubyanka* ✛ *F3*.

$ ✕ **Mu-Mu (Му-Му).** Join the masses for pancakes and kebabs at this
RUSSIAN   popular cafeteria-style chain. This location is just a block away from the Lubyanka, once the home of the KGB, and still the main building of that notorious agency's successor. Compared to the offerings at similar Russian fast food joints, the food here is of a higher quality. Even so, unless you love mayonnaise, skip the mystery salads for simpler meats and sides that include stuffed and fried cutlets and dumplings, grilled meat and fish, and classic Russian soups, including borsch and *schi,* made from cabbage. The staff doesn't speak much English, but you can generally get by with gestures. [$] *Average main: 350R* ✉ *14 ul. Myas-nitskaya, Kitai Gorod* ☎ *495/623–4503* ⊕ *www.cafemumu.ru* ⊟ No credit cards [M] *Lubyanka* ✛ *F2*.

$ ✕ **Propaganda (Пропаганда).** This may be one of Moscow's most popu-
ECLECTIC   lar clubs, but before the dance floor opens up, it lays out the tables for its own hearty, delicious food, for some of the most reasonable prices in the city center. The cuisine ranges over all the continents, from Indian to Thai to Russian, but the dishes are kept simple, and service is quick. The filling sandwiches and pastas, with such accompaniments as curried chicken and porcini mushrooms, are particularly good val-ues. Warning: the place gets smokey at night. [$] *Average main: 400R* ✉ *7 per. Bolshoi Zlatoustinsky, Kitai Gorod* ☎ *495/624–5732* ⊕ *www.propagandamoscow.com* ⊟ *No credit cards* [M] *Kitai Gorod* ✛ *F2*.

$$$ ✕ **Vogue Café.** One of the most fashionable restaurants in town is dis-
ECLECTIC   tinctly Russian, serving a menu that's a throwback to Soviet times, with items such as Russian cured sausage and kefir, a sour-milk drink. The interior is sophisticated and understated, with gold-and-black-suede booths and walls lined with photos of fashion models, many of whom are regulars. [$] *Average main: 800R* ✉ *9 ul. Kuznetsky Most, bldg. 7, Kitai Gorod* ☎ *495/623–1701* ⊕ *www.novikovgroup.ru* [M] *Kuznetsky Most* ✛ *E2*.

$ ✕ **Volkonsky (Волконский).** Moscow has waited years for the arrival of
BAKERY   a sophisticated French-style bakery like this. In addition to the mouth-watering choice of pastries, biscuits, and cakes, this is also an ideal place to pick up a sandwich or a freshly prepared salad, or to simply grab a coffee. There are lines out the door at all three locations, and this branch has a small seating area and a range of quiches and pastas for a sit-down lunch. [$] *Average main: 400R* ✉ *2 ul. Maroseyka, bldg. 4, Kitai Gorod* ☎ *903/185–3291* ⊕ *www.wolkonsky.ru* [M] *Kitai Gorod* ✛ *F3*.

$ ✕ **Yolki Palki (Ёлки Палки).** With hanging chickens and waitresses
RUSSIAN   dressed in national costume, the decor at one of the first chain res-taurants in Russia is more kitsch than traditional. But you might find

yourself saying "yolki palki," a light curse akin to "gee whiz," when you see the assortment here. There's a good selection of blini as well as other delicious pancakes called *olady,* which are thicker and often made with potatoes, and at the salad bar you can also try numerous types of marinated and

WORD OF MOUTH

"Red caviar is a good bet. I recommend it on warm blinis, covered with a generous layer of butter, and red caviar on top."
—echnaton

pickled vegetables. You'll find outlets throughout Moscow. ⑤ *Average main: 350R* ✉ *1 ul. Solyanka, bldg. 1/2, Kitai Gorod* ☎ *495/628–5539* ⊕ *www.elki-palki.ru* Ⓜ *Kitai Gorod* ⊹ *E2.*

ULITSA TVERSKAYA

$ ✕ **Bavarius (Баварнус).** Oompah music plays in the background, dirndl-
GERMAN clad waitresses carry fistfuls of liter-size mugs, and the smell of sauer-kraut lingers in the air. Whether you fancy a snack of knockwurst or just want to sample German and Czech beers, this is the place. Instead of sitting indoors, head through the arch to the left of the main entrance to reach the quiet courtyard that holds the biggest beer garden in Moscow. Food is served in both areas, but credit cards are accepted only in the restaurant. ⑤ *Average main: 500R* ✉ *30 ul. Sadovaya-Triumfalnaya, bldg. 2, Ulitsa Tverskaya* ☎ *495/699–4211* ⊕ *www.bavarius.ru* Ⓜ *Mayakovskaya* ⊹ *C1.*

$$$$ ✕ **Café Pushkin (Кафе Пушкин).** In a mansion meant to recall the days
RUSSIAN when the writer Pushkin strolled the 19th-century avenues of Moscow, staff members dress like household servants; the menu resembles an old newspaper, with letters no longer used in the Russian alphabet; and the food is fit for a tsar. All the favorites can be found here—blini, caviar, *pelmeni* (meat dumplings)—and there's a fine, if over-priced wine list. Prices rise with each floor (there are three) of the house. If you don't want to splurge on dinner, the three-course business lunch is an excellent way to sample Pushkin's food without breaking the bank. Open daily, 24 hours, Pushkin is popular for breakfast after a night of clubbing. In summer you can dine on the rooftop patio. ⑤ *Average main: 1200R* ✉ *26a bulvar Tverskoi, Ulitsa Tverskaya* ☎ *495/739–0033* ⊕ *www.cafe-pushkin.ru* ⌫ *Reservations essential* Ⓜ *Pushkinskaya* ⊹ *D2.*

$$ ✕ **Chaikhona No. 1 (Чайхона Но. 1).** This massive Uzbek café and
ASIAN lounge on ploshchad Pushkin is part of a chain with almost 20 locations around the city and offers diners the chance to sample traditional dishes like *plov,* a rice pilaf with lamb, and succulent kebabs. Each pillow, light fixture, painting, and plate is worthy of note. The only downside is that hookahs are a major part of the concept, so don't be surprised if the flavor of your neighbor's aromatic tobacco smoke infuses your meal. ⑤ *Average main: 500R* ✉ *2 pl. Pushkinskaya, Ulitsa Tverskaya* ☎ *495/234–0233* ⊕ *www.cha1.ru* Ⓜ *Pushkinskaya* ⊹ *D2.*

$$$$ ✕ **Chekhonte (Чехонте).** The modern takes on Russian classics served
RUSSIAN in chic, contemporary surroundings in the InterContinental Moscow Tverskaya are truly inventive. A trio of Russian salads is a barely recognizable version of the mayo-heavy Soviet standards and the *schi* is a rich

cabbage soup that's unlike the ubiquitous variety served elsewhere—this one contains suckling pig and is baked under puff pastry. Busy ulitsa Tverskaya provides a nice backdrop. $ *Average main: 1200R* ✉ *22 ul. Tverskaya, Ulitsa Tverskaya* ☎ *495/787–6211* Ⓜ *Tverskaya* ✜ *D1.*

$$$ ✕ **Correa's.** An expat from the United States, chef Isaac Correa has stood
ITALIAN out throughout his long Moscow career. This is his first major independent venture in the city, an intimate family restaurant that's become a favorite. The great pizzas and other simple, good Italian food with contemporary touches come in large portions and are served by friendly waitstaff, many of whom speak English. Correa's has several locations around Moscow and offers great lunch and dinner buffets and good breakfasts. $ *Average main: 700R* ✉ *7 ul. Gasheka, Ulitsa Tverskaya* ☎ *495/789–9654* ⊕ *www.correas.ru* Ⓜ *Mayakovskaya* ✜ *C1.*

$$$ ✕ **Delicatessen.** As if to reward you for locating the place (it's hidden
ECLECTIC in a courtyard with a front sign that says "Thanks for finding us"), staff members seem driven to make you join in their revelry. Greetings come first from the pirate-moustached owner, then from the team of gregarious bartenders, who will soon cajole you into trying one of the house-made liquors. Fresh flowers brighten the windowless space; menus are presented on clipboards; and the drink list is written in chalk across a wall. The casual fare includes well-prepared pizzas and pastas, and a selection of juicy burgers. $ *Average main: 700R* ✉ *1 ul. Sadovaya-Karetnaya, bldg. 20, Ulitsa Tverskaya* ☎ *495/699–3952* ⊕ *www.newdeli.ru* Ⓜ *Tstvetnoi Bulvar* ✜ *D1.*

$$ ✕ **Donna Klara** (**Донна Клара**). The menu consists mostly of classic
CAFÉ Continental salads, sandwiches, and other light fare, though the real attraction is the pastry case, which holds house-made cakes and other sweets that pair perfectly with a steaming cup of coffee. The tranquil atmosphere with comfy window seats is ideal for a break from sightseeing or for whiling away a rainy afternoon. It's a few minutes away from Patriarch's Ponds. $ *Average main: 500R* ✉ *13 ul. Malaya Bronnaya, bldg. 21, Ulitsa Tverskaya* ☎ *495/690–6974* Ⓜ *Mayakovskaya* ✜ *C2.*

$ ✕ **Fresh** (**Фреш**). The minimalist interior isn't necessarily welcoming,
VEGETARIAN but this a great place for a quick, healthy lunch near the city sights. There are lots of fresh salads with some ingredients that are quite rare in Russia, like quinoa and soy sprouts, and the sweet potato fries are a great indulgence. While here, try one of the many vitamin-packed mixed vegetable juices. $ *Average main: 450R* ✉ *11 ul. Bolshaya Dmitrovka, Ulitsa Tverskaya* ☎ *965/278–9089* ⊕ *www.freshrestaurant.ru* Ⓜ *Teatralnaya* ✜ *E1.*

$$$$ ✕ **Galereya** (**Галерея**). Most nights of the week, large Mercedes, Hum-
EUROPEAN mers, and Bentleys are parked outside this place, one of Moscow's hippest restaurants, owned by Moscow nightlife magnate Arkady Novikov. The interior has slick leather upholstery and the kitchen sends out sophisticated contemporary food that rarely hits a false note. The lamb dishes are always tender, and the desserts are some of the best in the city. The name is the Russian word for "gallery" and the walls are lined with edgy contemporary art. $ *Average main: 1200R* ✉ *27 ul. Petrovka, Ulitsa Tverskaya* ☎ *495/937–4504* ⊕ *www.gallerycafe.ru* Ⓜ *Pushkinskaya* ✜ *E1.*

$ ✕**Hachapuri** (Хачапури). This modern chain of cafes shares a name
GEORGIAN   with Georgia's most beloved culinary export, a crispy pie filled with
Fodor'sChoice   a creamy, tangy cheese (six varieties of this Caucasus pizza are on the
★   menu). The brick walls and track lighting at this popular branch create a bright and airy space, and the cooking displays a refreshing contemporary sensibility, with the always-luscious *chanakhi* (a lamb stew,
light with fragrant cilantro) and the *hinkali* (large dumplings you eat
with your hands) available with salmon or pumpkin in addition to the
traditional ground beef. Go for lunch to get the best value. $ *Aver-
age main: 450R* ✉ *10 per. Bolshoi Gnezdnikovsky, Ulitsa Tverskaya*
☎ *495/629–6656* ⊕ *www.hacha.ru* Ⓜ *Tverskaya* ✛ *D2.*

$$ ✕**Mari Vanna** (Мари Ванна). Find the unmarked entrance, ring the
RUSSIAN   right doorbell, and you will be taken back half a century to an ideal-
ized Soviet home. It could be Red Army Day, the way the tables are
garnished with white cloth and water goblets—and the flour-and-water
baranki crackers on the table evoke bygone scarcity. Stolid, apron-clad
waitresses glide from table to table delivering beet salads, mushroom
soup, and other nostalgic fare. Wooden shelves and the bric-a-brac on
them—glass cookie jars, an old radio, a deer figurine—make this place
feel truly homey. The experience isn't entirely homespun, though—Mari
Vanna has branches as far afield as New York and Los Angeles. $ *Aver-
age main: 700R* ✉ *10a per. Spiridonevsk, Ulitsa Tverskaya* ☎ *495/650–
6500* ⊕ *www.marivanna.ru* Ⓜ *Pushkinskaya* ✛ *C2.*

$$$$ ✕**Pavilion** (Павильон). If you've ever wondered how Soviet officials
RUSSIAN   dined, head to this retro eatery in an old mansion with views onto
Fodor'sChoice   Patriarch's Ponds, immortalized in Mikhail Bulgakov's Soviet-era novel
★   *The Master and Margarita*. Black-and-white photos cover the walls,
and the servers are dressed in typical Soviet garb. The kitchen turns
out updated versions of classic Russian dishes, including house-pickled
vegetables, smoked fish, and crispy chicken Kiev. Sip homemade vodkas
like *hrenovukha*, infused with horseradish, while enjoying live music
in the evenings. The desserts are memorable and beautifully presented.
$ *Average main: 900R* ✉ *7 per. Bolshoi Patriarshy, Ulitsa Tverskaya*
☎ *495/697–5110* ⊕ *www.restsindikat.com* Ⓜ *Mayakovskaya* ✛ *C2.*

$ ✕**Pizza Express** (Пицца Экспресс). This British pizza chain has slowly
ITALIAN   cornered the market for inexpensive Italian fare in Moscow with sev-
eral branches. The Tverskaya location is the largest, serving decent
pizzas and pasta dishes to local business people, students, and foreign-
ers who pack into the two floors of dining rooms. Reasonably priced
wines are available by the glass. $ *Average main: 400R* ✉ *17 ul. Tver-
skaya, Ulitsa Tverskaya* ☎ *495/629–7003* ⊕ *www.pizzaexpress.ru.com*
Ⓜ *Tverskaya* ✛ *D2.*

$$$ ✕**Ragout** (Рагу). A short and frequently changing menu features dishes
EUROPEAN   rooted in Continental and Eastern European traditions and often
Fodor'sChoice   includes a selection of pâtés, gratins, savory pies, and confits. A sweet
★   beetroot and black bread ice cream duo is usually on the dessert list. The
metal-and-wood surroundings are quiet and relaxing. $ *Average main:
700R* ✉ *69 ul. Bolshaya Gruzinskaya, Ulitsa Tverskaya* ☎ *495/662–
6458* ⊕ *www.caferagout.ru* Ⓜ *Belorusskaya* ✛ *B1.*

$$$$ ✗ **Scandinavia (Скандинавия).** One
SCANDINAVIAN   of the most serene dining rooms in
the city, with comfortable wooden
chairs and upholstered benches,
this spot also has a nice terrace and
beer garden for summer dining. The
Swedish chef mixes modern European and Scandinavian choices. If
you're interested in purely Scandinavian fare, try the herring with
boiled potatoes, which comes with
a shot of aquavit; for casual dining,
the burgers are considered to be the
best in Moscow. $ *Average main:
1000R* ✉ *7 per. Maly Palashevsky,
Ulitsa Tverskaya* ☎ *495/937–5630*
⊕ *www.scandinavia.ru* Ⓜ *Pushkinskaya* ✛ *D2.*

> ### HOW TO DRINK VODKA LIKE A RUSSIAN
>
> Vodka is drunk socially all over
> Russia to produce a state of
> conviviality referred to as *dusha-
> dushe* (soul-to-soul). When a Rus-
> sian taps his throat, be prepared
> to join in for a round. The "vodka
> procedure" is as follows: Prepare
> a forkful of food (pickles, herring,
> boiled potatoes) or a chunk of
> bread, inhale and exhale quickly,
> then breathe in and tip the vodka
> down your throat all at once (no
> sipping here). Finally, breathe out
> and eat.

$ ✗ **Starlite Diner (Старлайт).** This
AMERICAN   chain scattered throughout Moscow serves sandwiches and burgers
FAMILY   in brightly lit 1950s settings and is popular with late-night workers,
early-morning partygoers, and American travelers and expats looking
for a taste of home. This location is especially busy because of the city-
center location and secluded summertime patio. Waiters are young and
friendly, speak English, and serve fast. $ *Average main: 450R* ✉ *16 ul.
Bolshaya Sadovaya, in garden by Mossovet Theatre, Ulitsa Tverskaya*
☎ *495/650–0246* ⊕ *www.starlite.ru* Ⓜ *Mayakovskaya* ✛ *C1.*

$$$$ ✗ **Turandot (Турандот).** Ornate decor and elaborate, modern interpre-
ECLECTIC   tations of Russian, Continental, and Asian Fusion fare make quite an
impression—which is the point, and why this over-the-top rendition of
a baroque palace is one of the preferred eateries of the city's power elite.
Beneath elaborate frescoes, domes, and columns, a waitstaff in bro-
caded waistcoats serves everything from dim sum to smoked venison;
there's something for just about everyone willing to pay the bank-break-
ing prices. Weekend brunches are an expensive indulgence, while the
pre-theater set menus are quite a bargain. $ *Average main: 1500R* ✉ *5
bulvar Tverskoi, bldg. 26, Ulitsa Tverskaya* ☎ *495/739–0011* ⊕ *www.
turandot-palace.ru* ⌂ *Reservations essential* Ⓜ *Pushkinskaya* ✛ *D2.*

$$$ ✗ **Uryuk (Урюк).** The tangy and savory Uzbek food here is served in a
ASIAN   palatial dining room that appears to have been decorated by a particu-
larly extravagant sultan. Walls are swathed in Persian rugs, transparent
curtains, embroidered pillows, and turquoise-and-white tiles, and the
food selection is just as lush. On the menu is a choice of more than 20
fresh salads, plus grilled meats, tandoori breads, and such classics as
plov, the Central Asian take on rice pilaf, served with lamb and dried
fruit. Another choice is a hearty lamb-and-noodle soup called *lagman*.
Servers are friendly but can be a bit pushy, so be firm if they offer
something you don't want. $ *Average main: 700R* ✉ *1 bulvar Tsvet-
noi, bldg. 30, Ulitsa Tverskaya* ☎ *495/694–2450* ⊕ *www.urukcafe.ru*
Ⓜ *Tsvetnoi Bulvar* ✛ *E1.*

$$$$ ✕ **Varvary** (Варвары). Anatoly
RUSSIAN Komm, the only Russian chef to
receive a Michelin star (it was at a
restaurant in Geneva), has returned
home to present his innovative creations in baroque and theatrical
surroundings, where dabs of Russian folk patterns show up amid
the gray velvet armchairs and crim-
son trim. The intricate cuisine fuses
"molecular gastronomy" techniques
with down-home ingredients, all of
which come from within Russia. All
the foams and jellies may leave you
bewildered at times, but the two-bite
borscht and the "salade Olivier ice
cream" are truly inspired. Nothing
is à la carte here but there are many
prix-fixe options. Ⓢ *Average main:*
8500R ✉ *8a bulvar Strastnoi, Ulitsa Tverskaya* ☎ *495/229–2800* ⊕ *www.*
anatolykomm.ru ⏬ *Reservations essential* Ⓜ *Pushkinskaya* ✠ *D2.*

> **FROM FACTORY**
> **TO FOOD HALL**
>
> The redbrick compound on an
> island in the Moskva River across
> from the Kremlin was once one of
> the Soviet Union's beloved choco-
> late factories, Krasny Oktyabr, or
> Red October. Wafts of sweet choc-
> olate used to fill the air around
> the factory, and its chocolate
> bars were presented as gifts to
> visiting dignitaries to the Kremlin.
> Today the factory is closed, and
> the sprawling complex has been
> renovated to house a dozen or so
> restaurants, cafés, and bars.

ULITSA BOLSHAYA NIKITSKAYA

$ ✕ **Kvartira 44** (Квартира 44). Bookshelves line the walls of this two-
CAFÉ floor café, popular with students and intellectuals who enjoy good food
at budget prices—salads, braised and grilled meat and fish, vegetable
dishes, and seasonal selections, such as roasted pumpkin in fall and gaz-
pacho come June. It can get smoky, but there's a small nonsmoking area.
Ⓢ *Average main: 450R* ✉ *2 ul. Bolshaya Nikitskaya, bldg. 22, Ulitsa*
Bolshaya Nikitskaya ☎ *495/291–7503* ⊕ *www.kv44.ru* Ⓜ *Arbatskaya,*
Pushkinskaya, or Okhotny Ryad ✠ *D3.*

$$ ✕ **Vatrushka** (Ватрушка). The name comes from a popular Russian
RUSSIAN pastry, but there's nothing common or traditional about the presenta-
Fodor's Choice tions in this old mansion stripped down to its bare-brick walls. Head
★ Chef Dmitry Shurshakov lets fresh, locally sourced ingredients shine
through in dishes like stewed turkey necks with pearl barley and spiced
carrot puree, and cauliflower and cod liver crème brûlée. You can
enjoy the namesake *vatrushka*, a cottage cheese–filled pie, for dessert.
Ⓢ *Average main: 700R* ✉ *5 ul. Bolshaya Nikitskaya, Ulitsa Bolshaya*
Nikitskaya ☎ *495/530–5511* ⊕ *www.vatrushka-cafe.ru* Ⓜ *Biblioteka*
Imeni Lenina ✠ *D3.*

ARBAT

$$$ ✕ **Jean-Jacques** (Жан-Жак). This cheap and cheerful replica of a classic
FRENCH Parisian bistro, open 24 hours a day, is almost always busy, and little
wonder: the selection of wines by the glass is the best in Moscow; the
daily lunch special, with a choice of soup, salad, and main, is a great
value; and water is free, an unusual treat in Moscow. Some of the
mains are hit or miss, but the steak is reliably good. Ⓢ *Average main:*

700R ⊠ *12 bulvar Nikitsky, Arbat* ☎ *495/690–3886* ⊕ *www.jan-jak. com* Ⓜ *Arbatskaya* ✛ *D3.*

$$$$
EUROPEAN

✕ **Les Menus Par Pierre Gagnaire.** French Michelin-star holder Pierre Gagnaire has created dishes, such as lobster with mango sorbet, that can seem almost fanciful, and they're served in plush environs where the richly upholstered furniture, in tones of cream to beige to dark slate, is laced with gold trim. Oenophiles will be happy with the wine list, overseen by a French-trained sommelier. $ *Average main: 1200R* ⊠ *Lotte Hotel, 2 bulvar Novinsky, bldg. 8, Arbat* ☎ *495/745–1000* ⊕ *www. lottehotel.ru* Ⓜ *Smolenskaya* ✛ *B4.*

$
ASIAN FUSION

✕ **Zu Cafe** (Зю Кафе). Recently Pan-Asian cuisine has become quite popular in Moscow, and this small chain of affordable fusion cafés has done its part in introducing it to Muscovites. This location was Zu's first and remains the most popular, with a light, airy interior and only about ten tables (if you come during lunch time don't be surprised if you're asked to wait). Reliable dumplings, spring rolls, and wok-fried noodles at reasonable prices make up for the sometimes-indifferent service. Each month the café introduces a new menu of traditional dishes from an Asian country. $ *Average main: 350R* ⊠ *17 ul. Novy Arbat, Arbat* ☎ *495/989–6573* Ⓜ *Arbatskaya* ✛ *C4.*

KROPOTKINSKY DISTRICT

$$
RUSSIAN

✕ **Genatsvale VIP** (Генацвале). After entering through a tunnel of vine leaves, you're seated at oak tables in a somewhat Disneyfied version of an old country house in Georgia (the country). The food—rich stews, aromnatic rice dishes, grilled meats and kebabs—is genuine, however, and in the evenings you can enjoy an authentic Georgian choir and traditional dancing. $ *Average main: 700R* ⊠ *2 ul. Ostozhenka, bldg. 14, Kropotkinsky District* ☎ *495/695–0393* ⊕ *www.restoran-genatsvale.ru* Ⓜ *Kropotkinskaya* ✛ *C5.*

$
EUROPEAN

✕ **Gogol-Mogol** (Гоголь-Моголь). Sink into folds of burgundy velour with a plate of chocolates and a cappuccino at this indulgent dessert spot off the Boulevard Ring. Unapologetically frilly and romantic, the two rooms are adorned with pink ribbons on gauzy white curtains and floral-patterned cushions atop wrought-iron chairs; gold-framed still lifes line the walls. The menu is about two-thirds sweets—truffles, praline, mille-feuille, cookies, cakes, pies—but it also includes a weekday lunch selection of soups, pastas, and pancakes, and a handful of dinner items. Service is genial and almost courtly. $ *Average main: 450R* ⊠ *6 per. Gagarinsky, Kropotkinsky District* ☎ *495/695–1131* ⊕ *www.gogol-mogol.ru* Ⓜ *Kropotkinskaya* ✛ *C4.*

$$
ECLECTIC

✕ **Strelka Bar** (Стрелка Бар). A row of windows and the blond-wood patio provide you with a panorama of the Moskva River, the Kremlin, and the white marble monolith of Christ the Savior cathedral. Though the location alone warrants a visit, a reliable menu offers an interesting mix of salads, pastas, and grilled meats, and service is solicitous. The place buzzes with hipster youth and a velvet rope appears on Friday and Saturday nights, but, as at many Moscow clubs, foreigners don't usually have a problem getting in. $ *Average main: 600R* ⊠ *5 nab. Bersenevskaya, bldg. 14, Kropotkinsky District* ☎ *495/771–7416* ⊕ *www. strelka.com/bar* Ⓜ *Kropotkinskaya* ✛ *D4.*

MOSCOW'S OPEN-AIR MARKETS

Convenience stores and gargantuan supermarket chains have come to dominate food sales in Moscow, and the authorities don't allow the already congested roads to close for open-air markets, even on weekends. Instead, most markets have retreated to the outskirts; there are prominent clusters of vegetable vendors along almost every spoke of the metro system. Two of the best are upscale **Dorogomilovsky Rynok** ("rynok" is the Russian word for "market"), near the Kievskaya metro station, and lively **Danilovsky Rynok,** across from the Tulskaya metro. Both have alternately pushy and charming hawkers selling exotic produce, such as apricots from the mountains of Tajikistan and bulbous tomatoes from Azerbaijan, as well as fish, meat, dried fruit and nuts, and locally made cheeses—perhaps most notably, the tangy Georgian *suluguni.*

NORTHERN OUTSKIRTS

$$$$
ITALIAN
✕ **L'Albero.** This is one of the few truly excellent Italian restaurants in a city full of pretenders. Brand chef Nicola Canuti is a pupil of French great Alain Ducasse, and his creative Mediterranean cuisine has an artistic flair. The menu is large, with standouts that include foie gras with a sangria sauce and a signature 36-hour braised lamb. Potted plants dot the sumptuous glassed-in dining room, making it feel like a modern noble's playhouse/greenhouse. ⑤ *Average main: 1000R* ✉ *7 ul. Delegatskaya, Northern Outskirts* ☎ *495/650–1674* ⊕ *www.albero.su* Ⓜ *Novosloboskaya* ✛ *E1.*

SOUTHERN OUTSKIRTS

$$$$
GEORGIAN
✕ **U Pirosmani** (У Пиросмани). Copies of works by namesake Georgian artist Niko Pirosmani decorate the whitewashed walls that, along with wood-paneled ceilings, create the aura of an artist's studio. Try to sit by the window in the main hall or on the balcony so you can enjoy beautiful views of New Maiden's Convent, across the pond. The menu reads like a Georgian cookbook, though some complain that the food can be a bit hit or miss. But order the *hachapuri,* Georgian cheese pie, and a kebab and you can't go wrong. ⑤ *Average main: 900R* ✉ *4 proyezd Novodevichy, Southern Outskirts* ☎ *499/255–7926* ⊕ *www. upirosmani.ru* Ⓜ *Sportivnaya* ✛ *B6.*

EASTERN OUTSKIRTS

$
GEORGIAN
Fodor's Choice
★
✕ **Dukhan Chito-Ra** (Духан Чито-Ра). This one-room café has homestyle Georgian food so good that you'll feel you've found your way to a tavern deep in the Caucasus hinterlands. The house specialty is succulent *hinkali,* fist-sized dumplings filled with ground meat that you eat with your hands; the variety with herbs is best, and all the better if you add crisp-crusted *hachapuri* (cheese bread) to the order. There are many vegetarian-friendly options on the menu, including

pkhali, assorted vegetables blended with herbs and walnuts. Ordering might be difficult unless you or someone in your party has at least a moderate knowledge of Russian. ⑤ *Average main: 300R* ✉ *10 ul. Kazakova, Eastern Outskirts* ☎ *499/265–7876* ▭ *No credit cards* Ⓜ *Kurskaya* ✛ *H2.*

$$$$
RUSSIAN
Fodor'sChoice
★

✕ **Gusyatnikoff** (Гусятникоff). Feast on exquisite traditional Russian fare in what was once (and still feels like) a private mansion. On the four floors, there are spaces to fit every mood: a Middle Eastern room with hookahs; a billiard room; intimate, plush dining rooms; and a chandeliered main hall with lots of natural light. Try the *ukha*, a fish soup, and a basket of their excellent *pirozhki*, savory filled pastries; the beef Stroganoff is outstanding. The lightning-quick waitstaff is unassuming and attentive. ⑤ *Average main: 1500R* ✉ *2a ul. Aleksandra Solzhenitsyna, Eastern Outskirts* ☎ *495/632–7558* ⊕ *www.gusyatnikoff. ru* Ⓜ *Taganskaya* ✛ *H5.*

WESTERN OUTSKIRTS

$$$$
ITALIAN

✕ **Buono** (Боно). It's all about the view atop this Stalin-era skyscraper that also houses the Radisson Royal hotel. The cuisine takes few chances, hewing to classics, such as lemony octopus salad and sea bream with tomato and fennel, while the desserts are fanciful and fantastic. ⑤ *Average main: 1500R* ✉ *1 Kutuzovsky pr., bldg. 2/1, Western Outskirts* ☎ *495/221–5555* ⊕ *www.ginzaproject.ru* Ⓜ *Kievskaya* ✛ *A4.*

$$$$
EASTERN
EUROPEAN
Fodor'sChoice
★

✕ **Shinok** (Шинок). Meals at Moscow's best Ukrainian restaurant often include a plate of assorted *salo*—a specialty of cured pork fat. If such traditional country favorites seem out of keeping with the sleek interior, take a look at the far side of the main dining hall for a glimpse of a quaint Ukrainian farm scene, complete with rabbits, a cow, and even a milkmaid and a pair of beautiful peacocks. ⑤ *Average main: 900R* ✉ *2a ul. 1905 Goda, Western Outskirts* ☎ *495/651–8101* ⊕ *www.shinok.ru* Ⓜ *Ulitsa 1905 Goda* ✛ *A3.*

MOSCOW
WHERE TO STAY

Updated by
Anna Coppola

For years, Moscow hotels were plagued by the same Soviet-bequeathed deficiencies the city's other service industries had: poor value, inconsistent service, and a limited selection. These days, the situation has improved over what it was five or even three years ago, but progress is still slow. Four- and five-star luxury behemoths still dominate, although there's also a growing number of unfrilly, steel-and-Plexiglas business hotels that fill their rooms with exhibition-goers and salespeople. Unfortunately, only a handful of places in the center could be called both intimate and affordable.

That said, the glitzy affairs that crowd ulitsa Tverskaya and other boulevards downtown are world-class, with soaring marble foyers, celestial spas, and increasingly gracious and well-trained staff. Many of them replaced or transformed old Soviet *gostinitsas* (hotels) beyond recognition—both architecturally and service-wise. The magnificent Radisson Royal spread red carpets over the remains of the former Hotel Ukraine and became the top luxury business hotel in the city. A sparkling InterContinental (the first in Russia) arrived at the site of former Minsk hotel on Tverskaya. The Moscow Ritz formerly known as Intourist and steps from the Kremlin, still sets the gold standard for opulence and fine service in the city. All eyes are on a much-anticipated opening of the Four Seasons on Manezh Square, designed to be a replica of the iconic Soviet Hotel Moskva, famous for having its image on the label of Stolichnaya vodka.

Moscow's hotels live up to their dubious reputation as the most expensive in Europe. A major shortage of worthy choices still plagues the midrange segment, especially inside the Garden Ring. Within those bounds, you might have to scour every side street to find a room for under 6,000R a night, and for that price, you typically won't get the breakfast spread and heated pool you could expect at a typical chain place in the U.S. However, amenities are improving rapidly. Once the norm was plywood furniture and tarnished polyester upholstery, but now furnishings are sturdier and there are softer linens on firmer beds. (Plenty of hotels still haven't taken up that ubiquitous mouse-brown carpeting, though.)

A glaring Soviet carryover is in the approach to service. The customer is not always right at many midrange hotels, so it helps to treat the staff with extra care when making requests and even when asking questions. And ask questions you should; because standards vary widely, it's advisable to ask about everything you might want—including turndown service, assistance with concert tickets, and no-smoking rooms—before booking. Another pitfall to keep in mind when booking is the 18% VAT Russian hotels impose. Although in most cases the amount is already added to the room price, some hotels (particularly the upscale ones) prefer to charge that on top of the listed price. Read the fine print and rate rules.

At hotels in Moscow, someone on staff usually speaks English, so you can almost always find someone who can help you. However, English-speakers typically aren't fluent, so be patient when explaining anything complicated. In general, very few people will be offended if you speak English with them—in fact, many are eager for the practice—but do ask whether someone knows the language first (*Vi gavar, itye pa-angliisky?*).

If you're a confident traveler, you might consider renting a short-term apartment like those provided by Four Squares Apartments, as they often provide the best value. You might even be able to find living quarters near the Red Square that dwarf the suites of a luxury hotel next door. But if you want to be central, expect to pay a hefty sum no matter where you stay; for now, that's what Moscow demands.

Prices in the reviews are the lowest cost of a standard double room in high season.

4

LODGING REVIEWS

Hotel reviews have been abbreviated in this book. For expanded reviews, please visit Fodors.com. Use the coordinate (✛ B2) at the end of each review to locate a property on the Where to Stay in Moscow map.

KREMLIN/RED SQUARE

$$$$ ⛢ **Ararat Park Hyatt.** One of the most luxurious of Moscow's hotels
HOTEL combines the traditional and modern, with a sparkling lobby, light and spacious rooms elegantly done with beige furniture and glass tables, and beautifully equipped bathrooms. **Pros:** central location; great city view from rooftop Conservatory Lounge; plush linens; free fruit in rooms every day. **Cons:** restaurants are overpriced; room rates are among highest in the city. $ *Rooms from: 14900R* ✉ *4 ul. Neglinnaya, Kremlin/ Red Square* ☎ *495/783–1234* ⊕ *www.moscow.park.hyatt.com* ⛁ *216 rooms, 21 suites* ⧫ No meals Ⓜ *Okhotny Ryad or Teatralnaya* ✛ *E2.*

$$ ⛢ **Metropol** (**Метрополь**). Built between 1899 and 1903, Moscow's
HOTEL most fabled hotel transports you back in a time—whether it's the art
Fodor's Choice nouveau facade, the opulent restaurants, the guest rooms with hard-
★ wood floors topped with Oriental carpets, or the antiques-filled suites. **Pros:** superb location; beautiful interiors; great buffet breakfast. **Cons:** some guest rooms need updating (renovations are ongoing). $ *Rooms from: 9900R* ✉ *2 proyezd Teatralny, Kremlin/Red Square* ☎ *499/501– 7800* ⊕ *www.metropol-moscow.ru* ⛁ *363 rooms, 72 suites* ⧫ No meals Ⓜ *Ploshchad Revolutsii or Teatralnaya* ✛ *E3.*

$$$$ ⛢ **Savoy** (**Савой**). Gilded chandeliers, ceiling paintings, and polished
HOTEL paneling invoke the spirit of prerevolutionary Russia, as do the best of the high-ceilinged rooms and spacious marble bathrooms. **Pros:** great location; beautiful interiors; swimming pool open 24 hours. **Cons:** some rooms are small, especially given the price; can be overrun by business people and bureaucrats on weekdays. $ *Rooms from: 14200R* ✉ *3/6 ul. Rozhdestvenka, bldg. 1, Kremlin/Red Square* ☎ *495/620–8500* ⊕ *www. savoy.ru* ⛁ *67 rooms, 11 suites* ⧫ No meals Ⓜ *Kuznetsky Most* ✛ *E2.*

BEST BETS FOR MOSCOW LODGING

Fodor's offers a selective listing of quality lodging experiences in every price range, from the city's best budget beds to its most sophisticated luxury hotels. Here, we've compiled our top recommendations by price and experience. The very best properties—in other words, those that provide a particularly remarkable experience in their price range—are designated in the listings with the Fodor's Choice logo.

Fodor's Choice ★

Baltschug Kempinski, p. 133
Danilovskaya, p. 134
Hotel National, p. 130
Metropol, p. 125
Radisson Royal, p. 135

By Price

$

Arbat House, p. 131
Danilovskaya, p. 134
Gamma-Delta Izmailovo, p. 135
Hotel Universitet, p. 135
Krasnaya Zarya, p. 132
Ozerkovskaya, p. 133
Medea, p. 133
Sleepbox Hotel Tverskaya, p. 131
Sovietsky Historical, p. 134

$$

Courtyard Marriott, p. 131
Golden Apple, p. 130
Metropol, p. 125

$$$

InterContinental Moscow Tverskaya, p. 130
Katerina–City, p. 133

$$$$

Baltschug Kempinski, p. 133
Hotel National, p. 130
Lotte Hotel, p. 132
Mamaison Pokrovka, p. 127
Savoy, p. 125

By Experience

BEST SPA

Lotte Hotel $$$$, p. 132
Ritz-Carlton Moscow $$$$, p. 131

HISTORICAL INTEREST

Metropol $$, p. 125
Hotel National $$$$, p. 130
Savoy $$$$, p. 125
Sovietsky Historical $, p. 134

BUILDING ARCHITECTURE

Metropol $$, p. 125
Hotel National $$$$, p. 130
Peking $, p. 130
Radisson Royal $$$, p. 135

BEST VALUE

Danilovskaya $, p. 134
Four Squares Apartments $, p. 127

COOL BARS

Ritz-Carlton Moscow $$$$, p. 131
Swissôtel Krasnye Holmy $$$$, p. 133

BUSINESS HOTELS

InterContinental Moscow Tverskaya, $$$, p. 130
Katerina–City $$$, p. 133
Novotel Moscow Center $, p. 134
Sheraton Palace $$, p. 131

SPACIOUS ROOMS

Mamaison Pokrovka $$$$, p. 127
Medea $, p. 133
Peking $, p. 130

TOP-FLIGHT FOOD

Lotte Hotel $$$$, p. 132
Sheraton Palace $$, p. 131
Swissôtel Krasnye Holmy $$$$, p. 133

SMALL AND INTIMATE

Kebur Palace $$$, p. 132
Krasnaya Zarya $, p. 132
Medea $, p. 133
Ozerkovskaya $, p. 133

BEST VIEWS

Baltschug Kempinski $$$$, p. 133
Gamma-Delta Izmailovo $, p. 135
Hotel National $$$$, p. 130
Peking $, p. 130

KITAI GOROD

$$ ⬚ **Budapest** (Будапешт). What opened in 1876 as a club for noblemen
HOTEL became a hotel for visiting Soviet bureaucrats to stay while on official
business and now is a homey if somewhat outdated place to stay in the
city center with high ceilings, skirted bedspreads, and tasseled lampshades.
Pros: great location; nice Old World ambience. **Cons:** Soviet-style service
can be a bit indifferent; dated decor. ⑤ *Rooms from: 9800R* ✉ *18 Petro-
vsky Linii, bldg. 2, Kitai Gorod* ☎ *495/925–3050* ⊕ *www.hotel-budapest.
ru* ⤶ *116 rooms, 8 suites* ⦿ *No meals* Ⓜ *Kuznetsky Most* ⊹ *E2.*

$ ⬚ **Four Squares Apartments.** This outfit offers a good variety of serviced
RENTAL apartments ranging from studios to spacious two-bedrooms, all with
modern furnishings, Wi-Fi, and full kitchens—and all for about half of
what you typically pay at a hotel. **Pros:** spacious, modern accommoda-
tions; full kitchens. **Cons:** lack of on-site service staff. ⑤ *Rooms from:
5600R* ✉ *18a per. Milyutinsky, ste. 37, Kitai Gorod* ☎ *495/937–5572*
⊕ *www.foursquares.com* ⤶ *26 apartments* ⦿ *No meals* Ⓜ *Chekhovs-
kaya* ⊹ *G1.*

$$$$ ⬚ **Mamaison Pokrovka.** Rooms at this rather puzzling place at the end of
HOTEL winding ulitsa Pokrovka, all of them suites, pull off that elusive combina-
tion of poshness and comfort; there's lots of empty square feet to stretch
out in and many have well-equipped kitchens. **Pros:** stylish, comfort-
able rooms; close to many restaurants and metro stations. **Cons:** poor
views; impersonal service. ⑤ *Rooms from: 10643R* ✉ *40 ul. Pokrovka,
bldg. 2, Kitai Gorod* ☎ *495/229–5757* ⊕ *www.mamaison.com/moscow-
pokrovka.html* ⤶ *84 suites* ⦿ *No meals* Ⓜ *Krasniye Vorota* ⊹ *H2.*

$$$$ ⬚ **Marriott Royal Aurora** (Марриотт Ройал Аврора *Marriott Rojal
HOTEL Avrora*). Rooms meet Marriott's typical standards of corporatized
comfort, but stellar service sets the bland surroundings—a product of
Moscow's mid-'90s construction boom—apart from most business-
oriented lodgings. **Pros:** perfect location; helpful staff. **Cons:** rather
monotonous surroundings; overpriced Internet access, breakfast, and
executive car service. ⑤ *Rooms from: 9200R* ✉ *20 ul. Petrovka, bldg.
11, Kitai Gorod* ☎ *495/937–1000* ⊕ *www.marriott.com* ⤶ *227 rooms,
36 suites* ⦿ *No meals* Ⓜ *Okhotny Ryad or Kuznetsky Most* ⊹ *E2.*

$$$ ⬚ **Sretenskaya** (Сретенская). Surround yourself in the atmosphere of
HOTEL an old Russian fairy tale: there's massive carved oak furniture, stained-
glass windows, and wall paintings depicting popular tales like "Little
Scarlet Flower" (the Russian version of "Beauty and the Beast"). **Pros:**
helpful staff; excellent restaurant. **Cons:** long walk to Red Square; small
rooms; expensive. ⑤ *Rooms from: 9986R* ✉ *15 ul. Sretenka, Kitai
Gorod* ☎ *495/933–5544* ⊕ *www.hotel-sretenskaya.ru* ⤶ *38 rooms*
⦿ *No meals* Ⓜ *Sukharevskaya or Kitai Gorod* ⊹ *F1.*

$ ⬚ **Ulanskaya** (Уланская). Functional rooms in the back of a mono-
HOTEL lithic government building have drab modern furnishings and cover
all the shades of beige and gray, colored only by 17th-century-style
lithographs, at this hotel. **Pros:** lots of dining options and bars nearby;
steps from the metro; cheerful service. **Cons:** standard rooms are small;
bouncy beds; drab decor. ⑤ *Rooms from: 5248R* ✉ *16 per. Ulansky,
bldg. 1A, Kitai Gorod* ☎ *495/151–1103* ⊕ *www.ulanskaya.com* ⤶ *61
rooms* ⦿ *No meals* Ⓜ *Turgenevskaya or Sretensky Bulvar* ⊹ *G1.*

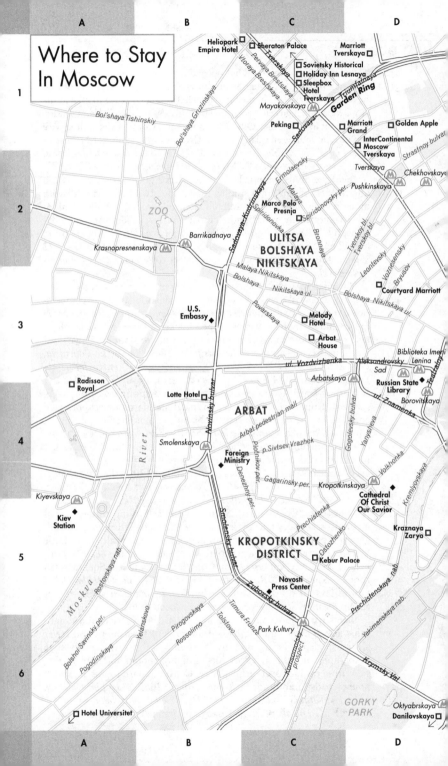

Where to Stay In Moscow

A

Bol'shaya Tishinskiy

Bol'shaya Gruzinskaya

ZOO

Krasnopresnenskaya Ⓜ

River

Moskva

Kiyevskaya Ⓜ

Kiev Station ◆

Rostovskaya nab.

Bol'shoi Savinsky per.

Pogodinskaya

Velarskovo

□ Hotel Universitet

B

Heliopark Empire Hotel □

□ Sheraton Palace

Vtoraya Brestskaya

Pervaya Brestskaya

Barrikadnaya

Spiridonovka

Ermolaevsky

Marco Polo Presnja □

Spiridonovka

Malaya Nikitskaya

Bolshaya

Povarskaya

U.S. Embassy ◆

Novinsky bulvar

Lotte Hotel □

Smolenskaya Ⓜ

ARBAT

Arbat pedestrian mall

p.Sivtsev Vrazhek

Foreign Ministry ◆

Plotnikov per.

Denezhny per.

Smolenskaya bulvar

Pirogovskaya

Rossolimo

Tolstovo

Timura Frunze

Zubovskiy bulvar

Park Kultury Ⓜ

C

Tverskaya

Tverskaya

Sadovaya

□ Sovietsky Historical

□ Holiday Inn Lesnaya

□ Sleepbox Hotel Tverskaya

Mayakovskaya Ⓜ

Garden Ring

Peking □

Malaya

Bronnaya

ULITSA BOLSHAYA NIKITSKAYA

Malaya Nikitskaya

Nikitskaya ul.

Bolshaya Nikitskaya ul.

Melody Hotel □

Arbat House □

ul. Vozdvizhenka

Arbatskaya Ⓜ

Aleksandrovsky Sad

Gogolevsky bulvar

Yanysheva

Arbatskaya

Russian State Library

Borovitskaya

ul. Znamenka

Kropotkinskaya Ⓜ

Gagarinsky per.

Kropotkinskaya

Cathedral Of Christ Our Savior ◆

Volkhonka

Prechistenka

KROPOTKINSKY DISTRICT

Ostozhenko

Kebur Palace □

Navosti Press Center ◆

Zubovskiy bulvar

prospect

Krymsky Val

D

Marriott Tverskaya □

Traunfalnaya

Garden Ring

□ Marriott Grand

□ Golden Apple

InterContinental Moscow Tverskaya □

Strastnoy bulvar

Tverskaya Ⓜ

Chekhovskaya Ⓜ

Pushkinskaya Ⓜ

Tverskoy bl.

Tverskoy bl.

Leontevsky

Voznesensky

Bryusov

Courtyard Marriott □

Biblioteka Imeni Lenina Ⓜ

Teatral...

◆

Kremlyovskaya

Kraznaya Zarya □

Prechistenskaya nab.

Yakimanskaya nab.

GORKY PARK

Oktyabrskaya Ⓜ

Danilovskaya □

A   **B**   **C**   **D**

1

2

3

4

5

6

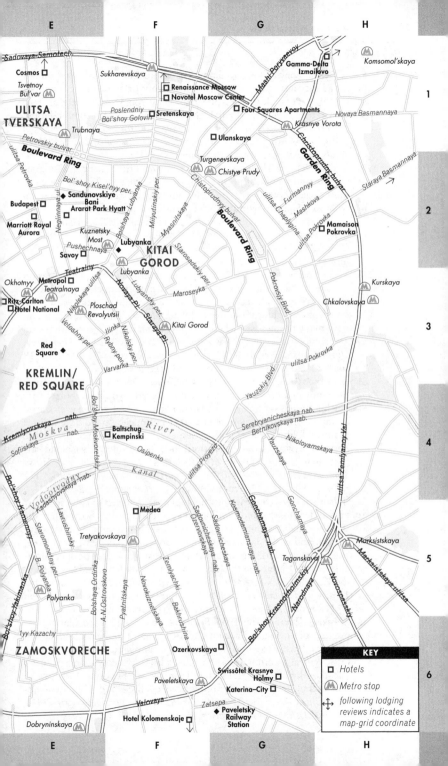

ULITSA TVERSKAYA

$$
HOTEL
🏨 **Golden Apple.** These accommodations are cozy, stylish, and quirky all at the same time, designed with plenty of color and contemporary flair. **Pros:** chocolate appears in guest rooms daily; helpful staff. **Cons:** some rooms are small; high rate for the level of accommodation. Ⓢ *Rooms from: 9700R* ✉ *11 ul. Malaya Dmitrovka, Ulitsa Tverskaya* ☎ *495/980–7000* ⊕ *www.goldenapple.ru* ⇨ *92 rooms, 2 suites* ⵠ *No meals* Ⓜ *Chekhovskaya or Pushkinskaya* ✛ *D1.*

$$$$
HOTEL
Fodor'sChoice
★
🏨 **Hotel National** (Националь). If you seek historical splendor, assiduous service, and plenty of plush comforts, this 1903 landmark, the city's most elegant hotel, is for you. **Pros:** outstanding location across a plaza from Red Square; helpful concierge staff; stunning room decor. **Cons:** some rooms overlook nearby roofs; pool is small; the health club is dull. Ⓢ *Rooms from: 12825R* ✉ *1 ul. Mochovaya, bldg. 15, Ulitsa Tverskaya* ☎ *495/258–7000* ⊕ *www.national.ru* ⇨ *202 rooms, 56 suites* ⵠ *No meals* Ⓜ *Okhotny Ryad* ✛ *E3.*

$$$
HOTEL
🏨 **InterContinental Moscow Tverskaya.** These distinctive new lodgings on the site of the demolished Soviet Minsk hotel pamper guests in contemporary luxury, accented by an enthusiastically helpful staff. **Pros:** excellent central location; free minibar; good in-house restaurants and bars; many business services. **Cons:** no swimming pool; somewhat cold and gaudy public areas. Ⓢ *Rooms from: 10620R* ✉ *22 ul. Tverskaya, Ulitsa Tverskaya* ☎ *495/787–8887* ⊕ *www.ihg.com* ⇨ *184 rooms, 19 suites* ⵠ *No meals* Ⓜ *Tverskaya or Mayakovskaya* ✛ *D2.*

$$
HOTEL
🏨 **Marriott Grand** (Марриотт Грандъ-Отель). Once you step inside, past the renovated turn-of-the-20th-century facade, you'll likely feel very much at home—if home is the United States and if you've ever stayed at any of this ubiquitous chain's other business-oriented hotels. **Pros:** beautiful lobby bar area with piano; excellent fitness center; extensive business services. **Cons:** overpriced food and drink; rather bland surroundings. Ⓢ *Rooms from: 8000R* ✉ *26 ul. Tverskaya, bldg. 1, Ulitsa Tverskaya* ☎ *495/937–0000* ⊕ *www.marriottmoscowgrand.com* ⇨ *372 rooms, 15 suites* ⵠ *No meals* Ⓜ *Mayakovskaya or Tverskaya* ✛ *C1.*

$
HOTEL
🏨 **Marriott Tverskaya** (Марриотт Тверская). A haven of calm in an art noveau landmark amid bustling ulitsa Tverskaya, this hotel offers the standard chain amenities and more—a small, peaceful lobby, four-story atrium, and understated guest rooms done in a palette of ivory, rose, and olive with dark-wood furnishings. **Pros:** spacious rooms; comfortable beds; 24-hour health club. **Cons:** long walk from Red Square and the Kremlin. Ⓢ *Rooms from: 7500R* ✉ *34 ul. Tverskaya-Yamskaya 1-ya, Ulitsa Tverskaya* ☎ *495/258–3000* ⊕ *www.marriotthotels.com* ⇨ *119 rooms, 43 suites* ⵠ *No meals* Ⓜ *Belorusskaya* ✛ *D1.*

$
HOTEL
🏨 **Peking** (Пекин). This 1955, Soviet-era tower is a Moscow landmark, offering old-fashioned accommodations that, though upgraded, still evoke Stalinist Russia, as may the service and amenities. **Pros:** convenient central location across the street from Moscow Conservatory's Tchaikovsky Hall; several nice restaurants nearby. **Cons:** beds can be bouncy and service surly. Ⓢ *Rooms from: 6400R* ✉ *5 ul. Bolshaya Sadovaya, Ulitsa Tverskaya* ☎ *495/650–2442* ⊕ *www.hotelpeking.ru* ⇨ *119 rooms, 21 suites* ⵠ *No meals* Ⓜ *Mayakovskaya* ✛ *C1.*

$$$$ **Ritz-Carlton Moscow.** What many
HOTEL travelers consider to be the city's finest luxury hotel—and with these rates, it ought to be—does its best to dazzle guests with sumptuously and traditionally furnished guest quarters that evoke tsarist Russia, as do the views of the onion domes of St. Basil's. **Pros:** prime location; exquisite surroundings and service. **Cons:** pricey. Ⓢ *Rooms from: 19500R* ✉ *3 ul. Tverskaya, Ulitsa Tverskaya* ☎ *495/225–8888* ⊕ *www.ritzcarltonmoscow.ru*
🛏 *334 rooms, 35 suites* ⦿ *No meals* Ⓜ *Okhotny Ryad* ✛ *E3.*

**NO CYRILLIC,
NO PROBLEM**

Some of the websites throughout this book are in Russian only. If you don't read Cyrillic, you can get a rough-and-ready version of such sites using **Google Translate** ⊕ *translate.google.com/#.* Just type in the Web address or original text you want translated and hit the Translate button.

$$ **Sheraton Palace** (**Шератон Палас**). The European business commu-
HOTEL nity loves this place, thanks to amenities that include a chauffeur-driven fleet of cars, though most rooms are small and crammed with chain-standard furnishings. **Pros:** well-organized transportation from airports; delicious breakfast (not included in most rates); helpful staff. **Cons:** a long walk from the Kremlin. Ⓢ *Rooms from: 8990R* ✉ *19 ul. Tverskaya-Yamskaya 1-ya, Ulitsa Tverskaya* ☎ *495/931–9700, 7502/256–3000 outside Russia* ⊕ *www.starwood.com/sheraton* 🛏 *221 rooms, 18 suites* ⦿ *No meals* Ⓜ *Belorusskaya* ✛ *C1.*

$ **Sleepbox Hotel Tverskaya.** The first capsule hotel in Russia is made
HOTEL up of compact, windlowless capsules, much like train compartments, each with one to three beds, limited storage space, and shared facili-ties (though several standard rooms with bathrooms are also avail-able). **Pros:** spotless; fun for George and Jane Jetson types into futuristic design. **Cons:** shared facilities in most units; lack of space and win-dows might invoke claustrophobia. Ⓢ *Rooms from: 2900R* ✉ *27 ul. Tverskaya-Yamskaya 1-ya, Ulitsa Tverskaya* ☎ *495/989–4104* ⊕ *www.sleepbox-hotel.ru* 🛏 *61 rooms, 5 with bath* ⦿ *No meals* Ⓜ *Belorusskaya* ✛ *C1.*

ULITSA BOLSHAYA NIKITSKAYA

$ **Arbat House.** Rooms in this former guesthouse for the Georgian
HOTEL embassy are a mix of the basic and the updated, with brown wall-to-wall carpeting and cramped bathrooms, but also plasma TVs and large beds. **Pros:** excellent location; spacious rooms; attractive restaurant. **Cons:** odd atmosphere and decor; negligible views. Ⓢ *Rooms from: 6726R* ✉ *13 per. Skatertny, Ulitsa Bolshaya Nikitskaya* ☎ *495/660–7178* ⊕ *www.melody-hotel.com* 🛏 *72 rooms, 3 suites* ⦿ *Breakfast* Ⓜ *Arbatskaya or Tverskaya* ✛ *C3.*

$$ **Courtyard Marriott** (**Кортъярд Марриотт**). These spacious, functional,
HOTEL and comfortable guest rooms, some with views of the Kremlin, are in the heart of the historical center, across from St. Andrew's Angli-can Church and near the Moscow Conservatory. **Pros:** wide selection of restaurants and coffee shops in the area; very comfortable beds. **Cons:** small fitness room and no pool. Ⓢ *Rooms from: 9775R* ✉ *7 per.*

4

Voznesensky, Ulitsa Bolshaya Nikitskaya ☎ *495/981–3300* ⊕ *www. marriott.com* ⤳ *208 rooms, 10 suites* ⦿ *No meals* Ⓜ *Pushkinskaya or Tverskaya* ✛ *D3.*

$$$ ⛾ **Marco Polo Presnja** (**Марко Поло Пресня**). Once a former residence HOTEL for English teachers then later the exclusive domain of the Communist Party, this hotel has many rooms with balconies overlooking a quiet green residential neighborhood near Patriarch's Ponds. **Pros:** art-lined halls and rooms; near cafés and bars. **Cons:** some unfriendly staff; some guest rooms are small and a bit dark; room rates rather high for amenities offered. Ⓢ *Rooms from: 10152R* ✉ *9 per. Spiridonevsky, Ulitsa Bolshaya Nikitskaya* ☎ *495/660–0606, 499/244–3631* ⊕ *www. presnja.ru* ⤳ *54 rooms, 16 suites* ⦿ *Breakfast* Ⓜ *Mayakovskaya or Pushkinskaya* ✛ *C2.*

ARBAT

$$$$ ⛾ **Lotte Hotel.** With towering black marble columns and a spiky crystal HOTEL chandelier, the lobby feels like the palace of a fashionable but villainous monarch, while guest rooms surrounding an atrium are warm, plush, and fully equipped. **Pros:** impressive restaurants; unique spa; luxurious marble bathrooms. **Cons:** standard rooms are on the small side; so-so views. Ⓢ *Rooms from: 22225R* ✉ *8 bul. Novinsky, bldg. 2, Arbat* ☎ *495/745–1000, 495/287–0500 for reservations* ⊕ *www.lottehotel.ru* ⤳ *304 rooms, 38 suites* ⦿ *No meals* Ⓜ *Arbtaskaya* ✛ *B4.*

KROPOTKINSKY DISTRICT

$$$ ⛾ **Kebur Palace** (**Кебур Палас** *Kebur Palas*). In this small, attractive HOTEL hotel built in the style of an old Georgian town house, guest rooms are large and have views of a small square and a fountain through floor-to-ceiling windows. **Pros:** excellent location; lots of natural light. **Cons:** some rooms are noisy due to a Georgian restaurant attached to the hotel; some room decor is a bit staid and dark. Ⓢ *Rooms from: 10660R* ✉ *32 ul. Ostozhenka, Kropotkinsky District* ☎ *495/733–9070* ⊕ *www.keburpalace.ru* ⤳ *79 rooms, 7 suites* ⦿ *Breakfast* Ⓜ *Kropotkinskaya* ✛ *C5.*

$ ⛾ **Krasnaya Zarya** (**Красная Заря**). The slick and minimalist rooms HOTEL that line two floors of what was once an employee club at the Krasny Oktybr chocolate factory on an island in the Moskva River still give out an industrial vibe, softened with stylish contemporary furnishings. **Pros:** surrounded by trendy bars and restaurants; spacious, comfortable rooms; central location. **Cons:** minimal support staff; interiors are rather bare; noise from the bar next door on weekends. Ⓢ *Rooms from: 5740R* ✉ *3/10 per. Bersenevsky, bldg. 8, Kropotkinsky District* ☎ *495/980–4774* ⊕ *www.red-zarya.ru* ⤳ *8 rooms* ⦿ *No meals* Ⓜ *Borovitskaya* ✛ *D5.*

ZAMOSKVORECHE

$$$$ ☷ **Baltschug Kempinski** (Балчуг Кемпински). Many of the stately and
HOTEL well-equipped rooms at this deluxe hotel, perched on the banks of
FAMILY the Moskva River, have extraordinary views of the Kremlin and Red
Fodor's Choice Square. **Pros:** close to Red Square; best breakfast in town (extra with
★ most rates); kid friendly; gracious service. **Cons:** far from metro.
⑤ *Rooms from: 17600R* ⊠ *1 ul. Baltchug, Zamoskvoreche* ☎ *495/287–*
2000 ⊕ *www.kempinski-moscow.com* ⇲ *190 rooms, 40 suites* ⊚| *No*
meals Ⓜ *Novokuznetskaya or Tretyakovskaya* ✥ *F4.*

$$$ ☷ **Katerina–City** (Катерина Сити *Katerina Siti*). Comfortable, modern
HOTEL rooms occupy this renovated prerevolutionary mansion and a modern
eight-story annex, complemented by nice views and friendly service.
Pros: tasty breakfast (extra); smoke-free; complimentary coffee and
minibar. **Cons:** businesslike and functional. ⑤ *Rooms from: 10700R*
⊠ *6 nab. Shlyuzovaya, Zamoskvoreche* ☎ *495/795–2444* ⊕ *www.*
katerinahotels.com ⇲ *120 rooms, 10 suites* ⊚| *No meals* Ⓜ *Pavelets-*
kaya ✥ *G6.*

$ ☷ **Medea** (Медея *Medeja*). If you're looking for privacy and quiet in
HOTEL the very heart of the city, these spacious, clean, and functional guest
rooms in a 19th-century mansion are the place for you. **Pros:** steps
from the metro; helpful staff; kitchens in most rooms. **Cons:** on a
grungy side street; negligible views. ⑤ *Rooms from: 6500R* ⊠ *4 per.*
Pyatnitsky, bldg. 1, Zamoskvoreche ☎ *495/232–4898* ⊕ *www.medea-*
hotel.ru ⇲ *21 rooms, 15 suites* ⊚| *No meals* Ⓜ *Tretyakovskaya or*
Novokuznetskaya ✥ *F5.*

$ ☷ **Ozerkovskaya** (Озерковская). In this refreshingly homey place,
HOTEL hallways are lined with Oriental rugs and the plainly furnished guest
rooms are large and some have tremendous views of the tower and
onion-domed church of Novospassky Monastery to the east. **Pros:**
helpful staff; decent location; great views from some rooms. **Cons:**
small common areas; unexciting decor; linens could use an update.
⑤ *Rooms from: 5800R* ⊠ *50 nab. Ozerkovskaya, bldg. 2, Zamoskvore-*
che ☎ *495/951–9582* ⊕ *www.ozerkhotel.ru* ⇲ *27 rooms* ⊚| *No meals*
Ⓜ *Paveletskaya* ✥ *G6.*

$$$$ ☷ **Swissôtel Krasnye Holmy** (Swissôtel Красные Холмы). This tallest
HOTEL luxury hotel in town, a 34-story sleek glass-and-metal cylinder that
holds its own with Stalin's Seven Sisters, also has some of the largest
guest rooms in town, warmly done with chestnut-wood walls. **Pros:**
stunning view of Moscow from top-floor City Space bar; caviar and
champagne for breakfast (not included in most rates); beautiful pool
and spa. **Cons:** not the most convenient location if you're planning to
use the metro; expensive everything. ⑤ *Rooms from: 13500R* ⊠ *52*
nab. Kosmodamianskaya, bldg. 6, Zamoskvoreche ☎ *495/787–9800*
⊕ *www.swissotel.com* ⇲ *233 rooms, 27 suites* ⊚| *No meals* Ⓜ *Pave-*
letskaya or Taganskaya ✥ *G6.*

NORTHERN OUTSKIRTS

$ 🖼 **Cosmos (Космос).** Years of heavy tourist traffic have dulled the shine
HOTEL on the French-furnished interiors here—the 26-floor complex was built
by the French for the 1980 Olympics—but the rooms are adequate and
clean, and some have been recently renovated. **Pros:** bargain prices; funky
retro Soviet-era flavor; several restaurants and bars on premises. **Cons:**
Soviet-style service; full of tour groups; far from many sights. *⑤ Rooms
from: 3567R ✉ 150 Mira pr., Northern Outskirts ☎ 495/234–1206
⊕ www.hotel-cosmos.ru ⇨ 1,777 rooms* ⑩ *No meals* Ⓜ *VDNKh ✛ E1.*

$$ 🖼 **Heliopark Empire Hotel.** Fresh decor, with cream-colored walls, button
HOTEL leather sofas, and good, firm beds, make up for the rather small rooms
here, while soundproof windows ward off incessant street noise from
the narrow, traffic-jammed ulitsa Brestskaya. **Pros:** central location;
pleasant, attentive staff. **Cons:** poor views; no gym or pool. *⑤ Rooms
from: 7913R ✉ 60 ul. Brestskaya 1, Northern Outskirts ☎ 499/251–
6413 ⊕ www.heliopark.ru ⇨ 33 rooms, 1 junior suite, 5 deluxe rooms*
⑩ *Breakfast* Ⓜ *Belorusskaya ✛ C1.*

$ 🖼 **Novotel Moscow Center (Новотель Москва-Центр** *Novotel Moskva-
HOTEL Centr).* Functional and efficient, if a bit unimaginative, rooms here come
with all the usual amenities, and some of them have rather interesting
shapes (the building itself is cylindrical). **Pros:** lots of cafés and bars in
the area; reasonably priced. **Cons:** staff isn't well-versed in tourist infor-
mation. *⑤ Rooms from: 6290R ✉ 23 ul. Novoslobodskaya, Northern
Outskirts ☎ 495/780–4000 ⊕ www.novotel.com ⇨ 255 rooms, 1 suite*
⑩ *No meals* Ⓜ *Mendeleyevskaya ✛ F1.*

$$ 🖼 **Renaissance Moscow Olympic (Ренессанс Москва Олимпик).** Rooms
HOTEL are large and equipped with every amenity at this hotel, busy with
conferences and meetings but far from the city center. **Pros:** attentive staff; comfortable beds; shuttle bus service to city center every
hour. **Cons:** far from Kremlin; closest metro is 15-minute walk away.
*⑤ Rooms from: 7800R ✉ 1 Olympisky pr., bldg. 18, Northern Out-
skirts ☎ 495/931–9000 ⊕ www.marriott.com ⇨ 475 rooms, 12 suites*
⑩ *No meals* Ⓜ *Prospekt Mira ✛ F1.*

$ 🖼 **Sovietsky Historical (Отель Советский).** Plunge into Soviet-era gran-
HOTEL deur at what even Russian guests consider to be a "time machine," with
marble columns, comfortable sofas, Socialist realist art, grand chandeliers, and a "shabby chic" ethos in the high-ceilinged guest rooms. **Pros:**
very spacious, clean, and well-lit rooms; famous Russian restaurant,
Yar, on premises. **Cons:** a 15-minute walk to the metro; a bit noisy.
*⑤ Rooms from: 5776R ✉ 2 Leningradsky pr., bldg. 32, Northern Out-
skirts ☎ 495/960–2000 ⊕ www.sovietsky.ru ⇨ 106 rooms, 24 suites*
⑩ *Breakfast* Ⓜ *Dinamo or Belorusskaya ✛ C1.*

SOUTHERN OUTSKIRTS

$ 🖼 **Danilovskaya (Даниловская).** A serene and lovely setting inside the
HOTEL walls of the Danilovsky (St. Daniel) Monastery provides a backdrop
Fodor'sChoice of fountains, religious-themed paintings, and domes for these simple,
★ tidy guest quarters with crisp new linens, lacquered-wood furnishings,
and polished parquet floors. **Pros:** nice grounds; clean (though plain)

rooms; excellent *pirozhki* (traditional Russian pastries). **Cons:** remote location; staff can be a bit stern. $ *Rooms from: 5166R* ⊠ *5 per. Bolshoi Starodanilovsky, Southern Outskirts* ☎ *495/954–0503* ⊕ *www. danilovsky.ru* ⇆ *131 rooms, 25 suites* ⦿| *Breakfast* Ⓜ *Tulskaya* ⊹ *D6.*

$ ⬚ **Hotel Kolomenskoye** (Коломенское). Accommodations are bare
HOTEL   bones, with linoleum floors, plain furnishings, and low beds, but the price is right, and as a bonus, a sense of elegance prevails in this estate-like setting on the grounds of the sprawling park of the same name. **Pros:** spotless; basic in-house restaurant; no-smoking rooms available. **Cons:** outside center in rather dull area; basic, institutional surroundings. $ *Rooms from: 3800R* ⊠ *39 Andropova pr., Southern Outskirts* ☎ *499/725–1174* ⊕ *www.hotel-kolomenskoye.ru* ⇆ *22 rooms* ⦿| *No meals* Ⓜ *Kolomenskaya* ⊹ *F6.*

$ ⬚ **Hotel Universitet** (Университетская). Quarters are small but much
HOTEL   more comfortable and attractive than you might expect in this bargain-priced, dorm-like setting near the prestigious Moscow State University. **Pros:** very attractive accommodations for the price; a lot of big-hotel amenities. **Cons:** rather staid; a lot of groups; not in center and a distance from metro. $ *Rooms from: 4000R* ⊠ *8/29 Michurinsky pr., Southern Outskirts* ☎ *499/147–2062* ⊕ *www.hotel-universitet.ru* ⇆ *264 rooms* ⦿| *No meals* Ⓜ *Universitet* ⊹ *A6.*

EASTERN OUTSKIRTS

$ ⬚ **Gamma-Delta Izmailovo** (Гамма-Дельта Измайлово). This mammoth
HOTEL   complex comprises four hotels: Alfa, Beta, Gamma, and Delta, with the last two most commonly used by foreigners and, though the Soviet past is much in evidence, offering well-maintained rooms with modern furnishings. **Pros:** excellent views of the city and the neighboring pond from upper floors; bargain prices. **Cons:** far away from the center and most tourist sights; standard rooms are small. $ *Rooms from: 3000R* ⊠ *71 shosse Izmailovskoye, Eastern Outskirts* ☎ *495/166–4490, 495/737–7000* ⊕ *www.izmailovo.ru* ⇆ *2,000 rooms, 28 suites* ⦿| *No meals* Ⓜ *Partizanskaya* ⊹ *H1.*

WESTERN OUTSKIRTS

$$$ ⬚ **Radisson Royal** (Украина). One of the famed Seven Sisters skyscrap-
HOTEL   ers commissioned by Stalin in the 1950s pampers present-day capital-
Fodor's Choice   ists in luxurious Italianate guest rooms, jauntily decorated lounges,
★   and a world-class spa. **Pros:** friendly service; great views; diverse dining options; impressive swimming pool area with hot tub and *hamam* (Turkish bath). **Cons:** far from metro and the Kremlin; expensive. $ *Rooms from: 11000R* ⊠ *2/1 Kutuzovsky pr., bldg. 1, Western Outskirts* ☎ *495/221–5555* ⊕ *www.radisson.ru/royalhotel-moscow* ⇆ *497 rooms, 38 suites* ⦿| *No meals* Ⓜ *Kievskaya* ⊹ *A4.*

MOSCOW
NIGHTLIFE AND
THE ARTS

Updated by
Natasha Doff

St. Petersburg may be known as Russia's cultural capital, but Moscow easily rivals its northern neighbor. Ballet at the Bolshoi, concerts at the Tchaikovsky Conservatory, and theaters packed for Chekhov plays are among the highlights of the intense arts scene in this city with dozens of theaters and concert halls and many prestigious acting schools. From raucous, boho joints like Kitaisky Lyotchik to sophisticated "minigarch" (wannabe oligarch) hangouts, Moscow's nightlife scene has a little bit of something for everyone. Almost all the major hotels have upscale bars: those at the Baltschug Kempinski, Ararat Park Hyatt, and Golden Ring are elegant and have majestic views of the city. But you'll likely have more fun if you head out on the town and taste a little Russian hedonism, be it sipping a cocktail on the rooftop at Rolling Stone or jumping about to a guitar band at Krizis Zhanra. For those after something calmer, there are several English-style pubs like Sixteen Tons that are great for a quiet pint and a bite to eat.

THE ARTS

Muscovites' love of culture spills over into the arena of visual arts, and a growing number of private galleries sell works by Russian artists, many cuts above the kitsch available at most of the tourist markets. The Friday edition of the *Moscow Times* carries reviews of current art exhibits; most galleries are closed on Sunday and Monday.

Moscow's musical life has always been particularly rich; the city has several symphony orchestras as well as song-and-dance ensembles. Moiseyev's Folk Dance Ensemble is well known in Europe and America, but the troupe is on tour so much of the year that when it performs in Moscow (generally at the Tchaikovsky Concert Hall), tickets are very difficult to obtain. Other renowned companies include the State Symphony Orchestra and the Armed Forces Song and Dance Ensemble. With the exception of special performances, tickets are usually easily available and inexpensive.

Although in the past Moscow was too far off the beaten track to attract top-name Western stars, in the last year the city has seen performances by everyone from Madonna to Muse to Elton John. Also be sure to catch the many talented Russian musicians playing jazz and blues, as well as ethnic folk acts from other regions in Russia, such as the Tuvan throat singers, who frequently appear at festivals.

Even if you don't speak Russian, you might want to explore the intense world of Russian dramatic theater. Unfortunately, headphones providing English translations are virtually unheard of, so it's best to stick to something you already know in English (Shakespeare is, of course, widely performed, as are many plays based on classic works that would be familiar to readers of Russian literature, such as *The Master and Margarita* and *Brothers Karamazov*). The increasingly popular Chekhov International Theater Festival usually takes place mid-May through mid- to late July.

Two free English-language newspapers, the daily *Moscow Times* (⊕ *www.themoscowtimes.com*) and the weekly *Moscow News* (⊕ *themoscownews.com*), publish schedules of cultural events for the coming week. Both can be picked up at the airport when you arrive or at a hotel, restaurant, or bar in the city center. Most theater tickets can be obtained on the theaters' websites, at the theaters themselves, or at the box offices (*teatralnaya kassa*) scattered throughout the city. Note that some theaters charge different prices for Russians and foreigners. If you're intimidated by the language barrier, ask your hotel's concierge for help. The prices are inflated, but a concierge can often get you tickets to otherwise sold-out performances. Scalpers usually can be found selling tickets outside theaters immediately prior to performances, but they've been known to rip off tourists, either charging exorbitant prices or selling fake tickets. Note that evening performances begin at 7 pm *sharp*.

KREMLIN/RED SQUARE

OPERA AND BALLET

State Kremlin Palace (Государственный кремлевский дворец *Gosudarstvenniy Kremlevsky Dvorets*). Formerly the hall where Soviet Communist Party congresses were held, this modern concert venue now hosts regular performances by opera and ballet troupes, including those from the Bolshoi and Mariinsky. Of late it has also become the stage for international performers such as Elton John, Mariah Carey, and Cirque du Soleil. Entrance is through the whitewashed Kutafya Gate. ✉ *1 ul. Vozdvizhenka, in Kremlin, Kremlin/Red Square* ☎ *495/620–7831* ⊕ *www.kremlinpalace.org* Ⓜ *Aleksandrovsky Sad.*

KITAI GOROD

This commercial district north and east of the Kremlin is known for its banks and offices, but it also houses many theaters, including the famous Bolshoi.

ART GALLERIES

Dom Nashchokina Gallery (Дом Нащокина Галарея). A mixture of classic Russian art and crowd-pulling exhibitions by celebrity artists can be found at this established space. ✉ *12 per. Vorotnikovsky, Kitai Gorod* ☎ *495/699–1178, 495/699–4774* ⊕ *www.domnaschokina.ru* Ⓜ *Mayakovskaya.*

FILM

35mm (35мм *Tridtsat Pyat Milimetrov*). An artsy crowd frequents this simple movie theater with top-quality projection and sound. The films are always shown in their original language, usually with Russian subtitles. ✉ *47/24 ul. Pokrovka, Kitai Gorod* ☎ *495/917–5492* ⊕ *www.kino35mm.ru* Ⓜ *Krasniye Vorota or Kurskaya.*

OPERA AND BALLET

Fodor's Choice ★ **Bolshoi Opera and Ballet Theatre** (Большой Театр). This world-renowned theater continues to produce innovative shows, despite a string of recent scandals—including the resignation of its two ballet stars and an acid attack on its artistic director. The Russian flair for set and costume design alone can often be enough to keep an audience enthralled. Performances on the main stage sell out quickly, so order tickets far in advance. Tickets for the second stage next to the main theater are easier to come by. ✉ *1 pl. Teatralnaya, Kitai Gorod* ☎ *495/455–5555 tickets* ⊕ *www.bolshoi.ru* Ⓜ *Teatralnaya.*

THEATER

Maly Theater (Малый Театр). Moscow's first dramatic theater, opened in 1824, is famous for its staging of Russian classics, especially those of the 19th-century satirist Alexander Ostrovsky—his statue stands outside the building. ✉ *1 proyezd Teatralny, bldg. 1, Kitai Gorod* ☎ *495/624–4046* ⊕ *www.maly.ru* Ⓜ *Teatralnaya.*

Operetta Theater (Московская Оперетта *Moskovskaya Operetta*). The theater stages lighthearted, and much humbler, versions of Western musicals, as well as the latest Russian musicals. ✉ *6 ul. Bolshaya Dmitrovka, Kitai Gorod* ☎ *495/925–5050 tickets* ⊕ *www.mosoperetta.ru* Ⓜ *Teatralnaya or Okhotny Ryad.*

Sovremennik Theater (Московский Театр Современник). This well-respected theater housed in a columned white stone building on leafy bulvar Chistoprudny stages a mix of Russian classics and foreign adaptations. ✉ *19 bulvar Chistoprudny, Kitai Gorod* ☎ *495/628–7749* ⊕ *www.sovremennik.ru* Ⓜ *Chistiye Prudy.*

WORD OF MOUTH

"A ballet performance is a mandatory experience wherever you are in Russia. Attending a Moscow ballet is . . . a stylish event. People dress up, and in the pauses, you consume drinks and snacks, some of them of outstanding quality."

—Echnaton

ULITSA TVERSKAYA

The lovely, wide boulevard, a grandiose product of the Stalinist era, is lined with cafés, banks, and hotels, and the neighborhood is a hotbed of Moscow culture, with the city's greatest concentration of theaters and concert halls.

ART GALLERIES

Fine Art (Файн Арт). This was one of the first private galleries in post-Soviet Russia. Today it displays contemporary art from the best of the previous generation's nonconformists to current names. ✉ *10 ul. Bolshaya Sadovaya, bldg. 3, Ulitsa Tverskaya* ☎ *499/251–7649* ⊕ *www.galleryfineart.ru* Ⓜ *Mayakovskaya.*

MUSIC

Kollony Zal (Коллоный Зал). This 18th-century building hosts regular concerts and music festivals from top international orchestras. ✉ *1 ul. Bolshaya Dmitrovka, Ulitsa Tverskaya* ☎ *495/692–0736* ⊕ *www.domsojuzov.ru* Ⓜ *Okhotny Ryad.*

Tchaikovsky Concert Hall (Концертый зал Чайковского *Kontsertny Zal Chaikovskovo*). With seating for more than 1,500, this huge hall is home to the State Symphony Orchestra, but also hosts concerts by other renowned Russian and international musicians. ✉ *31 pl. Triumfalnaya p, bldg. 4, Ulitsa Tverskaya* ☎ *495/232–0400* ⊕ *www.meloman.ru* Ⓜ *Mayakovskaya.*

OPERA AND BALLET

Kolobov Novaya Opera (Новая Опера). After opening in 1991, the Novaya ("New") opera house quickly established itself as one of the best and most innovative in Moscow. The surrounding Hermitage Garden is perfect for a pre- or post-theater stroll and bite to eat. The choir is ranked as the best in the city. ✉ *Hermitage Garden, 2 Karetny Ryad, bldg. 3, Ulitsa Tverskaya* ☎ *495/694–0868* ⊕ *www.novayaopera.ru* Ⓜ *Tverskaya or Mayakovskaya.*

THEATER

LenKom Theater (Ленком). Good, often flashy productions are on the bill at this large theater. Tickets can be bought online but are frequently very hard to get. ✉ *6 ul. Malaya Dmitrovka, Ulitsa Tverskaya* ☎ *495/699–0708* ⊕ *www.lenkom.ru* Ⓜ *Pushkinskaya.*

Teatr.doc (Театр.doc). This noncommercial project run mainly by volunteers specializes in documentary theater. Plays in this tiny basement theater are very experimental and provide a good insight into modern Russian life. The theater has no telephone number, so it's best to book tickets via the website. ✉ *11/13 per. Tryokhprudny, bldg. 1, Ulitsa Tverskaya* ☎ *No phone* ⊕ *www.teatrdoc.ru* Ⓜ *Pushkinskaya.*

Moscow Art Theater (МХТ им. А. П. Чехова *MKhAT*). Founded in 1898, the MKhAT is famous for its well-funded productions of the Russian classics, but it also stages plenty of modern and foreign performances. The theatre's American Studio Six presents performances, typically Russian classics, in English a few times a year. ✉ *3 per. Kamergersky, Ulitsa Tverskaya* ☎ *495/692–6748* ⊕ *www.art.theatre.ru* Ⓜ *Okhotny Ryad.*

5

Moscow Theater for Young Viewers (Московский Театр Юного Зрителя *Moskovsky Teatr Yunovo Zritelya*). Despite its name, this acclaimed theater mainly stages adult productions. It is famed for well-directed dramatizations of Chekhov short stories, staged by director Kama Ginkas. ✉ *10 per. Mamonovsky, Ulitsa Tverskaya* ☎ *495/699–4995* ⊕ *www.moscowtyz.ru* Ⓜ *Pushkinskaya.*

Praktika (Практика). An intimate space shows a wide selection of contemporary and experimental theater by some of Russia's best modern directors. ✉ *30 per. Bolshoi Kozikhinskoi, Ulitsa Tverskaya* ☎ *495/554–5545* ⊕ *www.praktikatheatre.ru* Ⓜ *Mayakovskaya or Pushkinskaya.*

Stanislavsky Music Theater (Музыкальный театр имени К. С. Станиславского *Muzikalniy Teatr imeni K. S. Stanislavskovo*). A wide range of well-produced operas and ballets are performed at the Stanislavsky, with tickets generally easier to come by than those for the Bolshoi or Novaya Opera. ✉ *17 ul. Bolshaya Dmitrovka, Ulitsa Tverskaya* ☎ *495/723–7325* ⊕ *www.stanmus.ru* Ⓜ *Pushkinskaya.*

ULITSA BOLSHAYA NIKITSKAYA

MUSIC

Fodor's Choice ★ **Tchaikovsky Conservatory** (Московская Консерватория имени П. И. Чайковского *Moskovskaya Konservatoriya imeni P. I. Chaikovskovo*). Rachmaninoff, Scriabin, and Tchaikovsky are among the famous composers who have worked here. The acoustics of the magnificent Great Hall are superb, and portraits of the world's great composers hang above the high balcony. The adjacent Small Hall is usually reserved for chamber-music concerts. ✉ *16 ul. Bolshaya Nikitskaya, bldg. 13, Ulitsa Bolshaya Nikitskaya* ☎ *495/629–9401* ⊕ *www.mosconsv.ru* Ⓜ *Okhotny Ryad or Arbatskaya.*

ARBAT

MUSIC

Scriabin Museum Hall (Мемормальный Музей А. Н. Скрябина *Memoralniy Muzei A. N. Skryabina*). Classical concerts are held four to five times a week in a small concert hall in the apartment building where the composer Alexander Scriabin lived. ✉ *11 per. Bolshoi Nikolopeskovsky, Arbat* ☎ *499/241–1901* ⊕ *www.anskriabin.ru* Ⓜ *Smolenskaya.*

OPERA AND BALLET

Helikon Opera (Геликон Опера). In addition to delivering consistently appealing and critically acclaimed opera performances, the Helikon troupe is equally talented in space management: even the grandest of classics are fitted with ease onto the small stage. ✉ *11 ul. Novy Arbat, Arbat* ☎ *495/690–6592* ⊕ *www.helikon.ru* Ⓜ *Arbatskaya.*

KROPOTKINSKY DISTRICT

ART GALLERIES

Zurab Tsereteli Art Gallery (Галерея Искусств Зураба Церетели *Galereya Iskustv Zuraba Tsereteli*). The giant sculptures of one of Russia's wackiest artists are on show at this neoclassical building, along with other temporary exhibits. Don't miss—not that you could— Tsereteli's giant metal apple. ✉ *19 ul. Prechistenka, Kropotkinsky District* ☎ *495/637–4150, 495/637–2569* ⊕ *www.museum.ru/M3027* Ⓜ *Kropotkinskaya.*

ZAMOSKVORECHE

ART GALLERIES

Central House of Artists (Центральный Дом Художника *Tsentralniy Dom Khudozhnika*). Many different galleries are housed within this vast exhibition center and if you wander long enough you're likely to find something to fit your taste, from traditional landscapes to the latest avant-garde outrage. In front, a huge art market snakes its way along the river. Among the piles of kitsch and banal landscapes you can find some real gems. Be prepared to bargain. ✉ *10 ul. Krymsky Val, Zamoskvoreche* ☎ *499/238–9634* ⊕ *www.cha.ru* Ⓜ *Park Kultury or Oktyabrskaya.*

MUSIC

Moscow International Performing Arts Center (Московский Международный Дом Музыки *Moscovsky Mezhdunarodniy Dom Muziki*). Opened in 2002, this architecturally striking center stages major classical concerts in its Svetlanov Hall, which contains Russia's largest organ. Concerts are also held in two other sizable halls and on the venue's summer terrace. ✉ *52 nab. Kosmodamianskaya, bldg. 8, Zamoskvoreche* ☎ *495/730–1011* ⊕ *www.mmdm.ru* Ⓜ *Paveletskaya.*

NORTHERN OUTSKIRTS

ART GALLERIES

FAMILY
Fodor'sChoice ★
Garage Center for Contemporary Culture (Гараж Центр Современной Культуры *Garazh Tsentr Sovremennoi Kulturi*). Buoyed with funding from oligarchs like Chelsea Football Club owner Roman Abramovich, the center has become one of Moscow's hottest venues for international and Russian contemporary art. There's a good café here, too. ✉ *Gorky Park, 9 ul. Krimsky Val, Yakimanka* ☎ *495/645–0520* ⊕ *www.garageccc.ru* Ⓜ *Park Kultury or Oktyabrskaya.*

MUSIC

Russian Army Theater (Театр Российской Армии *Teatr Rossiiskoi Armii*). The Armed Forces Song and Dance Ensemble calls this venue home. If nothing else, this theater is worth a visit for the architecture— a giant star-shaped construction with columns and marble floors. ✉ *2 pl. Suvorovskaya, Northern Outskirts* ☎ *495/681–2110* ⊕ *www.catra. su* Ⓜ *Dostoyevskaya.*

SOUTHERN OUTSKIRTS

MUSIC

Tsaritsyno Museum (Музей Заповедник "Царицыно" *Muzei Zapovednik Tsaritsino*). The music hall at Catherine the Great's restored Moscow palace regularly holds classical-music concerts in its four small halls. ✉ *1 ul. Dolskaya, Southern Outskirts* ☎ *495/725–7287* ⊕ *www.tsaritsyno.net* Ⓜ *Orekhovo or Tsaritsyno.*

THEATER

FAMILY **Tereza Durova Clown Theater** (Театриум на Серпуховке *Teatrium na Serpukhovke*). Attracting children and adults, the shows here, based on the commedia dell'arte, are filled with music, dance, and acrobatics. ✉ *6 ul. Pavlovskaya, inside DK Zavoda Ilyicha, Southern Outskirts* ☎ *495/958–5950* ⊕ *www.durova.org* Ⓜ *Serpukhovskaya or Tulskaya.*

EASTERN OUTSKIRTS

ART GALLERIES

Artplay (Артплей). Housed in the brightly painted brick buildings of a Soviet silk spinning mill, this vast design center has everything from photography and modern art exhibitions to architecture bureaus, design showrooms, and a roof-top ice rink in winter. ✉ *10 ul. Nizhnyaya Siromyatnicheskaya, Eastern Oustkirts* ☎ *495/620–0883* ⊕ *www.artplay.ru* Ⓜ *Chkalovskaya.*

Guelman Gallery (Гельман Галерея). One of Moscow's first galleries, this is also one of its most controversial, due to the attention-loving nature of owner Marat Guelman. There's a definite shock value to many of the modern and avant-garde exhibits. It's a good bet for performance art. ✉ *Winzavod, 1 per. 4th Syromantichesky, bldg. 6, Eastern Outskirts* ☎ *495/228–1159* ⊕ *www.guelman.ru* Ⓜ *Kurskaya or Chkalovskaya.*

Winzavod (Винзавод). What was a massive wine factory in Soviet times is now the epicenter of Moscow's burgeoning contemporary arts scene, housing more than a half-dozen galleries, as well as two restaurants, a bookstore, and several fashion showrooms. ✉ *1 per. 4th Syromantichesky per., bldg. 6, Eastern Outskirts* ☎ *495/917–4646* ⊕ *www.winzavod.ru* Ⓜ *Kurskaya or Chkalovskaya.*

XL-Gallery (XL Галерея). Russia's most renowned conceptual artists exhibit drawings, photographs, and installations, and occasionally put on performances in this intimate space. ✉ *Winzavod, 1 per. 4th Syromantichesky, bldg. 6, Eastern Outskirts* ☎ *495/775–8373* ⊕ *www.xlgallery.ru* Ⓜ *Kurskaya or Chkalovskaya.*

FILM

Dome Cinema (Кинотеатр "Под Куполом" *Kinoteatr "Pod Kupolom"*). A hotel movie house caters to the expatriate community with recent original-language Hollywood releases. ✉ *Renaissance Moscow hotel, 1 Olympiisky pr., bldg. 18, Eastern Outskirts* ☎ *495/931–9873* ⊕ *www.domecinema.ru* Ⓜ *Prospekt Mira.*

THEATER

Fodor's Choice ★ **Gogol Center** (Гогол центр). Opened in 1923 as a theater for railroad workers, this revamped, stunningly creative space is the hub of Moscow's contemporary theater scene. The schedule includes plays directed by top Russian directors as well as dance, film, and music. ⊠ *8 ul. Kazakova, Eastern Oustkirts* ☏ *499/262–9214* ⊕ *www.gogolcenter. com* Ⓜ *Kurskaya.*

Taganka Theater (Театр на Таганке *Teatr na Taganke*). What was once considered to be one of Moscow's best theaters is worth visiting for the troupe's most famed dramatization, of Mikhail Bulgakov's novel *The Master and Margarita.* ⊠ *21 ul. Zemlyanoy Val, bldg. 76, Eastern Outskirts* ☏ *495/915–1217* ⊕ *www.taganka.theatre.ru* Ⓜ *Taganskaya.*

NIGHTLIFE

As much progress as the Moscow bar scene has made in recent years, many of the capital's bartenders have not yet mastered the art of mixology, resulting in the occasional mangled martini (though nothing explosive yet). Unless there's live music, there's no cover charge for most bars.

Moscow's vibrant clubbing scene means there are plenty of great places to go. The ranks of Mercedes outside certain city clubs make it clear that Moscow is a city for big spenders. But you don't have to be one to have a good time sampling Moscow's bars and clubs. A more bohemian crowd gathers at many that offer live concerts by local bands, and demand from a rapidly growing middle class has ensured the emergence of dozens of stylish yet affordable clubs.

Face control (or a velvet-rope mentality) is common at most high-end clubs. Most clubs don't get busy until between midnight and 2 am. Live music is popular, and some larger clubs put on shows by famous foreign DJs and musicians. At some of the high-end places, there's a fee to be seated at a table.

No other part of Moscow's clubbing scene is more subject to closings than the tiny gay circuit, so these listings are far from definitive. A good way to keep up with the scene is by checking ⊕ *www.gay.ru,* which has regular updates in English. Gay clubbers should exercise caution when entering and leaving clubs, as random homophobic attacks have been reported in recent years.

The *Moscow Times* (⊕ *www.themoscowtimes.com*), *The Moscow News* (⊕ *themoscownews.com*), and *Element* (⊕ *www.elementmoscow.ru*), available for free at hotels, bars, and restaurants, publish up-to-date calendars of events in English.

⚠ **Foreigners make easy crime targets: take special precautions at night. You're safest venturing out with other people. Don't drive under any circumstances after drinking; Russia has a zero-tolerance drunk-driving law, and traffic police can and do stop cars at will.**

5

GETTING PAST THE VELVET ROPES

Although clubs the world over reserve the right to be choosy about who gets in and who gets left out in the cold, few doormen have a reputation for being as stringent—or as sadistic—as the ones working Moscow's night spots. The truth is many of the places listed here can easily be called *demokratichny*, meaning that they maintain an egalitarian door policy. If you do find yourself in a run-in with the face-control goons, however, there are a few strategies that can help you skip the velvet rope:

Dress to impress: Try to find out the type of crowd your club attracts, and wear the right clothes. Keep in mind, however, that "right" and "formal" are two different things. A pair of Prada jeans may get you a lot farther than a three-piece suit.

Speak English: Although foreigners seldom create the impression that they did, say, 15 years ago, many clubs consider it desirable to have an international clientele. Speaking some English, flashing your passport, and saying you'll tell everybody back in Boise how cool the club is might be enough for you to waltz right in.

Let your money do the talking: If you really want to get in and are still getting the cold shoulder, call the club's PR manager over and ask to buy a club card. The card makes you face-control proof and may also get you a discount on drinks and food, but it won't come cheap. Club cards can cost anywhere from a few thousand to tens of thousands of rubles.

KITAI GOROD

This center for Moscow commerce isn't all business—some of the city's hottest bars and clubs are also here.

BARS

Bilingua (Билингва). Young, creative types frequent this smoky bar-club-bookshop, which also has inexpensive food, live rock and pop music, and weekend club nights. ✉ *10 per. Krivokolenny, bldg. 5, Kitai Gorod* ☎ *495/623–9660* ⊕ *www.bilinguaclub.ru* Ⓜ *Chistiye Prudy or Lubyanka.*

Glavpivtorg (Главпивторг). Live musicians perform songs from the Soviet era at this enormous retro eatery with a big choice of beers, including its own brand. The traditional Russian dishes are expensive but served up with style. Book ahead, as it gets busy even on weeknights. ✉ *5 ul. Bolshaya Lubyanka, Kitai Gorod* ☎ *495/628–2591, 495/624–1996* ⊕ *www.glavpivtorg.ru* Ⓜ *Lubyanka.*

Kitaiysky Lyotchik Jao Da (Китайский Летчик Джао Да). Live music and tasty, affordable food draw a bohemian crowd to this cellar, whose name translates as "Chinese Pilot." ✉ *25 proyezd Lubyansky, bldg. 1, Kitai Gorod* ☎ *495/624–5611, 495/623–2896* ⊕ *msk.jao-da. ru* Ⓜ *Kitai Gorod.*

Krizis Zhanra (Кризис Жанра). An easygoing but stylish clientele fills this café-bar. In the evenings, the staff pushes away the tables to create a small dance floor. Live music on the weekends is mostly indie-rock, but DJs through the week play an eclectic mix of pop, rock, reggae, and funk. ✉ *16/16 ul. Pokrovka, bldg. 1, Chistiye Prudy* ☎ *495/623–2594* ⊕ *krisis.narod.ru* Ⓜ *Chistiye Prudy.*

CLUBS

Club Che (Клуб "Че"). A Latin American–theme involves occasional live Latino music, though music is usually provided by DJs playing Eurodance. Drink service can be slow at night, when the staff often dances with the crowd. Show up early or you'll never get in. ✉ *2 ul. Nikolskaya, bldg. 10, Kitai Gorod* ☎ *495/621–0668, 495/621–7477* ⊕ *www.clubche.ru* Ⓜ *Lubyanka.*

Cult (Культ). A cavernous venue with free entry and cheap drinks, which caters to lovers of reggae, funk, and soul. ✉ *5 ul. Yauzskaya, Kitai Gorod* ☎ *495/917–5706* ⊕ *www.cultmoscow.com* Ⓜ *Taganskaya or Kitai Gorod.*

Karma Bar (Карма Бар). R&B and hip hop hits, live music, and hookah pipes make this club a popular night spot for expats and Russian alike. Lenient face control also helps bring in the crowds. ✉ *3 ul. Pushechnaya, Kitai Gorod* ☎ *495/731–7538* ⊕ *www.karma-bar.ru* Ⓜ *Kuznetsky Most.*

Papa's Place (Папас Плейс). Themed nights, daily happy hours, and disco music ensure there is always a party atmosphere at this lively club. Entrance is free during the week and expat nights are held every Wednesday. ✉ *22 ul. Myasnitskaya, Kitai Gorod* ☎ *495/755–9554* ⊕ *www.papas.ru* Ⓜ *Chistiye Prudy.*

Propaganda (Пропаганда). This is probably the city's most reliable club for trendy, yet laid-back crowds and good DJs. It's *the* place to be on Thursday night. On Sunday night it turns into one of the city's most popular gay clubs. ✉ *7 per. Bolshoi Zlatoustinsky, Kitai Gorod* ☎ *495/624–5732* ⊕ *www.propagandamoscow.com* Ⓜ *Kitai Gorod.*

Solyanka (Солянка). Several rooms in this high-ceilinged converted mansion double up as a great café and restaurant during the day and a dance club after hours. Thursday through Saturday are laid-back techno and funk club nights, a top choice among Moscow's hipster youth, with free entry on Thursdays. ✉ *11/6 ul. Solyanka, bldg. 1, Kitai Gorod* ☎ *495/221–7557* ⊕ *www.s-11.ru* Ⓜ *Kitai Gorod.*

GAY AND LESBIAN CLUBS

7freedays (7 Фри Дейс). With its homely atmosphere, film nights, and tasty food, this club has become the top refuge of Moscow's gay and lesbian community and offers dancing and a good range of cultural events. Visitors should exercise caution when entering and leaving, though, as the bar has been subject to homophobic attacks in recent years. ✉ *6 per. Milyutinsky, bldg. 1, Kitai Gorod* ☎ *495/627–3101, 905/529–4463* ⊕ *www.7freedays.com* Ⓜ *Lubyanka.*

ULITSA TVERSKAYA

BARS

Denis Simachev Bar (Бар Дениса Симачева). A club opened by the renowned Russian designer of the same name combines kitsch, elegance, and a hot crowd for a unique experience that can be a treat for those keen on people-watching. Here's where Moscow's "Zolotaya Molodyozh," or "Gilded Youth," go for their pre-party drinks. ✉ *12 per. Stoleshnikov, bldg. 2, Ulitsa Tverskaya* ☎ *495/629–8085* ⊕ *denissimachev.blogspot.com* Ⓜ *Teatralnaya.*

Gogol (Гоголь). Cheap beer and a buzzing atmosphere attract a young crowd at Gogol. Head here for a quiet drink and a game of foosball during the week or join the packs of students for a rock gig on the weekend. ✉ *11 per. Stoleshnikov, Ulitsa Tverskaya* ☎ *495/514–0944* ⊕ *www.gogolclubs.ru* Ⓜ *Teatralnaya.*

Masterskaya (Мастерская). With its high ceilings, rickety furniture, and buzz of intellectual conversation, this bar and restaurant attracts an arty crowd. DJs and bands play most evenings in the main room. There's also a theater in the back, which shows mostly modern Russian plays. ✉ *3 proyezd Teatralny, bldg. 3, Ulitsa Tverskaya* ☎ *495/625–6836* ⊕ *www.mstrsk.ru* Ⓜ *Teatralnaya or Kuznetsky Most.*

Mendeleev (Менделеев). A black curtain to the right of the counter in a cheap eatery, Lucky Noodles, conceals an atmospheric underground boîte with chandeliers, a dance floor, and a creative assortment of cocktails. ✉ *1 ul. Petrovka, bldg. 20, Ulitsa Tverskaya* ☎ *495/625–3385* ⊕ *mendeleevbar.ru* Ⓜ *Teatralnaya.*

Silvers (Силверс). This is the place to go for an authentic Irish pub atmosphere and a pint of Guinness. Wood-paneled walls, shamrocks, and tons of expatriates are enough to make even the weariest traveler feel at home. ✉ *6 per. Nikitsky, bldg. 5, Ulitsa Tverskaya* ☎ *495/690–4222* ⊕ *www.silverspub.com* Ⓜ *Okhotny Ryad.*

CLUBS

B-2 (Клуб "Б2" *Klub Bi Dva*). One of the best places in Moscow for live rock performances, this enormous five-story club includes a restaurant, a pool hall, a dance club, and several bars. ✉ *8 ul. Bolshaya Sadovaya, bldg.1, Ulitsa Tverskaya* ☎ *495/650–9918, 495/650–9909* ⊕ *www.b2club.ru* Ⓜ *Mayakovskaya.*

GAY AND LESBIAN CLUBS

12 Volt (12 Вольт *Dvenadtsat Volt*). This gay club for both men and women is tricky to find, but has a welcoming atmosphere. It has DJs, film screenings, karaoke, and cheap drink deals. ✉ *12 ul. Tverskaya, bldg. 2, entrance in yard off Kozitsky per., Ulitsa Tverskaya* ☎ *495/933–2815* ⊕ *12voltclub.ru* Ⓜ *Tverskaya.*

ULITSA BOLSHAYA NIKITSKAYA

BARS

Fodor'sChoice ★ **Ryumochnaya** (**Рюмочная**). For a true Russian vodka-drinking experience, head to this 125-year-old tavern whose name literally translates
as "shot bar." Drinks are amazingly affordable and there's a large
variety of zakuski, tasty bites that help the booze go down, like salmon
sandwiches, boiled prawns, and fried potatoes. ✉ *22/2 ul. Bolshaya
Nikitskaya, bldg. 1, Ulitsa Bolshaya Nikitskaya* ☎ *495/691–5474*
Ⓜ *Okhotny Ryad.*

ARBAT

BARS

Hard Rock Cafe (**Хард Рок Кафе**). It may be an international chain,
but somehow the Moscow branch manages to maintain its own flavor.
Locals come for the pop-music classics, and Westerners stop by for a
taste of home. ✉ *44 ul. Arbat, Arbat* ☎ *499/241–9853, 499/241–4342*
⊕ *www.hardrockcafe.ru* Ⓜ *Smolenskaya.*

Tinkoff (**Тинкофф**). A lively microbrewery with a wide range of tasty
home-brewed beers and hearty German-style food is popular with
diplomats working in nearby embassies. ✉ *11 per. Protochny, Arbat*
☎ *495/780–5888* ⊕ *www.tinkof.ru* Ⓜ *Smolenskaya.*

ZAMOSKVORECHE

BARS

Balchug 5 (**Балчуг 5** *Balchug Pyat*). This place is not cheap, and the face
control gets strict from time to time, but if you're looking for an elite bar
scene, it's hard to beat. This is where Moscow's upper crust—everyone
from upwardly mobile execs to almost-oligarchs—comes to grab its
after-work drink, or a bite in one of the three lavishly appointed dining
halls. ✉ *5 ul. Baltchug, Zamoskvoreche* ☎ *495/956–7775* ⊕ *novikov-
group.ru/restaurants/balchug* Ⓜ *Novokuznetskaya.*

Bar Strelka (**Бар Стрелка**). The superbly positioned summer terrace
overlooking the Moscow River and the Cathedral of Christ Our Savior
is the main attraction of this upscale bar, which is part of the innovative Institute of Architecture and Design. The open-air theatre out
the back hosts film screenings and lectures. ✉ *14 nab. Bersenevskaya,
bldg. 5, Zamoskvoreche* ☎ *495/771–7416* ⊕ *www.barstrelka.com*
Ⓜ *Kropotkinskaya.*

CLUBS

Gipsy (**Джипси**). Music at this stylishly decorated and very popular
venue in the city's trendy Krasnaya Oktyabr complex varies from pop to
techno. Some 400 disco balls hang over the club's large and lively dance
floor. The club is well worth a visit for its roof terrace with stunning views
over the Moskva River. ✉ *3/4 nab. Bolotnaya, bldg. 2, Zamoskvoreche*
☎ *495/669–8693* ⊕ *www.bargipsy.ru* Ⓜ *Kropotkinskaya.*

5

Rolling Stone (Роллинг Стоун). What's considered by many to be Moscow's best night out presents an eclectic mix of all the best bits of the city's unique nightlife: bar-top dancing, creative cocktails, a huge roof terrace, and, of course, rigid face control. Some 3,000 clubbers are said to pass through this joint on an average weekend, so expect to have to wait to get in. ⊠ *3 nab. Bolotnaya, bldg. 1, Zamoskvoreche* ☎ *495/504–0932* Ⓜ *Kropotkinskaya.*

NORTHERN OUTSKIRTS

BARS

Help (Хелп Бар). More than 200 drink options range from classics like the Long Island Iced Tea to more exotic but well-made local creations. ⊠ *27 ul. 1st Tverskaya-Yamskaya, bldg. 1, Northern Outskirts* ☎ *495/995–5395* ⊕ *www.helpbar.ru* Ⓜ *Belorusskaya.*

CLUBS

Arena (Арена). With the biggest club stage in Moscow and a dance floor capacity of 3,500 people, this live music venue is a prime spot to see big and up-and-coming Russian groups, as well as foreign acts and DJs. ⊠ *31 Leningradsky pr., bldg. 4, Northern Outskirts* ☎ *495/940–6755* ⊕ *www.arenamoscow.ru* Ⓜ *Dinamo.*

GAY AND LESBIAN CLUBS

Central Station (Центральная Станция). This popular spot with students is one of the most well established gay clubs in town, with a regular rotation of good DJs. Mostly men come here, but women are welcome. ⊠ *4 proyezd Yuzhny, Northern Outskirts* ☎ *495/988–3585* ⊕ *www.centralclub.ru* Ⓜ *Komsomolskaya.*

JAZZ AND BLUES

BB King Blues Club (Клуб Би Би Кинг). The man himself came for the opening, and visiting Western stars have continued to make appearances here, often for post-concert jams. Call ahead to book a table for concerts as the small hall fills up fast. ⊠ *4 ul. Sadovaya-Samotyochnaya, bldg. 2, Northern Outskirts* ☎ *495/699–8206* ⊕ *www.bbkingclub.ru* Ⓜ *Tsvetnoy Bulvar.*

SOUTHERN OUTSKIRTS

BARS

City Space Bar (Сити Спейс Бар). Perched 140 meters above the city and with stunning panoramic views, this upscale cocktail bar is the perfect spot to watch the sun set over Moscow. ⊠ *Floor 34, 52 nab. Kosmodamianskaya, bldg. 6, Southern Outskirts* ☎ *495/221–5357* ⊕ *www.swissotel.com/hotels/moscow/bars/city-space-bar* Ⓜ *Paveletskaya.*

EASTERN OUTSKIRTS

CLUBS

Arma 17 (Арма 17 *Arma Semnadtsat*). A vast warehouse to the east of the center makes a refreshing change from the city's glitzy clubbing scene. The club regularly hosts big international techno DJs and its raucous parties have been known to carry on long into the afternoon. ✉ *5 per. Nizhny Susalny, bldg. 3a, Eastern Outskirts* ☎ *495/410–0414* ⊕ *www.arma17.ru* Ⓜ *Kurskaya.*

WESTERN OUTSKIRTS

BARS

Sixteen Tons (16 Тонн *Shestnadtsat Tonn*). A popular pub with a club upstairs, this spot serves its own home-brewed beer and hosts regular rock and indie gigs. ✉ *6 ul. Presnensky Val, bldg. 1, Western Outskirts* ☎ *499/253–5300* ⊕ *www.16tons.ru* Ⓜ *Ulitsa 1905 Goda.*

CLUBS

Crocus City Hall (Крокус Сити Холл). Sting and Elton John have played at this huge complex on the Moscow ring road with a 6,200-seat auditorium. Check ahead and you might catch your favorite group from home. ✉ *65–66 km Moscow Ring Road (MKhAD), Crocus City, Crocus Expo, Pavilion 3, Western Outskirts* ☎ *499/550–0055* ⊕ *www.crocus-hall.ru* Ⓜ *Myakinino.*

5

MOSCOW
SHOPPING

Updated by
Anna Coppola

These days, shopping is a national sport in Moscow. Locals shop in brand new mega-malls, revamped department stores, designer boutiques, and busy food markets. Display windows in parts of historical shopping districts in downtown Moscow, such as pereulok Stoleshnikov, Kuznetsky Most, and proyezd Tretyakovsky, are filled with brands like Hermès, Louis Vuitton, Dior, Brioni, Prada, and Fendi.

Big emporia such as GUM showcase midrange Western brands like Levi's and Nike. Russian designers also have a presence: some names to look for include Alena Akhmadullina, Alexander Terekhov, Igor Chapurin, Denis Symachev, Kira Plastinina, and Sultanna Frantsuzova. If you're simply on the hunt for souvenirs, the best bets are shops in the Arbat district or the Izmailovsky Flea Market in the Eastern Outskirts.

Stores are generally open Monday through Saturday 10 to 7, and many are open seven days a week; shopping malls are open daily from 10 or 11 in the morning to 9 or 10 at night. Some specialty stores and many supermarkets may operate 24/7.

KREMLIN/RED SQUARE

The political heart of Russia is best known for its corridors of power and many landmarks, but it's also a shopping district with modern malls and exclusive shops lining lively avenues.

DEPARTMENT STORES AND MALLS

Fodor's Choice
★

GUM (ГУМ). A series of shops and boutiques inside a 19th-century arcade, this shopping emporium sits on Red Square, across from the Kremlin. GUM, which stands for Gosudarstvenny Universalny Magazin, or State Department Store, now stocks only a handful of Russian brands in the upper-level stores. On the first floor you will find an arcade of upscale boutiques, including MaxMara, Hugo Boss, Louis Vuitton, and La Perla. Also here is the elegant Bosco restaurant, which overlooks Red Square and has a summer terrace. Cheaper eats are available at fast-food outlets on the top floor. A "historic toilett," with pre-revolutionary interiors made of marble and Murano glass, is located at the first floor (Lane 1). ⌧ *3 Red Sq., Kremlin/Red Square* ☎ *495/788–4343* ⊕ *www.gum.ru* Ⓜ *Ploshchad Revolutsii.*

Okhotny Ryad (Охотный Ряд). This underground shopping mall offers standards like Aldo, Benetton, Tommy Hilfiger, BeeFree, Motivi, and MEXX. Set under the main square adjacent to the Kremlin, the mall attracts crowds of Russian out-of-towners, who stroll, photograph the intricate cupola that extends aboveground, and window-shop. ⌧ *Trade Center Okhotny Ryad, 1 pl. Manezhnaya, bldg. 2, Kremlin/Red Square* ☎ *495/737–8449* Ⓜ *Okhotny Ryad.*

SPECIALTY STORES
ARTS AND CRAFTS

Ikonnaya Lavka (Иконная лавка). The Cathedral of Our Lady of Kazan houses this compact icon shop. In addition to icons, you can purchase religious books, silver crosses, and other Orthodox religious items. ✉ *3 ul. Nikolskaya, at Red Sq., Kremlin/Red Square* ☎ *495/698–2678* Ⓜ *Ploshchad Revolutsii.*

Salon Naslediye (Салон "Наследие"). The Historical Museum's art shop Naslediye (Heritage) deals in many sorts of souvenirs, including jewelry, T-shirts, handmade crafts, replicas of museum pieces, and Russian- and Ukrainian-style embroidered shirts, Gzhel ceramics, and more. Wooden bowls and spoons decorated in *khokhloma* style—with bright oils painted on a black-and-golden background—fill the shelves. The store is next to entrance number 1 of the museum; enter Red Square through the Resurrection Gates. ✉ *1/2 Red Sq., Kremlin/Red Square* ☎ *495/692–1320* Ⓜ *Ploshchad Revolutsii.*

SOUVENIRS

Shaltai-Boltai (Шалтай-Болтай). Located on the ground floor of Novinsky shopping center (just behind the U.S. Embassy) this quirky store with a name that translates as "Humpty-Dumpty" sells modern art turned into gifts and souvenirs. Works of renowned contemporary Russian designers and artists appear on T-shirts, cards, and cups. Imitation Soviet schoolchildren's star badges fashioned from fake gemstones are a distinctively Russian jewelry gift. ✉ *31 bulvar Novinsky, Novinsky shopping center, Kremlin/Red Square* ☎ *495/768–7850* ⊕ *shaltai-boltai. ru/eng* Ⓜ *Barrikadnaya.*

> **BUYING ANTIQUES**
>
> Russian law forbids taking out of the country anything of "cultural value." In practical terms, this means that you're not allowed to export art and craft items older than 30 to 40 years without special permission from the Ministry of Culture or its local agent; the item may be confiscated at the border if you lack the necessary papers.If you're buying paintings or art objects, consult with the seller regarding the proper documentation of sale for export. Always ask for a spravka (certificate) about the item to prove it's not of cultural heritage, and keep your receipt.

KITAI GOROD

This neighborhood of banks and offices north and east of Red Square also houses many shops; as befits this powerhouse of Russian commerce, many of them specialize in luxury goods.

DEPARTMENT STORES AND MALLS

Petrovsky Passazh (Петровский Пассаж). MaxMara, Nina Ricci, Givenchy, Kenzo, and Bally boutiques and an antiques store are in this chic, glass-roofed space, a top contender for the most luxurious shopping *passazh* (arcade) in town. ✉ *10 ul. Petrovka, Kitai Gorod* ☎ *495/928–5012* Ⓜ *Kuznetsky Most.*

Fodor's Choice ★ **Tsvetnoy Central Market** (Универмаг «Цветной» *Univermag «Cvetnoj»*).
What was once a central market selling food and utilitarian household
items is now an upscale mall, offering everything from furniture to
fashion to imported gourmet delicacies. Upper floors house fashion collections from Vivienne Westwood, Helmut Lang, Elizabeth and James,
and others; you may want to keep an eye out for offerings from such
Russian designers as Alexander Terekhov, Alena Akhmadullina, and
Andrei Artemov. The food market on the fifth floor is especially enticing, with organic vegetables sitting alongside such rarities as lavender
chocolate from France and Japanese wasabi-flavored chewing gum.
✉ *15 bulvar Tsvetnoy, bldg.1, Kitai Gorod* ☎ *495/737–7773* ⊕ *www.
tsvetnoy.com/en/* Ⓜ *Tsvetnoy Bulvar.*

TsUM (ЦУМ). TsUM (Central Department Store), a historical rival of
GUM, has upgraded itself to an expensive emporium with collections
of nearly all the top European designers. Although TsUM is nowhere
near as stunning as GUM architecturally, it usually has the larger
choice. ✉ *2 ul. Petrovka, Kitai Gorod* ☎ *495/933–7300* ⊕ *www.tsum.
ru* Ⓜ *Kuznetsky Most.*

SPECIALTY STORES

ARTS AND CRAFTS

Art boutiques of the ulitsa Varvarka churches (Церковные лавки на
Варварке). These boutiques are inside the Church of St. Maxim the
Blessed and the Church of St. George on Pskov Hill. They carry a fine
selection of handicrafts, jewelry, ceramics, and other types of native-
Russian art. ✉ *6 ul. Varvarka, Kitai Gorod* Ⓜ *Kitai Gorod.*

PERFUME/COSMETICS

Novaya Zarya. Novaya Zarya is one of Russia's oldest perfume manufacturers and makes its own line of fragrant essences, which you can
add to banya water (you can get your own tub at a public banya). The
shop in Kitai Gorod is one of many outlets throughout the city. ✉ *4 ul.
Ilinka, in Gostiny Dvor, Kitai Gorod* ☎ *495/698–1269* ⊕ *www.novzar.
ru* Ⓜ *Ploshchad Revolutsii.*

SPAS

Fodor's Choice ★ **Sandunovskiye Bani.** Dating from the late 1800s, this is probably the city's
most elegant bathhouse, with a lavish interior. Prices start at 1,700R for
a three-hour visit in the female section and 2,100R for two-hour visits
in the men's section. Prices go up from there, depending on which level
of service you chose. On-site facilities include a beauty parlor, a restaurant and, of course, massage. The facilities are closed on Tuesday for
cleaning. ✉ *14 ul. Neglinnaya, str. 3-7, Kitai Gorod* ☎ *495/625–4631,
495/628–4633* ⊕ *www.sanduny.ru* Ⓜ *Kuznetsky Most.*

ULITSA TVERSKAYA

Ulitsa Tverskaya is Moscow's main shopping artery and some of the city's best and biggest stores line the wide boulevard and adjacent streets.

SPECIALTY STORES

ARTS AND CRAFTS

Novodel (Новодел). This small store sells quirky contemporary crafts from local artists, including unique felt jewelry, toys, clocks, greetings cards, and T-shirts. ⊠ *9 per. Bolshoi Palashevsky, Ulitsa Tverskaya* ☎ *495/626-45-38* ⊕ *www.novodel.net* Ⓜ *Mayakovskaya or Tverskaya.*

CLOTHING

Denis Simachev Shop & Bar. This Russian celebrity designer is known for his humorous reinventions of traditional Russian fashion—think enormous fur accessories and enlarged folk art patterns. The store is located on the second floor of a building decorated with designs based on red-and-gold *khokhloma* (lacquered and painted bowls). The tiny bar downstairs becomes a hot spot at night. ⊠ *12 per. Stoleshnikov, bldg. 1, Ulitsa Tverskaya* ☎ *495/629–5702* Ⓜ *Teatralnaya.*

FOOD

Volkonsky (Волконский). This French-owned chain now has three branches in Moscow, where you can buy freshly baked cookies, pastries, and bread, and also drink coffee in a small café. This branch is a perfect place to stop after a walk around Patriarch's Ponds. ⊠ *46 ul. Bolshaya Sadovaya, bldg. 2, Ulitsa Tverskaya* ☎ *495/699–3620* Ⓜ *Tverskaya.*

Fodor'sChoice ★ **Yeliseyevsky (Елисеевский** *yeli'seyefskiy*). Historic, sumptuous, upscale—this turn-of-the-20th-century grocery store is the star of ulitsa Tverskaya, and even if you're not feeling hungry, the spectacle makes it well worth a visit. An art nouveau interior in a late-18th-century classical mansion sparkles with chandeliers, stained glass, and gilt wall decorations. Among the fine products here are cognac, Armenian berry juices, Russian chocolate, and candy of all sorts. This is one of the best places to buy freshly baked goods, caviar, and sturgeon. You'll find favorite Russian rye breads and a wide variety of croissants, brioches, and seven-grain loaves. A separate souvenir department offering traditional crafts such as lacquered boxes and toys is located at the back of the store. ⊠ *14 ul. Tverskaya, Ulitsa Tverskaya* ☎ *495/650–4643* Ⓜ *Pushkinskaya or Tverskaya.*

ARBAT

Two streets radiating out of the Kremlin to the west provide different shopping experiences: ulitsa Stary Arbat is a cobblestone pedestrian street with cafés and souvenir shops, and ulitsa Novy Arbat is a modern thoroughfare with many shopping malls.

SPECIALTY STORES

ARTS AND CRAFTS

Arbatskaya Lavitsa (Арбатская Лавица). In this large, old-fashioned store you can find Gzhel china, linen tablecloths, nesting dolls, ivory work, wooden toys, and national Russian costumes at reasonable prices and without the hard sell. ⊠ *27 ul. Arbat, Arbat* ☎ *495/290–5689* Ⓜ *Arbatskaya or Smolenskaya.*

CLOSE UP

Russian Food and Spirits

CAVIAR

Caviar in Russia? Who can resist? Unfortunately, the black variety became scarce after restrictions on sturgeon fishing were put in place to save this species in the Caspian Sea. However, black caviar that's imported or produced by individual farmers who rear sturgeons in artificial reservoirs is slowly making its way back into stores, at exorbitant prices. Red caviar is much cheaper and ubiquitous.

LIQUOR

Alcohol counterfeiting is a big problem in Russia; according to various estimates, illegally produced vodka accounts for 40% to 70% of what's available on the market. If you don't follow safe buying practices, you could end up with a brutal hangover or worse, a severe case of alcohol poisoning. Your best bet is to buy well-known brands such as Beluga, Russky Standart, or Zelenaya Marka (Green Mark) at reputable supermarkets. An amusing deviation from purified brands is Nemiroff's, infused with honey pepper. Note that every bottle of vodka sold in Russia must bear a white excise stamp, glued over the cap, and those sold in Moscow must also bear a bar-code stamp.

CHOCOLATE

Many Russians consider nationally produced brands to be "the real chocolate" and far superior to imported varieties. Babayevsky, Krasny Oktyabr, and Rot Front are popular varieties. Alenka, in a retro wrapper depicting a girl in babushka scarf, is the favorite milk chocolate of Russian kids. Aside from candy bars, Russians eat tons of individually wrapped konfety (chocolate covered sweets with fudge, crunchy waffles, nuts, or other fillings) or chocolate covered zefir (type of marshmallow) with tea.

BREAD

Nearly all supermarkets now run their own bakeries offering good freshly baked bread including round rye *stolichny* loaves with a crisp crust and a variety of international types like Italian ciabatta and French baguettes. Of Russian black rye varieties, *borodinsky* and *khamovnichesky* are the tastiest.

Chasy (Часы). *Chasy* is "watch" in Russian, and this small shop offers a wide choice of Russian men's brands, such as Raketa, Komadirskie, and Sturmanskie—Yuri Gagarin was wearing this last one when he became the first person to venture into outer space in April 1961. ⊠ *15 ul. Novy Arbat, Arbat* ☎ *495/517–4345* Ⓜ *Arbatskaya.*

Fodor's Choice
★

Russkaya Vyshivka (Русская вышивка). Specializing in traditional Russian linen, this old store stocks beautiful embroidered christening gowns as well as table linens, rag rugs, and fine cotton lace collars and cuffs from different parts of the country. ⊠ *31 ul. Arbat, Arbat* ☎ *495/241–2841* Ⓜ *Arbatskaya or Smolenskaya.*

Russkiye suveniry (Русские сувениры *'ruskiye suve'neery*). This pleasant souvenir shop sells the best of locally produced folk art, including *palekh* (colorful, lacquered wood with folklore designs), chess sets, cocktail glasses, coffee sets made of amber, and copies of Faberge eggs (including earings and pendants). ⊠ *12 ul. Novyy Arbat, Arbat* ☎ *495/691-53-74* Ⓜ *Arbatskaya or Smolenskaya.*

BOOKS

Dom Knigi (Дом Книги *House of Books*). One of the country's largest bookstores has an English-language section on the second floor. This is also a good place to get books for Russian-language learners. The chain has other stores around the city and a website where you can order online. ⊠ *8 Novy Arbat, Arbat* ☎ *495/789–3591* ⊕ *www.mdk-arbat. ru* ☺ *Weekdays 9 am–11 pm, weekends 10 am–11 pm* Ⓜ *Arbatskaya.*

FOOD

Krasny Oktyabr chocolate factory (Красный Октябрь). Russian-made chocolates make a great, unexpected souvenir from Russia, and those from Moscow's Krasny Oktyabr (Red October) factory are the best. You can buy various kinds of individually wrapped candies—*Krasnaya Shapochka* (Little Red Riding Hood), *Mishka Kosolapy* (Little Clumsy Bear), *Alyonka* (whose wrapper features a girl wearing a scarf), and *Yuzhnaya Noch* (Southern Night). Most of them retain Soviet-style wrappers. The chocolates are widely available in supermarkets and kiosks, but the best assortment, including gift boxes and chocolate animal figures, is at the main store, just north of the Arbat district. ⊠ *36 ul. Povarskaya, bldg. 29, Krasnaya Presnya District* ☎ *495/691–0937* Ⓜ *Krasnopresnenskaya or Barricadnaya.*

SOUVENIRS

Art. Lebedev Shop and Café (Лавка и кафе Артемия Лебедева). Artemiy Lebedev is probably the most successful graphic designer, style guru, and blogger in Russia. At this outlet you can find wittily designed apparel, accessories, and office supplies that make great gifts. They're also a revealing look into the concerns and obsessions of Russian intellectuals. Enter the coffee shop and go down the spiral stairs. ⊠ *35 ul. Bolshaya Nikitskaya, Arbat* ☎ *495/778–7015* ⊕ *store.artlebedev.com* Ⓜ *Arbatskaya or Biblioteka im. Lenina.*

SPAS

Bani na Presne. With a gym, salon, bar, pool, and massage service, this casual banya is popular with both locals and expats. Prices start at 1200R for a two-hour visit. Banyas are separate for men and women, but it's possible to reserve private, VIP banyas for four or more people. ⊠ *7 per. Stolyarny, str. 1, Arbat* ☎ *495/609–3550* ⊕ *baninapresne.ru* Ⓜ *Ulitsa 1905 Goda.*

ZAMOSKVORECHE

The old twisting streets of Zamoskvoreche give the neighborhood an Old World feel, accented by the presence of many Orthodox churches. It's a perfect setting for small specialty shops and galleries.

SPECIALTY STORES

ARTS AND CRAFTS

Moscow Culture Fund's Salon (Салон Московского Фонда культуры *Salon Moskovskogo Fonda kul'tury*). It's worth seeking out this out-of-the-way shop for their plentitude of handmade crafts. The choice of souvenirs, jewelry, and dolls by Moscow craftspeople and artists will make you dizzy. ⊠ *16 ul. Pyatnitskaya, Zamoskvoreche* ☎ *495/951–3302* Ⓜ *Novokuznetskaya.*

CLOSE UP

Russian Markets

Rynoks (outdoor markets) are good places to find strange and delicious foods. Look for lumpy red *church-khela*, a kind of Georgian candy made from walnuts and grape juice. Stalls sell piles of bright-pink pickled garlic, peppers, and grape leaves, strings of dried wild mushrooms, and dried and salted fresh-water fish. In fall, the berry selection might include rose hips; orange *oblepikha*, or sea buckthorn; and *brusnika*, or cowberry. You can also sample unfamiliar fruits, including the small red plum, *kizil*, or Cornelian cherry, and aromatic green *feikhua* (feijoa), a citrus fruit with an interior that tastes like strawberry.

Usually no price is shown for goods. Ask "*SkOlko stOit?*" or "how much is it?" If the price sounds too high, say the number of rubles you think is reasonable. If the offer is refused, and you don't like the price, say "*nyet, dorogo,*" or "no, it's expensive," and turn away. The trader may then tell you, "*dlya vas skidka,*" or "you get a discount." You'll likely receive a realistic price then.

FOOD AND SPIRITS

Globus Gourmet (Глобус Гурмэ *Globus Gurmje*). Gourmands flock to this 24-hour grocery store that supplies Moscow with high-quality imported foodstuffs. Among the wide array of deli foods are wild boar sausages, vinegars aged for 50 years, chocolates from Belgium, fish from Norway, ham from Spain, and special local dairy products—the cheese department is a memorable sight in itself. ⊠ *22 ul. Bolshaya Yakimanka, Gimenei trade center, Zamoskvoreche* ☎ *495/995–2170* ⊕ *globusgurme.ru* Ⓜ *Oktyabrskaya or Polyanka.*

Konditersky (Кондитерский на Пятницкой). This cozy, old-fashioned candy store, which will weigh out chocolates for you, has a good choice of Russian brands, including Krasny Oktyabr. The *pryaniki* are festive gingerbread cookies shaped as hearts, human figures, and animals with colorful frosting and inscriptions in Russian, such as "To my best friend" and "To my mother-in-law." ⊠ *22 ul. Pyatnitskaya, Zamoskvoreche* ☎ *495/951–3764* Ⓜ *Novokuznetskaya or Tretyakovskaya.*

CLOTHING

Mir Shersti (Мир Шерсти). Tucked away in a side street, this store specializes in *valenki,* Russian-made felt boots, which it stocks in children's and adult sizes. You can also buy ribbon-trimmed felt slippers and fleece-lined clothing. A small valenki museum is next door. ⊠ *12 per. 2nd Kozhevnichesky, Zamoskvoreche* ☎ *495/645–8464* Ⓜ *Paveletskaya.*

NORTHERN OUTSKIRTS

What is most likely to draw you out of the city center on a shopping excursion is the chance to find specialty items, such as crafts at the Soviet-era Culture Pavilion in the Northern Outskirts and dinnerware and figurines at the Imperial Porcelain outlet in the East. Many shops in outlying districts are concentrated in huge shopping malls, and colorful markets still operate throughout the outskirts.

SPECIALTY STORES

ARTS AND CRAFTS

Culture Pavilion (Павильон "Культура" *avilon Kultura*). Part of the Soviet showpiece that's now called the All-Russian Exhibition Center (abbreviated VVC in Russian), the elegant, white Pavilion No. 66 stocks a huge range of crafts, including Turkmen embroidery, earthenware pots from Suzdal, and carved stone animals from Perm. Enter the VVC through the main entrance and walk straight to the People's Friendship Fountain and continue walking a little more on the right side of the road. ⊠ *All-Russian Exhibition Center, 115 Mir pr., Northern Outskirts* ☎ *495/544–3400* Ⓜ *VDNKh.*

Flacon Design Factory (Дизайн-завод Флакон *Dizajn-zavod Flakon*). This former industrial complex is now a center of design studios, showrooms, advertising agencies, and workshops for all sorts of creative types. There's a two-level market full of shops offering handmade souvenirs, jewelry, urban fashions, books, and music. ⊠ *4 ul. Bolshaya Novodmitrovskaya, bldg. 36, Northern Outskirts* ☎ *495/790–7901* ⊕ *flacon.ru* Ⓜ *Dmitrovskaya.*

SPAS

Seleznyovskiye Bani. One of the better banya bargains in town combines quality service with low prices. A two-hour visit starts at 400R. It's closed on Mondays. ⊠ *15 ul. Seleznyovsky, Northern Outskirts* ☎ *499/978–9430, 499/978–8491* Ⓜ *Novoslobodskaya.*

UGG, MEET VALENKI

Perfect for a cold climate, *valenki* are traditional (and bulky) boots made of wool felt. They traditionally come in gray, black, or white with detachable rubber galoshes to keep out the snow. While they're not Moscow high fashion—you'd get funny looks if you wore these on the metro—Russians wear them at their *dachas* (country cottages) and traffic police pull them on for winter shifts. You can buy them at Moscow markets and specialty stores. You should purchase a pair two sizes larger than normal because the wool shrinks when it gets wet.

6

SOUTHERN OUTSKIRTS

SPECIALTY STORES
FARMERS' MARKETS
Danilovsky Rynok (Даниловский рынок). This bustling outdoor market surrounds a covered circus-shaped hall. Inside are meats, spices, vegetables, pickles, flowers, and pyramid-shaped displays of goods from Central Asia, especially dried fruit in extravagant quantity and combinations. In the outdoor stalls you're likely to come across porcelain Uzbek tea sets, woven baskets, and hand-knit wool socks. ⊠ *74 ul. Mytnaya, Southern Outskirts* ☎ *495/958–1725, 495/958–5319* Ⓜ *Tulskaya.*

EASTERN OUTSKIRTS

DEPARTMENT STORES AND MALLS
Atrium (Атриум). One of the most popular shopping malls among Muscovites is in front of the Kursk station and is yet another symbol of modern Moscow. Everything is under one roof, including numerous mass-brand clothing stores (H&M, Camper, UNIQLO, Zara, Karen Millen), a perfume "supermarket," a huge grocery store, and the Formula Kino movie theater. You can also find a trendy Italian café and a sushi bar here. ⊠ *33 ul. Zemlyanoi Val, Eastern Outskirts* ☎ *495/970–1555* ⊕ *www.atrium.su* Ⓜ *Kurskaya.*

SPECIALTY STORES
SOUVENIRS
Izmailovsky Flea Market (Измайловский рынок). In terms of choice and value, this is really the best stop for those looking for traditional Russian souvenirs in Moscow. *Matryoshki* (nesting dolls) come in a variety of styles here, and the stalls are also stacked high with amber, lacquer boxes, linens, used books, and Soviet memorabilia (such as authentic army belts and gas masks). Connoisseurs may find the real treasures in the antique aisles, such as Soviet porcelain figures or fully functional 19th-century music boxes. The flea market is open daily 9–6, but many stalls are only open on weekends. It's best to go early. ⊠ *schosse Izmailovskoe, bldg. 73-G, Eastern Outskirts* ⊕ *www. moscow-vernisage.com* Ⓜ *Preobrazhenskaya.*

WESTERN OUTSKIRTS

SPECIALTY STORES
CLOTHING
Evropeisky (Европейский). This huge, well-laid-out mall has a European theme that expresses itself in the form of a conspicuously vulgar sculpture of a euro sign in the front of a department store. You'll find branches of Britain's Marks & Spencer and Topshop as well as Spain's Bershka and Zara here. Affordable Russian brands So French by Sultanna Frantsuzova and Kira Plastinina both have stores here. ⊠ *2 pl. Kievskogo Vokzala, Western Outskirts* ☎ *495/921–3444* ⊕ *europe-tc. ru* Ⓜ *Kievskaya.*

MATRYOSHKI

Perhaps surprisingly, nesting dolls, or *matryoshki*, date only to the 19th century; they're said to be based on a Japanese tradition. The center for matryoshka-making is Sergiyev Posad, outside Moscow. In Soviet times, a matryoshka was used as the symbol of the state-owned travel agency, Intourist, which had a monopoly on organizing trips for foreigners (its name is short for *inostranny*, or foreign) and ran its own hotels. It still exists as a travel agency. In many Russian homes, you'll find a "classic Soviet" matryoshka doll wearing a yellow head scarf; the elaborately decorated dolls on sale in souvenir shops in the Arbat district are strictly for export.

Valentin Yudashkin Trading House (Торговый дом Валентина Юдашкина). Many Russian celebrities prefer Yudashkin's clothes to those of Western designers. Look for extravagant evening dresses, jeans embellished with Swarowski crystals, and golden accessories, all tailored to attract the eye of Russia's rich and fabulous. ⊠ *19 Kutuzovsky pr., Western Outskirts* ☎ *495/785–1055* Ⓜ *Kievskaya or Kutuzovskaya.*

CRAFTS

Fodor's Choice ★ **Imperial Porcelain** (Императорский фарфор *impi'ratorskiy far'for*). Founded in the 18th century by the order of Queen Elizaveta, daughter of Peter the Great, this firm (also known as Lomonosov) sold porcelain to the Russian royal families before the revolution. Dining tableware and collectible sculptures come in styles that include a classic cobalt fishnet design as well as prints inspired by Malevich, Kandinsky, and other members of the Russian avant-garde. ⊠ *17 Kutuzovsky pr., Western Outskirts* ☎ *499/678–0248* ⊕ *www.ipm.ru/enstart* Ⓜ *Kievskaya.*

FARMERS' MARKETS

Dorogomilovsky Rynok (Дорогомиловский рынок). This large covered hall is next to the outdoor Veshchevoy Rynok (literally, "Market of Things," which is certainly an apt name). Inside are rows of vendors hawking homemade cheese and milk products, honey, flowers, and produce of all kinds. Against one wall are sellers of pickled goods, an understandably popular form of conservation in this land of long winters; you may want to sample some of their cabbage and carrot slaws, salted cucumbers, or spiced eggplant or garlic. Many Moscow chefs buy ingredients here. ⊠ *10 ul. Mozhaisky Val, near Kiev station, Western Outskirts* Ⓜ *Kievskaya.*

SIDE TRIPS FROM MOSCOW

Visit Fodors.com for advice, updates, and bookings

Updated
by Khristina
Narizhnaya

Easy day trips into the Moscow environs bring you to some fascinating monasteries, including Russia's most popular place of pilgrimage, Troitse-Sergieva Lavra, and several important cultural sights, among them novelist Leo Tolstoy's estate in Yasnaya Polyana. Trips a bit farther afield into river valleys north and east of Moscow bring you to ancient Russian towns that make up what is commonly called the "Golden Ring."

They seem quite unassuming today in comparison to the sprawling, bustling capital, but before the Mongol invasion, Rostov, Vladimir, Suzdal, and Yaroslavl were the centers of Russian political, cultural, and economic life. In fact, you might call this historic realm Russia's Capital-That-Might-Have-Been. These small towns, all within easy striking distance of Moscow, were where the Russian nation was born nearly a millennium ago and, consequently, are home to some of the country's most beautiful churches and monasteries, romantic kremlins (fortresses), and famous works of art, such as Andrei Rublyov's frescoes in the cathedral at Vladimir. Although these towns may lack some of the amenities you can easily find in Moscow, they have a provincial charm and aura of history that make them an important stop for anyone seeking to become acquainted with Russian history.

ORIENTATION AND PLANNING

GETTING ORIENTED

With some exceptions, what you'll be traveling to see are churches and monasteries—the statement-making structures that princes, metropolitans (leaders of the Orthodox church), and merchants in old Russia built to display their largesse and power. Because most civil and residential buildings until the 18th century were constructed from wood, these religious buildings, constructed of stone, have best survived the ravages of time, invading armies, and fire. Today, many are being returned to their original, ecclesiastical purposes, but most are still museums. In either instance, neglect and funding shortages have taken their toll on preservation and restoration efforts, and at times it can be difficult to imagine these historic monuments in their original glory.

Moscow Environs. Don't worry if your schedule's tight. Day trips from Moscow bring spectacular sites within easy reach. At Sergiev Posad, a working monastery, you can see how Russian Orthodoxy has clawed back a place for itself in post-Soviet society. Tolstoy admirers will get a better measure of the man with a visit to his peaceful estate at Yasnaya Polyana.

TOP REASONS TO GO

Appreciate architecture: These towns are home to some of the finest examples of Russian architecture; the oldest, most beautiful kremlins; and religious buildings decorated with ancient frescoes.

Experience the "Real" Russia: A visit to a quiet provincial town like Vladimir or Rostov is markedly different from the bustle of Moscow's city. The towns' proximity to Moscow makes them easy for day or overnight trips.

Gaze at onion domes: The Troitse-Sergieva Lavra's Cathedral of the Assumption has some of the most beautiful and most photographed blue and gold onion domes, and is also the main pilgrimage site for all of Russia.

Honor Tchaikovsky and Tolstoy: Visit the home in Klin where Russia's best-known classical music composer wrote *The Nutcracker* and *Sleeping Beauty*. See the desk where Tolstoy penned *Anna Karenina* and *War and Peace* at his estate in Yasnaya Polyana.

Soak up some Russian history: Get to know the heritage of this land of princes: it's one of the birthplaces of modern Russia and a cradle of the Russian Orthodox religion.

The Northern Golden Ring. Here lies a scattering of ancient towns—Pereslavl-Zalessky, Rostov, and Yaroslavl. The first two are pretty and small, and the third is a lively city where the centuries of sights can be rooted out among all the trappings of modern, urban Russia.

The Eastern Golden Ring. Rich in stunningly varied churches and monasteries, Suzdal (population 12,000) is a strong contender for most beautiful town in Russia. Vladimir is a worthy neighbor, especially given the presence of the Church of the Intercession on the Nerl, a few miles away.

PLANNING

WHEN TO GO

To see the monasteries, churches, and kremlins of the region to the best advantage, you should try to make your visits in spring or summer. Winter visits to the Golden Ring can be magical, but in December and January it gets dark not long after 3 pm. Avoid late March, when the melting snow turns into slush.

PLANNING YOUR TIME

A few of the attractions of the Moscow Environs section, such as the Abramtsevo Estate Museum and Sergiev-Posad, can be combined in one visit, but most of the sights of this region will require individual day trips. The towns of the Golden Ring lie on two main routes that most visitors travel as two separate excursions—north of Moscow to Sergiev-Posad, Pereslavl-Zalessky, Rostov, and Yaroslavl; and east of Moscow to Vladimir and Suzdal.

GETTING HERE AND AROUND

BOAT TRAVEL

Cruises from Moscow to St. Petersburg, along the Moscow-Volga canal, visit one city of the Golden Ring, Yaroslavl.

BUS TRAVEL

You can get to most sights in the environs of Moscow by commuter train, sometimes with a local bus connection, while you have a choice of train or bus to reach most of the towns of the Golden Ring. You'll use the bus for short-distance travel between towns. Be sure to check schedules before you leave Moscow to see when the return bus runs.

Bus Contacts **Central Bus Station** (Центральный автовокзал *Tsentralny avtovokzal*). ⊠ *2 ul. Uralskaya, Moscow* ☎ *499/748–8029* ⊕ *Avtovokzaly.ru.*

CAR TRAVEL

For the towns of the Golden Ring, which lie relatively close to one another and are connected by some of Russia's best-paved roads, travel by car is by far the most flexible option. There's no problem getting gas in these towns.

TAXI TRAVEL

You'll usually have no trouble getting a taxi at a train or bus station in these towns, which is important, because the stations are often far from the town center. Most of the towns are small enough to be navigated easily on foot, but a taxi may be a desirable alternative to short bus trips (such as from Vladimir out to Bogolyubovo, from Vladimir to Suzdal, or from Tula to Yasnaya Polyana).

TRAIN TRAVEL

The easiest way to get to the towns of the Golden Ring is by train. Trains going from Moscow's Yaroslavsky train station will take you to Yaroslavl and Rostov. Trains from Moscow's Kursky train station run to Vladimir several times a day, while trains for Nizhny Novgorod always stop in Vladimir. Unless you speak some Russian you might find it easier to ask a hotel concierge to check the train schedule for you; buying the tickets at a train station is hardly ever a problem even for foreigners.

There are plenty of trains running on the main routes (Moscow–Yaroslavl and Moscow–Nizhny Novgorod) on which all the towns in this region lie, so it's quite easy to travel between towns here, as well as to and from Moscow. Two types of trains will get you to most of these towns: *elektrichkas* (suburban commuter trains) and normal long-distance trains. In addition to being cheaper, elektrichkas run more frequently. But they are also a bit less comfortable, and there's no reserved seating. Check with a local travel agent in Moscow or at the station itself for train schedules. You can also find the schedules online on the Russian Railways website ⊕ *www.rzd.ru.* With the exception of traveling by elektrichka at busy times (Friday evenings and weekends), you shouldn't have trouble getting a ticket the same day you wish to travel.

RESTAURANTS

You'll find relatively few restaurants in many of these towns, largely because Russians don't dine out that frequently. The most reliable restaurants are in hotels catering to tourists or, occasionally, in downtown locations near main tourist sights. This is slowly changing, and some of the restaurants outside hotels can be quite cozy. *Happily, restaurant prices here are considerably lower than those in Moscow.*

HOTELS

None of the towns covered in this section has a long list of hotels, let alone good, tourist-class options, although it won't be a problem to find lodging with basic amenities. The one exception is Suzdal, which has almost a dozen small private guesthouses. As with restaurants, hotel prices here are far below those in Moscow.

Hotel reviews have been abbreviated in this book. For expanded reviews, visit Fodors.com.

TOURS

Several local and international travel agents specialize in tours to the Golden Ring and Moscow environs.

Tour Contacts **Mir Corporation.** This Seattle-based operator is geared to individual travelers and also conducts regular tours to Russia that include the Golden Ring. ☎ *800/424–7289 in U.S.* ⊕ *www.mircorp.com.* **Patriarshy Dom Tours.** This Moscow-based company offers a variety of one-day and multiday tours throughout the Golden Ring at very reasonable rates. ☎ *495/795–0927 in Moscow, 650/678–7076 in the U.S.* ⊕ *www.toursinrussia.com.*

VISITOR INFORMATION

There's no regional tourist office dealing with the Golden Ring region. Any questions should be directed to travel agencies and guided tour companies in Moscow.

MOSCOW ENVIRONS

Within easy distance of Moscow are several sights of interest, including two monasteries: the New Jerusalem Monastery near Istra and the Troitse-Sergieva Lavra in Sergiev-Posad. Russian-culture buffs may want to explore Tchaikovsky's former home in Klin; Tolstoy's estate in Yasnaya Polyana; and the Abramtsevo Estate Museum, a beacon for Russian artists in the 19th century.

TCHAIKOVSKY'S HOUSE MUSEUM IN KLIN
ДОМ-МУЗЕЙ ЧАЙКОВСКОГО В КЛИНУ

84 km (52 miles) northwest of Moscow via shosse Leningradskoye and M10.

Pyotr Tchaikovsky (1840–93) spent a total of eight years in Klin, where he wrote Symphony No. 6 (Pathétique) and two of his three ballets, Sleeping Beauty and The Nutcracker. He resided at a series of addresses, but his last home, a typical, wooden residential building of the late 19th

GREAT ITINERARIES

IF YOU HAVE 1 OR 2 DAYS

The **Tchaikovsky's House Museum in Klin**, Leo Tolstoy's Museum in Yasnaya Polyana, Sergiev-Posad, and **Abramtsevo Estate Museum** can all be easily visited as separate day trips from Moscow.

If you have two days to explore the towns of the Golden Ring, drive or take a morning train to **Vladimir**. Explore the town, being sure to take in the Church of the Intercession on the Nerl, then travel on to **Suzdal**, where you can stay overnight and spend a day tackling its delightful—and walkable—sights. Return to Moscow via Vladimir late in the day.

Alternatively, take a morning train to **Yaroslavl** and spend the day and night there. The next morning catch a return train on the same route, stopping off in **Rostov** (1½ hours from Yaroslavl) to spend the day before catching a late-afternoon train back to Moscow.

IF YOU HAVE 3 OR 4 DAYS

Follow any of the itineraries above. But for the Vladimir and Suzdal trip, devote another full day to Suzdal. For the Yaroslavl and Rostov trip, overnight in Rostov and then stop for several hours in Pereslavl-Zalessky before returning to Moscow.

century, eclectic in style, is now a museum that pays tribute to one of Russia's greatest composers.

GETTING HERE AND AROUND

To get here from Moscow, take Bus 437 from the Rechnoy Vokzal metro stop, or a commuter train from Leningradsky railway station to Klin.

From Klin railway station it's about a 20-minute walk to the Tchaikovsky's House Museum or you can take Bus 5, 30, 37, or 40.

EXPLORING

Tchaikovsky's House Museum in Klin (Дом-музей П.И. Чайковского *Dom-muzei P.I. Chaikovskogo*). Russia's best-known composer left this house for the last time on October 7, 1893, for St. Petersburg, where he performed his last concert before his death on November 6 of that year. Less than a year after his death, the composer's brother, Modest Tchaikovsky, transformed the house into a museum. A gifted playwright and translator, Modest also played an outstanding role in preserving his brother's heritage. He maintained the original appearance of the second-floor rooms, and secured personal belongings, photographs, and a unique library of some 2,000 volumes. Some of the original scores, drafts, and letters that Modest collected are now displayed in Klin. The centerpiece of the museum is Tchaikovsky's Becker piano, on which only renowned musicians are permitted to play on special occasions. During World War II the house suffered major damage when the Nazis turned the first floor into a bike garage, and the second-floor rooms into soldiers' barracks. In the late 1940s the museum underwent major renovations, and a brick building with a concert hall was constructed next to the composer's house. The finalists of the annual Tchaikovsky International Competition of Young Musicians (held in May or June) perform in this Soviet-era

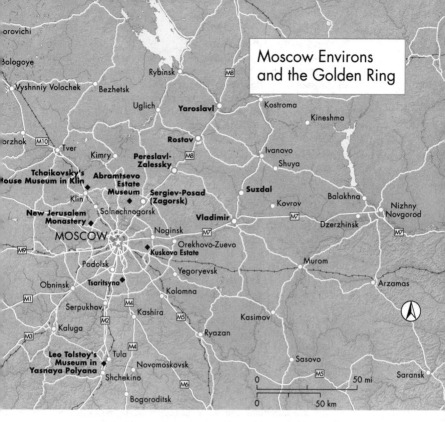

hall. Additionally, on the anniversary of the composer's birth (May 7) and death (November 6) memorial concerts are held in the hall. Tchaikovsky's music plays continuously in the museum. ■ TIP→ **The museum cafeteria provides a traditional Russian tea service from a samovar.** ✉ *48 ul. Tchaikovskovo* ☎ *49624/58196* ⊕ *www.tchaikovsky-house-museum.ru* 🎫 *300R* ⊗ *Mon., Tues., and weekends 10–6, Fri. 10–8; closed last Mon. of month.*

NEW JERUSALEM MONASTERY
НОВО-ИЕРУСАЛИМСКИЙ МОНАСТЫРЬ

65 km (40 miles) northwest of Moscow via Volokolamskoye shosse and the M9.

Far from the crowds, yet enticingly close to Moscow, this grandiose monastery is surrounded by captivating Russian countryside, a marvelous setting for walks. On a long summer's day, this would be an ideal afternoon outing from Moscow. It's close enough that you could devote the morning to seeing city sights, then spend the afternoon here in the country.

GETTING HERE AND AROUND

The monastery is near the town of Istra, at a bend in the river of the same name. This isn't the most visited locale in Russia, and it's included in the standard offerings of tourist agencies only in summer. If you can't book a tour and are feeling adventurous, you can reach the monastery by commuter train—take one from the Rizhsky railway station to Istra or Novy Ierusalim station. From either, it's a 20-minute walk, or a short bus ride.

Trains leave from Riga station and take about an hour and a half. Or, you could ask your concierge to arrange for a car and driver to drive you there.

EXPLORING

Fodor's Choice ★ **New Jerusalem Monastery** (Новоерусалимский Монастырь *Novoyerusalimsky Monastyr*). Nikon (1605–81), patriarch of the Russian Orthodox Church, founded this monastery in 1652. It lies on roughly the same longitude as Jerusalem, and its main cathedral, **Voskresensky Sobor** (Resurrection Cathedral), is modeled after the Church of the Holy Sepulchre in Jerusalem. Nikon's objective in re-creating the original Jerusalem in Russia was to glorify the power of the Russian Orthodox Church and at the same time elevate his own position as its head. Nikon initiated the great church reforms in the 17th century that eventually led to the *raskol* (schism) that launched the Old Believer sects of the Russian Orthodox faith. As a reformer he was progressive and enlightened, but his lust for power was his undoing. In 1658, before the monastery was even finished, the patriarch quarreled with Tsar Alexei Mikhailovich, claiming that the Church was ultimately superior to the State. Nikon was ultimately defrocked and banished to faraway Ferapontov Monastery, in the Vologda region, some 400 km (246 miles) north of Moscow. He died in virtual exile in 1681, and was buried in the monastery that was supposed to have glorified his power. You can find his crypt in the Church of St. John the Baptist, which is actually inside the Resurrection Cathedral. Ironically, the same church commission that defrocked Patriarch Nikon later voted to institute his reforms. Far from the crowds, the captivating Russian countryside surrounding the monastery is a marvelous setting for walks and excursions. ⊠ *On the banks of the river Istra, 2 ul. Sovetskaya* ☎ *495/994–6170* ⊕ *www.n-jerusalem.ru* 🗐 *Monastery grounds free; small fees for exhibits* ☉ *Tues.– Sun. 10–5; closed last Fri. of month.*

WHERE TO EAT

$$
RUSSIAN
✕ **Surozhsky Stan** (Сурожский Стан). This cosy café with blue domed ceilings serves moderately priced Russian specialties made on the premises. *Vareniki* and *pelmeni*, or dumplings with meat and other fillings, *rasstegai*, or pie with different fillings, can be paired with borscht for a filling lunch. ⑤ *Average main: 300R* ⊠ *13 ul. Sovetskaya* ☎ *495/994–6093.*

LEO TOLSTOY'S MUSEUM IN YAŞNAYA POLYANA
МУЗЕЙ ЛЬВА ТОЛСТОГО В ЯСНОЙ ПОЛЯНЕ

190 km (118 miles) south of Moscow via shosse Simferopolskoye and the M2.

Leo Tolstoy (1828–1910) spent 50 years of his life at Yasnaya Polyana, where he was born, wrote his most significant works, undertook social experiments, and was buried. Here he freed his serfs and taught peasant children at a school that he opened, attempting to transfer his ideal of a perfect world of universal equality to reality. Disappointed with his way of life and nobleman status, he decided at the age of 82 to depart from home forever, venturing out shortly before his death in October 1910.

GETTING HERE AND AROUND

A visit to the estate requires the whole day, because the trip from Moscow takes 2½ to 3 hours. If you're traveling by car, first head to the industrial town of Tula, some 170 km (105 miles) south of Moscow along shosse Simferopolskoye. After you pass through Tula's southern outskirts, Tolstoy's estate, 14 km (9 miles) away, is easy to find, thanks to clear signs in Russian and English; the roads, however, are notoriously bad. If you're traveling in the summer, avoid driving on Saturday morning as there's often heavy traffic due to hordes of Muscovites traveling to their *dachas* (summer cottages). You can also get to Tula by commuter train from Moscow's Kursk station, or by bus from metro stations Domodedovskaya, Prazhskaya, or ulitsa Akademika Yangelya; once in Tula, take a bus traveling to Shchyokino from the station at Lenina prospekt.

If you plan to explore the grounds of Yasnaya Polyana independently you should strive to arrive there as early in the morning as possible, especially on Friday and weekends, to avoid busloads of tourists and crowds of newlyweds who flock to places such as this on their wedding day. A guided tour of the museums and the grounds, however, does give a better idea of all the important sights and Tolstoy's favorite spots.

EXPLORING

Fodor's Choice ★ **Leo Tolstoy's Museum in Yasnaya Polyana** (**Ясная Поляна**). You'll begin your tour of the great writer's estate in the upstairs dining room, where you're greeted by numerous portraits of the Tolstoy aristocratic dynasty. Under their eyes, Tolstoy held significant social discussions with his family and his many visitors. Next door is the study where Tolstoy wrote *Anna Karenina* and *War and Peace* at his father's Persian desk. Tolstoy seemed to prefer moving around his house to work on different books, however: another room downstairs was also used as a study. This is usually the last room on a visit to the main house. In November 1910, the writer's body lay here in state as some 5,000 mourners passed to pay their last respects.

The far wing of the building houses a literary museum dedicated to Tolstoy's writing career. Drawings and prints produced by Tolstoy's contemporaries, derived from the plots and characters of his novels, as well as Tolstoy's original manuscripts are displayed in the six halls. A path from the main house into the forest leads to Tolstoy's simple, unadorned grave. On the edge of a ravine in the Stary Zakaz forest, the site was a favorite place of Tolstoy's and is now a popular pilgrimage destination for wedding parties. The walk to the grave takes about 20 minutes.

The estate-turned-museum is run by Tolstoy's great-great-grandson Vladimir Tolstoy, who is striving to turn it into a major cultural center. A restaurant, Noble's Estate, serves Russian food cooked using recipes from Tolstoy's wife Sophia that include sour cabbage soup and cow tongue with horseradish. There's also a hotel on the grounds. ✉ *Near Tula* ☎ *487/517–6146, 487/247–6712* 🌐 *www.ypmuseum.ru* 🎟 *20R, foreign-language guided tours 2,400R (3,600R at weekends) for a group of up to 8 people. Lower prices apply for bigger groups. Tours run throughout the day, until 3:30 pm* ⏲ *Tues.–Sun. 10–4; closed last Wed. of month.*

WHERE TO EAT AND STAY

$$$ RUSSIAN ✕ **Skovoroda (Сковорода).** Ukrainian food is the specialty at this pleasant eatery not far from the Tolstoy estate. Try borscht, the traditional Ukrainian soup served here with garlic bread, and follow with cherry-filled *vareniki*, or dumplings, for dessert. The colorful interior, designed by the same Moscow studio that decorated several properties of famed restauranteur Arkady Novikov, adds to the pleasant dining experience. $ *Average main: 500R* ✉ *57 Lenina pr., Tula* ☎ *487/236–4707* 🌐 *vk.com/club_skovoroda.*

$$$$ B&B/INN **Premiera (Премьера).** Comfortable rooms are clean, spacious, and colorful with rainbow-like striped curtains that match the bedspreads, and most welcome in the summer is the air-conditioning. **Pros:** good service; sauna on the premises. **Cons:** few dining options in the area; no restaurant in the hotel (a bar serves breakfast). $ *Rooms from: 3700R* ✉ *3 ul. Maksimovskovo, Tula* ☎ *487/249–0262, 487/249–0368* 🌐 *www.premieratula.ru/eng* 🛏 *10 rooms* 🍽 *Breakfast.*

SERGIEV-POSAD (ZAGORSK, СЕРГИЕВ ПОСАД (ЗАГОРСК))

Fodor's Choice ★ *75 km (47 miles) northeast of Moscow via shosse Yaroslavskoye and the M8.*

Sergiev-Posad is a comfortable and popular day trip from Moscow. The town's chief attraction is the Troitse-Sergieva Lavra, which for 500 years has been the most important center of pilgrimage in Russia and remains one of the most beautiful of all monasteries—the fairy-tale gold and azure onion domes of its Cathedral of the Assumption are among the most photographed in the country. Until 1930 the town was known as Sergiev, after the monastery's founder, and in 1991 it was officially renamed Sergiev-Posad. But the Soviet name of Zagorsk—in honor of a Bolshevik who was assassinated in 1919—has stuck, and you're likely to hear both names used interchangeably.

The ride to Sergiev-Posad takes you through a lovely stretch of Russian countryside, dotted with colorful wooden cottages. As you approach the town, you see the sad and monolithic apartment buildings of more recent times. Then, peeking out above the hills, the monastery's golden cupolas and soft-blue bell tower come into view.

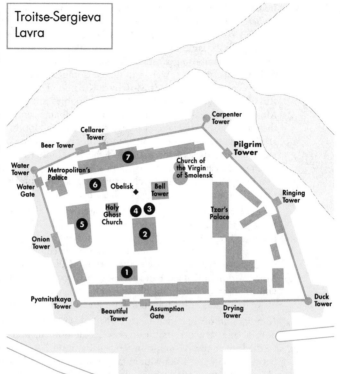

Troitse-Sergieva
Lavra

GETTING HERE AND AROUND

The best way to visit the town is to join an organized tour, because it's a full-day affair out of Moscow. The cost usually includes lunch in addition to a guided tour and transportation. You can also visit on your own by taking the commuter train from Moscow's Yaroslavsky station. The ride takes about two hours. This is much less expensive than an organized tour, but far from hassle-free. You can also take bus 388 from VDNKh metro station. If you choose either of these options, be sure to pack your own lunch because Sergiev-Posad's few restaurants fill up fast with prebooked tourist groups, especially in summer.

EXPLORING

FAMILY **Toy Museum** (Музей Игрушки *Muzey Igrushki*). The world's first *matryoshka* (that colorful, wooden nesting doll) was designed in Sergiev-Posad at the beginning of the 20th century, and most of the matryoshkas you see for sale in Moscow and St. Petersburg are made here. Although the Toy Museum is rarely included on organized tours, it is well worth an hour of your time and is within walking distance of the Troitse-Sergieva Lavra monastery. Its toys have amused, educated, and illuminated the lives of Russian children for generations. ✉ *123 Krasnoy Armii pr.* ☎ *496/540–4101* ⊕ *www.museumot.ru* 💰 *150R* ⊗ *Wed.–Sun. 10–5; closed last Fri. of month.*

Fodor's Choice   **Troitse-Sergieva Lavra** (Троице-Сергиева Лавра *Trinity Monastery of*
★   *St. Sergius*). Sergius of Radonezh (1314–92), who would later become
         Russia's patron saint, founded this famous monastery in 1340. The
         site rapidly became the nucleus of a small medieval settlement, and
         in 1550 the imposing white walls were built to enclose the complex
         of buildings, whose towers and gilded domes make it a smaller, but
         still spectacular, version of Moscow's Kremlin. The monastery was a
         Russian stronghold during the Time of Troubles (the Polish assault on
         Moscow in the early 17th century), and, less than a century later, Peter
         the Great (1672–1725) took refuge here during a bloody revolt of the
         streltsy (Russian militia), which took the lives of some of his closest
         relatives and advisers. It remained the heart of Holy Russia until 1920,
         when the Bolsheviks closed down most monasteries and shipped many
         monks to Siberia. Today the churches are again open for worship, and
         there's a flourishing theological college here.

         You enter the monastery through the archway of the **Gate Church of
         St. John the Baptist,** which was erected in the late 17th century and is
         decorated with frescoes telling the life story of St. Sergius. One of the
         most important historic events in his life occurred prior to 1380, when
         the decisive Russian victory in the Battle of Kulikovo led to the end of
         Mongol rule in Russia. Before leading his troops off to battle, Prince
         Dmitri Donskoy sought the blessing of the peace-loving monk Sergius, a
         move that's generally thought to have greatly aided the Russian victory.

         Although all of the monastery's cathedrals vie for your attention, the
         dominating structure is the massive, blue-domed, and gold-starred
         Cathedral of the Assumption (Uspensky Sobor) in the center. Built
         between 1554 and 1585 with money donated by Tsar Ivan the Terrible
         (1530–84)—purportedly in an attempt to atone for killing his own son
         in a fit of rage—it was modeled after the Kremlin's Uspensky Sobor. Its
         interior contains frescoes and an 18th-century iconostasis. Among the
         artists to work on it was Simon Ushakov, a well-known icon painter
         from Moscow. The cathedral is open for morning services.

         The small building just outside the Cathedral of the Assumption (near
         the northwest corner) is the **tomb of Boris Godunov and his family.** Boris
         Godunov, who ruled as regent after Ivan the Terrible's death, died suddenly
         in 1605 of natural causes. This was during the Polish attack on Moscow
         led by the False Dmitri, the first of many impostors to claim he was the son
         of Ivan. The death of Godunov facilitated the invaders' victory, after which
         his family was promptly murdered. This explains why Godunov wasn't
         bestowed the honor of burial in the Kremlin, as normally granted to tsars.

         Opposite Boris Godunov's tomb is a tiny and colorful chapel, the **Cha-
         pel-at-the-Well,** built in 1644 above a fountain that's said to work mir-
         acles. According to legend, the spring here appeared during the Polish
         Siege (1608–10), when the monastery bravely held out for 16 months
         against the foreign invaders (this time led by the second False Dmitri).
         You can make a wish by washing your face and hands in its charmed
         waters. Towering 86 meters (285 feet) next to the chapel is the five-tier
         baroque belfry. It was built in the 18th century to a design by the master
         of St. Petersburg baroque, Bartolomeo Rastrelli.

Along the southern wall of the monastery, to your far left as you enter, is the 17th-century **Refectory and Church of St. Sergius.** The church is at the eastern end, topped by a single gilt dome. The long building of the refectory, whose colorful facade adds to the vivid richness of the monastery's architecture, is where, in times past, pilgrims from near and far gathered to eat on feast days. The pink building just beyond the refectory is the metropolitan's residence.

Across the path from the residence is the white-stone **Cathedral of the Holy Trinity** (Troitsky Sobor), built in the 15th century over the tomb of St. Sergius. Over the centuries it's received many precious gifts from the powerful and wealthy rulers who've made the pilgrimage to the church of Russia's patron saint. The icons inside were created by famous master Andrei Rublyov and one of his disciples, Danil Chorny. Rublyov's celebrated *Holy Trinity,* now on display at the Tretyakov Gallery in Moscow, originally hung here; the church's version is a copy. The interior's beauty is mainly due to its 17th-century gilded iconostasis (which separates the sanctuary from the altar and body of the church). The upper tier of the church was once used by monks as a manuscript library. A continual service in memoriam to St. Sergius is held all day, every day.

The vestry, the building behind the Cathedral of the Holy Trinity, houses the monastery's **Museum of Ancient Russian Art.** It's often closed for no apparent reason or open only to groups, which is yet another reason to visit Sergiev-Posad on a guided tour. The museum contains a spectacular collection of gifts presented to the monastery over the centuries. On display are precious jewels, jewel-encrusted embroideries, chalices, and censers. Next door to the vestry are two more museums, which are open to individual tourists. The first museum contains icons and icon covers, portrait art, and furniture. The other museum (on the second floor) is devoted to Russian folk art, with wooden items, toys, porcelain, and jewelry. There's also a gift shop here. ☎ *496/540–5721* ⊕ *www.stsl.ru* 🖃 *Lavra free for Russians, 280R for foreign tourists; museum 150R* 🕙 *Lavra daily 5 am–9 pm; museum daily 10–5.*

■ TIP→ **Be sure to dress appropriately for your visit to the functioning monastery: men are expected to remove their hats, and women are required to wear below-knee-length skirts or slacks (never shorts) and bring something to cover their heads.**

WHERE TO EAT AND STAY

$$$$
RUSSIAN

✕ **Grillage (Грильяж).** Live music, a decent alcohol selection, and a menu of traditional Russian food makes this place popular with locals. Favorites include borscht, meat dumplings, and salmon steak. Be prepared for slow service. ⑤ *Average main: 800R* ✉ *7 st. Karla Marksa* ☎ *496/547–0706* ⊕ *www.grillage-sp.ru.*

$$$$
EASTERN
EUROPEAN
Fodor'sChoice
★

✕ **Russky Dvorik (Русский Дворик).** This spot right across from the Lavra draws lots of tour groups, who are served traditional fare, including *golubtsi*, meat cooked inside cabbage leaves, and several types of vodka by waiters dressed in peasant costumes. Service is pleasant but can be slow when the big groups pack in for lunch. ⑤ *Average main: 1500R* ✉ *2 ul. Krasnoy Armii, bldg. 134,* ☎ *496/540–5114* ⊕ *www.russky-dvorik-restaurant.ru.*

$$$$
HOTEL
⛅ **Hotel Imperial Village** (Царская Деревня *Tsarskaya Derevnya*). Here you have a choice of cozy accommodations in the historical center of the city, near the Lavra, in a number of character-filled houses spread across nice grounds. **Pros:** best hotel in town. **Cons:** slow service. ⑤ *Rooms from: 5400R* ✉ *2 ul. Mitkina, bldg. 14,* ☎ *496/547–5392* ⊕ *www. imperial-village.ru* ⮐ *64 rooms* 🍽 *No meals.*

ABRAMTSEVO ESTATE
MUSEUM МУЗЕЙ-УСАДЬБА АБРАМЦЕВО

61 km (38 miles) northeast of Moscow via shosse Yaroslavskoye and the M8.

The 18th-century, wooden Abramtsevo Estate was at the center of Russia's cultural life in two different periods of the 19th century. It's easier to name the cultural figures of the early 19th century who didn't visit Abramtsevo than all of those who did. Among the latter are the writers Nikolai Gogol and Ivan Turgenev. The artists Valentin Serov, Mikhail Vrubel, Ilya Repin, Viktor Vasnetsov, and Vasily Polenov were just a few of the artists who lived and worked at the estate when it was an artists' colony in the late 19th and early 20th centuries.

GETTING HERE AND AROUND

The estate can easily be visited on the way back from Sergiev-Posad. For Russian art aficionados, however, it may be worth making it a single one-day trip. You can visit the estate on a tour or head there yourself by commuter train from Yaroslavsky station to Sergiev-Posad or Alexandrov; get off at the Abramtsevo station. From the station the museum is a 15-minute walk or a short bus or taxi trip.

EXPLORING

Fodor's Choice
★

Abramtsevo Estate (Абрамцево). Until 1870 Abramtsevo belonged to Sergei Aksakov, a Slavophile who advocated the exportation of Orthodox Christianity to the West. A very religious man, Aksakov chose Abramtsevo as his residence because it was close to the Troitse-Sergieva Lavra. He opened his home to sympathetic writers and intellectuals of the 1840s.

After Aksakov's death, railway tycoon Savva Mamontov purchased the estate in 1870 and turned it into an artists' colony. Here Mamontov and a community of resident artists tried to revive traditional Russian arts, crafts, and architecture to stimulate interest in Russian culture and make arts more accessible to the people.

In the 1880s half a dozen resident artists participated in the construction of the prettiest structure on Abramtsevo's grounds, the diminutive **Tserkov Ikony Spasa Nerukotvornovo** (Church of the Icon of the Savior Not Made by Hands). The idea to build a church was born when a flood prevented the local community from attending the festive Easter church service. The artist Polenov chose a 12th-century church outside Novgorod as a model. He and fellow artists Repin and Nesterov painted the gilt iconostasis; Vasnetsov laid the mosaic floor he'd designed in the shape of a giant blooming flower. Some of the resident artists created their finest works in Abramtsevo. Serov painted his *Girl with*

Peaches, an 1870 portrait of Mamontov's daughter, Vera, which now decorates Mamontov's dining room. Vasnetsov worked on his 1898 *Bogatyri* (Russian epic heroes) in Abramtsevo as well. Other structures on Abramtsevo's grounds include the wooden Izbushka Na Kuryikh Nozhkakh (House on Chicken Legs), a rendering of the residence of the witch Baba-Yaga from Russian fairy tales; Polenov's dacha; and an artists' workshop. In 1889 the troubled artist Mikhail Vrubel joined the Abramtsevo colony to participate in the ceramics workshop, where his provocative grotesque designs are still evident in the tile stoves, ceramic inlay, and furniture. The estate has been a museum since 1918, when it was nationalized. ✉ *Sergiev-Posad district, Abramtsevo station, 1 ul. Muzeunaya, Abramtsevo* ☎ *496/543–2470* ⊕ *www.abramtsevo.net* 🎟 *525R* ☽ *Wed.–Sun. 10–6; closed last Thurs. of month.*

WHERE TO EAT

$$ ✕ **Galereya** (Галерея). The extensive menu of traditional Russian food
EASTERN served at this stylish inn makes it a solid choice for lunch or dinner,
EUROPEAN and so does the fact that it's right across the street from the central gate of the Abramtsevo estate. If you don't feel like dining in, order a few *pirozhki* (small pies of cabbage, apple, or potatoes) to go. They're particularly delicious with *mors*, a traditional Russian cranberry drink. ⑤ *Average main: 300R* ✉ *3 ul. Muzeynaya, Abramtsevo* ☎ *495/989–1052* ⊕ *www.clubgalereya.ru.*

THE NORTHERN GOLDEN RING

Within this historic region northeast of Moscow are ancient towns, venerable churches, and the magnificent Rostov kremlin and Monastery of St. Ipaty. There are plenty of guided-tour options, ranging from one-day outings to 1,000-km (620-mile) bus tours. If you want to visit this region on your own, you're in luck: these towns are tourist-friendly.

PERESLAVL-ZALESSKY ПЕРЕСЛАВЛЬ-ЗАЛЕССКИЙ

127 km (79 miles) northeast of Moscow via the M8.

Pereslavl-Zalessky was founded in 1157 by Prince Yuri Dolgoruky, son of Vladimir Monomakh, the Grand Prince of Kiev. Yuri was given control over the northeastern outpost of what was then Kievan Rus' (the early predecessor of modern-day Russia and Ukraine), and Pereslavl-Zalessky served two very important functions. The first was political: Yuri sought to draw parallels between the power base he was building in the Rus' region and the center of power in Kiev, to the southeast. So he named this town Pereyaslavl (meaning "to achieve glory"; the "ya" was later dropped) after a town outside of Kiev, and he named the river alongside the town Trubezh, just as in the Kievan Pereyaslavl. The "Zalessky" appellation, added in the 15th century, means "beyond the forests" and was used to distinguish the town from many other Pereyaslavls (not least the one near Kiev).

The second reason was economic. The location of the town on the southern shore of Lake Pleshcheyevo was ideal for defending the western approaches to vital trade routes along the Nerl River to the Klyazma, Oka, and Volga rivers. The topography only accentuates this role. From the hills, the impressive Danilovsky and Goritsky monasteries peer down on the low wooden and stone buildings of the town.

As the birthplace of Alexander Nevsky (1220–63), Pereslavl-Zalessky has yet another claim to fame. Nevsky entered the pantheon of Russia's great heroes when, as Prince of Novgorod, he beat back invading Swedes in 1240 at the Battle of the Neva (thus his last name). For his victory, the Mongol Khan awarded Nevsky the title of Grand Prince of Vladimir. There's a small church in town honoring Nevsky.

GETTING HERE AND AROUND

■ TIP→ **Note that the town can be reached by bus or car, but not by train.**

A bus leaves from Moscow's Shchelkovskaya metro station and reaches Pereslavl-Zalessky in two and a half to three hours.

EXPLORING

Botik museum (Музей Ботик). Pereslavl-Zalessky was the birthplace of the Russian navy. The Botik museum, 3 km (2 miles) outside of town, houses the only remaining boat of the more than 100 Peter the Great built for the fleet he sailed on Lake Pleshcheyevo. The *botik,* a small sailboat, usually single-mast, is often called the grandfather of the Russian fleet. The museum also displays several naval guns, a triumphal arch, and a monument to Peter the Great. To get to the museum, take a taxi or a bus from the bus station. ⊠ *Near Veslevo village* ☎ *485/356–2116* ⊕ *www.museumpereslavl.ru* 🎫 *150R* ☉ *Tues.–Sun. 10–5; closed last Thurs. of month.*

Cathedral of the Transfiguration (Спасо-Преображенский Собор *Spaso-Preobrazhensky Sobor*). Construction began on this 12th-century limestone cathedral in the center of town the same year as workers started constructing the Church of Saints Boris and Gleb in Kideksha, near Suzdal, making it one of the oldest stone buildings standing in Russia. ⊠ *pl. Krasnaya* ☎ *485/353–8100* ⊕ *www.museumpereslavl.ru* 🎫 *40R* ☉ *May–Oct., Wed.–Mon. 10–6.*

Goritsky Monastyr (Горитский Монастырь). This fortresslike monastery, high on a hill south of the town center, was founded in the first half of the 14th century and is now an art and history museum. It displays ancient manuscripts and books found in this area, jewelry, and sculptures. An impressive collection of icons includes the 15th-century treasure, *Peter and Paul Apostles,* the oldest icon in the region, and a small collection of paintings with works of Konstantin Korovin. Outside the entrance to the museum is a proud monument to the T-34 tank, which saved Russia from the Germans in World War II. Inside is the large Uspensky Sobor (Cathedral of the Assumption), built in 1544. ⊠ *4 per. Muzeyny* ☎ *48535/381–00* ⊕ *www.museumpereslavl.ru* 🎫 *20R for monastery grounds, other small fees to enter different parts of museum.* ☉ *Wed.–Mon. 10–4:30; closed last Mon. of month.*

WHERE TO STAY

$$$
RESORT
🏠 **Botik Tourist Complex** (**Туристический Комплекс Ботик**). Seven pretty, newly renovated wooden houses that accommodate two people each are down the path from the Botik museum, on the bank of Pleshcheyevo Lake. **Pros:** great views of the lake; beachfront location. **Cons:** rooms must be booked in advance. $ *Rooms from: 3000R* ✉ *77 ul. Petra I, near Veskovo village* ☎ *485/359–8085* ⊕ *www.tkbotik.ru* ➦ *7 houses* ▤ *No credit cards* ⦿ *No meals.*

$$$
HOTEL
🏠 **Hotel Pereslavl** (**Переславль**). A Soviet-era lodging in the town center offers clean and light rooms with nice furniture and decent bathrooms, and a bit of a surprise bonus: a staff that prides itself on service. **Pros:** convenient location; nice basic comforts. **Cons:** bar can get loud on weekends. $ *Rooms from: 2600R* ✉ *27 ul. Rostovskaya* ☎ *485/353–1788, 485/353–2687* ⊕ *www.hotelpereslavl.ru* ➦ *59 rooms* ⦿ *No meals.*

$$$
HOTEL
🏠 **West Hotel** (*Hotel Zapadnaya*). Clean and spacious rooms enjoy a superb, picturesque location in the historic center of town and a number of them look on to the Trubezh River, the old city ramparts, and the Cathedral of the Transfiguration. **Pros:** great location; helpful staff. **Cons:** a bit overpriced; decor is a bit basic. $ *Rooms from: 2990R* ✉ *1-A ul. Pleshcheyevskaya* ☎ *485/353–4378, 485/353–4395* ⊕ *www. westhotel.ru* ➦ *12 rooms* ⦿ *No meals.*

ROSTOV ПОСТОВ

225 km (140 miles) northeast of Moscow via the M8, 58 km (36 miles) southwest of Yaroslavl.

Rostov, also known as Rostov-Veliky ("the Great") so as not to confuse it with Rostov-on-the-Don, is one of the oldest towns in Russia. Founded even before Riurik, a semi-legendary Viking prince, came to rule Russia in the 9th century, Rostov is first mentioned in historical chronicles in 862. It became an independent principality at the beginning of the 13th century and soon became one of the most prosperous and influential political centers of ancient Russia. However, the city was destroyed when the Mongols invaded in 1238. In the 15th century Rostov ultimately lost its political independence but retained its influence as a major religious center. It became the seat of the metropolitan, the leader of the Orthodox Church, in the late 16th century.

The town, with a population of 36,000, is on the edge of Lake Nero, with earthen ramparts and radial streets.

GETTING HERE AND AROUND

From Moscow you can take a three-hour "express" train from Yaroslavsky station or get a bus from the Shchelkovskaya or Komsomolskaya metro stations. The bus takes about four hours.

EXPLORING

Avraamiyev (Abraham) Monastery. Founded at the end of the 11th century on the site of a former pagan temple to Veles, god of cattle, this monastery claims to be the oldest in Russia. The five-dome Epiphany Cathedral in the monastery complex dates from 1553 and is the oldest standing building in Rostov. The nuns' cloister, which is still working, is on the lakefront, northeast of the kremlin. ✉ *32 ul. Zhelyabinskaya* ☎ *485/366–3712* ⌨ *Free* ☉ *Daily 9–5.*

Rostov kremlin (Ростовский Кремль). At the center of Rostov is the incomparable Rostov kremlin, a fortress with 6-foot-thick white-stone walls and 11 circular towers topped with wood-shingle cupolas. The kremlin dates from 1631, but it was built to its current glory between 1670 and 1690 by Rostov Metropolitan Jonah. Its main purpose was to serve as court and residence for the metropolitan, though Jonah saw himself as creating an ideal type of self-enclosed city focused on spiritual matters. As such, it was Russia's first planned city.

The huge, blue-dome **Cathedral of the Assumption** (Uspensky Sobor) stands just outside the walls of the kremlin. Inside are frescoes dating to 1675. But the truly memorable site is the adjacent four-tower **belfry.** The famous 13 bells of Rostov chime on the half hour and full hour and can play four tunes. It's said that the largest of the bells, which weighs 32 tons and is named Sysoi, for Jonah's father, can be heard from 19 km (12 miles) away.

You enter the kremlin through the richly decorated northern entrance, past the **Gate Church of the Resurrection** (Nadvratnaya Voskresenskaya Tserkov). Well-groomed pathways and a pleasant, tree-lined pond lend themselves to a contemplative walk. Just to the right of the entrance into the kremlin is the **Church of the Mother of God Hodegetria** (Tserkov Bogomateri Odigitrii), whose faceted baroque exterior rises to a single onion dome.

The **Church of John the Theologian** (Tserkov Ioanna Bogoslova), another gate church, is on the west side of the kremlin. Adjacent to this church is the two-story **Red Palace** (Krasnaya Palata), once known as the Chamber for Great Sovereigns. Built first for Ivan the Terrible for his visits to the town, it was later used by Peter the Great and Catherine the Great.

The tall **Church of Grigory the Theologian** (Tserkov Grigoria Bogoslova) dominates the southern portion of the kremlin. ☎ *48536/61717* ⊕ *www.rostmuseum.ru* ⌨ *450R for all churches and palaces inside the kremlin* ☉ *Daily 10–6; churches: May–Oct., daily 10–5.*

White Palace (Белая Палата *Belaya Palata*). The metropolitan's residence, adjacent to the kremlin, is most notable for its large hall (3,000 square feet) supported by a single column. Connected to the residence is the private church of the metropolitan, the Church of the Savior on the Stores, which was built over a food-storage shelter. This church has the most beautiful wall paintings in the entire complex, as well as gilded columns and handsome brass doors. The metropolitan's residence now houses a museum of icons and Rostov enamel (*finift*), a craft the town is famous for throughout Russia. ☎ *485/366-1717 Tourism department of the museum* ⊕ *www.rostmuseum.ru* ⌨ *50R* ☉ *May–Oct., daily 10–5*

Torgoviye Ryady (Торговые Ряды *trade rows*). In the early 19th century, after Rostov had lost its metropolitanate to nearby Yaroslavl, it became an extremely important trading center. Rostov's annual market, across the square from Uspensky Sobor, was the third largest in Russia. Today the town's central market, where food, clothes, and household goods are sold, occupies the site.

St. Jacob's Dmitriyev Monastery (Яковлевский Монастырь *Spaso-Yakovlevsky Dmitriev Monastyr*). Dominating the ensemble along the lakefront and southwest of the kremlin is the huge Romanesque Dmitriyev Church, crowned by a large spherical central dome and four smaller corner domes. The monastery was founded in 1389. Take the guided tour for access to the premises of the working monastery. ☎ *485/367–4369, 485/367–7004* ⊕ *www.rostov-monastir.ru* 🎫 *Free* ☉ *Daily 9–5.*

WHERE TO EAT AND STAY

$$ ✕ **Teremok (Теремок).** Borscht, solyanka, and blini with caviar are

EASTERN among the good Russian dishes served at this cozy spot in front of the

EUROPEAN kremlin. ⑤ *Average main: 260R* ⊠ *1 ul. Moravskovo* ☎ *48536/61648* 🚫 *No credit cards.*

$$ 🏨 **Boyarsky Dvor (Боярский Двор).** Just steps from the kremlin, this

HOTEL 18th-century, two-story historic mansion-turned-hotel has all the amenities you could ask for from a provincial hotel, especially the clean, spacious rooms cheerfully decorated in pastel colors. **Pros:** great location; comfortable beds. **Cons:** advance booking required in summer. ⑤ *Rooms from: 2100R* ⊠ *4 ul. Kammeny Most* ☎ *48536/60446, 48536/64800* ⊕ *www.reinkap-hotel.ru* 🛏 *53 rooms.*

$$ 🏨 **Dom na Pogrebakh (Дом на Погребах).** If you've ever wanted to

HOTEL stay overnight in a kremlin, here's your chance: these wooden-walled rooms of varying sizes are built over the food stores, or *pogreba*. **Pros:** the opportunity to stay inside a 17th-century kremlin. **Cons:** rooms are a bit shabby. ⑤ *Rooms from: 2500R* ⊠ *Rostov Kremlin, in Red Palace* ☎ *485/366–1244* ⊕ *www.domnapogrebah.ru* 🛏 *16 rooms* 🚫 *No credit cards* 🍽 *No meals.*

YAROSLAVL ЯРОСЛАВЛЬ

282 km (175 miles) northeast of Moscow on the M8.

Yaroslavl has a very storied history, beginning with an apocryphal founding. It's said that local inhabitants set loose a bear to chase away Prince Yaroslav the Wise (978–1054). Yaroslav wrestled and killed the bear and founded the town on the spot. It's historical fact that Yaroslav decreed the town's founding as a fortress on the Volga in 1010. About 600 years later, in 1612, during the Time of Troubles, the town was the center of national resistance against the invading Poles, under the leadership of Kuzma Minin and Dmitri Pozharsky.

The town rests at the confluence of the Volga and Kotorosl rivers, which made it a major commercial center from the 13th century until 1937, when the Moscow–Volga canal was completed, allowing river traffic to proceed directly to the capital. This commercial heritage bequeathed the city a rich legacy that offers a glimpse of some of the finest church architecture in Russia. The center of Yaroslavl, which is a UNESCO World Heritage site, has 21st-century additions including a 3-meter tall metal statue of a bear on the banks of the Kotorosl River and a statue of Yarslovai, staring off in the direction of Moscow, on ulitsa Nakhimsona.

In the town center, proceed northwest along ulitsa Pervomaiskaya, a favorite pedestrian route that follows the semicircular path of the town's former earthen ramparts. Peruse the impressive, colonnaded **trade rows** and walk on to the Znamenskaya watchtower, which in the middle of the 17th century marked the western edge of the town. Another watchtower stands on the Volga embankment. The yellow building directly across the square is the **Volkov Theater.** The theater and square are named for Fyodor Volkov, who founded Russia's first professional drama theater here in 1750—the theater was the first to stage *Hamlet* in Russia. Continue along Pervomaiskaya and it'll take you to the banks of the Volga, which is 1 km (half a mile) wide at this point. Look for the monument to the great Russian poet Nikolai Nekrasov, who came from nearby Karabikha.

GETTING HERE AND AROUND

You can take a train from Moscow's Yaroslavsky train station to Yaroslavsky Glavny. It takes four hours.

EXPLORING

Candle of Yaroslavl (Ярославская Свеча *Yaroslavskaya Svecha*). The 100-foot-tall "candle" is actually a belfry for two churches, Ioann Zlatoust (St. John Chrysostom, 1649) and the miniature Tserkov Vladimirskoi Bogomateri (Church of the Vladimir Virgin, 1678). The former is a larger summer church, ornately decorated with colorful tiles; the latter is the more modest and easy-to-heat winter church. From the Monastery of the Transfiguration of the Savior, it's a 1-km (½-mile) walk (or two stops on bus 4) across the bridge and along the mouth of the Kotorosl to the churches and belfry.

Church of Elijah the Prophet (Церковь Ильи Пророка *Tserkov Ilyi Proroka*). The mid-17th-century Church of Elijah the Prophet (*Tserkov Ilyi Proroka*) stands at the center of town on ploschad Sovetskaya (Soviet Square), some say on the site of Yaroslav's alleged wrestling match with the bear. Tall, octagonal belfry and faceted green onion domes make the church the focal point of the town. Inside the ornamental church are some of the best-preserved frescoes (1680) by Gury Nikitin and Sila Savin, whose works also adorn Moscow Kremlin cathedrals, as well as churches throughout the region. The frescoes depict scenes from the Gospels and the life of Elijah and his disciple Elisha. ✉ *7 pl. Sovetskaya* ☎ *4852/304072* ⊕ *www.yarmp.yar.ru* ☞ *70R* ☽ *May–Oct., daily 8:30–7:30.*

Church of the Epiphany (Церковь Богоявления *Tserkov Bogoyavleniya*). The large, redbrick, blue-cupola Church of the Epiphany (Tserkov Bogoyavleniya) is renowned for its fine proportions, enhanced by splendid decorative ceramic tiles and unusually tall windows. Inside are eight levels of wall paintings in the realistic style that began to hold sway in the late 1600s. The church is directly west of the Monastery of the Transfiguration of the Savior. ✉ *12 pl. Bogoyavlenskaya* ☎ *4852/303429, 4852/725623* ⊕ *www.yarmp.yar.ru* ☞ *60R* ☽ *Wed.–Sun 9–4.*

Church of St. John the Baptist (Церковь Иоанна Предтечи *Tserkov Ioanna Predtechi*). Although it looks as though it's made from wood, the 17th-century five-dome Church of St. John the Baptist (*Tserkov Ioanna Predtechi*) is actually fashioned from carved red brick. The church is on the same side of the Kotorosl River as the Candle of Yaroslavl, but it's west of the bridge by about 1 km (½ miles). The church is the biggest in Yaroslavl and is depicted on the 1,000 ruble note. ⌧ *69 nab. Kotoroslnaya* ☎ *4852/304072* ⊕ *www.yarmp.yar.ru* ⌫ *60R* ☾ *Wed.–Sun. 10–5.*

Monastery of the Transfiguration of the Savior (Спасо-Преображенский Монастырь *Spaso-Preobrazhensky Monastyr*). Surrounded by white, 10-foot-thick walls, this attractive complex was the site of northern Russia's first school of higher education, dating to the 13th century. It houses several magnificent churches and is where Ivan the Terrible took refuge in 1571, when the Mongols were threatening Moscow. Dating to 1516, the **Holy Gates** entrance to the monastery, on the side facing the Kotorosl River, is the oldest extant structure in the compound. A six-story **belfry** rises high above the round-dome Cathedral of the Transfiguration of the Savior. The clock in the belfry hung in the famous Spasskaya Tower of the Moscow Kremlin until 1624, when it was purchased by the merchants of Yaroslavl. ⌧ *25 pl. Bogoyavlenskaya* ☎ *4852/304072* ⊕ *www.yarmp.yar.ru* ⌫ *25R, small fee for individual churches and belfry within monastery* ☾ *Tues.–Sun. 10–5:30; closed 1st Wed. of month.*

WHERE TO EAT AND STAY

$$$$
EASTERN
EUROPEAN
✕ **Skver 20/10** (Сквер 20/10). St. Petersburg–brewed Baltika beer accompanies the traditional Russian dishes served at this trendy café behind the Volkov Theater. ⑤ *Average main: 600R* ⌧ *5 bul. Pervomaiskiy* ☎ *4852/202010.*

$$$$
HOTEL
⌂ **Kotorosl** (Короросль). These rooms are basic but streamlined, clean, and decently equipped, and they aren't far from the city center, near the railway station. **Pros:** close to train station. **Cons:** some bathrooms are shared between two rooms. ⑤ *Rooms from: 3600R* ⌧ *87 ul. Bolshaya Oktyabrskaya* ☎ *485/221–1581, 485/221–2415* ⊕ *www.kotorosl. yaroslavl.ru* ⇋ *181 rooms* ⑩ *No meals.*

$$$$
HOTEL
⌂ **Ring Premier Hotel.** The most luxurious accommodations in town are reasonably large, nicely furnished, air-conditioned, and have such amenities as satellite television and Internet access. **Pros:** staff speaks excellent English; great sauna and pool. **Cons:** hotel bar and restaurant are a bit overpriced. ⑤ *Rooms from: 4425R* ⌧ *55 ul. Svobody* ☎ *485/258–1158, 485/258–0858* ⊕ *www.ringhotel.ru* ⇋ *122 rooms* ⑩ *No meals.*

$$$$
HOTEL
⌂ **Yubileynaya** (Юбилейная). Plain but adequate rooms have the advantage of being near the monastery and overlook the Kotorosl River and the historic town center. **Pros:** central location on the riverbank; nice buffet breakfast. **Cons:** a bit overpriced. ⑤ *Rooms from: 3650R* ⌧ *26 nab. Kotoroslnaya* ☎ *485/272–6565* ⊕ *www.yubilyar.com* ⇋ *220 rooms* ⑩ *Breakfast.*

CLOSE UP

Moscow's Age-Old Rival

In the mid–12th century, Andrei Bogolyubsky amassed considerable power within Kievan Rus', centered on his inherited lands of Suzdalia. He made Vladimir his capital and built up its churches and monasteries to rival those of Kiev, the capital of Kievan Rus'. In 1169, unhappy with the pattern of dynastic succession in Kiev, Bogolyubsky sent his and allied troops to sack Kiev and placed his son on the throne as grand prince. From that point forward, political and ecclesiastical power began to flow toward the northeastern region of Rus'.

If a Mongol invasion hadn't arrived a century later in 1237, Vladimir might have continued to grow in power and be the capital of Russia today. But invade the Mongols did, and within three years every town in the region was nearly destroyed; the region remained subjugated for more than 200 years. Moscow, meanwhile, with the cunning it's still known for today, slowly rose to prominence by becoming tax (or tribute) collector for the Mongols. Ivan Kalita ("Ivan Moneybags") was a particularly proficient go-between, and, as Mongol power receded in the 14th century, he began gathering together the lands surrounding Moscow, beginning with Vladimir.

THE EASTERN GOLDEN RING

Vladimir and Suzdal, which together make up a World Heritage site, hold some of Russia's most beautiful medieval kremlins, churches, and monasteries. The towns lie to the east of Moscow.

VLADIMIR ВЛАДИМИР

190 km (118 miles) east of Moscow via the M7.

Although this city of 350,000 seems unassuming today, half a millennium ago it was the cultural and religious capital of northeastern Rus'. Several of the monuments dating to this time of prosperity and prestige remain, and a visit to this city, and nearby Suzdal, is vital to understanding the roots of contemporary Russian culture.

Vladimir was founded in 1108 on the banks of the Klyazma by Vladimir Monomakh, grandson of Yaroslav the Wise and father of Yuri Dolgoruky. As Yuri increased his power en route to taking the throne in Kiev, he made Suzdal his de facto capital in 1152. Upon Yuri's death five years later, his son, Andrei Bogolyubsky, moved the capital of Suzdalia to Vladimir and began a massive building campaign.

GETTING HERE AND AROUND
From Moscow, take the express train from Kursky train station or a bus from Shchelkovskaya metro station. Once you're in Vladimir you can get bus number 18 or 152 to visit Bogolyubovo village or find a taxi to take you.

EXPLORING

Bogolyubovo (Боголюбово). Most of Andrei Bogolyubsky's construction projects were in Bogolyubovo, 10 km (6 miles) east of Vladimir. Near the convergence of the Nerl and Klyazma rivers, he built an impressive fort and living compound. The dominant building in the compound today is the richly decorated **Cathedral of the Assumption** (Uspensky Sobor), rebuilt in the 19th century. Remnants of his quarters—a tower and an archway—still stand. It was on the stairs of this tower that Andrei, despised by many for his authoritarian rule, was stabbed to death by several members of his inner circle. In the 13th century, Bogolyubovo became a convent, which it remains today. In 1702 Andrei was canonized. ⊠ *Bogolyubovo village* 🕾 *4922/3242–63 tour reservations* ⊕ *www.vladmuseum.ru* 🔁 *Free* ⊙ *Daily 10–5.*

Cathedral of the Assumption (Успенский Собор *Uspensky Sobor*). The huge, boxy outline and golden domes rise high above the Klyazma River. After a fire in 1185, the cathedral was rebuilt, only to burn down again in 1237 when the Mongols attacked the city. The town's residents took refuge in the church, hoping for mercy. Instead, the invaders burned them alive. The cathedral was again restored, and in 1408 the famous medieval painter Andrei Rublyov repainted the frescoes of the Last Judgment, which in themselves make this impressive monument worth a visit. Ivan the Great (1440–1505) had his architects use this cathedral as a model to build the Assumption Cathedral in the Moscow Kremlin. The cathedral also houses a replica of Russia's most revered icon, the Virgin of Vladimir; the original was moved from here to Moscow in 1390. Andrei Bogolyubsky is entombed here. ⊠ *pl. Sobornaya* 🕾 *4922/324263, 4922/325201* ⊕ *www.vladmuseum.ru* 🔁 *150R* ⊙ *Tues.–Sun. 1–4:45.*

Cathedral of St. Dmitri (Дмитриевский Собор *Dmitriyevsky Sobor*). Andrei Bogolyubsky was succeeded by Vsevolod III, also known as "the Great Nest" because of the great number of his progeny. Although he focused much of his energy in the neighboring regions of Ryazan and Murom, he was instrumental in rebuilding Vladimir's town center in 1185 after a fire caused much damage. He also built the remarkable Cathedral of St. Dmitri (completed in 1197). The cathedral stands adjacent to Vladimir's much larger Cathedral of the Assumption, where Andrei is buried, and is covered in ornate carvings with both secular and religious images. The lower images are quite precise and detailed; the upper ones have fewer details but deeper grooves for better visibility. ⊠ *pl. Sobornaya* 🕾 *4922/324263* ⊕ *www.vladmuseum.ru* 🔁 *50R* ⊙ *Mon. and Wed.–Sun. 11–5; closed last Wed. of month.*

Church of the Intercession on the Nerl (Храм Покрова на Нерли *Khram Pokrova Na Nerli*). Andrei's greatest creation and arguably the most perfect medieval Russian church ever built is less than 2 km (1 miles) from Bogolyubovo. On a massive limestone foundation covered with earth, the church sits near the confluence of the Nerl and Klyazma rivers and appears to be rising out of the water that surrounds it. Andrei built the church, completed in 1165, in memory of his son Izyslav, who was killed in a victorious battle with the Bulgars. Look for the unique carvings of King David on the exterior, the earliest such iconographic carvings in this region. Inside, the high, narrow arches give an impressive feeling of space and light. To get to the church from Bogolyubovo, walk a few hundred yards west of the monastery, down ulitsa Frunze and under a railway bridge; then follow the path through a field.

Golden Gates (Золотые Ворота *Zolotye Vorota*). Originally, Vladimir had four gates guarding the main approaches to the town. The 12th-century Golden Gates, which stand in the middle of ulitsa Moskovskaya, a few hundred yards west of the Cathedral of the Assumption, guarded the western approach. The main road from Moscow to Siberia passed through these gates, which, starting in the 1800s, became a significant monument on the infamous Vladimirka—the road that prisoners took east to Siberia. ⊠ *ul. Nikitskaya* ☎ *492/232–4263* ⊕ *www.vladmuseum.ru* 🎟 *50R.*

<aside>
WORD OF MOUTH

"The attractions in the Golden Ring are not so much the urban architecture but the towns' kremlins and monasteries, which are superb. Suzdal is small, more village than town, and is quite delightful."

—wasleys
</aside>

WHERE TO EAT AND STAY

$$$

EASTERN
EUROPEAN

✕ **Stary Gorod (Старый Город).** This "Old Town" restaurant serving Russian and European cuisine is a good option for a meal, in part because it's just steps away from the cathedrals on ploshchad Sobornaya. The place is quiet, the staff is friendly, and the summer terrace, open May through September, is a delightful place to linger. ⑤ *Average main: 500R* ⊠ *41 ul. Bolshaya Moskovskaya* ☎ *492/232–5101* ▭ *No credit cards.*

$$$$

HOTEL

▦ **Monomah Hotel (Мономах).** These cozy rooms in a rambling apartment are some of the best accommodations in the city, filled with nice old wooden furnishings and colorful fabrics; some are tucked under the eaves. **Pros:** central location; slippers and other nice amenities in each room; room service. **Cons:** a bit overpriced; no elevator. ⑤ *Rooms from: 3500R* ⊠ *20 ul. Gogolya* ☎ *492/244–0444* ⊕ *www.monomahhotel.ru* ⇘ *16 rooms* ❙❙ *Some meals.*

$$$

HOTEL

▦ **U Zolotykh Vorot (У Золотых Ворот).** Tastefully decorated rooms done in restful shades of beige and pink are in a recently renovated 19th-century building, next to the Golden Gates. **Pros:** central location; great breakfast. **Cons:** rooms with a street view can be noisy. ⑤ *Rooms from: 2800R* ⊠ *15 ul. Bolshaya Moskovskaya* ☎ *492/242–0823* ⊕ *www. golden-gate.ru* ⇘ *13 rooms, 1 suite* ❙❙ *Breakfast.*

SUZDAL СУЗДАЛЬ

190 km (118 miles) east of Moscow on the M7 via Vladimir, then 26 km (16 miles) north on the A113.

Suzdal is the crown jewel of the Golden Ring, with more than 200 historic monuments and some of the most striking churches in Russia. This quiet tourist town of 12,000 on the Kamenka River is compact enough to be explored entirely on foot, but to do it justice, give it two days.

One of the earliest settlements in central Russia, Suzdal has been inhabited since the 9th century and was first mentioned in the *Russian Chronicle* (Russia's ancient historical record) in 1024. In 1152 Yuri Dolgoruky made Suzdal the capital of his growing fiefdom in north-eastern Russia. He built a fortress in nearby Kideksha. That town, 4 km (2½ miles) to the east, is the site of the oldest stone church in northeastern Russia, the Church of Saints Boris and Gleb, built in 1152. His son, Andrei Bogolyubsky, preferred nearby Vladimir and focused much of his building efforts there. Still, Suzdal remained a rich town, largely because of donations to the many local monasteries and church-building commissions. Indeed, medieval Suzdal had only about 400 families, but some 40 churches.

GETTING HERE AND AROUND

Buses to Suzdal go from Moscow's Shchelkovskaya metro station. Or you can get the Moscow–Vladimir express from Kursky train station and then catch a bus to Suzdal.

EXPLORING

Churches of St. Lazarus and St. Antipy (Церковь Святого Лазаря и Церковь Святого Антипия *Tserkov Svyatovo Lazarya and Tserkov Svyatovo Antipiya*). Walking north from the kremlin on ulitsa Lenina, you'll pass several churches on your left and the pillared trading arcades. Just beyond the arcades are the beautiful Churches of St. Lazarus and St. Antipy, their colorful bell tower topping the unique, concave tent-roof design. This ensemble is a good example of Russian church architecture, where a summer church (St. Lazarus, with the shapely onion domes, built in 1667) adjoins a smaller, easier-to-heat, and more modest winter church (St. Antipy, built in 1745). ✉ *ul. Staraya* 🎫 *Free*.

Convent of the Intercession (Покровский Монастырь *Pokrovsky Monastyr*). In addition to being a religious institution, this convent was also a place for political incarcerations. Basil III divorced his wife Solomonia in 1525 and banished her here when she failed to produce a male heir. Basil may have chosen this monastery because, in 1514, he had commissioned the splendid octagonal, three-dome cathedral in the complex as supplication for a male heir. Local legend has it that Solomonia subsequently gave birth to a boy and then staged the child's death to hide him from Basil.

Basil subsequently married Yelena Glinskaya, who did give him an heir: Ivan IV, who would be known as "the Terrible." Ivan, in turn, banished his wife Anna here. And when Peter the Great, after returning from Europe in 1698, finally decided that he wanted to rid himself of his wife, Yevdokia, he forced her to take the veil and live out the rest of her life in this convent. A fine view of the monastery can be had from across the river, from the sparse remains of the Alexander Nevsky monastery. The convent sits across the Kamenka River from Spaso Yefimsky, in an oxbow bend of the river. To get here, turn east off ulitsa Lenina onto ulitsa Stromynka, and then go north on Pokrovskaya ulitsa. ✉ *76 ul. Pokrovskaya* 🕾 *49231/20609* ⊕ *www. spokrov.ru* 🎫 *Free* ☉ *Daily 7–7*.

Monastery of the Feast of the Deposition of the Robe (Ризоположенский Монастырь *Rizopolozhensky Monastyr*). Rising 236 feet high, the bell tower in the Monastery of the Feast of the Deposition of the Robe complex is the tallest building in Suzdal. It was built by local residents in 1819 to commemorate Russia's victory over Napoléon. ⊠ *1 ul. Lenina.*

Fodor'sChoice **Monastery of St. Yefim** (Спасо-Ефимский Монастырь *Spaso-Yefimsky*
★ *Monastyr*). The tall brick walls and 12 towers of this monastery, completed in 1350, have often been the cinematic stand-in for the Moscow Kremlin. The main church, the 16th-century **Church of the Transfiguration of the Savior,** is distinctive for its extremely pointed onion domes and its New Testament frescoes by Gury Nikitin and Sila Slavin, 17th-century painters from the city of Kostroma. A museum in the monastery is devoted to their lives and work. The church also houses the tomb containing the remains of Dmitri Pozharsky, one of the resistance leaders against the Polish invaders in the Time of Troubles. Adjoining the church is a single-dome nave church, which is actually the original Church of the Transfiguration; it was built in 1509, constructed over the grave of St. Yefim, the monastery's founder; its bells chime melodically every hour on the hour. The adjacent 16th-century **Church of the Assumption** (Uspenskaya Tserkov) is one of the earliest examples of tent-roof architecture in Russia.

In the middle of the 18th century, part of the monastery became a place for "deranged criminals," many of whom were actually political prisoners. The prison and hospital are along the north wall and closed to visitors. ⊠ *ul. Lenina* ☎ *4922/324263* ⊕ *www.vladmuseum.ru* ✉ *Monastery grounds 70R, with museums 350R* ☉ *Tues.–Sun. 10–6; closed last Thurs. of month.*

Museum of Wooden Architecture (Музей Деревянного Зодчества *Muzey Derevyannovo Zodchestva*). These wooden buildings have been moved here from throughout the region and restored. Of particular interest is the ornate **Church of the Transfiguration,** dating from 1756; it was moved here from the village of Kozlyatievo. The buildings can be viewed from the outside any time of year, but from the inside only from May to October. ⊠ *ul. Pushkarskaya* ☎ *49231/20784* ⊕ *www.vladmuseum.ru* ✉ *200R* ☉ *May–Oct., Thurs.–Tues. 9–7; Nov.–Apr., daily 9–4.*

Fodor'sChoice **Suzdal kremlin** (Суздальский Кремль). The dominant monument in the
★ kremlin, which may have first been built in the 10th century and sits on an earthen rampart with the Kamenka River flowing around all but the east side, is the mid-13th-century **Cathedral of the Nativity of the Virgin** (Sobor Rozhdestva Bogorodnitsy), topped by deep-blue cupolas festooned with golden stars.

Original limestone carvings can still be found on its corners and on its facade, and its exquisite bronze entry doors are the oldest such doors in Russia, from the 13th century. Inside, the brilliant and colorful frescoes dating from the 1230s and 1630s are without compare.

The long, white, L-shaped three-story building that the cathedral towers over is the **Archbishop's Chambers.** Behind its broad windows you'll find the superb "cross chamber" (named for its shape), which is a large hall without any supporting pillars—the first hall of its type in all Russia. The kremlin also holds museums of antique books and art. ✉ *ul. Kremlevskaya* ☎ *49231/20–937* ⊕ *www.vladmuseum.ru* 🎫 *250R* ☉ *Wed.–Sun. 10–6; closed last Fri. of month.*

WHERE TO EAT AND STAY

Suzdal has a wider range of hotels that other towns in the Golden Ring.

$$$$
EASTERN
EUROPEAN
Fodor'sChoice
★

× **Trapeznaya Kremlya (Трапезная Кремля).** Not to be confused with the restaurant of the same name in the Convent of the Intercession (which is now open only to pilgrims), this pleasant Russian-style eatery within the Suzdal kremlin is arguably the best restaurant in town. Even so, the quality of your meals may depend on the day of the week you visit; it's likely to be better on weekdays, when the crowds are thinner. If you don't want to order a full meal, consider trying some tea and *keks* (cakes) or *pirozhnoye* (pastries), all-day selections in Russia. ⑤ *Average main: 700R* ✉ *Archbishop's Chambers, Suzdal kremlin* ☎ *492/312–1763* ⊕ *www.trapeznaya.ru* ▭ *No credit cards.*

$$$$
HOTEL

🛏 **Sokol Hotel (Сокол).** Located in the historic part of town (a pleasant 10-minute walk to the kremlin), the rooms here are simple, but have great views of the nearby churches. **Pros:** hearty breakfast included. **Cons:** some staff may not speak English. ⑤ *Rooms from: 4200R* ✉ *2A pl. Torgovaya* ☎ *492/312–0987* ⊕ *www.hotel-sokol.ru* ⇆ *39 rooms* ⦿ *Breakfast.*

$
B&B/INN

🛏 **Tatyana's House (Татьянин Дом** *Tatyanin Dom***).** Tatyana, the owner, welcomes guests to her home in a white-brick two-story building, a five-minute walk from the Museum of Wooden Architecture and the kremlin. **Pros:** cozy; central location; warm welcome. **Cons:** guests share bathrooms. ⑤ *Rooms from: 2000R* ✉ *46B ul. Lenina* ☎ *905/057–7453* ⊕ *ann.05@mail.ru* ⇆ *5 rooms with shared bath* ▭ *No credit cards* ⦿ *Breakfast.*

$$$$
RESORT

🛏 **Tourcenter (Суздальский Туристический Центр** *Suzdalskiy Turistichesky Center***).** This large former Soviet complex includes the Hotel Suzdal and a separate motel-style section with two-story rooms with separate street entrances; some even have garages. **Pros:** nice pool; extremely good service in hotel. **Cons:** the huge complex can get crowded with tour groups on some weekends and public holidays. ⑤ *Rooms from: 3100R* ✉ *7 ul. Korovniki* ☎ *492/312–0908* ⊕ *www.suzdaltour.ru* ⇆ *430 rooms* ⦿ *No meals.*

EXPLORING
ST. PETERSBURG

Updated by
Irina Titova

Commissioned by Tsar Peter the Great (1672–1725) as "a window looking into Europe," St. Petersburg is a planned city whose elegance is reminiscent of Europe's most alluring capitals. Little wonder it's the darling of fashion photographers and travel essayists today: built on more than a hundred islands in the Neva Delta linked by canals and arched bridges, it was called the "Venice of the North" by Goethe, and its stately embankments are reminiscent of those in Paris. A city of golden spires and gilded domes, of pastel palaces and candlelit cathedrals, this city conceived by a visionary emperor is filled with pleasures and tantalizing treasures.

With its strict geometric lines and perfectly planned architecture, so unlike the Russian cities that came before it, St. Petersburg is almost too European to be Russian. And yet it's too Russian to be European. The city is a powerful combination of both East and West, springing from the will and passion of its founder to guide a resistant Russia into the greater fold of Europe, and consequently into the mainstream of history. That he accomplished, and more.

With a population of nearly 5 million, St. Petersburg is the fourth largest city in Europe after Paris, Moscow, and London. Without as many of the fashionably modern buildings that a business center like Moscow acquires, the city has managed to preserve much more of its history. Here, you can imagine yourself back in the time of the tsars and Dostoyevsky. Although it's a close race, it's safe to say that most visitors prefer St. Petersburg's culture, history, and beauty to Moscow's glamour and power.

That said, St. Petersburg has begun to play a more active role in politics in recent years, as if it were the country's northern capital. It may be because of the affection the city holds in the heart of the country's political elite, many of whom are natives of the city. New high-speed trains now travel between Moscow and St. Petersburg, a new international airport and metro stations have just opened, and some crumbling parts of the city are undergoing reconstruction. St. Petersburg revels in its historic beauty but also embraces the new.

TOP REASONS TO GO

Be awed by the Hermitage: In one of the world's premier historical and art collections, you can see works by Monet, Picasso, and Matisse, the opulence of tsarist Russia, Egyptian mummies, and Scythian gold.

Take in the view from St. Isaac's Cathedral: The third largest cathedral in the world, with a gilded dome covered in 100 kilograms (220 pounds) of pure gold, dominates St. Petersburg skyline and affords great views from its colonnade.

Bask in the White Nights: If you're planning to visit in May through July you'll be witness to this romantic and beautiful phenomenon: the city is aglow in daylight throughout the night.

Enjoy the Mariinsky Opera and Ballet Theatre: Ballet stars such as Anna Pavlova, Vaslav Nijinsky, Rudolf Nureyev, and Mikhail Baryshnikov once graced this theater's stage; now it turns out great modern ballet and opera performances.

Pay homage at Peter and Paul Fortress: St. Petersburg was founded at this citadel, built by Peter the Great. It never saw battle, and instead became a political prison for Peter's rebellious son, Alexei. It later held Dostoyevsky, Gorky, and Trotsky to name a few. The dynasty of Russian tsars is buried within the fortress.

ORIENTATION AND PLANNING

GETTING ORIENTED

It's easy to find your way around St. Petersburg's center. The major sights, such as the Hermitage Museum, Palace Square, Peter and Paul Fortress, St. Isaac's Cathedral, the Admiralty, and Strelka, are all mainly along or near the Neva River, and within sight of each other. The city's main avenue, Nevesky prospekt, leads directly to the river and to the Dvortsovyi, one of its major bridges. Most streets run straight, except in places where they curve along canals or small rivers. It's helpful to keep in mind that addresses on streets that begin at the Neva go higher as they go away from the river. The smaller the number, the closer the address is to the river and to most of the major sights.

One of the city's weak points for foreign tourists is the rarity of signs in general as well as signs in English (an exception is the metro, however, where stops are identified in English). The names of the streets are written in Cyrillic, so it's well worth spending some time familiarizing yourself with its letters before you arrive. In any case, don't forget your city map. Finally, although a lot fewer people in St. Petersburg speak English than in cities in Western Europe, there are still more and more of those who do. It's always worth asking a passerby for directions (the young or middle-aged are most likely to understand).

City Center. The City Center embraces Palace Square, the Hermitage, and the northern end of Nevsky prospekt, with the Fontanka River as its southeastern border. Most of St. Petersburg's major attractions are within this area.

Admiralteisky and Vasilievsky Island. To the west of the City Center is the smaller neighborhood of the Admiralteisky, surrounding the Admiralty building. Second in number of sights, including the Chamber of Art and the Rostral Columns, is Vasilievsky Island, opposite the Admiralty and set off from the City Center by the Little and Great Neva rivers.

The Petrograd Side. North of the City Center and the Neva River is the Petrograd Side, which holds Peter and Paul Fortress and the sights of Petrograd Island.

Vladimirskaya (Lower Nevsky Prospekt). On the mainland, Vladimirskaya is an area south of the Fontanka, taking in the lower part of Nevsky prospekt and bordered by the Obvodny Canal.

Liteiny/Smolny. This region lies to the northeast of Vladimirskaya and includes the Smolny cathedral. Still farther afield, the Kirov Islands (north of the city) and the Vyborg Side (in the northeast corner of the city) have a few sights.

PLANNING

WHEN TO GO

St. Petersburg's weather is the most pleasant from early May through August. May ushers in the White Nights, when night brings only a couple hours of twilight. It's an incredibly romantic time to visit, although the high hotel rates can also make it a costly time.

GETTING HERE AND AROUND

Although St. Petersburg is spread out over 650 square km (250 square miles), most of its historic sites are concentrated in the downtown section and are best explored on foot. These sites are often not well served by the extensive public transportation system, so be prepared to do a lot of walking. Bilingual city maps with bus routes marked on them are sold at bookstores and newsstands. *St. Petersburg In Your Pocket* (a monthly visitor's guide) prints valuable info about *marshrutki* (minibus) routes in every issue.

AIR TRAVEL

St. Petersburg is served by new facilities at Pulkovo Airport, about 17 km (11 miles) south of central St. Petersburg.

Pulkovo serves domestic and foreign airlines. St. Petersburg air carrier Rossiya, Russia's second-largest airline after Aeroflot, offers direct flights to and from 27 countries. Aeroflot only flies between St. Petersburg and Moscow, where passengers must take connecting flights to other destinations. Its tough competitor, Transaero, offers both domestic and international flights to such destinations as Egypt, Thailand, Japan, the Dominican Republic, and India.

Airport Information Pulkovo Airport ☎ *812/337–3444 information* ⊕ *www.pulkovoairport.ru.*

TRANSFERS

Municipal buses (in Russian, the word to look for is "avtobus") and minibuses ("marshrutka") run between the airport and the Moskovskaya metro stop on Moskovsky prospekt. The commercial bus ride costs about 35R. If you're traveling with a tour package, all transfers will have been arranged. If you're traveling alone, you're strongly advised to make advance arrangements with your hotel. There are plenty of taxis available, but you'd be ill-advised to pick up a cab on your own if you don't speak Russian. Foreign tourists, especially passengers arriving at train stations and airports, are prime targets for scams, so be skeptical about offers.

If you want to take a cab, look for a desk with a "TAXI Pulkovo" sign at the airport exit. A clerk there will tell you the price you need to pay for your destination in the city. He or she will also give you two pieces of paper, one for you and one for a taxi driver, on which the price is stated. The driver won't be able to charge you more than that. As you exit the airport, look for a person in a reflective yellow vest, who will direct you to a vacant taxi. A taxi ride to the City Center will cost 700R–1,000R and take about 40 minutes. When you return to the airport, a regular cab that you order by phone will cost you between 750R and 1,250R.

Taxi777 ☎ *812/777–1777.*

BOAT AND FERRY TRAVEL

In summer, you can enjoy a lovely one- or two-hour boat trip along the city's Neva River, seeing all the major sights from the water. Boats leave from piers in front of the Hermitage Museum, the Medny Vsadnik (Bronze Horseman) monument, and Peter and Paul Fortress. The pier at the Hermitage also docks hydrofoils that go to Peterhof, one of St. Petersburg's most attractive suburbs, which is famous for its fountains. A hydrofoil, which leaves every 15–30 minutes, takes you there in half an hour. You can take a hydrofoil to Kronshtadt, a suburb famous for its navel history, as well as Lomonosov. Both trips depart from Finland Station. Tours to the latter are rare, so expect a long wait in line. To take the ferry Princess Maria, which travels between St. Petersburg and Helsinki, make arrangements at the Sea Passenger Port Marine Facade terminal, which is on Vasilievsky Island. The trips takes a day to reach Helsinki and gives you a day to explore before returning. Inland trips to places such as Valaam Island, Kizhi Island, and Moscow depart from Neva River piers at 195 Obukhovskoi Oborony prospekt and 31 naberezhnaya Oktyabrskaya. One of many companies organizing these trips is Vodohod, with offices at the Obukhovskoi Oborony pier. Passenger cruise ships arrive at the new Port Marine Facade, where four terminals have facilities that include a tourist information center and currency exchange office.

Boat and Ferry Contacts Sea Passenger Port Marine Facade ✉ *1 ul. Bereg Nevskoi Gubi, Vasilievsky Island* ☎ *812/303–6740 information* ⊕ *www.portspb. ru* Ⓜ *Primorskaya.*

St. Petersburg History

"The most abstract and intentional city on earth"—to quote Fyodor Dostoyevsky—became the birthplace of Russian literature, the setting for his *Crime and Punishment* and Pushkin's *Eugene Onegin*. From here, Tchaikovsky, Rachmaninov, Prokofiev, and Rimsky-Korsakov went forth to conquer the world of the senses with unmistakably Russian music. It was in St. Petersburg that Petipa invented—and Pavlova, Nijinsky, and Ulanova perfected—the ballet. Later, at the start of the 20th century, Diaghilev enthralled the Western world with the performances of his Ballets Russes. Great architects were summoned to the city by 18th-century empresses to build palaces of marble, malachite, and gold. A century later it was here that Fabergé craftsmen created those priceless objects of beauty that have crowned the collections of royalty and billionaires ever since.

The grand, new capital of the budding Russian empire was built in 1703, its face to Europe, its back to reactionary Moscow, which had until this time been the country's capital. It was forcibly constructed, stone by stone, under the might and direction of Peter the Great, for whose patron saint the city is named. Building this city on such marshy ground was nearly an impossible achievement— so many men, forced into labor, died laying the foundations of this city that it was said to have been built on bones, not log posts. As one of 19th-century France's leading lights, the writer Madame de Staël, put it: "The founding of St. Petersburg is the greatest proof of that ardor of the Russian will that does not know anything is impossible." But if

Peter's exacting plans called for his capital to be the equal of Europe's great cities, they always took into account the city's unique attributes. Peter knew that his city's source of life was water, and whether building palace, fortress, or trading post, he never failed to make his creations serve it. Being almost at sea level (there's a constant threat of flooding), the city appears to rise straight up from its embracing waters. Half of the Neva River lies within the city's boundaries. As it flows into the Gulf of Finland, the river subdivides into the Great and Little Neva and the Great and Little Nevka. Together with numerous tributaries, they combine to form an intricate delta. Water weaves its way through the city's streets as well. Incorporating more than 100 islands and crisscrossed by more than 60 rivers and canals, St. Petersburg is often compared to that other great maritime city, Venice.

St. Petersburg's gleaming imperial palaces emphasize the city's regal bearing, even more so in the cold light of the Russian winter. The colorful facades of riverside estates glow gently throughout the long days of summer, contrasting with the dark blue of the Neva's waters. Between May and July, the city falls under the spell of the White Nights, or *Belye Nochy*. During this time following the summer solstice (from June to early July), night is banished, replaced by a twilight that usually lasts no more than 30 to 40 minutes. To honor this magical phenomenon, music festivals and gala events adorn the city's cultural calendar.

St. Petersburg isn't just about its fairy-tale setting, however, for its history is integrally bound up in Russia's dark side, too—a centuries-long procession of wars and revolutions. In the 19th century, the city witnessed the struggle against tsarist oppression. Here the early fires of revolution were kindled, first in 1825 by a small band of starry-eyed aristocratic officers—the Decembrists—and then by organized workers' movements in 1905. The full-scale revolutions of 1917 led to the demise of the Romanov dynasty, the foundation of the Soviet Union, and the end of St. Petersburg's role as the nation's capital, as Moscow reclaimed that title. But the worst ordeal by far came during World War II, when the city—then known as Leningrad—withstood a 900-day siege and blockade by Nazi forces. Nearly 1.1 million civilians were killed in air raids, as a result of indiscriminate shelling, or died of starvation and disease.

St. Petersburg has had its name changed three times during its brief history. With the outbreak of World War I, it became the more Russian-sounding Petrograd. After Lenin's death in 1924, it was renamed Leningrad in the Soviet leader's honor. Following the failed coup d'etat of August 1991, which hastened the demise of the Soviet Union and amounted to another Russian revolution, the city reverted to its original name—it was restored by popular vote, the first time the city's residents were given a choice in the matter. There were some who opposed the change, primarily because memories of the siege of Leningrad and World War II

had become an indelible part of the city's identity. But for all the controversy surrounding the name, residents have generally referred to the city simply—and affectionately— as Piter.

In fits and starts, the city goes about restoring its prerevolutionary splendor. It doesn't really seem to matter how glossy a face St. Petersburg presents to the world. Busloads, planeloads, boatloads of tourists come to feast their eyes on pastel palaces, glittering churches, and that great repository of artwork, the Hermitage.

8

Several firms operate bus routes between St. Petersburg and central Europe. A bus trip can be a reasonably comfortable way to connect with the Baltic states, Scandinavia, and Germany, although as with train travel in and out of the country, it entails a bit of waiting at the border for everyone to clear customs. The Gorodskoi Avtobusny Vokzal (City Bus Station), open from 6:30 am until 11:30 pm, sells tickets for international and domestic routes. It takes about 5–7 minutes to walk to the station from Obvodny Kanal metro station, but you might find it more convenient to go through a travel agent.

Lux Express runs coaches to Tallinn and Riga (and from these cities to destinations all over Europe). The Finnish company Finnord runs coaches between Helsinki and St. Petersburg via the border town of Vyborg. The service runs twice daily, leaving from Finnord's offices at 37 ulitsa Italyanskaya, and then stopping at half a dozen Finnish towns before reaching Helsinki.

When traveling by bus, tram, or trolley within the city, you must purchase a ticket from the conductor. A ticket valid for one ride costs 25R, regardless of the distance you intend to travel; if you change buses, you must pay another fare. You can also buy a smart card called "Podorozhnik;" costs vary, but some sample prices are 265R for a maximum of 10 rides over 7 days and 485R for 20 rides over 15 days. Buses, trams, and trolleys operate from 5:30 am to midnight, although service in the late evening hours and on Sunday tends to be unreliable.

Note that all public transportation vehicles tend to be extremely overcrowded during rush hours. It's very much the Russian philosophy that there's always room for one more passenger. Make sure you position yourself near the exits well before the point at which you want to disembark, or risk missing your stop. Buses tend to be new and reasonably comfortable. Trolleys and trams, on the other hand, sometimes give the impression that they're held together with Scotch tape and effort of will, and can be extremely drafty.

Bus, Tram, and Trolley Contacts The City Bus Station ⊠ *36 nab. Obvodnovo kanala, Vladimirskaya* ☎ *812/766–5777 information* ⊕ *www.avokzal.ru* Ⓜ *Obvodny Kanal.* **Finnord** ⊠ *37 ul. Italyanskaya* ☎ *812/314–8951 information* Ⓜ *Nevsky Prospekt.* **Lux Express** ☎ *812/441–3757* ⊕ *www.luxexpress.eu.*

You can reach St. Petersburg from Finland via the Helsinki–St. Petersburg Highway through the border town of Vyborg; the main street into and out of town for Finland is Kamennoostrovsky prospekt. To reach Moscow, take Moskovsky prospekt; at the Hotel Pulkovskaya roundabout, take shosse Mosvoskoye (M–10/E–95), slightly to the left of the road to the airport. Bear in mind that it may sometimes take more than an hour to clear customs and immigration at the border, and at busy times (e.g., Friday night and weekends) it may take much longer.

METRO TRAVEL

St. Petersburg's metro is straight-forward, efficient, and inexpensive, but its stops tend to be far apart. Stations are deep underground—the city's metro is the deepest in the world—necessitating long escalator rides. All central stations are infamous for theft and rank high in the city's list of pickpocket hot spots. Although the city police regularly trumpet successes and report arrests of more gangs, it doesn't seem to get any safer. The metro operates from 5:30 am to 12:30 am, but is best avoided during rush hours. You can pick up a metro map printed in English at most hotels.

FARES AND SCHEDULES

To use the metro, you must pur-

SAFETY TIP

St. Petersburg is a large city of 5 million inhabitants, and petty crime is a problem. As a foreigner, you're an even more likely target for pickpockets, especially in the metro and in and around Nevsky prospekt. Watch belongings carefully in such areas, and be careful when using your phone. Thieves have been known to grab mobiles and similar devices while their owners are distracted. Be attentive, leave valuables in the hotel safe if you can, and carry those you need to take with you in a money belt or at least in a front pocket, preferably zippered.

chase a token or a magnetic card (available at stations). The fare (28R) is the same regardless of distance. Alternatively, you may purchase a pass valid for unlimited travel for two weeks (1020R) and good for all modes of city public transportation. Or you can buy a smart card ("Podorozhnik") for 265R for a maximum of 10 rides over 7 days or 485R for 20 rides over 15 days. Other variations are available.

TAXI TRAVEL

Although taxis roam the city quite frequently, it's far easier—and certainly safer—to order a cab through your hotel (if you call on your own, keep in mind that getting an English-speaking operator is hit or miss). Most taxi companies will give you a price in advance. There's sometimes a delay, but usually the cab arrives within 15 to 20 minutes unless it's late at night or rush hour; the company will phone you back when the driver is nearby. If you order a cab this way, you pay the official state fare, which is quite reasonable by U.S. standards. No tip is expected beyond rounding up the amount on the meter.

If you flag down a taxi in the street, fares vary according to the driver's whim; you're expected to negotiate. Foreigners can often be charged much more than Russians, and oblivious tourists tend to be gouged. Make sure that you agree on a price before getting into the car, and try to have the correct money handy.

Taxi Contacts Petersburg Taxi (*Peterburgskoye Taxi*). ☎ *068.*
Taxi Million ☎ *812/700–0000.*

TRAIN TRAVEL

St. Petersburg has several train stations, the most important of which are Baltic station (Baltiysky Vokzal), for trains to the Baltic countries; Finland station (Finlandsky Vokzal), for trains to Finland, Karelia, and other points north; Moscow station (Moskovsky Vokzal), at ploshchad

Vosstania, off Nevsky prospekt, for trains to Moscow and points east; and Vitebsk station (Vitebsky Vokzal), for trains to the Ukraine and points south. All the major train stations have a connecting metro stop.

Train tickets may be purchased through the tourist bureau in your hotel or at the Central Railway Agency Office (Tsentralnoye Zheleznodorozhnoye Agenstvo) off Nevsky prospekt, adjacent to the Kazan Cathedral. The Central Airline Ticket Agency on Nevsky has two train-ticket desks and is a far quieter option. It's possible to buy tickets at the stations themselves, but this is best attempted only by the brave or bilingual. You can also buy electronic tickets online.

FARES AND SCHEDULES

Several trains run daily between Moscow and St. Petersburg, including the *Krasnaya Strela* (Red Arrow), a night train that departs from one end at 11:55 pm and arrives at the other at 8:25 am the next day. Its Empire-style rival, *Nikolayevsky Express*, departs the city at 11:24 am and gets to Moscow at 7:10 pm. Designed to resemble a typical early-20th-century train and named after Russia's last tsar, Nicholas II, this romantic train has staff dressed in turn-of-the-20th-century costumes, oak settings in its restaurant, and brass details in compartments. The most popular trains between St. Petersburg and Moscow are the high-speed Sapsan trains. At least five trips are scheduled each day, traveling the 800 km (500 miles) between the two cities in 3½ to 4¼ hours. The Sapsans let you leave St. Peterburg as early as 6:45 am and arrive in Moscow by 10:30 am, or leave Moscow at 7:45 pm and arrive in St. Petersburg at 11:30 pm. The trains are modern, with amenities that include TV, food service, and the ability to order a taxi ahead of time. Check ⊕ *www.trainsrussia.com* for availability, pricing, and booking for all trains between St. Petersburg and Moscow. Another good website is ⊕ *www.rzd.ru*, although it's easier to use if you know some Russian. There's also a train that travels twice daily to and from Helsinki; the trip, which leaves from Finland Station, takes 3½ hours.

Train Contacts Central Airline Ticket Agency ⊠ *16 ul. Malaya Morskaya, City Center* ☎ *812/571–5669 information, booking* ⊕ *www.cavs.ru* Ⓜ *Admiralteiskaya.* **Central Railway Booking Offices** (*Tsentralnye zheleznodorozhnye kassy*). The office has three information points that can point you in the direction of the correct desks. ⊠ *24 Kanal Griboyedova, City Center* ☉ *Mon.–Sat 8–8, Sun. 8–4* Ⓜ *Nevsky Prospekt.* **Train information** ☎ *812/768–3344* ⊕ *www.trainsrussia. com or www.rzd.ru.*

TOUR OPTIONS

TRAVEL AGENCIES

In addition to the scores of private agencies that operate in the city, every major hotel has a tourist bureau that can help you book individual and group tours, make restaurant reservations, or purchase theater tickets. Even if you're not a hotel guest, you're usually welcome to use these facilities, provided you're willing to pay the hefty fees for their services.

Tour Contacts Mir Travel Agency ⊠ *1½ ul. Marata, Liteiny/Smolny* ☎ *812/325–7122* ⊕ *mir-travel.com* Ⓜ *Mayakovskaya.* **Reisebuero-Welt** ⊠ *Northern Capital business center, 3 nab. Reki Moyki, 6th fl., City Center* ☎ *812/449–4564* ⊕ *www.reisebuero-welt.com* Ⓜ *Nevsky Prospekt.*

BOAT TOURS

A float down the Neva or through the city's twisting canals—*Exkursii na katere po rekam i kanalam*—is always a pleasant way to spend a summer afternoon or a White Night. For trips through the canals, take one of the boats at the pier near Anichkov most on Nevsky prospekt. Boats cruising the Neva and the canals leave from the piers outside the State Hermitage Museum; outside the Admiralty Building (2 naberezhnaya Admiralteiskaya) at the Dvortsovsy most; from the corner of naberezhnaya Reki Fontanki and Nevsky prospekt (27 naberezhnaya Reki Fontanki), and a number of other spots. Boat trips have departures from the early morning to the late afternoon from mid-May through mid-September. In warmer months, typically May through October, you can find many boats offering such trips along the Neva, and travel agents can help with booking.

> ### WORD OF MOUTH
>
> "We were very glad we hired a private tour guide. We could have done it on our own, but she saved us a lot of time and provided excellent commentary in English (she, too, spoke better English than ours!) everywhere we went…. We communicated often prior to our trip, and she was invaluable in helping us plan our time."
>
> —Djkbooks

Boat Tour Contacts Astra Marine ⊠ *Central Pier, 2 nab. Admiralteyskaya, Admiralteisky* ☎ *812/647–0017* ⊕ *www.boattrip.ru.* **Vodohod** ⊠ *209 Obukhovskoy Oborony pr., South of the city center* ☎ *812/335–1778* ⊕ *www.vodohod.spb.ru.*

PRIVATE TOUR GUIDES

There are many private tour guides who can provide detailed tours in English at the many sights within and outside of St. Petersburg. They can be very helpful, especially in places like the Hermitage. Many of them are highly educated in history and art, and they must also go through a rigorous training process before becoming licensed. Rates begin at about $20 an hour. *Below is a sampling of a few trusted names.*

Private Tour Contacts Ksenia Belous ☎ *905/229–1907* ✎ *bel-ksenia@yandex.ru.* **Natalia Velikaya** ☎ *905/277–5394* ✎ *natour@mail.ru.*

WALKING TOURS

If you prefer to plunge into city life instead of observing it from the window of your tour bus, the best bet is to take an excursion (from 650R) with one of the city's best-known walking tour companies, Peter's Walking Tours. Founded by inveterate local backpacker Peter Kozyrev, the company turns, walks, and pub crawls through memorable experiences that interweave history, current affairs, mystery, and gossip.

Walking Tour Contacts Peter's Walking Tours ☎ *812/943–1229 information, booking* ⊕ *www.peterswalk.com.*

VISITOR INFORMATION

The staff members of the City Tourist Information Center (Gorodskoi Turistichesky Tsentr Informatsii ot Soveta po Turismu) are generally friendly, although they have a tendency to thrust maps and booklets at you rather than offering advice. The center has a database on cultural

GREAT ITINERARIES

IF YOU HAVE 3 DAYS

If you have only three days, begin your visit of the city on Vasilievsky Island and the Left Bank. Most of the city's historic sites are here, including the Rostral Columns, the Admiralty (Admiralteistvo), and the elegant St. Isaac's Cathedral. After lunch, dedicate some time to the State Museum of Russian Art, one of the country's most important art galleries. On your second day, rise early to tackle the gargantuan Hermitage, one of the world's richest repositories of art. Don't try to see it all in one visit; instead, cross the river to the Petrograd Side and have lunch by the Peter and Paul Fortress. After lunch, spend the afternoon touring the Peter and Paul Fortress. On your third day, consider an excursion to Pushkin (formerly Tsarskoye Selo), south of St. Petersburg, once the summer residence of the Imperial family and a popular summer resort for the Russian aristocracy. The main attraction here is the Catherine Palace, with its magnificent treasures, including the famed Amber Room. If you have the energy, take in a performance at the Mariinsky Theatre.

IF YOU HAVE 5 DAYS

Follow the three-day itinerary described above. Devote your fourth day to St. Petersburg's inner streets, squares, and gardens. Begin with the grandeur of ploshchad Iskusstv, or Square of the Arts. Here you can visit the State Museum of Russian Art before moving on to the colorful Church of the Savior on Spilled Blood. Finish your walk at the Summer Garden with its famous railing designed by Yuri Felten in 1779. After lunch, visit the Kazan Cathedral. On the fifth day, if it's summer season, head west of St. Petersburg to Peterhof (*Petrodvorets*), accessible by hydrofoil. The fountains, lush parks, and the magnificent Great Palace are at their best in the summer.

and sports events, hotels, major tourist attractions, and so on. The center also runs information booths in the most-visited spots of the city, including Palace Square, St. Isaac's Square, Pulkovo Airport, in front of Gostinyi Dvor metro station, and at Moskovsky railway station. At these booths, which have a big letter "I" on top, operators speak English, German, French, and Spanish. The booths are open daily 10–7. On the center's tourist help line, staffed daily 9–11, English-speaking operators can help with typical tourist questions, book hotels, get you a table in a restaurant, or even order flowers upon your request. They can also call police or an ambulance and help translate in case of emergency. The center also runs the Angels Service (Sluzhba Angelov), in which young Russian students help visitors at the Gostinyi Dvor metro station, the Moskovsky railway station, and other busy locations. The "angels" are dressed in uniforms that include a red jacket, a white baseball cap with letter "I" on it, and blue bags. In summer they work 10–10 and in winter noon–6.

Visitor Information City Tourist Information Center ⊠ *52 ul. Sadovaya, bldg. 14, City Center* ☎ *812/310–2831 information center, 812/300–3333 tourist help line* ⊕ *eng.ispb.info* ⊗ *Weekdays 10–7, Sat. noon–6* Ⓜ *Sennaya Ploshchad.*

EXPLORING ST. PETERSBURG

The city's focal point is the Admiralteistvo, or Admiralty, a spire-top golden-yellow building; a stone's throw away is the Winter Palace, the city's most visited attraction (it houses the Hermitage). Three major avenues radiate outward from the Admiralty: Nevsky prospekt (St. Petersburg's main shopping street), ulitsa Gorokhovaya, and Voznesensky prospekt. Most visitors begin at Palace Square, site of the fabled Hermitage. The square housed not only the center of power—the tsar's residence and the great offices of state—but also the splendid art collections of the imperial family. In the twilight of the tsar's empire, it was here that troops were ordered to disperse a workers' demonstration on Bloody Sunday in 1905—a decision that may have made the Revolution of 1917 inevitable.

> **WORD OF MOUTH**
>
> "I was in St. Petersburg without a guide and saw the sights with relative ease. The only place I regretted not having a guide was during the visit to The Hermitage, and this is why: it was the summer, crowded beyond belief, and the museum is ENORMOUS. Even if you are going in December, take a guided visit at a minimum to get the highlights, and then go back on your own. BTW, I never felt unsafe."
>
> —Viajero2

Wherever you go exploring in the city, remember that an umbrella can come in handy. In winter be prepared for rather cold days that alternate with warmer temperatures, often resulting in the famous Russian snowfalls.

CITY CENTER ДВОРЦОВАЯ ПЛОЩАДЬ И ЭРМИТАЖ

The best place to get acquainted with St. Petersburg is the elegant ploshchad Dvortsovaya, or Palace Square. Its scale alone can hardly fail to impress—the square's great Winter Palace was constructed to clearly out-Versailles Versailles—and within the palace is the best reason to come to St. Petersburg: the Hermitage. Renowned as one of the world's leading art museums, it also served as a residence of the Russian Imperial family, and provides a setting of unparalleled opulence for its dazzling collections, which include some of the greatest old master paintings in the world. As a relief from all this impressive glitz and grandeur and tucked away in the shadows of the great Imperial complex is the moving apartment museum of Alexander Pushkin, that most Russian of writers, set in a neighborhood that still conjures up early-19th-century Russia.

Some of St. Petersburg's prettiest inner streets, squares, and gardens start at ploshchad Iskusstv (Square of the Arts). Along the route to the Field of Mars are several squares and buildings of historic interest: it was in this part of the city that several extremely important events in Russian history took place, including the murder of tsars Paul I, who was assassinated in the Engineer's Castle by nobles opposed to his rule, and Alexander II, killed when a handmade bomb was lobbed at him by revolutionary terrorists as he was riding in a carriage along Kanal Griboyedova.

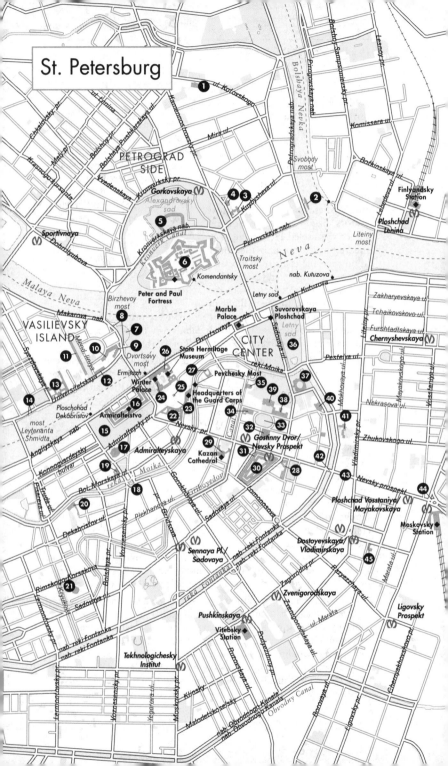

St. Petersburg

PETROGRAD SIDE

Gorkovskaya Ⓥ

Alexandrovsky sad

Sportivnaya Ⓥ

Finlyandsky Station

Ploshchad Lenina

Svobody most

Komissara ul.

Liteiny most

Neva

nab. Kutuzova

Troitsky most

Letny sad

Komendantsky

Peter and Paul Fortress

Birzhevoy most

Makarova nab.

VASILIEVSKY ISLAND

Mend. linia

Dvortsovy most

Ermitazh

Marble Palace

State Hermitage Museum

Winter Palace

CITY CENTER

Suvorovskaya Ploshchad

Letny sad

Chernyshevskaya Ⓥ

Zakharyevskaya ul.

Tchaikovskovo ul.

Furshtadtskaya ul.

Pestelya ul.

reki Moika

Peychesky Most

Ploschad Dekábristov

most Leytenanta Shmidta

Angliysky nab.

Admiralteistvo

Admiralteyskaya Ⓥ

Headquarters of the Guard Corps

Kazan Cathedral

Bol. Morskaya ul.

reki Moika

Konnogvardeysky bulvar

Plekhanova ul.

Gorokhovaya ul.

Sadovaya ul.

Sennaya Pl. / Sadovaya Ⓥ

Gostinny Dvor / Nevsky Prospekt

Nevsky pr.

Mokhovaya ul.

Nekrasova ul.

Zhukovskogo ul.

Nevsky prospekt

Ploshchad Vosstaniya Mayakovskaya Ⓥ

Moskovsky Station

Dostoyevskaya / Vladimirskaya Ⓥ

Ligovsky Prospekt Ⓥ

Zvenigorodskaya Ⓥ

Rimskovo-Korsakova

Sadovaya ul.

nab. reki Fontanka

reka Fontanka

nab. reki Fontanka

Zagorodny pr.

ul. Marata

Pushkinskaya Ⓥ

Vitebsky Station

Tekhnologichesky Institut

Klinsky pr.

Moskovshosse

nab. Obvodnogo Kanala

nab. Obvodnogo Kanala

Obvodny Canal

Bolshaya Nevka

Malaya Neva

Kronverksky pr.

Kronverksky Canal

Kronverkskaya nab.

Petrovskaya nab.

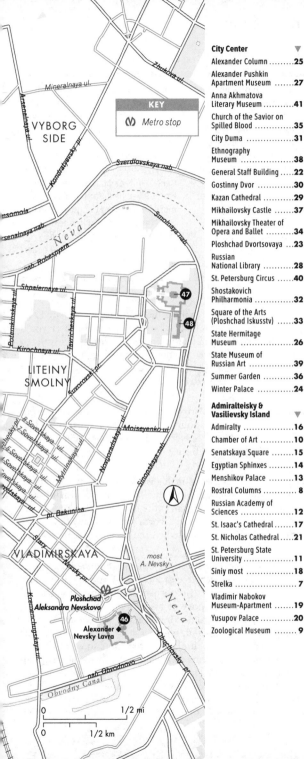

Mineralnaya ul.

KEY

Ⓜ Metro stop

VYBORG SIDE

Sverdlovskaya nab.

Neva

Shpalernaya ul.

Kirochnaya ul.

LITEINY SMOLNY

Moiseyenko ul.

pr. Bakunina

VLADIMIRSKAYA

most A. Nevsky

Ploshchad Aleksandra Nevskovo

Alexander Nevsky Lavra ◆

Neva

Obvodny Canal

0   1/2 mi

0   1/2 km

A Walk Through the Historic District

Begin at **ploshchad Dvortsovaya** (Palace Square). Extending the length of the western side of the square, with its back to the river, is the **Winter Palace,** which houses the legendary **State Hermitage Museum.** In the center of the square is the **Alexander Column,** commemorating the Russian victory over Napoléon in 1812. Dominating the eastern side of the square is the **General Staff Building,** formerly the army's general staff headquarters and now part of the Hermitage.

Next to it is the **Headquarters of the Guard Corps;** leave by its right-hand side and cross the Pevchesky most, or Singing Bridge, to enter one of the most charming parts of the city, enchantingly threaded by the Zimnaya Kanavka, or the Little Winter Canal. On the opposite side of the Moika River, head for the moving museum honoring the great Pushkin, the **Alexander Pushkin Apartment Museum,** a short walk from the corner of Nevsky prospekt and naberezhnaya Moiki.

GETTING HERE AND AROUND

You can get close to the area by taking the metro to the Nevsky Prospekt station and exiting at the Kanal Griboyedova end. However, you'll still have to walk for 10–15 minutes along noisy Nevsky prospekt to reach the quiet of Palace Square. (It's not worth taking the bus for this distance, though—just walk.) Once you've reached the area, you'll find that the sites are all quite close to each other.

TIMING

Strolling through ploshchad Dvortsovaya and taking in the sights from the outside may only take an hour or so, but it's a great introduction to St. Petersburg. The entire Hermitage can't be seen in one day; you'll want to devote anywhere from a morning to two days to wander through it.

Touring the Square of the Arts section might take between two and three hours, unless you want to linger at the State Museum of Russian Art, in which case you might want to plan an entire day here. Outdoor attractions, such as the Summer Garden, are worth visiting at any time of the year. Note that the Neva is very close here, so it's windy year-round.

TOP ATTRACTIONS

Alexander Column (Александровская Колонна *Aleksandrovskaya Kolonna*). The 156-foot-tall centerpiece of Ploschad Dvortsovaya (Palace Square) is a memorial to Russia's victory over Napoléon, commissioned in 1830 by Nicholas I in memory of his brother, Tsar Alexander I, and designed by Auguste Ricard de Montferrand. The column was cut from a single piece of granite and, together with its pedestal, weighs more than 650 tons. It stands in place by the sheer force of its own weight; there are no attachments fixing the column to the pedestal. When the memorial was erected in 1832, the entire operation took only an hour and 45 minutes, but 2,000 soldiers and 400 workmen were required, along with an elaborate system of pulleys and ropes. Crowning the column is an angel (symbolizing peace in Europe) crushing a snake, an allegorical depiction of Russia's defeat of Napoléon. ✉ *Pl. Dvortsovaya, City Center* Ⓜ *Nevsky Prospekt.*

Church of the Savior on Spilled Blood (Храм Спаса на Крови *Khram Spasa na Krovi*). The highly ornate, old-Russian style of this colorful church seems more Moscow than St. Petersburg, where the architecture is generally more subdued and subtle; indeed, the architect, Alfred Parland, was consciously aiming to copy Moscow's St. Basil's. The drama of the circumstances leading to the church's inception more

than matches the frenzy of its design, however. It was commissioned by Alexander III to memorialize the death of his father, Alexander II, who was killed on the site in 1881 by a terrorist's bomb. The height of the cathedral, 81 meters, symbolizes the year of Alexander II's death.

The church opened in 1907 but was closed by Stalin in the 1930s. It suffered damage over time, especially throughout World War II, but underwent meticulous reconstruction for decades and finally reopened at the end of the 20th century. The interior is as extravagant as the exterior, with glittering stretches of mosaic from floor to ceiling (70,000 square feet in total). Stone carvings and gold leaf adorn the walls, the floors are made of pink Italian marble, and the remarkable altar is constructed entirely of semiprecious gems and supported by four jasper columns. Blinded by all this splendor, you could easily overlook the painted scenes of martyrdom, including one that draws a parallel between the tsar's death and the crucifixion of Christ. Across the road there's an exhibit that takes a compelling look at the life of Alexander II. ✉ *2a Kanal Griboyedova, City Center* ☎ *812/315–1636* 🎟 *250R* 🕓 *Thurs.–Tues. 11–7* Ⓜ *Nevsky Prospekt.*

Ploshchad Dvortsovaya (Дворцовая Площадь *Palace Square*). One of the world's most magnificent plazas is a stunning ensemble of buildings and open space, a combination of several seemingly incongruous architectural styles in perfect harmony. It's where the city's imperial past has been preserved in all its glorious splendor, but it also resonates with the history of the revolution that followed. Here, the fate of the last Russian tsar was effectively sealed, on Bloody Sunday in 1905, when palace troops opened fire on peaceful demonstrators, killing scores of women and children. It was across Palace Square in October 1917 that Bolshevik revolutionaries stormed the Winter Palace and overthrew Kerensky's Provisional Government, an event that led to the birth of the Soviet Union. Almost 75 years later, during tense days, huge crowds rallied on Palace Square in support of perestroika and democracy. Today, the beautiful square is a bustling hub of tourist and market activity. ✉ *City Center* Ⓜ *Nevsky Prospekt.*

8

FAMILY **Ethnography Museum** (Этнографический Музей *Etnograficheskii Muzey*). Costumes, crafts, and other artifacts provide a look at the various ethnic groups of the former Soviet Union. If you're traveling with kids, the best time for a visit may be Sunday afternoons, when they can attend workshops and learn how to paint on wood and clay, model something out of birch bark, or make folk dolls. ✉ *1 ul. Inzhenernaya, bldg. 4, City Center* ☎ *812/570–5421* ⊕ *www.ethnomuseum.ru* 💴 *350R* ⊙ *Tues.– Sun. 11–6; closed last Fri. of month* Ⓜ *Nevsky Prospekt.*

Gostiny Dvor (Гостиный Двор). Taking up an entire city block, this is St. Petersburg's answer to the GUM department store in Moscow.

> **HEROIC MUSIC**
>
> During Hitler's siege of Leningrad, the conductor Karl Eliasberg managed to put an orchestra together for the premiere of Dmitri Shostakovich's Seventh Symphony ("Leningrad"), despite some of the musicians being too weak from starvation to hold their instruments. The performance went on as scheduled at the Philharmonic on August 9, 1942—the day that Hitler had predicted would mark the success of the German siege. Batteries of loudspeakers were arranged outside the hall and at the edge of the city so it could be heard across German lines.

Initially constructed by Rastrelli in 1757, it was not completed until 1785, by Vallin de la Mothe, who was responsible for the facade with its two tiers of arches. At the time the structure was erected, traveling merchants were routinely put up in guesthouses (called *gostiny dvor*), which, like this one, doubled as places for doing business. This arcade was completely rebuilt in the 19th century, by which time it housed some 200 general-purpose shops that were far less elegant than those in other parts of the Nevsky. It remained a functional bazaar until alterations in the 1950s and 1960s connected most of its separate shops into St. Petersburg's largest department store. Today Gostiny Dvor houses fashionable boutiques, and you can also find currency-exchange kiosks and ATMs here. On its ground floor there is a souvenir shop where you can buy all kinds of Russian traditional souvenirs such as matryoshka dolls, khokhloma painted bowls, spoons and cutting boards, as well as magnets with St. Petersburg sights and many other things to bring home as gifts. Virtually across the street, at 48 Nevsky prospekt, is the city's other major "department store," also an arcade, called **Passazh**, built in 1848. ✉ *35 Nevsky pr., City Center* ☎ *812/710–5408 information desk* ⊙ *Daily 10–10* Ⓜ *Gostiny Dvor.*

Mikhailovsky (Inzhenernyi) Castle (Инженерный Замок *Mikhailovsky Zamok*). This orange-hued building belonged to one of Russia's strangest and most pitiful leaders. Paul I grew up in the shadow of his powerful mother, Catherine the Great, whom he despised; no doubt correctly, he held her responsible for his father's death. By the time Paul became tsar, he lived in terror that he, too, would be murdered. He claimed that shortly after ascending the throne, he was visited in a dream by the Archangel Michael, who instructed him to build a church on the site of his birthplace—hence the name of this landmark: Mikhailovsky Castle. Paul built not just a church but a castle, which he tried to make into an

The Fate of Rembrandt's Danaë

One of the most celebrated of Rembrandt's works, and among the most beautiful examples of European painting, the *Danaë* was almost irreparably damaged in 1985 when a mentally deranged man twice knifed and then splashed sulfuric acid on the painting in front of a stunned tour group. Acquired by Catherine the Great in 1772, it was one of the jewels of her collection. After the shocking act of vandalism, the canvas, completed by the Dutch master in 1636, was a mess of brown spots and splashes. The process of restoration began the same day, when after consulting chemists, the Hermitage restorers washed the canvas with water to stop the chemical reaction. It then took 12 years to reconstruct the picture, which was finally placed on view again in 1997. It's now covered with armored glass to prevent any further damage. The painting isn't 100 percent Rembrandt anymore, but the original spirit of the work remains intact.

impenetrable fortress. Out of spite toward his mother, he took stones and other materials from castles that she had built. The Fontanka and Moika rivers cut off access from the north and east; and for protection everywhere else, he installed secret passages, moats with drawbridges, and earthen ramparts. All of Paul's intricate planning, however, came to nothing. On March 24, 1801, a month after he began living there, he was suffocated with a pillow in his bed. Historians speculate that his son Alexander I knew of the murder plot and may even have participated. After Paul's death, the castle stood empty for 20 years, then was turned over to the Military Engineering Academy. One of the school's pupils was Fyodor Dostoyevsky, who may have absorbed something of the castle while he studied here: as a novelist he was preoccupied with themes of murder and greed. The castle is now part of the State Museum of Russian Art; it houses temporary exhibits from the museum, plus an exhibit on the history of the castle. ⊠ *2 ul. Sadovaya, City Center* ☎ *812/570–5112, 812/570–5173 tours* ⊕ *www.rusmuseum.ru* ⊠ *300R* ⊙ *Mon. 10–4, Wed. 1–8, Thurs.–Sun. 10–5* Ⓜ *Nevsky Prospekt.*

Kazan Cathedral (Казанский Собор *Kazansky Sobor*). After a visit to Rome, Tsar Paul I (1754–1801) commissioned this magnificent cathedral, wishing to copy—and perhaps present the Orthodox rival to—that city's St. Peter's. You approach the huge cathedral, erected between 1801 and 1811 from a design by Andrei Voronikhin, through a monumental, semicircular colonnade. Inside and out, the church abounds with sculpture and decoration, including statues of such sanctified Russian heroes as Grand Prince Vladimir (who advanced the Christianization of Russia) and Alexander Nevsky. The enormous bronze front doors are exact copies of Ghiberti's *Gates of Paradise* in Florence's Baptistery.

The cathedral was closed after the revolution and turned into the Museum of Religion and Atheism, with an emphasis on the latter. Religion was presented from the Marxist point of view, essentially as an archaeological artifact. It's once again a place of worship.

At each end of the square in front of the cathedral are statues of military leaders Mikhail Barclay de Tolly and Mikhail Kutuzov. They reflect the value placed in the 19th century on the cathedral as a place of military tribute, especially following Napóléon's invasion in 1812. Kutuzov is buried in the cathedral's northern chapel, where he's supposed to have prayed before taking command of the Russian forces. ⊠ *2 pl. Kazanskaya, City Center* ☎ *812/314–4663 information desk* ☉ *Daily 8:30–8; services weekdays at 10 am and 6 pm, weekends at 7 am, 10 am, and 6 pm* Ⓜ *Nevsky Prospekt.*

Nevsky prospekt (Невский проспект). St. Petersburg's most famous street, the Russian Champs-Élysées, was laid out in 1710, beginning and ending at different bends of the Neva River and just short of 5 km (3 miles) long. The street starts at the foot of the Admiralty building and runs in a perfectly straight line to the Moscow station, where it curves slightly before ending a short distance farther at the Alexander Nevsky Lavra. Because St. Petersburg was once part of the larger lands of Novgorod, the road linking the city to the principality was known as Great Novgorod Road; it was an important route for trade and transportation. By the time Peter the Great built the first Admiralty, however, another major road was needed to connect the Admiralty directly to the shipping hub. Originally this new street was called the Great Perspective Road; later it was called the Nevskaya Perspektiva, and finally Nevsky prospekt.

On the last few blocks of Nevsky prospekt as you head toward the Neva are some buildings of historic importance. No. 18, on the right-hand side, was once a private dwelling before becoming a café called Wulf and Beranger; it's now the **Literary Café.** It was reportedly here that Pushkin ate his last meal before setting off for his fatal duel. **Chicherin's House,** at No. 15, was one of Empress Elizabeth's palaces before it became the Nobles' Assembly and, in 1919, the House of Arts. Farther down, at No. 14, is one of the rare buildings on Nevsky prospekt built *after* the Bolshevik Revolution. The blue sign on the facade dates from World War II and the siege of Leningrad; it warns pedestrians that during air raids the other side of the street is safer. The city was once covered with similar warnings; this one was left in place as a memorial, and on Victory Day (May 9 in Russia) survivors of the siege lay flowers here. ⊠ *City Center* Ⓜ *Nevsky Prospekt, Gostinny Dvor, Mayakovskaya, Ploschad Vosstaniya, or Ploshchad Alexandra Nevskovo.*

Russian National Library (Российская Национальная Библиотека *Rossiiskaya Natsionalnaya Biblioteka*). Opened in 1814, Russia's first public library is still known fondly as the "Publichka." It holds more than 20 million books and claims to have a copy of every book ever printed in Russia. Among the treasures are Voltaire's library and the only copy of *Chasovnik* (1565), the second book printed in Russia. The main section, on the corner of Nevsky Prospekt and ulitsa Sadovaya, was designed by Yegor Sokolov and built between 1796 and 1801. Another wing, built between 1828 and 1832, was designed by Carlo Rossi as an integral part of Ploshchad Ostrovskovo. The facade is adorned with statues of philosophers and poets, including Homer and Virgil, and the Roman goddess of wisdom, Minerva. Using the library requires a passport, registration note (a note from a hotel, in the case of tourists), and two photos, which can be taken during the registration in the library. You may be able to get in for a quick look if you show your passport and ask nicely. ⊠ *18 ul. Sadovaya, City Center* ☎ *812/310–7137 information* ⊕ *www.nlr.ru* ☉ *Weekdays 9–9, weekends 11–7; closed last Tues. of month* Ⓜ *Gostiny Dvor, Nevsky Prospekt.*

Shostakovich Philharmonia (**Филармония имени Шостаковича**). What was once the Nobles' Club before the revolution is now home to the **St. Petersburg Philharmonic.** Its main concert hall, the Bolshoi Zal, with its impressive marble columns, has been the site of many celebrated performances, including the premiere (in 1893) of Tchaikovsky's Sixth (*Pathétique*) Symphony, with the composer conducting. (This was his final masterpiece; he died nine days later.) More recently, in 1942, when Leningrad was completely blockaded, Dmitri Shostakovich's Seventh (*Leningrad*) Symphony premiered here, an event broadcast in the same spirit of defiance against the Germans in which it was written. Later the concert hall was officially named for this composer. ⊠ *2 ul. Milkhailovskaya, City Center* ☎ *812/710–4257 kassa, 812/710–4290 information desk* Ⓜ *Nevsky Prospekt.*

Abrikosov. At this soothing place to take a break with a good view of Nevsky prospekt, you can enjoy coffee, ice cream, and scrumptious cakes, or a whole range of traditional Russian and European dishes. Out of the Russian menu try borscht (beetroot soup) with sour cream or pickled herring and mushrooms. In summer Abrikosov offers an open terrace. ⊠ *40 Nevsky pr., City Center* ☎ *812/312–2457* Ⓜ *Nevsky Prospekt.*

Zhyly-Byly. The name of this restaurant comes from the phrase used to open every Russian folktale, similar to "Once upon a time" in English. The clean, cool interior displays a smattering of folk-related objects and serves mainly excellent salads, as well as pastries and delicious and beautiful cakes. In summer the café is open around the clock. ⊠ *52 Nevsky pr., City Center* ☎ *812/314–6230* Ⓜ *Nevsky Prospekt.*

Fodor'sChoice
★ **State Hermitage Museum** (**Государственный Эрмитаж** *Gosudarstvenny Ermitazh Muzey*). Leonardo's *Benois Madonna,* Rembrandt's *Danaë,* Matisse's *The Dance*... one of the world's most famous museums is virtually wallpapered with celebrated paintings, part of the former private art collection of the tsars. In addition, the walls are works of art themselves, for parts of this collection are housed in the lavish Winter Palace, one of the most outstanding examples of Russian baroque magnificence. The museum takes its name from Catherine the Great (1729–96), who used the palace for her private apartments, intending them to be a place of retreat and seclusion. "Only the mice and I can admire all this," the empress once declared.

Between 1764 and 1775, the empress undertook, in competition with rulers whose storehouses of art greatly surpassed Russia's, to acquire some of the world's finest works of art. Sometimes acquiring entire private collections outright, she quickly filled her gallery with masterpieces from all over the world. This original gallery section of the Hermitage, completed in 1770 by Vallin de la Mothe, is now known as the Maly (Little) Hermitage. It's attached to the Stary (Old) Hermitage, which was built in 1783 by Yuri Felten to house the overflow of art (it also contained conference chambers for the tsarina's ministers). Attached to the Hermitage by an arch straddling the Winter Canal is the **Hermitage Theater,** built between 1783 and 1787 by the Italian architect Giacomo Quarenghi. Yet another addition, the New Hermitage, was built between 1839 and 1852 under Catherine's grandson, Nicholas I; it became Russia's first public museum, although admission was by royal invitation only until 1866. Its facade is particularly striking, with 10 male figures cut from monolithic gray granite supporting the portico. Today's Hermitage is one of the world's richest repositories of art; it was continually enlarged with tsarist treasures and acquisitions, all later confiscated and nationalized, along with numerous private collections, by the Soviet government after the 1917 Bolshevik Revolution.

The entrance to the museum is through the main gates on Palace Square; during peak tourist season and at times of special exhibitions you may encounter long lines. Note that ticket-takers are strict about checking oversize bags and about foreigners trying to enter on Russian-rate tickets.Those experienced employees can easily tell foreigners even if you try to keep silent.

With more than 400 exhibit halls and gilded salons, it's impossible to see everything here in a single day. Since you probably only have a few hours, be sure to take in the major attractions, which include Egyptian mummies and Scythian gold; the splendid halls of Russian tsars; the Peacock Clock; the great paintings of Leonardo, Rembrandt, Van Dyck, and Velázquez; and the outstanding collection of Impressionists and Postimpressionists.

The museum's eight sections are not clearly marked, and the floor plans available are not very useful, though they are in English as well as Russian. To orient yourself before your trip, you can go on a virtual tour of the museum on the website. Don't be shy about asking the guards to point you in the right direction. There's also a helpful information desk in the main hall, before you go into the museum, where you can ask specific questions.

Ground Floor

There are three floors to wander through: the ground, first, and second. The ground floor covers prehistoric times, displaying discoveries made on former Soviet territory, including Scythian relics and artifacts; art from the Asian republics, the Caucasus, and their peoples; and Greek, Roman, and Egyptian art and antiquities. On the ground floor, head for the Hall of Ancient Egypt, the Pazyryk exhibition, and the Hall of the Big Vase. The first contains the remains of a mummified priest; the second, a mummified Scythian tsar and his horses as well as the most ancient carpet in the world; the third, a magnificent example of Russian stone-carving—the huge Kolyvan vase in the center of the hall. It's 2.57 meters (2.81 yards) high and weighs 19 tons.

Possibly the most prized section of the Hermitage—and definitely the most difficult to get into—is the ground floor's **Treasure Gallery,** also referred to as the Zolotaya Kladovaya (Golden Room). This spectacular collection of gold, silver, and royal jewels is well worth the hassle and additional extrance fee. The collection is divided into two sections. The first section, covering prehistoric times, includes Scythian gold and silver treasures of striking simplicity and refinement recovered from the Crimea, Ukraine, and Caucasus. The second section contains a dizzying display of precious stones, jewelry, and such extravagances as jewel-encrusted pill-boxes and miniature clocks, all from the 16th through the 20th centuries.

First Floor

Through the entrance hall you can reach the first-floor galleries by way of the Jordan Staircase, a dazzling 18th-century creation of marble, granite, and gold. One of the first rooms you pass through on the first floor is the Malachite Room, with its displays of personal items from the imperial family. In the White Dining Room the Bolsheviks seized power from the Provisional Government in 1917. Balls were staged in the Great Hall and in the smaller Concert Hall (which now also holds the silver coffin—but not the body—of the hero Alexander Nevsky). The Pavilion Hall on the first floor is known for the wondrous Peacock Clock. Every Wednesday at 7 pm you can usually see the clock's figures move and sound; the event attracts large crowds. The hall itself, with 28 crystal chandeliers, is impressive in its own right. The Knights' Room is also on this floor, displaying armor that includes a child-size version and one made for a horse. The first floor also has many rooms that have been left as they were when the imperial family lived in the Winter Palace.

A wealth of Russian and European art is also on this floor: Florentine, Venetian, and other Italian art through the 18th century, including Leonardo's *Benois Madonna* and *Madonna Litta* (Room 214), Michelangelo's *Crouching Boy* (Room 229), two Raphaels, eight Titians, and works by Tintoretto, Lippi, Caravaggio, and Canaletto. The Hermitage also houses a superb collection of Spanish art, including works by El Greco, Velázquez, Murillo, and Goya. Its spectacular presentation of Flemish and Dutch art contains roomfuls of Van Dycks, including portraits done in England when he was court painter to Charles I. Also here are more than 40 canvasses by Rubens (Room 247) and an equally impressive number of Rembrandts, including *Flora, Abraham's Sacrifice,* and *The Prodigal Son* (Room 254). His famous *Danaë,* which was mutilated by a knife- and acid-wielding lunatic in 1985, was put back on display in 1997. A smattering of excellent British paintings, extending also to the next floor, includes works by Joshua Reynolds, Thomas Gainsborough, and George Morland.

Reflecting the Francophilia of the empresses Elizabeth and Catherine, the museum is second only to the Louvre in its collection of French art. The scope is so extraordinary that the collection must be housed on both the first and second floors. Along with masterpieces by Lorrain, Watteau, and Poussin—including Poussin's *Tancrède et Herminie* (Room 279)—there are also early French art and handicrafts, including some celebrated tapestries.

Second Floor

On the second floor, you can start with the French art of the 19th century, where you'll find Delacroix, Ingres, Corot, and Courbet. You then come to a stunning collection of Impressionists and Postimpressionists, originally gathered mainly by two prerevolutionary industrialists and art collectors, Sergei Shchukin and Ivan Morozov. They include Monet's deeply affecting *A Lady in the Garden*, Degas's *Woman at Her Toilette* and *After the Bath*, and works by Sisley, Pissarro, and Renoir. Sculptures by Auguste Rodin and a host of pictures by Cézanne, Gauguin, and van Gogh are followed by Picasso and a lovely room of Matisse, including one of the amazing *Joys*. Somewhat later paintings—by the Fauvist André Derain and by Cubist Fernand Léger, for example—are also here. Rounding out this floor is the museum's collection of Asian and Middle and Near Eastern art, a small American collection, and two halls of medals and coins.

■TIP➡ The best deal is to buy a two-day combined-entrance ticket, which allows you to visit the State Hermitage Museum and three other museums: the original, wooden Winter Palace of Peter the Great, accessible through a tunnel from the museum (historians believe this tunnel is the site where Peter died); the General Staff Building; and Menshikov Palace.

■TIP➡ Tours in English (of several sections of the museum or just the Treasure Gallery) are available. Tours are normally given once or twice a day around noon, 1, or 2 pm, but make sure to call a day before to figure out the exact time. Tours tend to be rushed and you may want to return on your own. Consider hiring a private guide from outside the museum instead—their licensing requires a year of study and training and they'll take their time explaining the artwork to you. ⊠ *2 pl. Dvortsovaya, City Center* ☎ *812/710–9625 recorded information in Russian, 812/710–9079 information desk, 812/571–8446 tours* ⊕ *www.hermitagemuseum.org* 🎟 *400R, free 1st Thurs. of month; Treasure Gallery 300R; two-day combined entrance ticket, 780R* ☉ *Tues., Thurs.–Sun. 10:30–6; Wed. 10:30–9* Ⓜ *Nevsky Prospekt.*

Fodor'sChoice
★ **State Museum of Russian Art** (Государственный Русский Музей *Gosudarstvenny Russky Muzey*). In 1898 Nicholas II turned the stupendously majestic neoclassical **Mikhailovsky Palace** (Mikhailovsky Dvorets) into what has become one of the country's most important art galleries. He did so in tribute to his father, Alexander III, who had a special regard for Russian art and regretted, after seeing Moscow's Tretyakov Gallery, that St. Petersburg had nothing like it.

The Peacock Clock

The Peacock Clock (*Tchasy Pavlin*), one of the most delightful pieces on display at the State Hermitage Museum, is in the Pavilion Hall, on the first floor. The clock consists of a gilded peacock on a branch, a rooster, and an owl in a cage. Designed by the famous London jeweler and goldsmith James Cox and brought in pieces to St. Petersburg for Russian empress Catherine the Great in 1781, the clock is still in working order. Over the past decades it's been wound once a week (normally on Wednesday evenings at 7, but the time can be changed, occasionally) to activate the moving pieces—the peacock spreads its wings and turns in a circle, the rooster crows, and the owl opens and closes its eyes. Even without motion the clock is a must-see. If you have kids with you, ask them to count all the creatures on the clock. Hint: there are more than just the three birds; for instance, a dragonfly acts as the tiny second hand on the mushroom dial.

The collection at what's sometimes just called the Russian Museum is now four times greater than that at the Tretyakov Gallery, with scores of masterpieces on display. Outstanding icons include the 14th-century *Boris and Gleb* and the 15th-century *Angel Miracle of St. George*. Both 17th- and 18th-century paintings are also well represented, especially with portraiture. One of the most famous 18th-century works here is Ivan Nikitin's *The Field Hetman*. By far the most important works are from the 19th century—huge canvases by Repin, many fine portraits by Serov (his beautiful *Countess Orlova* and the equally beautiful, utterly different portrait of the dancer Ida Rubinstein), and Mikhail Vrubel's strange, disturbing *Demon Cast Down*. For many years much of this work was unknown in the West, and it's fascinating to see the stylistic parallels and the incorporation of outside influences into a Russian framework. Painters of the World of Art movement—Bakst, Benois, and Somov—are also here. There are several examples of 20th-century art, with works by Kandinsky and Kazimir Malevich. Natan Altman's striking portrait of the poet Anna Akhmatova is in Room 77. The museum usually has at least one excellent special exhibit in place, and there's a treasure gallery here as well (guided tours only; you need a special ticket that you can only get before noon). The Marble Palace, Engineer's Castle, and Stroganov Palace are all branches of the museum.

The square in front of the palace was originally named Mikhailovsky Ploshchad for Grand Duke Mikhail Pavlovich (1798–1849), the younger brother of Alexander I and Nicholas I and resident of the palace. The square's appearance is the work of Carlo Rossi, who designed the facade of each building encircling it as well as the Mikhailovsky Palace. Each structure, as well as the plaza itself, was made to complement Mikhail's residence on its north side. The palace, which was built between 1819 and 1825, comprises a principal house and two service wings. The central portico, with eight Corinthian columns, faces a large courtyard now enclosed by a fine art nouveau railing, a late (1903) addition. The statue of Alexander Pushkin in the center of the plaza was designed by Mikhail Anikushin and erected in 1957. ⊠ *2 ul. Inzhenernaya, bldg. 4, City Center* ☎ *812/595–4248 information* ⊕ *www.rusmuseum.ru* ⌑ *350R* ⊙ *Mon. 10–5, Thurs. 1–9, Wed., Fri. –Sun. 10–6; kassa closes 1 hr before closing* Ⓜ *Nevsky Prospekt.*

Summer Garden (**Летний Сад** *Letny Sad*). One of Peter the Great's passions was inspired by Versailles. When first laid out in 1704, the garden was given the regular, geometric style made famous by Louis XIV's gardener, Andre Le Nôtre, and decorated with statues and sculptures as well as with imported trees and plants. Grottoes, pavilions, ponds, fountains, and intricate walkways were placed throughout, and the grounds are bordered on all sides by rivers and canals. In 1777, floods did so much damage (entirely destroying the system of fountains) that the Imperial family stopped using the garden for entertaining, and the fountains were not restored. When the family decamped for environs farther afield, they left the Summer Garden for use by the upper classes. Today it's a popular park accessible to everyone. The graceful wrought-iron fence that marks the entrance to the garden was designed in 1779 by Yuri Felten; it's supported by pink granite pillars decorated with vases and urns.

Just inside this southeastern corner is Peter's original **Summer Palace,** Letny Dvorets. Designed by Domenico Trezzini and completed in 1714, the two-story building is quite simple, as most of Peter's dwellings were. The walls are of brick covered in stucco and painted primrose yellow. Open since 1934 as a museum, it has survived without major alteration. Currently the palace is closed for a long-needed restoration that is expected to last for several years. Two other attractive buildings nearby are the **Coffee House** (Kofeinyi Domik), built by Carlo Rossi in 1826, and the **Tea House** (Tchainyi Domik), built by L.I. Charlemagne in 1827. Neither of them serves the beverage they are named for: they're both used for expositions these days. As you walk through the park, take a look at some of its more than 80 statues. *Peace and Abundance,* sculpted in 1722 by Pietro Baratta, an allegorical depiction of Russia's victory in the war with Sweden, is one of the two original statues left in the garden after a recent renovation; the others are in Mikhailovsky Palace. The other original statue, just off the main alley, is of Ivan Krylov, a writer known as "Russia's La Fontaine." Peter Klodt, who also did the Anichkov Bridge horse statues, designed this sculpture, which was unveiled in 1855. Scenes from Krylov's fables, including his version of "The Fox and the Grapes," appear on the pedestal. ⊠ *2 nab. Kutozova, City Center* ⌑ *free* ⊙ *May 1–Sept. 30, Wed.–Mon. 10–10; Oct. 1–Mar. 31, Wed.–Mon. 10–7; closed last Mon. of month* Ⓜ *Chernyshevskaya or Nevsky Prospekt.*

Fodor's Choice ★ **Winter Palace** (**Зимний Дворец** *Zimny Dvorets*). With its 1,001 rooms swathed in malachite, jasper, agate, and gilded mirrors, the residence of Russia's rulers from Catherine the Great (1762) to Nicholas II (1917) is the grandest monument of Russian rococo, that eye-popping mix of the old-fashioned 17th-century baroque and the newfangled 18th-century neoclassical style. The palace is now part of the State Hermitage Museum, and the only parts you may tour are the relatively few rooms open to museumgoers. Among these are three of the most celebrated rooms in the palace: the Gallery of the 1812 War, where portraits of Russian commanders who served against Napoléon are on display; the Great Throne Room, richly decorated in marble and bronze; and the Malachite Room, designed by the architect Alexander Bryullov and decorated with columns and pilasters of malachite.

The exterior—adorned with rows of columns and outfitted with 2,000 heavily decorated windows—is particularly successful and pleasing; note the way the enormous horizontal expanses of outer wall are broken up by vertical lines and variations of lines, pediments, and porches, all topped with a roof balustrade of statues and vases.

The palace was created by the Italian architect Bartolomeo Francesco Rastrelli and stretches from Palace Square to the Neva River embankment. It was the fourth royal residence on this site, the first having been a wooden palace for Peter the Great (today, a remnant of this palace exists and has been restored; it can be visited separately within the State Hermitage Museum). Oddly enough, the all-powerful tsar had to observe some bureaucratic fine print himself. Because it was forbidden to grant land from this site to anyone not bearing naval rank, Peter had to obtain a shipbuilder's license before building his palace. The current palace was commissioned in 1754 by Peter the Great's daughter Elizabeth. By the time it was completed, in 1762, Elizabeth had died and the craze for the Russian rococo style had waned. Catherine the Great left the exterior unaltered but had the interiors redesigned in the neoclassical style of her day. In 1837, after the palace was gutted by fire, the interiors were revamped once again. ⊠ *34 pl. Dvortsovaya, City Center* ⊕ *www.hermitagemuseum.org* Ⓜ *Nevsky Prospekt.*

> ## PUSHKIN: RUSSIA'S POETIC LOVE
>
> Alexander Pushkin is undoubtedly the most beloved poet in Russia, and most any citizen can quote from his poetry the way Westerners may quote Shakespeare. *"Moroz I solntse! Den chudesnyi!"* ("Snow, frost, and sunshine. Lovely morning!") Russians exclaim on a clear winter day, reciting lines from "Winter Morning" ("Zimneye Utro"). Though he only lived to be 37, he had many loves, was exiled by Tsar Alexander I for his criticism of the monarchy, and married one of the most beautiful women of his time, Natalya Goncharova.

WORTH NOTING

Alexander Pushkin Apartment Museum (Музей-квартира Александра Пушкина *Muzey Kvartira Alexandra Pushkina*). After fighting a duel to defend his wife's honor, the beloved Russian poet Alexander Pushkin died in a rented apartment in this building on January 27, 1837. The poet lived out the last act of his illustrious career here, and what a life it was. Pushkin (b. 1799) occupies in Russian literature the position enjoyed by Shakespeare and Goethe in the respective literatures of England and Germany. He is most famous as the author of *Eugene Onegin*, the ultimate tale of unrequited love, whose Byronic hero is seen more as the victim than as the arbiter of his own fate (a new sort of "hero" who cleared the path for the later achievements of Tolstoy and Chekhov). At the heart of this story—which involves a young genteel girl who falls in love with Onegin only to be rejected, then years later winds up rejecting Onegin when he falls in love with her—is a sense of despair, which colored much of Pushkin's own life and death. The poet was killed by a dashing count who had openly made a play for Pushkin's wife, Natalya Goncharova, reputedly "the most beautiful woman in Russia."

Pushkin actually lived at this address less than a year (and could afford it only because the palace owners, the noble Volkhonsky family, were co-sympathizers with the poet for the Decembrist cause). The apartment museum has been

> ### BEST BETS
>
> ■ **For Architecture**: Ploshchad Dvortsovaya, St. Isaac's Cathedral
>
> ■ **For Art**: State Hermitage Museum
>
> ■ **For Romance**: Strelka
>
> ■ **For Kids**: Zoological Museum
>
> ■ **For Military Sights**: *Avrora* cruiser ship
>
> ■ **For History**: Peter and Paul Fortress

restored to give it the appearance of an upper-middle-class dwelling typical of the beginning of the 19th century. (Pushkin had to support a family of six with his writing, so his apartment was less luxurious than it looks now.) Although few of the furnishings are authentic, his personal effects (including the waistcoat he wore during the duel) and those of his wife are on display. Recently, St. Petersburg forensic experts verified that the bloodstains on the sofa here were indeed left by the poet's gunshot wound. The library, where Pushkin actually expired, has been rebuilt according to sketches made by his friend and fellow poet Vasily Zhukovsky, who was holding vigil in his last hours. A moving tape-recorded account leads you through the apartment and retells the events leading up to the poet's death. ✉ *12 nab. Moika, City Center* ☏ *812/314–0006, 812/571–3531* ⊕ *www.museumpushkin.ru* ✉ *100R; audioguide in English, German, French, or Italian 100R* ☽ *Wed.–Mon. 10:30–5; closed last Fri. of month* Ⓜ *Nevsky Prospekt.*

QUICK BITES

Pushka Inn. The extensive menu includes *blini* (pancakes) with caviar, homemade *pelmeni* (meat dumplings), borscht, and *vareniki* (a Ukrainian dish—dumplings filled with all kinds of stuffing, such as cabbage, cherries, and mushrooms). The name is both a play on Pushkin's name and the Russian word for cannon—which explains the military-theme paintings and the miniature cannon near the entrance. ✉ *14 nab. Moika, City Center* ☏ *812/312–0957 reception* ⊕ *www.pushkainn.ru* Ⓜ *Nevsky Prospekt.*

Anna Akhmatova Literary Museum (Музей Анны Ахматовой *Muzey Anny Akhmatovoy*). The famous St. Petersburg poet lived for many years in a communal apartment in a wing of this former palace of Count Sheremetyev. Akhmatova was born in 1888 in Odessa and was published for the first time in 1910. She did not leave Petrograd after the October Revolution, but remained silent between 1923 and 1940. She died in 1966 and is remembered as one of the greatest successors to Pushkin. Her museum is also the venue for occasional poetry readings, other literary events, and temporary exhibitions—in short, a slice of the old-style Russian intelligentsia. ✉ *34 nab. Fontanki, also entered at 53 Liteiny pr., City Center* ☎ *812/272–2211 kassa, 812/579–7239 tours* ⊕ *www.akhmatova.spb. ru* 🎫*80R* ☉ *Tues.–Sun. 10:30–6:30, Wed. 11:30–8* Ⓜ *Nevsky Prospekt.*

Grand Hotel Europe. You can enjoy a pot of tea or a glass of champagne, served with bowls of strawberries, in this lovely mezzanine café. You can also order unique chocolates made at the hotel's own factory. Take a peek at the art-nouveau lobby, furnished with stained-glass windows and antique furnishings. ✉ *7 ul. Mikhailovskaya, bldg. 1, City Center* ☎ *812/329–6000* Ⓜ *Nevsky Prospekt.*

City Duma (Городская Дума *Gorodskaya Duma*). The city hall under the tsars has a notable red-and-white clock tower, meant to resemble those in Western European cities and erected by Ferrari between 1799 and 1804. It was originally equipped with signaling devices that sent messages between the Winter Palace and the royal summer residences. The tower looks particularly beautiful when illuminated. ✉ *1 ul. Dumskaya, City Center* Ⓜ *Nevsky Prospekt, Gostiny Dvor.*

Dom Knigi (Дом Книги). This is where you'll find Petersburgers engaged in one of their favorite pursuits: buying books. The city's largest bookstore, which offers more than 150,000 titles, occupies one of the most exquisite buildings on Nevsky Prospekt. Until 1917 it belonged to the Singer sewing-machine company, for which Russia was the biggest market after the United States. In the first decade of the 20th century the company wanted to erect a skyscraper similar to the one it was building at the time in New York City, but in old St. Petersburg no structure other than a cathedral could be taller than the Winter Palace. To solve the dilemma, Singer's architect erected an elegant tower above the six-story building and topped it with a glass globe nearly 10 feet in diameter. ✉ *28 Nevsky pr., City Center* ☎ *812/448–2355 information* ⊕ *www.spbdk.ru* ☉ *Daily 9 am–midnight* Ⓜ *Nevsky Prospekt.*

General Staff Building (Главный Штаб *Glavny Shtab*). The eastern side of ploshchad Dvortsovaya (Palace Square) is formed by the huge arc of this building; its form and size give the square its unusual shape. During tsarist rule this was the site of the army headquarters and the ministries of foreign affairs and finance. Created by the architect Carlo Giovanni Rossi in the neoclassical style and built between 1819 and 1829, the huge assemblage is actually two structures connected by a monumental archway. Together they form the longest building in Europe. The arch itself is another commemoration of Russia's victory over Napoléon. Topping it is an impressive 33-foot-tall bronze of Victory driving a six-horse chariot, created by the artists Vasily Demut-Malinovsky and Stepan Pimenov. The passageway created by the arch leads from the square to St. Petersburg's most important boulevard, Nevsky prospekt. Part of the Hermitage, the building has a permanent display on its history and architecture, plus temporary exhibits of local and international artwork. ✉*pl. Dvortsovaya, City Center* ☎ *812/710–9079 information desk* ⊕ *www.hermitagemuseum.org* 🎫*780R for multi-access ticket to several branches of State Hermitage Museum* ☉ *Tues.–Sun. 10:30–6* Ⓜ *Nevsky Prospekt.*

Mikhailovsky Theatre of Opera and Ballet (Михайловский Театр Оперы и Балета имени Мусоргского). This historic theater, built in 1833, is St. Petersburg's second-most-important opera and ballet theater after Mariinsky. The repertoire is concentrated on the most important works of European opera and ballet theater of the 19th and 20th centuries. The theater also pays significant attention to works composed for children. ⊠ *1 pl. Iskusstv, City Center* ☎ *812/595–4305 kassa* ⊕ *www. mikhailovsky.ru* Ⓜ *Nevsky Prospekt.*

Square of the Arts (*ploshchad Iskusstu*). If you stand in front of the magnificent State Museum of Russian Art and turn to survey the entire square, the first building on your right, with old-fashioned lanterns adorning its doorways, is the Mikhailovsky Theatre of Opera and Ballet. Bordering the square's south side, on the east corner of ulitsa Mikhailovskaya, is the former Nobles' Club, now the Shostakovich Philharmonia, home to the St. Petersburg Philharmonic. The buildings on the square's remaining sides are former residences and school buildings. ⊠ *pl. Iskusstu, City Center* Ⓜ *Gostinyi Dvor or Nevsky Prospekt.*

FAMILY **St. Petersburg Circus** (Большой Санкт-Петербургский Государственный Цирк *Bolshoi Sankt-Peterburgskii Gosudarstvennyi Tsirk*). Though not as famous as the Moscow Circus, St. Petersburg's version of this popular Russian form of entertainment dates from 1867 and remains a popular treat for children. Avid young circus fans get a kick out of its adjacent **Circus Art Museum**, founded in 1928. ⊠ *3 nab. Fontanki, City Center* ☎ *812/570–5390 kassa, 812/570–5413 museum* ⊕ *www.circus. spb.ru* ✉ *500R–2,000R, free for children under 5* ☉ *Performances: Fri. 7, Sat. 3 and 6, Sun. 1 and 5; museum weekdays noon–5* Ⓜ *Gostinyi Dvor or Nevsky Prospekt.*

ADMIRALTEISKY АДМИРАЛТЕЙСТВО

The Admiralteisky is the area just west of the City Center. At its center is the famous golden-yellow Admiralteistvo, or Admiralty building. This neighborhood is also home to Decembrists' Square, the site where roughly 3,000 army officers revolted on December 14, 1825. The Bronze Horseman, one of the city's most famous monuments, is located in the middle of the square—it's dedicated to Peter the Great.

GETTING HERE AND AROUND

To get to the Admiralteisky, take a metro to Nevsky Prospekt station and leave it through the Canal Griboyedova exit. After a 15-minute walk down Nevsky prospekt, you'll reach the golden-spired Admiralty. You can take a 1 or 7 trolley from any stop on Nevsky prospekt. You can also take a taxi there or drive if you're far away.

TOP ATTRACTIONS

Admiralty (Адмиралтейство *Admiralteistvo*). The spire of this lovely golden-yellow building is visible throughout the city and is one of St. Petersburg's most renowned emblems. The first structure on this site was a shipyard of Peter the Great, followed by an earthen fortress that guarded the port; after this came the first Admiralty, made of stone and topped by the spire that's endured to grace each successive structure. As

St. Petersburg in Literature

"On an exceptionally hot evening early in July, a young man came out of the garret in which he lodged in S. Place and walked slowly, as though in hesitation, towards K. Bridge." Thus opens Fyodor Dostoyevsky's *Crime and Punishment*, one of the greatest crime stories ever written, with the protagonist Rodion Raskolnikov making his way through 19th-century St. Petersburg. Both the grand landmarks and miserable details of St. Petersburg were so powerfully inspiring to the giants of Russian literature that the city became as much an inseparable part of their writing as it was of their lives.

The beloved Russian poet Alexander Pushkin (1799–1837) lived and died in St. Petersburg, and he honored the mighty capital in his works. In his epic *Bronze Horseman*, he immortalized the equestrian statue of Peter the Great on Decembrists' Square. In the poem, a poor clerk imagines that the rearing statue—which evokes the creative energy and ruthlessness of Peter—comes to life and chases him though the streets. In his poetic novel *Eugene Onegin*, Pushkin writes of St. Petersburg's early-19th-century high society—of balls, receptions, theaters, and ballets.

In contrast, Dostoyevsky's St. Petersburg is a place of catastrophes, strange events, crimes, and dramas. His heroes live desperate lives in a dank city of slums, poverty, and hopelessness. Fyodor Dostoyevsky (1821–81) was born in Moscow but spent much of his life in St. Petersburg, and was so scrupulous about describing the city that you can find many of the places where his "brainchildren"—as he called his characters—lived. Dostoyevsky lived at 19 ulitsa Grazhdanskaya for a time, and many believe this is the apartment he used as a model for Raskolnikov's home. Dostoyevsky wrote that on his way to murder the elderly pawnbroker, Raskolnikov took 730 steps from his lodgings to the victim's lodging at 104 Kanal Griboyedova/25 ulitsa Rimskovo-Korsakova. You can re-create this walk, though it requires more than 730 steps.

Nikolai Gogol (1809–52) also portrayed a shadowy St. Petersburg—a city of nonsensical businesslike character and ridiculous bureaucratic fuss. In Gogol's short story "The Nose," the protagonist, low-ranking civil servant Kovalyov, loses his nose and must search through St. Petersburg to find it. The nose starts boosting its own bureaucratic career, obtains a higher rank than its owner, and ignores the desperate Kovalyov. To mark Gogol's satirical story, a bas-relief nose is displayed at the corner of Voznesenskii prospekt and ulitsa Rimskogo-Korsakova. The "memorial" regularly gets stolen.

The poetry of Anna Akhmatova (1889–1966) reflects the changing face of St. Petersburg during her lifetime. Born in the St. Petersburg suburb of Tsarskoye Selo, Akhmatova wrote romantic and nostalgic verse about her beloved city at the beginning of her career. As the city changed, so did her poetry, based in part on her firsthand experience of Stalin's repression. Her son was imprisoned, and her works were harshly denounced by government officials. Her poem "Requiem" describes the horrors of those times. During the siege of Leningrad, Akhmatova read on the city radio her poems of support for the hungry and dying city residents.

8

you walk through the park in front, you'll see various statues, mostly of artists such as the composer Mikhail Glinka and the writer Mikhail Lermontov; the figure accompanied by the delightful camel is of Nikolai Przhevalsky, a 19th-century explorer of Central Asia. ⊠ *Admiralteisky pr., Admiralteisky* Ⓜ *Admiralteyskaya.*

Senatskaya Square (Сенатская Площадь *Senatskaya Ploshchad*). One of St. Petersburg's best-known landmarks, a gigantic equestrian statue of Peter the Great, dominates this square that from 1925 through 2008 was known as "Decembrists' Square," a reference to the dramatic events that unfolded here on December 14, 1825. Following the death of Tsar Alexander I (1777–1825), a group of aristocrats, some of whom were army officers, staged a rebellion on the square in an attempt to prevent the crowning of Nicholas I (1796–1855) as the new tsar, and perhaps do away with the monarchy altogether. Their coup was suppressed with much bloodshed by troops who were loyal to Nicholas, and those rebels who were not executed were banished to Siberia. Although the Decembrists, as they came to be known, did not bring significant change to Russia in their time, their attempts at liberal reform were often cited by the Soviet regime as proof of deep-rooted revolutionary fervor in Russian society.

In the center of the square is the grand statue called the **Medny Vsadnik** (Bronze Horseman), erected as a memorial from Catherine the Great to her predecessor, Peter the Great. The simple inscription on the base reads, "To Peter the First from Catherine the Second, 1782." Created by the French sculptor Étienne Falconet and his student Marie Collot, the statue depicts the powerful Peter, crowned with a laurel wreath, astride a rearing horse that symbolizes Russia, trampling a serpent representing the forces of evil. The enormous granite rock on which the statue is balanced comes from the Gulf of Finland. Reportedly, Peter liked to stand on it to survey his city from afar. Moving it was a Herculean effort, requiring a special barge and machines and nearly a year's work. The statue was immortalized in a poem of the same name by Alexander Pushkin, who wrote that the tsar "by whose fateful will the city was founded beside the sea, stands here aloft at the very brink of a precipice, having reared up Russia with his iron curb." ⊠ *Pl. Senatskaya, Admiralteisky* Ⓜ *Sennaya Ploshchad.*

Fodor's Choice ★ **St. Isaac's Cathedral** (Исаакиевский Собор *Isaakievsky Sobor*). The grandly proportioned St. Isaac's is the world's third-largest domed cathedral and the first monument you see of the city if you arrive by ship. Its architectural distinction is up for debate; some consider the massive design and highly ornate interior to be excessive, but others revel in its opulence. Tsar Alexander I commissioned the construction of the cathedral in 1818 to celebrate his victory over Napoléon, but it took more than 40 years to actually build it. The French architect Auguste Ricard de Montferrand devoted his life to the project, and died the year the cathedral was finally consecrated, in 1858.

The interior of the cathedral is lavishly decorated with malachite, lazulite, marble, and other stones and minerals. Gilding the dome required 220 pounds of gold. At one time a Foucault pendulum hung here to demonstrate the axial rotation of the earth, but it was removed in the late 20th century. After the Revolution of 1917 the cathedral was closed to worshippers, and in 1931 was opened as a museum; services have since resumed. St. Isaac's was not altogether returned to the Orthodox Church, but Christmas and Easter are celebrated here (note that Orthodox holidays follow the Julian calendar and fall about 13 days after their Western equivalents).

When the city was blockaded during World War II, the gilded dome was painted black to avoid its being targeted by enemy fire. The cathedral nevertheless suffered heavy damage, as bullet holes on the columns on the south side attest. The outer colonnade beneath the dome affords an excellent view of the city, especially at twilight and during the famous White Nights.

To one side of the cathedral, where the prospekt meets Konnogvardeisky bulvar, is the early-19th-century **Konnogvardeisky Manège,** gracefully designed by Giacomo Quarenghi and decorated with marble statues of the mythological twins Castor and Pollux. This former barracks of the Imperial horse guards is used as an art exhibition hall. ⊠ *1 pl. Isaakievskaya, Admiralteisky* ☎ *812/315–9732* 🖙 *Cathedral 250R; colonnade 150R* ☉ *Cathedral May–Sept., Thurs.–Tues. 10 am–10:30 pm; Oct.–Apr., Thurs.–Tues. 11– 7; colonnade May and late Aug. and Sept., Thurs.–Tues. 10 am–11 pm, June 1–Aug. 20, Thurs.–Tues. and second Wed. of each month, 10 am–4:30 am* Ⓜ *Sennaya Ploshchad.*

St. Isaac's Square (Ст. Исаацьс Сяуаре *ploshchad Isaakievskaya*). In the center of this square in front of St. Isaac's Cathedral stands the **Nicholas Statue.** Unveiled in 1859, the statue of Tsar Nicholas I was commissioned by the tsar's wife and three children, whose faces are engraved (in the allegorical forms of Wisdom, Faith, Power, and Justice) on its base. It was designed, like St. Isaac's Cathedral and the Alexander Column, by Montferrand. The statue depicts Nicholas mounted on a rearing horse. Other engravings on the base describe such events of the tsar's reign as the suppression of the Decembrists' uprising and the opening ceremonies of the St. Petersburg–Moscow railway line. ⊠ *pl. Isaakievskaya, Admiralteisky* Ⓜ *Sennaya Ploshchad.*

QUICK BITES | **Idiot** (Идиот). A favorite among St. Petersburg expatriates, this restaurant serves hearty vegetarian Russian food, good seafood, and nice Italian coffee. The background music leans heavily on Charles Aznavour, Louis Armstrong, and Ella Fitzgerald. Add occasional art exhibits, chess and backgammon sets, and a small library, and you have several excuses to linger. ⊠ *82 nab. Moika, City Center* ☎ *812/315–1675 information* ⊕ *www.idiot-spb.com* Ⓜ *Admiralteiskaya.*

WORTH NOTING

St. Nicholas Cathedral (Никольский Собор *Nikolsky Sobor*). This turquoise-and-white extravaganza of a Russian baroque cathedral was designed by S.I. Chevakinsky, a pupil of Bartolomeo Francesco Rastrelli. It's a theatrical showpiece, and its artistic inspiration was in part derived from the 18th-century Italian prints of the Bibiena brothers, known for their opera and theater designs. Canals and green spaces surround the wedding-cake silhouette, a forest of white Corinthian pilasters and columns and flanked by an elegant campanile. Inside are a lower church (low, dark, and warm for the winter) and an upper church (high, airy, and cool for the summer), typical of Russian Orthodox sanctuaries. The interior is no less picturesque than the outside. This is one of the few Orthodox churches that stayed open under Soviet power. ⊠ *3 pl. Nikolskaya , bldg. 1, Admiralteisky* ☎ *812/714-6926* ☉ *Daily, 7–7; morning services at 7 and 10, vespers at 6 pm* Ⓜ *Sennaya Ploshchad.*

> ### NABOKOV
>
> Vladimir Nabokov was born in St. Petersburg to a rich noble family. The Nabokovs fled Russia soon after the Bolshevik Revolution and would never return. In 1940 they left Paris for the United States, where Nabokov began writing his novels and short stories, including Lolita (1955), in English. Never forgetting his roots, he once said of himself, "I am an American writer, born in Russia, educated in England, where I studied French literature before moving for 15 years to Germany…. My head speaks English, my heart speaks Russian, and my ear speaks French."

Siniy most (**Синий мост** *Blue Bridge*). This bridge spanning the Moika River is so wide (about 325 feet) and stubby that it seems not to be a bridge at all but rather a sort of quaint raised footpath on St. Isaac's Square. The "Blue Bridge" is named for the color of the paint on its underside. ⊠ *Pl. Isaakievskaya, Admiralteisky* Ⓜ *Sennaya Ploshchad.*

Vladimir Nabokov Museum-Apartment (**Музей-квартира Владимира Набокова** *Musei Kvartira Vladimira Nabokova*). Vladimir Nabokov (1899–1977), best known in America for the novel *Lolita,* was born and lived in this apartment until his 18th year. Judging from Nabokov's works, in which the author often describes his building in detail, it seems he had warm memories of his first home. When in exile, Nabokov lived in hotels or rented apartments in different cities but never owned his own home. When asked why he didn't want to settle into a permanent home, he would answer, "I already have one in St. Petersburg." On view are family photos; the writer's drawings and various editions of his books; some of his belongings; and his collection of butterflies, which was previously kept at Harvard University. Visitors can watch a tape of a 1962 interview with Nabokov, in English. ⊠ *47 ul. Bolshaya Morskaya, Admiralteisky* ☎ *812/315–4713* ⊕ *www.nabokovmuseum.org* ☜ *free* ☉ *Tues.–Fri. 11–6, weekends 12–5* Ⓜ *Sennaya Ploshchad.*

Yusupov Palace (**Юсуповский Дворец** *Yusupovsky Dvorets*). On the cold night of December 17, 1916, this elegant yellow palace on the banks of the Moika River became the setting for one of history's most melodramatic murders. Prince Yusupov and others loyal to the tsar spent several frustrating and frightening hours trying to kill Grigory Rasputin (1872–1916), who had strongly influenced the tsarina, who in turn influenced the tsar, during the tumultuous years leading up to the Bolshevik Revolution. An extended tour given once daily at 1:45

CLOSE UP

Rasputin the Mystic

Neither a monk nor a priest as commonly believed, Rasputin was a wandering peasant who eventually came to exert great power over Nicholas II, the last tsar of Imperial Russia. The royal family came under his spell when, claiming to have visions of the future and strange healing powers, he began to minister to Alexei, Nicholas's young son. Alexei suffered from hemophilia, but when Rasputin prayed over the child, the hemorrhaging mysteriously stopped. The tsarina, Alexandra, soon came to believe that without Rasputin, her son would die. He became a regular palace visitor, though his presence wasn't always welcome. He was accused of scandalous misdeeds, including rape, and of having too much political control over the royal family. A number of people eventually tired of Rasputin's influence and conspired to murder him. On one cold December night in 1916, the mad healer was lured to the palace of Prince Felix Yusupov, where he was fed cakes and drinks laced with cyanide. To the horror of the conspirators, however, Rasputin was unaffected by their poisons. In desperation, they shot him several times and beat him before dumping him into the icy waters of the Neva River. His body was later found and autopsied; the results purportedly showed that he died of hypothermia, not cyanide or gunshot wounds.

pm shows off the rooms in which Rasputin was (or began to be) killed, as well as a waxworks exhibit of Rasputin and Prince Yusupov (who was forced to flee the country when Rasputin's murder was uncovered). Another tour (scheduled on the hour) takes you through the former reception rooms of the second floor. Both tours are in Russian only, but an audioguide tour is available in English, French, German, Italian, Finnish, and Spanish or you may phone ahead at least ten days in advance to arrange an English-language tour. The palace's underground tunnel where Rasputin was actually poisoned is ostensibly off-limits, but you may be able to view it if you avail yourself of the bathroom facilities on the lower level of the mansion.

On a lighter note, the showpiece of the palace remains the jewel-like rococo theater, whose stage was once graced by Liszt and Chopin; concerts are still presented here, and also in the palace's august and elegant White-Columns Room (concert tickets usually have to be purchased just before performance time). ✉ *94 nab. Moika, Admiralteisky* ☏ *812/314-9883, 812/314–8893 tours* ⊕ *yusupov-palace.ru* ☏ *500R, additional 300R for extended tour* ⊙ *Daily 10:45–5; closed 1st Wed. of month* Ⓜ *Sennaya Ploshchad.*

8

VASILIEVSKY ISLAND ВАСИЛЬЕВСКИЙ

Across the Neva river is Vasilievsky Ostrov (Vasilievsky Island), the largest island in the Neva Delta and one of the city's oldest developed sections. Peter the Great wanted his city center there, and his original plans for the island called for a network of canals for the transport of goods from the main sea terminal to the city's commercial center at the opposite end of the island. These plans to re-create Venice never materialized, although some of the smaller canals were actually dug (and later filled in). These would-be canals are now streets, and are called "lines" (*liniya*). Instead of names they bear numbers, and they run parallel to the island's three main thoroughfares: the Great (Bolshoi), Middle (Sredny), and Small (Maly) prospekts. Now the island is a popular residential area, with most of its historic sites concentrated on its eastern edge. The island's western tip, facing the Gulf of Finland, houses the city's main sea terminals.

GETTING HERE AND AROUND

To reach Vasilievsky Island, from the Admiralty, cross Dvortsovy most (Palace Bridge), which starts between the Admiralty and the Hermitage. The bridge takes you to the island's end, near the island's easternmost tip, called Strelka ("arrow"). It's here that the Neva River splits into two parts, on either side of the island. As you stand in ploshchad Birzhevaya, as the park on the Strelka is called, you'll be between two thick, brick-red columns, known as the Rostral Columns, and have a magnificent view of the city's major sights.

TOP ATTRACTIONS

Chamber of Art (Кунсткамера *Kunstkammer*). This fine example of Russian baroque is painted bright azure with white trim and stands out from the surrounding classically designed architecture. Also known as the Kunstkammer (from the German *Kunst,* "art," and *Kammer,* "chamber") and the Chamber of Curiosities, the building was commissioned in 1718 to house the collection of oddities Peter the Great gathered during his travels. It was completed in 1734, destroyed by fire in 1747, and almost entirely rebuilt later. Today it houses the **Museum of Anthropology and Ethnography** but still includes a room with Peter's original collection, a truly bizarre assortment ranging from rare precious stones to preserved human organs and fetuses. The museum is enormously popular, so buy your entrance ticket early in the day. ✉ *3 nab. Universitetskaya, Vasilievsky Island* ☎ *812/328–1412 information, excursions* ⊕ *www.kunstkamera.ru* ✉ *200R* ☉ *Tues.–Sun. 11–6. Closed last Tues. of month* Ⓜ *Vasileostrovskaya.*

Rostral Columns (Ростральные Колонны *Rostralnyie Kolonny*). Swiss architect Thomas de Thomon designed these columns, which were erected between 1805 and 1810 in honor of the Russian fleet. The monument takes its name from the Latin *rostrum,* meaning "prow." Modeled on similar memorials in ancient Rome, the columns are decorated with ships' prows; sculptures at the base depict Russia's main waterways, the Dnieper, Volga, Volkhov, and Neva rivers. Although the columns originally served as lighthouses—until 1855 this was St. Petersburg's commercial harbor—they are now lit only on special occasions, such as City Day (May 27). The columns were designed to frame the architectural centerpiece of this side of the embankment—the old Stock Exchange, which now holds the Naval Museum. ✉ *Pl. Birzhevaya, Vasilievsky Island* Ⓜ *Vasileostrovskaya.*

WORTH NOTING

Egyptian Sphinxes (**Египетские Сфинксы** *Yegipetskiye Sfinksy*). Two of St. Petersburg's more magnificent landmarks stand on the landing in front of the Repin Institute, leading down to the Neva. These twin statues, which date from the 15th century BC, were discovered during an excavation at Thebes in the 1820s. They were apparently created during the era of Pharaoh Amenhotep III, whose features they supposedly bear. It took the Russians more than a year to transport the sphinxes from Thebes. ✉ *nab. Universitetskaya, Vasilievsky Island* Ⓜ *Vasileostrovskaya.*

Menshikov Palace (**Меншиковский Дворец** *Menshikovsky Dvorets*). Alexander Menshikov (1673–1729), St. Petersburg's first governor, was one of Russia's more flamboyant characters. A close friend of Peter the Great (often called his favorite), Menshikov rose from humble beginnings as a street vendor, reportedly getting his start when he sold a cabbage pie to the tsar—or so the legend goes. He eventually became one of Russia's most powerful statesmen, infamous for his corruption and political maneuvering. He's said to have incited Peter the Great against his son Alexei and later attempted to take power from Peter II by arranging the young tsar's engagement to his daughter. The marriage didn't take place, and Peter exiled Menshikov and his family to Siberia.

Menshikov's palace, the first stone building in St. Petersburg, was the city's most luxurious building at the time of its completion in 1720. Although only a portion of the original palace has survived, it easily conveys a sense of Menshikov's love of luxury. Particularly noteworthy are the restored bedrooms: the walls and ceilings are completely covered with handcrafted ceramic tiles that Peter the Great allegedly sent home from Delft for himself but were appropriated by Menshikov. After Menshikov's exile, his palace was turned over to a military training school and was significantly altered over the years. In June 1917 it served as the site of the First Congress of Russian Soviets. The Menshikov Palace is a branch of the Hermitage Museum. In addition to the restored living quarters of the Menshikov family, there's an exhibit devoted to early-18th-century Russian culture. ✉ *15 nab. Universitetskaya, Vasilievsky Island* ☎ *812/323–1112* 💷 *60R* ☾ *Tues.–Sun. 10:30–4:30* Ⓜ *Vasileostrovskaya.*

Russian Academy of Sciences (**Российская Академия Наук** *Rossiiskaya Akademiya Nauk*). Erected on strictly classical lines between 1783 and 1789, the original building of the Russian Academy of Sciences is considered to be Giacomo Quarenghi's grandest design, with an eight-column portico, a pediment, and a double staircase. The administrative offices of the academy, founded in 1724 by Peter the Great, were transferred to Moscow in 1934 and the building now houses the St. Petersburg branch of the academy. ✉ *32a nab. Universitetskaya, Vasilievsky Island* Ⓜ *Vasileostrovskaya.*

St. Petersburg State University (Санкт-Петербургский Государственный Университет *Sankt-Peterburgskii Gosudarstvenny Universitet*). Tsar Alexander I founded this university in 1819, and today it's one of Russia's leading institutions of higher learning with an enrollment of more than 20,000. Russian president Vladimir Putin and Prime Minister Dmitry Medvedev graduated from the university's law faculty. Much of the campus dates to the 18th-century reign of Peter the Great. The bright red baroque building on the right (if you're walking west along the embankment) is the **Twelve Colleges Building,** designed by Domenico Trezzini and completed in 1741. The next building in the university complex is the **Rector's Wing,** where a plaque attests that the great Russian poet Alexander Blok (d. 1921) was born here in 1880. The third building along the embankment is a former **palace** built for Peter II (1715–30), Peter the Great's grandson, who lived and ruled only briefly. ⊠ *7 nab. Universitetskaya, Vasilievsky Island* Ⓜ *Vasileostrovskaya.*

Strelka (Стрелка). This bit of land (the name means "arrow" or "spit") affords a dazzling view of the Winter Palace and the Peter and Paul Fortress and reveals the city's triumphant rise from a watery outpost to an elegant metropolis. Seen against the backdrop of the Neva, the brightly colored houses lining the embankment seem like children's toys—the building blocks of a bygone aristocracy. They stand at the water's edge, seemingly supported not by the land beneath them but by the panorama of the city behind them. Gazing here is a great way to appreciate the scope of Peter the Great's vision for his country. The view also makes clear how careful the city's founders were to build their city not despite the Neva but around and with it. The Strelka is very popular with wedding couples, who traditionally come to visit the sight on their wedding day and often break a bottle of champagne on the ground here. ⊠ *Vasilevsky Island, at the north end of Dvortsovy Most (Palace Bridge), Vasilievsky Island* Ⓜ *Vasileostrovskaya.*

FAMILY **Zoological Museum** (Зоологический Музей *Zoologichesky Muzey*). An unusual collection of more than 30,000 species includes a mammoth, now stuffed, recovered from Siberia in 1901, and it joins tigers, foxes, bears, goats, and many kinds of birds. The museum also has a large collection of butterflies and other insects. ⊠ *1 nab. Universitetskaya, Vasilievsky Island* ☎ *812/328–0112* 💲*200R; free last Thurs. of month* ⊙ *Wed.–Mon. 11–6* Ⓜ *Vasileostrovskaya.*

PETROGRAD SIDE ПЕТРОГРАДСКАЯ СТОРОНА

St. Petersburg was born in the battles of the Northern Wars with Sweden, and it was in this area, on Hare Island (Zayachy Ostrov), that it all began: in 1703 Peter laid the foundation of the first fortress to protect the mainland and to secure Russia's outlet to the sea. Ever since, the small hexagonal island forms, as it were, the hub around which the city revolves. The showpiece of the island is the magnificent Peter and Paul Fortress, the starting point for any tour of this section of the city, which actually consists of a series of islands, and is commonly referred to as the Petrograd Side (Petrogradskaya Storona). Hare Island and the fortress are almost directly across the Neva from the Winter Palace. Cut off from the north by the moatlike Kronverk Canal, the island is connected by a footbridge to ploshchad Troitskaya (Trinity Square, sometimes still referred to by its Soviet name, Revolution Square) on Petrogradsky Ostrov (Petrograd Island). Along with its famous monuments, this part of the city is also one of its earliest residential areas, and ploshchad Troitskaya, named for the church that once stood here (demolished in 1934), is the city's oldest square.

GETTING HERE AND AROUND

You can reach the area by walking across the Dvortsovyi (Palace) Bridge (it starts near the Hermitage), passing through the Strelka, and then across the smaller Birzhevoi Bridge. On your right you'll see the Peter and Paul Fortress: the walk will also give you a chance to take in a panorama of the city's grandest sites, including the Hermitage, the Neva River, and the Strelka. You can also take trolley 1 or 7 from Nevsky prospekt, or hire a taxi. Another option is to take the metro to Gorkovskaya station, and from there walk through the park in the direction of the fortress, which remains the major site in the area. The Artillery Museum is across from the Fortress. You'll recognize it at once by the World War II–era cannons.

> ### WORD OF MOUTH
>
> "Maybe the comparison is not fair, but if you have a choice between Moscow and St. Petersburg, the answer is quick and easy: St. Petersburg. Frankly, I consider it one of the most beautiful cities on the planet if not THE most beautiful one. [There's] an incredible wealth of palaces, museums, churches and, furthermore, [it] has a stunning architectural cohesiveness, with over 3,000 listed historical buildings."
>
> —Echnaton

TOP ATTRACTIONS

FAMILY **Avrora (Аврора).** This historic cruiser, moored in front of the **Nakhimov Academy of Naval Officers** and reopening in the summer of 2014 after an extensive restoration, saw action in the 1904–05 Russo-Japanese War as well as in World War II, but it's best known for its role in the Bolshevik Revolution. At 9:40 pm on November 7, 1917, the cruiser fired the shot that signaled the storming of the Winter Palace. On display are the crew's quarters and the radio room used to broadcast Lenin's victory address. ✉ *4 nab. Petrogradskaya, Petrograd Side* ☎ *812/230–8440* 💰 *300R* ☉ *Tues.–Thurs. and weekends 10:30–4, last tour at 3* Ⓜ *Gorkovskaya.*

Fodor's Choice **Peter and Paul Fortress** (**Петропавловская Крепость** *Petropavlovskaya*
★ *Krepost*). The first building in Sankt-Piter-Burkh, as the city was then called, was erected in just one year, between 1703 and 1704, during the Great Northern War against Sweden. It was never used for its intended purpose, however, as the Russian line of defense quickly moved farther north, and, in fact, the war was won before the fortress was mobilized. Instead, the fortress served mainly as a political prison, primarily under the tsars. The date on which construction began on the fortress is celebrated as the birth of St. Petersburg.

Cross the footbridge and enter the fortress through **St. John's Gate** (Ioannovskyie Vorota), the main entrance to the outer fortifications. Entrance to the inner fortress is through **St. Peter's Gate** (Petrovskiye Vorota). Designed by the Swiss architect Domenico Trezzini, it was completed in1718. After you pass through the gate, the first building to your right is the **Artilleriisky Arsenal,** where weaponry was stored. Just to your left is the **Engineer's House** (Inzhenerny Dom), which was built from 1748 to 1749. Now a branch of the Museum of the History of St. Petersburg (as are all exhibits in the fortress), it presents displays about the city's prerevolutionary history.

As you continue to walk down the main center lane, away from St. Peter's Gate, you soon come to the main attraction of the fortress, the **Cathedral of Saints Peter and Paul** (Petropavlovsky Sobor). Constructed between 1712 and 1733 on the site of an earlier wooden church, it was designed by Domenico Trezzini and later embellished by Bartolomeo Rastrelli. It's highly unusual for a Russian Orthodox church. Instead of the characteristic bulbous domes, it's adorned by a single, slender, gilded spire whose height (400 feet, 120 meters) made the church the city's tallest building—in accordance with Peter the Great's decree—until 1962, when a television tower was erected. The spire is identical to that of the Admiralty across the river, except that it's crowned by an angel bearing a golden cross.

The interior of the cathedral is also atypical. The baroque iconostasis, designed by Ivan Zarudny and built in the 1720s, is adorned by free-standing statues. Another uncommon feature is the pulpit. It's reputed to have been used only once, in 1901, to excommunicate Leo Tolstoy from the Russian Orthodox Church for denouncing the institution. You can exit the cathedral through the passageway to the left of the iconostasis. This leads to the adjoining **Grand Ducal Crypt** (Usypalnitsa), built between 1896 and 1908. You can identify Peter the Great's tomb by the tsar's bust on the railing on the far right facing the iconostasis.

As you leave the cathedral, note the small classical structure to your right. This is the **Boathouse** (Botny Domik), built between 1762 and 1766 to house Peter the Great's boyhood boat. The boat has since been moved to the Naval Museum on Vasilievsky Island, and the building is not open to the public.

The long pink-and-white building to your left as you exit the cathedral is the **Commandant's House** (Komendantsky Dom), erected between 1743 and 1746. It once housed the fortress's administration and doubled as a courtroom for political prisoners. The Decembrist revolutionaries were tried here in 1826. The room where the trial took place forms part of the ongoing exhibits, which deal with the history of St. Petersburg from its founding to 1917. Across the cobblestone yard, opposite the entrance to the cathedral, stands the **Mint** (Monetny Dvor), which was first built in 1716; the current structure, however, was erected between 1798 and 1806. The mint is still in operation, producing coins, medals, military decorations, and *znachki* (Russian souvenir pins). The coins that were taken along on Soviet space missions were made here. In the yard of the fortress there is the most unusual bronze **sculpture of Peter the Great**.

The first Russian emperor is featured sitting on a throne. His body is unproportionally long, the bold head looks too small and pressed into the shoulders. His long fingers are squeezing elbows of the throne. The sculpture was made by eccentric Russian dissident artist Mikhail Shemyakin, who used a living mask of the tsar made by Italian sculptor Karlo Rastrelli. Initially the body was made proportional to the head but then Shemyakin decided to make the body longer to meet the proportion traditional to the Russian icon painting. In the beginning the monument caused negative attitude of the city residents but then became a place of tourists' pilgrimage. Visitors rub the tsar's fingers hoping that it will bring them wealth and take pictures of themselves sitting on Peter's laps.

Take the pathway to the left of the Commandant's House (as you're facing it), and you'll be headed right for **Neva Gate** (Nevskiye Vorota), built in 1730 and reconstructed in 1787. As you walk through its passageway, note the plaques on the inside walls marking flood levels of the Neva. The gate leads out to the **Commandant's Pier** (Komendantskaya Pristan). Up above to the right is the **Signal Cannon** (Signalnaya Pushka), fired every day at noon.The honor to fire from the Signal Cannon is given now and then for Russia's known people or people who have done significant things for the city. From this side you get a splendid view of St. Petersburg. You may want to step down to the sandy beach, where even in winter hearty swimmers enjoy the Neva's arctic waters. In summer the beach is lined with sunbathers.

Trubetskoi Bastion

As you return to the fortress through the Neva Gate, you'll be following the footsteps of prisoners who passed through this gate on the way to their executions. Several of the fortress's bastions, concentrated at its far western end, were put to use over the years mainly as political prisons. One of them, Trubetskoi Bastion, is open to the public as a museum. Aside from a few exhibits of prison garb, the only items on display are the cells themselves, restored to their chilling, prerevolutionary appearance. The first prisoner confined in its dungeons was Peter the Great's own son, Alexei, who was tortured to death in 1718 for treason, allegedly under the tsar's supervision. The prison was enlarged in 1872, when an adjacent one, Alexeivsky Bastion, which held such famous figures as the writers Fyodor Dostoyevsky and Nikolai Chernyshevsky, became overcrowded with dissidents opposed to the tsarist regime. A partial chronology of revolutionaries held here includes some of the People's Will terrorists, who killed Alexander II in 1881; Lenin's elder brother Alexander, who attempted to murder Alexander III (and was executed for his role in the plot); and Leon Trotsky and Maxim Gorky, after taking part in the 1905 revolution. The Bolsheviks themselves imprisoned people here for a short period, starting with members of the Provisional Government who were arrested and "detained for their own safety" for a few days, as well as sailors who mutinied against the Communist regime in Kronshtadt in 1921. They were apparently the last to be held here, and in 1925 a memorial museum (to the prerevolutionary prisoners) was opened instead. Some casements close to the Neva Gate have been converted into a printing workshop (*pechatnya*), where you can buy good-quality graphic art in a broad range of prices. Original late-19th-century presses are used to create lithographs, etchings, and linocuts depicting, most often, urban St. Petersburg landscapes, which make nice alternatives to the usual souvenirs. In the basement, the original foundations were excavated; different layers of the history of the fortress can thus be seen. ✉3 *Petropavlovskaya Krepost, Petrograd Side* ☎812/230–6431 *information, 812/232–9454 excursions* 🎫 *Cathedral 160R (Nov.–Mar.), 220R (Apr.–Oct.); cathedral and other sights and exhibitions 280R (Nov.–Mar.), 370R (Apr.–Oct.); audio guide in English, French, German, Spanish, or Italian 250R* ⏰*Thurs.–Tues. 11–6, kassa closes at 5, at 4 on Tues; closed last Tues. of month* Ⓜ*Gorkovskaya.*

THE BURIAL PLACE OF TSARS

The Cathedral of Saints Peter and Paul is the final resting spot of nearly all the tsars, from Peter the Great on—including Nicholas II, who was executed with his family in Yekaterinburg (Siberia) in 1918 and whose remains, along with those of his wife and three of his daughters weren't buried in the cathedral until 1998. The remains of the tsarevitch Alexei and his sister Maria were then still missing and were found in Yekaterinburg only in 2007. There hasn't yet been any move to have them reburied with the rest of the royal family in the cathedral.

WORTH NOTING

FAMILY **Artillery Museum** (**Артиллерийский Музей** *Artilleriysky Muzey*). You can't miss St. Petersburg's main army museum—just look for the hundreds of pieces of artillery on the grounds outside. Exhibits have a distinctly Soviet penchant for detail—if you're interested in circuit boards inside ballistic missiles, for example, this is the place to come. ✉7 *Alexandrovsky Park, Petrograd Side* ☎812/232–0296 ⊕*www.artillery-museum.ru* 🎫*300R* ⏰*Wed.–Sun. 11–5; closed last Thurs. of month* Ⓜ*Gorkovskaya.*

FAMILY **LabirintUm** (**Лабиринтум**). About 60 exhibits provide visitors with the opportunity to learn the laws of physics, chemistry, and nature in an entertaining way, whether by making lightning, creating an artificial tornado, getting inside a huge bubble, or finding their way through a mirror labyrinth. The museum is a reinvention of similar displays installed here by the eminent scientist Yakov Perelman in 1935. These were destroyed during World War II, and Perelman and his wife starved to death during the Siege of Leningrad. ✉9A *ul. Lva Tolstogo, 6th floor of Tolstoi Skver Design House, Petrograd Side* ☎812/328–0001 ⊕*www.labirint-um.ru* 🎫*Weekdays 300R, weekends 350R* ⏰*Daily 11–7* Ⓜ*Petrogradskaya.*

Mosque (**Мечеть** *Mechet*). Built between 1910 and 1914, the city's center of Muslim worship is designed after the Gur Emir in Samarkand (in modern-day Uzbekistan), where Tamerlane, the 14th-century conqueror, is buried. The huge dome is flanked by two soaring minarets and covered with sky-blue ceramics, and the inside columns, which support the arches under the dome, are faced with green marble. ✉7 *Kronversky pr., Petrograd Side* ☎812/233–9819 ⏰*Services daily at 2:20* Ⓜ*Gorkovskaya.*

Russian Political History Museum (Государственный Музей Политической Истории России *Gosudarstvenny Muzey Politicheskoi Istorii Rossii*). Almost as interesting as the paintings, posters, flags, and porcelain tracing the history of Russia in the 20th century is the history of this elegant art-nouveau house itself, built in 1905 by Alexander Goguen. It was the home of Mathilda Kshesinskaya, a famous ballerina and the mistress of the last Russian tsar, Nicholas II, before he married Alexandra. Kshesinskaya left Russia in 1917 for Paris, where she married a longtime lover, Andrei Vladimirovich, another Romanov. One of Kshesinskaya's pupils was the great English ballerina Margot Fonteyn. The mansion served as Bolshevik committee headquarters in the months leading up to the October Revolution (an exhibit reconstructs Lenin's study from this period) and in 1957 was linked to the adjoining town house by a rather nondescript central wing and turned into the Museum of the Great October Socialist Revolution; it was given its current name in 1991. ✉ *4 ul. Kuybysheva, bldg. 2, Petrograd Side* ☎ *812/233–7052* 💲 *150R* 🕐 *Fri.–Tues. 10–6, Wed. 10–8; closed last Mon. of month* Ⓜ *Gorkovskaya.*

VLADIMIRSKAYA (LOWER NEVSKY PROSPEKT) (ВЛАДИМИРСКАЯ)

"There is nothing finer than Nevsky prospekt, not in St. Petersburg at any rate, for in St. Petersburg it is everything . . . " wrote the great Russian author Nikolai Gogol more than 150 years ago. Today Nevsky prospekt may not be as resplendent as it was in the 1830s, when noblemen and ladies strolled along the elegant avenue or paraded by in horse-drawn carriages, but it's still the main thoroughfare, and remains the pulse of the city. Through the 18th century it was built up with estates and manors of the gentry, most of which still stand as testimony to the city's noble past. The next century saw a boom of mercantile growth that added sections farther south as centers for commerce, finance, and trade. Under the Communists, few new sites were planned on the prospekt. Instead, old structures found new uses, and the bulk of the Soviets' building was directed outside the City Center. Today, Nevsky is a retail center, complete with souvenir shops, clubs, neon lights, and young kids sporting some outrageous clothes.

GETTING HERE AND AROUND

To reach Lower Nevsky, get off at Ploshchad Vosstaniya metro station. The Vladimirskaya area is best reached via the Vladimirskaya/Dostoyevskaya metro station.

TIMING

If you want to just see the sights on Nevsky prospekt, you need only plan for a few hours of walking. The top attractions you'll most likely want to visit are Kazan Cathedral, Alexander Nevsky Lavra, and Nevsky prospekt. If you want to do some shopping then you may spend another couple of hours at Gostiny Dvor department store. Most souvenir shops are on and around Nevsky prospekt.

8

TOP ATTRACTIONS

Fodor's Choice ★ **Alexander Nevsky Lavra (Александро-Невская Лавра)**. The word *lavra* in Russian is reserved for a monastery of the highest order, of which there are just four in all of Russia and Ukraine. Named in honor of St. Alexander Nevsky, this monastery was founded in 1710 by Peter the Great and given lavra status in 1797. Prince Alexander of Novgorod (1220–63), the great military commander, became a national hero and saint because he halted the relentless eastward drive for Russian territory by the Germans and the Swedes. Peter chose this site for the monastery, thinking that it was the same place where the prince had fought the battle in 1240 that earned him the title Alexander of the Neva (Nevsky); actually, the famous battle took place some 20 km (12 mi) away. Alexander Nevsky had been buried in Vladimir, but in 1724, on Peter's orders, his remains were transferred to the monastery that was founded in his honor.

Entrance to the monastery is through the archway of the elegant **Gate Church** (Tserkovnyye Vorota), built by Ivan Starov between 1783 and 1785. The walled pathway is flanked by two cemeteries—together known as the Necropolis of Masters of Arts—whose entrances are a short walk down the path. To the left lies the older **Lazarus Cemetery** (Lazarevskoye kladbische). The list of famous people buried here reads like a who's who of St. Petersburg architects; it includes Quarenghi, Rossi, de Thomon, and Voronikhin. The cemetery also contains the tombstone of the father of Russian science, Mikhail Lomonosov. The **Tikhvinskoye kladbische**, on the opposite side, is the final resting place of several of St. Petersburg's great literary and musical figures. The grave of Fyodor Dostoyevsky, in the northwestern corner, is easily identified by the tombstone's sculpture, which portrays the writer with his flowing beard. Continuing along the walled path you'll soon reach the composers' corner, where Rimsky-Korsakov, Mussorgsky, Borodin, and Tchaikovsky are buried. The compound includes an exhibition hall with temporary exhibits of "urban sculpture."

Church of the Annunciation

After this look at St. Petersburg's cultural legacy, return to the path and cross the bridge spanning the **Monastyrka River.** As you enter the monastery grounds, the Church of the Annunciation (Tserkov Blagovescheniya), greets you on your left. The red-and-white rectangular church was designed by Domenico Trezzini and built between 1717 and 1722. It now houses the Museum of City Sculpture (open daily 9:30–1 and 2–5), which contains models of St. Petersburg's architectural masterpieces as well as gravestones and other fine examples of memorial sculpture. Also in the church are several graves of 18th-century statesmen. The great soldier Generalissimo Alexander Suvorov, who led the Russian army to numerous victories during the Russo-Turkish War (1768–74), is buried here under a simple marble slab that he purportedly designed himself. It reads simply: "Here lies Suvorov." Opposite the church, a shop sells religious items and souvenirs.

Trinity Cathedral

Outside the church and continuing along the same path, you'll first pass a millennial monument celebrating 2,000 years of Christianity on your right, before reaching the monastery's main cathedral, the Trinity Cathedral (Troitsky Sobor). This was one of the few churches in St. Petersburg allowed to function during the Soviet era. Designed by Ivan Starov and completed at the end of the 18th century, it stands out among the monastery's predominantly baroque architecture for its monumental classical design. Services are held here daily, and the church is open to the public from 6 am until the end of the evening service around 8 pm. The magnificent interior, with its stunning gilded iconostasis, is worth a visit. The large central dome, adorned by frescoes designed by the great architect Quarenghi, seems to soar toward the heavens. The church houses the main relics of Alexander Nevsky.

St. Nicholas Cemetery

As you leave the church, walk down the steps and go through the gate on the right. A door on the left bears a simple inscription, written by hand: "Svezhy Khleb" (fresh bread). Here you can buy delicious bread baked on the premises. After the gate comes a courtyard and, at the back of the church, a gate to yet another burial ground: St. Nicholas Cemetery (Nikolskoye Kladbishche), opened in 1863 and one of the most prestigious burial grounds of the time; it's open daily 9–8 (until 7 in winter). In 1927 the cemetery was closed and the remains of prominent people buried here, including novelist Goncharov and composer Rubinstein, were transferred over the course of several years to the Volkovskoye Cemetery and the Necropolis of Masters of Arts. This movement went on until the 1940s, by which time valuable funeral monuments had been lost. As you reach the steps of the little yellow-and-white church in the center (which gave its name to the graveyard), turn right and walk to a derelict chapel of yellow brick, which has been turned into a makeshift **monument to Nicholas II.** Photocopies stand in for photographs of the Imperial family; pro-monarchy white, yellow, and black flags hang from the ceilings; and passionate adherents have added primitive frescoes to the scene. Nearby, in front of Trinity Cathedral, is yet another final resting place on the lavra's grounds—the **Communist Burial Ground** (Kommunisticheskaya Ploshchadka), where, starting in 1919, defenders of Petrograd, victims of the Kronshtadt rebellion, old Bolsheviks, and prominent scientists were buried. The last to receive that honor were people who took part in the siege of Leningrad.

Entrance to the monastery grounds is free, although you are asked to make a donation. You must purchase a ticket for the two cemeteries of the Necropolis of Masters of Arts and the museum, and (as with most Russian museums) it costs extra to take photos or use a video camera. There are ticket kiosks outside the two paying cemeteries, after the gate, and inside the Tikhvin Cemetery, on the right side. ✉ *1 pl. Alexandra Nevskovo, Vladimirskaya* ☎ *812/274–1612 information, tours* ⊕ *lavra. spb.ru* ✇ *Museum of City Sculpture 60R; Necropolis of Masters of Arts 200R* ☉ *Fri.–Wed. 9:30–5* Ⓜ *Ploshchad Alexandra Nevskovo.*

Anichkov most (Аничков мост *Anichkov bridge*). Each corner of this beautiful bridge on the Nevsky prospekt spanning the Fontanka River (the name means "fountain") bears an equestrian statue designed by Peter Klodt, erected in 1841. Removed and buried during World War II, the beautiful monuments were restored to their positions in 1945. The bridge was named for Colonel Mikhail Anichkov, whose regiment had built a wooden draw-bridge here in the 18th century; the bridge marked the city limits, and night guards carefully screened those entering the city. As you cross the bridge, pause for a moment to look back at No. 41, on the corner of Nevsky Prospekt and the Fontanka. This was formerly the **Palace of Prince Beloselsky-Belozersky**—a highly ornate, neobaroque pile designed in 1848 by Andrei Stackenschneider, who wanted to replicate Rastrelli's Stroganovsky Dvorets. The facade of blazing red stonework and whipped-cream stucco trim remains the showiest in St. Petersburg. The lavish building housed the local Communist Party headquarters during the Soviet era and is now the setting for classical music concerts. ✉ *Nevsky pr., Vladimirskaya* Ⓜ *Gostinyy.*

> **WORD OF MOUTH**
>
> "I went to the monastery Alexander Nevsky Lavra one day. The monks also sell bread here, which was interesting to see. The cemeteries are also full of famous musicians, novelists, etc. Follow the canal around a bit and get a feel for the solitude."
>
> —Lincasanova

WORTH NOTING

F.M. Dostoyevsky Literary-Memorial Museum (Литературно-мемориальный Музей Ф.М. Достоевского *Literaturno Memorialnyi Muzey Fyodora Dostoyevskovo*). Here, in the last place in which he lived, Fyodor Dostoyevsky (1821–81) wrote *The Brothers Karamazov.* Dostoyevsky preferred to live in the part of the city inhabited by the ordinary people who populated his novels. He always insisted that the windows of his workroom overlook a church, as they do in this simple little house that has been remodeled to look as it did at the time Dostoyevsky and his family lived here. Perhaps the most interesting section of the museum deals with the writer's stay in prison in the Peter and Paul Fortress, and his commuted execution. ✉ *2 per. Kuznechny, bldg. 5, Vladimirskaya* ☎ *812/571–4031 information, 812/571-4031 order excusions* ⊕ *www.md.spb.ru* 🎫 *160R* ☉ *Tues.–Sun. 11–6* Ⓜ *Dostoyevskaya or Vladimirskaya.*

Ploshchad Vosstaniya (Площадь Восстания *Insurrection Square*). The site of many revolutionary speeches and armed clashes with military and police forces is generally called by its former name, Insurrection Square (the adjacent metro station is still known by that name). The busy Moscow railroad station is here, and this part of Nevsky Prospekt is lined with many kinds of shops, including new stores like Stockmann and H&M, as well as art galleries and bookstores. A stroll here is not a casual affair, since Nevsky is almost always teeming with bustling crowds of shoppers and street artists. ✉ *Ploshchad Vosstaniya, Vladimirskaya* Ⓜ *Ploshchad Vosstaniya.*

White Nights

St. Petersburg is at 59 degrees north latitude, roughly the same latitude as Oslo, Norway; Stockholm, Sweden; and Anchorage, Alaska. Due to this northerly position, the summer months receive many more hours of sunlight, especially in June and July. The sun's short trip around this part of the earth creates an ethereal glow of twilight into the wee hours. During these White Nights, wrote the poet Joseph Brodsky, "it's hard to fall asleep because it's too light and because any dream will be inferior to this reality. Where a man doesn't cast a shadow, like water." If you're visiting St. Petersburg during this time, you should partake in the many festivals, such as the Mariinsky Theatre's Stars of the White Nights, and spend at least one late night outdoors. Take a walk around the historic center, by Peter and Paul Fortress, St. Isaac's Cathedral, and the State Hermitage Museum, which all face the Neva. Stroll along the banks of the river until you come across a bridge such as Dvortsovy most (Palace Bridge) next to the Hermitage and stop to watch the ships pass through the open bridge. Each bridge has its own time schedule, but they begin to open at approximately 1 am and close at about 5 am. If you don't want to stay out all night, be sure to stay on the side of the river where your hotel is located. However, getting trapped on the other side of the city is rather romantic and you'll see couples kissing on the embankment while "waiting" for the bridges to close.

LITEINY/SMOLNY

8

This region lies to the northeast of Vladimirskaya and includes the Smolny cathedral. The Kirov Islands (north of the city), the Southern Suburbs, and the Vyborg Side (in the northeast corner of the city) have just a few sights. Luckily, that gives visitors to this neighborhood less of a touristy experience and more of a unique taste of Russian life, including interesting music venues and funky shops.

Smolny (Смольный). Someone mentioning the Smolny may be referring to either the beautiful baroque church and convent or the classically designed institute that went down in history as the Bolshevik headquarters in the Revolution of 1917. The two architectural complexes are right next door to each other, on the Neva's left bank. Construction of the Smolny convent and cathedral began under Elizabeth I and continued during the reign of Catherine the Great, who established a school for the daughters of the nobility within its walls. The centerpiece of the convent is the magnificent five-domed **Cathedral of the Resurrection,** which was designed by Bartolomeo Rastrelli and which is, some historians say, his greatest creation. At first glance, the highly ornate blue-and-white cathedral seems to have leaped off the pages of a fairy tale. Its five white onion domes, crowned with gilded globes supporting crosses of gold, convey a sense of magic and power. Begun by Rastrelli in 1748, the cathedral was not completed until the 1830s, by the architect Vasily Stasov. Few traces of the original interior have survived. It's currently used for concerts, notably of Russian sacred music, and rather insignificant exhibits.The cathedral tower offers the highest viewing point in the city. ⊠ *1 pl. Rastrelli, bldg. 3, Liteiny/Smolny* ☎ *812/710–3159 information, 812/577–1421 automatic information* ⊕ *www.cathedral.ru* ✉ *Cathedral 150R, tower 100R, combined ticket to cathedral and the tower 200R* ☉ *Sept.16–Apr. 30, Thurs.–Tues. 11–7 (tower and kassa close at 6); May 1–Sept. 15, Thurs.–Tues. 10–7 (kassa closes at 6)* Ⓜ *Chernyshevskaya.*

OFF THE
BEATEN
PATH

Piskaryevskoye Cemetery (Пискаревское кладбище *Piskaryevskoye Kladbische*). The extent of the city's suffering during the 900-day siege by the Nazis between 1941 and 1944 becomes clear on a visit to this sobering place in the northeastern outskirts of the city, used as a mass burial ground for 500,000 World War II victims. The numbingly endless rows of common graves carry simple slabs indicating the year in which those below them died, some from shelling, but most from cold and starvation. Memorial monuments and an eternal flame commemorate the dead, but most moving of all is an inscription on the granite wall at the far end of the cemetery: a famous poem by radio personality Olga Bergholts ends with the oft-repeated phrase, "No one is forgotten, nothing is forgotten." The granite pavilions at the entrance house a small museum with photographs and memoirs documenting the siege. (Start with the one on the right side; the pavilions are open until 5 and admission is free.) On display is Tanya Savicheva's "diary," scraps of paper on which the young schoolgirl recorded the death of every member of her family. The last entry reads, "May 13. Mother died. Everyone is dead. Only I am left." (She, too, died as a result of the war.) To reach the cemetery go to Ploshchad Muzhestva metro station, then take a public bus 123 or 178 up Nepokoryonnykh prospekt to the stop marked "Piskaryovskoye Kladbische." ⊠ *74 Nepokorennykh pr., Vyborg Side* ☎ *812/247–5716 tours* ⊕ *www.pmemorial.ru* ✉ *Free* ☉ *Daily 10–6* Ⓜ *Ploshchad Muzhestva.*

State Museum "Smolny" (Государственный Музей). Giacomo Quarenghi designed this neoclassical building between 1806 and 1808 in the style of an imposing country manor. It's here where Lenin and his associates planned the overthrow of the Kerensky government in October 1917, and Lenin lived at the Smolny for 124 days. The rooms in which he resided and worked are now a memorial museum. The museum also has an exhibit on the Russian Institute of Noble Girls, which was in the building from 1808 through 1917. The school was founded by the decree of Catherine the Great in 1764 and aimed to turn out well-educated women and future mothers, who would go on to raise similarly worthy children. The Institute enrolled girls from noble families from six years of age, and they graduated when they turned 18, after intense instruction in science, crafts, and the arts. They were allowed to see their parents rarely, and only with special permission. Today the rest of the building houses the offices of the governor of St. Petersburg and can be visited only by special request. To see the museum, make an appointment at least a week in advance. Tours are in Russian only, so you may want to bring an interpreter.

■TIP→ **Admission to the Smolny is only through a tourist company or some other official or business organization and arrangements must be made at least four or five days in advance.** ✉ *1 Proletarskoy Diktatury, Liteiny/Smolny* ☎ *812/576–7461 tours, 812/576–7746 tours* 💳 *300R* ⊘ *Weekdays 10–5 by appointment* Ⓜ *Chernyshevskaya.*

Ulitsa Zodchevo Rossi (Улица Зодчего Росси). The street named for architect Carlo Rossi, the Italian architect who designed many of the classical buildings in St. Petersburg, has extraordinary proportions: it's bounded by two buildings of exactly the same height, its width (72 feet) equals the height of the buildings, and its length is exactly 10 times its width. A complete view unfolds only at the end of the street, where it meets ploshchad Lomonosov. The perfect symmetry is reinforced by the identical facades of the two buildings, which are painted the same yellow and both decorated with impressive white pillars. One of the buildings here, at Number 2, is the legendary **Vaganova Ballet School** (founded in 1738), whose pupils included Karsavina as well as Pavlova, Nijinsky, Ulanova, Baryshnikov, and Nureyev. ✉ *Liteiny/Smolny* Ⓜ *Nevsky Prospekt.*

> ## THE SONG OF GRIEF
>
> One of Anna Akhmatova's most famous poems is "Requiem," first published in 1963. It's in part about her son, historian Lev Gumilev, who spent many years imprisoned during Stalin's Terror. Akhmatova was asked to describe what was happening by another woman waiting in the visitors' line at the prison. She did just that in the haunting lines: "This happened when only the dead wore smiles— / they rejoiced at being safe from harm. / And Leningrad dangled from its jails / like some unnecessary arm."

8

ST. PETERSBURG
WHERE TO EAT

Updated by
Chris Gordon

More than two decades have passed since the fall of the Soviet Union and with it the days when dining choices in St. Petersburg, or any Russian city for that matter, were limited to traditional, often uninspired, but always inexpensive Russian-style eateries. In fact, dining is among the great pleasures in the city of Peter the Great these days. Yes, you can dine like a tsar, and in just about any other fashion and on any kind of cuisine you prefer. Top chefs have taken over the dining rooms of some of the best hotels—including the Grand Hotel Europe, the Kempinski, and the W—where they serve top-notch food in beautiful settings. You'll also find a growing number of ethnic choices, and even vegetarians, often at a loss to find a meat-free meal in Russian, have some options, too.

Traditionalists need not worry, however. Homey and jovial budget eateries serving quick, substantial, and good meals for less than 250 rubles have mushroomed around the city. Stands selling Russian blini, the hearty Russian cousin of the French crepe, are everywhere, and they make a great pit stop.

Here are a few things to keep in mind. Few restaurants in St. Petersburg have no-smoking sections; in fact, some places have cigarettes listed on the menu. But attitudes are changing and you'll sometimes be offered a seat in a no-smoking section. The dining sections of *St. Petersburg Times* and *St. Petersburg in Your Pocket* are worth checking out, for both the restaurant reviews and the ads for tempting business lunch deals, which are typically priced between 300R and 600R.

It's not necessary to plan ahead if you want to land a table in a nice establishment on weekdays, but it's generally a good idea to reserve ahead for weekend dining. Ask your hotel or tour guide for help making a reservation. Most restaurants stop serving food around 11 pm or midnight, although more and more 24-hour cafés are opening.

BEST BETS FOR ST. PETERSBURG DINING

With hundreds of restaurants to choose from, how will you decide where to eat? Fodor's writers and editors have selected their favorite restaurants by price, cuisine, and experience in the Best Bets lists below. In the first column, Fodor's Choice properties represent the "best of the best" in every price category. You can also search by neighborhood for excellent eats—just peruse our reviews on the following pages.

Fodor'sChoice★

Buddha Bar $$$$, p. 255
L'Europe $$$$, p. 247
Mechta Molokhovets $$$$, p. 256
miX $$$$, p. 252
Restoran $$$, p. 253
Taleon $$$$, p. 250
Terrassa $$, p. 250
Tsar $$$$, p. 251

By Price

$

Bizet, p. 255
Chainaya Lozhka, p. 246
Jean-Jacques, p. 254
Kilikia, p. 247
Pervoye, Vtorye i Kompot, p. 256
Stolle, p. 253
Teplo, p. 253

$$

Tandoor, p. 250
Tbiliso, p. 254
Terrassa, p. 250
Vostochny Ugolok, p. 251

$$$

Gastronom, p. 247
Macaroni, p. 256
Mops, p. 256

$$$$

1913, p. 251
Bellevue Brasserie, p. 246
Francesco, p. 255
L'Europe, p. 247
Mechta Molokhovets, p. 256
Russian Vodka Room No. 1, p. 252
Taleon, p. 250
Tsar, p. 251

By Cuisine

RUSSIAN

1913 $$$$, p. 251
Chekhov $$$, p. 254
Mechta Molokhovets $$$$, p. 256
Restoran $$$, p. 253
Russian Vodka Room No. 1 $$$$, p. 252
Tsar $$$$, p. 251

ITALIAN

Da Albertone $, p. 246
Francesco $$$$, p. 255
Il Grappolo $$$, p. 247

MIDDLE EASTERN

Caravan $$, p. 251
Kilikia $, p. 247
Tbiliso $$, p. 254
Vostochny Ugolok $$, p. 251

VEGETARIAN

Botanika $, p. 255
Francesco $$$$, p. 255
Pervoye, Vtorye i Kompot $, p. 256
Stolle $, p. 253
Tandoor $$, p. 250

By Experience

CHILD-FRIENDLY

Da Albertone $, p. 246
Botanika $, p. 255
Gastronom $$$, p. 247
Teplo $, p. 253
Via dell'Oliva $$, p. 251

GREAT VIEW

Bellevue Brasserie $$$$, p. 246
Café Singer $, p. 246
Ocean $$$$, p. 254
Terrassa $$, p. 250

MOST ROMANTIC

Bellevue Brasserie $$$$, p. 246
Il Grappolo $$$, p. 247
L'Europe $$$$, p. 247
Staraya Tamozhnya $$$$, p. 254
Tsar $$$$, p. 251

MOST AUTHENTIC

Mechta Molokhovets $$$$, p. 256
Restoran $$$, p. 253
Tandoor $$, p. 250
Tbiliso $$, p. 254
Tsar $$$$, p. 251

9

RESTAURANT REVIEWS

Use the coordinate (✣ B2) at the end of each review to locate a property on the Where to Eat in St. Petersburg map.

Prices in the reviews are the average cost of a main course at dinner or, if dinner is not served, at lunch.

CITY CENTER

$$$$
FRENCH
✕ **Bellevue Brasserie (Бельвью Брассери).** A meal atop the Kempinski Hotel is literally head and shoulders above any other dining experience in St. Petersburg, thanks to a breathtaking, 360-degree panorama. The menu fuses French classics with traditional Russian classics, such as beef Stroganoff. For dessert, there's the coupe Romanoff, an artfully presented concoction of strawberries, vanilla ice cream, and whipped cream. Bellevue welcomes those who just want to stop in for coffee or a drink and take in a view that includes the golden spire of the Admiralty, the top of the Church of the Savior on Spilled Blood, the roof of the Hermitage, and the dome of St. Isaac's Cathedral. ⑤ *Average main: 930R* ✉ *Kempinski Hotel, 22 nab. Reki Moiki, City Center* ☎ *812/335–9111* ⊕ *www.kempinski-st-petersburg.com* Ⓜ *Nevsky Prospekt* ✣ *D4.*

$
CAFÉ
✕ **Café Singer (Кафе Зингеръ).** The location, on the second floor of the Dom Knigi bookstore, is one of the best people-watching spots in St. Petersburg, and the food is a notch above that usually on offer in cafés. The menu includes traditional Russian dishes, including *pelmeni* (meat dumplings) and borscht, as well as lighter and sweeter fare, such as sandwiches and quiches and cakes and ice cream. ⑤ *Average main: 450R* ✉ *Dom Knigi, 28 Nevsky pr., City Center* ☎ *812/571–8223* ⊕ *www.singercafe.ru* Ⓜ *Nevsky Prospekt* ✣ *D4.*

$
EASTERN
EUROPEAN
✕ **Chainaya Lozhka (Чайная ложка).** Distinguishable by its white and orange teaspoon logo, this is an extremely cheap and cheerful counter-service *blini* chain with locations all over downtown. You may be put off by the plastic cutlery and the lackadaisical service, but the *blini* are authentic and filling, and they provide a great cheap meal when you are in a hurry. The two-course business lunch is also a good deal and very popular. ⑤ *Average main: 35R* ✉ *42 ul. Sadovaya, City Center* ☎ *812/310–1315* ⊕ *www.teaspoon.ru* ▭ *No credit cards* Ⓜ *Sadovaya* ✣ *D4.*

$
CAFÉ
✕ **Coffeehouse.** Starbucks clones have sprung up on almost every corner in St. Petersburg, and many belong to the Coffeehouse chain. At any you can grab a good and inexpensive lunch with soup, salad, and coffee or tea, and a full range of reasonably well-made coffee drinks are available. ⑤ *Average main: 350R* ✉ *9 Nevsky pr., bldg. 7, City Center* ☎ *812/570–4774* ⊕ *www.coffeehouse.ru* Ⓜ *Admiralteyskaya* ✣ *D4.*

$
ITALIAN
✕ **Da Albertone (Да Альбертоне).** More than 40 kinds of pizza are prepared by Italian cooks who know what they're doing. The house-made focaccia is also delicious, and other dishes worth looking out for are the *osso buco* (veal shank), seafood risotto, and any of the pastas. Though this cheerful place is always busy, service is friendly and prompt. ⑤ *Average main: 450R* ✉ *23 ul. Millionnaya, City Center* ☎ *812/315–8673* ⊕ *www.daalbertone.ru* Ⓜ *Admiralteyskaya* ✣ *D3.*

$$$$
EASTERN
EUROPEAN

✕ **Erivan** (Эривань). One of the city's few Armenian restaurants is calm and simply decorated, and nicely located along a quiet stretch of the Fontanka around the corner from the Alexandrinsky Theatre. Every element of the dining experience—from the food to the table linens—has been lovingly crafted: the *kufta* (stone-ground veal sirloin) and stuffed quail are authentic and delicious. Every night, except Sunday, live folk music adds to the atmosphere. $ *Average main: 900R* ⊠ *51 nab. Reki Fontanki, City Center* ☎ *812/703–3820* ⊕ *www.erivan.ru* Ⓜ *Gostiny Dvor* ✥ *E4.*

$$$$
RUSSIAN
Fodor's Choice
★

✕ **L'Europe** (Европа *Yevropa*). The breathtaking surroundings—there's an art-nouveau stained-glass roof, shining parquet floors, and private balconies—are fit for a tsar, as are the prices. The mouthwatering menu includes some dishes inspired by authentic royal recipes, among them beef filet with a bacon and mustard champagne sauce. The chef's tasting menu gets off to a memorable start with a pair of eggshells filled with truffle-flavored scrambled eggs topped with Osetra caviar. Reserve well ahead, especially in summer. $ *Average main: 1900R* ⊠ *Grand Hotel Europe, 1/7 ul. Mikhailovskaya, City Center* ☎ *812/329–6600* ⊕ *www.grandhoteleurope.com* ⌂ *Reservations essential* ⌷ *Jacket and tie* Ⓜ *Nevsky Prospekt or Gostinny Dvor* ✥ *D4.*

$$
MEDITERRANEAN

✕ **Freeman's.** Behind an unassuming facade down a quiet side street off Nevsky prospekt is this warm and comforting room that might transport you to Italy or the South of France, as will the cuisine. Updated versions of classic Mediterranean dishes include some inventive, simply prepared fish dishes, such as tuna with pesto and scallops with figs. The menu varies, as the chef selects from what's freshest at the market. $ *Average main: 600R* ⊠ *8 ul. Kazanskaya, City Center* ☎ *812/312–0540* ⊕ *www.freemans.su* Ⓜ *Nevsky Prospect* ✥ *D4.*

$$$
EUROPEAN

✕ **Gastronom** (Гастроном). This favorite for relaxed weekend lunches is especially popular in warm weather, when outdoor tables overlook the Field of Mars. The main dining room is done in French farmhouse style, with chunky wooden tables and soft cushions; walls lined with dusty wine bottles; and a long table along one wall groaning under mounds of cheese, freshly baked bread, and fruit. Salads come in generous sizes and can easily replace a main course; Italian and Russian dishes predominate. $ *Average main: 700R* ⊠ *7 nab. Reki Moiki, bldg. 1, City Center* ☎ *812/314–3849* ⊕ *www.gastronom.su* Ⓜ *Nevsky Prospekt or Gostinny Dvor* ✥ *D3.*

$$$
MODERN ITALIAN

✕ **Il Grappolo.** One of the city's best Italian restaurants serves deliciously fresh food, including a Caprese salad with buffalo mozzarella. Everything—from the fresh arugula salad with shrimp to the mushroom risotto, duck confit, and a stellar tiramisu—stands out. Downstairs at the wine bar, Probka, you can order wines by the glass from the well-chosen list and have an authentic Caesar salad. $ *Average main: 750R* ⊠ *5 ul. Belinskogo, City Center* ☎ *812/273–4904* ⊕ *www.probka.org* Ⓜ *Gostiny Dvor or Mayakovskaya* ✥ *E4.*

$
MIDDLE EASTERN

✕ **Kilikia** (Киликия). A haven for local Armenians, and named after an ancient region in modern-day Turkey, this restaurant serves sizzling beef stew and a tempting variety of expertly cooked kebabs in sprawling, dimly lit rooms. The seemingly endless menu may confuse the uninitiated, but the staff is ready to help. A bargain-priced, three-course business lunch is popular with locals and budget-minded travelers. $ *Average*

9

Where to Eat in St. Petersburg

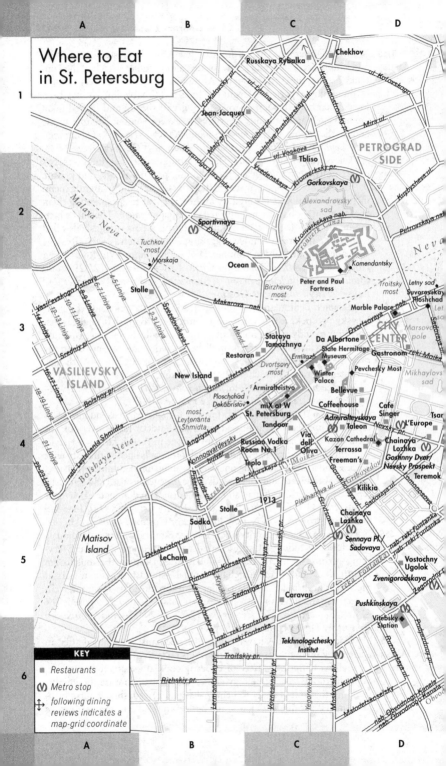

A   **B**   **C**   **D**

1

Chekhov

Russkaya Rybalka

Jean-Jacques

ul. Lenina

Chkalovsky pr.

Krasnogo kursanta ul.

ul. Voskova

Tbliso

Malty ul.

Bolshoy pr.

Bolshaya Pushkarskaya ul.

Kamennoostrovsky pr.

Mira ul.

Kuybysheva ul.

PETROGRAD SIDE

Vvedenskaya

Kronverksky pr.

Gorkovskaya Ⓜ

2

Zhdanovskaya ul.

Malaya Neva

Tuchkov most

Morskaya

Sportivnaya Ⓜ

Dobrolyubova

Ocean

Alexandrovsky sad

Kronverskaya nab.

Kronverk Canal

Komendantsky

Peter and Paul Fortress

Birzhevoy most

Petrovskaya nab.

Neva

Troitsky most

Letny sad

Suvorovskaya

Ploshchad

Let

3

Vasilevskaya Ostrova

4-5 Liniya

6-7 Liniya

8-9 Liniya

10-11 Liniya

12-13 Liniya

14 Liniya

Stolle

Sredny pr.

Sredkovskaya

2-3 Liniya

Makarova nab.

Mendi

Staraya Tamozhnya

Restoran

VASILIEVSKY ISLAND

Bolshoy pr.

18-19 Liniya

21 Liniya

New Island

Universitetskaya

Dvortsovy most

Ermitazh

Da Albertone

State Hermitage Museum

Marble Palace

Dvortsovaya

CITY CENTER

reki Moika

Gastronom

Mikhailovsky sad

Marsovo pole

Pevchesky Most

4

Bolshaya Neva

nab. Leytenanta Shmidta

Angliyskaya nab.

Ploschad Dekábristov

most Leytenanta Shmidta

Armiralteistvo

miX at W St. Petersburg

Tandoor

Via dell Oliva

Winter Palace

Bellevue

Coffeehouse

Admiralteyskaya Ⓜ

Taleon

Kazan Cathedral

Terrassa

Freeman's

Cafe Singer

L'Europe

Tsar

Nevsky pr.

Ⓜ

Chainaya Lozhka

Goshnny Dvor

Nevsky Prospekt Ⓜ

Teremok

Konnogvardeysky bulvar

Russian Vodka Room No.1

Teplo

Bol. Morskaya ul.

Moika

Gorokhovaya ul.

Griboyedot

Kilikia

Sadovaya

5

Matisov Island

Pryazhka

Dekabristov ul.

Stolle

Sadko

LeChaim

Rimskago-Korsakova

Kryukova

1913

Plekhanova ul.

Voznesensky

Sadovaya ul.

Caravan

Chainaya Lozhka

Ⓜ Sennaya Pl.

Sadovaya

reki Fontanka

nab. reki Fontanka

Vostochny Ugolok

Zvenigorodskaya Ⓜ

Pushkinskaya Ⓜ

Vitebsky Station

Zagarodny

Podezdhoy

6

Rizhskiy pr.

nab. reki Fontanka

Lermontovsky pr.

Kaznacheevsky ul.

Yegorova ul.

Troitskiy pr.

Tekhnologichesky Institut Ⓜ

Moskovsky pr.

Kinsky

Mladetskosełski

nab. Obrodnagô Kanala

nab. Obvodnogo Kanala

Obvod

KEY

▪ Restaurants

Ⓜ Metro stop

↕ *following dining reviews indicates a map-grid coordinate*

A   **B**   **C**   **D**

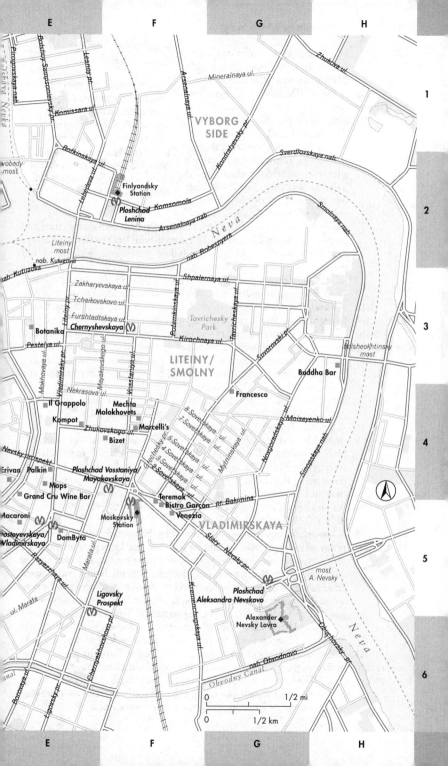

main: 420R ✉ *40 nab. Kanala Gri-boyedova, City Center* ☎ *812/327–2208* Ⓜ *Sennaya Ploshchad* ✣ *D4.*

$$$$
FRENCH
✕ **Palkin** (**Палкин**). A legendary restaurant of the same name was established on this spot in 1785. The formal and elegant interior evokes those bygone days, though the present incarnation has become a bit worn around the edges since its Yeltsin-era heyday. You'll still feast like an aristocrat, on such dishes as chicken with morel sauce, venison with pine-nut marmalade, fillet of turbot served with pistachio nuts and curry sauce, and a salad of smoked salmon with fresh oysters and beluga caviar. It's worth a visit for the window seats alone, which look out onto bustling Nevsky prospekt. Ⓢ *Average main: 1090R* ✉ *47 Nevsky pr., at Vladirmirsky pr., City Center* ☎ *812/703–5371* ⊕ *www.palkin.ru* ⟁ *Reservations essential* Ⓜ *Mayakovskaya or Nevsky Prospekt* ✣ *E4.*

$$$$
EASTERN
EUROPEAN
Fodor's Choice
★
✕ **Taleon** (**Талион**). Inside an opulent mansion connected to the Taleon Imperial Hotel you'll find the usual array of fun for the bodyguard-protected high-society set (cigars and cognac are much in evidence) in a glittering setting, with marble fireplaces and gilded ceilings. The menu is laden with hearty Russian classics with European inspiration, including caviar, consommé with fois gras ravioli, and sea bass with truffle risotto. Ⓢ *Average main: 1200R* ✉ *Taleon Imperial Hotel, 59 nab. Reki Moiki, City Center* ☎ *812/324–9911, 812/324–9944* ⊕ *www.taleon.ru* ⟁ *Reservations essential* 🏛 *Jacket and tie* Ⓜ *Admiralteyskaya* ✣ *C4.*

$$
INDIAN
✕ **Tandoor** (**Тандур**). Waiters dressed in traditional costumes and soft embroidered shoes move soundlessly in this comfortable and quiet little place across the street from St. Isaac's Cathedral. Reliable Indian classics such as those served here were hard to find in St. Petersburg before the downfall of the USSR. A generous business lunch is an especially good deal and includes a vegetarian option. Ⓢ *Average main: 600R* ✉ *10 Admiralteysky pr., City Center* ☎ *812/312–3886* ⊕ *www.tandoor-spb.ru* Ⓜ *Admiralteyskaya* ✣ *C4.*

$
CAFÉ
✕ **Teremok** (**Теремок**). Don't be put off by the spartan setting: the owners penny-pinch on furnishings and presentation but focus their attention on their famous blinis, deservedly considered to be the best in town. Stuffed with mushrooms, ham, pork, grilled chicken, cream, honey, and a dozen other fillings, they're rich in flavor and never over- or underdone. Be conservative when you order unless you're absolutely starving: a single blini is so rich and hefty that it may leave you stuffed. Teremok operates dozens of cafés and street stands throughout the city. Ⓢ *Average main: 110R* ✉ *60 Nevsky pr., City Center* ⊕ *www.teremok.ru* Ⓜ *Nevsky Prospekt* ✣ *F4.*

$$
ASIAN FUSION
Fodor's Choice
★
✕ **Terrassa**. It seems as if you could touch the cupola of the Kazan cathedral from the open-air terrace of this stylish and glamorous "place to be seen." The fusion cuisine shows heavy Asian influences, with such dishes as Peking-style roasted duck on the menu. Excellent service complements the fine food and memorable views. Ⓢ *Average main: 560R* ✉ *3 ul.*

Kazanskaya, 6th fl. of Vanity Opera boutique, City Center ☎ *812/937–6837* ⊕ *www.terrassa.ru* Ⓜ *Nevsky Prospekt or Gostiny Dvor* ✛ *D4.*

$$$$
RUSSIAN
Fodor's Choice
★

✕ **Tsar (Царь).** This large, bustling, and brightly lit dining room where oil paintings commemorate various Romanovs seems to be lifted right off the pages of *War and Peace,* and the dining experience is truly royal. A meal might begin with the classic Russian appetizer of layers of herring enclosing a beet vinaigrette and move on to beef Stroganoff or a Pozharskaya cutlet, served with sizzling hot potatoes, made in a copper pan. Despite the grandeur, the atmosphere is pleasantly relaxed and the service is anything but intimidating. Ⓢ *Average main: 2400R* ⊠ *12 ul. Sadovaya, City Center* ☎ *812/930–0444* ⊕ *www.tsar-project.ru* Ⓜ *Nevsky Prospekt* ✛ *D4.*

$$
MEDITERRANEAN
FAMILY

✕ **Via dell'Oliva.** Feta cheese delivered directly from Greece transports you directly to sunnier climes, as does everything about this stone and terra-cotta dining room that seems like the banquet hall of an Italian villa. Assorted souvlaki provide a taste of the Greek isles, while spaghetti carbonara and juicy steaks coud emerge from a trattoria kitchen in Florence. The servers are also international, and multilingual, and live folk music from many countries plays on most nights. Ⓢ *Average main: 500R* ⊠ *31 ul. Bolshaya Morskaya, City Center* ☎ *812/314–6563* ⊕ *www.viadelloliva.ru* Ⓜ *Admiralteyskaya* ✛ *C4.*

$$
MIDDLE EASTERN

✕ **Vostochny Ugolok (Восточный уголок).** The lamb, herbs, and other ingredients here are laudably fresh, and flown in several times a week from Baku, Azerbaijan. It is easy to get lost in the long menu, but much harder to be disappointed in your choice. Juicy kebabs, chops, and *khatchapuri* (cheese bread) are served in vast portions—a bowl of soup is a meal in itself. Not as appetizing is the music blaring in the three dining rooms, decorated with Oriental carpets, pillows, and pottery. Ⓢ *Average main: 600R* ⊠ *52 ul. Gorokhovaya, City Center* ☎ *812/407–5747* ⊕ *www.restoran-nzh.ru/halleasterncorner* Ⓜ *Sadovaya or Sennaya Ploshchad* ✛ *D5.*

ADMIRALTEISKY

$$$$
RUSSIAN

✕ **1913** (*Tisicha Dyevatsot Trinatsat*). The name evokes the last days of Imperial Russia, and the era is celebrated in low-key, comfortably elegant surroundings where a menu offers a huge selection of Russian favorites served in huge portions. The emphasis is on game and fish; an excellent and traditional meal might begin with mushroom soup or borscht, followed by sturgeon or salmon. Ⓢ *Average main: 1200R* ⊠ *2 Voznesensky pr., bldg. 13, Admiralteisky* ☎ *812/315–5148* ⊕ *www.restaurant-1913.spb.ru* ⚐ *Reservations essential* Ⓜ *Sadovaya or Ploshchad Sennaya* ✛ *C5.*

$$
MIDDLE EASTERN

✕ **Caravan (Караван).** The stuffed camel, Turkish carpets, and sizzling kebabs prepared in the middle of the room create an exotic ambience in which to enjoy what many aficionados consider to be the best Middle Eastern food in St. Petersburg. Whatever the variety of kebab you choose, begin a meal with *kutab,* a lightly fried pocket of dough filled with shrimp, pumpkin, or cheese. Ⓢ *Average main: 600R* ⊠ *46 Voznesensky pr., Admiralteisky* ☎ *812/310–5678* Ⓜ *Sadovaya or Tekhnologichesky Institut* ✛ *C5.*

9

$$$$
INTERNATIONAL

✕ **Grand Cru Wine Bar.** Wine lovers can choose from a huge list of French and Italian vintages, then select a bottle from the adjacent shop. Or, they can settle into the sleek and fashionably eclectic surroundings for an inventive and flavorful meal in which duck with rosemary and honey might be accompanied by black rice with a cappuccino of Mediterranean herbs and an extremely elegant take on borscht. $ *Average main: 1200R* ⊠ *52 nab. Reki Fontanki, Admiralteisky* ☏ *812/363–2511* ⊕ *www. grandcru.ru* Ⓜ *Gostiny Dvor, Dostoyevskaya, or Vladimirskaya* ✛ *E4.*

$$
RUSSIAN

✕ **LeChaim** (Лехаим). The kosher cuisine, served in the spacious basement of St. Petersburg's Great Choral Synagogue, is as popular with a nonreligious crowd as it is with dietary adherents. Such favorites as chicken schnitzel and trout fillet wrapped in grape leaves are served in generous portions and at very reasonable prices. Keep in mind that the restaurant can be difficult to find, since the doorway is discreetly marked, and is often booked for weddings and other events that take place in the synagogue, so call ahead. $ *Average main: 500R* ⊠ *2 Lermontovsky pr., Admiralteisky* ☏ *812/572–5616* ⊕ *www.jewishpetersburg.ru* ▭ *No credit cards* ⊘ *Closed Sat.* Ⓜ *Sennaya Ploshchad or Sadovaya* ✛ *B5.*

$$$$
MODERN FRENCH
Fodor's Choice
★

✕ **miX.** Michelin-starred chef Alain Ducasse's Russian outpost has shaken up the city's dining scene with its haute-cuisine interpretation of French classics. Using the best and freshest local produce—as well as specialty items flown in from abroad—the kitchen prepares satisfying and deceptively straightforward variations of such classics as oven-baked duck breast and seared beef fillet. Like the menu, the dining room manages to be ultra-fashionable while staying relaxed and comfortable at the same time. $ *Average main: 1500R* ⊠ *6 Voznesensky pr., Admiralteisky* ☏ *812/610–6160* ⊕ *www.mixinstpetersburg.com* ⌂ *Reservations essential* Ⓜ *Admiralteyskaya* ✛ *C4.*

$$$$
RUSSIAN

✕ **Russian Vodka Room No.1** (Русская Рюмочная №1 *Russkaya Ryumochnaya Nomer Odin*). Discreet and genteel, this spacious one-room venue could come straight out of one of Chekhov's stories and is the perfect place to try various vodkas and home-brewed liqueurs. Alcoholic sampling requires sustenance, and a menu offers many traditional choices, with an emphasis on fish dishes. A starter group platter features four types of smoked fish—including *omul* (cisco, a kind of whitefish) from Lake Baikal and *sig,* a whitefish from Russia's far east. A memorable main course is fried pike-perch from Lake Ladoga, served with mashed potatoes. $ *Average main: 900R* ⊠ *4 ul. Konnogvardeisky bulvar, Admiralteisky* ☏ *812/570–6420* ⊕ *www.vodkaroom.ru* Ⓜ *Sadovaya, Sennaya Ploshchad, or Admiralteyskaya* ✛ *C4.*

$$$
RUSSIAN

✕ **Sadko** (Садко). Ruby red chandeliers and modern interpretations of Russian folkloric motifs provide a perfect prelude to a night at the nearby Marrinsky Theatre. The menu, however, is as down to earth as the surroundings are fanciful, focusing on such popular Russian classics as borscht, breaded veal cutlets, and beef Stroganoff. The wine list is particularly well chosen. $ *Average main: 800R* ⊠ *2 ul. Glinka, Admiralteisky* ☏ *812/903–2373* ⊕ *www.sadko-rst.ru* Ⓜ *Sennaya Ploschad, Sadovaya, or Spasskaya* ✛ *B5.*

$ ✕ **Stolle** (Штолле *Shtolle*). This

CAFÉ casual eatery combines the best of the old and new: the fashionable surroundings are comfortable, clean, and spacious, while the kitchen turns out an old favorite—fresh-baked traditional pies. Choose from sweet or savory fillings that make the most of seasonal fruit, beef, salmon, cabbage, mushrooms, and rabbit. The salmon is a dream, and the apricot is a suitable follow-up, but all the choices are extremely good. If you have a hard time finding a seat at this popular spot, try the branch just down the street at number 33. $ *Average main: 240R* ✉ *19 ul. Dekabristov, Admiralteisky* ☎ *812/315–2383* ⊕ *www.stolle.ru* ▭ *No credit cards* Ⓜ *Sennaya Ploshchad* ✛ *C5.*

> **WORD OF MOUTH**
>
> "[The Georgian] style of food is known to be very flavorful, and it didn't disappoint. It was great having someone who speaks Russian order off the menu for us, with a sampling of dumplings, salads, and meats. (By the way, salads are not what you think. They are all a conglomeration of vegetables and marinade. Think potato salad with lots of different stuff in it, like beets, pickles, or cabbage)."
>
> —sdtravels

$ ✕ **Teplo.** The name means "warmth" in Russian, and this popular spot does

RUSSIAN indeed make guests feel warm all over, with a country-house atmosphere (a fire blazes and the main dining room is lined with bookshelves) and menu laden with cozy, expertly made classics, such as marinated beets, salted herring, meat pies, and borscht. The signature dish is a warm salad of juicy chicken livers and crispy strips of bacon surrounded by salad leaves, cherry tomatoes, and herby croutons. The three-course-plus-a-drink business lunch is an excellent value, and accordingly popular. $ *Average main: 420R* ✉ *45 ul. Bolshaya Morskaya, Admiratleisky* ☎ *812/570–1974* ⊕ *www.v-teple.ru* ⚞ *Reservations essential* Ⓜ *Admiralteyskaya* ✛ *C4.*

VASILIEVSKY ISLAND

9

$$$ ✕ **New Island** (Новыи Остров *Noviy Ostrov*). In summer this dinner

EASTERN cruise has stunning views as it sails along the Neva River, past the rows
EUROPEAN of colorful palaces lining the banks. The *New Island* sets sail promptly at 2, 6, 8, and 10:30 pm for 90-minute cruises. Inside, all is simple but refined, as is the menu. The Kamchatka crab salad makes an excellent starter, and is nicely followed with the veal Orloff with baked potatoes and dill or the fried fillet of trout with almonds. The wine list is extensive but pricey. $ *Average main: 740R* ✉ *15 nab. Universitetskaya, between Blagovyeshchensky and Dvortsovy bridges, Vasilievsky Island* ☎ *812/320–21100* ⊕ *www.concord-catering.ru* ⚞ *Reservations essential* Ⓜ *Vasileostrovskaya* ✛ *B3.*

$$$ ✕ **Restoran** (РесторанЪ). Spacious, with soft lighting and earth tones,

RUSSIAN the surroundings are at once stylish and traditional, and as straightfor-
Fodor's Choice ward as the name, which means "restaurant" in Russian. The menu of
★ traditional classics is as nonfussy as the decor; try the *sterlet* (sturgeon) baked in fragrant herbs with horseradish sauce, veal with mashed potatoes and chanterelles, or the house-made *pelmeni* (dumplings) filled with lamb, beef, or potatoes and dill. A long, wooden table at the entrance supports a wide selection of house-made flavored vodkas in rustic glass

decanters. $ *Average main: 800R* ⊠ *2 per. Tamozhenny, Vasilievsky Island* ☎ *812/327–8979* ⊕ *elbagroup.ru/restoran* ⌂ *Reservations essential* Ⓜ *Vasileostrovskaya* ✛ *C3.*

$$$$

EUROPEAN

✕ **Staraya Tamozhnya (Старая таможня** *Old Customs House*). What was for many years the best restaurant in St. Petersburg has been surpassed in recent years, but with open brickwork walls, ornate decor, and immaculately presented tables, the "Old Customs House" still puts on a good show for a memorable night on the town. Meals are exquisitely prepared, with such choices as duck breast, accompanied by pan-fried foie gras with white beans and black truffle, and black-cod fillet on a cushion of saffron and fennel that show just how sophisticated Russian cuisine can be. The wine list is excellent, and the service is friendly as well as top-notch. $ *Average main: 1600R* ⊠ *1 per. Tamozhenny, Vasilievsky Island* ☎ *812/327–8980* ⌂ *Reservations essential* Ⓜ *Admiralteyskaya or Vasileostrovskaya* ✛ *C3.*

PETROGRAD SIDE

$$$

RUSSIAN

✕ **Chekhov (Чеховъ**). Wicker furniture, handwoven napkins, and a birdcage with canaries and finches add to the flavor of an early-20th-century Russian country house, and the menu also lovingly re-creates Russian recipes of yesteryear. Emerging from the family-run kitchen are such carefully prepared dishes as roasted venison with warm fruit, Spanish garlic, and port wine sauce and Caspian sturgeon fillet with salmon roe, leek cream, and morel mushroom sauce. Libations include a nice selection of fruit liqueurs. $ *Average main: 700R* ⊠ *4 ul. Petropavlovskaya, Petrograd Side* ☎ *812/234–4511* ⊕ *www.restaurant-chekhov.ru* ⌂ *Reservations essential* Ⓜ *Petrogradskaya* ✛ *C1.*

$

FRENCH

✕ **Jean-Jacques (Жан-Жак**). Mirrored walls, red and mahogany furnishings, and tables topped with paper provide an authentic bistro ambience, a perfect setting for a classic French meal of onion soup, steak and bordelaise sauce, and crème brûlée. Fine wines are available by the glass, and attentive servers will help you with your choice. Seating is limited to only 25 people, so it's advisable to come early for dinner or take advantage of the excellent lunch, served from noon to 4 pm. $ *Average main: 390R* ⊠ *2 ul. Gatchinskaya, Petrograd Side* ☎ *812/232–9981* ⊕ *www.jan-jak.com* Ⓜ *Chkalovskaya or Petrogradskaya* ✛ *C1.*

$$$$

SEAFOOD

✕ **Ocean (Океан** *Okean*). This floating restaurant moored within sight of the Hermitage offers spectacular views as well as a buzzy dining scene on weekends. At other times, the glassed-in dining salons are calm oases in which to linger over a candlelit dinner of wonderfully fresh seafood before being whisked away to your hotel in one of the restaurant's water taxis. $ *Average main: 1200R* ⊠ *14a Dobrolyubova pr., Petrograd Side* ☎ *812/986–8600* ⊕ *www.okeanspb.ru* Ⓜ *Sportivnaya* ✛ *C2.*

$$

MIDDLE EASTERN

✕ **Tbiliso (Тбилисо**). A lot of thought was put into creating this busy and authentic Georgian restaurant, which evokes the atmosphere of old Tbilisi, the capital of Russia's southern neighbor. There may be political tensions between the nations these days, but Russians' love affair with Georgian cuisine, from *lobio* (bean salad) and grilled meat and fish *shashlyks* (shish kebabs) to *lavash* (flat bread) and *khatchapuri* (cheese-filled bread), remains passionate. Tbiliso satisfies this appetite and then some, with servers in national costume and a Georgian choir to serenade diners. If you visit only one Georgian restaurant in St. Petersburg, make it this one. Ⓢ *Average main: 500R* ⊠ *10 ul. Sytninskaya, Petrograd Side* ☎ *812/232– 9391* ⊕ *www.tbiliso.ru* Ⓜ *Petrogradskaya or Gorkovskaya* ✛ *C2.*

VLADIMIRSKAYA (LOWER NEVSKY PROSPEKT)

$$
FRENCH
✕ **Bistro Garçon (Бистро Гарсон).** Nevsky prospekt is St. Petersburg's version of a Parisian boulevard, and this comfortable, Parisian-style bistro fits right in. From the first bite of baguette you'll be transported, and the seasonably changing menu is full of soups, mussels, quiches, and other bistro favorites. With fluffy omelets, buttery croissants, and good strong coffee, the breakfast here is one of the best in the city. Ⓢ *Average main: 600R* ⊠ *95 Nevsky pr., Vladimirskaya* ☎ *812/717–2467* ⊕ *www. garcon.ru* Ⓜ *Ploshchad Vosstania* ✛ *F5.*

$
CAFÉ
✕ **Bizet (Бизе).** A youngish bohemian crowd flocks to this café furnished in pastel greens and creams and famous for its airy meringues—the Bizet, with chopped almonds and garnished with fresh raspberries, is especially popular. Some good soups and about a dozen salads are also available. Ⓢ *Average main: 400R* ⊠ *41 ul. Zhukovskogo, Vladimirskaya* ☎ *812/702– 7738* ⊕ *www.bize.spb.ru* Ⓜ *Mayakovskaya or Ploshchad Vosstania* ✛ *F4.*

$
VEGETARIAN
FAMILY
✕ **Botanika (Ботаника).** This haven for vegetarians and those seeking lighter dishes serves excellent soups, pastas, sandwiches, and dips. The airy dining room, done in shades of green, has an abundance of potted plants and is no-smoking; the only alcohol permitted is beer. Ⓢ *Average main: 350R* ⊠ *7 ul. Pestelya, Vladimirskaya* ☎ *812/272–7091* ⊕ *www. cafebotanika.ru* Ⓜ *Mayakovskaya* ✛ *E3.*

$$$$
ASIAN FUSION
Fodor's Choice
★
✕ **Buddha Bar.** Dining alcoves that line the mezzanine of a former red-brick textile factory on the Neva are an atmospheric setting for a meal of inspired cuisine accompanied by mellow jazz and lounge music. Portions of expertly prepared sushi and other Asian delights are big enough to share and the cocktails are perfectly calibrated. Ⓢ *Average main: 890R* ⊠ *78 nab. Sinopskaya, Vladimirskaya* ☎ *812/318–0707* ⊕ *www. buddha-bar.ru* Ⓜ *Aleksandra Nevskogo* ✛ *H3.*

$$
ECLECTIC
✕ **Dom Byta (Дом Быта).** A lively bar serving old-fashioned cocktails up front, a quirkily decorated dining room in the back, and a menu that ranges from Asian to European (and includes a great burger) provide a little something for everyone. The decor is thrift-shop chic; this popular and trendy place takes its name from a Soviet-era neighborhood center where it's located and is littered with old sewing machines, televisions, and retro lighting fixtures. Ⓢ *Average main: 500R* ⊠ *12 ul. Razyezhaya, Vladimirskaya* ☎ *812/975–5599* ⊕ *www.dombeat.ru* Ⓜ *Vladimirskaya or Dostoyevskaya* ✛ *E5.*

$$$$
ITALIAN
✕ **Francesco (Франческо).** Politicians, businesspeople, and television personalities are regulars at one of the city's busiest and most fashionable venues, where the two large, charmingly cluttered dining rooms are almost always packed. Whether it's a straightforward lasagna or more elegant fare, such as risotto with cuttlefish ink, everything the Italian chef sends out of the kitchen is delicious. The wine list is extensive. Ⓢ *Average main: 2000R* ⊠ *47 Suvorovsky pr., Vladimirskaya* ☎ *812/275–0552* ⊕ *www.restoran-francesco.ru* Ⓜ *Ploshchad Vosstania* ✛ *G4.*

9

$$$
MODERN ITALIAN

✕**Macaroni** (Макарони). Settle into one of the plush booths to enjoy simple Italian fare in friendly and comfortable surroundings. The pastas and pizzas are authentically delicious, as are the more ambitious meat and fish choices. A 15 percent discount for weekday dining between noon and 5 pm makes a meal here, reasonably priced at any time, a real bargain. $ *Average main: 700R* ✉ *23 ul. Rubinshteina, Vladimirskaya* ☎ *812/572–2849* Ⓜ *Dostoevskaya, Vladimirskaya, or Mayakovskaya* ✛ *E5.*

$$
ITALIAN

✕**Marcelli's** (Марчеллис). An unpretentious dining room decorated with Italian knickknacks and bare wooden tables is a good choice for an inexpensive lunch or post-theater dinner of pasta and salad (it's open until midnight). For an Italian shopping experience, stop at the retail counter to stock up on imported cheeses, cold meats, and coffees. $ *Average main: 600R* ✉ *15 ul. Vosstaniya, Vladimirskaya* ☎ *812/986–9111* ⊕ *www.marcellis.ru* Ⓜ *Ploshchad Vosstaniya* ✛ *F4.*

$$$$
RUSSIAN
Fodor's Choice
★

✕**Mechta Molokhovets** (Мечта Молоховецъ). This refined restaurant with prerevolutionary flair has a tantalizing menu based on a famous 19th-century cookbook, *A Gift to Young Housewives*, by Yelena Molokhovets. Cooking is elaborate and highly traditional here, along the lines of baked venison fillet in lingonberry and juniper sauce, pan-fried foie gras with orange-flavored brioche, or Astrakhan sturgeon braised in champagne. Waiters show deference to the guests, serving them in a pleasantly ceremonial, but not always genuine, manner. With only six tables, this dining experience is as intimate as it is expensive. $ *Average main: 1800R* ✉ *10 ul. Radischeva, Vladimirskaya* ☎ *812/929–2247* ⊕ *www.molokhovets.ru* ⚐ *Reservations essential* Ⓜ *Ploshchad Vosstania* ✛ *F4.*

$$$
ASIAN

✕**Mops** (Мопс). The city's most authentic Thai cuisine is served in modern black-and-white surroundings with a glass-enclosed terrace on the street that's great for people-watching. You can follow up a meal of spring rolls and Bangkok duck with another authentically Thai experience—the building houses a well-known massage spa of the same name. $ *Average main: 690R* ✉ *12 ul. Rubinshteina, Vladimirskaya* ☎ *812/572–3834* ⊕ *www.mopscafe.ru* Ⓜ *Mayakovskaya* ✛ *E4.*

$
CAFÉ

✕**Pervoye, Vtoroye i Kompot** (Первое, второе и компот). A glass of *kompot*, an infusion of stewed fruit, is served as a welcome drink at this funky café where two dining rooms are furnished with vintage lamps, surrealist paintings, and bizarre curio items. The menu focuses on light fare—hummus, falafels, curries, and sandwiches—and breakfast is available at any hour. On weekdays between noon and 4 pm, you get two meals for the price of one. $ *Average main: 400R* ✉ *10 ul. Zhukovskogo, Vladimirskaya* ☎ *812/719–6542* ⊕ *www.kompotcafe.ru* Ⓜ *Mayakovskaya or Ploshchad Vosstania* ✛ *E4.*

$
CAFÉ

✕**Venezia** (Венеция). This tiny café (just six tables) is hugely popular with the local Italian community, who reserve well in advance for weekends and evenings. The draw is the best Italian sorbet and gelato in St. Petersburg, with 20 different flavors that rotate every day. The chocolate gelato—bittersweet, smooth, and dizzyingly rich—is renowned. Soups, pastas, and snacks are also served. $ *Average main: 200R* ✉ *107 Nevsky pr., Vladimirskaya* ☎ *812/717–5218* ⚐ *Reservations essential* ▭ *No credit cards* Ⓜ *Ploshchad Vosstania* ✛ *F5.*

ST. PETERSBURG
WHERE TO STAY

Updated by
Chris Gordon

The former imperial capital still captivates, with accommodations that are often nothing short of sumptuous. In fact, as elsewhere in modern Russia, where luxury almost always means opulence, sophisticated minimalist interiors are few and far between here. Instead, heavy curtains, tapestries, ornate furniture, and deep carpeting grace the interiors of many of the top hotels, some of which are set in stately 19th-century mansions and charge prices to match the surroundings. One pervasive shortcoming is service, and in even in some of the grandest hotels you might encounter a somewhat haughty staff.

Like Moscow, St. Petersburg has a shortage of moderately priced hotels, and even economy-class hotels cost about twice the price you'd pay in almost any other European city. The best budget options are some of the guesthouses in former mansions that were converted to communal apartments during the Soviet era. Much nicer in this reincarnation, they're intimate, have a genial atmosphere, are often furnished with antiques, and charge rates that often include home-cooked breakfasts and modern comforts, such as free Wi-Fi.

On an organized tour, you're likely to land in one of the old standbys run by Intourist, the Soviet tourist agency monopoly. Most U.S. and British tour operators take advantage of the discounted rates at the Moskva or the Oktyabrskaya. If you're traveling on your own, the main reason to choose one of these hotels is their lower rates; many of them aren't convenient to major attractions.

An expanding number of realty agents like City Realty can organize a suitable and safe apartment rental, usually in the center of the city. The prices for such apartments usually run the level of three-star hotels, but accommodations often have much more space.

LODGING REVIEWS

Hotel reviews have been abbreviated in this book. For expanded reviews, please visit Fodors.com. Use the coordinate (⊹ B2) at the end of each review to locate a property on the Where to Stay in St. Petersburg map. Prices in the reviews are the lowest cost of a standard double room in high season.

CITY CENTER

$
RENTAL

🖼 **City Realty.** This American-owned company can help you locate a suitable mini-hotel, B&B, or centrally located apartment (which usually it owns). **Pros:** usually less expensive than the city's central hotels; can choose your own apartment; personalized service; downtown locations; more privacy. **Cons:** fewer services than a hotel; you're staying in a stranger's house. ⑤ *Rooms from: 4650R* ✉ *2 per. Muchnoi, City Center* ☎ *812/570–6342, 812/570-4709* ⊕ *www.cityrealtyrussia.com* ⊙ *Weekdays 9:30–6:30* Ⓜ *Sennaya Ploshchad, Sadovaya, or Spasskaya* ⊹ *D4.*

$$$$
HOTEL
Fodor'sChoice
★

🖼 **Grand Hotel Europe** (Гранд Отель Европа *Gran Otel Yevropa*). Behind the stunning neobaroque facade lies an art-nouveau interior with stained-glass windows, antique furnishings, and stylish and comfortable guest rooms done in pleasing shades of mauve, cream, and gold. **Pros:** the best in town combines the elegance of prerevolutionary St. Petersburg with loads of modern amenities; prime location; historic building. **Cons:** so expensive that if you have to ask the price, you can't afford it. ⑤ *Rooms from: 19500R* ✉ *7 ul. Mikhailovskaya, bldg. 1, City Center* ☎ *812/329–6000* ⊕ *www.grand-hotel-europe.com* 🛏 *212 rooms, 65 suites* ⑩ *Breakfast* Ⓜ *Nevsky Prospekt or Gostiny Dvor* ⊹ *D4.*

$$$$
HOTEL
Fodor'sChoice
★

🖼 **Kempinski Hotel Moika 22** (Отель Кемпински Мойка 22 *Otel Kempinski Moika Dvatsat Dva*). Behind a 1853 facade are sumptuous rooms furnished with substantial antiques, loaded with modern amenities, and, in many cases, overlooking the Hermitage. **Pros:** unbeatable views; unpretentious personal service; character-filled surroundings full of Old World charm; lavish breakfast. **Cons:** some rooms overlook busy atrium; no pool or gym; some street noise. ⑤ *Rooms from: 16055R* ✉ *22 nab. Reki Moiki, City Center* ☎ *812/335–9111* ⊕ *www. kempinski-st-petersburg.com* 🛏 *197 rooms, 23 suites* ⑩ *Breakfast* Ⓜ *Nevsky Prospekt or Admiralteyskaya* ⊹ *D4.*

$
B&B/INN

🖼 **Nevsky Inn 1.** It's a steep climb to these plain, sunny rooms on the fourth floor (there's no elevator), but this little inn is friendly and just opposite the Admiralteysky metro station. **Pros:** a good deal in city center; kitchen available for use. **Cons:** no phone in rooms; no elevator. ⑤ *Rooms from: 4100R* ✉ *2 per. Kirpichny, apt. 19, code 19B, City Center* ☎ *812/315–8836, 812/972–6873* ⊕ *www.nevskyinn.com* 🛏 *7 rooms* ⑩ *Breakfast* Ⓜ *Admiralteyskaya* ⊹ *C4.*

$$$
HOTEL

🖼 **Pushka Inn** (Отель Пушка Инн *Otel Pushka Inn*). The former home of Ivan Puschin, friend of Alexander Pushkin, retains much of its old character, offering comfortable, tastefully furnished guest rooms and excellent service in the heart of the city. **Pros:** a few minutes' walk from the

10

BEST BETS FOR
ST. PETERSBURG LODGING

Fodor's offers a selective listing of quality lodging experiences in every price range, from the city's best budget beds to its most sophisticated luxury hotels. Here, we've compiled our top recommendations by price and experience. The very best properties—in other words, those that provide a particularly remarkable experience in their price range—are designated in the listings with the Fodor's Choice logo.

Fodor's Choice ★

Alexander House, p. 261

Astoria, p. 264

Grand Hotel, p. 259

Kempinski Hotel Moika 22, p. 259

Sokos Hotel Palace Bridge, p. 266

Taleon Imperial Hotel, p. 261

Best By Price

$

Matisov Domik, p. 265

$$

Courtyard Marriott, p. 266

Herzen House, p. 264

Hotel Vera, p. 268

Petro Palace Hotel, p. 265

$$$

Alexander House, p. 261

Comfort Hotel, p. 264

Hotel Dostoyevsky, p. 267

Pushka Inn, p. 259

Rossi, p. 261

$$$$

Astoria, p. 264

Grand Hotel, p. 259

Kempinski Hotel Moika 22, p. 259

Novotel, p. 267

Sokos Hotel Palace Bridge, p. 266

Taleon Imperial Hotel, p. 261

Tradition, p. 266

By Experience

BEST SPA

Astoria $$$$, p. 264

Grand Hotel Europe $$$$, p. 259

Sokos Hotel Palace Bridge $$$$, p. 266

W St. Petersburg $$$$, p. 265

BEST FOR BUSINESS

Corinthia Hotel $$$$, p. 267

Courtyard Marriott $$, p. 266

Grand Hotel Europe $$$$, p. 259

Novotel $$$$, p. 267

BEST VIEWS

Astoria $$$$, p. 264

Courtyard by Marriott St. Petersburg Vasilievsky Ostrov $$, p. 266

Grand Hotel Europe $$$$, p. 259

Kempinski Hotel Moika 22 $$$$, p. 259

W St. Petersburg $$$$, p. 265

KID-FRIENDLY

Alexander House $$$, p. 261

Ambassador $$$$, p. 261

ROMANTIC HOTELS

Alexander House $$$, p. 261

Astoria $$$$, p. 264

Kempinski Hotel Moika 22 $$$$, p. 259

Pushka Inn $$$, p. 259

Taleon Imperial Hotel $$$$, p. 261

ECO-FRIENDLY

Alexander House $$$, p. 261

Astoria $$$$, p. 264

BEST DINING

Astoria $$$$, p. 264

Corinthia Hotel $$$$, p. 267

Grand Hotel $$$$, p. 259

Novotel $$$$, p. 267

Taleon Imperial Hotel $$$$, p. 261

W St. Petersburg $$$$, p. 265

ANTIQUE FURNISHINGS

Astoria $$$$, p. 264

Hotel Rachmaninov $$, p. 264

Kempinski Hotel Moika 22 $$$$, p. 259

Old Vienna $$, p. 265

Hermitage and Nevsky prospekt; beautiful views of the canal; friendly, English-speaking staff; nice modern bathrooms. **Cons:** quite expensive, even when compared to similar-quality hotels. $ *Rooms from: 9000R* ⊠ *14 nab. Reki Moiki, City Center* ☎ *812/312–0913, 812/312–0957* ⤺ *29 rooms, 4 family rooms* ⊘ *www.pushka-inn.com* ⦿ *Breakfast* Ⓜ *Gostinyy Dvor* ✛ *D3.*

$$$ 🏨 **Rossi (отель Росси).** Wooden
HOTEL ceiling beams and patches of open brickwork are among the engaging features of these elegant and spacious rooms just around the corner from Nevsky prospekt. **Pros:** great location; good restaurant; many rooms are large with great bathrooms; gym and spa. **Cons:** some rooms are small; some street noise. $ *Rooms from: 9000R* ⊠ *55 nab. Reki Fontanki, City Center* ☎ *812/635–6333* ⊕ *www.rossihotels.com* ⤺ *40 rooms, 10 suites* ⊘ *Otel Rossi* ⦿ *Breakfast* Ⓜ *Gostiny Dvor* ✛ *D3.*

$$$$ 🏨 **Taleon Imperial Hotel (Талион Империал Отель).** The former man-
HOTEL sion of Stepan Eliseev, a prominent 19th-century banker and arts
Fodor'sChoice patron, conjures up plenty of romance, with guest rooms awash in
★ light-gold wall coverings, marble-topped furniture, and loads of inlay and ornate plasterwork. **Pros:** prices are astronomical, but the mind-boggling grandeur just about justifies them; rich breakfast (extra) complete with caviar and champagne; palatial fitness center and spa. **Cons:** few rooms have views; a bit too formal and opulent for some tastes. $ *Rooms from: 38500R* ⊠ *15 Nevsky pr., City Center* ☎ *812/324–9911* ⊕ *www.taleonimperialhotel.com* ⤺ *80 rooms, 40 suites* ⦿ *No meals* Ⓜ *Admiraleyskaya* ✛ *C4.*

ADMIRALTEISKY

$$$ 🏨 **Alexander House (Отель Александр Хаус,** *Otel Alexander Haus***).**
HOTEL Each of the 20 airy guest rooms here shows off an original, somewhat
FAMILY quirky design that incorporates wood, brick, linen, and other natural
Fodor'sChoice materials in a style that evokes a different city or country, from Rome to
★ China. **Pros:** quiet and homey; environmentally friendly; good breakfast and restaurant; helpful multilingual staff; free loaner laptops. **Cons:** no gym or spa; some rooms are small; a bit out of the way. $ *Rooms from: 9000R* ⊠ *27 nab. Kryukova Canala, Admiralteisky* ☎ *812/334–3540* ⊕ *www.a-house.ru* ⤺ *20 rooms* ⦿ *Breakfast* Ⓜ *Sadovaya* ✛ *B6.*

$$$$ 🏨 **Ambassador (отеле Амбассадор** *Otel Ambasador***).** Modern com-
HOTEL fort prevails in the bright, stylish guest rooms at this hotel, some with
FAMILY views of the adjacent Yusupovsky Garden and the old city. **Pros:** modern building; quiet location; kid- and pet-friendly; nice pool. **Cons:** somewhat stark, bland surroundings; not quite central location: a seven-minute walk to the metro and a 20-minute walk to sights. $ *Rooms from: 18250R* ⊠ *5–7 Rimskovo-Korsakova pr., Admiralteisky* ☎ *812/331–8844* ⊕ *www.ambassador-hotel.ru* ⤺ *242 rooms, 9 suites* ⦿ *Breakfast* Ⓜ *Sadovaya or Sennaya Spasskaya* ✛ *C5.*

10

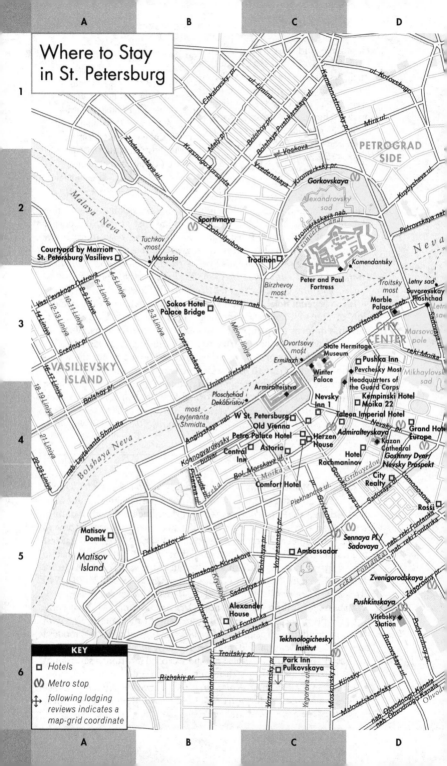

Where to Stay in St. Petersburg

PETROGRAD SIDE

Gorkovskaya

Alexandrovsky sad

Kronverkskaya nab.

Komendantsky

Neva

Peter and Paul Fortress

Letny sad

Troitsky most

Suvorovskay Ploschad

Marble Palace

Letni sad

Birzhevoy most

Dvortsovaya

Dvortsovy most

CITY CENTER

Marsovo pole

reki Moyka

Mikhailovsk sad

Sportivnaya

Dobrolyubova

Makarova nab.

Tuchkov most

Courtyard by Marriott St. Petersburg Vasilievs ☐

Morskaja

Tradition ◆

Mend. Inliya

Sokos Hotel Palace Bridge ☐

Zhdanovskaya ul.

Krasnogo kursanta

Maly pr.

Bolshoy pr.

Bolshaya Pushkarskaya ul.

ul. Voskova

Vvedenskaya

Kronverksky pr.

Mira ul.

Krybyshevaul.

Petrovskaya nab.

Matveevsky per.

Zhdanovskaya ul.

Malaya Neva

Vasilievskaya Ostrova

4-5 Liniya

6-7 Liniya

8-9 Liniya

10-11 Liniya

12-13 Liniya

14 Liniya

Sredny pr.

VASILIEVSKY ISLAND

18-19 Liniya

Bolshoy pr.

21 Liniya

nab. Leytenanta Shmidta

22-23 Liniya

Bolshaya Neva

Sredny pr.

Sezdovskaya

2-3 Liniya

Universitetskaya

Ploschad Dekábristov

most Leytenanta Shmidta

Angliyskaya nab.

Konnogvardeysky

Dvortsovy nab.

Dvortsovaya

Reki Moyka

Nevsky pr.

Nevsky pr.

Sadovaya

reki Fontanka

Ermitazh

State Hermitage Museum

Winter Palace

Armiralteistva ◆

Pushka Inn ☐

Pevchesky Most ◆

Headquarters of the Guard Corps ☐

Nevsky Inn 1 ☐

Kempinski Hotel Moika 22 ☐

Taleon Imperial Hotel ☐

W St. Petersburg ☐

Old Vienna ☐

Petro Palace Hotel ☐

Astoria ☐

Central Inn ☐

Herzen House ☐

Comfort Hotel ☐

Admiralteyskaya

Hotel Rachmaninov ☐

Kazan Cathedral ◆

Grand Hotel Europe ☐

Gostinny Dvor/Nevsky Prospekt

City Realty ☐

Rossi ☐

Sennaya Pl./ Sadovaya

Ambassador ☐

Zvenigorodskaya

Pushkinskaya

Vitebsky Station ◆

Matisov Domik ☐

Matisov Island

Dekabristov ul.

Rimskogo-Korsakova

Sadovaya ul.

Kryukova

Pryazhka

reka Fontanka

Bol. Morskaya ul.

Griboedov

Plekhanova ul.

Bolsh. Podyacheskaya

Gorstova

Alexander House ☐

nab. reki Fontanka

nab. reki Fontanka

Tekhnologichesky Institut

Troitskiy pr.

Rizhskiy pr.

Voznesenskiy

Yegorova ul.

Moskovsky pr.

Klinsky

Malodetskoselsky

Zagorodny pr.

Podyezdnoy per.

nab. Obvodnogo Kanala

nab. Obvodnogo Kanala

Park Inn Pulkovskaya ☐

KEY

☐ Hotels

Ⓜ Metro stop

✠ following lodging reviews indicates a map-grid coordinate

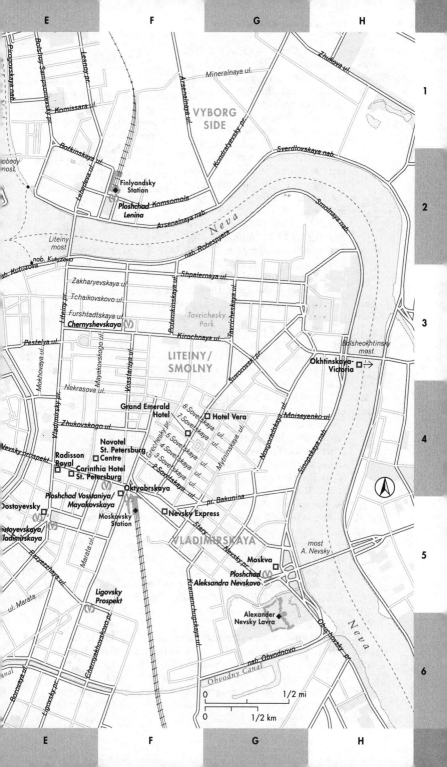

$$$$
HOTEL
Fodor's Choice
★

Astoria (Отель Аст *Otel Astoria*). An art-nouveau landmark, one of St. Petersburg's most renowned hotels before the Revolution, is once again a luxurious place to stay, with magnificently decorated guest quarters overlooking St. Isaac's Square through tall windows. **Pros:** beautiful location; classy dining; stylish surroundings. **Cons:** sky-high prices; frequent security checks due to VIPs; a bit far from the metro; no pool but use of one at nearby hotel. $ *Rooms from: 27500R* ✉ *39 ul. Bolshaya Morskaya, Admiralteisky* ☎ *812/494–5757* ⊕ *www.thehotelastoria.com* ⤴ *81 rooms, 87 suites* ⓘ⊙ *No meals* Ⓜ *Sennaya Ploshchad, Spasskaya, Sadovaya, or Admiralteyskaya* ⊹ *C4.*

THE ASTORIA AND HITLER

Legend has it that Adolf Hitler, on giving the order to lay siege to Leningrad in September 1941, claimed he'd be celebrating New Year's in the Astoria Hotel. The fact that the Soviets held back the Nazis at the cost of hundreds of thousands of lives, and that Hitler never got his party in the hotel, is a source of great local pride.

$
HOTEL

Central Inn (отене Central Inn *Otel Central Inn*). An excellent location next to St. Isaac's Cathedral and access to communal cooking facilities may or may not offset the plain rooms and basic comforts at this hotel. **Pros:** good price for the location (but slightly expensive for what's offered); easy to have some meals in your room. **Cons:** rooms aren't very large; room phones can't call outside hotel. $ *Rooms from: 4500R* ✉ *2 ul. Yakubovicha, Admiralteisky* ☎ *812/571–4516* ⊕ *www.central-inn. ru* ⤴ *15 rooms* ⓘ⊙ *Breakfast* Ⓜ *Admiralteyskaya* ⊹ *C4.*

$$$
HOTEL

Comfort Hotel (Комфорт Отель *Comfort Otel*). Don't look for luxury, but comfort really does abound in these slightly old-fashioned and quirkily charming rooms on the second and third floors of a 19th-century building close to St. Isaac's Cathedral, the Hermitage, and other sights. **Pros:** very convenient; friendly. **Cons:** some rooms are rather small; breakfast, served at a nearby restaurant, is less than lavish. $ *Rooms from: 7800R* ✉ *25 ul. Bolshaya Morskaya, Admiralteisky* ☎ *812/570–6700* ⊕ *www.comfort-hotel.ru* ⤴ *18 rooms* ⓘ⊙ *Breakfast* Ⓜ *Admiralteyskaya* ⊹ *C4.*

$$
HOTEL

Herzen House (Герцен Хаус Отель *Gerzen Haus Otel*). These lodgings are in the same building as the Comfort Hotel and offer the same level of basic comfort, though many rooms have been redone in a sleek but bland contemporary style. **Pros:** excellent location near Hermitage, Nevsky prospekt, and other sights; friendly staff and truly hospitable surroundings. **Cons:** some rooms are small; walls are a bit thin. $ *Rooms from: 6800R* ✉ *25 ul. Bolshaya Morskaya, Admiralteisky* ☎ *812/571–5098* ⊕ *www.herzen-hotel.ru* ⤴ *29 rooms* ⓘ⊙ *Breakfast* Ⓜ *Admiralteyskaya* ⊹ *C4.*

$$
HOTEL

Hotel Rachmaninov (отель Рахманинов). A piano in the lounge, a private art gallery, and cozy, Old-World guest rooms furnished with antiques handpicked by the owners lend a bohemian feel to these elegant quarters with views of Kazan Cathedral and Nevsky prospekt. **Pros:** tasteful and charming; friendly staff; excellent location near cafés, pubs, and restaurants. **Cons:** smallish rooms; no restaurant (but room

CLOSE UP

White Nights = High Rates

St. Petersburg's White Nights, during which time the sun hardly sets at all, may be even more popular with hoteliers than it is with everyone else. That's because the period's popularity means that hotels can ask for—and often get—rates that are triple or even quadruple low-season prices. If you're planning on visiting during the general White Nights period, from mid-May through early July, keep in mind that it pays to shop around. Every hotel schedules its "super-high" rates differently, and some may only run them for a couple weeks, while others may have them for as much as two months. Making the hotel situation even tighter is the mid-June, three- or four-day St. Petersburg Economic Forum, bringing with it politicians, business people, and another bump in already sky-high room rates. Planning your trip immediately before or after the White Nights period can result in significant savings.

service available). $ *Rooms from: 6900R* ✉ *5 ul. Kazanskaya, Admiralteisky* ☎ *812/571–7618* ⊕ *www.hotelrachmaninov.com* ⤹ *23 rooms, 2 suites* ᵒ❘ *Breakfast* Ⓜ *Nevsky Prospekt* ✛ *D4.*

$ 🏨 **Matisov Domik** (**Матисов Домик**). The small yard with maple and
HOTEL chestnut trees, flowers, and benches is the most charming aspect of this pleasant but rather bland modern lodging overlooking the Pryazhka River. **Pros:** a bit less expensive than more-central hotels; quiet, attractive neighborhood. **Cons:** inconvenient to many major sights; no air-conditioning in some rooms. $ *Rooms from: 4700R* ✉ *1 nab. Reki Pryazhki, bldg. 3, Admiralteisky* ☎ *812/495–0242 www.matisov.com* ⤹ *55 rooms* ᵒ❘ *Breakfast* Ⓜ *Sadovaya* ✛ *A5.*

$$ 🏨 **Old Vienna** (**отель Старая Вена**. *Otel Staraya Vena*). A stylish,
B&B/INN pseudo art-nouveau interior attempts to recapture some of the past glory of this location, on the first floor of a building that once housed a bohemian café of the same name and was popular with artists and writers. **Pros:** great location; stylish decor that may or may not appeal. **Cons:** no elevator; front desk isn't manned around the clock. $ *Rooms from: 6200R* ✉ *13 ul. Malaya Morskaya, entrance on ul. Gorokhovaya, Admiralteisky* ☎ *812/312–9339* ⊕ *www.vena.old-spb.ru* ⤹ *14 rooms* ᵒ❘ *Breakfast* Ⓜ *Admiralteyskaya* ✛ *C4.*

$$ 🏨 **Petro Palace Hotel** (**Петро Палас Отель**). Behind a 19th-century
HOTEL facade it's all business, with sleek, modern guest rooms, lots of business facilities, and many amenities that include a fitness center and indoor pool. **Pros:** central yet quiet and safe area; helpful staff speaks English. **Cons:** thin walls; windows in some rooms are sealed; room decor is pleasant but bland; some rooms overlook a dull courtyard. $ *Rooms from: 6750R* ✉ *14 ul. Malaya Morskaya, Admiralteisky* ☎ *812/571–3006* ⊕ *www.petropalacehotel.com* ⤹ *194 rooms* ᵒ❘ *No meals* Ⓜ *Admiralteyskaya* ✛ *C4.*

$$$$ 🏨 **W St. Petersburg** (**Отель W Санкт-Петербург** *Otel Dublevey Sankt*
HOTEL *Peterburg*). The hip international chain has treated the historic city center to some modern indulgence, along with spectacular views from

10

many of the stylish rooms that take in nearby sights: St. Isaac's Cathedral, the Hermitage, and other landmarks. **Pros:** superb location; nice pool and spa; beautiful rooftop terrace and other exciting public spaces. **Cons:** some rooms are small and not all have views; standards aren't as high as at some other W hotels; a bit sceney for those looking for a quiet retreat. ⑤ *Rooms from: 18390R* ✉ *6 Voznesensky pr., Admiralteisky* ☎ *812/610–6161* ⊕ *www.wstpetersburg.com* 🛏 *127 rooms, 10 suites* ⑩ *No meals* Ⓜ *Admiralty* ✛ *C4.*

VASILIEVSKY ISLAND

$$ | 🏨 **Courtyard Marriott St. Petersburg Vasilievsky Ostrov** (Кортъярд Марриотт Санкт-Петербург Васильевский Отель). Airy bedrooms, decked out in subdued gold, beige, and red shades, have highly comfortable beds, and from some it's possible to watch the traffic on the Neva River below through floor-to-ceiling windows. **Pros:** amazing river views; spacious rooms. **Cons:** 20-minute walk to the nearest metro stop; surroundings lack Russian character; extras are pricey. ⑤ *Rooms from: 6960R* ✉ *61/30, 2 Liniya, Vasilievsky Island* ☎ *812/380–4011* ⊕ *www.courtyardsaintpetersburg.ru* 🛏 *202 rooms, 12 suites* ⑩ *No meals* Ⓜ *Vasileostrovskaya* ✛ *A2.*

HOTEL

$$$$ | 🏨 **Sokos Hotel Palace Bridge** (Отел Сокос Двартсовиы Мост *Otel Sokos Dvartsoviy Most*). Spacious rooms furnished in modern Scandinavian style are delightful, but guests spend most of their time in the glass-roofed spa, with a pool in the style of an ancient Roman bath, hydromassage pools, a cold plunge pool, and eight types of saunas. **Pros:** comfortable and stylish rooms; superb spa and wellness center; good restaurants and bar in hotel. **Cons:** a bit off the beaten track; unappealing views from some rooms. ⑤ *Rooms from: 10500R* ✉ *4 per. Birzhevoi, Vasilievsky Island* ☎ *812/335–2200* ⊕ *www.sokoshotels.fi/ru/hotels/stpetersburg* 🛏 *287 room, 32 suites* ⑩ *No meals* Ⓜ *Vasileostrovskaya* ✛ *B3.*

HOTEL
Fodor's Choice
★

PETROGRAD SIDE

$$$$ | 🏨 **Tradition** (отель Традиция *Otel Traditsya*). Stylish rooms resemble those in a 19th-century mansion, have large bathrooms, are equipped with tea kettles and many other nice touches, and best of all, overlook the Neva River and the golden spire of the Peter and Paul Fortress. **Pros:** excellent location, handy to the Hermitage; extremely comfortable rooms with good beds. **Cons:** rooms facing the street can be noisy; no gym; no bar or restaurant, though many are nearby. ⑤ *Rooms from: 10500R* ✉ *2 Dobrolyubova pr., Petrograd Side* ☎ *812/405–8855* ⊕ *www.traditionhotel.ru* 🛏 *16 rooms, 1 suite* ⑩ *Breakfast* Ⓜ *Sportivnaya* ✛ *C2.*

HOTEL

VLADIMIRSKAYA (LOWER NEVSKY PROSPEKT)

$$$$ ⛻ **Corinthia Hotel (отел Corinthia** *Otel Corinthia*). An 1861 neoclassi-
HOTEL cal mansion, once home to the Samoilov acting family, has been com-
FAMILY pletely brought up to date, and along with an adjoining wing offers
sleek, contemporary rooms that suggest modern luxury more than historic heritage. **Pros:** central location; lavish breakfast (not included in
all rates); efficient service. **Cons:** crowded and noisy surroundings; a
bit cold and businesslike; many conventions. $ *Rooms from: 13500R*
⊠ *57 Nevsky pr., Vladimirskaya* ☎ *812/380–2001* ⊕ *www.corinthia.
com* ⇆ *388 rooms, 43 suites* ⏣ *No meals* Ⓜ *Mayakovskaya* ⊹ *E4.*

$$$ ⛻ **Hotel Dostoyevsky (Отель Достоевский,**). Fyodor Dostoyevsky once
HOTEL lived here, and now the hotel offers comfortable rooms in a busy loca-
tion with plenty of shops and cafés nearby. **Pros:** next to a metro sta-
tion; lots of good restaurants nearby; nice bar. **Cons:** next to a busy
intersection; rather drab surroundings; popular with European tour
groups. $ *Rooms from: 8484R* ⊠ *19 Vladimirsky pr., Vladimirskaya*
☎ *812/331–3200* ⊕ *www.dostoevsky-hotel.ru* ⇆ *204 rooms, 14 suites*
⏣ *Breakfast* Ⓜ *Vladimirskaya or Dostoyevskaya* ⊹ *E5.*

$$ ⛻ **Moskva (Отель Москва**). This gargantuan Soviet-era hostelry is a
HOTEL thowback to a different era, and though the rooms are hardly sophis-
ticated or fancy they're neat and clean—some have views of the Neva
River—and public areas are lively and filled with greenery. **Pros:** inexpensive; good transport links; many services in the hotel and nearby;
an interesting look at Soviet style. **Cons:** modest, functional, and aging
quickly; hardly any free extras beyond breakfast; some rooms are noisy.
$ *Rooms from: 6000R* ⊠ *2 pl. Alexandra Nevskogo, Vladimirskaya*
☎ *812/333–2444* ⊕ *www.hotel-moscow.ru* ⇆ *733 rooms, 67 suites*
⏣ *Breakfast* Ⓜ *Ploshchad Alexandra Nevskovo* ⊹ *C5.*

$$ ⛻ **Nevsky Express (Невский Экспресс**). If you arrive by train you'll
B&B/INN appreciate the fact that you only have to walk a few steps from Moscow
Station to plop your bags down in one of the cozy rooms spread over
three floors of this old apartment building. **Pros:** reasonably priced for
the central location; kitchen privileges; home-like atmosphere; friendly
staff. **Cons:** no elevator (staff can help with bags); some rooms face noisy
Nevsky prospekt (others face the quieter inner courtyard). $ *Rooms
from: 7380R* ⊠ *91 Nevsky pr., Vladimirskaya* ☎ *812/717–1888* ⊕ *www.
hon.ru* ⇆ *16 rooms* ⏣ *Breakfast* Ⓜ *Ploshchad Vosstaniya* ⊹ *F5.*

$$$$ ⛻ **Novotel St. Petersburg Centre (Новотель Санкт-Петербург Центр**).
HOTEL Business travelers especially like this smart chain, where they can count
on unremarkable but comfortable, attractive, and quiet accommoda-
tions with good beds and comfy lounge chairs; this one is just off Nevsky
prospekt and top-floor rooms have great views of domes and towers.
Pros: great location; comfortable rooms; good restaurant. **Cons:** some
rooms are small; not a lot of local flavor. $ *Rooms from: 10450R* ⊠ *3a
ul. Mayakovskogo, Vladimirskaya* ☎ *812/335–1188* ⊕ *www.novotel.
com* ⇆ *233 rooms, 16 suites* ⏣ *Breakfast* Ⓜ *Mayakovskaya or Plos-
chad Vosstaniya* ⊹ *E4.*

$$ ⛻ **Oktyaberskaya (Гостиница Октябрьская** *Gostinitsya Oktyaber-
HOTEL skaya*). It's hard to miss this monolith directly opposite Moscow
Station—a huge sign, "Leningrad–Gorod Geroi" (Leningrad–Hero City),

10

sits on top—but how you'll feel about the drearily functional rooms will depend on your tolerance of Soviet-era decor. **Pros:** next to main railway station; surrounded by shops and restaurants. **Cons:** huge and impersonal; on a noisy intersection; you might feel like a prisoner of the state in the drab rooms. ⑤ *Rooms from: 7140R* ⊠ *10 Ligovsky pr., Vladimirskaya* ☎ *812/578–1515* ⊕ *www.hoteloktiabrskaya.ru* ⇌ *567 rooms, 97 suites* ⦿ *Breakfast* Ⓜ *Ploshchad Vosstaniya* ✛ *F4.*

$$$$ ⛉ **Radisson Royal** (**Рэдиссон Ройал**). The late-19th-century playwright
HOTEL   Anton Chekhov stayed here during his visits to St. Petersburg, and he would probably be in awe of the current reincarnation, with luxurious quarters done in shades of navy blue and gold and filled with antique reproductions. **Pros:** loads of character; prime location; kids under 18 stay for free. **Cons:** some rooms are dark, others noisy; some of the rates don't include breakfast. ⑤ *Rooms from: 16900R* ⊠ *2 Nevsky pr., bldg. 49, Vladimirskaya* ☎ *812/322–5000* ⊕ *www.radisson.ru/en/hotel-stpetersburg* ⇌ *164 rooms, 17 suites* ⦿ *No meals* Ⓜ *Maya-kovskaya* ✛ *E4.*

LITEINY/SMOLNY

$$ ⛉ **Hotel Vera** (**Отель Вера**). You'll still find some art-nouveau touches
HOTEL   in this 1903 building, but the plain guest rooms are modern and filled with handy amenities that include refrigerators. **Pros:** reasonable prices; some nice architectural details; helpful staff. **Cons:** 20-minute walk to a metro station; fairly distant from most major sights; some street noise. ⑤ *Rooms from: 6109R* ⊠ *25 Suvorovsky pr., Liteiny/Smolny* ☎ *812/702–6190, 650/969–2939 U.S. office, 866/989–2939 toll free in U.S.* ⊕ *www.hotelvera.ru* ⇌ *69 rooms, 15 suites* ⦿ *Breakfast* ✛ *F4.*

ST. PETERSBURG NIGHTLIFE AND THE ARTS

Updated by
Chris Gordon

St. Petersburg's cultural life is one of its top attractions. The city oozes musical history, and there's a fascinating and thrilling concentration of the brightest names in classical music here. Russian classical ballet was also born in St. Petersburg and you can almost always catch a performance of *Swan Lake* at any time of the year.

The city's nightclubs and discos can't compete with Moscow's glamorous establishments in terms of grand scale, pomp, and attitude, but they offer a more laid-back environment and friendlier crowds.

Your best source for information about what's going on is the *St. Petersburg Times* (⊕ *www.sptimes.ru*), a free, local, independent English-language weekly that's published on Wednesdays. It can be found at airline offices, bars, clubs, hotels, cafés, and other places generally patronized by foreigners or students. The publication has a calendar of events in the Arts and Culture section, with theater and concert listings, a club guide, and a restaurant column.

THE ARTS

St. Petersburg may have one of the world's great museums, but it's not known for its contemporary art scene. Art is generally judged according to whether it fits in with the city's venerable artistic traditions, which can be stifling for younger artists. The temptation to preserve the historical center in its original state is so strong that contemporary sculpture is largely absent from the streets of St. Petersburg, and the installation of every new monument, especially in the City Center, provokes a massive debate. Even so, the contemporary art scene is growing, with galleries showcasing the work of a range of artists in many styles.

With so much 18th-century heritage in evidence, St. Petersburg makes the perfect setting to enjoy Russia's formidable musical tradition. The spiritual presence of Tchaikovsky, Mussorgsky, Prokofiev, and Shostakovich is strong here—they all studied at the St. Petersburg Conservatory.

The St. Petersburg Philharmonic publishes its schedule well in advance, but programming at other venues is often not determined until shortly before performances—websites for concert halls and theaters usually don't include info on events more than a month or two out. Only a few venues offer online ticket sales; among them are the Philharmonic (⊕ *www.philharmonia.spb.ru*) and the Mariinsky (⊕ *www.mariinsky.ru*). You can find information on musical events around town at ⊕ *www.classicalmusic.spb.ru.*

During the high tourist season, *Swan Lake,* a signature production for the Russian classical ballet, appears by the dozen each day on various stages. If purity is important to you, go to either the Mariinsky or Mussorgsky theaters, and beware of the clones: not all stages are fit for such a grand ballet and there's a high risk of being served a brutally cut version, with difficult bits omitted, a few swans missing, and even no live orchestra.

Russian opera is much less known than Russian dance, and much less appreciated abroad. Many potential spectators are frightened merely by the sound of them. St. Petersburg opera singers, who've long complained that Russian operas aren't performed in the West, are convinced that Tchaikovsky's *The Queen of Spades* is the greatest-ever dramatic opera and eager to make you change your mind. The Mariinsky's artistic director, Valery Gergiev, has declared it the company's policy to perform the obscure masterpieces of Russia's operatic legacy. Opera in Russia is about power, drama, depth, and philosophy. There's always a peasant riot, a doomed tsar, much chaos and insanity, and a lack of tuneful heroines. Among the works most likely to convert you are the philosophical and spiritual renditions of Rimsky-Korsakov's *The Legend of the Invisible City of Kitezh* or Glinka's *A Life for the Tsar.*

St. Petersburg has some excellent drama theaters; performances are almost exclusively in Russian. But don't except lots of new works: instead, you'll have a choice of multiple productions of such classics as *Antigone,* Gogol's *Marriage,* and Chekhov's *Uncle Vanya,* among others.

There are a number of ways to get the most from St. Petersburg's theater scene if you don't speak Russian. First, stick to English-language authors whose plays you already know. Plays by Shakespeare, Oscar Wilde, and Tennessee Williams are popular and appear at many of the city's theaters. Then there are Russian classics well-known outside Russia, usually by Chekhov, Dostoyevsky, Gogol, and Tolstoy. The Maly Drama Theater specializes in hosting foreign troupes and puts some effort into welcoming non-Russian-speaking audiences with English-language playbills and occasionally English subtitles projected above the stage.

Except for the most renowned theaters, tickets are easily available and inexpensive. You can buy them at the box offices of the theaters themselves, at *teatralnaya kassa* (theater kiosks) throughout the city, and at service bureaus in hotels, most of which post performance listings in their main lobby. The most useful website, ⊕ *www.theart.ru*, features listings and e-ticketing for all St. Petersburg theaters, but is in Russian only. You can also purchase tickets online through the website ⊕ *www. kassir.ru*; you can arrange for the tickets to be delivered, and if you want to avoid paying with your credit card, you can choose to pay in cash when you get your tickets.

The Mariinsky Theatre sells tickets online through its website (⊕ *www. mariinsky.ru*), at the theater itself, or at its own ticket office on the second floor of Gostiny Dvor, at the corner of Nevsky prospekt and ulitsa Dumskaya.

Note that many venues, including the Mariinsky Theatre, charge higher prices for foreigners than for Russians and that theater tickets purchased through hotels are the priciest of all, as most hotels tend to charge a markup on the foreigner price. All in all, your best option is to go in person to the theater concerned and buy the ticket there.

Most major theaters close down between mid-July and early August and start up again in mid-September or early October. However, summer is also the time for touring companies from other regions in Russia to come to town, so it's a rare day that there are no shows on at all. Sumptuous balls are thrown in the most famous palaces and concert halls in winter.

> A NOTE ABOUT FESTIVALS
>
> In English, a "festival" usually denotes a special season or group of events, such as the Cannes Film Festival. In Russia, however, the same word is often attached to random or run-of-the-mill presentations or even to a single performance in order to generate interest. Check ahead to verify that a "festival" you want to see is worthwhile.

FESTIVALS

The Arts Square Winter Festival (**Международный зимний фестиваль Площадь Искусств** *Mezhdunarodny zimni festival Ploshchad Iskusstv*). The brainchild of Yury Temirkanov, artistic director of the St. Petersburg Philharmonic, runs between Western Christmas (December 25) and Russian Orthodox Christmas (January 7) and showcases classical concerts and ballets with top-notch international stars. The State Russian Museum organizes special exhibitions and hosts receptions for the festival. ⊕ *www.artsquarewinterfest.ru.*

Early Music Festival. International soloists and ensembles gather for the festival, usually held late September through early October. ⊕ *www.earlymusic.ru.*

Musical Olympus (**Музыкальный Олимп** *Muzakalny Olimp*). Another attractive event is the Musical Olympus festival organized by acclaimed Russian pianist Irina Nikitina at the Philharmonic in May and June. The festival assembles winners and laureates of each year's most respected musical contests from all over the globe. Each musician is handpicked by Nikitina herself or members of the festival's honorary committee. The audiences often get to see rising talents immediately after they've claimed the fame but haven't yet been booked for years to come. ⊕ *www.musicalolympus.ru.*

Palaces of St. Petersburg (**Дворцы Санкт Петербурга** *Dvortsy Sankt Peterburga*). The Palaces of St. Petersburg festival presents an impressive series of classical concerts in more than two dozen magnificent palaces and mansions year-round. In the heyday of Imperial Russia, the social season, with its grand balls, masquerades, and concerts, occurred in winter. During the stuffy summers the pillars of high society escaped the heat and dust of the city by heading to their country estates. A century later, St. Petersburg is trying to restore the glories of the past—minus the serfs. ☎ *812/570–0515* ⊕ *www.palacefest.spb.ru.*

Petro Jazz (**Международный фестиваль ПетроДжаз** *Mezhdeyarodny festival PetroJazz*). Every year in July, the Peter and Paul Fortress hosts three days of performances of bands from Russia and beyond. ⊕ *www.petrojazz.com.*

Stars of the White Nights (Звёзды белых ночей *Zvyozdy belykh nochey*). St. Petersburg's premier arts event stretches from the end of May until the middle of July or longer. The event's founder and driving force is the Mariinsky's indefatigable artistic director Valery Gergiev, who brings together a lineup of international stars and orchestras that other Russian festivals can only dream of inviting. It helps that Gergiev, a principal guest conductor with the London Symphony Orchestra, is a regular with the world's most acclaimed orchestras. The festival interweaves opera, ballet, symphony, and chamber music in almost equal proportions and provides a rare opportunity to see the Mariinsky's most renowned soloists—who spend most of their time between La Scala, Opera Bastille, and the Met and include mezzo-soprano Olga Borodina, tenor Vladimir Galuzin, bass Ildar Abdrazakov, baritone Nikolai Putilin, and soprano Anna Netrebko. ☎ *812/326-4141* ⊕ *www.mariinsky.ru.*

CITY CENTER

ART GALLERIES

Gallery Borey (Галерея Борей). On display here are changing exhibitions of work by contemporary artists, including paintings, graphics, and decorative art. There is also a shop that sells artists prints and books, as well as unusual souvenirs. ✉ *58 Liteiny pr., City Center* ☎ *812/275–3837* ⊕ *www.borey.ru* Ⓜ *Mayakovskaya.*

Guild of Masters (Гильдия мастеров *Gildiya masterov*). You'll find paintings, graphics, decorative art, and various jewelry items made by local craftsmen for sale here. ✉ *82 Nevsky pr., City Center* ☎ *812/922–9914* ⊕ *www.guild-master.ru* Ⓜ *Nevsky Prospekt or Gostinny Dvor.*

Marina Gisich Gallery (Галерея Марины Гисич *Galereya Mariny Gisich*). One of the best small galleries in St. Petersburg hosts exhibitions by international and Russian artists in a former apartment. ✉ *121 nab. Reki Fontanki, no. 13, City Center* ☎ *812/314–4380* ⊕ *www.gisich.com* ☉ *Closed Sundays* Ⓜ *Tekhnologichesky Institute, Sadovaya, Spasskaya, or Sennaya Ploschad.*

The Russian Icon (Русская икона *Russkaya Ikona*). This gallery exhibits and sells contemporary Russian Orthodox icons. It's possible to order customized pieces. ✉ *15 ul. Bolshaya Konyushennaya, City Center* ☎ *812/314–7040* Ⓜ *Nevsky Prospekt.*

St. Petersburg Artists Union Gallery (Выставочный Центр Санкт-Петербургского Союза Художников *Vystavochny Tsenter Sankt-Peterburgskogo Soyuza Khudozhnikov*). The ground floor gallery hosts a program of temporary exhibitions, and works by artists are for sale upstairs. ✉ *38 ul. Bolshaya Morskaya, City Center* ☎ *812/314–3060* ⊕ *www.spb-uniart.ru* Ⓜ *Admiralteyskaya.*

MUSIC

CONCERT HALLS

Academic Capella (Академическая капелла *Akademicheskaya kapella*). One of St. Petersburg's best-kept secrets is its oldest concert hall, dating to the 1780s and presenting choral events as well as symphonic, instrumental, and vocal concerts. Many famous musicians, including Glinka

Music Groups

Russian Horn Capella (Русская роговая капелла *Russkaya rogovaya kapella*). The ensemble revives the traditions of 18th-century Russian horn music, and is the only one of its kind in Russia. Apart from baroque pieces written specifically for horn, the musicians perform a repertoire of arrangements of well-known classical works. ⊕ *www.horncapella.ru.*

St. Petersburg Male Choir (Мужской хор Санкт-Петербурга *Muzhskoi khor Sankt Peterburga*). This marvelous choir led by artistic director Vadim Afanasiev, is a must-see. Their favorite venues are the Capella and Petropavlovsky Cathedral in Peter and Paul Fortress, where the choir performs Orthodox chants and choral works by Russian composers. The sound can be mesmerizing. ⊕ *www.malechoir.cpa-sr.com.*

Terem Quartet (Терем Квартет). These famous local musicians have adapted classic works such as Oginsky's "Polonaise" and Schubert's "Ave Maria" for balalaika, bayan, domra, and alto domra to superb effect. Virtuosi in their instruments, and highly interactive in their performing style, which critics have branded "instrumental theater," they freely mix J.S. Bach's "Toccata and Fugue in D Minor" with Russian folk songs, and make every concert a fun experience. ⊕ *www.terem-quartet.ru.*

and Rimsky-Korsakov, have performed in this elegant space along the Moika, near the Alexander Pushkin Apartment Museum and the Winter Palace. The main entrance and the surrounding courtyards have been beautifully restored. ⊠ *20 nab. Reki Moiki, City Center* ☎ *812/314–1058* ⊕ *www.capella-spb.ru* Ⓜ *Nevsky Prospekt, Admiralteyskaya.*

Glinka Hall (Малый зал Филармонии *Maly zal filarmonii*). For chamber and vocal music, head to this small theater, part of the Shostakovich Philharmonic (it's just around the corner from the main hall of the Philharmonic). It's also known as the Maly Zal (Small Hall). ⊠ *30 Nevsky pr., City Center* ☎ *812/312–4585* ⊕ *www.philharmonia.spb. ru* Ⓜ *Nevsky Prospekt or Gostiny Dvor.*

Hermitage Theater (Эрмитажный театр *Ermitazhny teater*). This glorious and highly unusual theater in the Hermitage mainly hosts the St. Petersburg Camerata, a fine but often overlooked chamber ensemble. The theater doesn't have a box office, so purchase tickets at a theater kiosk or via your concierge. The entrance is reached via the museum's staff entrance at 34 Dvortsovaya embankment. ⊠ *32 nab. Dvortsovaya, City Center* ☎ *812/710–9030* ⊕ *www.hermitagemuseum.org* Ⓜ *Admiralteyskaya.*

House of Composers (Дом композиторов *Dom Kompozitorov*). Lovers of contemporary classical music flock here to hear pieces written by its members—look for names such as Sergei Slonimsky, Boris Tishchenko, and Andrey Petrov—and their students at the conservatory. ⊠ *45 ul. Bolshaya Morskaya, City Center* ☎ *812/571–3548* Ⓜ *Admiralteyskaya.*

11

Shostakovich Philharmonic (Большой зал Филармонии имени Д. Д. Шостаковича *Bolshoi zal filarmonii imeni Shostakovicha*). Two excellent symphony orchestras perform in the Philharmonic's newly refurbished grand concert hall (Bolshoy Zal): the St. Petersburg Philharmonic Orchestra and the Academic Philharmonic (a fine outfit, although it's officially the B-team). Both troupes have long, illustrious histories of collaboration with some of Russia's finest composers, and many famous works have premiered in this hall. ✉ *2 ul. Mikhailovskaya, City Center* ☎ *812/312–9871, 812/710–4085* ⊕ *www.philharmonia.spb.ru* Ⓜ *Nevsky Prospekt or Gostiny Dvor.*

OTHER CLASSICAL MUSIC VENUES

For a relaxing evening of classical music in a prerevolutionary setting, try the concert halls in some of St. Petersburg's museums, mansions, palaces, and churches.

Beloselsky-Belozersky Palace (Дворец Белосельских-Белозерских *Dvorets Beloselsky-Belozersky*). Once the home of Prince Beloselsky-Belozersky, a rose-color neobaroque palace, has a large mirrored ballroom that hosts concerts. ✉ *41 Nevsky pr., City Center* ☎ *812/315–5236, 812/570–3993* ⊕ *www.beloselskiy-palace.ru* Ⓜ *Gostiny Dvor or Mayakovskaya.*

Kochneva's House (Дом Кочневой *Dom Kochnevoi*). Chamber music concerts are held here in atmospheric salons. ✉ *41 nab. Reki Fontanki, City Center* ☎ *812/710–4062* ⊕ *www.petroconcert.spb.ru* Ⓜ *Gostiny Dvor.*

Peterburg Concert (Петербург концерт). Many of the concerts organized at St. Petersburg's most historic venues are run by Peterburg Concert. These concerts are not usually of the same high standard found at other musical events in the city, but they are a much better bet than most of the events organized especially for tourist groups. Tickets can be bought directly from the Peterburg Concert offices. ✉ *41 nab. Reki Fontanki, City Center* ☎ *812/310–2987* ⊕ *www.petroconcert.spb.ru* Ⓜ *Gostiny Dvor.*

Samoilov Family Museum (Музей-квартира Самойловых *Muzei kvartira Samoilovykh*). Charming evening concerts are held in authentic surroundings. The museum displays memorabilia related to Russia's greatest composers, musicians, conductors, and dancers. ✉ *8 ul. Stremyannaya, entrance from back side of Nevsky Palace Hotel, City Center* ☎ *812/764–1130* ⊕ *www.spbtheatremuseum.ru* Ⓜ *Mayakovskaya.*

Sheremetev Palace (Шереметевский дворец *Sheremetevsky Dvorets*). Chamber concerts are held in one of the grand rooms of this palace that also houses Russia's national collection of musical instruments. ✉ *34 nab. Reki Fontanki, City Center* ☎ *812/272–4441* ⊕ *www. spbtheatremuseum.ru/ru/brn_shr.html* Ⓜ *Mayakovskaya.*

OPERA AND BALLET

Fodor's Choice
★

Eifman Ballet Theater St. Petersburg (Театр балета Бориса Эйфмана *Teater baleta Borisa Eifmana*). Psychological drama reigns here. Most of the ballets in the repertoire of this internationally acclaimed troupe—one of the only professional contemporary ballet companies in St. Petersburg—have been inspired by the biographies of extraordinary Russians with a tragic fate or are based on Russian literature. A must-see is *Red*

Giselle, which tells the story of the great Russian ballerina Olga Spessivtseva, who fled Russia after the Bolshevik Revolution and spent 20 years in a psychiatric ward in New York. Also highly recommended are *Anna Karenina, Tchaikovsky,* and *The Russian Hamlet,* devoted to the doomed life of Russian tsar Paul I,

who was murdered in Mikhailovsky Castle. The troupe, founded in the late 1970s, has no permanent home, and spends most of its time abroad. When here, the company usually performs at the Alexandrinsky Theater, the Mariinsky, or the Mikhailovsky Theater. ☎ *812/232–0235* ⊕ *www.eifmanballet.ru.*

Mikhailovsky Theater (Михайловский театр). This charming theater puts on productions that, at their best, rival those at the Mariinsky. As far as opera is concerned, the Russian repertoire is the theater's strong suit, but it occasionally strikes gold with Italian works as well. Although the company hosted the world premieres of Shostakovich's *Lady Macbeth of Mtsensk* in 1934 and Prokofiev's *War and Peace* in 1946, the works of these composers are now absent from the repertoire, which focuses heavily on 19th-century classics. Highlights include Tchaikovsky's *The Queen of Spades,* Rimsky-Korsakov's *The Tsar's Bride*, Borodin's *Prince Igor,* and Tchaikovsky's *Iolanta.*

The company's strong dance division is deservedly rated the second-best in town. The classical fare includes *Swan Lake, Giselle, La Esmeralda,* and *Don Quixote* as well as some jewels of Soviet-era choreography, like Khachaturian's *Spartacus* and Prokofiev's *Romeo and Juliet.*

Spanish choreographer Nacho Duato became the artistic director of the ballet company in 2011 and stages several premieres of his new work each season. Ballet and opera are both generally performed September through June or July. ✉ *1 pl. Iskusstv, City Center* ☎ *812/595–4305* ⊕ *www.mikhailovsky.ru* Ⓜ *Nevsky Prospekt, Gostiny Dvor.*

THEATER

Alexandrinsky Theater (Александринский театр). Russia's oldest theater opened in 1756 and is one of the country's most elegant and comfortable. Its repertoire is dominated by 19th-century classics but with prominent Moscow director Valery Fokin at the helm, the company is enjoying a prolonged renaissance and staging new productions that have been critically acclaimed. Fokin's interpretations of Dostoyevsky's *The Double* and Gogol's *The Government Inspector* are thought-provoking and engaging. The theater also hosts an international drama festival in the early summer. ✉ *6 pl. Ostrovskovo, City Center* ☎ *812/312–1545, 812/710–4103* ⊕ *www.alexindrinsky.ru* Ⓜ *Gostinny Dvor or Nevsky Prospekt.*

Bolshoi Drama Theater (Большой драматический театр *Bolshoi Dramatichesky Teatr*). Known as BDT, this theater is one of the jewels in St. Petersburg's crown and with a repertoire that focuses on classics—from Chekhov and Ostrosky to Shakespeare and Albee—attracts Russia's top acting talent to its boards. With the appointment of one of Russia's most respected directors for the stage, Andrei Moguchi, as artistic director, big things are expected. ✉ *65 nab. Reki Fontanki, City Center* ☎ *812/310–9242* ⊕ *www.bdt.spb.ru* Ⓜ *Nevsky Prospekt.*

CHILDREN'S THEATER

A passing knowledge of Russian fairy tales, which can differ from other versions, may help children get more out of puppet shows, but the use of music, amusing animals, and stock villains is easy to follow.

Marionette Theater (Театр марионеток имени Е. С. Деммени *Teater marionetok imeni Demeni*). The company revels in an avant-garde and experimental tradition in which works by Swift and Andersen are adapted for marionettes. It has a varied repertoire of fairy tales and children's stories. ✉ *52 Nevsky pr., City Center* ☎ *812/310–5879* ⊕ *www. demmeni.ru* Ⓜ *Gostiny Dvor.*

ADMIRALTEISKY

ART GALLERIES

Matiss Club (Матисс Клуб). Underground art is the main focus of this gallery, which represents a number of well-known local artists. ✉ *6 pl. Nikolskaya, Admiralteisky* ☎ *812/572–5670* ⊕ *www.matissclub.com* Ⓜ *Sadovaya or Sennaya Ploshchad.*

S.P.A.S Gallery (Галерея С.П.А.С.). This spacious gallery exhibits a good collection of contemporary artists. ✉ *93 nab. Reki Moiki, Admiralteisky* ☎ *812/571–4260* ⊕ *www.spasgal.ru* Ⓜ *Admiralteyskaya.*

MUSIC

CONCERT HALLS

Mariinsky Concert Hall (Концертный зал Мариинского театра). The lobby of this theater converted from a redbrick warehouse isn't much to look at and brings to mind a faceless business hotel. The inside of the hall itself, however, is a different story. It's a large-scale, world-class venue with stellar classical-music performances that's extremely comfortable and boasts superb acoustics. In addition to concert performances, a number of operas have been staged especially for the venue. ✉ *37 ul. Dekabristov, Admiralteisky* ☎ *812/326–4141* ⊕ *www. mariinsky.ru* Ⓜ *Sadovaya, Sennaya Ploshchad, or Spasskaya.*

OPERA AND BALLET

Fodor's Choice ★ **Mariinsky Theatre** (Мариинский театр *Mariinsky Teatr*). The names Petipa, Pavlova, Nijinsky, and Nureyev—and countless others associated with the theater and the birth of ballet in St. Petersburg—are enough to lure ballet lovers here from around the globe. The Mariinsky is without a doubt one of the best ballet companies in the world, with a seemingly inexhaustible supply of stars.

The Imperial Ballet School was founded here on May 4, 1738, by the order of Empress Anna Ioannovna, to be run by Frenchman Jean-Baptiste Lande. French and Italian masters taught the first class of 12 boys and 12 girls. Works of another Frenchman, Marius Petipa, who arrived at the academy in 1847, still dominate the repertoire of the Mariinsky. Today the school is called the Vaganova Ballet Academy in honor of Agrippina Vaganova, who radically changed the way ballet was taught in Russia. The best students traditionally appear on the venerable Mariinsky stage around Christmas in *The Nutcracker* and then in May and June in graduation performances.

Between February and March, the company runs the impressive **Mariinsky International Ballet Festival,** which has at least one premiere and an array of guest performers from other renowned companies, such as London's Royal Ballet, Opera Bastille, and the American Ballet Theater.

The Mariinsky is also at the forefront of the world's opera companies, thanks largely to the achievements of the Mariinsky's artistic director, Valery Gergiev. The company's best operatic repertoire centers on Russian opera: Tchaikovsky's *The Queen of Spades,* Prokofiev's *Semyon Kotko,* Shostakovich's *The Nose,* Rimsky-Korsakov's *The Legend of the Invisible City of Kitezh,* and *The Snow Maiden* are particularly recommended.

Operas are all sung in their original language; Russian operas are all provided with English subtitles, while Russian subtitles are given for foreign operas. Verdi can be hit-or-miss, but Wagner is one of Gergiev's greatest passions, and the company now feels very much at home with the composer. The orchestra's rapport with the conductor is amazing, and the sound is nuanced and powerful.

Ballet and opera share the calendar throughout the year; the opera and ballet companies both tour, but at any given time one of the companies is performing in St. Petersburg. ⊠ *1 pl. Teatralnaya, Admiralteisky* ☎ *812/326–4141* ⊕ *www.mariinsky.ru* Ⓜ *Sadovaya, Sennaya Ploshchad, or Spasskaya.*

Mariinsky II (**Вторая сцена Мариинского театра** *Mariinsky Dva*). Set just across a small canal from the historic Mariinsky Theatre, Mariinsky II is the company's state-of-the-art opera, ballet, and concert hall. The massive theater, which opened in 2013, seats 2,000 spectators and features one of the world's most technologically advanced stages. ⊠ *34 ul. Dekabristov, Admiratleisky* ☎ *812/326–4141* ⊕ *www.mariinsky.ru* Ⓜ *Sadovaya.*

The Rimsky-Korsakov Conservatory (**Консерватория имени Н. А. Римского-Корсакова** *Konservatoriya imeni Romskogo-Korsakova*). The Conservatory is directly opposite the Mariinsky, but the opera and ballet performances come nowhere near the level of its famous neighbor—partly because the Mariinsky is so good at siphoning off the Conservatory's brightest talent. ⊠ *3 pl. Teatralnaya, Admiralteisky* ☎ *812/312–2519* ⊕ *www.conservatory.ru* Ⓜ *Sadovaya, Sennaya Ploshchad, or Spasskaya.*

St. Petersburg Opera (**Санкт Петербург Опера** *Sankt Peterburg Opera*). The company is based in the former mansion of Baron Derviz, where the famous theatrical director Vsevolod Meyerhold staged productions at the end of the 19th century. The company's repertoire is small and dominated by Russian classics and light Italian operas, with occasional experimental performances. ⊠ *33 ul. Galernaya, Admiralteisky* ☎ *812/312–3982* ⊕ *www.spbopera.ru* Ⓜ *Sadovaya, Sennaya Ploshchad, or Spasskaya.*

THEATER

Molodezhny Theater. Although most troupes in town tend to rely heavily on only their most seasoned players, this theater is brave enough to showcase younger talent. Shows are bursting with youthful energy and romanticism, yet there's no amateur-student feel to them; most are expertly staged by artistic director Semyon Spivak, a professor at the renowned St. Petersburg Academy for Theatre Art. The company's signature show is Alexei Tolstoy's *The Swallow*. Isaac Babel's *Cries From Odessa* and Alexander Ostrovsky's *Love Lace* are also among its hits. ✉ *114 nab. Reki Fontanki, Admiralteisky* ☎ *812/316–6870* ⊕ *www. mtfontanka.spb.ru* Ⓜ *Tekhnologichesky Institut.*

VASILIEVSKY ISLAND

ART GALLERIES

Erarta Contemporary Art Museum and Gallery (Музей и галереи современного искусства Эрарта). With 2,000 works by nearly 150 Russian artists on display, this mammoth five-floor complex is the country's largest contemporary art exhibition space. Conceived by Marina Varvarina, the widow of a powerful local businessman, Erarta is packed with artworks dating from the 1940s to the present day. The gallery has a team of enthusiastic curators who busily tour the country for up-and-coming talent. The place always has the name of an exciting new artist up its sleeve. In addition to the halls, where regular exhibitions are held, there is a gallery where artworks are sold. ✉ *2 29th Line, Vasilievsky Island* ☎ *812/324–0809* ⊕ *www.erarta.com* 💳 *300R* Ⓜ *Vasileostrovskaya.*

Novy Museum (Новый музей). Emphasizing the work of Soviet artists who opposed the officially approved socialist realism style during the years of the Iron Curtain, this gallery draws from the impressive collection of Aslan Chekhoyev, who purchased his first items several decades ago. He was personally acquainted with many of those at the forefront of Russian Nonconformist Art. The museum often holds lectures by these artists as well as film screenings and book presentations. ✉ *29 6th Line, Vasilievsky Island* ☎ *812/323–5090* ⊕ *www.novymuseum.ru* 💳 *100R–200R, depending on event* Ⓜ *Vasileostrovskaya.*

MUSIC

CLASSICAL MUSIC

For a relaxing evening of classical music in a prerevolutionary setting, try the concert halls in some of St. Petersburg's museums, mansions, palaces, and churches.

St. Catherine Lutheran Church (Церковь Св. Екатерины *Tserkov Svyatoi Ekateriny*). Popular with foreign worshippers, the church also hosts an engaging classical concert program that mixes secular and religious music. ✉ *1a Bolshoi pr., Vasilievsky Island* ☎ *812/323–1852* ⊕ *www. st-katherina-orgel.ru* Ⓜ *Vasileostrovskaya.*

PETROGRAD SIDE

THEATER

Baltiisky Dom Festival Theater (Театр-фестиваль Балтийский дом). An umbrella venue for a dozen experimental companies of various genres holds performances in its large hall and a variety of basements, attics, and backrooms. Once a full-fledged theater, it has turned into a modern art complex, where aspiring directors experiment with material by playwrights like Luigi Pirandello, Ivan Turgenev, and the Presnyakov Brothers. Each October the theater hosts an impressive four-week Baltic Theater Festival, attracting the best talent from the Baltic Sea region. ✉ *4 Alexandrovsky Park, Petrograd Side* ☎ *812/232–3539* ⊕ *www. baltic-house.ru* Ⓜ *Gorkovskaya.*

VLADIMIRSKAYA (LOWER NEVSKY PROSPEKT)

ART GALLERIES

Loft Project Etagi (Tserkov Svyatoi Ekateriny). Inside the five floors of what was once a bakery are galleries, exhibition halls, and designer boutiques. This arts and cultural center gets attention from the hip for its provocative shows, controversial artists, and unorthodox approches. Exhibitions on themes like urban biking, post-war Italian commercial design, or World Press photos are displayed on the rough-and-ready painted brick walls, concrete floors, and exposed pipes. ✉ *74 Ligovsky pr., Vladimirskaya* ☎ *812/458–5005* ⊕ *www.loftprojectetagi.ru* Ⓜ *Ligovsky Prospekt.*

Pushkinskaya 10 Arts Center (Арт-Центр Пушкинская 10). Also known as the Free Arts Foundation, this ramshackle maze of studios, galleries, yards, cafés, and performance spaces was once a legendary squat for the pioneering artists of the Nonconformist, unofficial, and Neo-Academy art movements that flowered here in the 1980s, as the Soviet Union's grip on cultural life began to loosen. Today the foundation receives state funds, but it has lost none of its thirst for exhibiting modern art that thumbs its nose at the establishment. Pushkinskaya 10 includes, among others, the New Academy Fine Arts Museum, the Museum of Nonconformist Art, the St. Petersburg Archive and Library of Independent Art, FOTOImage, Navicula Artis Gallery, GEZ-21, and Kino-FOT-703. ✉ *10 ul. Pushkinskaya, entrance at 53 Ligovsky pr., through the courtyard, Vladimirskaya* ☎ *812/764–5371* ⊕ *www.p10. ru* Ⓜ *Ploshchad Vosstaniya.*

THEATER

Fodor's Choice ★ **Maly Drama Theater** (Малый драматический театр *Maly Dramatichesky Teatr*). With a smattering of performances with English, French, and Italian subtitles, the MDT is home to one of the best theater companies in Russia and is well worth seeing. The repertoire includes productions of Chekhov, Dostoyevsky, Shakespeare, and Oscar Wilde. The theater is also one of the few companies in town to continue to stage the finest plays from the Soviet era. Seeing their whole repertoire has been compared to living through the entire 20th-century history of Russia. If you have a whole day to spare and lots of stamina, the nine-hour performance of Dostoyevsky's *The Possessed* makes for an incredible theatrical experience, although it can be a bit hard on the posterior and comes without translation. It takes two consecutive evenings to sit through the company's veteran show, Fyodor Abramov's *Brothers and Sisters*, but it's a great experience. Order tickets well in advance, because it's rare that the Maly plays to a less-than-packed house. ⊠ *18 ul. Rubinshteina, Vladimirskaya* ☎ *812/713–2078* ⊕ *www.mdt-dodin.ru* Ⓜ *Vladimirskaya.*

FAMILY **Zazerkalye Theater** (Театр Зазеркалье). This charming theater is a great place for parents and their children to catch a show together. Masterfully blending dramatic and musical elements, the captivating productions are famous for their daring experiments. The company is good at winning children over to opera with entertaining versions of serious repertoire such as Donizetti's *L'Elisir d'Amore*—during which Nemorino sings his famous aria while riding a bike—or Offenbach's *Les contes d'Hoffmann* and Puccini's *La Bohème*. Shows can last anywhere from 30 minutes to three hours. ⊠ *13 ul. Rubinshteina, Vladimirskaya* ☎ *812/570–3306* ⊕ *www. zazerkal.spb.ru* Ⓜ *Vladimirskaya, Dostoevskaya.*

> **RUSSIAN BEATLEMANIA**
>
> The Pushkinskaya 10 Arts Center is known for housing one of Russia's most famous fans of the legendary Beatles, Kolya Vasin. Vasin, who is now in his early 60s, has never worked and never married because, as he says, he only had time for the Beatles. The little apartment-museum he lives in at 10 ulitsa Pushkinskaya is called the "Office of John Lennon's Temple." Vasin dreams of building a temple to John Lennon in St. Petersburg, where thousands of people can worship the Liverpool Four.

LITEINY/SMOLNY

ART GALLERIES

Sol-Art. Next to the prestigious Mukhina Academy for Arts and Design, this gallery exhibits St. Petersburg's young artistic talents and some of the big names in the local contemporary art scene. ⊠ *15 per. Solyanoy, Liteiny/Smolny* ☎ *812/327–3082* ⊕ *www.solartgallery.com* Ⓜ *Nevsky Prospekt.*

NIGHTLIFE

St. Petersburg is hardly hip compared to the major capitals of Europe, but it's waking up to what hip really is. The city's vibrant and evolving club scene is diverse enough to incorporate funky theme clubs, bunker-style techno venues, cozy artsy basements, run-down discos, cool alternative spots, and elegant hedonist establishments to keep the clubbers up all night. A local claim to clubber fame is that Russia's rock movement was born in St. Petersburg, and almost all key names in the country's rock culture come from the city. The first bands emerged in the 1970s, when rock and roll was branded "alien music" and rock culture was repressed by the Soviet culture bosses. Underground musicians and artists refrained from contacts with state-run music organizations. They worked as night guards, boiler-room operators, or street cleaners and expressed their protest in rock ballads, which reached a wider audience only with the arrival of perestroika. Some of the most famous bands still play regular gigs—look for veteran bands like Akvarium, DDT, and Tequilajazzz. The strongest point of Russian rock ballads are the meaningful lyrics, but even without knowledge of the language, you can still feel the drive.

Even popular spots are well hidden and you need to know where to look. A good rule of thumb for tourists with little or no experience in Russia is to stick to the City Center, where you have several options: bohemian art clubs, trendy dance clubs, live-music venues, and simple pubs. Locals in the City Center are friendly and more than a few speak English—and foreigners aren't the novelty they once were. If you're seeking the company of expats, you'll find them in centrally located Irish and British pubs or at low-key artsy bars such as *Datscha*. The historical center is abundant with expensive strip clubs, but these are meant for deep-pocketed foreign tourists and ravenous Russian beauties hunting for them. Beware that if you venture to a place beyond the historical center, the risk of being robbed or attacked by one of the city's many skinhead and hooligan gangs increases significantly.

Russia has adopted the concept of "face control" (a strict door policy) enthusiastically, but in schizophrenic St. Petersburg its rules can either fall to the whim of a zealous doorman or be ignored altogether depending on the character of the place. Generally, dirty clothes or men going shirtless will be frowned upon, and in the more glamorous spots designer gear and displays of wealth are expected. That said, St. Petersburg's nightclubs are more typically bars or music venues, where just about anything goes. Women are expected to wear feminine clothes, nice shoes—preferably with heels—and makeup. Men can be more relaxed, but Russian men like to wear dark colors, sports coats, and dress shoes. Cover prices vary wildly, depending on the type of place, the day of the week, the time of night, and whether there's some sort of act on the bill. However, 500R is a fair average. Drink prices in a club are generally double what they are in a regular bar. Reliable, if pricey, taxis swarm around clubs until closing time. ■ TIP➔ **Note that there's no official "last call"—bars and clubs may choose to close anywhere from midnight to 6 am.**

The nightlife scene is ever changing, so it's always best to consult current listings. The most reliable English-language sources are the free *St. Petersburg Times* (⊕ *www.sptimes.ru*) or the monthly English-language issue of *St. Petersburg in Your Pocket* (⊕ *www.inyourpocket.com*). These publications include excellent unbiased club guides in addition to detailed listings. There are more comprehensive sources in Russian, such as the magazine *Time Out* (⊕ *www.timeout.ru*).

Unlike much of Europe and North America, Russia hasn't yet opened up to the idea of gay men and lesbians. The scene in St. Petersburg is still in its embryonic stage and the few friendly and unpretentious venues that are available keep a relatively low profile. New laws restricting gay

CLOSE UP

Bridge Schedules

11

St. Petersburg's mighty Neva River creates some of its most picturesque views, making it easy to forget that it's a working river for transporting many goods and raw materials. During the navigation season (April–November), the Neva is crowded with ships making up for the winter months. However, since its bridges are too low to allow ships to pass and it would cripple the city to lift them frequently during the day, the city's bridges remain raised at night from 1 am to about 5 am. There are published schedules for each bridge, some of which are lowered once during the night, but these are unreliable. If you don't want to get caught on the wrong side of the river from where you're staying and be stuck until morning, think about heading home before 1 am. What at first sounds like a terrific inconvenience for a large, busy city has been turned into something positive by St. Petersburgers: during White Nights the raising of the attractively illuminated bridges has become a crowd-pleasing ritual and "I missed the bridges" has become the perfect excuse to party until dawn.

"propaganda" that have recently come into force may have a chilling effect on the scene, but it's too early yet to tell what that may be. The best starting point into St. Petersburg's scene is ⊕ *www.gay.ru*, which has some English content, including a "Traveller's Guide."

CITY CENTER

BARS

Daiquiri Bar (Бар Дайкири). Cocktail bars are few and far between in St. Petersburg but for expertly mixed drinks, rely on the talented bartenders here. The music is geared to a young, hip crowd and can become a bit loud later in the evening, so go early if you want to have a conversation without shouting. ⊠ *1 ul. Bolshaya Konyushennaya, City Center* ☎ *812/943–8114* ⊕ *www.dbar.ru* Ⓜ *Admiralteyskaya.*

Datscha (Дача). A tremendously popular haunt of expats, bohemians, students, and night owls takes after the merry joints of the Reeperbahn in Hamburg (the owner is German). The galvanizing spirit of this eclectic art bar is hugely addictive—despite its claustrophobic size, low ceilings, shabby setting, horrific toilets, and lack of food beyond peanuts. The music, mainly rock and ska, is loud enough to make conversation barely possible. Reckless dance parties sometimes get out of hand and spill into the street, where neighboring bar Fidel soaks up the overflow. ⊠ *9 ul. Dumskaya, City Center* Ⓜ *Nevsky Prospekt.*

Hallelujah Bar. This little bar stands out from the rest by the young, attractive, and friendly crowd it draws in. Always packed on weekends, getting to the bar can be a bit of a chore but the retro 80s and 90s music makes the wait more bearable. ⊠ *7 ul. Inzhenernaya, City Center* ☎ *812/314–5926* Ⓜ *Gostiny Dvor.*

The Office Pub (Офис Паб). Style and elegance characterize the atmosphere of this Irish pub located next to Kazan cathedral. It is frequented by a fashionable crowd and is a favorite with the 20-somethings and local yuppies. The choice of beers on tap here is one of the widest in the city. ✉ *5 ul. Kazanskaya, City Center* ☏ *812/571–5428* ⊕ *www.molly. su/office* Ⓜ *Nevsky Prospekt.*

BAR HOPPING

A small street linking Nevsky prospekt and the Griboyedov canal has recently become the site of a cluster of hip and grungy bars that attract crowds of young people. Ulitsa Dumskaya, with its central location, disheveled colonnades, dance-till-you-drop attitude, and two of the city's gay venues has been dubbed the city's answer to London's Old Compton Street.

CLUBS

Purga (Пурга). They celebrate New Year's Eve every night here, and whatever season and the weather, you get the full holiday package, complete with decorated Christmas tree, the Russian version of Santa Claus and his granddaughter, champagne, and a dance party. An exhaustive collection of season's greetings recordings delivered by Soviet and Russian leaders is broadcast and mocked throughout the night. This ritual has become one of St. Petersburg's most memorable nights out. The food and beer is good and inexpensive, and the droll staff is dressed in white rabbit costumes. Each table has a unique design. Be sure to get there and fill your glass before midnight. Purga's clone next door throws wedding parties with the same regularity and similarly comic bent. ✉ *11 nab. Reki Fontanki, City Center* ☏ *812/570–5123* ⊕ *www.purga-club.ru* Ⓜ *Mayakovskaya or Gostiny Dvor.*

GAY AND LESBIAN CLUBS

Central Station (Центральная станция *Tsentralnaya Stantsia*). A youthful, fashionable, mixed crowd packs onto three floors, each with its own character, interlinked by a number of dark staircases. There are theme nights, drag shows, multiple lounge areas, karaoke, and a counter that serves food. ✉ *1 ul. Lomonosova, City Center* ☏ *812/312–3600* ⊕ *www.centralstation.ru* Ⓜ *Nevsky Prospekt.*

LIVE MUSIC CLUBS

Money Honey Saloon (Клуб Money-Honey *Club Money-Honey*). If rockabilly is your thing, or if you simply want to see a country-western saloon in Russia, head to this always-crowded bar for dancing and lots of fun. The live music usually starts at 8 pm. A minimal cover charge is collected sporadically. ✉ *13 Apraksin Dvor, enter via the courtyard at 28–30 ul. Sadovaya, City Center* ☏ *812/310–0549* ⊕ *www.money-honey.ru* Ⓜ *Gostinny Dvor or Sadovaya.*

ADMIRALTEISKY

11

BARS

Dickens (Диккенс). This outlet of a chain that originated in Riga, Latvia serves up a lot of Merrie Olde England kitsch. The food is pricey but good. ✉ *108 nab. Reki Fontanki, Admiralteisky* ☎ *812/702–6263* ⊕ *www.dickensrest.ru* Ⓜ *Sennaya Ploshchad.*

Kneipe Jager Haus. Designed as a cozy hunting lodge, this German pub is one of the quieter drinking venues in town. It has vaulted brick ceilings, antique bric-a-brac, and stuffed wild animals and game trophies. The spirited and highly herbal Jägermeister digestif pops up in just about every other drink offered here, including the popular Grizli and Jager-Cola cocktails. There's also a sauerkraut-heavy German menu available and a filling three-course business lunch on weekdays. The pub, open round the clock, also has branches at 17 ulitsa Pravdy and 64 Srednii prospekt. ✉ *34 ul. Gorokhovaya, Admiralteisky* ☎ *812/310–8270* ⊕ *www.jagerhaus.ru* Ⓜ *Sadovaya.*

> ### STRIPPED BARE
>
> St. Petersburg's "adult entertainment" sector promotes itself more vigorously and splashily than any other category of nightlife, particularly to foreign men, who are usually offered discounted entry. These gaudy strip palaces feature shows that range from full-on sex shows down to Moulin Rouge–style "erotic ballets"—often with real ballerinas who didn't quite make the grade. Vulgar, expensive, pushy, and sinister, St. Petersburg's strip clubs increasingly seem like a relic from a different age: the fast and loose 1990s.

Fodor's Choice ★ **Shamrock Irish Pub** (Шемрок Ирландский паб *Shamrock Irlandsky Pub*). A long-standing favorite of local expats, this jolly inn with great pub food, cozy wooden furnishings, and a reasonable selection of beer stands across the street from the Mariinsky Theatre. The company's younger talent can be often spotted having a quick bite or beers here at any time of day. Live Irish music is played every night, except Tuesday and Friday, and a bargain-priced set lunch is available weekdays. ✉ *27 ul. Dekabristov, Admiralteisky* ☎ *812/570–4625* Ⓜ *Sadovaya.*

Stirka (Стирка). This peculiar hybrid of a bar and a laundromat started life as the graduation project of a German design student. Here you'll find underground rock DJs, international bands, a good sound system, a small bar, and comfortable soft furnishings. Guests are welcome to follow in the footsteps of Led Zeppelin and the Rolling Stones—it's said they made use of the venue's washing machines and dryers while in town on tour. ✉ *26 ul. Kazanskaya, Admiralteisky* ☎ *812/314–5371* ⊕ *www.40gradusov.ru* Ⓜ *Sennaya Ploshchad, Sadovaya, or Spasskaya.*

CLUBS

Zal Ozhidaniya (Зал ожидания). This modern and minimalist club, whose name means "waiting room," is part of the Varshavsky Express shopping center and entertainment complex, next to the former railway station for trains to Warsaw and beyond. The club can accommodate up to 1,000 people, making it one of the largest venues of its kind in the city, but rarely fills up past the point of comfort. The bands that perform here are a mix of homegrown Russian talent and visiting indy bands from abroad, and cover lots of musical bases, including rock, jazz, pop, and electronic. VIP and Super VIP areas let you score a table and put you at stage height, for a price. ⊠ *118 nab. Obvodnogo Kanala, Admiralteisky* ☎ *812/333–1068* ⊕ *www.clubzal. com* Ⓜ *Baltiiskaya.*

VASILIEVSKY ISLAND

BARS

KwakInn (**Квакинн**). This pint-size Belgian pub—the only one in town—is one of the city's friendliest venues. Within its yellow walls you can get mouthwatering mussels and frites and a couple of dozen Belgian beers, both draft and bottled. In addition to the beers, Belgium is evoked with Tin-Tin cartoons and posters recalling Agatha Christie's Hercule Poirot and Audrey Hepburn. ⊠ *37 Bolshoi pr., Vasileostrovskaya* ☎ *812/493–2639* ⊕ *www.kwakinn.ru* Ⓜ *Vasileostrovskaya.*

VLADIMIRSKAYA (LOWER NEVSKY PROSPEKT)

CLUBS

Metro (**Метро**). An old standard is as popular as ever and continues to draw fashionable teenagers from all over the city and the suburbs. Each of the three floors plays different music. The door policy is very strict. ⊠ *174 Ligovsky pr., Vladimirskaya* ☎ *812/766–0204* ⊕ *www. metroclub.ru* Ⓜ *Ligovsky Prospekt.*

Mishka Bar (**Мишка бар**). Local celebrity DJs spin their favorite discs at this club, which is popular with expats for its international vibe. ⊠ *40 nab. Reki Fontanki, Vladimirskaya* ☎ *812/643–2550* ⊕ *www. mishkabar.ru* Ⓜ *Mayakovskaya.*

GAY AND LESBIAN CLUBS

Cabaret (**Кабаре**). This gay club has been going for years, in one incarnation or another. Attracting a friendly mixed crowd, the emphasis is on having a good time and everyone is welcome. Shows at the weekend start at 2 am and attract a loyal following. The club serves coffee and light snacks from noon on weekdays. ⊠ *43 ul. Razyezhaya, Vladimirskaya* ☎ *812/764–0901* ⊕ *www.cabarespb.ru* Ⓜ *Ligovskiy Prospekt.*

LIVE MUSIC CLUBS

Fish Fabrique. This is a favorite haunt of locals and expats who enjoy drinking and listening to local alternative musicians, or who just want to play table football. ⊠ *10 ul. Pushkinskaya, entrance through courtyard of 53 Ligovsky pr., Vladimirskaya* ☎ *812/764–4857* ⊕ *www. fishfabrique.ru* Ⓜ *Ploshchad Vosstaniya.*

Griboyedov (**Грибоедов**). The best underground (literally) club in the city, this small former bomb shelter is usually packed with friendly, down-to-earth hipsters. It's owned and operated by a local band. In addition to decent live music, there's a mix of talented DJs spinning house, techno, and funk; check listings for different nights. Upstairs is Griboyedov Hill, or GH, which houses a small cafe, a couple of terraces that offer outdoor seating in the summer, and music fare that is lighter than that to be heard in the club proper. ✉ *2a ul. Voronezhskaya, at the corner of ul. Konstantina Zaslonova, Vladimirskaya* ☎ *812/764–4355* ⊕ *www.griboedovclub.ru* Ⓜ *Ligovsky Prospekt.*

Jazz Philharmonic Hall (**Филармония джазовой музыки** *Filarmoniya jazovoy muzyki*). Russia's top jazz musicians, including the Leningrad Dixieland Band and the David Goloshchokin's Ensemble, regularly appear at this venue in a turn-of-the-20th-century building, as do visiting jazz luminaries. ✉ *27 Zagorodny pr., Vladimirskaya* ☎ *812/764–8565* ⊕ *www.jazz-hall.spb.ru* Ⓜ *Zinigorodskaya.*

LITEINY/SMOLNY

GAY AND LESBIAN CLUBS

Malevich Bar (**Бар Малевич**). Friendly and unpretentious, this club by night also offers a number of classes, such as tango and vocal training, during the early evenings to prepare clients for dance floor magic and karaoke. Not particularly easy to find or very well decorated, the club still manages to be welcoming and entertaining. ✉ *109 Moskovsky pr., entrance via the courtyard, Liteiny/Smolny* ☎ *812/920–3207* ⊕ *www. malevich-club.ru* Ⓜ *Moskovskiye Vorota.*

LIVE MUSIC CLUBS

Cafe Sunduk (**Кафе Сундук**). Head to this intimate and quiet little art café decorated in a British colonial style for live jazz, blues and rock. The menu is varied and good but inexpensive. Beware, though: the toilet, with its many large but defunct locks, is designed to confuse the guests. ✉ *42 ul. Furshtatskaya, Liteiny/Smolny* ☎ *812/272–3100* ⊕ *www.scafeunduk.ru* Ⓜ *Chernyshevskaya.*

JFC Jazz Club. The most popular jazz venue in town attracts top musicians performing all styles of jazz: acid funk, swing and blues, avant-garde, mainstream, improvisation. The only disadvantage is its modest size, so you may want to reserve a seat ahead of time. ✉ *33 ul. Shpalernaya, entry is via the courtyard, Liteiny/Smolny* ☎ *812/272–9850* ⊕ *www.jfc-club.spb.ru* Ⓜ *Chernyshevskaya.*

The Place. Inside an anonymous building in an industrial wasteland far from the center, this chic oasis is still well worth seeking out. Inside, things are cool and sophisticated, decked out in dark woods, chrome and steel fixtures, and clever lighting. There's a modern menu and a lively music program of international art rock, jazz, and experimental acts. They also offer the weekly film screenings. ✉ *47 ul. Marshala Govorova, south of the city center* ☎ *812/252–4683* ⊕ *www.placeclub. ru* Ⓜ *Narvskaya or Baltiiskaya.*

ST. PETERSBURG SHOPPING

Updated by
Chris Gordon

The vast majority of Russians are, by economic necessity, not big consumers. In fact, official figures suggest that only 10% of Russians earn more than $1,000 a month. You probably wouldn't realize this on a walk down Nevsky prospekt, lined with shops and, most noticeably, the city's big department stores and shopping arcades. While not all the goods are of the quality you might find in the big stores in New York or other European cities, plenty of jewelry, high fashion, and other luxury goods fill the shelves of shops that cater to those with the means to afford them.

For a distinctly Russian experience, try to seek out the fashion designs of Tatyana Parfinova, Sultanna Frantsuzova, Leonid Alexeev, and Larissa Pogoretskaya. Especially appealing to Westerners are typical Russian handicrafts, such as *gzhel* (blue-and-white and majolica pottery), shiny *khokhloma* tablewood (wood painted with flowery ornaments and imitation gilding), *zhostovo* metal trays (painted with elaborate enamel designs), and electric samovars—you'll find them in all the shops catering to tourists.

There are several things to keep in mind when shopping in St. Petersburg. For one, except for the Russian designers mentioned above, this isn't the place to stock up on fashion pieces. People tend to dress conservatively in St. Petersburg, often in plain dark clothes. Fashion as a means of self-expression hardly exists here yet except among the very young. When it comes to buying clothes, practical considerations hold sway, and that can make for a range of colors that doesn't go much beyond black, white, or gray. Also, most Western fashion brands sell for more than you'd expect to pay elsewhere in Europe and in the United States.

Don't be surprised by the number of supermarkets, pharmacies, and other stores that are now open 24 hours, seven days a week—they're fairly reliable and have emerged because of the hectic lives Russians lead.

If you want to take presents home, some of the best buys include fine porcelain, carved wooden goods such as toy soldiers or chess sets, and Russian-made silverware and linen. More than the goods on offer, one of the great delights of shopping St. Petersburg is the surroundings in which you'll find yourself, including 18th- and 19th-century shopping arcades, art-nouveau interiors, colorful food markets, and the other evocative settings of this romantically historic city.

CITY CENTER

The neighborhood that radiates from Palace Square and the Hermitage evokes all the city's historic grandeur and is also its bustling commercial center. Beautiful 18th- and 19th-century arcades provide especially atmospheric shopping experiences.

12

CRAFTS AND SOUVENIRS

Armeisky Magazin (Армейский магазин). Army surplus—belts, flasks, caps, pins, and marine shirts with Russian and Soviet army symbols—is a much better bargain here, at this state-run store, than in touristy souvenir markets. You'll find a huge variety. ✉ *24 ul. Kirochnaya, City Center* ☎ *812/579–2907* ⊕ *www.armygoods.ru* Ⓜ *Chernyshevskaya.*

DEPARTMENT STORES

DLT TSUM (ДЛТ ЦУМ *Dey El Tey Tsum*). What was once a dusty Soviet relic has emerged as one of the most glamorous department stores in all of St. Petersburg. With a focus on high fashion and rare perfumes, shopping here comes at a premium but it's worth it for the selection and service. ✉ *21–23 ul. Bolshaya Konushennaya, City Center* ☎ *812/648–0841* ⊕ *www.dlt.ru* Ⓜ *Nevsky Prospekt.*

Gostiny Dvor (Гостиный Двор). The city's oldest and largest shopping center was built in the mid-18th century. It has a few upscale boutiques and is also a good place to find souvenirs, such as *matryoshka* (nesting dolls), at some of the best prices in the city (look in the shops along Nevsky to the right of the metro entrance). The second floor houses a string of multibrand boutiques selling women's and men's clothes from famous European designers as well as housewares. *Gostinka,* as Gostiny Dvor is also known, also has some stores with cheaper prices; it can be a good place to buy winter clothing, such as fur hats. The store, open daily from 10 until 10, is in the center of town, and is easily reached by the metro—the station opening into the shop is named in its honor. ✉ *35 Nevsky pr., City Center* ☎ *812/710–5408* ⊕ *www.bgd.ru* Ⓜ *Gostiny Dvor.*

Grand Palace (Гранд Палас). Reigning at the top end of the boutique market and serving shoppers with the deepest pockets, this temple to consumption carries Woolford lingerie, Escada dresses, and Trussardi suits as well as perfume and jewelry at impressively high prices. The café on the first floor offers irresistible desserts and a wide assortment of high-end teas and coffees. ✉ *44 Nevsky pr., City Center* ☎ *812/449–9344* ⊕ *www.grand-palace.ru* Ⓜ *Gostiny Dvor.*

Passazh (Пассаж). Across the street from Gostiny Dvor, this mid-19th-century shopping arcade caters primarily to locals. The souvenir sections, however, are worth visiting, as prices, in rubles, are a bit lower here than in the souvenir shops around hotels and in other areas frequented by tourists. You can also pick up fine table linens at bargain prices. The antiques section in the center of the arcade is worth a look, too, and there's a reasonably sized supermarket in the basement. ✉ *48 Nevsky pr., City Center* ☎ *812/315–5209* ⊕ *www.passage.spb.ru* Ⓜ *Gostiny Dvor.*

Stockmann (Стокманн). One of the newest and largest department stores on Nevsky prospekt, this Finnish retailer specializes in quality clothes, lingerie, toys, kitchen gadgets, linens, and bathroom goods, much of it by Finnish and Scandinavian producers. A vast supermarket located on the lower level offers a wide range of hard-to-find delicacies (at least in Russia) from around the world and an extensive wine selection. ✉ *114–116 Nevsky pr., City Center* ☎ *812/313–6000* ⊕ *www. stockmann.ru* Ⓜ *Ploscshad Vosstaniya.*

Tatyana Parfinova (Татьяна Парфенова). St. Petersburg's most famous clothing designer offers her jewel-toned designs in flowing silk and velvet, as well as a line of housewares that includes linens, tableware, furniture, and even original paintings. ✉ *51 Nevsky pr., City Center* ☎ *812/713–1415* ⊕ *www.parfionova.ru* Ⓜ *Mayakovskaya.*

SPECIALTY STORES

ANTIQUES

Petersburg Antiques Salon (Антикварный салон Петербург). This shop stocks icons, Carl Fabergé jewelry, furniture, and vintage lamps. There is also Soviet propaganda porcelain, such as ashtrays in the shape of an Uzbek man reading a newspaper, or tea sets featuring the heroes of the Russian Revolution. Some are collectors' items that once belonged to some of Russia's finest museums. Keep in mind that it's against the law to export any item that's more than 100 years old. In theory, taking out even a rusted nail would be a breach of the law. With any antique purchase you make, you need an export certificate, which can be obtained only at the state-run Board for the Preservation of Cultural Valuables and only after an expert assessment that can take up to three days. ✉ *54 Nevsky pr., City Center* ☎ *812/571–4020* ⊕ *www.salon-petersburg.ru* Ⓜ *Nevsky Prospekt.*

Tertia (Терция). All things printed are the specialty of this snug shop, with original Soviet posters, prerevolutionary postcards bearing portraits of Romanov family members, and prints, maps, and books on offer. There is also some silverware and bric-a-brac. The store is popular with both serious collectors and museum researchers, who sometimes manage to fish out rare manuscripts. ✉ *5 ul. Italyanskaya, City Center* ☎ *812/571–8048* ⊕ *tertiaspb.ru* Ⓜ *Nevsky Prospekt.*

CRAFTS AND SOUVENIRS

Galereya Steklo (галерея Стекло). At this glass gallery, the city of St. Petersburg is reflected in carved Easter eggs, stained glass, vases, and candlesticks. Each work is handmade, and many are one-of-a-kind. ✉ *28 ul. Lomonosova, bldg. 1, City Center* ☎ *812/312–2214* ⊕ *www. glassdesign.ru* Ⓜ *Nevsky Prospekt.*

Guild of Masters (Гильдия мастеров *Gildia Masterov*). Jewelry, ceramics, and other types of Russian traditional art, all made by members of the Russian Union of Artists, are sold here. They can provide the documents necessary to export artwork. ✉ *82 Nevsky pr., City Center* ☎ *812/579–0979* ⊕ *www.guild-master.ru* Ⓜ *Mayakovskaya.*

Nado Zhe (НАДО ЖЕ). This artist-run collective offers some of the city's most unique souvenirs, from nostalgic Soviet kitsch to modern felt handbags in unusual shapes. The goods are both distinctive and reasonably priced. ✉ *11 ul. Rubinsteina, City Center* ☎ *812/314–3247* ⊕ *www.nadoje.ru* Ⓜ *Vladimirskaya.*

Russky Ljon (**Русский лен**). This is a good source for linen goods created in the traditional Russian style of the 19th century. There are several branches throughout the city. There's another branch nearby at 3 ulitsa Pushkinskaya. ✉ *151 Nevsky pr., City Center* ☎ *812/979–2929* ⊕ *www.linorusso.ru* Ⓜ *Ploshchad Alexandra Nevskovo.*

Vernisazh (**Vernisazh**). At this open-air market outside the Church of the Savior on Spilled Blood, more than 100 vendors sell nesting dolls, paintings, Soviet icons, and miscellaneous trinkets. It is probably the easiest and quickest market to locate if your time in St. Petersburg is limited; there are sure to be items here that make good gifts and keepsakes. Most vendors speak several languages but the prices can be rather inflated. Don't accept the first price quoted, and try to pay a third or so less than that. ✉ *1 Kanal Griboyedova, City Center* Ⓜ *Nevsky Prospekt.*

FARMERS' MARKETS

The fresh food markets (*rynok*) in St. Petersburg are lively places in which a colorful collection of goods and foods are sold by vendors, often from out of town and sometimes from outside the Russian republic. In addition to the fine cuts of fresh and cured meat, dairy products, and local honey, piles of fruits and vegetables are sold here, even in winter. You can also find many welcome surprises such as hand-knit scarves, hats, and mittens. In general, the markets are open daily from 8 am to 7 pm (until 5 pm on Sunday).

FARMERS' MARKETS

Apraksin Dvor (**Апраксин Двор**). St. Petersburg's less wealthy citizens come to this seething bazaar to shop for cheap clothes, shoes, DVDs, household items, and whatever else you can think of. The market is a chaotic relic of the Yeltsin years, and hardly befitting Russia's newfound love affair with Slavic glamour. As a result the city's rulers have decreed that Apraksin Dvor must go, although it's very popular with the locals, and the traders are a resourceful bunch who are fighting to remain in place. They are likely to win in the end. ✉ *28–30 ul. Sadovaya, City Center* Ⓜ *Nevsky Prospekt.*

Sennoi Rynok (**Сенной рынок**). This may be the biggest food market in the city; the entrance is just a short walk from ploshchad Sennaya. While this is one of the cheapest places in the city to buy fresh produce, the goods are mainly sold extremely close to their expiration date and anything bought here should be used within a day or two. ✉ *4 Moskovsky pr., City Center* Ⓜ *Sadovaya or Sennaya Ploshchad.*

FOOD

Gastronom 811 (**Гастроном**). This mini-supermarket is open 24 hours a day and sells the basics for a light lunch or breakfast, including a few fresh fruits and vegetables. It also contains a café where resonably priced, if uninspired, cakes and coffees can be had at all hours. ✉ *66 Nevsky pr., City Center* ⊕ *www.gastronom811.ru* Ⓜ *Gostiny Dvor.*

Food Stores in St. Petersburg

For cigarettes, snacks, drinks, and basic foodstuffs like bread, milk, and tea, look for a *produkty* shop. They also sell such popular local treats as rye bread, *vatrushka* (a kind of pastry), *pelmeni* (dumplings), smoked salmon, salted herring, and pickles. If you want to find a broad range of foreign food, there are well-stocked supermarkets in any large shopping mall. These stores are usually open daily, until at least 8 pm.

Black caviar, which once reigned as the food gift of choice in Russia, is hard to find in the shops these days. Its harvest and sale was banned for several years owing to massive sturgeon poaching. Due to conservation measures, caviar sales are expected to resume only fitfully and with very limited amounts.

Supermarkets with branches all over the city include Pyatyorochka (there's a figure 5 in its logo), Perekryostok ("Crossroads"; look for a cross), Lenta (featuring a daisy), and Diksi (a red disc on a yellow square with "Diksi" written in black). French-style markets include Mega, O'Key, and Giant. There's also a Finnish chain called Prisma (a red-orange-yellow triangle on a green square). If you see a red-and-white logo that reads Maksidom on what appears to be a superstore, don't go in looking for food—it's a home-improvement and furniture chain that competes with IKEA.

Nevsky prospekt itself doesn't have many food shops, but a short walk down its cross streets will usually yield one. Vladimirsky Passage on Vladimirskaya prospekt just a few minute's walk from Nevsky is a good bet, as it contains one of the city's best supermarkets in its basement. Large shopping centers around ploshchad Vosstania, such as Stockmann and Galeria, also have vast supermarkets. As farming in Russia is a very small industry, don't expect to see any private butcher shops, upscale organic fruit shops, or the like.

JEWELRY

Jewelry used to be an unlikely reason to come to St. Petersburg, but there are some good places to explore these days, particularly on Nevsky prospekt.

Russian Jewelry House (Российский Ювелирный Дом *Rossisky Yuvilrniy Dom*). This is a good bet for jewelry, particularly amber pieces. ⊠ *27 Nevsky pr., City Center* ☎ *812/312–8501* Ⓜ *Nevsky Prospekt*.

MUSIC STORES

Otkryty Mir (Открытый Мир). For a city that prides itself on its cultural legacy the selection of classical music on offer is surprisingly poor. While no one could accuse this CD and DVD store of being overstocked, it does hold the occasional hidden classical gem, particularly when it comes to Russian composers and artists and recordings on the old Melodiya label. Hunt around. ⊠ *32 Nevsky pr., City Center* ☎ *812/315–8222* ⊕ *www.cd-classic.ru* Ⓜ *Nevsky Prospekt*.

Phonoteca (Фонотека). This shop sells an eclectic selection of music and DVDs that tends toward the esoteric but still manages to cover most genres. Prices are good and there's also a choice of new and vintage vinyl. Friendly staff speak English and are always ready to offer suggestions or let you listen before buying. ✉ *28 ul. Marata, City Center* ☎ *812/712–3013* ⊕ *www.phonoteka.ru* Ⓜ *Vladimirskaya.*

Severnaya Lyra (Северная лира). Run by one of the biggest music publishers in Russia, this all-around music shop sells CDs, sheet music, and even musical instruments. The selection includes hard-to-find scores by contemporary Russian composers as well as traditional Russian musical instruments, all at very reasonable prices. ✉ *26 Nevsky pr., City Center* ☎ *812/312–0796* ⊕ *www.compozitor.spb.ru/eng* Ⓜ *Nevsky Prospekt.*

SPAS

Yamskie Bani. The fancier banya in St. Petersburg has a public banya and individual rooms for private groupds. There is also a bar, restaurant, massage, tanning facilities, and a fitness center. Prices start at 220R. ✉ *9 ul. Dostoyevskovo, City Center* ☎ *812/713–3580* ⊕ *www.yamskie. ru* Ⓜ *Vladimirskaya.*

SPORTS

Zenit Arena (Зенит Арена). This shop is devoted to St. Petersburg's hugely popular local soccer team, which has produced international stars that include Andrei Arshavin, who went on to play for London's Arsenal. Merchandise includes printed scarves, sweaters, balls, mugs, bed linens, and wallpaper. There are even jumpsuits and outfits for babies and toddlers emblazoned with the Zenit's light-blue colors. ✉ *54 Nevsky pr., City Center* ☎ *812/606–6516* ⊕ *www.shop.fc-zenit. ru* Ⓜ *Gostiny Dvor.*

ADMIRALTEISKY

Just west of the City Center and centered around the famous golden-yellow Admiralteistvo, or Admiralty building, the Admiralteisky neighborhood is largely residential with many specialty shops.

SPECIALTY STORES

JEWELRY

Russkie Samotsvety (Русские Самоцветы). Many items in these collections were inspired by St. Petersburg's architecture, history, literature, and artistic legacy. Jewelers play with familiar visual images, like ballet or shipbuilding, and incorporate city symbols in their designs. ✉ *1 ul. Krasnoarmeiskaya, Admiralteisky* ☎ *812/316–7646* ⊕ *www.russam.ru* Ⓜ *Tekhnologichesky Institut.*

SPAS

Kazachi Bani. Though located in a somewhat dilapidated building, this is a good place to try for a truly authentic banya. It's open 24 hours a day, and many locals use it regularly. Sunday, Monday, Wednesday and Friday nights are men only. Tuesday, Wednesday and Thursdays nights are women only. You can't beat the prices, which start at 100R for an hour. It has a private banya for 10 people. ✉ *11 per. Kazachiy, Admiralteisky* ☎ *812/315–0734* Ⓜ *Pushkinskaya.*

VASILIEVSKY ISLAND

Vasilievsky Island, across the Neva River from the Admiralteisky and the Winter Palace, is another historic district, and also a good stop for specialty shopping.

SPECIALTY STORES

CLOTHING

Rot Front Furs (Меха Рот Фронта *Mekha Rot Fronta*). At the large factory shop of this established and respected Russian furrier, founded in 1885, you can get elegant coats, hats, jackets, wraps, and accessories made of mink, polar fox, sheepskin, seal, and other furs, all of them from Russia. The prices are lower than they are in most other fur stores. ✉ *7 nab. Reki Smolenki, bldg. 5, Vasilievsky Island* ☎ *812/321–5726* ⊕ *www.meharf.ru* Ⓜ *Vasileostrovskaya.*

PETROGRAD SIDE

Almost directly across the Neva from the Winter Palace is Petrograd, one of the city's oldest residential neighborhoods, laced with streets and boulevards lined with monuments (including the Peter and Paul Fortress) and many shops.

SPECIALTY STORES

CLOTHING

Tatyana Kotegova Fashion House. For romantic collections with a note of restraint, this designer uses only natural materials, with an emphasis on wool, silk, and cashmere. Kotegova's soaring classical silhouettes capture the essence of St. Petersburg, and her velvet evening dresses, simple yet exquisite, are the dream of a good half of the local female population. ✉ *44 Bolshoi pr., 2nd fl., Petrograd Side* ☎ *812/346–3467* ⊕ *www.kotegova.com* Ⓜ *Petrogradskaya.*

JEWELRY

Ananov (Ананов). Head and shoulders above other jewelry shops in town, this quiet, dimly lit store is owned by former sailor and theater director Andrei Ananov, now famous as a jeweler following in the traditions of the great Karl Fabergé. Ananov is as much a gallery as a shop and prices are only available by asking the deferential staff; rings and necklaces can easily cost upwards of thousands of dollars. ✉ *7 ul. Michurinskaya, Petrograd Side* ☎ *812/235–8338* ⊕ *www.a-ananov.com* Ⓜ *Gorkovskaya.*

VLADIMIRSKAYA (LOWER NEVSKY PROSPECT)

Nevsky prospekt, the center's main thoroughfare, is lined with retail establishments for its length, all the way east into what's known as Lower Nevsky prospekt, or Vladimirskaya.

DEPARTMENT STORES

Galeria (Галерея). Containing 290 shops, this mammoth shopping center also has 24 cafés and restaurants, a 10-cinema multiplex including an IMAX screen, a supermarket, and a bowling alley. The fashion brands are primarily major European labels, such as M&S and Reiss from

Britain, Lindex from Finland, and France's Cacharel. There is a good children's section and a wealth of cosmetics shops selling mainly foreign brands. ✉ *30a Ligovsky pr., City Center* ☎ *812/643–3172* ⊕ *www.galeria-spb.ru* Ⓜ *Ploshchad Vosstania.*

Vladimirsky Passazh (Владимирский Пассаж). This modern and spacious four-story mall, just outside the Dostoyevskaya metro station, has numerous small boutiques selling jewelry, clothes, shoes, bags,

12

lingerie, and cosmetics at less than exorbitant prices. The basement houses a large, 24-hour supermarket that offers a wide selection and there's a great bakery on the ground floor—an excellent budget choice for a quick refuel. ✉ *19 Vladimirsky pr., City Center* ☎ *812/331–3232* ⊕ *www.vpassage.ru* Ⓜ *Dostoyevskaya or Vladimirskaya.*

SPECIALTY STORES

CRAFTS

OFF THE BEATEN PATH

Imperial Porcelain Manufactory (Императорский фарфоровый завод *Imperatorsky Farfory Zavod*). One of the most famous porcelain manufacturers in Russia, this factory was founded in St. Petersburg in 1744 to serve the imperial family. You'll come across Imperial Porcelain shops on Nevsky prospekt and elsewhere in the city, as well as in Moscow, but this shop at the factory is an especially well-stocked source for the world-famous hand-painted cobalt-blue china. There's also a porcelain museum here that's part of the Hermitage's holdings. ✉ *151 Obukhovskoy Oboroni pr., Southern Suburbs* ☎ *812/560–8544* ⊕ *www.ipm.ru* Ⓜ *Lomonosovskaya.*

FARMER'S MARKETS

Kuznechny Rynok (Кузнечный Рынок). This is the best and most expensive of St. Petersburg's food markets and one of the best places to find caviar, fresh dairy products, and an assortment of local honey. ✉ *3 per. Kuznechny, Vladimirskaya* Ⓜ *Vladimirskaya.*

FOOD

Land Supermarket (Супермаркет Лэнд). Hidden away on the lower level of Vladimirsky Passazh, this spacious well-stocked supermarket is open 24 hours a day and offers a wide selection of hard-to-find foreign products as well as fresh baked goods and even a few souvenirs. ✉ *19 Vladimirsky pr., City Center* ☎ *812/331–3233* ⊕ *www.supermarketland.ru* Ⓜ *Vladimirskaya.*

LITEINY/SMOLNY

Just east of Petrograd across yet another of the city's many waterways, the Bolshaya River, is another popular shopping district.

SPECIALTY STORES

CLOTHING

St. Petersburg Furs (Меха Петербурга *Mekha Peterburga*). Even fur-decorated wedding dresses can be found at this palace of a store that caters to modern-day "tsarinas." The many kinds of fur here include such rarities as lynx and Russia's famous sable (a type of the weasel-like marten that's found in Siberia). ⊠ *35 ul. Komsomola, Vyborg Side* ☎ *812/591–6448* ⊕ *www.spbmeh.ru* Ⓜ *Ploshchad Lenina.*

FARMERS' MARKETS

Polyustrovsky Rynok (Полюстровский рынок). On the weekend you can find a pet market, with puppies, kittens, chickens, and more. In a possibly surprising twist, the market also boasts an impressive fur department, with some good bargains on such items as rabbit-fur winter hats. ⊠ *45 Polyustrovsky pr., Vyborg Side* ☎ *812/540-3039* ⊕ *www.p45.ru* Ⓜ *Ploshchad Lenina.*

SIDE TRIPS FROM
ST. PETERSBURG

Updated by
Irina Titova

If St. Petersburg is the star of the show, then its suburbs are the supporting cast needed to tell the story. For every aspect of the city's past—the glamour and glory of its Imperial era, the pride and power of its military history, the splendor of its architecture, the beauty of its waterways—there's a park, a palace, a playground of the tsars somewhere outside the city limits with a corresponding tale to tell.

From the dazzling fountains of Peterhof on the shores of the Gulf of Finland, to the tranquil estate of Pavlovsk to the south, to the naval stronghold of Kronshtadt, what surrounds St. Petersburg is as important to its existence and identity as anything on Nevsky prospekt. It might seem odd to tell you to get out of the city almost as soon as you've arrived, but you'll understand why once you've strolled through palatial rooms and vast grounds in the footsteps of the aristocrats and officers who made Russia a world power.

What draws most visitors, and residents as well, out of St. Petersburg are the elaborate residences where royalty and aristocracy retreated for relaxation. Of all the palaces in Russia, the one that generally makes the most distinct and lasting impression on visitors is Peterhof, on the shore of the Baltic Sea, some 29 km (18 miles) west of St. Petersburg. More than a mere summer palace, it's an Imperial playground replete with lush parks, monumental cascades, and gilt fountains. Tsarskoye Selo, now renamed Pushkin, was a fashionable haunt of members of the aristocracy who were eager to be near the Imperial family. After the Revolution of 1905, Nicholas II and his family lived here, more or less permanently. Pavlovsk was the Imperial estate of Paul I. The estate of Lomonosov, on the Gulf of Finland, is perhaps the least commanding of the suburban Imperial palaces. It is, however, the only one to have survived World War II intact.

Two islands offer different experiences—Kronshtadt is a former naval stronghold, and Valaam is one of Russia's most sacred places.

ORIENTATION AND PLANNING

GETTING ORIENTED

The area around St. Petersburg is one big monument to its role as Russia's Imperial capital, from the time of Peter the Great (1672–1725) to the ill-fated Nicholas II, whose execution in Ekaterinburg in 1918 brought the Romanov dynasty to an end

While it's possible to reach all of the palaces by public transport, the simplest way to see them is to book an excursion (available through any tour company). The cost is reasonable and covers transportation, a guided tour, and admission fees. An organized excursion to any of

TOP REASONS TO GO

Make a splash in the Peterhof Fountains: The grounds surrounding Peterhof's Great Palace (nicknamed the "Russian Versailles") are filled with whimsical fountains. Beware, though: trick fountains in the Lower Park might douse you in a burst of water.

Let the glow of the Amber Room embrace you: The original carved amber panels that once filled a room in Catherine's Palace went missing during World War II and their whereabouts remain a mystery. The panels have been painstakingly re-created and are a wonder to behold.

Stroll in Ekaterininsky Park: The landscaped park on the grounds of Pushkin (Tsarskoye Selo) contains mirror-effect lakes, vast lawns, and impressive views of Catherine Palace. Enjoy a picnic lunch here in the summer.

Get a glimpse of Russian naval might in Kronshtadt: Experience a Russian navy town, taking in the Baltic Sea air as you tour.

Walk on the wild side in Gatchina Park: A lovely walk around Silver Lake is a charming escape from city fuss. You might see newlyweds attaching locks to a small bridge—a Russian wedding tradition.

13

the suburban palaces will take at least four hours; if you travel on your own, it's likely to take up the entire day. But whichever plan you opt for, you'll enjoy numerous sights filled with splendor and magic.

Connections between the palaces are limited, so it's not easy to see more than two at most in a day. Of all the places, the ones that make the most sense to do in tandem would be: Pushkin and Pavlovsk, Peterhof and Lomonosov, Peterhof and Kronshtadt, or Lomonosov and Kronshtadt.

Because this region is so close to St. Petersburg and most people visit on day trips, hotels are few and far between.

Summer Palaces. These status symbols of the royal elite—the Menshikov's Great Palace in Lomonosov, the Great Palace in Peterhof, the Catherine Palace and the Alexander Palace in Pushkin, the Great Palace in Pavlovsk, the Great Palace and Priorat Palace in Gatchina, and the Konstantine Palace in Strelna—are at the heart of any trip outside St. Petersburg. Even Russians who've already visited these tsarist wonders find themselves returning time and time again, drawn back not necessarily by the opulence but by the acres of beautiful parks and gardens, perfect for relaxing.

Kronshtadt and Valaam. The port of Kronshtadt is on an island connected to the city by a dam. Its landmarks include the grandiose Naval Cathedral and numerous forts in the waters around the island. The history of Kronshtadt embraces more than 300 years of Russian navy life. Valaam Island, a national park, is known for its virtually untouched natural surroundings, as well as for its religious history, which includes active monasteries. It's a very popular destination for Russian Orthodox pilgrims.

GREAT ITINERARIES

IF YOU HAVE 1 OR 2 DAYS

You can take your pick of the suburbs for any day trip, although your choice of destination will be influenced by the time of year. In summer, **Peterhof** is a must. At this time of year, **Pushkin** and **Pavlovsk** are also at their most attractive, and can be seen in a single day or, better still, over two days. If you have to choose, head to Pushkin.

IF YOU HAVE 3 OR 4 DAYS

In summer head to **Peterhof** and **Pushkin** on your first two days. On your third day, take a break from the palaces and visit the unforgettable **Valaam Archipelago.** To get to Valaam, on the evening of your second day catch the boat down the Neva River and up into Lake Ladoga. Spend the third day admiring the secluded monasteries and natural beauty of the islands, and return to the city overnight. On your final day, head for **Gatchina, Lomonosov,** or the **Konstantine Palace.** For a destination with a completely different historical feel, head for the naval town of **Kronshtadt.**

PLANNING

WHEN TO GO

To see the palaces and estates at their best, try to time your visits to coincide with spring or summer. Peterhof in particular is best visited in summer, so you can fully appreciate the fountains, statues, monumental cascades, and lush parks. From late September to early June the fountains and cascades are closed down and take on the depressing look of drained pools. Autumn can also be a pleasant time for viewing the palaces. The waterway along the Neva River and Lake Ladoga to Valaam is only open from the end of May through October.

If you're traveling in the extreme cold of winter or the hottest days of summer, dress carefully, as much of your time will probably be spent outdoors.

GETTING HERE AND AROUND

BUS TRAVEL

Bus is often the best way to reach most of the sights around St. Petersburg. Buses or minibuses run on direct routes to almost all of the suburbs, as well as to Kronshtadt. Minibuses (called *marshrutka*) from the city to the suburbs are more convenient than commuter trains (called *elektrichka*) because they usually take you directly to the sights.

HYDROFOIL TRAVEL

From June until roughly the end of September, the "meteor"-type hydrofoil is the best way of getting from St. Petersburg to Peterhof, and it's also one of the options for traveling to Kronshtadt.

TAXI TRAVEL

You'll usually have no trouble getting a taxi at a train or bus station in these towns. Most of the towns are small enough to be navigated easily on foot, but a taxi is an alternative to short bus or train trips (e.g., from Pushkin to Pavlovsk). It's also possible to take a taxi all the way back to St. Petersburg from most of these towns (about 1,000R–1,300R), if you speak Russian.

TRAIN TRAVEL

Though not as easy or convenient as traveling by bus, traveling by *elektrichka* (commuter train) provides a slice of authentic Russian life all on its own, but it's best attempted only if you have at least a little Russian under your belt. Fares are low, and the trip to most suburbs takes less than 45 minutes. Overall, it's worth the minor discomforts of the press of humanity and hard wooden seats. Check with a local travel agent or at the station for schedules. With the exception of traveling by elektrichka at busy times (Friday evening and weekends), you shouldn't have trouble getting a ticket on the same day you wish to travel. For the most part, ticket booths are easy to find; if you don't speak Russian, just say the name of your destination and hold up as many fingers as there are passengers. Bear in mind that there's a lull in departures between 10 am and noon.

RESTAURANTS

Because most of the suburbs are just a short trip from St. Petersburg, there hasn't been any real demand for tourist-oriented restaurants and cafés. There are some exceptions, notably in Pavlovsk and Pushkin, but on the whole it's best to pack some sandwiches. You will, however, find plenty of beer tents and ice-cream vendors.

TOUR OPTIONS

Several local tour companies operate out of kiosks on St. Petersburg's Nevsky prospekt. You can simply step up and buy a ticket, the price of which includes coach seating and a guided tour in English. You can also book in advance by visiting or phoning the tour-company offices.

Two of the most reliable excursion companies are MIR Travel and Davranov-Travel.

Tour Contacts MIR Travel ✉ *Office 1, 11 Nevsky pr., City Center* ☎ *812/325–2595* ⊕ *mir-travel.com.* **Davranov-Travel** ✉ *17 ul. Italianskaya, City Center* ☎ *812/571–8694, 812/312–4662* ⊕ *www.davranovtravel.ru.*

VISITOR INFORMATION

You can find a wealth of information about these suburban sights at St. Petersburg's City Tourism Information Center (where operators are very helpful and speak English, French, and German) and private travel agencies and guided-tour companies.

Visitor Information City Tourist Information Center ✉ *14/52 ul. Sadovaya, at Nevsky prospekt and ul. Sadovaya, City Center* ☎ *812/310–2822 information in English, 812/300–3333 tourist helpline* ⊕ *eng.ispb.info* Ⓜ *Nevsky Prospekt.*

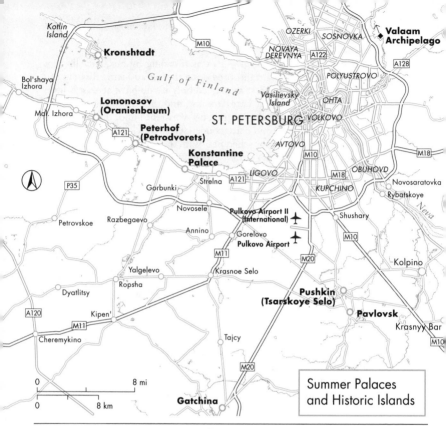

Summer Palaces
and Historic Islands

THE SUMMER PALACES

A visit to this region takes you through a lavish trail of evidence of the Imperial spirit. These majestic old palaces, estates, and former nobles' residences—all on lovingly tended grounds—are within easy reach of St. Petersburg.

LOMONOSOV (ORANIENBAUM)
ЛОМОНОСОВ (ОРАНИЕНБАУМ)

39 km (24 miles) west of St. Petersburg's City Center on the southern shore of the Gulf of Finland.

Alexander Menshikov (circa 1672–1729), the first governor of St. Petersburg, began building this luxurious summer residence on the shores of the Baltic Sea in 1710. Before construction was complete, however, Menshikov was stripped of his formidable political power and exiled, leaving his half-finished summer estate in the hands of Peter III, the ill-fated husband of Catherine the Great. Lomonosov was originally called Oranienbaum after the orangery attached to the main palace then renamed for the 18th-century scientist Mikhail Lomonosov and is the only imperial residence to have survived World War II entirely intact.

13

GETTING HERE AND AROUND

You can get to Lomonosov in an hour by taking the commuter train (elektrichka from Baltiisky railway station) and getting off at Oranienbaum-I (be sure not to get off at Oranienbaum-II). From there walk through a public garden down to the white St. Michael's Cathedral. In front of the cathedral you'll see the fence of the palace and its entrance. Minibus 300, which leaves from Avtovo metro station, is also an option. The trip will cost around 50R. Get off the minibus at the stop called Dvortsovyi Prospekt, cross the road, and walk towards the same cathedral until you see the entrance to the palace grounds. The public bus 200 also leaves from Avtovo metro station and takes you to Dvortsovyi Prospekt.

Lomonosov (Oranienbaum) (Ломоносов [Ораниенбаум]). The original palace on the property, **Menshikov's Great Palace** (Bolshoi Menshikovskii Dvorets), stands on a terrace overlooking the sea and offers visitors a look at a lavishly decorated dining room, study, bedroom, and a number of other rooms. Nearby is **Peterstadt Dvorets,** the modest palace that Peter III used. That it seems small, gloomy, and isolated is perhaps appropriate, as it was here in 1762 that the tsar was arrested, then taken to Ropsha, and murdered in the wake of the coup that placed his wife, Catherine the Great, on the throne. The building that most proclaims the estate's Imperial beginnings, however, is unquestionably Catherine's **Chinese Palace** (Kitaisky Dvorets), designed by Arnoldo Rinaldi. It's quite an affair—baroque outside, rococo inside, with ceiling paintings created by Venetian artists, inlaid-wood floors, and elaborate stucco walls. Down the slope to the east of the Great Palace is the curious **Katalnaya Gorka.** All that remains of the slide, which was originally several stories high, is the fanciful, dazzling pavilion, painted soft blue with white trim, that served as the starting point of the ride, where guests of the empress could catch their breath before tobogganing down again. ✉ 48 Dvortsovyi pr., Lomonosov ✢ exit train at Oranienbaum-I (not II) ☏ 812/422–8016 for tours (operators don't speak English) ⊕ www.peterhofmuseum.ru ✉ Menshikov's Great Palace 400R; Peterstadt Dvorets 200R; Chinese Palace 400R ☉ Menshikov's Great Palace: Wed.–Mon. 11–6 (closed last Wed. of month); Petershtadt Palace: Tues.–Sun. 11–6 (closed last Tues. of month); Chinese Palace: Wed.–Mon. 11–6 (closed last Tues. of month). Park daily 9–8.

PETERHOF (PETRODVORETS) ПЕТЕРГОФ (ПЕТРОДВОРЕЦ)

29 km (18 miles) west of St. Petersburg on the southern shores of the Gulf of Finland.

Peter the Great masterminded this complex of gardens and residences, starting around 1720. His motivation was twofold. First, he was proud of the capital city he was creating and wanted its evolving Imperial grandeur showcased with a proper summer palace. Second, he became attached to this spot while erecting the naval fortress of Kronshtadt on a nearby island across the Gulf of Finland. Half-encircled by the sea, filled with fountains and other water monuments, and with the Marine Canal running straight from the foot of the palace into the bay, Peter's palace was also intended as a tribute to the role of water in the life, and strength, of his city. The German name (Peter's Court) was changed to Petrodvorets after World War II.

GETTING HERE AND AROUND

From Baltiisky Railway Station, take minibus 404; from Avtovo metro station take minibus 224, 300, 401, 424, or 424a. The minibuses run from 6 am to midnight and cost 50R. On weekends, lines for the bus can be quite long, and it may take half an hour to board, unless you're willing to stand. A trip to Peterhof may take an hour on weekends, although it may take half that on weekdays. The bus will stop just next to the entrance to Peterhof's Upper Park. After walking through the park, you'll reach the Grand Palace and its booking offices. There you can buy tickets to the Palace and the Lower Park, site of Peterhof's famous fountains. You can also take the commuter train from Baltic station to Novy Peterhof station, approximately 40 minutes from St. Petersburg; from the station take one of the many buses (number 350, 351, 351a, 352, 353, 354, or 356) to the palace. Another good option for summer season is to take a hydrofoil from the Ermitazh Nizhny (Lower Hermitage) pier. Hydrofoils run from May to mid-September, every half hour from 10 to about 4. The trip will take 30 minutes, and on the way you'll be able to see Kronshtadt and Strelna, the presidential residence. A one-way ticket for a half-hour journey will cost you from 450R to 650R, depending on the time of the day. You may buy tickets on the pier.

EXPLORING

FAMILY

Fodor'sChoice

★

Peterhof (Petrodvorets) (Петергоф (Петродворец)). It's hard to believe that virtually all of Peterhof and the other palaces were almost completely in ruins toward the end of World War II. Many priceless objects had been removed to safety before the Germans advanced, but a great deal was left behind and was looted. Now, after decades of painstaking work, art historians and craftspeople have used photographs and other records to return the palaces to their former splendor. Peterhof and its neighboring palaces are so vast, however, that renovation work will continue for many years to come.

The Lower Park

The Lower Park is a formal baroque garden in the French style, adorned with statues and cascades. Peter's playful spirit is still very much in evidence here. The tsar installed "trick fountains"—hidden water sprays built into trees and tiny plazas. The fountains come to life when staff press hidden mechanisms, much to the surprise of the unsuspecting visitor and the delight of the squealing children who love to race through the resulting showers on hot summer days. Located in the eastern half of Lower Park is the oldest building at Peterhof, **Monplaisir** (literally "My Pleasure"), completed in 1721. This is where Peter the Great lived while overseeing construction of the main Imperial residence. As was typical with Peter, he greatly preferred this modest Dutch-style villa to his later, more extravagant living quarters. Some of its most interesting rooms are the Lacquered Study, decorated with panels painted in the Chinese style (these are replicas; the originals were destroyed during

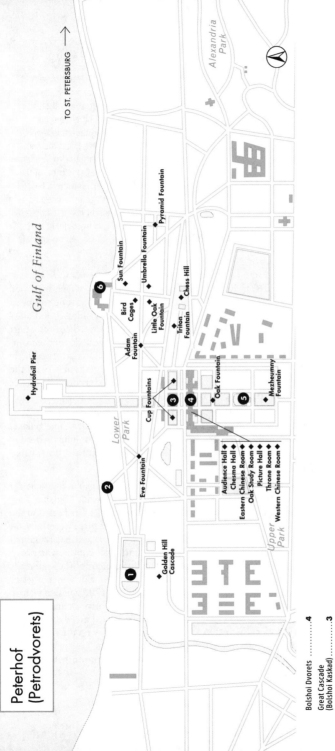

Peterhof (Petrodvorets)

TO ST. PETERSBURG →

Gulf of Finland

Hydrofoil Pier

Sun Fountain

Pyramid Fountain

Umbrella Fountain

Bird Cages

Little Oak Fountain

Triton Fountain

Chess Hill

Adam Fountain

Cup Fountains

Lower Park

Oak Fountain

Mezheumny Fountain

Eve Fountain

Golden Hill Cascade

Alexandria Park

Audience Hall
Chesma Hall
Eastern Chinese Room
Oak Study Room
Picture Hall
Throne Room
Western Chinese Room

Upper Park

Bolshoi Dvorets **4**

Great Cascade
(Bolshoi Kaskad) **3**

Hermitage **2**

Marly Palace **1**

Monplaisir **6**

Neptune Fountain **5**

World War II); Peter's Naval Study; and his bedroom, where some personal effects, such as his nightcap and a quilt made by his wife, are on display. Attached to Peter's villa is the so-called Catherine Wing, built by Rastrelli in the mid-18th century in a completely different style. The future Catherine the Great was staying here at the time of the coup that overthrew her husband and placed her on the throne; the space was later used mainly for balls.

In the western section of the Lower Park is another famous structure, the **Hermitage,** built in 1725. It may be the first of the great Imperial hermitages (the most famous, of course, still stands in St. Petersburg), or retreats, in Russia. This two-story pavilion, which was used primarily as a banquet hall for special guests, was at one time equipped with a device that would hoist the dining table area—diners and all—from the ground floor to the private dining room above. The center part of the table could be lifted out, and guests would write down their dinner preferences and then signal for their notes to be lifted away. Shortly thereafter, the separated section would be lowered, complete with the meals everyone had ordered. The only way to the Hermitage was over a drawbridge, so privacy was ensured.

Almost adjacent to the Hermitage is the **Marly Palace,** a modest Peter the Great construction that's more of a country retreat than a palace. As with Monplaisir, there's mostly Peter-related memorabilia on display here. The four ponds were used by Catherine the Great to stock fish.

The Great Cascade

A walk up the path through the center of the Lower Park (along the Marine Canal) leads you to the famous **Great Cascade** (Bolshoi Kaskad). Running down the steep ridge separating the Lower Park and the Great Palace towering above, the cascade comprises three waterfalls, 64 fountains, and 37 gilt statues. The system of waterworks has remained virtually unchanged since 1721. The ducts and pipes convey water over a distance of some 20 km (12 miles). The centerpiece of the waterfalls is a gilt Samson forcing open the jaws of a lion, out of which a jet of water spurts into the air. The statue represents the 1709 Russian victory over the Swedes at Poltava on St. Samson's day. The present figure is a meticulous replica of the original, which was carried away by the Germans during World War II. A small entrance halfway up the right-hand staircase (as you look at the palace above) leads to the grotto, where you can step out onto a terrace to get a bit closer to Samson before going inside to have a look under the waterworks.

13

Bolshoi Dvorets

Little remains of Peter's original two-story house, built between 1714 and 1725 under the architects Leblond, Braunstein, and Machetti and crowning the ridge above the cascade. The building was considerably altered and enlarged by Peter's daughter, Elizabeth. She entrusted the reconstruction to her favorite architect, Bartolomeo Rastrelli, who transformed the modest residence into a blend of medieval architecture and Russian baroque. Before you begin your tour of the palace interiors, pause for a moment to take in the breathtaking view from the marble terrace. From here a full view of the grounds below unfolds, stretching from the cascades to the Gulf of Finland and on to the city horizon on the shore beyond.

Main Palace

The lavish interiors of the main palace are primarily the work of Rastrelli, although several of the rooms were redesigned during the reign of Catherine the Great to accord with the more classical style that prevailed in her day. Of Peter's original design, only his **Oak Study Room** (Dubovy Kabinet) survived the numerous reconstructions. The entire room and all its furnishings are of wood, with the exception of the white-marble fireplace, above whose mantel hangs a long mirror framed in carved oak. The fine oak panels (some are originals) lining the walls were designed by the French sculptor Pineau.

The classically designed **Throne Room** (Tronny Zal) takes up the entire width of the building and was once the scene of receptions and ceremonies. The pale-green and dark-red decor is bathed in light, which pours in through two tiers of windows (28 in all) taking up the long sides of the room. Behind Peter the Great's throne at the eastern end of the room hangs a huge portrait of Catherine the Great. The empress, the epitome of confidence after her successful coup, is shown astride a horse, dressed in the uniform of the guard regiment that supported her bid for power.

Next to the Throne Room is the **Chesma Hall** (Chesmensky Zal), whose interior is dedicated entirely to the Russian naval victory over the Turks in 1770. The walls are covered with 12 huge canvases depicting the battles; they were created for Catherine by the German painter Phillip Hackert. Arguably the most dazzling of the rooms is the **Audience Hall** (Audients Zal). Rastrelli created the definitive baroque interior with this glittering room of white, red, and gold.

Other notable rooms include the **Chinese Study Rooms** (Kitaiskye Kabinety), designed by Vallin de la Mothe in the 1760s. Following the European fashion of the time, the rooms are ornately decorated with Chinese motifs. Finely carved black-lacquer panels depict various Chinese scenes. Between the two rooms of the study is the **Picture Hall** (Kartinny Zal), whose walls are paneled with 368 oil paintings by the Italian artist Rotari. The artist used just eight models for these paintings, which depict young women in national dress.

Upper Park

This symmetrical formal garden is far less imaginative than the Lower Park. Its focal point is the **Neptune Fountain,** made in Germany in the 17th century and bought by Paul I in 1782. During World War II this three-tier group of bronze sculptures was carried away by the Germans, but it was recovered and reinstalled in 1956.

You can reach the palace by commuter train from St. Petersburg but as long as you're visiting in the summer and there isn't too much fog, the best way to go is by hydrofoil. This way your first view is the panorama of the grand palace overlooking the sea. The lines to get into the palace can be excruciatingly long in summer, and sometimes guided tours get preferential treatment. The ticket office for foreigners is inside the palace, and although admission is more expensive than it is for Russians, the lines are significantly shorter. Some park pavilions are closed Wednesday and others on Thursday; visiting on the weekend is your best chance to see everything.

> **FIRE FOR ART'S SAKE**
>
> It's said that when Catherine the Great asked the painter Phillip Hackert to depict the naval battles between the Russians and the Turks in 1770, he replied that he couldn't paint a burning ship since he'd never seen one. The solution: Catherine arranged to have ships blown up for him to use as models.

■**TIP→** In the summer you can see the ceremony of the Great Cascade fountains at 11 am daily. ⊠ *2 ul. Razvodnaya* ☎ *812/450–5806 tours, 812/450–5287 information (English in summer)* ⊕ *peterhofmuseum.ru* 🖳 *Palace late-Apr.–mid-Oct. 550R, mid-Oct.–late Apr. 450R; Lower Park 450R (100R after the fountains are off); separate admission fees for park pavilions* ⊙ *Great Palace: Tues.–Fri. and Sun. 10:30–7, Sat. 10:30–9. Park daily 9–8; some park pavilions are closed Wed. and others on Thurs.; all closed last Tues. of month; fountains operate summer, weekdays 10–6, weekends 10–7.*

WHERE TO EAT

$$$
EUROPEAN

✕**Bolshaya Oranzhereya.** The best option on the grounds of the palace itself is in the palace's old *oranzhereya*, or garden house. A comfortable, quaint spot for a snack and cup of tea, it also serves prix-fixe Continental meals with various kinds of fish and meat, including venison and duck courses, or traditional Russian options such as borscht (beet soup) or *solyanka* (slightly spicy meat soup with pickles). The restaurant is open from 10 to 6 from May to October. ⑤ *Average main: 600R* ⊠ *Peterhof palace grounds, near Triton fountain, 2 ul. Razvodnaya* ☎ *812/450–6106* ⊕ *www.museumrestaurants.com* ⊙ *Closed Oct.–Apr.*

KONSTANTINE PALACE КОНСТАНТИНОВСКИЙ ДВОРЕЦ

19 km (12 miles) south of St. Petersburg on the southern shores of the Gulf of Finland.

In 1720 Peter the Great commissioned work on this maritime country residence that was to be a "Russian Versailles." Italian architect Nicolo Micketti designed not only the palace, but also beautiful fountains and waterworks meant to draw water from the Gulf of Finland. However, the fountains never worked, and the palace itself underwent several fires and was later redesigned. Nearly destroyed in World War II, this suburban palace dazzles once again. After years of renovation, based on old photographs and plans, the Italian-baroque, coffee-color palace is now officially the Palace of Congress and used to host government functions.

13

TRICKSTER'S FOUNTAINS

If you're traveling to Peterhof with small children in the summer, be sure to pack a bathing suit or an extra set of clothes for them and be prepared to get wet. The Lower Park's "trick fountains" are supposedly turned on by stomping on magic stones or pulling on levers, and kids love to try and figure out which one makes the fountains work. You won't want to point out the person sitting nearby who secretly makes them spray at just the right moment.

GETTING HERE AND AROUND

A great option to get to the palace is to join a special tourist bus (labeled "To Konstantine Palace") that leaves from Beloselsky-Belozersky Palace (located at Nevsky prospekt) in St. Petersburg. You can purchase a ticket from any theater box office. The excursion departs weekdays at 2 pm and at 11 am and 3 pm on weekends. You can also get to the palace by taking public bus 200 or 210 or taking minibus 424 or 424a from the Avtovo metro station. Another option is tram 36, from the same metro station. This is a slower method, and the train stops about 500 yards from the palace. The buses and minibuses stop near an entrance that's closed, so you'll have to backtrack a bit to get to a smaller gate. There you'll see a kiosk for an excursion bureau. Buy a ticket here. Security measures are high. In addition to being a tourist attraction, the palace is also an official residence of the Russian president; if you're traveling independently a Russian guide will lead you through a metal detector to reach the palace.

EXPLORING

Konstantine Palace (**Константиновский Дворец.**). Of the palace's 50-odd rooms, several are open to the public on guided tours when no state functions are taking place. Grandest of all is the central **Marble Hall,** used to host official events, which lives up to its name, with yellow marble pilasters framed by bluish marble walls. A balcony here affords a breathtaking view of the huge park and canals leading to the Gulf of Finland. In addition to the rooms, you can see various permanent exhibits: Russian state symbols from the Hermitage; naval memorabilia from St. Petersburg's Naval Museum; the famed Rostropovich-Vishnevskaya art collection; and the Naryshkins' treasure, found in 2011 during the reconstruction works in an old mansion that used to belong to the Russian noble family and including 2,000 silver objects like tea sets made by the best Russian and European jewelers of the 19th to early 20th centuries. The grounds include the Upper (English) Park, Big Pond, canals, drawbridges, and the monument to Peter the Great, which stands just in front of the palace.

Rostropovich-Vishnevskaya Collection

The Rostropovich-Vishnevskaya collection of some 850 Russian paintings, art, and crafts originally belonged to the Russian cellist Mstislav Rostropovich and his wife, opera star soprano Galina Vishnevskaya. The couple fled the Soviet Union in 1974 under fire for their support of dissident Alexander Solzhenitsyn. After her husband's death, Vishnevskaya decided to auction the collection, saying she didn't have enough money to maintain it and keep it safe. Russian steel magnate Alisher Usmanov preempted a Sotheby's auction by buying the collection outright, reportedly for more than the $40 million it was expected to fetch at auction. He said he chose Konstantine Palace as the collection's home because: "I wanted to obey the will of Galina Vishnevskaya, who would like the collection to find its place in one of the palaces of St. Petersburg. I learned that one of the beautifully and recently rebuilt palaces, the Konstantine Palace, has no collection of its own." The collection includes works by some of Russia's most renowned painters, including Ilya Repin and Boris Grigoryev, as well as furniture, porcelain, silver, and other items.

Before visiting, be sure to call ahead to make sure the palace will not be closed for state functions. ✉ *3 alleya Beryozovaya, Strelna, Strelna* ☎ *812/438–5360 information* ⊕ *www.konstantinpalace.ru* 🖃 *270R* ⊙ *Thurs.–Tues. 10–4.*

PUSHKIN (TSARSKOYE SELO) ПУШКИН (ЦАРСКОЕ СЕЛО)

Fodor'sChoice
★

24 km (15 miles) south of St. Petersburg's City Center via commuter train from Vitebsk station, 40 km (25 miles) southeast of Peterhof.

The town of Pushkin was a summer residence of the Imperial family from the days of Peter the Great to the last years of the Romanov dynasty. Pushkin was initially known as Tsar's Village (Tsarskoye Selo), but the town's name was changed after the Revolution of 1917, first to Children's Village (Detskoye Selo) and then to Pushkin, in honor of the great Russian poet who studied at the lyceum here. During the 18th and 19th centuries, Tsarskoye Selo was a popular summer resort for St. Petersburg's aristocracy and well-to-do citizens. Not only was the royal family close by, but it was here, in 1837, that Russia's first railroad line was opened, running between Tsarskoye Selo and Pavlovsk, to be followed three years later by a line between here and St. Petersburg.

GETTING HERE AND AROUND

From Vitebsky railway station take a suburban train to Deskoye Selo station (in the town of Pushkin), then Bus 371 or 382 or minibus ("marshrutka") 371, 377, or 382 to the Catherine Palace and Park. From Moskovskaya metro station, take minibus 342 or 545 to the Tsarskoye Selo. You can enter the park from the main entrance: there you'll see the magnificent Catherine Palace on your right. The Catherine Park will be on your left. From Moskovskaya metro station, take minibus 342 or 545 to the museum complex.

Pushkin
(Tsarskoye Selo)

Alexander Park

Catherine Park

Great Pond

Alexander Palace (Aleksandrovsky Dvorets) ..**4**	Chapel **1**
Amber Room.............**7**	Chesma Column **11**
Cameron Gallery **18**	Chinese Theater **2**
Cameron's Pyramid **19**	Chinese Village **3**
Catherine Palace (Ekaterininsky Dvorets) ...**5**	Concert Hall **20**
Canal **16**	English Garden **17**
	Great Hall **6**

Great Pond **14**	
Grotto....................**15**	
Lyceum **9**	
Marble Bridge **12**	
Picture Gallery **8**	
Pushkin Monument ...**10**	
Ruined Tower **13**	

EXPLORING

Fodor'sChoice ★ **Catherine Palace** (*Ekaterininsky Dvorets*). The dazzling 18th-century Catherine Palace is a perfect example of Russian baroque, its bright-turquoise exterior distinguished by row after row of white columns and pilasters with gold baroque moldings running the entire 985 feet of the facade. Although much of the palace's history and its inner architectural design bears Catherine the Great's stamp, it's for Catherine I, Peter the Great's second wife, that the palace is named. Under their daughter, Empress Elizabeth, the original modest stone palace was completely rebuilt. The project was initially entrusted to the Russian architects Kvasov and Chevakinsky, but in 1752 Elizabeth brought in the Italian architect Bartolomeo Rastrelli. Although Catherine the Great had the interiors remodeled in the classical style by a pair of noted architects, the Scottish Charles Cameron and the Italian Giacomo Quarenghi, she left Rastrelli's stunning facade untouched.

The Interior

You enter the palace grounds through the gilded black-iron gates designed by Rastrelli. The *E* mounted atop is for Catherine ("Ekaterina" in Russian). To your right, a visual feast unfolds as you walk the length of the long blue-and-gold facade toward the museum entrance. Sparkling above the palace at the northern end are the golden cupolas of the Palace Church. Entering the palace by the main staircase (not added until 1861), you'll see displays depicting the extent of the wartime damage and of the subsequent restoration work. Like Peterhof, the palace was almost completely destroyed during World War II. It was used by occupying Nazi forces as an army barracks, and as the Germans retreated, they blew up what remained of the former Imperial residence.

The largest and arguably most impressive room is the **Great Hall** (Bolshoi Zal), which was used for receptions and balls. The longer sides of the hall are taken up by two tiers of gilt-framed windows, with tall, elaborately carved, gilded mirrors placed between them. Light pouring in through the windows bounces off the mirrors and sparkles on the gilt, amplifying the impression of spaciousness and brilliance. The huge ceiling painting, depicting Russian military victories and accomplishments in the sciences and arts, makes the room seem even larger. Here it's easy to imagine the extravagant lifestyle of St. Petersburg's prerevolutionary elite.

On the north side of the State Staircase is one of the palace's most famous rooms, the **Amber Room** (Yantarnaya Komnata), so named for the engraved amber panels that line its walls. The room owes much of its fame to the mysterious disappearance of its amber panels in World War II. In 1979 the Soviet government finally gave up hope of ever retrieving the panels and began the costly work of restoring the room. Leaving the Amber Room, you'll come to the large **Picture Gallery** (Kartinny Zal), which runs the full width of the palace. The paintings are from Western Europe and date from the 17th to early 18th centuries.

The Blue Drawing Room, the Blue Chinese Room, and the Choir Anteroom face the courtyard. Each has pure-silk wall coverings—when the postwar restoration began, this extra supply of the original silk was discovered tucked away in a storage room of the Hermitage.

13

Catherine Park

The beautiful park, with its marble statues, waterfalls, garden alleys, boating ponds, pavilions, bridges, and quays, is split into two sections. The inner, formal section, the French Garden, runs down the terraces in front of the palace's eastern facade. The outer section encloses the Great Pond and is in the less-rigid style of an English garden. If you follow the main path through the French Garden and down the terrace, you'll eventually reach Rastrelli's Hermitage pavilion, which he completed just before turning his attention to the palace itself. Other highlights of the French Garden include the Upper and Lower Bath pavilions (1777–79) and Rastrelli's elaborate blue-domed grotto.

In the English-style garden, the **Cameron Gallery** (Galereya Kamerona) forms a continuation of the palace's park-side frontage. It's off to the right (with your back to the palace). Open only in summer, it contains a museum of 18th- and 19th-century costumes. From its portico you get the best views of the park and its lakes—which is exactly what Cameron had in mind when he designed it in the 1780s. The double-sided staircase leading down to the Great Pond is flanked by two bronze sculptures of Hercules and Flora. From here, descend the stairs to begin your exploration of the park. Just beyond the island in the middle of the artificially created Great Pond stands the Chesma Column, commemorating the Russian naval victory in the Aegean in 1770. At the far end of the pond is Cameron's Pyramid, where Catherine the Great is said to have buried her beloved greyhounds. If you walk around the pond's right side, you'll come to the pretty blue-and-white Marble Bridge, which connects the Great Pond with a series of other ponds and small canals. At this end, you can rent rowboats. Farther along, up to the right, you come to the Ruined Tower. This architectural folly was built in the late 18th century merely to enhance the romantic ambience of these grounds.

Alexander Palace

Outside the park stands yet another palace, Alexandrovsky Dvorets, a present from Catherine to her favorite grandson, the future Tsar Alexander I, on the occasion of his marriage. Built by Giacomo Quarenghi between 1792 and 1796, the serene and restrained classical structure was the favorite residence of Russia's last tsar, Nicholas II. The left wing of the building is open to the public and hosts topical exhibits. Most of the interior was lost, with the notable exception of Nicholas's cabinet, a fine example of art-nouveau furniture and design.

Lyceum

Built in 1791 and originally intended for the education of Catherine the Great's grandchildren, the Lyceum later became a school for the nobility. Its most famous student, enrolled the first year it opened, was the beloved poet Alexander Pushkin. The building now serves as a museum; the classroom, library, and Pushkin's bedroom have been restored to their appearance at the time he studied here. In the school's garden is a statue of the poet as a young man, seated on a bench, presumably deep in creative meditation.

■TIP➔ In summer you can enjoy carriage rides in the park (600R to 1200R), a Great Pond gondola ride (300R), and even electric car tours (250R). In winter you can enjoy sleigh rides in Alexander Park on weekends and holidays (600R-1200R). ⊠ *7 ul. Sadovaya* ☎ *812/465–2024 recorded information in Russian, 812/465–9424 administration of Catherine Palace, 812/476–6411 Lyceum information* ⊕ *www.tzar.ru* ✉ *Catherine Palace 320R, audioguide in English, German, and French 150R; Alexander Palace 250R; Lyceum 120R; Park 100R in summer, 300R with bathhouses and court carriage exhibition* ⊙ *Catherine Palace: Mon. 10–9, Wed.–Sun. 10–6; closed last Mon. of month. Alexander Palace: Wed.– Mon. 10–6; closed last Wed. of month. Lyceum: Wed.–Mon. 10–6; closed last Fri. of month.*

WHERE TO EAT

$$$$ ╳**Admiralteistvo.** This charming little restaurant is on the second floor
RUSSIAN   of an old redbrick pavilion across the lake from the Catherine Palace. Its nostalgic interiors are furnished with antique furniture and a number of partially enclosed seating areas that give you some isolation for a private dinner. The kitchen specializes in European and excellent Russian cuisine. For a genuine Russian dish, go for fish such as baked sturgeon or sterlet, which was very popular at the tsars' tables. You can also try traditional Russian homemade *pelmeni,* dumplings with various fillings, or different kinds of *kotleta,* a stuffed and breaded meat dish (also known as Kiev). ⑤ *Average main: 600R* ⊠ *7 ul. Sadovaya, in Ekaterininsky Park* ☎ *812/465–3549 reservations* ⊕ *admiral.gutsait.ru* ⚒ *Reservations essential.*

PAVLOVSK ПАВЛОВСК

30 km (19 miles) south of St. Petersburg's City Center, a 5-minute train journey from Tsarskoye Selo, 6 km (4 miles) south of Pushkin.

The land at Pavlovsk had always been the royal hunting grounds, but in 1777 Catherine the Great awarded them to her son, Paul I, upon the birth of his first son, the future Tsar Alexander I. (Pavlovsk comes from "Pavel," the Russian word for Paul.) Construction of the first wooden buildings started immediately, and in 1782 Catherine's Scottish architect Charles Cameron began work on the Great Palace and the landscaped park. In contrast to the dramatically baroque palaces of Pushkin and Peterhof, Pavlovsk is a tribute to the reserved beauty of classicism. Paul's intense dislike of his mother apparently manifested itself in determinedly doing exactly what she wouldn't—with, most visitors agree, gratifying results. The place is popular with St. Petersburg

The Story of the Amber Room

CLOSE UP

The original Amber Room panels, a masterpiece of amber carving, were presented to Peter the Great in 1716 by Prussian king Friedrich Wilhelm I in exchange for 55 "very tall" Russian soldiers (that was Friedrich's request). The panels were eventually incorporated in one of the numerous halls of Ekaterininsky Dvorets (Catherine Palace) in Tsarskoye Selo. After the Revolution of 1917, Catherine Palace was turned into a museum, and the public had its first chance to see the Amber Room. The Nazis looted the palace in 1941 and moved the contents of the Amber Room to what was then the German town of Königsberg. That town (soon to become the Russian town of Kaliningrad) was captured by the Soviets in 1945, but by the time the Soviet troops entered the city, the amber panels had disappeared.

It's believed that the panels were either destroyed by Allied bombing or were somehow hidden by the Nazis. For obvious reasons, the second theory has held the most appeal, and over the years it's given hope to eager treasure seekers. Some postulated that the amber could have been buried in a silver mine near Berlin, hidden on the shores of the Baltic Sea, or taken as far away as South America. Explorers have searched caves, jails, churches, salt mines, tunnels, bunkers, and ice cellars. For some, the quest was an obsession: Georg Stein, a former German soldier, searched for more than two decades, spent almost all his fortune, and in the end was found mysteriously murdered in a Bavarian forest in 1987. In 1991 the German magazine *Der Spiegel* organized its own archaeological expedition to search for the panels in the ruins of Lochstedt Castle in the Kaliningrad region. It failed to find them.

In 1979 the Soviet government gave up all hope of relocating the panels and initiated the reconstruction of the Amber Room, allocating about $8 million for the project. It would take another $3.5-million donation from the German company Ruhrgas AG in 1999 to complete the restoration work. More than 30 craftspeople worked tirelessly, some dedicating up to 20 years of their lives to the project. Using microscopes to make the tiniest engravings in the amber, many lost their vision over the years or suffered illness from inhaling amber dust. Ironically, most of the amber came from the world's largest deposit of the fossil resin, in Kaliningrad—the very place where the original amber panels had disappeared. After 25 years of work and 6 tons of amber (though 80% of this amber was waste product), the replica of the Amber Room was unveiled in 2003 in time for St. Petersburg's 300th-anniversary celebrations.

Covered with more than a ton of amber, the room embraces you with the warm glow of more than 13 hues of this stone, ranging from butter yellow to dark red. One panel, *Smell and Touch*, is an original, found in Bremen, Germany, in 1997; a German pensioner whose father had fought in the Soviet Union was caught trying to sell the panel.

13

residents, who come to stroll through its beautiful 1,500-acre park, full of woods, ponds, tree-lined alleys, and pavilions. If you have time to walk around the park you can bring along or buy in the park some nuts to feed local squirrels. Tours to Pavlovsk and Pushkin are often combined. However, it's difficult to do justice to each of these in a one-day visit. If you only have time to visit one of the two, pick Pushkin.

GETTING HERE AND AROUND

From the Moskovskaya metro station get minibus (marshrutka) 299, which will take you directly to the palace in Pavlovsk. After passing the palace stop, the minibus continues, so make sure to get off at the palace (it's an obvious stop). From Kupchino metro station take minibus 286, which also takes you directly to the palace. A less preferable option is to take a commuter train from Vitebsky Railway station, which takes about 40 minutes. But if you don't speak Russian you may feel a bit lost at the station, and as you arrive at Pavlovsk Railway Station you'll either have to walk through the museum's park for about half an hour to get to the palace or take minibus 513, 299, 286, or 521 to get there. If you reach the park first, buy tickets from a kiosk and enter it through a small iron gate. First walk straight, and then head a bit right to the palace grounds. The park has a rather thick forest and many lanes, but few signs, so you can get a bit lost. Don't hesitate to ask other tourists for directions to the palace.

EXPLORING

Pavlovsk (Павловск). The golden yellow **Great Palace** (Bolshoi Dvorets) stands on a high bluff overlooking the river and dominates the surrounding park. The stone palace was built between 1782 and 1786 as the summer residence of Paul, son of Catherine the Great, and his wife, Maria Fyodorovna, in imitation of a Roman villa. The architect Vincenzo Brenna enlarged the palace between 1796 and 1799 with the addition of a second story to the galleries and side pavilions. Despite a devastating fire in 1803 and further reconstruction by Andrei Voronikhin in the early 19th century, Cameron's basic design survives. The building is crowned with a green dome supported by 64 small white columns. In front of the palace stands a statue of the snub-nosed Paul I, a copy of the statue at Gatchina, Paul's other summer residence.

The splendid interiors, with their parquet floors, marble pillars, and gilt ceilings, were created by some of Russia's most outstanding architects, including Quarenghi, who designed the interiors of five rooms on the first floor, and Carlo Rossi, who was responsible for the library, built in 1824. The state apartments on the first floor include the pink-and-blue **Ballroom;** the formal **Dining Hall,** where the full dinner service for special occasions is set out; and the lovely **Corner Room,** with walls of lilac marble and doors of Karelian birch. On the first floor, on the way from the central part of the palace to the southern section, are the **Maria Fyodorovna Empress Rooms** (Komnaty Imperatritsy Marii Fyodorovny), six rooms that were designed for Maria Fyodorovna after the death of Paul I. The most impressive of these is the Small Lamp Study (Kabinet Fonarik), a light-green room that overlooks the Tsar's Little Garden. The empress's library and other belongings are on display here.

Among the lavishly decorated state rooms on the second floor is the famous **Greek Hall,** with a layout like that of an ancient temple. Its rich green Corinthian columns stand out against the white of the faux-marble walls. The hall, which also served as a small ballroom, linked the state chambers of Paul I to those of his wife. The last room on his side is the **Hall of War.** Maria's **Hall of Peace** was designed to correspond to it. The gilt stucco wall moldings of her suite are decorated with flowers, baskets of fruit, musical instruments, and other symbols of peace. Beyond Maria's apartments is the light-filled **Picture Gallery,** with floor-length windows and an eclectic collection of paintings. From the gallery, via a small, pink, marble waiting room, you reach the palace's largest chamber, **Throne Hall.** It once held the throne of Paul I, which was removed for a victory party after Napoléon's defeat and somehow never returned.

13

The Park

Like the palace, the design of the park was shared by the leading architects of the day—Brenna, Cameron, Voronikhin, and Rossi. The park differs greatly from park designs of other Imperial palaces, where the strict rules of geometrical design were followed; at Pavlovsk nature was left much less controlled.

The combined length of the park's paths and lanes is said to equal the distance between St. Petersburg and Moscow (656 km/407 miles). If you walk down the slope just behind the palace to the **Tsar's Little Garden** (Sobstvenny Sadik), you can see the Three Graces Pavilion, created by Cameron. The 16-column pavilion encloses a statue of Joy, Flowering, and Brilliance. Directly behind the palace, a stone staircase, decorated with lions, will take you to the Slavyanka Canal. On the canal's other side, down to the left, is the graceful **Apollo Colonnade,** built in 1783. Its feeling of ruin isn't just due to time: it was struck by lightning in 1817 and never restored. If you bear right at the end of the stairs, you come to the **Temple of Friendship,** meant to betoken the friendship between Empress Maria and her mother-in-law, Catherine the Great. Beyond it is a monument from Maria to her own parents; the center urn's medallion bears their likenesses. Of the other noteworthy pavilions and memorials dotting the park, the farthest one up the bank is the **Mausoleum of Paul I,** set apart on a remote and overgrown hillside toward the center of the park. Maria had the mausoleum built for her husband after he was murdered in a palace coup. Paul was never interred here, however, and though Maria is portrayed as inconsolable in a statue here, historical evidence indicates that she was well aware of the plot to kill her husband. ⊠ *20 ul. Revolutsii* ☎ *812/452–1536 tours* ⊕ *www.pavlovskmuseum.ru* ✉ *Palace 450R, tours in English 700R; park 150R* ⊗ *Sat.–Thurs. 10–6; closed 1st Mon. of month.*

WHERE TO EAT

$$$$
EASTERN
EUROPEAN
✕ **Grand Column Hall.** The former servants' quarters inside Pavlovsk Palace offer cafeteria-style and full-menu service. The European offerings include different kinds of salads and well-prepared trout and pike perch. If you want to go Russian, you can order traditional national dishes, such as pancakes with caviar, or fish or meat in aspic. The

savory pies are delicious. You can also order picnic items to eat on the palace's extensive grounds. $ *Average main: 600R* ⊠ *Pavlovsk Palace* ☎ *812/452–3809* ⊕ *www.palace-rest.ru* ☉ *Closed Fri. in winter.*

$$$$
RUSSIAN

✕ **Podvoriye.** This is one of St. Petersburg's most popular restaurants for traditional Russian food, and it's best to make a reservation. Past guests at this wooden restaurant built in the *terem* (folk or fairy tale) style include the former presidents of France and Russia as well as luminaries of Hollywood and fashion, including Michael Douglas and Georgio Armani. Inside, a stuffed bear greets you with samples of vodka. Traditional Russian fare includes pickled garlic and mushrooms, excellent sturgeon dishes, and cutlets of wild boar, bear, or elk. Among the less expensive mains are pelmeni and *golubtsy* (a mixture of rice and meat wrapped in cabbage or grape leaves). Drinks to try are *kvas* (a sweet, lightly fermented drink made from bread or grains) and *mors* (a sour-sweet cranberry juice). The delicious kids' menu has all kinds of pancakes and dozens of different jams—most of them are made of berries that grow at the restaurant owner's dacha in the Crimea Peninsula of Ukraine. $ *Average main: 900R* ⊠ *16 shosse Filtrovskoye* ☎ *812/454-5464 for reservations* ⊕ *www.podvorye.ru.* ⪪ *Reservations essential.*

GATCHINA ГАТЧИНА

45 km (28 miles) southwest of St. Petersburg's City Center.

Gatchina, which is the name of both the city and the park-palace complex, dates to the 15th century, when it was a small Russian village. The main attractions of the most distant of St. Petersburg's palace suburbs are an expansive park with a network of bridges for island-hopping and a grim-looking palace—resembling a feudal English castle—that has unfortunately deteriorated over the years. Probably because Gatchina lacks the splendor of the other suburban palaces, it's usually not included in prearranged tours, and thus is rarely visited by foreign tourists. Because it does offer a chance to escape from the crowds for a while, however, it's worth a visit. Keep in mind that few restaurants are available, so be sure to bring along a lunch that you can enjoy on the shores of Silver Lake.

The name Gatchina is a bit of a mystery. One popular suggestion is that it comes from the Russian expression *gat chinit*, meaning "to repair the road." Others believe it comes from the German phrase *hat schöne*, meaning "it's beautiful." In its current state, both expressions could apply.

GETTING HERE AND AROUND

From the city's Moskovskaya metro station take minibus 18A. It will take you just next to the palace and its park. Get off in front of the palace and walk towards its central entrance to buy tickets. From Baltiisky Railway Station take a commuter train to Gatchina Baltiiskaya station; the trip takes around 45 minutes. If the train brings you to the first platform, exit the train and head towards the palace grounds, which are visible from there—it's a five-minute walk. If the train brings you to the second platform, head through the underground passage; as you exit you'll see the palace.

EXPLORING

English Landscape Gardens. After touring the palaces, you may want to head down to the lakes for a little relaxation. Rowboats and catamarans are available for rent—look for the bare-chested, tattooed men standing along the lake (you may be asked to provide your passport as a deposit, to make sure you actually return the boat instead of fleeing to Finland). The Gatchina park is laid out around a series of lakes occupying about one third of its entire area. The English Landscape Gardens were built around the White and Silver lakes. On a clear day the mirrorlike water reflects the palace facade and pavilions. The gardens are dotted with little bridges, gates, and pavilions and include the Eagle (Orliny) Pavilion, built in 1792 on the shores of the Long Island, and the so-called Chesma Column, built by Rinaldi in honor of the Orlovs' military deeds. Keep in mind that the signs in the park are in Russian and point to eventual destinations, such as Berlin, but if you keep to the lakeshore, you shouldn't have any trouble. ⊠ *1 Krasnoarmeisky pr.* ☎ *813/719–3492 tours* ⌨ *included in admission to Gatchina Palace* ☉ *Tues.–Sun. 10–5; closed 1st Tues. of month.*

> ### COUNT ORLOV
>
> Count Grigory Orlov, young and handsome, was a favorite of Catherine the Great, and the feeling was mutual. Ready and willing to do anything for her, he headed the coup against Catherine's husband, Peter III, in 1762, which allowed Catherine to take the throne. Orlov was also supposedly the father of Catherine's illegitimate son Alexei.

13

Gatchina Palace (Гатчина). In 1712, following the final conquest of the area by Russia, Peter I gave Gatchina to his sister, the tsarevna Natalya Alexeyevna. The land changed hands several times over the years, eventually ending up as a possession of Catherine the Great. She gave it to one of her favorites, Count Grigory Orlov, in 1765. It was during this period that the architect Antonio Rinaldi designed and built the Grand Palace and laid out the park, which was eventually decorated with obelisks and monuments in honor of the Orlovs.

In 1783 Orlov died, and Gatchina passed to Catherine's son, Paul I, and his wife. At various times, Gatchina Palace was a residence of Nicholas I, Alexander II, and Alexander III, and it bears witness to many important historic events, as well as the political and personal secrets of the Romanov dynasty.

In contrast to the pastel colors and flashiness of the palaces of Pushkin and Peterhof, Gatchina Palace has the austere look of a military institution, with a restrained limestone facade and a blocky structure with little ornamentation. The palace, which is built on a ridge, is also surrounded by a deep moat, which emphasizes the castle design of the facade. Its northern side faces a green forest stretching for some distance. The southern facade opens up to the main parade grounds, which were once used for military displays. Along the outer edge of the parade grounds runs a short bastion with parapets cut out with openings for firing weapons. The palace is also accentuated by two five-sided, five-story towers: the Clock Tower and the Signal Tower.

Construction on the palace was carried out in three main phases. The first period began in 1766 under the guidance of Rinaldi. He built the three-story central part of the palace, as well as the service wings and the inner courtyards, known as the Kitchen Block and the Stable Block (later called the Arsenal Block). The second stage of construction began in 1783, when Brenna made the side blocks level with the galleries and installed cannons, adding to the palace's image as a feudal castle. Brenna also integrated new palatial halls, thus turning Rinaldi's chamberlike interiors into ceremonial rooms.

The third stage took place under Nicholas I. He hired the architect Roman Kuzmin to reconstruct both side blocks between 1845 and 1856. He also built a new chapel, and living rooms were arranged in the Arsenal Block. Kuzmin's work also eventually led to the restoration of the 18th-century rooms, the construction of a new main staircase in the central section, and the reshaping of the bastion wall in front of the palace.

> **ECHO**
>
> It was during Count Orlov's control of the complex that a subterranean passage was created between Silver Lake and the halls of the Grand Palace. The 130-yard passage was built to emphasize echoes, repeating up to four words. Today visitors of the palace stand at the start of the passage, and guides ask them to speak a few special questions. The last word in the question becomes the echo's "answer." For example, after asking "Kto boitsya moroza?" (Who is afraid of frost?), the echo answers: "rosa" (rose).

The palace was badly damaged during World War II, and restoration is still underway. Fortunately, a collection of watercolors by the artists Luigi Premazzi and Edward Hau survived. Painted during the 1870s, these watercolors have been a helpful guide for restoring the palace to its prewar condition. Within the palace you can see some partially restored rooms and exhibits of 19th-century arms and clothing. Some rooms are now restored to the appearance they had when they belonged to the family of Alexander III. ⊠ *1 Krasnoarmeisky pr.* ☎ *812/958–0366 administrator (can answer in English)* ⊕ *www.gatchinapalace.ru* 📧 *250R* ☉ *Tues.–Sun. 10–6; closed 1st Tues. of month.*

Prioratsky Palace. A 10-minute walk from Gatchina Palace brings you to Black Lake and this white palace, a unique construction made of rammed earth (compressed clay, sand, and gravel, and other materials). It was built at the end of the 18th century by architect Nikolai Lvov, the first person in Russia to introduce cheap, fireproof construction of this type. The palace was meant for the great French prior Prince Condé (though he never lived here). The southern part of the palace suggests a Gothic chapel, but the rest resembles a fortification. On the first floor are exposed samples of the rammed earth; the second floor has displays on the palace's construction. To reach the palace directly, you can take minibus 18 or 18a and get off at the bus stop for ulitsa Chkalova. ⊠ *Ul. Chkalova, Prioratsky Park* 📧 *120R* ☉ *Tues.–Sun. 10–5; closed 1st Tues. of month.*

KRONSHTADT AND VALAAM

Two islands, one to the west and one to the northeast o͏͏
set a different tone than the palace suburbs but are still o͏
icance. The town of Kronshtadt, on Kotlin Island, has a l͏
naval tradition, while the monasteries of Valaam Archipe͏
to the earliest days of Christianity, more than a millennium ago.

KRONSHTADT КРОНШТАДТ

30 km (19 miles) west of St. Petersburg.

Kronshtadt (Kotlin Island), to the west of St. Petersburg, was developed between 1703 and 1704 by Peter the Great as a base from which to defend St. Petersburg and to attack the long-standing enemy of the Russian empire, the Swedish navy. For a long time it was the only military harbor of the empire, which is why it was off-limits to all but its permanent residents; visitors were stopped at special checkpoints as late as 1996. Today anyone can visit, either by taking a "Meteor" hydrofoil, which departs from St. Petersburg, or by taking an excursion from one of the agencies on St. Petersburg's Nevsky prospekt.

In the first half of the 20th century the Kronshtadt Commune aimed to break the monopoly of the Communist Party and to give back to peasants the right to use their land freely. The revolt lasted two weeks, seriously jeopardizing Lenin's hold on power, but was finally bloodily repressed. Despite this uprising, the streets of Kronshtadt are still named after Marx and Lenin, and the town still seems to live in the past, as if to hold on to the mighty era of the Soviet military machine. Meanwhile, once closed for foreign and even Soviet public access because of its military status, Kronshtadt is still proud of its naval pedigree. Its significance was gradually diminished by the development of St. Petersburg throughout the 19th century, but there are still military and scientific vessels using its harbors. Sights include Naval Cathedral; a lovely embankment overlooking the Gulf of Finland and the modern Russian navy ships moored at the piers; the Gostinny Dvor (one of Kronshtadt's first buildings and now a department store in need of renovation); the Summer Garden; and the Menshikov Palace, now a club for the island's sailors. Off the shore are several forts that were constructed during the Crimean War (1853–56). The most interesting of these is Fort Aleksandr, which in the 19th century was turned into a laboratory to research the bubonic plague. These days it's a favorite stop-off point for yachters.

GETTING HERE AND AROUND

Take minibus 405 from the Chyornaya Rechka metro station (as you exit the metro station go to your left, cross the road, and you'll see the row of various minibuses). From Prospekt Prosveshcheniya metro station, take minibus 407. The cost of the trip will be approximately 60R and it takes about 40 minutes. Get off at the stop next to the Naval Cathedral (Morskoi Sobor). If you'd rather skip the Cathedral, head by the same minibus to Kronshtadt's embankment, another attraction here. Tickets for bus tours are sold at the excursion kiosks at the corner of Nevsky prospekt and ulitsa Sadovaya, and buses depart from a location nearby.

CLOSE UP

Hydrofoils: Ships on Wings

Hydrofoils, or *meteory*, are a popular mode of transport in St. Petersburg, especially for visiting the city suburbs of Peterhof and Kronshtadt near the Gulf of Finland. A hydrofoil is essentially a ship that works on underwater wings, or hydrofoils, below the hull. As the ship picks up speed, the hull lifts off the water, creating less drag and allowing for even greater speed—they can go as fast as 80 kph (about 43 knots). Travel by hydrofoil from St. Petersburg to Peterhof takes about half an hour. By car, the same trip may take up to an hour and a half to two hours with traffic. Hydrofoils are only available in the summer months, as the Neva River freezes in winter.

In summer you can also take a hydrofoil or an aquabus (a water taxi) from the pier at Arsenalnaya Embankment, in front of Finlyandsky Railway Station or from the pier at Lower Hermitage (Dvortsovaya Embankement 38), in front of the major exit from the Hermitage Museum. The trip costs 130R. Keep in mind that the hydrofoils travel infrequently (usually at 10 am, 1 pm, and 7 pm) and the schedule for an aquabus can change (check the schedule at ⊕ *www.vodohodspb. ru*). There can be long lines, especially in good weather. Arriving by boat, you disembark on a pier near a number of military ships. From the pier walk straight for about 10–15 minutes to reach the Naval Cathedral. (You may need to ask directions on the way.) A boat tour to Kronshtadt, four to five hours round-trip, leaves from Lower Hermitage pier at 10:45 am.

EXPLORING

Naval Cathedral. One of Kronshtadt's highlights is the finest example of neo-Byzantine architecture in Russia, built between 1902 and 1913 by Vassili Kosyakov. The **Naval Cathedral** (Morskoi Sobor) honors all sailors who ever died in tragic circumstances and also served as a landmark for ships. In 1913, the blessing of the 230-foot-high (70-meter-high) cathedral that could seat up to 5,000 parishioners was attended by the family of the last Russian tsar, Nicholas II. However, in 1927 the Bolshevik authorities closed the cathedral and turned it into a cinema, naming it Maxim after Soviet writer Maxim Gorky. Later the cathedral also housed a club and a concert hall, with a stage replacing the altar. After a major interior and exterior renovation, the richly colored and decorated cathedral celebrated its centennial in 2013. ⊠ *pl. Yakornaya* ☎ *812/576–9000* ⊗ *Daily 8–6.*

VALAAM ARCHIPELAGO ВАЛААМСКИЙ АРХИПЕЛ

170 km (105 miles) north of St. Petersburg, east along and up into Lake Ladoga.

An overnight trip by boat from St. Petersburg delivers bustle of the city and into the Republic of Karelia. The of the 83 federal subjects of the Russian Federation; though its language is Russian, it has close cultural ties to its neighbor, Finland. One of its most tranquil and beautiful settings is Valaam, a cluster of islands in the northwestern part of Lake Ladoga, Europe's largest freshwater lake. The southern part of the lake borders Russia. The archipelago consists of Valaam Island and about 50 other isles.

Valaam Island is the site of an ancient monastery said to have been started by Saints Sergey and German, missionaries who came to the region (probably from Greece) sometime in the 10th century—perhaps even before the "official" conversion of the land of the Rus' to Christianity. The next 1,000 years are a sorry story of Valaam and its monks battling to survive a regular series of catastrophes—including plague, fire, invasion, and pillage—only to bounce back and build (and rebuild) Valaam's religious buildings and way of life. In 1611 the monastery was attacked and razed by the Swedes; it languished for a century until Peter the Great ordered it rebuilt in 1715. Valaam was also to pass into the hands of Finland on more than one occasion, the longest period being from the end of World War I to 1940. After World War II, during which the islands were evacuated and then occupied by Finnish and German troops, the monasteries fell into almost total disrepair, and it was only in 1989 that the monks returned.

GETTING HERE AND AROUND
You can visit Valaam only from June through September or early October, when the waterway along the Neva River and Lake Ladoga is open. Ferries leave from the piers of former Rechnoi Vokzal (River Passenger Station) at 195 Obukhovskoy Oborony prospekt, near Proletarskaya metro station in the south of St. Petersburg. The journey takes around 10 hours. Usually ferries leave at 9 pm and arrive in Valaam by 8 am. You can contact a tourist agent, such as MIR, to order a tour to Valaam. The 10-hour ferry journey to Valaam isn't luxurious—you'll be witnessing a real throwback to the Soviet era. The rooms are very plain, but are perfectly manageable for two nights' sleep. In any case, you can spend much of the journey sitting on the sundeck; watch the industrial south of St. Petersburg give way to the rural setting of the lower Neva, before you pass the ancient fort of Petrakrepost on your right as the ferry sails into Lake Ladoga. On the return journey, you'll see the golden spires and cupolas of the monasteries poke out of the tree line and glint in the setting sun. Take some food with you: although three meals are included in the price of most tours, they're best avoided. Instead, pack some sandwiches, fruit, and perhaps some wine.

EXPLORING
Valaam monasteries (Валаамский Архипелаг). A guided tour of Valaam takes about six hours, including a break for lunch. You can also buy a map of the island from one of the tourist shops and strike out on your

own. But the tour guides, most of whom live on the island throughout the summer, have an enormous amount of interesting information to impart about Valaam (most, however, don't speak English). The guides also know where the best shady spots to sit and relax are, and while you catch your breath they'll tell you everything about Valaam's history, prehistory, wildlife, geology and geography, religious life, and gradual renaissance as a monastic center. The island's beauty has also inspired the work of many Russian and foreign artists, composers, and writers; the second movement of Tchaikovsky's First Symphony is said to be a musical portrait of the island, and you'll hear it played over loudspeakers as your ferry departs.

Most tours spend the first half day on a small selection of the *skity*, a monastery in seclusion. Only four skity are currently used as places of worship, and some of them are in the archipelago's most remote areas. Closest to where the ferries dock is the **Voskresensky (Resurrection) Monastery**, consecrated in 1906. In the upper church, you can hear a performance of Russian liturgical music performed by a male quartet. Another monastery within easy walking distance is the **Getsemanskii (Gethsemene) Monastyr**, consisting of a wooden chapel and church built in a typically Russian style, and monastic cells, which are inaccessible to the public. The squat construction next door is a hostel for pilgrims, some of whom you may see draped in long robes.

After lunch, buy a ticket for the ferry that will take you to the 14th-century **Spaso-Preobrazhensky Valaamskii (Transfiguration of the Savior) Monastyr,** the heart of the island's religious life. You can walk the 6 km (4 miles) from the harbor in either direction, but if you walk back from the monastery, make sure you give yourself enough time to catch the ferry back to St. Petersburg (about 1¼ hours should be enough time to walk back). As you reach the monastery, you'll see tourist stands. The walk up the hill is well worth it, as you reach the splendid Valaamskii Monastyr cathedral (under ongoing restoration). The cathedral's lower floor is the **Church of St. Sergius and St. German,** finished in 1892, and is in the best condition. It's a living place of worship, as you'll see from the reverence of visitors before the large icon depicting Sergey and German kneeling before Christ. The upper **Church of the Transfiguration of the Savior,** consecrated in 1896, is in a terrible state, although the cavernous interior, crumbling iconostasis, and remaining frescoes are still impressive in their own right.

■ TIP➜ **Although drinking and smoking are permitted in most areas of the island, you should refrain while on the territory of the monasteries. Visitors must also follow a dress code on the grounds of the cathedral: women should wear a long skirt and cover their heads (scarves and inelegant black aprons are provided at the entrance for those who need them), and men must leave their heads uncovered and wear long trousers, not shorts.** You might want to poke your head into the rather severe bar on the island, but you're unlikely to want to linger. ⊠ *Ostrov Valaam, Sortavalsky raion, Republic of Karelia* ⊕ *www.valaam.ru.*

UNDERSTANDING MOSCOW & ST. PETERSBURG

RUSSIA AT A GLANCE

ENGLISH–RUSSIAN
VOCABULARY

RUSSIA AT A GLANCE

FAST FACTS

Type of government: Federation
Capital: Moscow
Administrative divisions: 89 administrative regions, broken down into 46 *oblastey* (districts), 21 *respubliky* (republics), 4 *avtonomnykh okrugov* (autonomous regions), 9 *krayev* (regions), 2 *goroda* (federal cities), 1 *avtonomnaya oblast* (autonomous oblast)
Independence: August 24, 1991 (following the collapse of the Soviet Union)

"I cannot forecast to you the action of Russia. It is a riddle wrapped in a mystery inside an enigma."
—Winston Churchill, 1939

Constitution: December 12, 1993
Legal system: Based on civil law, with judicial review of legislative acts
Legislature: Bicameral parliament: Duma (lower house) and Federation Council (upper house)
Population: 139,390,205 (est. July 2010)
Fertility rate: 1.41 children per woman
Language: Russian is the official state language; other languages are spoken by limited numbers of ethnic minorities, including Bashkir, Tatar, Yevnik (Evenk), Chuvash, Buryat, and numerous languages in the Caucasus.
Ethnic groups: Russian 79.8%, Tatar 3.8%, Ukrainian 2%, Bashkir 1.2%, Chuvash 1.1%, other 12.1% (2002 Census)
Life expectancy: Female 73, male 59
Literacy: Total population 99.4%; male 99.7%, female 99.2% (2002 Census)
Religion: Russian Orthodox 15%–20%, Muslim 10%–15%, Other Christian 2%
Inventions: Ice slide (precursor to the roller coaster, 17th century), periodic table (invented by Dmitry Mendeleev, 1869), Kalashnikov assault rifle (AK-47; invented by Mikhail Kalashnikov, 1947), magnetohydrodynamic power generator (1972)

ECONOMY

The Soviet Union is a long-forgotten memory for Russia's capitalists as the country's economy continues to surge ahead. The economy is largely dependent on commodities exports—mostly oil and natural gas.

"To believe that Russia has got rid of the evils of capitalism takes a special kind of mind. It is the same kind of mind that believes that a Holy Roller has got rid of sin."
—H. L. Mencken, mid-20th century

Annual growth: 4% in 2010
Inflation: 6.7% in 2010
Unemployment: 7.6% in 2010
Per capita income: $15,900
GDP: $2.229 trillion
Services: 62%
Agriculture: 4.2%
Industry: 33.8%
Work force: 75.55 million; agriculture 10%, industry 31.9%, services 58.1%
Currency: Ruble
Exchange rate: 30 rubles per U.S. dollar
Major industries: Petroleum, natural gas, coal, chemicals, steel, mining, lumber, transportation equipment (aircraft, ships, railways), communications equipment, medical and scientific instruments, consumer goods, textiles
Agricultural products: Wheat, potatoes, livestock, sugar beets
Exports: $376.7 billion in 2010
Major export products: Crude oil and refined oil products, natural gas, wood and wood products, metals, chemicals, military equipment
Export partners: Netherlands 10.62%, Italy 6.46%, Germany 6.24%, China 5.69%, Turkey 4.3%, Ukraine 4.01%
Imports: $237.3 billion in 2010
Major import products: Machinery, medicine, meat, sugar, consumer goods, metal products
Import partners: Germany 14.39%, China 13.98%, Ukraine 5.48%, Italy 4.84%, United States 4.46%

POLITICAL CLIMATE

A guerilla conflict with militants in the Chechen Republic continues to dominate headlines, despite government claims that the situation is under control. Other unresolved conflicts include a dispute with Japan over the Kuril Islands south of Sakhalin in the Pacific Ocean. The biggest dispute between Russia and the European Union is over travel and visa regulations for Kaliningrad residents (Kaliningrad, formerly Konigsberg, was captured from Germany by the Soviet Union in World War II). A 1990 maritime boundary agreement between the United States and the Soviet Union regarding the Bering Sea has yet to be ratified by Russia.

"A Russian is wise after the event."
—Russian proverb

DID YOU KNOW?

■ Russia contains the greatest mineral reserves of any country in the world.

■ The world's only freshwater seals live in Russia, at Lake Baikal in Siberia.

■ Russia's population density is a mere eight people per square mile.

■ More than 100 languages are spoken in Russia.

■ In the Soviet Union, the richest 10% of the population earned only four times more than the poorest 10%. By the mid-1990s, the richest 10% earned as much as 15 times more than the poorest 10%.

■ More than 20 million Russian civilians died as a result of World War II.

THE RUSSIAN ALPHABET AND SOUNDS

LETTER	SOUND	SOUND IN ENGLISH WORD
А а	ah	father
Б б	b	boy
В в	v	voice
Г г	g	go
Д д	d	day
Е е	yeh, eh	yet, keg
Ё ё	yo	yolk
Ж ж	zh	measure
З з	z	zero
И и	ee, e	feel, me
Й й	y	boy
К к	k	kit
Л л	l	lamp
М м	m	map
Н н	n	now
О о	oh	folk
П п	p	pan
Р р	r, rr (rolled)	roll
С с	s	see
Т т	t	top
У у	oo	boot
Ф ф	f	fun
Х х	kh, h	hush
Ц ц	ts	cats
Ч ч	ch	chair
Ш ш	sh	shut
Щ щ	shch	fresh
ъ	hard sign	short pause after a consonant
ы	y	it
ь	soft sign	often preceding consonant
Э э	eh	elk
Ю ю	yoo	Yule
Я я	yah	yacht

Adapted from "The Russian Alphabet and Sounds" table in Living Language: Ultimate Russian Beginner-Intermediate.

RUSSIAN VOCABULARY

ENGLISH	CYRILLIC	TRANSLITERATION

COMMON GREETINGS

Hello!	Здравствуйте!	**Zdrahst**-vooy-tyeh!
Good morning!	Доброе утро!	**Dohb**-rah-yeh **oot**-rah!
Good afternoon!	Добрый день!	**Dohb**-ree **dyehn**!
Good evening!	Добрый вечер!	**Dohb**-ree **vyeh**-cherr!
Good-bye.	До свидания.	**Dah** svee-**dah**-nya.
Pleased to meet you!	Очень рад с вами познакомиться!	**Oh**-chen **rahd** s **vah**-mee pah-znah-**koh**-meet-sah!
How are you?	Как дела?	**Kahk** dee-**lah**?
Fine, thanks.	Хорошо, спасибо.	Hah-rah-**shoh**, spah-**see**-bah
What is your name?	Как вас зовут?	**Kahk vahs** zah-**voot**?
My name is . . .	Меня зовут . . .	Men-**yah** zah-**voot** . . .
Nice to meet you.	Очень приятно.	**Oh**-chen pree-**yaht**-nah!
I'll see you later.	До встречи.	Dah **fstreh**-chee.

POLITE EXPRESSIONS

Please / You're welcome	пожалуйста	pah-**zhah**-loos-tah
Thank you	спасибо	spah-**see**-bah
Yes	да	**dah**
No	нет	**nyet**
Perhaps	может быть	**moh**-zhet **bweet**
I do not understand.	Я не понимаю.	**Yah nee** pah-nee-**mah**-yoo.
I am from USA (America, Britain).	Я из США (Америки, Англии).	**Yah** is **Seh Sheh Ah** (Ah-**myeh**-ree-kee, **Ahn**-glee-ee).
I speak only English.	Я говорю только по-английски.	**Yah** gah-vah-**ryoo tol'**-kah pah-ahn-**glees**-kee.
Do you speak English?	Вы говорите по-английски?	**Vwee** gah-vah-**ree**-tee pah-ahn-**glees**-kee?
Please, show (explain, translate)	Пожалуйста, покажите (объясните, переведите)	Pah-**zhah**-loos-tah, pah-kah-**zhee**-tee (ahb-yas-**nee**-tee, pee-ree-vee-**dee**-tee)

Excuse my poor pronunciation.	Извините меня за плохое произношение.	Eez-vee-**nee**-tee men-**yah** zah plah-**hoh**-ye prah-eez-nah-**sheh**-nye.
I don't know.	Я не знаю.	**Yah nee znah**-yoo.

QUESTIONS

Who?	Кто?	**Ktoh?**
What?	Что?	**Shtoh?**
Where?	Где?	**Gdyeh?**
When?	Когда?	Kahg-**dah**?
Why?	Почему?	Pah-chee-**moo**?
How do you say ... in Russian?	Как по-русски ?	**Kahk** pah-**roos**-kee ?
Do you understand?	Вы понимаете?	**Vwee** pah-nee-**mah**-ee-tye?
Please speak slowly.	Пожалуйста, говорите медленно.	Pah-**zhah**-loos-tah, gah-vah-**reet**-ye **myed**-lee-nah.
Please write it down.	Пожалуйста, напишите.	Pah-**zhah**-loos-tah, nah-pee-**shee**-tee.
Can you please repeat?	Повторите, пожалуйста.	Pahf-tah-**ree**-tee, pah-**zhah**-loos-tah

DIRECTIONS

Where is ...	Где ...	**Gdyeh** ...
... the metro station?	... метро (станция метро)?	... meet-**roh** (**stahn**-tsee-yah meet-**roh**)?
... the restroom?	... туалет?	... too-ahl-**yet**?
... the Internet cafe?	... Интернет-кафе?	... In-terr-**net** ca**fe**?
... the hotel?	... гостиница ... ?	... gahs-**tee**-nee-tsah ... ?
... restaurant?	... ресторан?	... rees-tah-**rahn**?
Here/there	тут/там	**toot/tahm**
Left/right	налево/направо	nah-**lyeh**-vah/ nah-**prah**-vah
Straight ahead	прямо	**pryah**-mah
Forward	вперед	**fpee-ryod**
Back	назад	nah-**zahd**

Turn right	поверните направо	pah-verr-**nee**-tee nah-**prah**-vah
Turn left	поверните налево	pah-verr-**nee**-tee nah-**lyeh**-vah
Turn around	развернитесь	rahz-verr-**nee**-tyes
Around the corner	за углом	**zah** oog-**lohm**
Is it near/far?	Это близко/ далеко?	**Eht**-tah **blees**-kah/ dah-lee-**koh**?

AT THE HOTEL

I would like a room...	Мне нужен номер...	Mn-**yeh noo**-zhen **noh**-mehr...
...for one person.	...на одного.	...nah ahd-nah-**voh**.
...for two people.	...на двоих.	...nah dvah-**eekh**.
...for tonight.	...на сутки.	...nah soot-kee.
...for two nights.	...на двое суток/ на два дня.	...nah **dvoh**-ye **soo**-tok/ nah **dvah dnyah**.
How much does it cost?	Сколько стоит?	**Skohl**-kah **stoh**-eet?
Do you have another room?	У вас есть другой номер?	Oo **vahs** yest droo-**goy noh**-mehr?
...with a private bathroom?	...с ванной и туалетом?	...s **vah**-noy **ee** too-ahl-**yeh**-tahm?
Is there a larger room?	Есть номер побольше?	**Yest noh**-mehr pah-**bohl**-she?

MEALS

breakfast	завтрак	**zahft**-rahk
lunch	обед	ah-**byehd**
dinner	ужин	**oo**-zheen
appetizers	закуски	zah-**koos**-kee
dessert	десерт	dee-**sehrt**
bar	бар	**bar**
café	кафе	kah-**fe**
restaurant	ресторан	rees-tah-**rahn**
menu	меню	men-**yoo**

The menu, please.	Меню, пожалуйста.	Men-**yoo**, pah-**zhah**-loos-tah.
I would like to order.	Примите заказ.	Pree-**mee**-tee zah-**kahz**.
Do you have a vegetarian dish?	У вас есть вегетари-анские блюда?	Oo **vahs yest** veh-geh-tah-**ryahn**-skee **blyoo**-dah?
The check, please.	Счет, пожалуйста.	**Schyot**, pah-**zhah**-loos-tah.
To your health!	За ваше здоровье!	Zah **vah**-she zdah-**rohv**-yeh!

TOURING

tourist	турист	too-**reest**
guide	гид	**geed**
museum	музей	moo-**zay**
church	церковь	**tsair**-kahv
monestary	монастырь	mah-nah-**styrr**
palace	дворец	**dvah**-ryehts
open	открыто	aht-**kree**-tah
closed	закрыто	zah-**kree**-tah
admission fee	плата за вход	**plah**-tah zah **fhoht**

DAYS OF THE WEEK

Monday	понедельник	pah-nee-**dyel**-neek
Tuesday	вторник	**ftorr**-neek
Wednesday	среда	sree-**dah**
Thursday	четверг	chet-**vyerk**
Friday	пятница	**pyaht**-neet-sah
Saturday	суббота	soo-**boh**-tah
Sunday	воскресенье	vahs-kree-**syeh**-nye
Holiday, feast	праздник	**prahz**-neek
Today	сегодня	see-**vohd**-nyah
Tomorrow	завтра	**zahf**-trah
Yesterday	вчера	fchee-**rah**

NUMBERS

How many?	Сколько?	**Skohl**-kah?
1	один	ah-**deen**
2	два	**dvah**
3	три	**tree**
4	четыре	che-**teer**-ee
5	пять	**pyaht**
6	шесть	**shest**
7	семь	**syem**
8	восемь	**voh**-syem
9	девять	**dehv**-yat
10	десять	**dehs**-yat
11	одиннадцать	ah-**dee**-nah-tset
12	двенадцать	dvee-**nah**-tset
13	тринадцать	tree-**nah**-tset
14	четырнадцать	che-**teer**-nah-tset
15	пятнадцать	pyat-**nah**-tset
16	шестнадцать	shest-**nah**-tset
17	семнадцать	seem-**nah**-tset
18	восемнадцать	vah-seem-**nah**-tset
19	девятнадцать	dee-vet-**nah**-tset
20	двадцать	**dvah**-tset
30	тридцать	**tree**-tset
40	сорок	**soh**-rahk
50	пятьдесят	pyat-dee-**syaht**
60	шестьдесят	shest-dee-**syaht**
70	семьдесят	**syem**-dee-syaht
80	восемьдесят	**voh**-syem-dee-syaht
90	девяносто	dee-vee-**noh**-stah
100	сто	**stoh**
1000	тысяча	**tee**-se-chah

SIGNS

Toilet (Gentlemen) (Ladies)	Туалет (М), (Ж)	too-ahl-**yeht** (M), (Zh)
No smoking!	Не курить!	**Nee** koo-**reet!**
Taxi stand	стоянка такси	stah-**yahn**-kah tahk-**see**
Entrance	вход	**fhohd**
Exit	выход	**vwee**-hahd
No exit	нет выхода	**nyet vwee**-hah-dah
Emergency exit	запасной выход	zah-pahs-**noy vwee**-hahd
Stop!	Стоп!	**Stohp!**

DRINKS

beverages	напитки	nah-**peet**-kee
cold water	холодная вода	hah-**lohd**-nah-ya vah-**dah**
mineral water	минеральная вода	mee-nee-**rahl**-nah-ya vah-**dah**
grape, tomato, orange juice	виноградный, томатный, апельсиновый сок	vee-nahg-**rahd**-nee, tah-**maht**-nee, ah-peel-see-nah-vee **sohk**
whisky, vodka	виски, водка	**vees**-kee, **voht**-kah
liqueur	ликер	lee-**kyorr**
lemonade	лимонад	lee-mah-**nahd**
beer	пиво	**pee**-vah
tea, coffee, cocoa	чай, кофе, какао	**chai**, **koh**-fe, kah-**kah**-oh
with sugar/ without sugar	с сахаром/ без сахара	s **sah**-khah-rahm/ **behs sah**-kha-rah
milk, skim	молоко, обезжиренное	mah-lah-**koh**, ah-be-**zzhee**-re-nah-ye
fruit juice	сок	**sohk**
ice	лед	**lyod**

MEAT

meat	мясо	**myah**-sah
steak	стейк	**steak**
roast beef	ростбиф	**rohst**-beef
veal	телятина	teel-**yah**-tee-nah
pork	свинина	svee-**nee**-nah
ham	ветчина	veet-chee-**nah**
sausage	колбаса	kahl-bah-**sah**

POULTRY

chicken	курица	**koo**-reet-sah
hazel-grouse	рябчик	**ryahp**-cheek
partridge	куропатка	koo-rah-**paht**-kah
duck	утка	**oot**-kah

FISH

fish	рыба	**rwee**-bah
red caviar	красная икра	**krahs**-nah-yah eek-**rah**
black caviar	черная икра	**chyorr**-nah-yah eek-**rah**
salmon	лосось, лососина	lah-**sohs**, lah-sah-**see**-nah
sturgeon	осетр, осетрина	ahs-**yotr**, ah-see-**tree**-nah

VEGETABLES

vegetables	овощи	**oh**-vah-schee
green peas	горошек	gah-**roh**-shek
radishes	редиска	ree-**dees**-kah
tomatoes	помидоры	pah-mee-**doh**-rwee
potatoes	картошка	kahrr-**tohsh**-kah
cucumbers	огурцы	ah-goorr-**tsee**
onions	лук	**look**
salad	салат	sah-**laht**

DESSERTS

desserts	десерт	dee-**syert**
cake	торт	**tohrrt**
fruit	фрукты	**frook**-te
apple	яблоко	**yahb**-lah-kah
orange	апельсин	ah-peel-**seen**
pear	груша	**groo**-shah
tangerine	мандарин	mahn-dah-**reen**
grapes	виноград	vee-nahg-**raht**
banana	банан	bah-**nahn**
rye bread	черный хлеб	**chyorr**-nee **khlehp**
white bread	белый хлеб	**beh**-lee **khlehp**
butter	масло	**mahs**-lah
cheese	сыр	**seer**
fried eggs	яичница	ya-**eesh**-nee-tsah
omelet	омлет	ahm-**let**
yogurt	йогурт	**yo**-gurrt

SHOPPING

shopping	шопинг	**shoh**-ping
good	хороший	hah-**roh**-shee
bad	плохой	plah-**hoy**
beautiful	красивый	krah-**see**-vee
dear	дорогой	dah-rah-**goy**
cheap	дешевый	dee-**shoh**-vee
old	старый	**stah**-ree
new	новый	**noh**-vee
How much is it?	Сколько стоит?	**Skohl**-kah **stoh**-eet?
It's expensive/cheap	Это дорого/дешево.	**Eht**-tah **doh**-rah-gah/**dyo**-she-vah.
I would like this.	Вот это, пожалуйста.	**Voht eht**-tah, pah-**zhah**-loos-tah.

I'd like to pay by credit card.	Я заплачу кредитной картой.	**Yah** zah-plah-**choo** kree-**deet**-noy **kahrr**-toy.
Bakery	булочная	**boo**-lahch-nah-yah
Supermarket	супермаркет	**soo**-perr-**marr**-ket
Store	магазин	mah-gah-**zeen**
Market	рынок, базар	**ree**-nahk, bah-**zaar**
Bookstore	книжный магазин	**kneezh**-nee mah-gah-**zeen**
Drugstore	аптека	ahp-**tyeh**-kah
Wine and Spirits	вино-водочный магазин	**vee**-nah **voh**-dah-chnee mah-gah-**zeen**
Fruit and Vegetables	фрукты и овощи	**frook**-te ee **oh**-vah-schee

EMERGENCIES

Can you help me?	Помогите мне, пожалуйста?	Pah-mah-**geet**-ye men-**yeh**, pah-**zhah**-loos-tah?
I've lost my baggage.	Мой багаж потерялся.	**Moy** bah-**gahzh** pah-teer-**yahl**-syah.
I've lost my wallet.	Я потерял бумажник.	**Yah** pah-teer-**yahl** boo-**mahzh**-neek.
Help!	Помогите!	Pah-mah-**geet**-ye!
Police!	Милиция!	Mee-**lee**-tsee-yah!
Fire!	Пожар!	Pah-**zhahrr**!
I've been robbed.	Меня ограбили.	Men-**yah** ahg-**rah**-bee-lee.
I'm hurt.	Мне больно.	Men-**yeh** **bohl**-nah.
I need a doctor.	Мне нужен доктор.	Men-**yeh** **noo**-zhin dohk-torr.

TRAVEL SMART
MOSCOW AND
ST. PETERSBURG

GETTING HERE AND AROUND

▌ AIR TRAVEL

Major U.S. and European carriers have a number of nonstop flights to Russia, making flying here a lot more convenient than it used to be. Two Russian airlines, Aeroflot and Transaero, also make nonstop flights from North America and Europe. Flying time to Moscow is 9½ hours from New York, 10 hours from Washington, D.C., 11–13 hours from Chicago, 10½ hours from Atlanta, 12½ hours from Los Angeles, and 11 hours from Miami. From Europe, it's 4 hours from London and 3 hours from Frankfurt. Moscow is 24–30 hours from Sydney, depending on which airline you choose.

Nonstop flights from the United States to Moscow originate in New York; Atlanta; Washington, D.C.; Miami; and Los Angeles. To St. Petersburg from the U.S., your options are either a direct flight, which requires at least one stop (usually in Moscow), or a connecting flight, which requires a change of airplanes in Moscow or another European city. Some flights, especially those that are nonstop, may be scheduled only on certain days of the week and at certain times of the year.

Two airlines may operate a connecting flight jointly, so ask whether your airline operates every segment of the trip; you may find that the carrier you prefer flies you only part of the way. To find more booking tips and to check prices and make online flight reservations, visit ⊕ *www.fodors.com.*

If you're flying as an independent traveler within the CIS (Commonwealth of Independent States, a quasi-confederation of states that includes most of the former Soviet Union), it's best to purchase your ticket with a credit card via an agent in your home country or a reputable one in Russia. This will allow you the best chance for refunds if your flight is canceled. Russian airlines have a habit of permitting refunds only at the office where the ticket was purchased. If you book from abroad, you should reconfirm your reservation in person as soon as you arrive in the country.

Note that in Russia, check-in officially ends 40 minutes before departure, and if you arrive late you may need to do some serious begging to be allowed on to the plane.

Smoking is prohibited on all international flights, but some of the smaller Russian carriers may have designated smoking areas partitioned off by a curtain on some of their domestic flights. Ask your carrier about its policy.

Within Russia, you don't normally need to reconfirm your outbound flight or intra-destination flights.

Airlines and Airports Airline and Airport Links.com. This handy site has links to many of the world's airlines and airports. ⊕ *www.airlineandairportlinks.com.*

Airline Security Issues Transportation Security Administration. The agency has answers for almost every security question that might come up. ⊕ *www.tsa.gov.*

AIRPORTS

The major international airports are Sheremetyevo II Airport (airport code SVO), which also handles some domestic flights, and Domodedovo (DME) in Moscow. Pulkovo Airport (LED) is the international airport in St. Petersburg.

For domestic travel, Moscow has three airports in addition to Sheremetyevo II: Sheremetyevo I (for flights to the north and west), Domodedovo (for eastern destinations and for the carriers British Airways, United Airlines, and Transaero), and Vnukovo (VKO) (for southern destinations). Even though the departing or arriving airport may be printed on your ticket, double-check this information with your local travel agent.

GROUND TRANSPORTATION

⇨ *For information on getting to Moscow and St. Petersburg from the airport, see the Transfers sections in Chapter 2 for Moscow and Chapter 8 for St. Petersburg.*

FLIGHTS

When flying internationally, you must usually choose among a domestic carrier, the national flag carrier of the country you're visiting (Aeroflot-Russian International Airlines), and a foreign carrier from a third country. National flag carriers have the greatest number of non-stop flights. Domestic carriers may have better connections to your hometown and serve a greater number of gateway cities. Third-party carriers may have a price advantage.

Within Russia, in addition to Aeroflot, there are several smaller, regional airlines (sometimes called "babyflots"). Aeroflot offers good international service between Russia and some 200 destinations, and it also flies several domestic routes. Babyflots are slowly bringing their service up to international standards, with especially good service between St. Petersburg and Moscow. Two airlines that stand head and shoulders above the rest are Transaero, which flies to several destinations in Europe and the CIS, and has internal flights to major Russian cities; and Rossiya (formerly known as Pulkovo), which also has a number of international flights as well as good domestic service. Both have established partnerships with international airlines in order to increase their reach—Transaero has links to the United States with Continental, Virgin, and Lufthansa, for example.

Delays and cancellations are more frequent in winter, particularly in those places where the climate is severe.

Airline Contacts Aeroflot-Russian International Airlines ✉ *10 Rockefeller Plaza, Suite 1015, New York, New York, USA* ☎ *888/340-6400 toll-free in U.S., 212/944-2300 in U.S., 495/223-5555 in Moscow, 812/438-5583 in St. Petersburg* ⊕ *www.aeroflot.ru/cms/en.*

Air France ☎ *800/237-2747 in U.S., 495/937-3839 in Moscow, 812/336-2900 in St. Petersburg* ⊕ *www.airfrance.com.* **British Airways** ☎ *800/247-9297 in U.S., 495/363-2525 in Moscow, 812/336-0626 in St. Petersburg* ⊕ *www.britishairways.com.* **Czech Airlines** ☎ *810/42023-900-7261 Call center in Prague, 499/973-1847 in Moscow, 812/315-2240 in St. Petersburg* ⊕ *www.czecharlines.com.* **Delta Airlines** ☎ *800/241-4141 for international reservations, 495/937-9090 in Moscow, 800/700-0990 all other Russian cities* ⊕ *www.delta.com.* **Finnair** ☎ *800/950-5000 in U.S., 495/933-0056 in Moscow, 812/676-9898 in St. Petersburg* ⊕ *www.finnair.com.* **KLM** ☎ *800/618-0104 in U.S., 495/258-3600 in Moscow, 812/346-6868 in St. Petersburg* ⊕ *www.klm.com.* **Lufthansa** ☎ *800/645-3880 in U.S., 495/980-9999 in Moscow* ⊕ *www.lufthansa.com.* **SAS** ☎ *800/221-2350 in U.S., 495/961-3060 in Moscow, 812/326-2600 in St. Petersburg* ⊕ *www.flysas.com.* **United Airlines** ☎ *800/538-2929 for international reservations, 495/980-0882 in Moscow* ⊕ *www.united.com.*

Within Russia Rossiya (formerly known as Pulkovo) ☎ *973/884-5952 in U.S., 800/333-3800 toll-free in Russia, 495/956-5019 in Moscow, 812/633-3800 in St. Petersburg* ⊕ *www.rossiya-airlines.com.* **S7 (formerly known as Sibir)** ☎ *800/200-0007 toll-free in Russia, 495/777-9999 in Moscow, 812/718-6876 in St. Petersburg* ⊕ *www.s7.ru.* **Transaero** ☎ *877/747-1191 in U.S., 800/200-2376 toll-free in Russia, 495/788-8080 in Moscow* ⊕ *www.transaero.ru.*

CRUISES

All the major cruise lines listed *below* visit Russia, but they only dock at St. Petersburg. Crystal Cruises has tours that go between Copenhagen and Stockholm and between London and Stockholm with three days in St. Petersburg. Cunard has a Russian Rendezvous tour that goes from Southampton and stops off in St. Petersburg for two days. It also visits Poland and Estonia. Princess Cruises sails a round-trip from Copenhagen that stops in Berlin and spends two days in St. Petersburg. Regent Seven Seas has a tour from Stockholm to Copenhagen. Its visit to St. Petersburg includes a day at the Hermitage and its restoration workshops and an onboard lecture from a Russian art expert.

International cruise lines offering tours to Russia usually disembark in St. Petersburg and continue to Moscow by land. Some cruises follow the Volga River between Moscow and St. Petersburg on a journey of up to two weeks. It's also possible to take longer trips calling at destinations such as the southern cities of Volgograd and Astrakhan and east to Kazan.

Cruise Lines Celebrity Cruises ☎ 800/647–2251 ⊕ www.celebrity.com. **Costa Cruises** ☎ 800/462–6782 ⊕ www.costacruise.com. **Crystal Cruises** ☎ 310/785–9300, 888/722–0021 ⊕ www.crystalcruises.com. **Cunard Line** ☎ 800/728–6273 ⊕ www.cunard.com. **Holland America Line** ☎ 877/932–4259 in U.S., 495/234–6272 in Moscow ⊕ www.hollandamerica.com. **Mediterranean Shipping Cruises** ☎ 800/666–9333 ⊕ www.msccruises.com. **Norwegian Cruise Line** ☎ 866/234–7350 ⊕ www.ncl.com. **Oceania Cruises** ☎ 800/531–5619 toll-free, 305/514–2300 ⊕ www.oceaniacruises.com. **Princess Cruises** ☎ 800/774–6237 ⊕ www.princess.com. **Regent Seven Seas Cruises** ☎ 800/477–7500 toll-free, 954/776–6123 ⊕ www.rssc.com. **Royal Caribbean International** ☎ 866/562–7625 toll-free, 305/341–0204 ⊕ www.royalcaribbean.com. **Seabourn Cruise Line** ☎ 866/755–5619 toll-free, 206/626–9179 ⊕ www.seabourn.com. **Silversea Cruises** ☎ 954/522–2299, 800/722–9955 ⊕ www.silversea.com.

River Cruises Amadeus Waterways ✉ 21625 Prairie St., Chatsworth, California, USA ☎ 800/626–0126 ⊕ www.amawaterways.com. **GlobeQuest** ☎ 877/610–6300 ⊕ www.globequesttravelclub.com. **Infoflot** ✉ 6/1 per. Chapayevsky ☎ 495/363–2060 in Moscow, 812/456–2256 in St. Petersburg ⊕ www.infoflot.com. **Orthodox Cruise Company** ✉ 5 ul. Alabyana ☎ 499/943–8560 ⊕ www.cruise.ru. **Smithsonian**

Journeys ☎ 855/330–1542 🖷 202/633–6088 ☎ 800/338–8687 ⊕ www.smithsonianjourneys.org. **Uniworld** ✉ 17323 Ventura Blvd., Encino, California, USA ☎ 800/733–7820 toll-free, 818/382–7820 ⊕ www.uniworld.com. **Viking River Cruises** ✉ 5700 Canoga Ave., Suite 200, Woodland Hills, California, USA ☎ 800/304–9616 toll-free, 818/227–1234 ⊕ www.vikingrivers.com.

▮ BUS TRAVEL

Traveling by bus can be daunting in Russia if you don't speak the language. When you can, you should travel by train or suburban train (*elektrichka*). But for some smaller towns and suburban destinations, this may be the only way to travel, and bus is an especially easy and convenient way to make day trips from Moscow and St. Petersburg.

Ticket offices tend to have long hours of operation, and you can typically purchase your bus ticket ahead of time at the city *avtovokzal*, or bus station. Payment is accepted only in rubles.

If you have any contact who will help negotiate the purchase for you, avail yourself of him or her. Handwritten seating charts and tickets are the norm, but tickets are sold even when there are no seats left (even for longer rides). This leads to some very crowded conditions (and, on hot days, quite stuffy situations, as these buses, although reasonably comfortable, don't have air-conditioning and only sometimes do their windows open). It's recommended that you buy advance tickets for peak long-distance travel days—Friday, Saturday, and Sunday.

Long-distance international buses operate from Moscow and St. Petersburg to the Baltic States, several CIS countries, and some points in Europe including Helsinki, Berlin, and Warsaw. The trips are long and often require extensive waiting times at the border.

▌ CAR TRAVEL

If you're visiting only Moscow and St. Petersburg, you'll have no need to drive. If you don't speak Russian and don't have local knowledge, don't drive: the poor roads, reckless drivers, and unwanted police attention all make doing so dangerous. Even if you plan to make extensive side trips from these cities, you'll find it much easier to do so by train, bus, or boat, or on organized tours. If you do decide to rent a car and drive, keep in mind that you must be comfortable driving on roads marked only with Cyrillic and/or international symbols; you must be willing to deal with the bribe-hungry traffic inspectors; and you must be prepared for poor and sometimes even dangerous road conditions. Even the main highways have potholes and are in poor condition. Repair stations are few and far between, and many places sell poor-quality gasoline. In addition, you shouldn't underestimate the risk of crime: highway robbery and car theft are common, and foreign drivers are often targets. Don't stop to help motorists whose cars appear to have broken down, even if they wave at you for help—this is a classic ambush technique. Never leave anything of value inside your car. In light of these concerns, you may wish to hire a car and driver rather than driving yourself (⇨ *See Car Rental below*).

Your driver's license isn't acceptable in Russia. You'll need an International Driver's Permit and, if traveling into the country by car, an international certificate of registration of the car in the country of departure. You'll also need a certificate of obligation (which should be registered with customs at the point of entry; consult your rental company about this) if you have plans for driving a rental car in over the border. International Driving Permits (IDPs) are available from the American and Canadian automobile associations and, in the United Kingdom, from the Automobile Association and Royal Automobile Club.

All of these documents will need to have a certified Russian translation, which you can obtain at a Russian consulate or embassy before you leave.

GASOLINE

More and more stations bearing the names of major oil companies have opened, and it's easy to find somewhere to fill up, even outside of major towns. However, you may not be able to pay with a credit card. Always ask for a *chek*, or receipt. Gas prices are comparable to those in the United States. It's also fairly easy to find unleaded gasoline; for leaded gas, foreign cars should be filled only with 95-octane gas. Russian-made cars run on 92-octane. Gas is sold by the liter. Some stations provide full service, while at others you pump your own gas.

PARKING

Paid parking has recently been implemented in Moscow to relieve the city's notorious traffic jams. Parking costs 50R per hour and payments are made through a special machine called a "parkomat," marked with a "P." Currently, Moscow has some off- street parking in the big shopping malls. Sometimes, random sections of curb will be cordoned off and you'll be expected to pay a guard—who may or may not be acting in an official capacity—to park there. The "official" city parking guards should wear uniforms with the parking price—currently 50R per hour in the city center—printed on the back. Cars parked illegally will be fined heavily and run the risk of being towed away. The driver then has to spend hours filling in official documents and pay a fine. Expect to see stricter parking rules in Moscow as the current mayor, Sergey Sobyanin, has made improving transportation in the capital a top priority.

ROAD CONDITIONS

Around Moscow and St. Petersburg, most of the country roads have been paved with asphalt. Nonetheless, driving in winter can be dangerously slippery, and the spring thaw can turn roadways into lakes. Driving in snowy conditions in the cities is only for the experienced—Russian drivers see fallen snow as an obstacle to be overcome, not as a reason to take the metro.

ROADSIDE EMERGENCIES
Because service stations are few and poorly stocked, it's recommended that for long distances you carry a complete emergency repair kit, including a set of tools, a towing cable, a pressure gauge, a pump, a spare tire, a repair outfit for tubeless tires, a good jack and one or two tire levers, a gasoline can, a spare fan belt, spare windshield-wiper blades, and spark plugs. You should also have a set of headlight bulbs and fuses, a set of contact-breaker points for the ignition distributor, a spare condenser, a box of tire valve interiors, and a roll of insulating tape. There's no national emergency service to call, but if you're in the Moscow area, consider joining the Angel Club (☎ 495/747–0022 ⊕ *angel-club.ru*), an autoclub that offers some emergency services.

RULES OF THE ROAD
Traffic keeps to the right. The speed limit on highways is 90 kph (56 mph); in towns and populated areas it's 60 kph (37 mph), although on the wide streets of Moscow few people observe this rule. It's illegal to use a mobile phone while driving, but again you're likely to see many drivers on their phones. You can proceed at traffic intersections only when the light is green—this includes left and right turns. You must wait for a signal—an arrow—permitting the turn, and give way to pedestrians crossing. Wearing front seat belts is compulsory; driving while intoxicated carries very heavy fines, including imprisonment. Don't consume any alcohol at all if you plan to drive. You should also keep your car clean—you can be fined for having a dirty car.

Traffic control in Russia is exercised by traffic inspectors (GIBDD, but still commonly known as GAI), who are stationed all over cities and at permanent posts out of town; they also patrol in cars and on motorcycles and like to sit in ambush.

They may stop you for no apparent reason other than to check your documentation. In this event, you're not required to exit your vehicle. Don't ignore attempts by a traffic cop—known colloquially as *gaishnik*—to flag you over. Remember that the GIBDD is regarded as a confounded nuisance by most Russians, and the friendly cop who will provide directions to gas stations or garages is rare. Traffic cops are also good at finding *something* wrong with your documentation and/or your driving; this may be nothing more than an attempt to secure a bribe.

CAR RENTAL
Some hotels will make car-rental arrangements for you. Otherwise, several international car-rental agencies have offices in Moscow; be sure to reserve at least three days in advance.

Car-rental rates are all over the map in Russia, but if you shop around you should be able to get rates from the major chains for as low as $60 a day for a Russian car (manual, no air) with at least 100 free km (60 miles) per day. If you want a foreign car, automatic transmission, or air-conditioning, they'll cost you more. These prices usually include the tax on car rentals, which is 18%. Insurance is mandatory (Russian rentals usually include the cost of insurance).

All agencies require advance reservations (at least two to three days is a good idea), and you'll have to show your driver's license, an International Driving Permit (IDP), and a credit card.

Children's car seats aren't mandatory in Russia, but agencies are able to provide them. Ask for one when you book your car. You'll pay about 125R per day for a seat, and some places may do it for free. If you're returning a car to Sheremetyevo II, bear in mind that shosse Leningradskoye leading to the airport is notoriously slow. Allow two hours for the drive from the center.

If you'd rather hire a car with driver—and we think it's a way to avoid a lot of potential hassle—you can do so for about 400R–1500R per hour. Major hotels will arrange this service for their guests. Some local tour companies, such as Patriarshy Dom Tours, or Western travel agents specializing in independent travel, such as Mir Corporation, can arrange daily-rate car-and-driver options, which are less expensive. ⇨ *For more information, see the Tour Options sections in Chapter 2 for Moscow and Chapter 8 for St. Petersburg.*

■TIP➔ **Make sure that a confirmed reservation guarantees you a car. Agencies sometimes overbook, particularly for busy weekends and holiday periods.**

Your driver's license may not be recognized outside your home country. You may not be able to rent a car without an International Driving Permit (IDP), which can be used only in conjunction with a valid driver's license and which translates your license into 10 languages. Check the AAA website for more info as well as for IDPs ($15) themselves.

▌ TRAIN TRAVEL

In Russia trains are reliable, convenient, and comfortable. Remarkably, most trains leave exactly on time; there's a broadcast warning five minutes before departure, but no whistle or "all aboard!" call, so be careful not to be left behind.

There are numerous day and overnight trains between St. Petersburg and Moscow. The new Sapsan express train makes the trip in just over four hours and has several departures a day from each city. The Siemans-built trains travel at speeds of 150 mph. Other fast day trains include the *Avrora* and *Nevsky Express,* which take around four hours, 30 minutes, and also have comfortable compartments. The *Grand Express,* which runs overnight, has showers in the compartments of the higher classes, and hand basins in lower classes, as well as satellite television and other amenities.

Train travel in Russia offers an unrivaled opportunity to glimpse the Russian countryside, which is dotted in places with colorful wooden cottages and fog-covered lakes, dubbed "mirror lakes," for their stillness. If you're traveling by overnight train, set your alarm and get up an hour or so before arrival so that you can watch at close hand the workers going about their morning rounds in the rural areas just outside the cities.

To make your train trip more comfortable, be sure to carry bottled water. Vendors run up and down train cars at and between stops, selling drinks and sandwiches. You may, however, want to bring a packed meal; most Russians do so, and your compartment mates may offer to share (beware of offers of vodka, however; poison bootleg vodka is a big problem in Russia). The communal bathrooms at both ends of each car can be dirty, so bring premoistened cleansing tissues for washing up. You may want to pack toilet paper just to be on the safe side, although it's rare now for train bathrooms to be without it. Also be sure to pack a heavy sweater in winter. The cars are often overheated and toasty warm, but sometimes they're not heated at all. (Note: smoking in the cars isn't acceptable, but smokers will find plenty of company in between cars.)

You should stick to the usual security precautions. To be on the safe side when sharing a compartment on overnight trips you should sleep with your money, passport, and other important items.

On the more expensive trains (the lower the train number, the faster and more expensive the journey), you're likely to share compartments with businessmen or families. Many travelers to Russia say their trips on overnight trains have proven to be some of their most memorable experiences. For many, it's a chance to get to know real Russians, despite language barriers.

Trains are divided into four classes. The deluxe class offers two-berth compartments with soft seats and private washrooms; the other classes have washrooms at the end of the cars. First-class service—the highest class for domestic routes—is called "soft-seat," with spring-cushion berths (two berths to a compartment). When buying your ticket, ask for "SV."

There's rarely segregation of the sexes (although this has been introduced as an experiment on a few train services), and no matter what class of service you choose, you could end up sharing a compartment with someone of the opposite sex. Never fear. There's an unspoken system on Russian trains that allows each passenger to change into comfortable train clothes in privacy. Your traveling partner will most likely signal this by exiting the compartment for you to change. When he or she returns 15 minutes later, consider that your signal to do the same.

Second-class service, or "hard-seat" service—ask for *coupé*—has a cushion on wooden berths, with four berths to a compartment. The third class—wooden berths without compartments—is not the most comfortable choice but sometimes necessary. Known in Russian as *platskart*, this class entails an almost complete surrender of privacy in an open compartment. If you have to travel in this class, be sure to keep your valuables on you at all times.

Most compartments have a small table, limited room for baggage (including under the seats), and a radio that can be turned down, but not off. In soft-seat compartments there are also table lamps. The price of the ticket may or may not include use of bedding; sometimes this fee

(which will not be much more than 150R) is collected by the conductor.

All of the cars are also equipped with samovars. It's not uncommon in soft-seat class to be offered tea in the evening and morning, plus a small boxed meal. For second- or third-class travel, you may want to bring some tea bags or instant coffee and a mug, since you can take hot water from the samovar at any time.

Russian Railways is experimenting with online ticket purchases. At this writing, this can only be done easily if you have Russian language skills; the English version of the Russian Railways website shows timetables of trains, but doesn't allow the purchase of tickets. Also, foreign credit card holders may experience problems with purchases on Russian websites. In the meantime, there are several online services, such as Way To Russia, Visit Russia, and Russian Passport, who will buy the tickets for you for a nominal service fee. Tickets go on sale 45 days prior to departure, and for popular routes during peak travel times (summer and winter holidays), it's advisable to buy them as far in advance as possible. Note that you must show your passport or a photocopy when purchasing train tickets. Your best bet is to go to Moscow or St. Petersburg's central booking office, although you can buy tickets for any destination at any mainline train station. Telephone inquiries for train services usually involve poor lines and clerks who speak only Russian. Try to get your hotel, a Russian acquaintance, or an independent travel agency to help you book tickets. A one-way ticket between Moscow and St. Petersburg on the Sapsan express train start at 2,300R. The Grand Express overnight train starts at 6,000R for the luxury class. ⇨ *For more information, see Train Travel in Chapter 2 for Moscow and Chapter 8 for St. Petersburg.*

Train Support Visit Russia ⊕ *www.visitrussia. com.* **Way to Russia** ⊕ *www.waytorussia.net.*

ESSENTIALS

■ COMMUNICATIONS

INTERNET

Checking your email or surfing the web can often be done in the business centers of major hotels, which usually charge an hourly rate; most hotels now also provide Wi-Fi, at least in public areas. Web access is also available at many fax and copy centers, many of which are open 24 hours and on weekends. The easiest way to get online in Moscow and St. Petersburg is to visit one of the plentiful cafés, many of which offer free Wi-Fi. Some require you to pay an hourly rate, which can run from about 60R, or $2, per hour and up. Some parks and metro stations in Moscow offer free Wi-Fi access, as well.

PHONES

The good news is that you can now make a direct-dial telephone call from virtually any point on earth. The bad news? You can't always do so cheaply. Calling from a hotel is almost always the most expensive option; hotels usually add huge surcharges to all calls, particularly international ones. In some countries you can phone from call centers or even the post office. Calling cards usually keep costs to a minimum, but only if you purchase them locally. And then there are mobile phones (⇨ see below), which are sometimes more prevalent—particularly in the developing world—than landlines; as expensive as mobile phone calls can be, they're still usually a much cheaper option than calling from your hotel.

The country code for Russia is 7. Moscow has two city codes, 495 and 499; St. Petersburg's is 812. When dialing a Russian number from abroad, drop the initial 0 from the local area code.

The country code is 1 for the United States and Canada, 61 for Australia, 64 for New Zealand, and 44 for the United Kingdom.

CALLING WITHIN RUSSIA

Direct dialing is the only way to go. Russian phone numbers have 10 digits (including the area code). To use your North American cell phone in Russia, it must be tri or quad band. If it's an unlocked GSM cell phone, purchase and install a SIM card so that you'll be charged Russian rates for usage while there.

Throughout the country you can dial 09 for directory assistance. However, because directory workers and operators are underpaid, overworked, and speak only Russian, you probably have a better chance of getting telephone information from your hotel concierge or a friendly assistant at a business center.

Public phones, which are similar to those found in most other European countries, can be harder to find these days, as most Russians have mobile phones. The modern public phones are all card-operated, and the line tends to be atrocious. You can buy cards at kiosks.

City centers have telephone centers handy for making all sorts of calls: in Moscow, try the Central Telegraph office at 7 ulitsa Tverskaya, and St. Petersburg has one located at 2 ulitsa Bolshaya Morskaya.

For long-distance calls within Russia, simply dial 8, wait for another dial tone, and then dial the rest of the number as listed.

CALLING OUTSIDE RUSSIA

The country code for the United States is 1.

Most hotels have satellite telephone booths where, for several dollars a minute, you can make an international call in a matter of seconds. If you want to economize, you can visit the main post or telegraph office and order a call for rubles (but you'll still pay about a dollar or two a minute). From your hotel room or from a private residence, you can dial direct. To place your call, dial 8, wait for the dial tone, then dial 10, then the country code (1 for the United States) followed by

LOCAL DO'S AND TABOOS

CUSTOMS OF THE COUNTRY

In general, there's no such thing as being overdressed in Russia. Bring some urban, dressy clothes. Russians believe that keeping shoes clean is particularly important, even when the weather makes it difficult.

SIGHTSEEING

Russia is far stricter about enforcing dress codes at religious sites than are most similar places in Europe. Men are expected to remove their hats, and women are required to wear below-knee-length skirts or slacks (*never* shorts) and bring something to cover their heads. It's considered disrespectful to put your hands inside your pockets when visiting an Orthodox church.

OUT ON THE TOWN

When entering a restaurant, you'll be asked to leave your coat in a cloakroom. This is virtually compulsory in more formal, upscale establishments. To hail a male waiter, catch his eye and say *molodoi chelovik*; to attract a waitress, say *devushka*. To ask for the check, say *chek, pozhaluista*. A new law banning smoking in restaurants and bars will come into effect in June 2014.

Diners usually dress smartly, although it's rare for a restaurant to insist on a jacket and tie.

At a dinner, usually a carafe or bottle of vodka will be ordered for the whole table and shots will be gulped down whole (not sipped) after repeated toasts throughout the meal. Shots will usually be poured for women even if they don't want any. Although it's quite acceptable for a woman to not drink vodka and to have wine or champagne instead, men are obliged. It's not good form to drink vodka without food.

If you're invited to a home, be ready to remove your shoes and put on some of the household's communal slippers.

If you meet any Russians socially, chances are they'll give you something; Russians tend to give small gifts even on short acquaintance. You may want to be prepared to reciprocate with small souvenirs from your hometown or state. One of the great taboos, however, is to present someone with a gift, shake hands, or kiss across the threshold or doorway. Wait until you're inside. If the hosts have children, it's appropriate to bring them some small sweets or trinkets.

DOING BUSINESS

Gift-giving is also the norm in business relations—as is drinking. Personal trust and personal relations are more important in Russian business than in the West, so businesspeople should be willing to take part in all sorts of bonding sessions, from vodka drinking to visiting the *banya*, or Russian-style sauna. That said, vodka-drinking sessions with strangers should be avoided, especially on trains.

LANGUAGE

Try to learn a little of the local language. You need not strive for fluency; mastering just a few basic terms is bound to make chatting with the locals more rewarding.

If you make an effort to learn the Russian (Cyrillic) alphabet, you'll be able to decipher many words; a rudimentary knowledge of the alphabet can help you to navigate the streets and subways on your own. Hotel staff almost always speak good English. If you need to find an English-speaking person on the street, the younger generation tends to speak more English than the older.

The following terms pop up in this book and may help you in your travels: *dom*, or house; *dvor*, or courtyard; *dvorets*, or palace; *khram*, or church; *monastyr*, or monastery or convent; *muzey*, or museum; *palata*, or palace; *passazh*, or arcade; *sobor*, or cathedral; *stantsiya*, or metro station; *teatr*, or theater; *tserkov*, or church; *vokzal*, or train/bus station; and *vorota*, or gateway.

the number you're trying to reach. In the Western-managed hotels, rooms are usually equipped with international, direct-dial (via satellite) telephones, but beware that the rates are hefty.

If you want to save money, computer and smartphone applications such as Skype and the voice and video chat services offered by Facebook and Google are good ways to stay in contact with people back home. If you didn't bring your computer with you, such services are also frequently available in Internet cafés. Another option is to set up an international call-back account in the United States before you go. This service can often save you as much as half off the rates of the big carriers. To use the call-back account, you must dial a pre-established number in the United States from any phone in Moscow or St. Petersburg, let the call ring a few times, then hang up. In a few minutes, a computer calls you back and makes a connection, giving you a U.S. dial tone, from which you dial any number in the United States.

ACCESS CODES

AT&T Direct ☎ *495/363–2400 from Moscow to U.S., 8/10–800–120–1011 from within other cities in Russia, 812/363–2400 from St. Petersburg to U.S..*

MCI WorldPhone ☎ *495/747–3322 in Moscow, 812/346–8022 in St. Petersburg.*

Sprint International Access ☎ *8/10–800–120–2011 from Russia to U.S.*

Callback Company Kallback ☎ *877/777–5242 ⊕ www.kallback.com.*

CALLING CARDS

Phone cards can be bought at street kiosks that also sell cards for dial-up Internet access. You stick the card in the pay phone (there's a picture showing you the right way) and wait for the dial tone. Then press 8 and wait for another dial tone, then dial the number. A number will flash on the screen showing you how many units you have left; as you speak, units are subtracted from your total.

MOBILE PHONES

If you have a multiband phone (some countries use different frequencies from those used in the United States) and your service provider uses the world-standard GSM network (as do T-Mobile, AT&T, and Verizon), you can probably use your phone abroad. Roaming fees can be steep, however. When overseas you normally pay the toll charges for incoming calls. It's almost always cheaper to send a text message than to make a call, since text messages have a very low set fee (often 15¢).

If you just want to make local calls, consider buying a new SIM card (note that your provider may have to unlock your phone for you to use a different SIM card) and a prepaid service plan in the destination. You'll then have a local number and can make local calls at local rates. If your trip is extensive, you could also simply buy a new cell phone in your destination, as the initial cost will be offset over time.

■ TIP→ **If you travel internationally frequently, save one of your old mobile phones or buy a cheap one on the Internet; ask your cell phone company to unlock it for you, and take it with you as a travel phone, buying a new SIM card with pay-as-you-go service in each destination.**

To get around the problem of unlocking a U.S. cell phone, you could buy a cell phone in Russia. The country has embraced cell phones with enthusiasm, and you can buy them in stores on every corner. Basic models can be found for less than $50. Handsets aren't usually sold as a package with a service provider, so you simply choose which network you want to join. Offices for the main providers, Beeline, MTS, and Megafon, are ubiquitous. They may ask to see your registration card and passport before signing you up. The country uses GSM.

Contacts Cellular Abroad. The company rents and sells GSM phones and sells SIM cards that work in many countries. ☎ *800/287–5072 ⊕ www.cellularabroad.com.* **Mobal.** Mobiles and sells GSM phones that will operate in 190 countries are for rent and sale. ☎ *888/888–9162 ⊕ www.mobal.com.*

■ CUSTOMS AND DUTIES

You're always allowed to bring goods of a certain value back home without having to pay any duty or import tax. But there's a limit on the amount of tobacco and liquor you can bring back duty-free, and some countries have separate limits for perfumes; for exact figures, check with your customs department. The values of so-called duty-free goods are included in these amounts. When you shop abroad, save all your receipts, as customs inspectors may ask to see them as well as the items you purchased. If the total value of your goods is more than the duty-free limit, you'll have to pay a tax (most often a flat percentage) on the value of everything beyond that limit.

Upon arrival in Russia, you first pass through passport control, where a border guard will carefully examine your passport and visa.

It's very important that you fill out a migration card and get it stamped while passing though passport control. These white cards are automatically issued on some flights, but not all. It's possible to enter the country without one, but lack of a card can cause all manner of headaches, from hotel registration problems to document checks by police. If you're not given a card, ask for one (*migratsionnaya karta* for one, *migratsionnye karty* for several) or look for them on stands in the arrivals hall.

If you haven't been given a customs form on the plane, look for the forms on a table or stand at customs after retrieving your luggage. You must keep it until your departure, when you'll be asked to present it again (along with a second, identical form noting any changes). You may import free of duty and without special license any articles intended for personal use, including clothing, food, tobacco, up to 200 cigarettes, two liters of alcoholic drinks, perfume, sports equipment, and camera equipment. One video camera and one laptop computer per person are allowed. Importing weapons and ammunition, as well as opium, hashish, and pipes for smoking them, is prohibited. The punishment for carrying illegal substances is severe. You're allowed to bring up to $10,000 in cash without declaring it. It's important to include any valuable items, such as musical instruments, and the like, on the customs form to ensure that you'll be allowed to take them back with you out of Russia (note that you're expected to take them with you, so you cannot leave them behind as gifts). If an item included on your customs form is stolen, you should obtain a police report to avoid being questioned upon departure. Technically you're allowed to bring into the country only up to $3,000 of consumer items for personal use and gifts. But customs agents at the airport have been enforcing this rule sporadically at best, and won't likely challenge you on this front unless you have an excessive amount of luggage. For information about bringing domestic animals in and out of Russia, see ⊕ *www.moscowanimals.org.*

Anything that's likely to be considered valuable art or an antique (this could include coins, manuscripts, or icons) by customs officials requires a receipt from the Committee for Culture showing that you've paid a special tax on it. Art and antique dealers usually have updated information about this, but for more details call ☎ *495/975–1918* in Moscow and ☎ *812/311–5196* in St. Petersburg.

INFORMATION IN RUSSIA
Russian Federal Customs Service.
The site includes some information in English.
⊕ www.eng.customs.ru.

U.S. Information U.S. Customs and Border Protection ⊕ www.cbp.gov.

■ EATING OUT

MEALS AND MEALTIMES
At traditional Russian restaurants, the main meal of the day is served in midafternoon and consists of a starter, soup, and a main course. Russian soups, which are excellent, include borscht, *shchi*

(cabbage soup), and *solyanka,* a spicy, thick stew made with vegetables and meat or fish. Delicious and filling main courses include Siberian *pelmeni* (tender dumplings, usually filled with minced pork and beef, and sometimes also lamb) or beef Stroganoff. If you're looking for Russian delicacies, try the excellent smoked salmon, blini with caviar, or the famous *kotlety po-Kievski* (chicken Kiev), a garlic-and-butter-filled chicken breast encased in a crispy crust. Consider ordering a shot of vodka or a glass of local beer to accompany your meal.

Restaurants are typically open from noon until midnight, and late at night many nightclubs serve good food. There are also several 24-hour restaurants in both cities. During the week, many restaurants are nearly empty, but there's no hard and fast rule about this—an ordinary Wednesday can find even an off-the-beaten-path eatery packed, because more and more Russians eat out regularly.

Unless otherwise noted, the restaurants listed in this guide are open daily for lunch and dinner.

PAYING

Restaurants are now required by law to list their prices in rubles. There are some restaurants that cater to tourists that still list their prices in "conditional units" (YE in Cyrillic), which are pegged to an exchange rate of their own devising (usually the dollar or euro). They're required to also list the ruble equivalent, as payment can only be accepted in rubles. Many restaurants accept credit cards, though you should always double-check with the staff, even if the restaurant has a sign indicating that it accepts cards. ⇨ *Also see Tipping, below.*

RESERVATIONS AND DRESS

For the trendiest restaurants, it's a good idea to book in advance, particularly for groups of four or more. Regardless of where you are, it's a good idea to make a reservation if you can. In some places, it's expected. We only mention reservations specifically when they're essential (there's no other way you'll ever get a table) or when they're not accepted. We mention dress only when men are required to wear a jacket or a jacket and tie. In general, reservations are a good idea in popular restaurants.

WINES, BEER, AND SPIRITS

Drinks are normally ordered by milliliters (50, 100, or 200) or by the bottle. In upscale establishments you'll often find an impressive wine list with imported wine and foreign liquors. Most hotel restaurants and smaller restaurants have some imported wines, as well as cheaper wines from Moldova and Eastern Europe. Even the less-expensive restaurants can serve a bewildering array of vodkas and other spirits. Make any non-restaurant alcohol purchases from a proper shop, as wine and spirits counterfeiting is a problem. In Moscow, you won't be able to buy any alcohol after 10 pm, so it's best to make your purchases in advance. In the past few years, sales of beer have really taken off. Perhaps the most famous national brand is Baltika, which produces numbered beers—0 being the lightest, and 9 being difficult to distinguish from rocket fuel. But there are dozens of other companies producing ales, lagers, porters, and flavored and unfiltered beers, making it a drink that's become almost as ubiquitous as vodka.

Note that public intoxication is strictly punished. It's okay to become inebriated within an establishment as long as you don't fall over or become aggressive. However, if you walk along the streets in a drunken state, you'll be a target for police document checks and could possibly be arrested for public drunkenness. It's also technically illegal to drink alcoholic beverages on the street or in the metro. Although many people do this, you risk being fined by police.

ELECTRICITY

The electrical current in Russia is 220 volts, 50 cycles alternating current (AC); wall outlets take Continental-type plugs, with two round prongs.

Consider making a small investment in a universal adapter, which has several types of plugs in one lightweight, compact unit. Most laptops and mobile phone chargers are dual voltage (i.e., they operate equally well on 110 and 220 volts), so they require only an adapter. These days the same is true of small appliances such as hair dryers. Always check labels and manufacturer instructions to be sure. Don't use 110-volt outlets marked "for shavers only" for high-wattage appliances such as hair dryers.

Contacts Walkabout Travel Gear. The site includes information about electricity around the world and offers adapters and other products for sale. ⊕ www.walkabouttravelgear.com.

EMERGENCIES

In case of emergency, the U.S. and U.K. consulates have consular officers on call at all times. This can be useful if a shakedown on the part of the local police goes too far, and—heaven forbid—if you land in jail. Insist on your right to call your consulate. There's a Canadian consulate in St. Petersburg; Australians and New Zealanders should check with the U.K. consulate first and the Canadian one if that doesn't work. A word of warning: phone lines to the U.S. consulate are constantly busy. It may take hours of persistent dialing to get through. In Moscow, unless you have official business or are met by embassy personnel or a compound resident, the U.S. embassy is off-limits, even to Americans.

FOREIGN EMBASSIES IN MOSCOW

Contact Canada ⊠ 23 per. Starokonyush-enny, Kropotkinsky District ☎ 495/925–6000 ⊕ www.russia.gc.ca Ⓜ Kropotkinskaya. **United Kingdom** ⊠ 10 nab. Smolenskaya, Arbat ☎ 495/956–7200 ⊕ ukinrussia.fco. gov.uk Ⓜ Smolenskaya. **United States** ⊠ 21

bul. Novinsky, Ulitsa Bolshaya Nikitskaya ☎ 495/728–5577 American Citizen Services ⊕ moscow.usembassy.gov Ⓜ Barrikadnaya.

FOREIGN EMBASSIES IN ST. PETERSBURG

Contact United Kingdom ⊠ 5 pl. Prolet-arskoi Diktatury, Liteiny/Smolny, St. Peters-burg ☎ 812/320–3200 ⊕ ukinrussia.fco. gov.uk Ⓜ Ploshchad Vosstaniya. **United States** ⊠ 15 Furstadtskaya ul., Cherny-shevskaya, St. Petersburg ☎ 812/331–2600 24-hours, 317/472–2328 U.S. State Dept. ⊕ www.stpetersburg-usconsulate.ru Ⓜ Chernyshevskaya.

GENERAL EMERGENCY CONTACTS

Ambulance ☎ 03. **Fire** ☎ 01. **Police** ☎ 02.

HEALTH

The most common types of illnesses are caused by contaminated food and water. Drink only bottled, boiled, or purified water and drinks; don't drink from public fountains or use ice. You should even consider using bottled water to brush your teeth. Make sure food has been thoroughly cooked and is served to you fresh and hot; avoid vegetables and fruits that you haven't washed (in bottled or purified water) or peeled yourself.

SPECIFIC ISSUES IN MOSCOW AND ST. PETERSBURG

A visit to Russia poses no special health risk, but the country's medical system is far below world standards, a fact you should consider if you have chronic medical conditions that may require treatment during your visit. There are, however, Western-style clinics in Moscow and St. Petersburg. Bear in mind that treatment at these clinics will be expensive unless you have traveler's health insurance. You should also purchase insurance that covers medical evacuation. Sometimes even minor conditions can't be treated adequately because of the severe and chronic shortage of basic medicines and medical equipment. Tuberculosis is a serious problem in Russian prisons, but the short-term visitor to Russia needn't worry about infection.

You should drink only boiled or bottled water. The water supply in St. Petersburg contains giardia, an intestinal parasite that can cause diarrhea, stomach cramps, and nausea. The gestation period is two to three weeks, so symptoms usually develop after an infected traveler has already returned home. The condition is easily treatable, but be sure to let your doctor know that you may have been exposed to this parasite. Avoid ice cubes and use bottled water to brush your teeth, particularly in St. Petersburg. In Moscow and St. Petersburg, imported and domestic bottled water is widely available in shops. It's a good idea to buy a liter of this water whenever you can. Hotel floor attendants always have a samovar in their offices and will provide boiled water if asked. Many top-end hotels filter their water, but it's best to double-check with reception. Mild cases of traveler's diarrhea may respond to Imodium (known generically as loperamide) or Pepto-Bismol, both of which can be purchased over the counter. Drink plenty of purified water or tea—chamomile is a good folk remedy. In severe cases, rehydrate yourself with a salt-sugar solution—½ teaspoon salt and 4 tablespoons sugar per quart of water.

Fruits and vegetables served in restaurants are generally washed with purified water and are thus safe to eat. However, food poisoning is common in Russia, so be wary of dairy products and ice cream that may not be fresh. The *pierogi* (meat- or cabbage-filled pies) sold everywhere on the streets are cheap and tasty, but they can give you a nasty stomachache.

SHOTS AND MEDICATION

Foreigners traveling to Russia are often advised to get vaccinated against diphtheria—in the early 1990s, both Moscow and St. Petersburg had outbreaks of this disease, and cholera isn't unknown either. These outbreaks are now rare, but in particular, children should be immunized against diphtheria, measles, mumps, rubella, and polio, as well as hepatitis A and typhus. A flu shot is also recommended for winter travel for people of all ages.

■ TIP→ **If you travel a lot internationally— particularly to developing nations—refer to the CDC's Health Information for International Travel (aka Traveler's Health Yellow Book). Information from it is posted on the CDC website (⊕ wwwnc.cdc.gov/travel), or you can buy a copy from a bookstore for $24.95.**

Health Warnings National Centers for Disease Control and Prevention (*CDC*). ☎ *800/232-4636 international travelers' health line* ⊕ *www.cdc.gov/travel.* **World Health Organization** (*WHO*). ⊕ *www.who.int.*

OVER-THE-COUNTER REMEDIES

Just about everything is available in pharmacies without a prescription, and many pharmacies stock Western painkillers and cold medicines, which mostly come from Germany and France. If you can't find your favorite brand, just ask for either aspirin or Panadol, which is another brand name for acetaminophen, the active ingredient in Tylenol. However, there's a good chance of buying a counterfeit medicine as well. According to official statistics, up to 30% of the most popular drugs in Russian pharmacies are fake or made illegally with inadequate technology. Large chains—including 36.6, PetroFarm, Natur Produkt, Pharmacy Doctor, and Pervaya Pomoshch—as well as the pharmacies of international clinics are believed to be free of such fakes. The chains are also more likely to stock Western brands.

■ HOURS OF OPERATION

General hours for most businesses and banks are from 10 am to 6 pm. They're usually closed on weekends, and many take an hour off for lunch. In Moscow, there are many 24-hour shops, grocery stores, and restaurants.

Consulates, government offices, ticket agencies, and exchange offices tend to close for an hour in the afternoon for lunch. Nothing stands between Russian businesses and public holidays, and the major holidays often involve a break of at least two days—three if they coincide with a weekend. ⇨ *See Holidays, below, for national holidays and Mail and Shipping for post office hours.*

Most gas stations are open 24 hours.

Museum hours vary, but many are closed on Monday. Many museums close for one extra day (on which they'd normally be open) at the end of the month.

In general, pharmacies are open from 9 am or 10 am until 9 pm. There are, however, some 24-hour pharmacies in the major cities—check with the staff at your hotel to find those that are closest. Most shops and department stores are open from 10 am until 7 pm or even as late as 9 pm seven days a week. Fewer and fewer break for lunch for an hour in the afternoon. Restaurants and shopping arcades and malls are rarely closed at that time.

HOLIDAYS

Here's a list of Russia's major holidays, most of which entail closures of many businesses; note that religious holidays like Christmas and Easter are celebrated according to the Russian Orthodox calendar. In addition, from May 1 through May 9 and from December 31 through January 13, the entire country shuts down. These are major holiday periods when absolutely nobody does anything: even medical clinics close. These weeks can pose a real problem for visitors, so try not to travel to Russia during these special holiday periods. Be aware, too, that on the day before a public holiday, everything tends to close early:

January 1–5 (New Year's), January 7 (Russian Orthodox Christmas), February 23 (Defenders of the Fatherland Day), March 8 (International Women's Day), May 1 (Day of Spring and Labor), May 9 (Victory Day), June 12 (Russia Day), November 4 (Day of Reconciliation and Agreement).

■ MAIL

The Russian postal service is more reliable than it once was, and many travelers report letters, postcards, and even packages arriving safe and sound abroad within a reasonable time. Post offices, or *pochta,* are open approximately from 8:30 am to 7 pm and mailboxes are painted blue. WestPost in St. Petersburg, which whisks mail off to Finland and sends it from there using European postal services, is another option if you don't want to risk it with the Russian post. There are also DHL and Federal Express offices in Moscow and St. Petersburg.

You can buy international envelopes and postcards at post offices and in hotel-lobby kiosks.

Sending mail from Russia to the United States, Europe, or Australia starts at 20R for a postcard or letter and is priced according to weight.

Mail from outside Russia takes approximately four weeks to arrive, sometimes longer, and sometimes it never arrives at all. The postal service will often open large packages and envelopes to inspect them, and sometimes things go missing.

Contacts DHL ⊠ *11 ul. 1st Tverskaya-Yamskaya ul., Mayakovskaya* ☎ *495/933–1001* ⊕ *www.dhl.ru* Ⓜ *Mayakovskaya.* **Federal Express** ⊠ *22/24 nab. Ovchinnikovskaya, str. 1, Novokuznetskaya* ☎ *495/788–8881* ⊕ *www.fedex.com/ru* Ⓜ *Novokuznetskaya.* **WestPost** ⊠ *86 Nevsky pr., City Center, St. Petersburg* ☎ *812/336–63-52* ⊕ *www.westpost.ru.*

SHIPPING PACKAGES

Stores don't offer shipping, so you should use DHL, Federal Express, or another mailing service. Don't attempt to send a work of art without the correct accompanying documents from the store where you bought it, proving that you're allowed to take it out of the country.

▌ MONEY

Today the ruble is reasonably stable at around 30R to the dollar. Talk of a growing middle class aside, the majority of Russians can only dream of buying Western-made cars and clothes, dining out, and traveling abroad for their holidays.

ITEM	AVERAGE COST
Cup of Coffee	150R
Glass of Wine	300R
Glass of Beer	250R
Sandwich	300R
One-Mile Taxi Ride in Capital City	150R–200R
Museum Admission	50R–750R

Prices here are given for adults. Substantially reduced fees are almost always available for children, students, and senior citizens.

Goods and services aimed at foreigners are as expensive as anywhere in Western Europe. Public transport is cheap; a ride on the metro costs 28R one-way, less if you buy many trips. Taxi rates are generally low, but as soon as the driver realizes that you're a foreigner, the rate goes up. Some museums and theaters, such as the Armory Palace in the Moscow Kremlin and the Hermitage Museum in St. Petersburg, have instituted special, higher fees for foreign tourists. For example, a "foreign ticket" for an opera or ballet at the Mariinsky (Kirov) Theatre costs from 4000R to 6000R for some performances, whereas a Russian price ranges from 1500R to 4000R.

▌TIP➔ Banks never have every foreign currency on hand, and it may take as long as a week for them to get it. If you're planning to exchange funds before leaving home, don't wait until the last minute.

ATMS AND BANKS

Your own bank will probably charge a fee for using ATMs abroad; the foreign bank you use may also charge a fee. Nevertheless, you'll usually get a better rate of exchange at an ATM than you will at a currency-exchange office or even when changing money in a bank. And extracting funds as you need them is a safer option than carrying around a large amount of cash.

▌TIP➔ PIN codes with more than four digits aren't recognized at ATMs in Russia. If yours has five or more, remember to change it before you leave.

Bankomaty (bank machines) have cropped up all over the place in Moscow and St. Petersburg, and in the city centers they're not difficult to find: hotels and banks are the most obvious (and safest) places to look, but there are some on the streets as well. In addition, many metro stations now have them—but have a partner watch your back when you take money out, and remember that pickpockets often hang around such places.

ATM Locations Cirrus ☎ *800/424–7787 Global customer service number* ⊕ *mastercard.com.*

CREDIT CARDS

It's a good idea to inform your credit card company before you travel. Otherwise, the credit card company might put a hold on your card owing to unusual activity—not a good thing halfway through your trip. Record all your credit card numbers—as well as the phone numbers to call if your cards are lost or stolen—in a safe place, so you're prepared should something go wrong. Both MasterCard and Visa have general numbers you can call (collect if you're abroad) if your card is lost, but you're better off calling the number of your issuing bank, since

MasterCard and Visa usually just transfer you to your bank; your bank's number is usually printed on your card.

If you plan to use your credit card for cash advances, you'll need to apply for a PIN at least two weeks before your trip. Note that some credit card companies *and* the banks that issue them add substantial percentages to all foreign transactions, whether they're in a foreign currency or not. Check on these fees before leaving home, so there won't be any surprises when you get the bill.

Many shops, restaurants, and hotels within Moscow and St. Petersburg accept credit cards, though you should always double-check with the staff, despite any signs you may see. Establishments outside the cities are less likely to accept credit cards.

To report lost or stolen credit cards, the U.S. Embassy in Russia advises that you call your credit-card company collect through AT&T Direct. From Moscow, dial ☎ 363–2400; from St. Petersburg, it's the same number, with the St. Petersburg area code 812.

When you use your credit card to make travel purchases you may get free travel-accident insurance, collision-damage insurance, and medical or legal assistance, depending on the card and the bank that issued it. American Express, MasterCard, and Visa provide one or more of these services, so get a copy of your credit card's travel benefits policy. If you're a member of an auto club, always ask hotel and car-rental reservations agents about auto-club discounts. Some clubs offer additional discounts on tours, cruises, and admission to attractions.

Reporting Lost Cards American Express
☎ 800/528–4800 in the U.S., 336/393–1111 collect from abroad ⊕ www.americanexpress. com. **Diners Club** ☎ 800/234–6377 in the U.S., 514/877–1577 collect from abroad ⊕ www.dinersclub.com. **MasterCard** ☎ 800/627–8372 in the U.S., 636/722–7111 collect from abroad ⊕ www.mastercard.com. **Visa** ☎ 800/847–2911 in the U.S., 866/654–0164 Toll free customer service number from Moscow and St. Petersburg ⊕ www.visa.com.

CURRENCY AND EXCHANGE

The national currency in Russia is the ruble (R). There are paper notes of 10, 50, 100, 500, 1,000, and 5,000, and there are 1-, 2-, 5-, and 10-ruble coins. There are 100 kopeks in a ruble and there are coins for 1, 5, 10, and 50 kopeks.

Russians and resident expats have gotten used to thinking in both rubles and dollars—that is, talking in rubles but mentally pegging prices to the dollar. This can create a certain amount of confusion for the tourist, so bear the following in mind. First, remember that payment, by law, can only be made in rubles or by credit card. Nonetheless, some stores, restaurants, travel agencies, and retailers list prices in dollars, or "conditional units" (*uslovnye yedinitsy*, often marked on menus and price lists as *YE*), a euphemism for the dollar (or in some cases the euro). This practice is thankfully diminishing and you'll most often see prices in rubles. In this book prices are listed in rubles for everything, including sights, attractions, hotels, and restaurants. Bear in mind that the sum in rubles will be high for hotels especially, so it may be helpful to carry around a small pocket calculator for conversions that are difficult to do in your head.

At this writing one U.S. dollar equaled 31 rubles; one euro equaled 41 rubles; one U.K. pound equaled 47 rubles; one Canadian dollar equaled 31 rubles; one Australian dollar equaled 33 rubles; and one New Zealand dollar equaled 26 rubles.

Rubles can rarely be obtained at banks outside Russia, but if you somehow acquire them (through friends or acquaintances) it's legal to import or export them. There's no limit on the amount of foreign currency you may bring in with you, but you have to declare more than $10,000. ATMs are the way to go, but traveler's checks are a better option than bringing lots of currency. You should have at least $100 in cash (in 10s and 20s). If you don't mind the risk of theft or loss, bring more; you're bound to need it. For the most favorable rates, change money through banks. Although ATM transaction fees may be higher abroad than at home, ATM rates are excellent because they're based on wholesale rates offered only by major banks. You can also exchange foreign currency for rubles (and vice versa) at state-run exchange offices—where you'll get the worst rate—or at any of the numerous currency-exchange booths (*obmen valyuty*). Try to bring newer bills with you to Russia, as older versions (as well as worn or torn foreign bills) are frequently rejected by exchange offices. On your way out of Russia you can change excess rubles back into dollars at any bank or at the airport. For this you'll need your passport.

■ TIP→ Even if a currency-exchange booth has a sign promising no commission, rest assured that there's some kind of huge, hidden fee. (Oh...that's right. The sign didn't say no fee.) And as for rates, you're almost always better off getting foreign currency at an ATM or exchanging money at a bank.

EXCHANGE RATES

Google does currency conversion. Just type in the amount you want to convert and an explanation of how you want it converted (e.g., "14 Swiss francs in dollars"), and then voilà. **Oanda.com** also allows you to print out a handy table with the current day's conversion rates. **XE.com** is another good currency conversion website.

Conversion sites **Google** ⊕ *www.google.com*. **Oanda.com** ⊕ *www.oanda.com*. **XE.com** ⊕ *www.xe.com*.

TRAVELER'S CHECKS

Some consider this the currency of the caveman, and it's true that fewer establishments accept traveler's checks these days. Using an ATM is preferable, but traveler's checks remain a cheap and secure way to carry extra money, particularly on trips to urban areas. Both Citibank (under the Visa brand) and American Express issue traveler's checks in the United States, but Amex is better known and more widely accepted;

you can also avoid hefty surcharges by cashing Amex checks at Amex offices. Whatever you do, keep track of all the serial numbers in case the checks are lost or stolen.

Traveler's checks can be cashed at the state-run offices, at private banks, and at most major hotels within the cities (note that some exchange counters and many stores won't accept traveler's checks). If you're going to rural areas and small towns, convert your traveler's checks to rubles before you go. Lost or stolen checks can usually be replaced within 24 hours. To ensure a speedy refund, buy your own traveler's checks—don't let someone else pay for them: irregularities like this can cause delays. The person who bought the checks should make request the refund.

■ PACKING

No matter what time of year you visit, bring a sweater. St. Petersburg especially can be unexpectedly cold in summer. A raincoat and fold-up umbrella are also musts. You'll probably be doing a lot of walking outdoors, so bring warm, comfortable clothing, and be sure to pack a pair of sturdy walking shoes.

Russians favor fashion over variety in their wardrobes, and it's perfectly acceptable to wear the same outfit several days in a row. Be sure to pack one outfit for dress-up occasions, such as the theater. The layer system works well in the unpredictable weather of fall and spring; wear a light coat with a sweater that you can put on and take off as the weather changes. In winter, bring heavy sweaters, warm boots, a wool hat, a scarf and mittens, and a heavy coat. Woolen tights or long underwear are essential during the coldest months. Russian central heating can be overly efficient, so again, use the layer system to avoid sweltering in an overheated building or train.

Russian pharmacies, supermarkets, and hotels all have reasonable stocks of the essential toiletries and personal hygiene products, but bring your own supplies of medicines and prescription drugs you take regularly. Although some well-known Western brands are easily available, you may not recognize the Russian equivalent of certain medicines. Consider whether you might want to bring any items that can be difficult to find in Russia, such as insect repellent (in summer and fall mosquitoes can be a serious problem), camera batteries, laxatives, anti-diarrhea pills, travel-sickness medicine, and the like.

Toilet paper is plentiful in hotels but less so in public buildings, so bring small packages of tissues to carry around with you. Premoistened cleansing tissues will also come in handy, especially if you're traveling by train. A small flashlight may also prove useful, particularly if visiting someone's apartment—stairwells are often dimly lit.

Within Russia, the rules regulating carry-on luggage are strict disregarded. Checked luggage is frequently lost and/or pilfered, so pack as much as you can in your carry-on, including all of your valuables, for internal flights.

∎ PASSPORTS AND VISAS

You must have a valid passport and visa to enter Russia. Within Russia you should carry your passport, visa, migration card, and registration card at all times. ∎TIP➔ **Make two photocopies of the data page of your passport (one for someone at home and another for you, carried separately from your passport). If you lose your passport, promptly call the nearest embassy or consulate and the local police.**

PASSPORTS

U.S. citizens, even infants, need a valid passport to enter Russia for stays of any length, plus a visa. The passport should be valid for at least six months after the date you apply for the visa and must have at least two clear pages. U.S. passports are valid for 10 years. You must apply in person if you're getting a passport for the first time; if your previous passport was lost, stolen, or damaged; or if your

previous passport has expired and was issued more than 15 years ago or when you were under 16. All children under 18 must appear in person to apply for or renew a passport. Both parents must accompany any child under 14 (or send a notarized statement with their permission) and provide proof of their relationship to the child.

There are 13 regional passport offices, as well as 7,000 passport acceptance facilities in post offices, public libraries, and other governmental offices. If you're renewing a passport, you can do so by mail. Forms are available at passport acceptance facilities and online.

The cost to apply for a new passport is $110 for adults, $80 for children under 16, plus a $25 execution fee; renewals for adults are $110. Allow six weeks for processing, both for first-time passports and renewals. For an expediting fee of $60 you can reduce this time to about two weeks. If your trip is less than two weeks away, you can get a passport even more rapidly by going to a passport office with the necessary documentation. Private expediters can get things done in as little as 48 hours, but charge hefty fees for their services.

VISAS

You must have a valid visa to enter Russia for any length of time. Visa application procedures change frequently, so check the Russian Consulate's website for the latest information. At this writing, visa applicants must submit the following items to the Russian Consulate at least 21 days before departure: a printout of the visa application, your passport, two passport photos, confirmation letters and official itineraries from a Russian travel agency, hotel, or cruise line you'll be using (to prove that you have confirmed reservations) or a properly endorsed business invitation from a host organization, a self-addressed stamped envelope, and the application fee (between $140 and $450 for U.S. citizens, depending on what kind of visa—tourist, business, or multi-entry).

The fee is higher if you need a faster turn-around time. Requirements vary slightly if you'll be staying as a guest in a private home or if you're traveling on business. Travel agencies have ways of getting around the advance hotel reservations requirement, but usually you must pay for at least one night's accommodation. Go To Russia (⊕ *www.gotorussia.net*) is a useful resource for obtaining a visa.

Once in Russia, you'll need to register your visa within 72 hours (three days) of your arrival (excluding weekends and official holidays). If you're staying at a hotel, they can register your visa for a small fee, usually around 300R, but they may charge up to 1,000R. If you're staying in an apartment, your visa must be registered by your landlord. The landlord will need to fill out a notification form indicating your passport and migration card details and present his or her passport registered at the same apartment to the local police precinct (in Moscow) or FMS office (commonly known as OVIR) in other cities. ■ TIP➜ **If you don't register your visa, you may be detained by police, fined on departure, and possibly even prevented from boarding your plane.** Citizens of Australia, Canada, and the United Kingdom must also obtain a visa to enter Russia. The procedures are similar to those for American citizens.

U.S. Passport Information U.S. Department of State ☎ 877/487–2778 ⊕ *travel.state.gov/passport.*

U.S. Passport and Visa Expediters
A. Briggs Passport & Visa Expeditors ☎ 800/806–0581 toll-free, 202/338–0111 ⊕ *www.abriggs.com.* **American Passport Express** ☎ 800/455–5166, 800/841–6778 ⊕ *www.americanpassport.com.* **Passport Express** ☎ 800/362–8196 ⊕ *www.passportexpress.com.* **Travel Document Systems** ☎ 800/874–5100 toll-free, 202/638–3800 ⊕ *www.traveldocs.com.*
Travel the World Visas ☎ 866/886–8472 toll-free, 301/495–7700 ⊕ *www.world-visa.com.*

Russian Consulates General
Australia. Australia ⊠ 7–9 Fullerton St., Woollahra, Australia ☎ 2/9326-1702, 2/9326–1866 ⊕ *www.sydneyrussianconsulate.com.* **Canada** ⊠ 175 Bloor St. E., South Tower, Suite 801, Toronto, Ontario, Canada ☎ 416/962–9911 ⊕ *www.toronto.mid.ru.* **New Zealand.** New Zealand ⊠ 57 Messines Rd., Karori, Wellington, New Zealand ☎ 4/476–9548 Visa officer, 4/476–6742 ⊕ *www.newzealand.mid.ru.* **U.K** ⊠ 5 Kensington Palace Gardens, London, Great Britain ☎ 0203/668-7474 ⊕ *www.rusemb.org.uk.* **U.S.** ⊠ 9 E. 91st St., New York, USA ☎ 212/348–0926 ⊕ *www.ruscon.org.*

■ RESTROOMS

Public restrooms do exist, but they're mostly poorly marked and difficult to spot, and many are crumbling and not up to Western standards of hygiene. Blue chemical toilets on the street have no washbasin, and toilets in train stations and other public buildings are often the squat type. Your best bet is to buy a snack in a café or bar and avail yourself of its facilities. With the exception of some restrooms in stores, you always have to pay to use the facilities, usually around 20R. The attendant sometimes has a dish for tips. It's also a good idea to carry a package of tissues with you into public restrooms.

■ SAFETY

Travel to Russia is fraught with many unusual challenges, in addition to the normal safety and security issues you would associate with travel to any large city. Terrorist acts such as bombings have occurred in large Russian cities. In January 2011, a suicide bomber set off an explosion in the arrivals hall of Moscow's Domodedovo Airport, killing 35 people. A year before, some 40 people died after two bombs exploded on the capital's metro system during rush hour. Russian authorities have attributed such attacks to an increase in the Islamist insurgency in Russia's troubled North Caucasus region.

Be alert for any unusual behavior or packages left unattended in public. Consult government-issued travel advisories (⇨ Visitor Information) before your trip.

Never change money on the street; as with con artists everywhere, counterfeit money, sleights of hand, and the old folded-note trick are practiced by people standing outside official exchange offices. When using money-exchange booths, thoroughly check that you've received the full amount. As well as avoiding taxis that already have occupants and avoiding gypsy cabs, never allow your driver to stop to take an extra passenger after you've gotten in. It's possible that this is indeed a random passerby; it's also possible that he's an accomplice of the driver who has been waiting around the corner. If your driver attempts to take another fare, say "*nyet*" (no) and/or "*nye nado*" (literally "not necessary," meaning here "I'd rather not"). Better still, team up with a fellow lone traveler and split the fare.

Tourists are a common target for thieves in Moscow and St. Petersburg, so stay alert, particularly in places commonly frequented by visitors (outside hotels, for example, and at bars). If you get in trouble, don't expect much help from the police, who are often called *bandity* (gangsters) by natives.

Although police in the West are usually considered keepers of the peace, those in uniform don't enjoy this image in Russia. The reason is partly because of their habit of shaking people down to supplement their meager salaries. The Russian government is attempting to improve relations between the police and the public. Pay special attention when leaving a nightclub—the cops know that these are hangouts for foreigners and have been known to lie in wait to extract "fines" for alleged drunken behavior. If you find yourself in any tricky situations with the police, be prepared to show your passport, migration card, registration card, and visa. In all situations, be

polite, allow the police to search you if they require, and stay cool. This is by no means the way all Russian police act, but it happens too frequently to be dismissed as the actions of a minority.

Exercise the same precautions you would in any major city. In the metro, avoid very crowded cars where you could get your pocket picked. If you go to a street market, keep an expensive camera or phone out of sight. In cafés, don't hang your bag on the back of your chair where you can't see it. Moscow has well-lit central streets, and many stores, clubs, and cafés are open 24 hours, so as long as you avoid deserted areas, you should be fine. It's best to stick with a companion if you're out at night.

■TIP→ **Distribute your cash, credit cards, ID, and other valuables between a deep front pocket, an inside jacket or vest pocket, and a hidden money pouch. Don't reach for the money pouch when you're in public.**

GOVERNMENT INFORMATION AND ADVISORIES

Advisories U.S. Department of State ⊕ *travel.state.gov*.

■ TAXES

Airport departure taxes are almost always included in the price of the airline ticket. Hotels charge an 18% value-added tax if you pay in cash or by credit card upon arrival; if you pay in advance, then you don't get charged these taxes (at least that's the general rule). Moscow hotels add an extra 1% tax to your bill.

Russia's 18% value-added tax (V.A.T.) is charged on most everything and refundable on almost nothing (interestingly, the V.A.T. law specifically says the V.A.T.

doesn't apply to exported goods, but there's no mechanism worked out for handling refunds at the airport, nor do stores have V.A.T. refund forms). Goods bought at duty-free shops in the airport are free of V.A.T.

▌ TIME

Russia, the largest country in the world, has 9 official time zones. There used to be 11, but they were reduced in 2010. Moscow and St. Petersburg share one and are both three hours ahead of London, eight hours ahead of New York City, 11 hours ahead of Los Angeles, and six hours behind Sydney. Time differences vary with daylight savings time, which was abolished in Russia in 2011.

▌ TIPPING

Tipping is the norm in Russia. Waiters and porters will all expect a tip, and cloakroom and restroom attendants will appreciate them. A tour guide may be given a tip by the group as a whole after an excursion, although depending on the situation, it may be more appropriate to give a small souvenir. Whether you should tip the bartender depends on the establishment, but it's not the norm. Add an extra 10% to 15% to a restaurant bill. If you have negotiated a taxi fare ahead of time, there's no need to tip on top of that payment. Some restaurants add a service charge to the bill automatically, so double-check before you leave a big tip. If you're paying by credit card, leave the tip in cash—the waiter is less likely to see it if you add it to the credit-card charge. Moreover, some restaurants actively refuse to allow tips being added on to the bill by credit card. The only places with bellhops who carry your bags are Moscow and St. Petersburg's five-star hotels; in such establishments, a 100R tip—more if you have many heavy bags—is a decent thank-you.

TIPPING GUIDELINES FOR MOSCOW AND ST. PETERSBURG	
Bartender	50R, or round up the bill on simple orders; leave more for larger or special orders
Bellhop	100R per bag, depending on the level of the hotel
Hotel Concierge	150R to 300R or more, if he or she performs a service for you
Hotel Doorman	50R to 100R if he helps you get a cab
Hotel Maid	100R per day (either daily or at the end of your stay, in cash)
Hotel Room-Service Waiter	10%–15% per delivery, even if a service charge has been added
Porter at Airport or Train Station	100R per bag
Tour Guide	10% of the cost of the tour
Waiter	15%–20%, with 20% being the norm at high-end restaurants; nothing additional if a service charge is added to the bill
Restroom and coat-check attendants	Restroom attendants in more expensive restaurants expect some small change. Tip coat-check personnel at least 100R per item checked unless there's a fee, then nothing.

▌ TOURS

GUIDED TOURS

Among companies that sell tours to Moscow and St. Petersburg, the following are nationally known, have a proven reputation, and offer plenty of options. The classifications used here represent different price categories, and you'll probably encounter these terms when talking to a travel agent or tour operator. The key difference is usually in accommodations, which run from budget to better, and better-yet to best.

CONTACTS

Budget Cosmos ✉ 5301 South Federal Circle, Littleton, Colorado, USA ☎ 800/276–1241 ⊕ www.cosmos.com. **ITS Tours** ✉ 707 Texas Ave., Suite 101A, College Station, Texas, USA ☎ 800/533–8688 toll-free ⊟ 979/693–9673 ⊕ supersavertours.com.

First-Class Brendan Tours ✉ 17323 Ventura Blvd., Los Angeles, California, USA ☎ 800/428–6000 ⊕ www.brendanvacations. com. **General Tours** ✉ 53 Summer St., Keene, New Hampshire, USA ☎ 800/221–2216 ⊕ www.generaltours.com. **Insight Vacations** ✉ 801, E. Katella Ave., Anaheim, California, USA ☎ 800/582–8380 ⊕ www. insightvacations.com. **Intourist** ⊕ www. intourist.com. **Isram World of Travel** ✉ 233 Park Ave. S., 10 Fl., New York, New York, USA ☎ 800/223–7460, 212/661–1193 ⊕ www. isram.com. **Mir Corporation** ✉ 85 S. Washington St., Suite 210, Seattle, Washington, USA ☎ 800/424–7289, 206/624–7289 ⊕ www. mircorp.com. **Trafalgar Tours** ✉ 11 E. 26th St., New York, New York, USA ☎ 866/513–1995 ⊕ www.trafalgar.com.

Deluxe Exeter International ✉ 111 S. Dakota Ave., Tampa, Florida, USA ☎ 800/633–1008, 813/251–5355 ⊕ www. exeterinternational.com. **Globus** ✉ 5301 S. Federal Circle, Littleton, Colorado, USA ☎ 800/276–1241 ⊕ www.globusandcosmos. com. **Maupintour** ✉ 2690 Weston Rd, Ste. 200, Weston, Florida, USA ☎ 800/255–4266 ⊕ www.maupintour.com.

Super-Deluxe Abercrombie & Kent ✉ 1411 Opus Pl., Suite 300, Downer's Grove, Illinois, USA ☎ 800/554–7016 toll-free, 630/725–3400 ⊕ www.abercrombiekent.com. **Travcoa** ✉ 100 N. Sepulveda Blvd., Suite 1700, El segundo, California, USA ☎ 800/992–2003, 800/992–2003 ⊟ 946/476–2538 ⊕ www.travcoa.com.

▮ TRIP INSURANCE

Comprehensive trip insurance is valuable if you're booking a very expensive or complicated trip (particularly to an isolated region) or if you're booking far in advance. Comprehensive policies typically cover trip cancellation and interruption, letting you cancel or cut your trip short because of illness, or, in some cases, acts of terrorism in your destination. Such policies might also cover evacuation and medical care. (For trips abroad you should have at least medical-only coverage. ⇨ See *Medical Insurance and Assistance, under Health.*) Some also cover you for trip delays because of bad weather or mechanical problems as well as for lost or delayed luggage.

Another type of coverage to consider is financial default—that is, when your trip is disrupted because a tour operator, airline, or cruise line goes out of business. Generally you must buy this when you book your trip or shortly thereafter, and it's available to you only if your operator isn't on a list of excluded companies.

Always read the fine print of your policy to make sure that you're covered for the risks that most concern you. Compare several policies to be sure you're getting the best price and range of coverage available.

Insurance Comparison Info
Insure My Trip ☎ 800/487–4722 ⊕ www. insuremytrip.com. **Square Mouth** ☎ 800/240–0369 ⊕ www.squaremouth.com.

Comprehensive Insurers
Allianz ☎ 866/884–3556 ⊕ www. allianztravelinsurance.com. **AIG Travel Guard** ☎ 800/826–4919 ⊕ www.travelguard.com. **CSA Travel Protection** ☎ 800/711–1197 ⊕ www.csatravelprotection.com. **Travel Insured International** ☎ 800/243–3174 ⊕ www.travelinsured.com. **Travelex Insurance** ☎ 800/228–9792 ⊕ www. travelexinsurance.com.

▌ VISITOR INFORMATION

Russia doesn't have major tourism board offices in Moscow and St. Petersburg or abroad, but many commercial travel agencies can help you plan your trip. The Moscow Committee for Tourism has an office in Moscow on Red Square.

Contacts **The Moscow Committee for Tourism** ☎ *800/220–0001 Call center for tourists in Moscow, 495/690-7711 office in Moscow* ⊕ *www.moscomtour.mos.ru.* **Travel.SPB.Ru** ⊕ *www.travel.spb.ru.*

ONLINE TRAVEL TOOLS

Media **Johnson's Russia List** ⊕ *www.russialist.org.* **The Moscow Times** ⊕ *www.themoscowtimes.com.* **Radio Free Europe** ⊕ *www.rferl.org.* **Russia!** ⊕ *www.readrussia.com.* **Russia Today** ⊕ *www.rt.com.* **The St. Petersburg Times** ⊕ *www.sptimes.ru.*

The following websites provide interesting historical background as well as current statistics about Russia and its language.

Other Resources **Bucknell Russian Program** ⊕ *www.bucknell.edu/russian.* **CIA World Factbook** ⊕ *www.cia.gov.*

INDEX

PHOTO CREDITS

Front cover: SIME/eStock Photo [Description: Cathedral of Assumption, Kremlin, Moscow]. Back cover (from left to right): Stanislav Zaburdaev/Shutterstock; stocker1970/Shutterstock; OlegDoroshin/ Shutterstock. Spine: Vladitto/Shutterstock.. 1, Leonid Serebrennikov / age fotostock. 2 and 4, José Fuste Raga / age fotostock. 5 (top), Alex Segre / Alamy. 5 (bottom), José Fuste Raga / age fotostock. 6 (top left), Natalia Bratslavsky/Shutterstock. 6 (top right), (c) Toxawww | Dreamstime.com. 6 (bottom left), Ferdinand Hollweck / age fotostock. 6 (bottom right), Schwabe Kai / age fotostock. 7 (top), Walter Bibikow / age fotostock. 7 (bottom), Sergey Petrov/Shutterstock. 8 (top left), Travel Pictures / Alamy. 8 (top right), Yadid Levy / age fotostock. 8 (bottom), Greg Balfour Evans / Alamy. Chapter 1: Experience Moscow and St. Petersburg: 13, Dmitry Berkut/Shutterstock.15 (left), Dmitry Mordvint- sev/iStockphoto. 15 (right), Pavel Losevsky/iStockphoto. 17 (left), Kremlin Domes. by Ashley Good www.fl ickr.com/photos/kmndr/2790420745/ Attribution License. 17 (right), Sailorr/Shutterstock. 18, Moscow - Red Square by Andrew Bossi www.fl ickr.com/photos/thisisbossi/2913668763/ Attribution- ShareAlike License. 19, Rd/Shutterstock. 20, Russian Look/viestiphoto.com. 21, Sylvain Grandadam/ age fotostock. 22, Vladimir Sazonov/Shutterstock. 23, Ismailovsky Market Matryoshkas by Andrew Currie www.flickr.com/photos/andrewcurrie/4589175746/Attribution-ShareAlike License. 24, At the St. Petersburg canals by David Orban www.fl ickr.com/photos/davidorban/2637449715/ Attribution License. 25, Iakov Filimonov/iStockphoto. 27 (left), Th1234/Wikimedia Commons. 27 (right), William- borg/Wikimedia Commons. 28, Klaas Lingbeek- van Kranen/iStockphoto. 29, Red Square. by Ashley Good www.fl ickr.com/photos/kmndr/2793414193/Attribution License. 35, Waiting for the married couple by Maarten www.flickr.com/photos/superchango/3145465832/ Attribution License. Chapter 2: Exploring Moscow: 37, Reidl/Shutterstock. Chapter 3: Moscow Where to Eat: 107, Tips Images / Tips Italia Srl a socio unico / Alamy. Chapter 4: Moscow Where to Stay: 123, Starwood Hotels & Resorts Worldwide, Inc. Chapter 5: Moscow Nightlife and the Arts: 137, anshar/Shutterstock. Chapter 6: Mos- cow Shopping: 153, Jaume/Shutterstock.com. Chapter 7: Side Trips from Moscow: 165, Boris Stroujko/ Shutterstock. Chapter 8: Exploring St. Petersburg: 193, Solodov Alexey/Shutterstock. Chapter 9: St. Petersburg Where to Eat: 243, Anna Moskvina/Shutterstock. Chapter 10: St. Petersburg Where to Stay: 257, Starwood Hotels & Resorts Worldwide, Inc. Chapter 11: St. Petersburg Nightlife and the Arts: 269, Sergey Petrov/Shutterstock. Chapter 12: St. Petersburg Shopping: 289, Northfoto / Shutterstock. com. Chapter 13: Side Trips from St. Petersburg: 299, cTermit/Shutterstock.

NOTES

3 7834 00207213 9

Fodor's MOSCOW & ST. PETERSBURG

Publisher: Amanda D'Acierno, *Senior Vice President*

Editorial: Arabella Bowen, *Executive Editorial Director*; Linda Cabasin, *Editorial Director*

Design: Fabrizio La Rocca, *Vice President, Creative Director*; Tina Malaney, *Associate Art Director*; Chie Ushio, *Senior Designer*; Ann McBride, *Production Designer*

Photography: Melanie Marin, *Associate Director of Photography*; Jessica Parkhill and Jennifer Romains, *Researchers*

Maps: Rebecca Baer, *Senior Map Editor*; David Lindroth and Mark Stroud (Moon Street Cartography) *Cartographers*

Production: Linda Schmidt, *Managing Editor*; Evangelos Vasilakis, *Associate Managing Editor*; Angela L. McLean, *Senior Production Manager*

Sales: Jacqueline Lebow, *Sales Director*

Marketing & Publicity: Heather Dalton, *Marketing Director*; Katherine Fleming, *Senior Publicist*

Business & Operations: Susan Livingston, *Vice President, Strategic Business Planning*; Sue Daulton, *Vice President, Operations*

Fodors.com: Megan Bell, *Executive Director, Revenue & Business Development*; Yasmin Marinaro, *Senior Director, Marketing & Partnerships*

Copyright © 2014 by Fodor's Travel, a division of Random House LLC.

Writers: Sabra Ayres, Catherine Blanchard, Anna Coppola, Natasha Doff, Chris Gordon, Khristina Narizhnaya, Irina Titova

Lead Editors: Amanda Sadlowski, Caroline Trefler

Editor: Stephen Brewer

Production Editor: Jennifer DePrima

10th Edition

ISBN 978–0–7704–3205–8

ISSN 1538–6082

All details in this book are based on information supplied to us at press time. Always confirm information when it matters, especially if you're making a detour to visit a specific place. Fodor's expressly disclaims any liability, loss, or risk, personal or otherwise, that is incurred as a consequence of the use of any of the contents of this book.

SPECIAL SALES

This book is available at special discounts for bulk purchases for sales promotions or premiums. For more information, e-mail specialmarkets@randomhouse.com

PRINTED IN THE UNITED STATES OF AMERICA

10 9 8 7 6 5 4 3 2 1

ABOUT OUR WRITERS

Sabra Ayres is a journalist who has spent more than seven years working in the former Soviet Union. She was based in Moscow for four years as a correspondent for the Cox Newspapers. Her articles on Russia and beyond have appeared in the *International Herald Tribune*, the *Columbia Journalism Review*, the *Baltimore Sun*, *Newsweek Japan*, and the *Economist Intelligence* Unit. Before becoming a journalist, she spent two years as a Peace Corps volunteer in Ukraine, and she has taught aspiring young journalists in Afghanistan and India. She worked on the Experience Moscow and St. Petersburg and Exploring Moscow chapters.

Catherine Blanchard has been an editor and freelance writer in Russia since 2009. She covers fashion for *Women's Wear Daily* and food, nightlife, and the music scene for the English-language newspaper *element* in Moscow. She worked on the Moscow Where to Eat chapter.

Anna Coppola, a native of Russia, has spent more than four years in the United States as a journalist and media producer. Since 2007 she has been working as a Culture Fluent for the global market research publication *Iconoculture*, where she translates cultural differences of the Russian consumer market for American marketing professionals. She is also a contributing writer of Moscow's business magazine *Kompania* and a self-proclaimed tour guide for her visiting foreign friends and family in Moscow and St. Petersburg. She updated the Moscow Shopping and Moscow Where to Stay chapters this edition.

Natasha Doff is a British journalist and writer currently based in Moscow. As one of the first (adopted) Muscovites to cycle the bustling streets of Russia's capital to work every day, she has developed an intimate knowledge of the city. Formerly the news editor at a local English-language newspaper, Natasha has covered breaking news stories for a number of U.S. and European publications. When not scoping out Moscow's newest cafés and exhibitions, she can be found swimming in the mighty Volga River or exploring the wonders of Siberia and the former Soviet Union. She updated the Moscow Nightlife chapter.

Chris Gordon is a journalist and editor who has lived in St. Petersburg since 2002. He is currently the editor-in-chief of the *St. Petersburg Times*, following several years as editor-in-chief of *Hermitage* magazine. With a background in contemporary art (gained as a curator of international exhibitions), he specializes in reporting on luxury travel, fine dining, and the arts. He contributed to the St. Petersburg Where to Eat, Where to Stay, Nightlife, and Shopping chapters.

Khristina Narizhnaya is a Moscow-based writer who updated our Side Trips from Moscow and Travel Smart chapters.

A reporter at the *St. Petersburg Times*, Irina Titova has written everything from daily-news articles to unusual feature stories. She also studied for a year at St. Michael's College in Vermont, which first introduced her to American journalism. Irina worked on Exploring St. Petersburg and Side Trips from St. Petersburg this edition.